CompTIA Security+:
Get Certified Get Ahead

SY0-501 Study Guide

Darril Gibson

CompTIA Security+: Get Certified Get Ahead SY0-501 Study Guide
Copyright © 2017 by Darril Gibson

YCDA, LLC books may be purchased for educational, business, or sales promotional use. For information, please contact Darril Gibson at darril@darrilgibson.com.

Copy editor: Karen Annett
Technical editor: Chris Crayton
Proofreader: Karen Annett
Compositor: Susan Veach

ISBN-10: 1-939136-05-9
ISBN-13: 978-1-939136-05-3

Dedication

To my wife, who even after 25 years of marriage continues to remind me how wonderful life can be if you're in a loving relationship.
Thanks for sharing your life with me.

Acknowledgments

Books of this size and depth can't be done by a single person, and I'm grateful for the many people who helped me put this book together. First, thanks to my wife. She has provided me immeasurable support throughout this project. The technical editor, Chris Crayton, provided some great feedback on each of the chapters and the online labs. If you have the paperback copy of the book in your hand, you're enjoying some excellent composite editing work done by Susan Veach.

I'm extremely grateful for all the effort Karen Annett put into this project. She's an awesome copy editor and proofer and the book is tremendously better due to all the work she's put into it.

Last, thanks to my assistant Jaena Nerona who helped with many of the details behind the scenes. She helped me with some quality control and project management. More, she managed most of the daily tasks associated with maintaining online web sites.

While I certainly appreciate all the feedback everyone gave me, I want to stress that any errors that may have snuck into this book are entirely my fault and no reflection on anyone who helped. I always strive to identify and remove every error, but they still seem to sneak in.

Special thanks to:
- Chief Wiggum for bollards installation.
- Nelson Muntz for personal physical security services.
- Martin Prince for educating us about downgrade attacks.
- Comp-Global-Hyper-Mega-Net for intermittent HTTP services.
- Edna Krabapple for her thoughtful continuing education lessons.
- Apu Nahasapeemapetilon for technical advice on secure coding concepts.
- Moe Szyslak for refreshments and uplifting our spirits with his talks about RATs.

About the Author

Darril Gibson is the CEO of YCDA, LLC (short for You Can Do Anything). He has contributed to more than 40 books as the author, coauthor, or technical editor. Darril regularly writes, consults, and teaches on a wide variety of technical and security topics and holds several certifications, including CompTIA A+, Network+, Security+, and CASP; (ISC)2 SSCP and CISSP; Microsoft MCSE and MCITP; and ITIL Foundations.

In response to repeated requests, Darril created the *http://gcgapremium.com/* site where he provides study materials for several certification exams, including the CompTIA Security+ exam. Darril regularly posts blog articles at *http://blogs.getcertifiedgetahead.com/*, and uses the site to help people stay abreast of changes in certification exams. You can contact him through either of these sites.

Additionally, Darril publishes the Get Certified Get Ahead newsletter. This weekly newsletter typically lets readers know of new blog posts and about updates related to CompTIA certification exams. You can sign up at *http://eepurl.com/g44Of*.

Darril lives in Virginia Beach with his wife and two dogs. Whenever possible, they escape to a small cabin in the country on over twenty acres of land that continue to provide them with peace, tranquility, and balance.

Table of Contents

Introduction

Congratulations on your purchase of *CompTIA Security+: Get Certified Get Ahead* study guide. You are one step closer to becoming CompTIA Security+ certified. This certification has helped many individuals get ahead in their jobs and their careers, and it can help you get ahead, too.

It is a popular certification within the IT field. One IT hiring manager told me that if a résumé doesn't include the Security+ certification, or a higher-level security certification, he simply sets it aside. He won't even talk to applicants. That's not the same with all IT hiring managers, but it does help illustrate how important security is within the IT field.

Who This Book Is For

If you're studying for the CompTIA Security+ exam and want to pass it on your first attempt, this book is for you. It covers 100 percent of the objectives identified by CompTIA for the Security+ exam.

The first target audience for this book is students in CompTIA Security+ classes. My goal is to give students a book they can use to study the relevant and important details of CompTIA Security+ in adequate depth for the challenging topics, but without the minutiae in topics that are clear for most IT professionals. I regularly taught from the earlier editions of this book, and I'll continue to teach using this edition. I also hear from instructors around the United States and in several other countries who use versions of the book to help students master the topics and pass the Security+ exam the first time they take it.

Second, this book is for those people who like to study on their own. If you're one of the people who can read a book and learn the material without sitting in a class, this book has what you need to take and pass the exam.

Additionally, you can keep this book on your shelf (or in your Kindle) to remind yourself of important, relevant concepts. These concepts are important for security professionals and IT professionals in the real world.

Based on many conversations with students and readers of the previous versions of this book, I know that many people use the Security+ certification as the first step in achieving other security certifications. For example, you may follow Security+ with one of these cybersecurity certifications:

- (ISC)2 Systems Security Certified Practitioner (SSCP)
- (ISC)2 Certified Information Systems Security Professional (CISSP)
- CompTIA Advanced Security Practitioner (CASP)
- CompTIA Cybersecurity Analyst (CSA+)

If you plan to pursue any of these advanced security certifications, you'll find this book will help you lay a solid foundation of security knowledge. Learn this material, and you'll be a step ahead on the other exams.

About This Book

Over the past several years, I've taught literally hundreds of students, helping them to become CompTIA Security+ certified. During that time, I've learned what concepts are easy to grasp and what concepts need more explanation. I've developed handouts and analogies that help students grasp the elusive concepts.

Feedback from students was overwhelmingly positive—both in their comments to me and their successful pass rates after taking the certification exam. When the objectives changed in 2008, I rewrote my handouts as the first edition of this book. When the objectives changed again in 2011 and 2014, I rewrote the book to reflect the new objectives. This book reflects the objective changes released in 2017.

Gratefully, this book has allowed me to reach a much larger audience and share security and IT-related information. Even if you aren't in one of the classes I teach, this book can help you learn the relevant material to pass the exam the first time you take it.

How to Use This Book

Over the years, I've taught the Security+ course many times. During this process, I learned the best way to present the material so that students understand and retain the most knowledge. The book is laid out the same way.

For most people, the easiest way to use the book is by starting with the pre-assessment exam (after the intro) to gauge your initial understanding of the topics. Then, go through each chapter sequentially, including the end-of-chapter practice test questions. Doing so, you'll build a solid foundation of knowledge. This helps make the more advanced topics in later chapters easier to understand.

If you have a high level of IT security knowledge and only want to study the topics that are unclear to you on this exam, you can review the objective map listed at the end of the introduction. This lists all the objectives and identifies the chapter where the objective topics are covered. Additionally, you can look at the index to locate the exact page for these topics. If you have the Kindle version, it includes an excellent search feature you can use to find a specific topic.

When practicing for any certification exam, the following steps are a good recipe for success:

- **Review the objectives.** The objectives for the SY0-501 exam are listed in the "Objective to Chapter Map" section in this Introduction.
- **Learn the material related to the objectives.** This book covers all the objectives, and the introduction includes a map showing which chapter (or chapters) covers each objective. Along those lines, my goal when writing the book was to cover the objectives at sufficient depth to help you pass the exam. However, these topics all have a lot more depth. When I study for a certification exam, I typically dig in much deeper than necessary, often because the topics interest me. You can, too, if you want, but don't lose site of the exam objectives.
- **Take practice questions.** A key step when preparing for any certification exam is to make sure you can answer the exam questions. Yes, you need the knowledge, but you also must be able to read a question and select the correct answer. This simply takes practice. When using practice test questions, ensure they have explanations. Questions without explanations often encourage rote memorization without understanding and sometimes even give you the wrong answers.

- **Achieve high scores on practice exams.** I typically tell people that they should get scores of at least 90 percent on practice tests for the CompTIA Security+ exam. However, don't focus on only your scores.
- **Read and understand the explanations.** Ideally, you should be able to look at any practice test question and know why the correct answers are correct and why the incorrect answers are incorrect. Within this book, you'll find this information in the explanations. When you understand the explanations, you have the best chance of accurately interpreting the questions on the live exam and answering them correctly no matter how CompTIA words or presents them.

This book has over 300 practice test questions you can use to test your knowledge and your ability to correctly answer them. Every question has a detailed explanation to help you understand why the correct answers are correct and why the incorrect answers are incorrect.

You can find the practice questions in the following areas:

- **Pre-assessment exam.** Use these questions at the beginning of the book to get a feel for what you know and what you need to study more.
- **End-of-chapter practice questions.** Each chapter has practice questions to help you test your comprehension of the material in the chapter.
- **Post-assessment exam.** Use this as a practice exam to test your comprehension of the subject matter and readiness to take the actual exam.

It's OK if you do the practice questions in a different order. You may decide to tackle all the chapters in the book and then do the pre-assessment and post-assessment questions. That's fine. However, I strongly suggest you review all the questions in the book. Also, make sure you check out the additional free online resources at *http://gcgapremium.com/501-extras.*

The glossary provides a short definition of key terms. If you want more details on any topic, check out the index to identify the page numbers. Many index entries also list related topics.

Conventions

While creating this book, I've followed specific conventions to give you insight into the content. This includes the following items:

- **Glossary terms.** Important glossary items are presented in ***bold italics*** the first time they are mentioned, and/or when they are defined. The objectives include an extensive Security+ Acronyms list. Some of these are relevant to the current exam, so I've included them in Appendix A, "Glossary." However, irrelevant acronyms are not included in the Glossary.
- **Commands.** Some chapters include specific commands that I encourage you to enter so that you can see how they work. These are shown in **bold**.
- **File names.** File names such as *md5sum.exe* are shown in italics.
- **Web site URLs.** URLs such as *http:/gcgapremium.com* are shown in italics.

Remember This

Throughout the book, you'll see text boxes that highlight important information you should remember to successfully pass the exam. The surrounding content provides the additional information needed to fully understand these key points, and the text boxes summarize the important points.

These text boxes will look like this:

> ### *Remember this*
>
> I strongly encourage you to repeat the information in the text boxes to yourself as often as possible. The more you repeat the information, the more likely you are to remember it when you take the exam.

A tried-and-true method of repeating key information is to take notes when you're first studying the material and then rewrite the notes later. This will expose you to the material a minimum of three times.

Another method that students have told me has been successful for them is to use an MP3 player. Many MP3 players can record. Start your MP3 recorder and read the information in each text box for a chapter and the information in the Exam Topic Review section of each chapter. Save the MP3 file and regularly listen to it. This allows you to reaffirm the important information in your own voice.

You can play it while exercising, walking, or just about any time when it's not dangerous to listen to any MP3 file. You can even burn the MP3 files to a CD and play them back from a CD player.

If the MP3 method is successful for you, you can also record and listen to exam questions. Read the question, only the correct answer, and the first sentence or two of the explanation in each practice question.

If you don't have time to create your own MP3 recordings, check out the companion web site (*http://gcgapremium.com*) for this book. You can purchase MP3 recordings there that you can download and use.

Vendor Neutral

CompTIA certifications are vendor neutral. In other words, certifications are not centered on any single vendor, such as Microsoft, Apple, or Linux distributions. However, you can expect to see questions that are focused on specific vendors or operating systems.

For example, many of the topics in this version of the CompTIA Security+ exam are specific to Microsoft operating systems. Group Policy is one of many examples. More and more security devices use Linux as their operating system and this version of the exam has some specific topics on Linux. Command-line tools such as dig, ifconfig, and ip are a few examples. Most mobile devices use either the Apple iOS operating system or the Android operating system and some of the objectives (such as rooting and jailbreaking) focus on these operating systems.

Free Online Resources

There are many additional free resources available to you at *http://gcgapremium.com/501-extras/*, including:

- Free online labs
- Sample performance-based questions
- Additional free multiple-choice practice test questions
- Other free resources such as links to additional content

I created this online content with a couple of goals. First, this version of the objectives was significantly longer than the last version. There was a lot I wanted to include in the book, but there just wasn't room. As an example, if I included all the labs in the book, it would have inflated the page count of the book to an unmanageable level. Second, I wanted to give myself a way to update the book content. If it'll be helpful to readers, I can easily add additional labs and/or additional resources.

These materials are valuable free supplements, so you'll need to register to access this content and prove that you have the book by answering a question. As an example, you may have to answer a question such as this:

Locate the "Vendor Neutral" section in the introduction of the book. What is the last word in that section?

The "Vendor Neutral" section is right before this section ("Free Online Resources") and the last word in that section is **systems**. You will then need to enter the word **systems**. People guessing (or who don't have the book) won't be able to answer the question. You will.

Be careful, though. If you don't answer the question correctly the first time, you won't get another chance for several days. It's important that you take the time to enter the correct word the first time.

Additional Web Resources

Check out *http://GetCertifiedGetAhead.com* for up-to-date details on the CompTIA Security+ exam. This site includes additional information related to the CompTIA Security+ exam and this book.

Although many people have spent a lot of time and energy trying to ensure that there are no errors in this book, errors occasionally slip through. This site includes an errata page listing any errors we've discovered.

If you discover any errors, please let me know through the Contact Us page on the web site. I'd also love to hear about your success when you pass the exam. I'm constantly getting good news from readers and students who are successfully earning their certifications.

In response to all the requests I've received for additional materials, such as online practice test questions, flash cards, and audio files, I created this site: *http://gcgapremium.com/*. It includes access to various study materials at an additional cost. Packages include all the materials in the book and in the free online resources area, plus additional materials such as flash cards, audio, and additional performance-based questions.

Last, I've found that many people find cryptography topics challenging, so I've posted some videos on YouTube (*http://www.youtube.com/*). As time allows, I'll post additional videos, and you can get a listing of all of them by searching YouTube with "Darril Gibson."

Assumptions

The CompTIA Security+ exam assumes you have the following experience and knowledge:
- "A minimum of two years' experience in IT administration with a focus on security"
- "Day-to-day technical information security experience"
- "Broad knowledge of security concerns and implementation, including the topics in the domain list"

However, I'm aware that two years of experience in a network could mean many different things. Your two years of experience may expose you to different technologies than someone else's two years of experience.

When it's critical that you understand an underlying network concept to master the relevant exam material, I have often included the concept within the background information.

Set a Goal

Look at a calendar right now and determine the date 45 days from today. This will be your target date to take this exam. Set this as your goal to complete studying the materials and to take the exam.

This target allows you to master about one and a half chapters per week. It may be that some of the chapters take you less time and some of the chapters take you more time. No problem. If you want to modify your target date later, do so. However, a recipe for success in almost any endeavor includes setting a goal.

When I teach CompTIA Security+ at a local university, I often help the students register for the exam on the first night. They pick a date close to the end of the course and register. I've found that when we do this, about 90 percent of the students take and pass the exam within one week after completing the course. On the other hand, when I didn't help the students register on the first night, more than half of them did not complete the exam in the same time frame. Setting a goal helps.

About the Exam

CompTIA first released the Security+ exam in 2002, and it has quickly grown in popularity. They revised the exam objectives in 2008, 2011, 2014, and again in 2017. The 2017 exam is numbered as SY0-501. The English version of the SY0-401 exam is scheduled to retire in July 2018.

Here's a summary of the exam details:
- **Number of questions:** Maximum of 90 questions
- **Length of test:** 90 minutes
- **Passing score:** 750
- **Grading criteria:** Scale of 100 to 900 (about 83 percent)
- **Question types:** Multiple choice and performance-based
- **Exam format:** Traditional—can move back and forth to view previous questions
- **Exam prerequisites:** None required but Network+ is recommended
- **Exam test provider:** Pearson VUE (*https://home.pearsonvue.com/*)

Passing Score

A score of 750 is required to pass. This is on a scale of 100 to 900. If you take the exam but don't get a single question correct, you get a score of 100. If you get every question correct, you get a score of 900. A passing score of 750 divided by 900 equals .8333 or 83.33 percent.

Also, a score of 83 percent is higher than many other certification exams, so you shouldn't underestimate the difficulty of this exam. However, many people regularly pass it and you can pass it, too. With this book and the free online resources, you will be well prepared.

Exam Prerequisites

All that is required for you to take the exam is money. Other than that, there are no enforced prerequisites. However, to successfully pass the exam, you're expected to have "a minimum of two years' of experience in IT administration with a focus on security." If you have more than that, the exam materials will likely come easier to you. If you have less, the exam may be more difficult.

Beta Questions

Your exam may have some beta questions. They aren't graded but instead are used to test the validity of the questions. If everyone gets a beta question correct, it's probably too easy. If everyone gets it incorrect, there's probably something wrong with the question. After enough people have tested a beta question, CompTIA personnel analyze it and decide if they want to add it to the test bank, or rewrite and test it as a new beta question.

The good news is that CompTIA doesn't grade the beta questions. However, you don't know which questions are ungraded beta questions and which questions are live questions, so you need to treat every question equally.

Exam Format

The exam uses a traditional format. You start at question 1 and go to the last question. During the process, you can skip questions and mark any questions you want to review when you're done. Additionally, you can view previous questions if desired. For example, if you get to question 10 and then remember something that helps you answer question 5, you can go back and redo question 5.

Question Types

You will see two primary question types on the exam: multiple-choice and performance-based. Each type is described in the following sections.

Multiple Choice

Most questions are multiple-choice types where you select one answer or multiple answers. When you need to select multiple answers, the question will include a phrase such as "Select TWO" or "Select THREE."

You may also see questions that use phrases such as "BEST choice," "BEST description," or "MOST secure." In these examples, don't be surprised if you see two answers that could answer the question, while only one is the best choice. As an example, consider this simple question:

Q. Which one of the following numbers is between 1 and 10 and is the HIGHEST?

A. 2
B. 8
C. 14
D. 23

Clearly, 2 and 8 are between 1 and 10, but 14 and 23 are not. However, only 8 is both between 1 and 10 and the highest.

Performance-Based Questions

You can expect as many as 10 performance-based questions. These include matching, drag and drop, and data entry questions. CompTIA refers to these as performance-based questions and instead of picking from a multiple-choice answer, you're often required to perform a task. CompTIA's goal is to provide more accurate testing to verify people have a full understanding of a topic.

People often ask if they get partial credit. CompTIA has said that you may get partial credit on some questions, but other questions may not give you partial credit. However, you'll never know which questions give you partial credit and which questions don't give you partial credit. It's best to do the best you can with each question.

The following sections cover the different types of performance-based questions you can expect. You can also check out some of the blogs on performance-based questions that I've written here: *http://blogs.getcertifiedgetahead.com/security-blog-links/*.

Matching

In a matching performance-based question, you will see two lists and you need to match them. As an example, one list might include control types such as technical, administrative, and physical and the second list might include specific controls such as risk assessments, security guards, and encryption. You would match technical with encryption, administrative with risk assessments, and physical with security guards. If you understand the common security control types, this becomes trivial. Then again, if you don't understand the control types, this can be quite difficult.

Drag and Drop

In some questions, you might need to drag items from one location on the screen to another location to answer a question. You can think of these as multiple-choice questions with multiple answers that are correct. However, instead of selecting the check boxes to indicate a correct answer, you drag it to somewhere else on the screen.

As an example, consider this question:

Q. Arrange the following list in order from most volatile to least volatile:
- Paging file
- Local drive
- Archive media
- RAM
- Cache

You would drag and drop the items until they were in the following order:
- Cache
- RAM
- Paging file
- Files on local drive
- Archive media

Data Entry

Some performance-based questions might ask you to analyze a scenario and then enter appropriate data. For example, Chapter 4, "Securing Your Network," discusses the configuration of wireless access points and wireless routers. A related question might ask you to configure an access point to work with WPA2 Enterprise mode. The Configuring a Wireless Router Lab mentioned in Chapter 4 and available online (*http://gcgapremium.com/labs/*) shows you relevant settings that you would enter.

Performance-Based Questions Strategy

You'll see the performance-based questions first and they take much longer than typical multiple-choice questions. If the answer is clear to you, then take the time to answer it. However, if the question isn't clear, mark the question and skip it. You can come back to it later. It's entirely possible that the question is a poorly worded beta question that doesn't even count. However, if you spend 45 minutes on it, you might run out of time before you finish the multiple-choice questions.

Performance-based questions have occasionally caused problems for the test systems. A common problem is that instead of displaying the question, the screen is mostly blank. If this happens, you can often just use the reset button for the question. This allows you to move past the problem and continue with the test. However, resetting the question erases any answer you've entered, so you'll have to come back to it after you finish other questions.

It's common for people to be nervous when thinking about these performance-based test questions. However, most people who take the test say that these questions usually aren't that difficult. If you understand the concepts from the exam objectives, you won't have any problem. I do recommend you check out the posts on performance-based questions that I've posted here: *http://blogs.getcertifiedgetahead.com/security-blog-links/*.

Question Complexity

In the past, the Security+ test questions were relatively straightforward. For example, a question may be like this "What is 5 × 5?" Either you know the answer is 25 or you don't. The exam questions tested your knowledge of the material, not necessarily your ability to dissect the question so that you could figure out what the question was really trying to ask.

However, CompTIA has made these questions progressively more complex. Consider this example:

Q. You are driving a bus from Springfield to Shelbyville at 55 mph with 22 passengers. The bus is painted blue. At the same time, a train is traveling from Shelbyville to Springfield at 40 mph. The train has a yellow caboose. What color are the bus driver's eyes?

Notice that the question adds a lot of superfluous information. The actual question is in the last sentence and only one comment is directly related to this question. The question starts by saying, "You are driving a bus..." and then ends by asking, "What color are the bus driver's eyes?" You're required to put the two together and weed through the irrelevant information to come to the correct answer.

Many people memorize practice test questions and answers. However, this is not a successful path to success because CompTIA often modifies the questions. Ideally, you should know why the correct answers are correct and why the incorrect answers are incorrect. This will give you a much better chance of interpreting the questions and answering them correctly. Consider this question from Chapter 5:

Q. Managers within your organization want to implement a secure boot process for some key computers. During the boot process, each computer should send data to a remote system to check the computer's configuration. Which of the following will meet this goal?

    A. Trusted Platform Module

    B. Hardware root of trust

    C. Remote attestation

    D. Trusted operating system

The answer is **C**. A remote attestation process checks a computer during the boot cycle and sends a report to a remote system. The remote system attests, or confirms that the computer is secure. None of the other answers sends data to a remote system. A Trusted Platform Module (TPM) is a hardware chip on a motherboard and provides a local secure boot process. A TPM includes an encryption key burned into the CPU, which provides a hardware root of trust. A trusted operating system meets a set of predetermined requirements typically enforced with the mandatory access control (MAC) model.

If someone memorizes a few key words to the previous question along with the answer, they will likely have problems if CompTIA modifies the question. As an example, consider the following question:

Q. Managers within your organization want to implement a secure boot process for some key computers. During the boot process, each computer should send data to an internal system to check the computer's configuration. Which of the following will meet this goal?

    A. Trusted Platform Module

    B. Hardware root of trust

    C. Remote attestation

    D. Trusted operating system

Notice that only one word in the question is different. The word remote (as in remote system) was changed to internal (as in internal system). If someone memorized questions and answers, they might jump on Remote attestation without giving it any thought. However, the one-word change changes the correct answer to a Trusted Platform Module.

Video

Some people learn better with a combination of a study guide and watching videos. If that's you, I strongly encourage you to check out some excellent videos created by my good friend Mike Chapple. They're available on Lynda.com and you can often get a free peek at online videos by signing up for a free trial. Go to Lynda.com and enter Mike Chapple into the search. You'll find that he's created a lot of quality content, including videos on the CompTIA Security+ SY0-501 exam.

Exam Test Provider

You can take the exam at a Pearson VUE testing site. Some testing sites provide testing and nothing else. However, most testing sites are part of another company, such as a training company, college, or university. You can take an exam at the training company's testing site even if you haven't taken a course with them.

The Pearson VUE web site includes search tools you can use to find a testing site close to you. Check them out at *https://home.pearsonvue.com/*.

Voucher Code for 10 Percent Off

The cost of the CompTIA Security+ exam is $320 in the United States if you purchase it at full price, though CompTIA may raise the price at some time in the future. However, you can get a 10 percent discount using a discount code. This code changes periodically, so you'll need to go to this page to access the current code: *http://gcgapremium.com/discounted-comptia-vouchers/*.

When you purchase a voucher, you'll get a voucher number that you can use to register at a testing site. A word of caution: Some criminals sell bogus vouchers on Internet sites such as eBay. You won't know you've been ripped off until you try to use it and by that time, the criminal will probably have disappeared. In contrast, if you use the discount code, you buy the voucher directly from CompTIA.

Exam Domains

The exam objectives are divided into the following domains, or general topic areas. Additionally, CompTIA publishes the percentage of questions you can anticipate in any of the domains:

- **1.0 Threats, Attacks and Vulnerabilities.** 21 percent of examination content
- **2.0 Technologies and Tools.** 22 percent of examination content
- **3.0 Architecture and Design.** 15 percent of examination content
- **4.0 Identity and Access Management.** 16 percent of examination content
- **5.0 Risk Management.** 14 percent of examination content
- **6.0 Cryptography and PKI.** 12 percent of examination content

CompTIA publishes a listing of the objectives on its web site. They also include these comments:

> *"The lists of examples provided in bulleted format are not exhaustive lists. Other examples of technologies, processes or tasks pertaining to each objective may also be included on the exam although not listed or covered in this objectives document. CompTIA is constantly reviewing the content of our exams and updating test questions to be sure our exams are current and the security of the questions is protected.*
>
> *"When necessary, we will publish updated exams based on existing exam objectives. Please know that all related exam preparation materials will still be valid. The lists of examples provided in bulleted format below each objective are not exhaustive lists. Other examples of technologies, processes or tasks pertaining to each objective may also be included on the exam although not listed or covered in this objectives document."*

This indicates that you may see something that isn't on the objective list. As an example, the objectives clearly show an increased emphasis on Linux, including Linux commands. You won't find the chmod command or the chroot command in the objective lists. However, it's entirely possible that you'll see these commands in questions on the live exam.

I've done my best to predict how test item writers will interpret these objectives when writing test questions. However, there may be some surprises. Make sure you look at the free online materials at *http://gcgapremium.com/501-extras/*.

Additionally, you can check this book's companion site at *http://GetCertifiedGetAhead. com* for up-to-date information on the exam, and read blogs about various topics, including the CompTIA Security+ exam, at *http://blogs.GetCertifiedGetAhead.com*. Also, online practice test questions, flash cards, and other study materials are available at *http://gcgapremium.com/*.

Objective to Chapter Map

This following list shows the SY0-501 objectives published by CompTIA. Next to each objective, you'll also see the chapter or chapters where the objective is covered within this book.

1.0 Threats, Attacks and Vulnerabilities 21%

1.1 Given a scenario, analyze indicators of compromise and determine the type of malware. (Chapter 6)

- Viruses (Chapter 6)
- Crypto-malware (Chapter 6)
- Ransomware (Chapter 6)
- Worm (Chapter 6)

- Trojan (Chapter 6)
- Rootkit (Chapter 6)
- Keylogger (Chapter 6)
- Adware (Chapter 6)
- Spyware (Chapter 6)
- Bots (Chapter 6)
- RAT (Chapter 6)
- Logic bomb (Chapter 6)
- Backdoor (Chapter 6)

1.2 Compare and contrast types of attacks. (Chapters 3, 4, 6, 7, 9, 10)
- Social engineering (Chapter 6)
- Phishing (Chapter 6)
  - Spear phishing (Chapter 6)
  - Whaling (Chapter 6)
  - Vishing (Chapter 6)
  - Tailgating (Chapter 9)
  - Impersonation (Chapter 6)
  - Dumpster diving (Chapter 6)
  - Shoulder surfing (Chapter 6)
  - Hoax (Chapter 6)
  - Watering hole attack (Chapter 6)
  - Principles (reasons for effectiveness) (Chapter 6)
    - Authority (Chapter 6)
    - Intimidation (Chapter 6)
    - Consensus (Chapter 6)
    - Scarcity (Chapter 6)
    - Familiarity (Chapter 6)
    - Trust (Chapter 6)
    - Urgency (Chapter 6)
- Application/service attacks (Chapters 3, 6, 7)
  - DoS (Chapter 6)
  - DDoS (Chapter 6)
  - Man-in-the-middle (Chapter 7)
  - Buffer overflow (Chapter 7)
  - Injection (Chapter 7)
  - Cross-site scripting (Chapter 7)
  - Cross-site request forgery (Chapter 7)
  - Privilege escalation (Chapter 7)
  - ARP poisoning (Chapters 3, 7)
  - Amplification (Chapter 7)
  - DNS poisoning (Chapter 3)
  - Domain hijacking (Chapter 7)
  - Man-in-the-browser (Chapter 7)
  - Zero day (Chapter 7)
  - Replay (Chapter 7)
  - Pass the hash (Chapter 7)

- o Hijacking and related attacks (Chapter 7)
  - ▪ Clickjacking (Chapter 7)
  - ▪ Session hijacking (Chapter 7)
  - ▪ URL hijacking (Chapter 7)
  - ▪ Typo squatting (Chapter 7)
- o Driver manipulation (Chapter 7)
  - ▪ Shimming (Chapter 7)
  - ▪ Refactoring (Chapter 7)
- o MAC spoofing (Chapter 7)
- o IP spoofing (Chapter 7)
- Wireless attacks (Chapter 4)
  - o Replay (Chapter 4)
  - o IV (Chapter 4)
  - o Evil twin (Chapter 4)
  - o Rogue AP (Chapter 4)
  - o Jamming (Chapter 4)
  - o WPS (Chapter 4)
  - o Bluejacking (Chapter 4)
  - o Bluesnarfing (Chapter 4)
  - o RFID (Chapter 4)
  - o NFC (Chapter 4)
  - o Disassociation (Chapter 4)
- Cryptographic attacks (Chapters 7, 10)
  - o Birthday (Chapter 7)
  - o Known plain text/cipher text (Chapter 7)
  - o Rainbow tables (Chapter 7)
  - o Dictionary (Chapter 7)
  - o Brute force (Chapter 7)
  - o Online vs. offline (Chapter 7)
  - o Collision (Chapter 7)
  - o Downgrade (Chapter 10)
  - o Replay (Chapter 7)
  - o Weak implementations (Chapter 10)

1.3 Explain threat actor types and attributes. (Chapter 6)
- Types of actors (Chapter 6)
  - o Script kiddies (Chapter 6)
  - o Hacktivist (Chapter 6)
  - o Organized crime (Chapter 6)
  - o Nation states/APT (Chapter 6)
  - o Insiders (Chapter 6)
  - o Competitors (Chapter 6)
- Attributes of actors (Chapter 6)
  - o Internal/external (Chapter 6)
  - o Level of sophistication (Chapter 6)
  - o Resources/funding (Chapter 6)
  - o Intent/motivation (Chapter 6)

o Use of open-source intelligence (Chapter 6)

1.4 Explain penetration testing concepts. (Chapter 8)
- Active reconnaissance (Chapter 8)
- Passive reconnaissance (Chapter 8)
- Pivot (Chapter 8)
- Initial exploitation (Chapter 8)
- Persistence (Chapter 8)
- Escalation of privilege (Chapter 8)
- Black box (Chapter 8)
- White box (Chapter 8)
- Gray box (Chapter 8)
- Penetration testing vs. vulnerability scanning (Chapter 8)

1.5 Explain vulnerability scanning concepts. (Chapter 8)
- Passively test security controls (Chapter 8)
- Identify vulnerability (Chapter 8)
- Identify lack of security controls (Chapter 8)
- Identify common misconfigurations (Chapter 8)
- Intrusive vs. non-intrusive (Chapter 8)
- Credentialed vs. non-credentialed (Chapter 8)
- False positive (Chapter 8)

1.6 Explain the impact associated with types of vulnerabilities. (Chapters 2, 5, 6, 7, 9, 10)
- Race conditions (Chapter 7)
- Vulnerabilities due to: (Chapter 5)
  - o End-of-life systems (Chapter 5)
  - o Embedded systems (Chapter 5)
  - o Lack of vendor support (Chapter 5)
- Improper input handling (Chapter 7)
- Improper error handling (Chapter 7)
- Misconfiguration/weak configuration (Chapter 5)
- Default configuration (Chapter 5)
- Resource exhaustion (Chapter 6)
- Untrained users (Chapter 6)
- Improperly configured accounts (Chapter 2)
- Vulnerable business processes (Chapter 9)
- Weak cipher suites and implementations (Chapter 10)
- Memory/buffer vulnerability (Chapter 7)
  - o Memory leak (Chapter 7)
  - o Integer overflow (Chapter 7)
  - o Buffer overflow (Chapter 7)
  - o Pointer dereference (Chapter 7)
  - o DLL injection (Chapter 7)
- System sprawl/undocumented assets (Chapter 9)
- Architecture/design weaknesses (Chapter 9)
- New threats/zero day (Chapter 7)
- Improper certificate and key management (Chapter 10)

2.0 Technologies and Tools 22%

2.1 Install and configure network components, both hardware- and software-based, to support organizational security. (Chapters 3, 4, 5, 6, 8, 9)
- Firewall (Chapter 3)
  - o ACL (Chapter 3)
  - o Application-based vs. network-based (Chapter 3)
  - o Stateful vs. stateless (Chapter 3)
  - o Implicit deny (Chapter 3)
- VPN concentrator (Chapter 4)
  - o Remote access vs. site-to-site (Chapter 4)
  - o IPSec (Chapter 4)
    - Tunnel mode (Chapter 4)
    - Transport mode (Chapter 4)
    - AH (Chapter 4)
    - ESP (Chapter 4)
  - o Split tunnel vs. full tunnel (Chapter 4)
  - o TLS (Chapter 4)
  - o Always-on VPN (Chapter 4)
- NIPS/NIDS (Chapter 4)
  - o Signature-based (Chapter 4)
  - o Heuristic/behavioral (Chapter 4)
  - o Anomaly (Chapter 4)
  - o Inline vs. passive (Chapter 4)
  - o In-band vs. out-of-band (Chapter 4)
  - o Rules (Chapter 4)
  - o Analytics (Chapter 4)
    - False positive (Chapter 4)
    - False negative (Chapter 4)
- Router (Chapter 3)
  - o ACLs (Chapter 3)
  - o Antispoofing (Chapter 3)
- Switch (Chapter 3)
  - o Port security (Chapter 3)
  - o Layer 2 vs. Layer 3 (Chapter 3)
  - o Loop prevention (Chapter 3)
  - o Flood guard (Chapter 3)
- Proxy (Chapter 3)
  - o Forward and reverse proxy (Chapter 3)
  - o Transparent (Chapter 3)
  - o Application/multipurpose (Chapter 3)
- Load balancer (Chapter 9)
  - o Scheduling (Chapter 9)
    - Affinity (Chapter 9)
    - Round-robin (Chapter 9)
  - o Active-passive (Chapter 9)
  - o Active-active (Chapter 9)

- o   Virtual IPs (Chapter 9)
- Access point (Chapter 4)
  - o   SSID (Chapter 4)
  - o   MAC filtering (Chapter 4)
  - o   Signal strength (Chapter 4)
  - o   Band selection/width (Chapter 4)
  - o   Antenna types and placement (Chapter 4)
  - o   Fat vs. thin (Chapter 4)
  - o   Controller-based vs. standalone (Chapter 4)
- SIEM (Chapter 8)
  - o   Aggregation (Chapter 8)
  - o   Correlation (Chapter 8)
  - o   Automated alerting and triggers (Chapter 8)
  - o   Time synchronization (Chapter 8)
  - o   Event deduplication (Chapter 8)
  - o   Logs/WORM (Chapter 8)
- DLP (Chapter 5)
  - o   USB blocking (Chapter 5)
  - o   Cloud-based (Chapter 5)
  - o   Email (Chapter 5)
- NAC (Chapter 4)
  - o   Dissolvable vs. permanent (Chapter 4)
  - o   Host health checks (Chapter 4)
  - o   Agent vs. agentless (Chapter 4)
- Mail gateway (Chapter 3)
  - o   Spam filter (Chapters 3, 6)
  - o   DLP (Chapter 3)
  - o   Encryption (Chapter 3)
- Bridge (Chapter 3)
- SSL/TLS accelerators (Chapter 4)
- SSL decryptors (Chapter 4)
- Media gateway (Chapter 3)
- Hardware security module (Chapter 5)

2.2 Given a scenario, use appropriate software tools to assess the security posture of an organization. (Chapters 1, 3, 4, 8, 9, 10, 11)
- Protocol analyzer (Chapter 8)
- Network scanners (Chapter 8)
  - o   Rogue system detection (Chapter 8)
  - o   Network mapping (Chapter 8)
- Wireless scanners/cracker (Chapter 8)
- Password cracker (Chapter 8)
- Vulnerability scanner (Chapter 8)
- Configuration compliance scanner (Chapter 8)
- Exploitation frameworks (Chapter 8)
- Data sanitization tools (Chapter 11)
- Steganography tools (Chapter 10)

- Honeypot (Chapter 4)
- Backup utilities (Chapter 9)
- Banner grabbing (Chapter 8)
- Passive vs. active (Chapter 8)
- Command line tools (Chapters 1, 8)
    - ping (Chapter 1)
    - netstat (Chapter 1)
    - tracert (Chapter 1)
    - nslookup/dig (Chapter 3)
    - arp (Chapter 1)
    - ipconfig/ip/ifconfig (Chapter 1)
    - tcpdump (Chapter 8)
    - nmap (Chapter 8)
    - netcat (Chapter 8)

2.3 Given a scenario, troubleshoot common security issues. (Chapters 2, 3, 4, 5, 6, 8, 9, 10, 11)
- Unencrypted credentials/clear text (Chapters 2, 8)
- Logs and events anomalies (Chapter 8)
- Permission issues (Chapter 5)
- Access violations (Chapter 5)
- Certificate issues (Chapter 10)
- Data exfiltration (Chapter 5)
- Misconfigured devices (Chapters 3, 4)
    - Firewall (Chapter 3)
    - Content filter (Chapter 3)
    - Access points (Chapter 4)
- Weak security configurations (Chapter 5)
- Personnel issues (Chapter 6, 11)
    - Policy violation (Chapter 11)
    - Insider threat (Chapter 6, 11)
    - Social engineering (Chapter 6, 11)
    - Social media (Chapter 6, 11)
    - Personal email (Chapter 11)
- Unauthorized software (Chapter 5)
- Baseline deviation (Chapter 5)
- License compliance violation (availability/integrity) (Chapter 5)
- Asset management (Chapter 9)
- Authentication issues (Chapter 2)

2.4 Given a scenario, analyze and interpret output from security technologies. (Chapters 3, 4, 5, 6)
- HIDS/HIPS (Chapter 4)
- Antivirus (Chapter 6)
- File integrity check (Chapter 6)
- Host-based firewall (Chapter 3)
- Application whitelisting (Chapter 5)
- Removable media control (Chapter 5)
- Advanced malware tools (Chapter 6)

- Patch management tools (Chapter 5)
- UTM (Chapter 3)
- DLP (Chapter 5)
- Data execution prevention (Chapter 6)
- Web application firewall (Chapter 3)

2.5 Given a scenario, deploy mobile devices securely. (Chapter 5)
- Connection methods (Chapter 5)
    - Cellular (Chapter 5)
    - WiFi (Chapter 5)
    - SATCOM (Chapter 5)
    - Bluetooth (Chapter 5)
    - NFC (Chapter 5)
    - ANT (Chapter 5)
    - Infrared (Chapter 5)
    - USB (Chapter 5)
- Mobile device management concepts (Chapter 5)
    - Application management (Chapter 5)
    - Content management (Chapter 5)
    - Remote wipe (Chapter 5)
    - Geofencing (Chapter 5)
    - Geolocation (Chapter 5)
    - Screen locks (Chapter 5)
    - Push notification services (Chapter 5)
    - Passwords and pins (Chapter 5)
    - Biometrics (Chapter 5)
    - Context-aware authentication (Chapter 5)
    - Containerization (Chapter 5)
    - Storage segmentation (Chapter 5)
    - Full device encryption (Chapter 5)
- Enforcement and monitoring for: (Chapter 5)
    - Third-party app stores (Chapter 5)
    - Rooting/jailbreaking (Chapter 5)
    - Sideloading (Chapter 5)
    - Custom firmware (Chapter 5)
    - Carrier unlocking (Chapter 5)
    - Firmware OTA updates (Chapter 5)
    - Camera use (Chapter 5)
    - SMS/MMS (Chapter 5)
    - External media (Chapter 5)
    - USB OTG (Chapter 5)
    - Recording microphone (Chapter 5)
    - GPS tagging (Chapter 5)
    - WiFi direct/ad hoc (Chapter 5)
    - Tethering (Chapter 5)
    - Payment methods (Chapter 5)
- Deployment models (Chapter 5)

- o BYOD (Chapter 5)
- o COPE (Chapter 5)
- o CYOD (Chapter 5)
- o Corporate-owned (Chapter 5)
- o VDI (Chapter 5)

2.6 Given a scenario, implement secure protocols. (Chapters 2, 3, 10)
- Protocols (Chapters 2, 3, 10)
  - o DNSSEC (Chapter 3)
  - o SSH (Chapter 3)
  - o S/MIME (Chapter 10)
  - o SRTP (Chapter 3)
  - o LDAPS (Chapter 2)
  - o FTPS (Chapter 3)
  - o SFTP (Chapter 3)
  - o SNMPv3 (Chapter 3)
  - o SSL/TLS (Chapter 3)
  - o HTTPS (Chapter 3)
  - o Secure POP/IMAP (Chapter 3)
- Use cases (Chapter 3)
  - o Voice and video (Chapter 3)
  - o Time synchronization (Chapter 3)
  - o Email and web (Chapter 3)
  - o File transfer (Chapter 3)
  - o Directory services (Chapter 3)
  - o Remote access (Chapter 3)
  - o Domain name resolution (Chapter 3)
  - o Routing and switching (Chapter 3)
  - o Network address allocation (Chapter 3)
  - o Subscription services (Chapter 3)

3.0 Architecture and Design 15%

3.1 Explain use cases and purpose for frameworks, best practices and secure configuration guides. (Chapters 7, 9)
- Industry-standard frameworks and reference architectures (Chapter 7)
  - o Regulatory (Chapter 7)
  - o Non-regulatory (Chapter 7)
  - o National vs. international (Chapter 7)
  - o Industry-specific frameworks (Chapter 7)
- Benchmarks/secure configuration guides (Chapter 7)
  - o Platform/vendor-specific guides (Chapter 7)
    - ▪ Web server (Chapter 7)
    - ▪ Operating system (Chapter 7)
    - ▪ Application server (Chapter 7)
    - ▪ Network infrastructure devices (Chapter 7)
  - o General purpose guides (Chapter 7)
- Defense-in-depth/layered security (Chapter 9)

- o Vendor diversity (Chapter 9)
- o Control diversity (Chapter 9)
  - ▪ Administrative (Chapter 9)
  - ▪ Technical (Chapter 9)
- o User training (Chapter 9)

3.2 Given a scenario, implement secure network architecture concepts. (Chapters 1, 3, 4, 8)
- Zones/topologies (Chapters 3, 4)
  - o DMZ (Chapter 3)
  - o Extranet (Chapter 3)
  - o Intranet (Chapter 3)
  - o Wireless (Chapter 4)
  - o Guest (Chapter 4)
  - o Honeynets (Chapter 4)
  - o NAT (Chapter 3)
  - o Ad hoc (Chapter 4)
- Segregation/segmentation/isolation (Chapters 1, 3)
  - o Physical (Chapter 3)
  - o Logical (VLAN) (Chapter 3)
  - o Virtualization (Chapter 1)
  - o Air gaps (Chapter 3)
- Tunneling/VPN (Chapter 4)
  - o Site-to-site (Chapter 4)
  - o Remote access (Chapter 4)
- Security device/technology placement (Chapters 3, 4, 8)
  - o Sensors (Chapter 4)
  - o Collectors (Chapter 4)
  - o Correlation engines (Chapter 8)
  - o Filters (Chapter 3)
  - o Proxies (Chapter 3)
  - o Firewalls (Chapter 3)
  - o VPN concentrators (Chapter 4)
  - o SSL accelerators (Chapter 4)
  - o Load balancers (Chapter 3)
  - o DDoS mitigator (Chapter 3)
  - o Aggregation switches (Chapter 3)
  - o Taps and port mirror (Chapter 4)
- SDN (Chapter 4)

3.3 Given a scenario, implement secure systems design. (Chapters 2, 3, 5)
- Hardware/firmware security (Chapter 5)
  - o FDE/SED (Chapter 5)
  - o TPM (Chapter 5)
  - o HSM (Chapter 5)
  - o UEFI/BIOS (Chapter 5)
  - o Secure boot and attestation (Chapter 5)
  - o Supply chain (Chapter 5)
  - o Hardware root of trust (Chapter 5)

- o EMI/EMP (Chapter 5)
- Operating systems (Chapters 2, 3, 5)
    - o Types (Chapter 5)
    - o Network (Chapter 5)
    - o Server (Chapter 5)
    - o Workstation (Chapter 5)
    - o Appliance (Chapter 5)
    - o Kiosk (Chapter 5)
    - o Mobile OS (Chapter 5)
    - o Patch management (Chapter 5)
    - o Disabling unnecessary ports and services (Chapter 3)
    - o Least functionality (Chapter 5)
    - o Secure configurations (Chapter 5)
    - o Trusted operating system (Chapter 5)
    - o Application whitelisting/blacklisting (Chapter 5)
    - o Disable default accounts/passwords (Chapter 2)
- Peripherals (Chapter 5)
    - o Wireless keyboards (Chapter 5)
    - o Wireless mice (Chapter 5)
    - o Displays (Chapter 5)
    - o WiFi-enabled MicroSD cards (Chapter 5)
    - o Printers/MFDs (Chapter 5)
    - o External storage devices (Chapter 5)
    - o Digital cameras (Chapter 5)

3.4 Explain the importance of secure staging deployment concepts. (Chapter 5)
- Sandboxing (Chapter 5)
- Environment (Chapter 5)
    - o Development (Chapter 5)
    - o Test (Chapter 5)
    - o Staging (Chapter 5)
    - o Production (Chapter 5)
- Secure baseline (Chapter 5)
- Integrity measurement (Chapter 5)

3.5 Explain the security implications of embedded systems. (Chapter 5)
- SCADA/ICS (Chapter 5)
- Smart devices/IoT (Chapter 5)
    - o Wearable technology (Chapter 5)
    - o Home automation (Chapter 5)
- HVAC (Chapter 5)
- SoC (Chapter 5)
- RTOS (Chapter 5)
- Printers/MFDs (Chapter 5)
- Camera systems (Chapter 5)
- Special purpose (Chapter 5)
    - o Medical devices (Chapter 5)
    - o Vehicles (Chapter 5)

      o Aircraft/UAV (Chapter 5)

3.6 Summarize secure application development and deployment concepts. (Chapter 7)
- Development life-cycle models (Chapter 7)
    - o Waterfall vs. Agile (Chapter 7)
- Secure DevOps (Chapter 7)
    - o Security automation (Chapter 7)
    - o Continuous integration (Chapter 7)
    - o Baselining (Chapter 7)
    - o Immutable systems (Chapter 7)
    - o Infrastructure as code (Chapter 7)
- Version control and change management (Chapter 7)
- Provisioning and deprovisioning (Chapter 7)
- Secure coding techniques (Chapter 7)
    - o Proper error handling (Chapter 7)
    - o Proper input validation (Chapter 7)
    - o Normalization (Chapter 7)
    - o Stored procedures (Chapter 7)
    - o Code signing (Chapter 7)
    - o Encryption (Chapter 7)
    - o Obfuscation/camouflage (Chapter 7)
    - o Code reuse/dead code (Chapter 7)
    - o Server-side vs. client-side execution and validation (Chapter 7)
    - o Memory management (Chapter 7)
    - o Use of third-party libraries and SDKs (Chapter 7)
    - o Data exposure (Chapter 7)
- Code quality and testing (Chapter 7)
    - o Static code analyzers (Chapter 7)
    - o Dynamic analysis (e.g., fuzzing) (Chapter 7)
    - o Stress testing (Chapter 7)
    - o Sandboxing (Chapter 7)
    - o Model verification (Chapter 7)
- Compiled vs. runtime code (Chapter 7)

3.7 Summarize cloud and virtualization concepts. (Chapters 1, 5)
- Hypervisor (Chapter 1)
    - o Type I (Chapter 1)
    - o Type II (Chapter 1)
    - o Application cells/containers (Chapter 1)
- VM sprawl avoidance (Chapter 1)
- VM escape protection (Chapter 1)
- Cloud storage (Chapter 5)
- Cloud deployment models (Chapter 5)
    - o SaaS (Chapter 5)
    - o PaaS (Chapter 5)
    - o IaaS (Chapter 5)
    - o Private (Chapter 5)
    - o Public (Chapter 5)

- ○ Hybrid (Chapter 5)
- ○ Community (Chapter 5)
- On-premise vs. hosted vs. cloud (Chapter 5)
- VDI/VDE (Chapter 1)
- Cloud access security broker (Chapter 5)
- Security as a Service (Chapter 5)

3.8 Explain how resiliency and automation strategies reduce risk. (Chapters 1, 5, 8, 9)
- Automation/scripting (Chapters 5, 8)
    - ○ Automated courses of action (Chapter 5)
    - ○ Continuous monitoring (Chapter 8)
    - ○ Configuration validation (Chapter 8)
- Templates (Chapter 5)
- Master image (Chapter 5)
- Non-persistence (Chapter 1)
    - ○ Snapshots (Chapter 1)
    - ○ Revert to known state (Chapter 1)
    - ○ Rollback to known configuration (Chapter 1)
    - ○ Live boot media (Chapter 5)
- Elasticity (Chapter 1)
- Scalability (Chapter 1)
- Distributive allocation (Chapter 9)
- Redundancy (Chapter 9)
- Fault tolerance (Chapter 9)
- High availability (Chapter 9)
- RAID (Chapter 9)

3.9 Explain the importance of physical security controls. (Chapters 6, 9)
- Lighting (Chapter 9)
- Signs (Chapter 9)
- Fencing/gate/cage (Chapter 9)
- Security guards (Chapter 9)
- Alarms (Chapter 9)
- Safe (Chapter 9)
- Secure cabinets/enclosures (Chapter 9)
- Protected distribution/Protected cabling (Chapter 9)
- Airgap (Chapter 9)
- Mantrap (Chapter 9)
- Faraday cage (Chapter 9)
- Lock types (Chapter 9)
- Biometrics (Chapter 9)
- Barricades/bollards (Chapter 9)
- Tokens/cards (Chapter 9)
- Environmental controls (Chapter 9)
    - ○ HVAC (Chapter 9)
    - ○ Hot and cold aisles (Chapter 9)
    - ○ Fire suppression (Chapter 9)
- Cable locks (Chapter 9)

- Screen filters (Chapter 6)
- Cameras (Chapter 9)
- Motion detection (Chapter 9)
- Logs (Chapter 9)
- Infrared detection (Chapter 9)
- Key management (Chapter 9)

4.0 Identity and Access Management 16%

4.1 Compare and contrast identity and access management concepts. (Chapter 2)
- Identification, authentication, authorization and accounting (AAA) (Chapter 2)
- Multifactor authentication (Chapter 2)
    - Something you are (Chapter 2)
    - Something you have (Chapter 2)
    - Something you know (Chapter 2)
    - Somewhere you are (Chapter 2)
    - Something you do (Chapter 2)
- Federation (Chapter 2)
- Single sign-on (Chapter 2)
- Transitive trust (Chapter 2)

4.2 Given a scenario, install and configure identity and access services. (Chapters 2, 4)
- LDAP (Chapter 2)
- Kerberos (Chapter 2)
- TACACS+ (Chapter 4)
- CHAP (Chapter 4)
- PAP (Chapter 4)
- MSCHAP (Chapter 4)
- RADIUS (Chapter 4)
- SAML (Chapter 2)
- OpenID Connect (Chapter 2)
- OAUTH (Chapter 2)
- Shibboleth (Chapter 2)
- Secure token (Chapter 2)
- NTLM (Chapter 2)

4.3 Given a scenario, implement identity and access management controls. (Chapters 2, 4, 5, 9)
- Access control models (Chapter 2)
    - MAC (Chapter 2)
    - DAC (Chapter 2)
    - ABAC (Chapter 2)
    - Role-based access control (Chapter 2)
    - Rule-based access control (Chapter 2)
- Physical access control (Chapter 9)
    - Proximity cards (Chapter 9)
    - Smart cards (Chapter 9)
- Biometric factors (Chapter 2)
    - Fingerprint scanner (Chapter 2)

- o Retinal scanner (Chapter 2)
- o Iris scanner (Chapter 2)
- o Voice recognition (Chapter 2)
- o Facial recognition (Chapter 2)
- o False acceptance rate (Chapter 2)
- o False rejection rate (Chapter 2)
- o Crossover error rate (Chapter 2)
- Tokens (Chapter 2)
  - o Hardware (Chapter 2)
  - o Software (Chapter 2)
  - o HOTP/TOTP (Chapter 2)
- Certificate-based authentication (Chapters 2, 4)
  - o PIV/CAC/smart card (Chapter 2)
  - o IEEE 802.1x (Chapter 4)
- File system security (Chapter 5)
- Database security (Chapter 5)

4.4 Given a scenario, differentiate common account management practices. (Chapters 2, 8, 11)

- Account types (Chapter 2)
- User account (Chapter 2)
  - o Shared and generic accounts/credentials (Chapter 2)
  - o Guest accounts (Chapter 2)
  - o Service accounts (Chapter 2)
  - o Privileged accounts (Chapter 2)
- General Concepts (Chapters 2, 11)
  - o Least privilege (Chapter 2)
  - o Onboarding/offboarding (Chapter 11)
  - o Permission auditing and review (Chapter 8)
  - o Usage auditing and review (Chapter 8)
  - o Time-of-day restrictions (Chapter 2)
  - o Recertification (Chapter 2)
  - o Standard naming convention (Chapter 2)
  - o Account maintenance (Chapter 2)
  - o Group-based access control (Chapter 2)
  - o Location-based policies (Chapter 2)
- Account policy enforcement (Chapter 2)
  - o Credential management (Chapter 2)
  - o Group policy (Chapter 2)
  - o Password complexity (Chapter 2)
  - o Expiration (Chapter 2)
  - o Recovery (Chapter 2)
  - o Disablement (Chapter 2)
  - o Lockout (Chapter 2)
  - o Password history (Chapter 2)
  - o Password reuse (Chapter 2)
  - o Password length (Chapter 2)

5.0 Risk Management 14%

5.1 Explain the importance of policies, plans and procedures related to organizational security. (Chapter 11)
- Standard operating procedure (Chapter 11)
- Agreement types (Chapter 11)
    - o BPA (Chapter 11)
    - o SLA (Chapter 11)
    - o ISA (Chapter 11)
    - o MOU/MOA (Chapter 11)
- Personnel management (Chapter 11)
    - o Mandatory vacations (Chapter 11)
    - o Job rotation (Chapter 11)
    - o Separation of duties (Chapter 11)
    - o Clean desk (Chapter 11)
    - o Background checks (Chapter 11)
    - o Exit interviews (Chapter 11)
    - o Role-based awareness training (Chapter 11)
        - ▪ Data owner (Chapter 11)
        - ▪ System administrator (Chapter 11)
        - ▪ System owner (Chapter 11)
        - ▪ User (Chapter 11)
        - ▪ Privileged user (Chapter 11)
        - ▪ Executive user (Chapter 11)
    - o NDA (Chapter 11)
    - o Onboarding (Chapter 11)
    - o Continuing education (Chapter 11)
    - o Acceptable use policy/rules of behavior (Chapter 11)
    - o Adverse actions (Chapter 11)
- General security policies (Chapter 11)
    - o Social media networks/applications (Chapter 11)
    - o Personal email (Chapter 11)

5.2 Summarize business impact analysis concepts. (Chapter 9)
- RTO/RPO (Chapter 9)
- MTBF (Chapter 9)
- MTTR (Chapter 9)
- Mission-essential functions (Chapter 9)
- Identification of critical systems (Chapter 9)
- Single point of failure (Chapter 9)
- Impact (Chapter 9)
    - o Life (Chapter 9)
    - o Property (Chapter 9)
    - o Safety (Chapter 9)
    - o Finance (Chapter 9)
    - o Reputation (Chapter 9)
- Privacy impact assessment (Chapter 9)

- Privacy threshold assessment (Chapter 9)

5.3 Explain risk management processes and concepts. (Chapters 5, 8)

- Threat assessment (Chapter 8)
  - o Environmental (Chapter 8)
  - o Manmade (Chapter 8)
  - o Internal vs. external (Chapter 8)
- Risk assessment (Chapter 8)
  - o SLE (Chapter 8)
  - o ALE (Chapter 8)
  - o ARO (Chapter 8)
  - o Asset value (Chapter 8)
  - o Risk register (Chapter 8)
  - o Likelihood of occurrence (Chapter 8)
  - o Supply chain assessment (Chapter 8)
  - o Impact (Chapter 8)
  - o Quantitative (Chapter 8)
  - o Qualitative (Chapter 8)
  - o Testing (Chapter 8)
    - ▪ Penetration testing authorization (Chapter 8)
    - ▪ Vulnerability testing authorization (Chapter 8)
  - o Risk response techniques (Chapter 8)
    - ▪ Accept (Chapter 8)
    - ▪ Transfer (Chapter 8)
    - ▪ Avoid (Chapter 8)
    - ▪ Mitigate (Chapter 8)
- Change management (Chapter 5)

5.4 Given a scenario, follow incident response procedures. (Chapter 11)

- Incident response plan (Chapter 11)
  - o Documented incident types/category definitions (Chapter 11)
  - o Roles and responsibilities (Chapter 11)
  - o Reporting requirements/escalation (Chapter 11)
  - o Cyber-incident response teams (Chapter 11)
  - o Exercise (Chapter 11)
- Incident response process (Chapter 11)
  - o Preparation (Chapter 11)
  - o Identification (Chapter 11)
  - o Containment (Chapter 11)
  - o Eradication (Chapter 11)
  - o Recovery (Chapter 11)
  - o Lessons learned (Chapter 11)

5.5 Summarize basic concepts of forensics. (Chapter 11)

- Order of volatility (Chapter 11)
- Chain of custody (Chapter 11)
- Legal hold (Chapter 11)
- Data acquisition (Chapter 11)
  - o Capture system image (Chapter 11)

- o Network traffic and logs (Chapter 11)
- o Capture video (Chapter 11)
- o Record time offset (Chapter 11)
- o Take hashes (Chapter 11)
- o Screenshots (Chapter 11)
- o Witness interviews (Chapter 11)
- Preservation (Chapter 11)
- Recovery (Chapter 11)
- Strategic intelligence/counterintelligence gathering (Chapter 11)
  - o Active logging (Chapter 11)
- Track man-hours (Chapter 11)

5.6 Explain disaster recovery and continuity of operation concepts. (Chapter 9)
- Recovery sites (Chapter 9)
  - o Hot site (Chapter 9)
  - o Warm site (Chapter 9)
  - o Cold site (Chapter 9)
- Order of restoration (Chapter 9)
- Backup concepts (Chapter 9)
  - o Differential (Chapter 9)
  - o Incremental (Chapter 9)
  - o Snapshots (Chapter 9)
  - o Full (Chapter 9)
- Geographic considerations (Chapter 9)
  - o Off-site backups (Chapter 9)
  - o Distance (Chapter 9)
  - o Location selection (Chapter 9)
  - o Legal implications (Chapter 9)
  - o Data sovereignty (Chapter 9)
- Continuity of operation planning (Chapter 9)
  - o Exercises/tabletop (Chapter 9)
  - o After-action reports (Chapter 9)
  - o Failover (Chapter 9)
  - o Alternate processing sites (Chapter 9)
  - o Alternate business practices (Chapter 9)

5.7 Compare and contrast various types of controls. (Chapter 1)
- Deterrent (Chapter 1)
- Preventive (Chapter 1)
- Detective (Chapter 1)
- Corrective (Chapter 1)
- Compensating (Chapter 1)
- Technical (Chapter 1)
- Administrative (Chapter 1)
- Physical (Chapter 1)

5.8 Given a scenario, carry out data security and privacy practices. (Chapter 11)
- Data destruction and media sanitization (Chapter 11)
  - o Burning (Chapter 11)

- o Shredding (Chapter 11)
- o Pulping (Chapter 11)
- o Pulverizing (Chapter 11)
- o Degaussing (Chapter 11)
- o Purging (Chapter 11)
- o Wiping (Chapter 11)
- Data sensitivity labeling and handling (Chapter 11)
    - o Confidential (Chapter 11)
    - o Private (Chapter 11)
    - o Public (Chapter 11)
    - o Proprietary (Chapter 11)
    - o PII (Chapter 11)
    - o PHI (Chapter 11)
- Data roles (Chapter 11)
    - o Owner (Chapter 11)
    - o Steward/custodian (Chapter 11)
    - o Privacy officer (Chapter 11)
- Data retention (Chapter 11)
- Legal and compliance (Chapter 11)

6.0 Cryptography and PKI 12%

6.1 Compare and contrast basic concepts of cryptography. (Chapters 1, 2, 7, 10)
- Symmetric algorithms (Chapter 10)
- Modes of operation (Chapter 10)
- Asymmetric algorithms (Chapter 10)
- Hashing (Chapter 10)
- Salt, IV, nonce (Chapter 10)
- Elliptic curve (Chapter 10)
- Weak/deprecated algorithms (Chapter 10)
- Key exchange (Chapter 10)
- Digital signatures (Chapter 10)
- Diffusion (Chapter 10)
- Confusion (Chapter 10)
- Collision (Chapter 7)
- Steganography (Chapter 10)
- Obfuscation (Chapter 10)
- Stream vs. block (Chapter 10)
- Key strength (Chapter 10)
- Session keys (Chapter 10)
- Ephemeral key (Chapter 10)
- Secret algorithm (Chapter 10)
- Data-in-transit (Chapter 10)
- Data-at-rest (Chapter 10)
- Data-in-use (Chapter 10)
- Random/pseudo-random number generation (Chapter 10)
- Key stretching (Chapter 10)

- Implementation vs. algorithm selection (Chapter 10)
    - o Crypto service provider (Chapter 10)
    - o Crypto modules (Chapter 10)
- Perfect forward secrecy (Chapter 10)
- Security through obscurity (Chapter 10)
- Common use cases (Chapter 1)
    - o Low power devices (Chapter 10)
    - o Low latency (Chapter 10)
    - o High resiliency (Chapter 10)
    - o Supporting confidentiality (Chapter 1)
    - o Supporting integrity (Chapter 1)
    - o Supporting obfuscation (Chapter 1)
    - o Supporting authentication (Chapter 2)
    - o Supporting non-repudiation (Chapter 1)
    - o Resource vs. security constraints (Chapter 1)

6.2 Explain cryptography algorithms and their basic characteristics. (Chapter 10)
- Symmetric algorithms (Chapter 10)
    - o AES (Chapter 10)
    - o DES (Chapter 10)
    - o 3DES (Chapter 10)
    - o RC4 (Chapter 10)
    - o Blowfish/Twofish (Chapter 10)
- Cipher modes (Chapter 10)
    - o CBC (Chapter 10)
    - o GCM (Chapter 10)
    - o ECB (Chapter 10)
    - o CTM (Chapter 10)
    - o Stream vs. block (Chapter 10)
- Asymmetric algorithms (Chapter 10)
    - o RSA (Chapter 10)
    - o DSA (Chapter 10)
    - o Diffie-Hellman (Chapter 10)
        - ▪ Groups (Chapter 10)
        - ▪ DHE (Chapter 10)
        - ▪ ECDHE (Chapter 10)
    - o Elliptic curve (Chapter 10)
    - o PGP/GPG (Chapter 10)
- Hashing algorithms (Chapter 10)
    - o MD5 (Chapter 10)
    - o SHA (Chapter 10)
    - o HMAC (Chapter 10)
    - o RIPEMD (Chapter 10)
- Key stretching algorithms (Chapter 10)
    - o BCRYPT (Chapter 10)
    - o PBKDF2 (Chapter 10)
- Obfuscation (Chapter 10)

- o User (Chapter 10)
- o Root (Chapter 10)
- o Domain validation (Chapter 10)
- o Extended validation (Chapter 10)
- Certificate formats (Chapter 10)
  - o DER (Chapter 10)
  - o PEM (Chapter 10)
  - o PFX (Chapter 10)
  - o CER (Chapter 10)
  - o P12 (Chapter 10)
  - o P7B (Chapter 10)

Recertification Requirements

The CompTIA Security+ certification was previously a lifetime certification. You passed the exam once and you were certified for life. However, for anyone taking the exam after January 1, 2011, the certification expires after three years unless it is renewed.

You can renew the certification by either taking the next version of the exam or by enrolling in CompTIA's new Continuing Education (CE) program. You will be required to pay an annual fee of $50 and earn a minimum of 50 Continuing Education Units (CEUs). You can earn CEUs through a variety of activities. Some examples include presenting or teaching topics to others, attending training sessions, participating in industry events or seminars, or writing relevant articles, white papers, blogs, or books.

For full details, check out the CompTIA web site: *http://certification.comptia.org/*. Unfortunately, CompTIA frequently changes their URLs so I didn't list the specific URL for CEU policies. However, you can usually find it by searching on their site or using their Contact Us page.

Becoming a CompTIA Certified IT Professional is Easy

It's also the best way to reach greater professional opportunities and rewards.

Why Get CompTIA Certified?

Growing Demand

Labor estimates predict some technology fields will experience growth of over 20% by the year 2020.* CompTIA certification qualifies the skills required to join this workforce.

Higher Salaries

IT professionals with certifications on their resume command better jobs, earn higher salaries and have more doors open to new multi-industry opportunities.

Verified Strengths

91% of hiring managers indicate CompTIA certifications are valuable in validating IT expertise, making certification the best way to demonstrate your competency and knowledge to employers.**

Universal Skills

CompTIA certifications are vendor neutral— which means that certified professionals can proficiently work with an extensive variety of hardware and software found in most organizations.

Learn more about what the exam covers by reviewing the following:

- Exam objectives for key study points.

- Sample questions for a general overview of what to expect on the exam and examples of question format.

- Visit online forums, like LinkedIn, to see what other IT professionals say about CompTIA exams.

Purchase a voucher at a Pearson VUE testing center or at CompTIAstore.com.

- Register for your exam at a Pearson VUE testing center:

- Visit pearsonvue.com/CompTIA to find the closest testing center to you.

- Schedule the exam online. You will be required to enter your voucher number or provide payment information at registration.

- Take your certification exam.

Congratulations on your CompTIA certification!

- Make sure to add your certification to your resume.

- Check out the CompTIA Certification Roadmap to plan your next career move.

Learn more: **Certification.CompTIA.org/securityplus**

* Source: CompTIA 9th Annual Information Security Trends study: 500 U.S. IT and Business Executives Responsible for Security

** Source: CompTIA Employer Perceptions of IT Training and Certification

Pre-Assessment Exam

Use this assessment exam to test your knowledge of the topics before you start reading the book, and again before you take the live exam. An answer key with explanations is available at the end of the assessment exam.

1. Management within your organization has defined a use case to support confidentiality of PII stored in a database. Which of the following solutions will BEST meet this need?
   A. Hashing
   B. Digital signature
   C. Encryption
   D. Smart card

2. Management has implemented a policy stating that messages sent between upper-level executives must arrive without any changes. The IT department is tasked with implementing technical controls to meet this need. Which security goal does this policy address?
   A. Confidentiality
   B. Integrity
   C. Availability
   D. Authentication

3. Your organization recently implemented two servers that act as failover devices for each other. Which security goal is your organization pursuing?
   A. Obfuscation
   B. Integrity
   C. Confidentiality
   D. Availability

4. You are tasked with improving the overall security for a database server. Which of the following is a preventive control that will assist with this goal?
   A. Disabling unnecessary services
   B. Identifying the initial baseline configuration
   C. Monitoring logs for trends
   D. Implementing a backup and restoration plan

5. An IT department recently had its hardware budget reduced, but the organization still expects them to maintain availability of services. Which of the following choices would BEST help them maintain availability with a reduced budget?
    A. Failover clusters
    B. Virtualization
    C. Bollards
    D. Hashing

6. You want to test new security controls before deploying them. Which of the following technologies provides the MOST flexibility to meet this goal?
    A. Baselines
    B. Hardening techniques
    C. Virtualization technologies
    D. Patch management programs

7. You suspect that traffic in your network is being rerouted to an unauthorized router within your network. Which of the following command-line tools would help you narrow down the problem?
    A. ping
    B. tracert
    C. ipconfig
    D. netstat

8. The First Bank of Springfield has been experiencing widespread fraud recently. Attackers are transferring funds out of customer accounts to other banks. The bank began requiring customers to obtain credentials in person at the bank. However, this hasn't reduced the number of fraudulent transactions. After reviewing available logs, investigators determined that these fraudulent transactions are conducted with the customer's actual credentials. Which of the following security controls should be strengthened to reduce these incidents?
    A. Authentication
    B. Identification
    C. Accounting
    D. Authorization

9. An outside security auditor recently completed an in-depth security audit on your network. One of the issues he reported was related to passwords. Specifically, he found the following passwords used on the network: Pa$$, 1@W2, and G7bT3. Which of the following should be changed to avoid the problem shown with these passwords?
    A. Password complexity
    B. Password length
    C. Password history
    D. Password reuse

10. When you log on to your online bank account, you are also able to access a partner's credit card site, check-ordering services, and a mortgage site without entering your credentials again. Which of the following does this describe?
    A. SSO
    B. Same sign-on
    C. SAML
    D. Kerberos

11. Your network uses an authentication service based on the X.500 specification. When encrypted, it uses TLS. Which authentication service is your network using?
    A. SAML
    B. Diameter
    C. Kerberos
    D. LDAP

12. You're asked to identify who is accessing a spreadsheet containing employee salary data. Detailed logging is configured correctly on this file. However, you are unable to identify a specific person who is accessing the file. Which of the following is the MOST likely reason?
    A. Shared accounts are not prohibited.
    B. Guest accounts are disabled.
    C. Permissions for the file were assigned to a group.
    D. Account lockout has been enabled.

13. Interns from a local college frequently work at your company. Some interns work with the database developers, some interns work with the web application developers, and some interns work with both developers. Interns working with the database developers require specific privileges, and interns working with the web application developers require different privileges. Which of the following is the simplest method to meet these requirements?
    A. Use generic accounts.
    B. Create user-based privileges.
    C. Use group-based privileges.
    D. Grant the interns access to the Guest account.

14. You are configuring a file server used to share files and folders among employees within your organization. However, employees should not be able to access all folders on this server. Which of the following choices is the BEST method to manage security for these folders?
    A. Assign permissions to each user as needed.
    B. Wait for users to request permission and then assign the appropriate permissions.
    C. Delegate authority to assign these permissions.
    D. Use security groups with appropriate permissions.

15. The Retirement Castle uses groups for ease of administration and management. They recently hired Jasper as their new accountant. Jasper needs access to all the files and folders used by the Accounting department. Which of the following should the administrator do to give Jasper appropriate access?

    A. Create an account for Jasper and add the account to the Accounting group.

    B. Give Jasper the password for the Guest account.

    C. Create an account for Jasper and use rule-based access control for accounting.

    D. Create an account for Jasper and add the account to the Administrators group.

16. You need to send several large files containing proprietary data to a business partner. Which of the following is the BEST choice for this task?

    A. FTP

    B. SNMPv3

    C. SFTP

    D. SRTP

17. Your organization is planning to establish a secure link between one of your mail servers and a business partner's mail server. The connection will use the Internet. Which protocol is the BEST choice?

    A. TLS

    B. SMTP

    C. HTTP

    D. SSH

18. Bart is adding a DMZ into his organization's network. Which of the following is the BEST description of why he would do so?

    A. To increase security for servers accessed from public networks

    B. To provide a secure physical location for networking equipment

    C. To lure attackers to a fake server or fake network

    D. To cache data retrieved from a web server

19. Your organization wants to prevent employees from accessing file sharing web sites. Which of the following choices will meet this need?

    A. Content inspection

    B. Malware inspection

    C. URL filter

    D. Web application firewall

20. Your organization hosts several web servers in a web farm. They have recently been attacked, resulting in unacceptable downtime. Management wants to implement a solution that will provide protection for the web farm and include load balancing to improve the overall performance of the web farm. Which of the following will BEST meet this need?

    A. Stateless firewall

    B. Stateful firewall

    C. Web application firewall

    D. Host-based firewall

21. Management suspects that employees have been sending proprietary data out of the network via email. They want to implement a solution that will detect and block similar incidents in the future. Which of the following is the BEST choice to meet this need?
    A. Mail gateway
    B. UTM appliance
    C. Forward proxy
    D. Reverse proxy

22. You are tasked with configuring a switch so that it separates VoIP and data traffic. Which of the following provides the BEST solution?
    A. NAC
    B. DMZ
    C. SRTP
    D. VLAN

23. Your organization hosts an e-commerce business that has become quite successful recently. It includes a web farm and a database server within the DMZ. IT management is concerned that there isn't enough staff working around the clock to protect these servers. Which of the following would provide the BEST automated protection for these servers?
    A. NIDS and HIDS
    B. NIPS and HIPS
    C. SIEM and NIPS
    D. SIEM and NIDS

24. Management is concerned about malicious activity and wants to implement a security control that will detect unusual traffic on the network. Which of the following is the BEST choice to meet this goal?
    A. Network-based firewall
    B. Signature-based IDS
    C. Anomaly-based IDS
    D. Honeynet

25. Of the following choices, what can you use to divert malicious attacks on your network away from valuable data to worthless, fabricated data?
    A. IPS
    B. Proxy server
    C. Web application firewall
    D. Honeypot

26. Your organization frequently has guests visiting in various conference rooms throughout the building. These guests need access to the Internet via the wireless network, but should not be able to access internal network resources. Employees need access to both the internal network and the Internet. Which of the following would BEST meet this need?
    A. NAT
    B. DMZ
    C. VPN
    D. 802.1x

27. Management asks you if you can modify the wireless network to prevent users from easily discovering it. Which of the following would you modify to meet this goal?
    A. CCMP
    B. WPA2 Enterprise
    C. SSID broadcast
    D. MAC address filter

28. Marge, a security administrator, is tasked with ensuring that all devices have updated virus definition files before they can access network resources. Which of the following technologies would help her accomplish this goal?
    A. NIDS
    B. NAC
    C. DLP
    D. DMZ

29. Your organization is hosting a wireless network with an 802.1x server using PEAP. On Thursday, users report they can no longer access the wireless network, but they could access it on the previous day. Administrators verified the network configuration matches the baseline, there aren't any hardware outages, and the wired network is operational. Which of the following is the MOST likely cause for this problem?
    A. The RADIUS server certificate expired.
    B. DNS is providing incorrect host names.
    C. DHCP is issuing duplicate IP addresses.
    D. MAC filtering is enabled.

30. Lisa has created an application on her development computer. She wants to test it on a Linux-based computer she commonly uses for testing. However, she wants to ensure it is isolated when she tests it. Which of the following is the BEST solution to meet her needs?
    A. Use chroot.
    B. Sideload the application.
    C. Use FDE.
    D. Use chmod.

31. Your organization recently purchased some laptops that include a TPM. Which of the following BEST identifies what the TPM provides?
    A. Detection of unauthorized data transfers
    B. A hardware root of trust
    C. Sandboxing
    D. An external security device used to store cryptographic keys

32. Your organization has recently rented access to computing resources via a cloud. Administrators within your organization apply patches to the operating system. Which of the following choices BEST describes this cloud deployment model?
    A. Community
    B. Software as a Service
    C. Infrastructure as a Service
    D. Hybrid

33. Homer noticed that several generators within the nuclear power plant have been turning on without user interaction. Security investigators discovered that an unauthorized file was installed, causing these generators to start at timed intervals. Further, they determined this file was installed during a visit by external engineers. What should Homer recommend to mitigate this threat in the future?

    A. Create an internal CA.
    B. Implement WPA2 Enterprise.
    C. Implement patch management processes.
    D. Configure the SCADA within a VLAN.

34. Management wants to ensure that employees do not print any documents that include customer or employee PII. Which of the following solutions would meet this goal?

    A. HSM
    B. TPM
    C. VLAN
    D. DLP

35. A tech company recently discovered an attack on its organization, resulting in a significant data breach of customer data. After investigating the attack, they realized it was very sophisticated and likely originated from a foreign country. Which of the following identifies the MOST likely threat actor in this attack?

    A. Hacktivist
    B. APT
    C. Competitors
    D. Insiders

36. A recent antivirus scan on a server detected a Trojan. A technician removed the Trojan, but a security administrator expressed concern that unauthorized personnel might be able to access data on the server. The security administrator decided to check the server further. Of the following choices, what is the administrator MOST likely looking for on this server?

    A. Backdoor
    B. Logic bomb
    C. Rootkit
    D. Botnet

37. After Marge turned on her computer, she saw a message indicating that unless she made a payment, her hard drive would be formatted. What does this indicate?

    A. Keylogger
    B. Ransomware
    C. Backdoor
    D. Trojan

38. An organization's security policy requires employees to place all discarded paper documents in containers for temporary storage. These papers are later burned in an incinerator. Which of the following attacks are these actions MOST likely trying to prevent?
    A. Shoulder surfing
    B. Tailgating
    C. Vishing
    D. Dumpster diving

39. Users in your organization have reported receiving a similar email from the same sender. The email included a link, but after recent training on emerging threats, all the users chose not to click the link. Security investigators determined the link was malicious and was designed to download ransomware. Which of the following BEST describes the email?
    A. Phishing
    B. Spear phishing
    C. Spam
    D. Vishing

40. Your local library is planning to purchase new computers that patrons can use for Internet research. Which of the following are the BEST choices to protect these computers? (Select TWO.)
    A. Mantrap
    B. Anti-malware software
    C. Cable locks
    D. Disk encryption

41. You are troubleshooting an intermittent connectivity issue with a web server. After examining the logs, you identify repeated connection attempts from various IP addresses. You realize these connection attempts are overloading the server, preventing it from responding to other connections. Which of the following is MOST likely occurring?
    A. DDoS attack
    B. DoS attack
    C. Amplification attack
    D. Salting attack

42. You are reviewing security controls and their usefulness. You notice that account lockout policies are in place. Which of the following attacks will these policies thwart? (Select TWO.)
    A. DNS poisoning
    B. Replay
    C. Brute force
    D. Buffer overflow
    E. Dictionary

43. Security analysts recently discovered that users in your organization are inadvertently installing malware on their systems after visiting the comptai.org web site. Users have a legitimate requirement to visit the comptia.org web site. Which of the following is the MOST likely explanation for this activity?
    A. Smurf
    B. Typo squatting
    C. Fuzzing
    D. Replay

44. An attacker recently attacked a web server hosted by your company. After investigation, security professionals determined that the attacker used a previously unknown application exploit. Which of the following BEST identifies this attack?
    A. Buffer overflow
    B. Zero-day attack
    C. Man-in-the-browser
    D. Session hijacking

45. While reviewing logs for a web application, a developer notices that it has crashed several times reporting a memory error. Shortly after it crashes, the logs show malicious code that isn't part of a known application. Which of the following is MOST likely occurring?
    A. Buffer overflow
    B. ARP poisoning
    C. Privilege escalation
    D. Replay

46. Management at your organization is planning to hire a development firm to create a sophisticated web application. One of their primary goals is to ensure that personnel involved with the project frequently collaborate with each other throughout the project. Which of the following is an appropriate model for this project?
    A. Waterfall
    B. SDLC
    C. Agile
    D. Secure DevOps

47. Your organization is preparing to deploy a web-based application, which will accept user input. Which of the following will BEST test the reliability of this application to maintain availability and data integrity?
    A. Model verification
    B. Input validation
    C. Error handling
    D. Dynamic analysis

48. An attacker has launched several successful XSS attacks on a web application within your DMZ. Which of the following are the BEST choices to protect the web server and prevent this attack? (Select TWO.)
    A. Dynamic code analysis
    B. Input validation
    C. Code obfuscation
    D. WAF
    E. Normalization

49. Ziffcorp is developing a new technology that they expect to become a huge success when it's released. The CIO is concerned about someone stealing their company secrets related to this technology. Which of the following will help the CIO identify potential dangers related to the loss of this technology?
    A. Threat assessment
    B. Vulnerability assessment
    C. Privacy threshold assessment
    D. Privacy impact assessment

50. You are performing a risk assessment and you need to calculate the average expected loss of an incident. Which of the following value combinations would you MOST likely use?
    A. ALE and ARO
    B. ALE and SLE
    C. SLE and ARO
    D. ARO and ROI

51. You recently completed a vulnerability scan on your network. It reported that several servers are missing key operating system patches. However, after checking the servers, you've verified the servers have these patches installed. Which of the following BEST describes this?
    A. False negative
    B. Misconfiguration on servers
    C. False positive
    D. Non-credentialed scan

52. You want to identify all the services running on a server in your network. Which of the following tools is the BEST choice to meet this goal?
    A. Penetration test
    B. Protocol analyzer
    C. Sniffer
    D. Port scanner

53. Lisa needs to identify if a risk exists within a web application and identify potential misconfigurations on the server. However, she should passively test the security controls. Which of the following is the BEST choice to meet her needs?
    A. Perform a penetration test.
    B. Perform a port scan.
    C. Perform a vulnerability scan.
    D. Perform traffic analysis with a sniffer.

54. A network administrator needs to identify the type of traffic and packet flags used in traffic sent from a specific IP address. Which of the following is the BEST tool to meet this need?
    A. SIEM
    B. Netcat
    C. Protocol analyzer
    D. Vulnerability scan

55. Lisa has been hired as a penetration tester by your organization to test the security of a web server. She wants to identify the operating system and get some information on services and applications used by the server. Which of the following tools will BEST meet this need?
    A. SIEM
    B. Netcat
    C. Tcpdump
    D. Gray box test

56. An organization wants to provide protection against malware attacks. Administrators have installed antivirus software on all computers. Additionally, they implemented a firewall and an IDS on the network. Which of the following BEST identifies this principle?
    A. Implicit deny
    B. Layered security
    C. Least privilege
    D. Flood guard

57. A security professional needs to identify a physical security control that will identify and authenticate individuals before allowing them to pass, and restrict passage to only a single person at a time. Which of the following should the professional recommend?
    A. Tailgating
    B. Smart cards
    C. Biometrics
    D. Mantrap

58. Your company's web site experiences a large number of client requests during certain times of the year. Which of the following could your company add to ensure the web site's availability during these times?
    A. Fail-open cluster
    B. Certificates
    C. Web application firewall
    D. Load balancing

59. Which of the following is the LOWEST cost solution for fault tolerance?
    A. Load balancing
    B. Round-robin scheduling
    C. RAID
    D. Warm site

60. Employees access a secure area by entering a cipher code, but this code does not identify individuals. After a recent security incident, management has decided to implement a key card system that will identify individuals who enter and exit this secure area. However, the installation might take six months or longer. Which of the following choices can the organization install immediately to identify individuals who enter or exit the secure area?
    A. Mantrap
    B. Access list
    C. CCTV
    D. Bollards

61. An organization has decided to increase the amount of customer data it maintains and use it for targeted sales. The privacy officer has determined that this data is PII. Which type of assessment should be completed to ensure the organization is complying with applicable laws and regulations related to this data?
    A. Privacy impact assessment
    B. Privacy threshold assessment
    C. Threat assessment
    D. Supply chain assessment

62. A security technician runs an automated script every night designed to detect changes in files. Of the following choices, what are the MOST LIKELY protocols used in this script?
    A. PGP and SHA
    B. ECC and HMAC
    C. AES and Twofish
    D. SHA and HMAC

63. An application requires users to log on with passwords. The application developers want to store the passwords in such a way that it will thwart rainbow table attacks. Which of the following is the BEST solution?
    A. SHA
    B. Blowfish
    C. ECC
    D. Bcrypt

64. Which of the following cryptography concepts indicates that ciphertext is significantly different than plaintext after it has been encrypted?
    A. Diffusion
    B. Obfuscation
    C. Collision
    D. Confusion

65. Your organization is investigating possible methods of sharing encryption keys over a public network. Which of the following is the BEST choice?
    A. CRL
    B. PBKDF2
    C. Hashing
    D. ECDHE

66. An application developer is working on the cryptographic elements of an application. She needs to implement an encryption algorithm that provides both confidentiality and data authenticity. Which of the following cipher modes supports these goals?
    A. CTM
    B. CBC
    C. ECB
    D. GCM

67. An organization hosts several web servers in a web farm used for e-commerce. Due to recent attacks, management is concerned that attackers might try to redirect web site traffic, allowing the attackers to impersonate their e-commerce site. Which of the following methods will address this issue?
    A. Stapling
    B. Perfect forward secrecy
    C. Pinning
    D. Key stretching

68. Users within an organization frequently access public web servers using HTTPS. Management wants to ensure that users can verify that certificates are valid even if the public CAs are temporarily unavailable. Which of the following should be implemented to meet this need?
    A. OCSP
    B. CRL
    C. Private CA
    D. CSR

69. A security auditor discovered that several employees in the Accounting department can print and sign checks. In her final report, she recommended restricting the number of people who can print checks and the number of people who can sign them. She also recommended that no one should be authorized to print and sign checks. Which security policy does this describe?
    A. Discretionary access control
    B. Rule-based access control
    C. Separation of duties
    D. Job rotation

70. Your organization includes a software development division within the IT department. One developer writes and maintains applications for the Sales and Marketing departments. A second developer writes and maintains applications for the Payroll department. Once a year, they have to switch roles for at least a month. What is the purpose of this practice?
    A. To enforce a separation of duties policy
    B. To enforce a mandatory vacation policy
    C. To enforce a job rotation policy
    D. To enforce an acceptable use policy

71. Your organization is considering storage of sensitive data with a cloud provider. Your organization wants to ensure the data is encrypted while at rest and while in transit. Which type of interoperability agreement can your organization use to ensure the data is encrypted while in transit?
    A. SLA
    B. BPA
    C. MOU
    D. ISA

72. You work as a help-desk professional in a large organization. You have begun to receive an extraordinary number of calls from employees related to malware. Using common incident response procedures, which of the following should be your FIRST response?
    A. Preparation
    B. Identification
    C. Eradication
    D. Recovery

73. An incident response team is following typical incident response procedures. Which of the following phases is the BEST choice for analyzing an incident with a goal of identifying steps to prevent a reoccurrence of the incident?
    A. Preparation
    B. Identification
    C. Eradication
    D. Lessons learned

74. You are helping your organization create a security policy for incident response. Which of the following choices is the BEST choice to include when an incident requires confiscation of a physical asset?
    A. Ensure hashes are taken first.
    B. Ensure witnesses sign an AUP.
    C. Maintain the order of volatility.
    D. Keep a record of everyone who took possession of the physical asset.

75. Security personnel confiscated a user's workstation after a security incident. Administrators removed the hard drive for forensic analysis, but left it unattended for several hours before capturing an image. Which of the following could prevent the company from taking the employee to court over this incident?
    A. Witnesses were not identified.
    B. A chain of custody was not maintained.
    C. An order of volatility was not maintained.
    D. A hard drive analysis was not complete.

Assessment Exam Answers

When checking your answers, take the time to read the explanations. Understanding the explanations will help ensure you're prepared for the live exam. The explanation also shows the chapter or chapters where you can get more detailed information on the topic.

1. **C.** Encryption is the best choice to provide confidentiality of any type of information, including Personally Identifiable Information (PII) stored in a database. Hashing will support a use case of supporting integrity. Digital signatures will support a use case of supporting non-repudiation. A smart card will support a use case of supporting authentication. See Chapter 1.

2. **B.** Integrity provides assurances that data has not been modified and integrity is commonly enforced with hashing. Confidentiality prevents unauthorized disclosure of data, but doesn't address modifications of data. Availability ensures systems are up and operational when needed and uses fault tolerance and redundancy methods. Authentication provides proof that users are who they claim to be. See Chapter 1.

3. **D.** Failover devices increase availability. A failover cluster uses redundant servers to ensure a service will continue to operate even if one of the servers fails. Obfuscation methods attempt to make something unclear or difficult to understand and are not related to failover devices. Integrity methods ensure that data has not been modified. Confidentiality methods such as encryption prevent the unauthorized disclosure of data. See Chapter 1.

4. **A.** Disabling unnecessary services is one of several steps you can take to harden a server. It is a preventive control because it helps prevent an incident. Identifying the initial baseline configuration is useful to determine the security posture of the system, but by itself it doesn't prevent attacks. Monitoring logs and trend analysis are detective controls, not preventive controls. A backup and restoration plan is a corrective control. See Chapter 1.

5. **B.** Virtualization provides increased availability because it is much easier to rebuild a virtual server than a physical server after a failure. Virtualization supports a reduced budget because virtual servers require less hardware, less space in a data center, less power, and less heating and air conditioning. Failover clusters are more expensive. Bollards are physical barriers that block vehicles. Hashing provides integrity, not availability. See Chapter 1.

6. **C.** Virtualization provides a high degree of flexibility when testing security controls because testers can easily rebuild virtual systems or revert them using a snapshot. Baselines provide a known starting point, but aren't flexible because they stay the same. Hardening techniques make systems more secure than their default configuration. Patch management programs ensure patches are deployed, but do not test security controls. See Chapter 1.

7. **B.** You can use tracert to track packet flow through a network and if an extra router has been added to your network, tracert will identify it. You can use ping to check connectivity with a remote system, but it doesn't show the route. The ipconfig command will show the network settings on a Windows computer, but it doesn't identify failed routers. Netstat shows active connections and other network statistics on a local system, but it doesn't identify network paths. See Chapter 1.

8. **A.** Authentication should be increased, such as by forcing users to use stronger passwords. The scenario indicates that attackers are somehow obtaining customer credentials and using them to conduct the fraudulent transactions. Identification is simply claiming an identity, and having customers come into the bank to obtain their credentials increases identification, but this didn't help. Accounting is typically performed by reviewing logs, but the current logs are documenting the fraud. Authorization indicates what customers can do, but there isn't any indication that authorization is a problem. See Chapter 2.

9. **B.** The password policy should be changed to increase the minimum password length of passwords. These passwords are only four and five characters long, which is too short to provide adequate security. They are complex because they include a mixture of at least three of the following character types: uppercase letters, lowercase letters, numbers, and special characters. Password history and password reuse should be addressed if users are reusing the same passwords, but the scenario doesn't indicate this is a problem. See Chapter 2.

10. **A.** This is an example of single sign-on (SSO) capabilities because you can log on once and access all the resources without entering your credentials again. Same sign-on requires you to reenter your credentials for each new site, but you use the same credentials. Security Assertion Markup Language (SAML) is an SSO solution used for web-based applications and the bank might be using SAML, but other SSO solutions are also available. Kerberos is used in an internal network. See Chapter 2.

11. **D.** Lightweight Directory Access Protocol (LDAP) uses X.500-based phrases to identify components and Secure LDAP can be encrypted with Transport Layer Security (TLS). Security Assertion Markup Language (SAML) is an Extensible Markup Language (XML) used for single sign-on (SSO), but it is not based on X.500. Diameter is an alternative to RADIUS used in some remote access solutions. Kerberos is not based on X.500. See Chapter 2.

12. **A.** The most likely reason of those given is that shared accounts are not prohibited, allowing multiple users to access the same file. For example, if the Guest account is enabled and used as a shared account by all users, the logs will indicate the Guest account accessed the file, but it won't identify specific individuals. It doesn't matter how permissions are assigned in order for a log to identify who accessed the file. Account lockout stops someone from guessing a password, but it doesn't affect file access logs. See Chapter 2.

13. **C.** Using group-based privileges is the best choice to meet the needs of this scenario. For example, you can create a DB_Group and a Web_Group, assign appropriate privileges to the groups, and add intern accounts to the groups based on their assignments. Generic accounts such as the Guest account should not be used. User-based privileges take too much time to manage because you'd have to implement them separately. See Chapter 2.

14. **D.** You can create security groups, place users into these groups, and grant access to the folders by assigning appropriate permissions to the security groups. For example, the security groups might be Sales, Marketing, and HR, and you place users into the appropriate group based on their job. This is an example of using group-based privileges. Assigning permissions to each user individually has a high administrative overhead.

Waiting for users to ask will also increase administrative overhead. Although delegating authority to assign permissions might work, it doesn't provide the same level of security as centrally managed groups, and without groups, it will still have a high administrative overhead for someone. See Chapter 2.

15. **A.** The administrator should create an account for Jasper and add it to the Accounting group. Because the organization uses groups, it makes sense that they have an Accounting group. The Guest account should be disabled to prevent the use of generic accounts. This scenario describes role-based access control, not rule-based access control. Jasper does not require administrator privileges, so his account should not be added to the Administrators group. See Chapter 2.

16. **C.** Secure File Transfer Protocol (SFTP) is the best choice. File Transfer Protocol (FTP) is the best choice to send large files if they don't contain sensitive data. These files contain proprietary data so they should be encrypted and SFTP encrypts the files using Secure Shell (SSH). Simple Network Management Protocol version 3 (SNMPv3) is used to manage network devices, not transfer files. The Secure Real-time Transport Protocol (SRTP) provides encryption, message authentication, and integrity for streaming media. See Chapter 3.

17. **A.** Transport Layer Security (TLS) is a good choice to create a secure connection between two systems over the Internet. Although the mail servers will likely exchange mail using Simple Mail Transfer Protocol (SMTP), SMTP by itself will not create a secure link. Similarly, Hypertext Transfer Protocol (HTTP) doesn't create a secure link. Although Secure Shell (SSH) creates a secure connection, it isn't used with SMTP. See Chapter 3.

18. **A.** A demilitarized zone (DMZ) is a logical buffer zone for servers accessed from public networks such as the Internet, and it provides a layer of security for servers in the DMZ. A wiring closet or server room provides physical security for networking equipment. A honeypot is a fake server used to lure attackers and a honeynet is a fake network. Proxy servers cache data retrieved from web servers. See Chapter 3.

19. **C.** A URL filter blocks access to specific web sites based on their URLs. Proxy servers and unified threat management (UTM) devices include URL filters. UTM devices also include content inspection to identify and filter out different types of files and traffic, and malware inspection to identify and block malware. A web application firewall (WAF) protects a web server from incoming attacks. See Chapter 3.

20. **C.** A web application firewall (WAF) is the best choice. You can place it in the demilitarized zone (DMZ) and the web farm servers in the internal network. In addition to protecting the web servers, the WAF also provides load balancing. None of the other solutions provides load balancing. A stateless firewall filters traffic using an access control list. A stateful firewall filters traffic based on the state of a packet within a session. A host-based firewall provides protection for a single host. See Chapter 3.

21. **A.** A mail gateway is placed between an email server and the Internet and mail gateways typically include data loss prevention (DLP) capabilities. They can inspect the contents of outgoing traffic looking for key words and block any traffic containing proprietary data. A unified threat management (UTM) device includes content inspection, but this most

often blocks specific types of traffic, or specific file types. A mail gateway is more focused on email. Proxy servers are typically used for web traffic. They don't include the ability to filter email. See Chapter 3.

22. **D.** A virtual local area network (VLAN) provides separation for traffic and can be configured to separate Voice over IP (VoIP) traffic and data traffic. Network access control (NAC) solutions inspect clients for health after they connect to a network. A demilitarized zone (DMZ) provides a layer of protection for Internet-facing systems, while also allowing clients to connect to them. Secure Real-time Transport Protocol (SRTP) provides encryption and authentication for Real-time Transport Protocol (RTP) traffic. RTP is used for audio/video streaming, such as in video teleconferencing applications. See Chapter 3.

23. **B.** The best automated solution of the available choices is a network-based intrusion prevention system (NIPS) protecting the demilitarized zone (DMZ), and host-based intrusion prevention systems (HIPSs) on the database server and web servers. An intrusion detection system (IDS) detects intrusions and reports them, but it does not provide automated responses to protect the systems. A security information and event management (SIEM) system provides aggregation and correlation services for log entries, but it doesn't provide automated protection. See Chapter 4.

24. **C.** An anomaly-based (also called heuristic-based or behavior-based) intrusion detection system (IDS) compares current activity with a previously created baseline to detect any anomalies or unusual traffic on a network. A network-based firewall will block and allow traffic, but it does not detect unusual traffic. Signature-based IDS systems use signatures similar to antivirus software. A honeynet is a group of servers configured as honeypots. A honeynet is designed to look valuable to an attacker and can divert attacks. See Chapter 4.

25. **D.** A honeypot can divert malicious attacks to a harmless area of your network, such as away from production servers holding valid data. An intrusion prevention system (IPS) can block attacks, but it doesn't divert them. A proxy server can filter and cache content from web pages, but it doesn't divert attacks. A web application firewall (WAF) is an additional firewall designed to protect a web application. See Chapter 4.

26. **D.** An 802.1x server provides port-based authentication and can authenticate clients. Clients that cannot authenticate (the guests in this scenario) can be redirected to the guest network, which grants them Internet access but not access to the internal network. None of the other solutions provides port security or adequate network separation. Network Address Translation (NAT) translates private IP addresses to public IP addresses. A demilitarized zone (DMZ) provides a buffer zone between a public network and a private network for public-facing servers. A virtual private network (VPN) provides access to a private network via a public network. See Chapter 4.

27. **C.** You can disable service set identifier (SSID) broadcasting to prevent users from easily discovering the wireless networks. None of the other methods hide the network. Counter Mode Cipher Block Chaining Message Authentication Code Protocol (CCMP) provides stronger security for Wi-Fi Protected Access II (WPA2) and WPA2 Enterprise adds authentication for a wireless network. Media access control (MAC) address filtering can restrict access to the wireless network. See Chapter 4.

28. **B.** Network access control (NAC) inspects clients for health, including having up-to-date virus definition files and can restrict network access to unhealthy clients to a remediation network. A network intrusion detection system (NIDS) can detect incoming attacks, but doesn't inspect internal clients. A data loss prevention (DLP) system typically examines outgoing traffic looking for confidential data. A demilitarized zone (DMZ) is a buffer zone between the Internet and an internal network. See Chapter 4.

29. **A.** The most likely cause is that the Remote Authentication Dial-In User Service (RADIUS) server certificate expired. An 802.1x server is implemented as a RADIUS server and Protected Extensible Authentication Protocol (PEAP) requires a certificate, which is a key clue in this question. If Domain Name System (DNS) or Dynamic Host Configuration Protocol (DHCP) failed, it would affect both wired and wireless users. Media access control (MAC) address filtering might cause this symptom if all MAC addresses were blocked, but the scenario states that there weren't any network configuration changes. See Chapter 4.

30. **A.** The best answer of the available choices is to use the chroot command to isolate the application within a sandbox. Sideloading is the process of copying an application to a mobile device, not a Linux-based computer. Full disk encryption (FDE) is associated with mobile devices and would not isolate an application. The chmod command is used to change permissions on a Linux system. See Chapter 5.

31. **B.** A Trusted Platform Module (TPM) includes an encryption key burned into the chip, and this key provides a hardware root of trust. Data loss prevention (DLP) systems detect unauthorized data transfers. Sandboxing provides an isolated area on a system, typically used for testing. A hardware security module (HSM) is an external security device used to store cryptographic keys, but a TPM is a chip within the system. See Chapter 5.

32. **C.** Infrastructure as a Service (IaaS) is a cloud computing option where the vendor provides access to a computer, but customers must manage the system, including keeping it up to date with current patches. A community cloud is shared among several organizations, but the scenario doesn't indicate the resources are shared. Software as a Service (SaaS) provides access to applications, such as email, but not to the operating system. An IaaS solution can be public, private, or a hybrid solution. A hybrid cloud is a combination of two or more public, private, and/or community clouds. See Chapter 5.

33. **D.** The generators are likely controlled within a supervisory control and data acquisition (SCADA) system and isolating them within a virtual local area network (VLAN) will protect them from unauthorized access. An internal Certificate Authority (CA) issues and manages certificates within a Public Key Infrastructure (PKI), but there isn't any indication certificates are in use. Wi-Fi Protected Access II (WPA2) secures wireless networks, but doesn't protect SCADA networks. Patch management processes help ensure systems are kept up to date with patches, but this doesn't apply in this scenario. See Chapter 5.

34. **D.** A data loss prevention (DLP) solution can detect documents sent to a printer that contain Personally Identifiable Information (PII) and prevent them from printing. A hardware security module (HSM) and a Trusted Platform Module (TPM) both provide full disk encryption, but cannot block documents sent to a printer. A virtual local area network (VLAN) segments traffic and can help protect a supervisory control and data acquisition (SCADA) system, but isn't selective about documents sent to a printer. See Chapter 5.

35. **B.** This was most likely an advanced persistent threat (APT) because it was a sophisticated attack and originated from a foreign country. A hacktivist launches attacks to further a cause, but the scenario didn't mention any cause. Competitors might launch attacks, but they would typically focus on proprietary data rather than customer data. An insider would not launch attacks from a foreign country. See Chapter 6.

36. **A.** The security administrator is most likely looking for a backdoor because Trojans commonly create backdoors, and a backdoor allows unauthorized personnel to access data on the system. Logic bombs and rootkits can create backdoor accounts, but Trojans don't create logic bombs and would rarely install a rootkit. The computer might be joined to a botnet, but a botnet is a group of computers. See Chapter 6.

37. **B.** Ransomware attempts to take control of user's system or data and then demands ransom to return control. Keyloggers capture a user's keystrokes and store them in a file. This file can be automatically sent to an attacker or manually retrieved depending on the keylogger. It's possible that Marge's computer was infected with a Trojan, which created a backdoor. However, not all Trojans or backdoor accounts demand payment as ransom. See Chapter 6.

38. **D.** Dumpster diving is the practice of looking for documents in the trash dumpsters, but shredding or incinerating documents ensures dumpster divers cannot retrieve any paper documents. Shoulder surfers attempt to view something on a monitor or other screen, not papers. Tailgating refers to entering a secure area by following someone else. Vishing is a form of phishing using the phone. See Chapter 6.

39. **B.** This email is a form of spear phishing because it is targeting users in the same organization. While it is a form of phishing, spear phishing is a better answer because the email targeted users in the same organization. It is also spam because it is unwanted email, but not all spam is malicious. Phishing and spear phishing are types of attacks using email. Vishing is similar to phishing, but it uses telephone technology. See Chapter 6.

40. **B, C.** Anti-malware software and cable locks are the best choices to protect these computers. Anti-malware software protects the systems from viruses and other malware. The cable locks deter theft of the computers. A mantrap prevents tailgating, but this is unrelated to this question. Disk encryption is useful if the computers have confidential information, but it wouldn't be appropriate to put confidential information on a public computer. See Chapters 6 and 9.

41. **A.** A distributed denial-of-service (DDoS) attack includes attacks from multiple systems with the goal of depleting the target's resources and this scenario indicates multiple connection attempts from different IP addresses. A DoS attack comes from a single system, and a SYN flood is an example of a DoS attack. While the DDoS attack may be an amplification attack (an attack that significantly increases the amount of traffic sent to the victim), the scenario doesn't give enough details to identify this as an amplification attack. Salting is a method used to prevent brute force attacks to discover passwords. See Chapter 7.

42. **C, E.** Brute force and dictionary attacks attempt to guess passwords, but an account lockout control locks an account after the wrong password is guessed too many times. The other

attacks are not password attacks, so they aren't mitigated using account lockout controls. Domain Name System (DNS) poisoning attempts to redirect web browsers to malicious URLs. Replay attacks attempt to capture packets to impersonate one of the parties in an online session. Buffer overflow attacks attempt to overwhelm online applications with unexpected code or data. See Chapter 7.

43. **B.** Typo squatting (or URL hijacking) uses a similar domain name to redirect traffic. In this scenario, the last two letters in comptia are swapped in the malicious domain name, and that site is attempting to download malware onto the user systems. A smurf attack is unrelated to web sites. Fuzzing tests an application's ability to handle random data. A replay attack attempts to replay data with the intent of impersonating one of the parties. See Chapter 7.

44. **B.** A zero-day attack takes advantage of an undocumented exploit or an exploit that is unknown to the public. A buffer overflow attack sends unexpected data to a system to access system memory or cause it to crash. Although some buffer overflow attacks are unknown, others are known. If the server isn't kept up to date with patches, it can be attacked with a known buffer overflow attack. A man-in-the-browser attack is a type of proxy Trojan horse that takes advantage of vulnerabilities in web browsers, not web servers. Session hijacking takes over a user's session and isn't related to an attack on a server. See Chapter 7.

45. **A.** Buffer overflow attacks often cause an application to crash and expose system memory. Attackers then write malicious code into the exposed memory and use different techniques to get the system to run this code. None of the other attacks insert malicious code into memory. An Address Resolution Protocol (ARP) poisoning attack attempts to mislead systems about the source media access control (MAC) address. Privilege escalation techniques attempt to give an attacker more rights and permissions. In a replay attack, the attacker intercepts data and typically attempts to use the intercepted data to impersonate a user or system. See Chapter 7.

46. **C.** The agile software development model is flexible, ensures that personnel interact with each other throughout a project, and is the best of the available choices. The waterfall model isn't as flexible and focuses instead on completing the project in stages. Both agile and waterfall are software development life cycle (SDLC) models, which is a generic concept designed to provide structure for software development projects. Secure DevOps is an agile-aligned development methodology that focuses on security considerations throughout a project. See Chapter 7.

47. **D.** Dynamic analysis techniques (such as fuzzing) can test the application's ability to maintain availability and data integrity for some scenarios. Fuzzing sends random data to an application to verify the random data doesn't crash the application or expose the system to a data breach. Model verification ensures that the software meets specifications and fulfills its intended purpose, but it doesn't focus on reliability or integrity. Input validation and error-handling techniques protect applications, but do not test them. See Chapter 7.

48. **B, D.** Input validation and a web application firewall (WAF) are the best choices of the available answers. Both provide protection against cross-site scripting (XSS) attacks. Input validation

validates data before using it to help prevent XSS attacks. A WAF acts as an additional firewall that monitors, filters, and/or blocks HTTP traffic to a web server. None of the other answers will directly prevent XSS attacks. Dynamic code analysis (such as fuzzing) can test code. Code obfuscation makes the code more difficult to read. Normalization refers to organizing tables and columns in a database to reduce redundant data and improve overall database performance. See Chapters 2 and 7.

49. **A.** A threat assessment evaluates potential dangers that can compromise the confidentiality, integrity, and/or availability of data or a system. It evaluates threats and attempts to identify the potential impact from threats. A vulnerability assessment evaluates vulnerabilities (or weaknesses), not potential dangers. A privacy threshold assessment helps an organization identify Personally Identifiable Information (PII) within a system and a privacy impact assessment attempts to identify potential risks related to PII. However, this scenario doesn't mention PII. See Chapter 8.

50. **A.** The expected loss is the single loss expectancy (SLE) and you can calculate it with the annual loss expectancy (ALE) and annual rate of occurrence (ARO), as ALE / ARO. The SLE is what you are trying to determine, so you don't have that value. The return on investment (ROI) will not help in identifying the SLE. See Chapter 8.

51. **C.** In this scenario, the vulnerability scanner reported a false positive indicating that the servers had a vulnerability, but in reality, the servers did not have the vulnerability. A false negative occurs if a vulnerability scanner does not report a known vulnerability. There isn't any indication that the servers are misconfigured. The scenario doesn't indicate if the scan was run under the context of an account (credentialed or non-credentialed), so this answer isn't relevant to the question. See Chapter 8.

52. **D.** A port scanner identifies open ports on a system and is commonly used to determine what services are running on the system. A penetration test attempts to exploit a vulnerability. A protocol analyzer (also called a sniffer) could analyze traffic and discover protocols in use, but this would be much more difficult than using a port scanner. See Chapter 8.

53. **C.** A vulnerability scan identifies vulnerabilities that attackers can potentially exploit, and vulnerability scanners perform passive testing. A penetration test actively tests the application and can potentially compromise the system. A port scan only identifies open ports. A sniffer can capture traffic for analysis, but it doesn't check for security controls. See Chapter 8.

54. **C.** A protocol analyzer (or sniffer) can capture traffic sent over a network and identify the type of traffic, the source of the traffic, and protocol flags used within individual packets. A security information and event management (SIEM) system provides a centralized solution for collecting, analyzing, and managing log data from multiple sources, but it doesn't collect and analyze packets. Netcat is useful for remotely administering servers, but it doesn't collect and analyze packets. A vulnerability scan identifies vulnerabilities on a network. See Chapter 8.

55. **B.** Netcat can easily be used for banner grabbing and banner grabbing will provide her information on the operating system and get some information on services and

applications used by the server. A security information and event management (SIEM) system provides a centralized solution for collecting, analyzing, and managing data from multiple sources. Tcpdump is a command-line tool used to capture packets, but it doesn't query systems for data. A gray box test indicates the tester has some knowledge of the target, but it doesn't indicate the type of test used by a tester. See Chapter 8.

56. **B.** Layered security (or defense in depth) implements multiple controls to provide several layers of protection. In this case, the antivirus software provides one layer of protection while the firewall and the intrusion detection system (IDS) provide additional layers. Implicit deny blocks access unless it has been explicitly allowed. Least privilege ensures that users are granted only the access they need to perform their jobs, and no more. A flood guard attempts to block SYN flood attacks. See Chapter 9.

57. **D.** A mantrap controls access to a secure area and only allows a single person to pass at a time. The scenario describes the social engineering tactic of tailgating, not the control to prevent it. Some sophisticated mantraps include identification and authorization systems, such as biometric systems or smart cards and PINs. However, biometrics and smart cards used for physical security do not restrict passage to one person at a time unless they are combined with a mantrap. See Chapter 9.

58. **D.** Load balancing shifts the load among multiple systems and can increase the site's availability by adding additional nodes when necessary. A failover cluster also provides high availability, but there is no such thing as a fail-open cluster. Certificates help ensure confidentiality and integrity, but do not assist with availability. A web application firewall helps protect a web server against attacks, but it does not increase availability from normal client requests. See Chapter 9.

59. **C.** A redundant array of inexpensive disks (RAID) subsystem is a relatively low-cost solution for fault tolerance for disks. RAID also increases data availability. Load balancing adds in additional servers, which are significantly more expensive than RAID. Round-robin scheduling is one of the methods used in load balancing. A warm site is a separate location, which can be expensive. See Chapter 9.

60. **C.** Closed-circuit television (CCTV) or a similar video surveillance system can monitor the entrance and record who enters and exits the area. A mantrap prevents tailgating, but it doesn't necessarily identify individuals. An access list is useful if a guard is identifying users and allowing access based on the access list, but the access list does not identify users. Bollards are a type of barricade that protects building entrances. See Chapter 9.

61. **A.** A privacy impact assessment attempts to identify potential risks related to Personally Identifiable Information (PII) and ensure the organization is complying with applicable laws and regulations. A privacy threshold assessment helps an organization identify PII within a system and determine if a privacy impact assessment is needed. A threat assessment is part of a risk assessment and helps identify potential threats. A supply chain assessment is part of a risk assessment and helps identify potential problems in the supply chain that might impact an organization's mission. See Chapter 9.

62. **D.** Hashing algorithms such as Secure Hash Algorithm (SHA) and Hash-based Message

Authentication Code (HMAC) can detect changes in files (or verify the files have not lost integrity). Pretty Good Privacy (PGP) is a method used to secure email communication. Elliptic curve cryptography (ECC), Advanced Encryption Standard (AES), and Twofish are all encryption algorithms. See Chapter 10.

63. **D.** Bcrypt is a key stretching technique designed to protect against brute force and rainbow table attacks and is the best choice of the given answers. Another alternative is Password-Based Key Derivation Function 2 (PBKDF2). Both salt the password with additional bits. Passwords stored using Secure Hash Algorithm (SHA) are easier to crack because they don't use salts. Bcrypt is based on Blowfish, but Blowfish itself isn't commonly used to encrypt passwords. Elliptic curve cryptography (ECC) is efficient and sometimes used with mobile devices, but not to encrypt passwords. See Chapter 10.

64. **D.** In the context of encryption, confusion means that the ciphertext is significantly different than the plaintext. In cryptography, diffusion ensures that small changes in the plaintext result in large changes in the ciphertext. Obfuscation techniques attempt to hide data or make something unclear, but they don't necessarily convert plaintext into ciphertext. A collision refers to a hashing algorithm vulnerability and is unrelated to encryption. See Chapter 10.

65. **D.** Elliptic Curve Diffie-Hellman Ephemeral (ECDHE) allows entities to negotiate encryption keys securely over a public network and is the best choice of the available answers. A certificate revocation list (CRL) identifies revoked certificates and is unrelated to sharing encryption keys. Password-Based Key Derivation Function 2 (PBKDF2) is a key stretching technique designed to make password cracking more difficult. Hashing methods do not support sharing encryption keys over a public network. See Chapter 10.

66. **D.** Galois/Counter Mode (GCM) combines the Counter (CTM) mode with hashing techniques to provide both confidentiality and data authenticity. None of the other modes listed provide data authenticity. CTM mode combines an initialization vector (IV) with a counter to encrypt blocks. Cipher Block Chaining (CBC) mode encrypts the first block with an IV. It then combines each subsequent block with the previous block using an XOR operation. The Electronic Codebook (ECB) mode of operation should not be used because it encrypts blocks with the same key, making it easier for attackers to crack. See Chapter 10.

67. **C.** Public key pinning provides clients with a list of public key hashes that clients can use to detect web site impersonation attempts. Stapling reduces Online Certificate Status Protocol (OCSP) traffic by appending a timestamped, digitally signed OCSP response to a certificate. Perfect forward secrecy ensures that the compromise of a long-term key does not compromise keys used in the past. Key stretching techniques add additional bits (salts) to passwords, making them harder to crack. See Chapter 10.

68. **B.** A certificate revocation list (CRL) can meet this need because CRLs are cached. If the public Certificate Authority (CA) is not reachable due to any type of connection outage or CA outage, the cached CRL can be used as long as the cache time has not expired. The Online Certificate Status Protocol (OCSP) works in real time where the client queries the CA with the serial number of the certificate. If the CA is unreachable, the certificate cannot be validated. A private CA is used within an organization and cannot validate certificates

from a public CA. You request a certificate with a certificate signing request (CSR), but the CSR doesn't validate an issued certificate. See Chapter 10.

69. **C.** This recommendation is enforcing a separation of duties principle, which prevents any single person from performing multiple job functions that might allow the person to commit fraud. Discretionary access control specifies that every object has an owner, but doesn't separate duties. Devices such as routers use a rule-based access control model, but it doesn't separate duties. Job rotation policies rotate employees into different jobs, but they don't necessarily separate job functions. See Chapter 11.

70. **C.** This practice enforces a job rotation policy where employees rotate into different jobs, and is designed to reduce potential incidents. A separation of duties policy prevents any single person from performing multiple job functions to help prevent fraud, but it doesn't force users to switch roles. A mandatory vacation policy requires employees to take time away from their job. An acceptable use policy informs users of their responsibilities when using an organization's equipment. See Chapter 11.

71. **D.** An interconnection security agreement (ISA) specifies technical and security requirements for secure connections and can ensure data is encrypted while in transit. None of the other agreements address the connection. A service level agreement (SLA) stipulates performance expectations of a vendor. A business partners agreement (BPA) is a written agreement for business partners. A memorandum of understanding (MOU) expresses an understanding between two parties to work together. See Chapter 11.

72. **B.** At this stage, the first response is incident identification. The preparation phase is performed before an incident, and includes steps to prevent incidents. After identifying this as a valid incident (malware infection), the next steps are containment, eradication, recovery, and lessons learned. See Chapter 11.

73. **D.** You should analyze an incident during the lessons learned phase of incident response with the goal of identifying steps to prevent reoccurrence. Preparation is a planning step done before an incident, with the goal of preventing incidents and identifying methods to respond to incidents. Identification is the first step after hearing about a potential incident to verify it is an incident. Eradication attempts to remove all malicious elements of an incident after it has been contained. See Chapter 11.

74. **D.** It's important to keep a chain of custody for any confiscated physical items and the chain of custody is a record of everyone who took possession of the asset after it was first confiscated. Hashes should be taken before capturing an image, but they are not required before confiscating equipment. Users, not witnesses, sign an acceptable use policy (AUP). Security personnel should be aware of the order of volatility, but there isn't any way to maintain the order. See Chapter 11.

75. **B.** A chain of custody was not maintained because the hard drive was left unattended for several hours before capturing an image. Witnesses were not mentioned, but are not needed if the chain of custody was maintained. The order of volatility does not apply here, but the hard drive is not volatile. Analysis would occur after capturing an image, but there isn't any indication it wasn't done or wasn't complete. See Chapter 11.

Chapter 1

Mastering Security Basics

CompTIA Security+ objectives covered in this chapter:

2.2   **Given a scenario, use appropriate software tools to assess the security posture of an organization.**
- Command line tools (ping, netstat, tracert, arp, ipconfig/ip/ifconfig)

3.2   **Given a scenario, implement secure network architecture concepts.**
- Segregation/segmentation/isolation (Virtualization)

3.7   **Summarize cloud and virtualization concepts.**
- Hypervisor (Type I, Type II, Application cells/containers), VM sprawl avoidance, VM escape protection, VDI/VDE

3.8   **Explain how resiliency and automation strategies reduce risk.**
- Non-persistence (Snapshots, Revert to known state, Rollback to known configuration), Elasticity, Scalability

5.7   **Compare and contrast various types of controls.**
- Deterrent, Preventive, Detective, Corrective, Compensating, Technical, Administrative, Physical

6.1   **Compare and contrast basic concepts of cryptography.**
- Common use cases (Supporting confidentiality, Supporting integrity, Supporting obfuscation, Supporting non-repudiation, Resource vs. security constraints)

**

Before you dig into some of the details of security, you should have a solid understanding of core security goals. This chapter introduces many of these core goals to provide a big picture of the concepts, and introduces basic risk concepts. Security controls reduce risks and you'll learn about different security control categories in this chapter. You'll also learn about virtualization and have a chance to do some labs to set up a virtual environment. Finally, this chapter includes some relevant commands that you can run on your primary computer or within a virtual machine.

Understanding Core Security Goals

Security starts with several principles that organizations include as core security goals. These principles drive many security-related decisions at multiple levels. Understanding these basic concepts will help you create a solid foundation in security. Confidentiality, integrity, and availability together form the CIA security triad, a model used to guide security principles within an organization. Each element is important to address in any security program.

What Is a Use Case?

CompTIA includes the term use case in multiple objectives. A *use case* describes a goal that an organization wants to achieve. Engineers use it in systems analysis and software development to identify and clarify requirements to achieve the goal. A common naming strategy for a use case is in the verb-noun format. As an example, consider a use case named "Place Order." Different departments within an organization might use it differently, but it can still retain the same name.

In Chapter 7, "Protecting Against Advanced Attacks," you'll read about development life-cycle models such as agile. The agile model uses a set of principles that can be shared by cross-functional teams—employees in different departments. Developers can use the steps in the use case to create software to support the goal. The use case can help marketing personnel understand where they need to focus their efforts to motivate the buyer to start the process of placing an order. Billing and Shipping departments use it to understand their responsibilities after the customer places the order.

Imagine that Lisa wants to place an order via an online e-commerce system. The Place Order use case for this might include the following elements:

- **Actors.** Lisa is one of the actors. She might have an account and be a registered user with her shipping and billing information in an existing database. Or, she might be a brand-new customer and her information needs to be collected. Other actors include the billing system that bills her for the order and a fulfillment system that processes and ships the order.
- **Precondition.** A precondition must occur before the process can start. For example, Lisa needs to select an item to purchase before she can place the order.
- **Trigger.** A trigger starts the use case. In this case, it could be when Lisa clicks on the shopping cart to begin the purchase process.
- **Postcondition.** Postconditions occur after the actor triggers the process. In this case, Lisa's order will be put into the system after she completes the purchase. She'll receive an acknowledgment for her order, the Billing department may take additional steps to bill her (if she wasn't billed during the purchase process), and the Shipping department will take steps to ship the product.
- **Normal flow.** A use case will typically list each of the steps in a specific order. In this example, you might see a dozen steps that start when Lisa picks an item to order and end when she completes the order and exits the purchase system.
- **Alternate flow.** All purchases won't be the same. For example, instead of using existing billing and shipping information, Lisa might want to use a different credit card or a different shipping address. It's also possible for Lisa to change her mind and abandon the process before completing the purchase or even cancel the purchase after she completes the process.

Note that these are not the only possible elements in a use case. There are many more.

However, you don't need to be an expert in agile to understand the overall concept of a use case.

If you want to be an expert in agile, you can pursue the Project Management Institute Agile Certified Practitioner (PMI-ACP) certification. It requires at least 2,000 hours of general project experience working on teams, 1,500 hours working on agile project teams or with agile methodologies, and at least 21 hours of in-classroom training. The point is that passing the CompTIA Security+ exam doesn't require you to have the PMI-ACP or to know all the elements of use cases. It does require you to understand the basic concept of a use case.

The following sections discuss some common use cases related to supporting confidentiality, integrity, availability, authentication, obfuscation, and non-repudiation.

Ensure Confidentiality

A common use case that any organization has is to support confidentiality. **Confidentiality** prevents the unauthorized disclosure of data. In other words, authorized personnel can access the data, but unauthorized personnel cannot access the data. You can ensure confidentiality using several different methods discussed in the following sections.

Encryption

Encryption scrambles data to make it unreadable by unauthorized personnel. Authorized personnel can decrypt the data to access it, but encryption techniques make it extremely difficult for unauthorized personnel to access encrypted data. Chapter 10, "Understanding Cryptography and PKI," covers encryption in much more depth, including commonly used encryption algorithms like Advanced Encryption Standard (AES).

As an example, imagine you need to transmit Personally Identifiable Information (PII), such as medical information or credit card data via email. You wouldn't want any unauthorized personnel to access this data, but once you click Send, you're no longer in control of the data. However, if you encrypt the email before you send it, you protect the confidentiality of the data.

Access Controls

Identification, authentication, and authorization combined provide access controls and help ensure that only authorized personnel can access data. Imagine that you want to grant Maggie access to some data, but you don't want Homer to be able to access the same data. You use access controls to grant and restrict access. The following bullets introduce key elements of access controls:

- **Identification.** Users claim an identity with a unique username. For example, both Maggie and Homer have separate user accounts identified with unique usernames. When Maggie uses her account, she is claiming the identity of her account.
- **Authentication.** Users prove their identity with authentication, such as with a password. For example, Maggie knows her password, but no one else should know it. When she logs on to her account with her username and password, she is claiming the identity of her account and proving her identity with the password.
- **Authorization.** Next, you can grant or restrict access to resources using an authorization method, such as permissions. For example, you can grant Maggie's account full access to some files and folders. Similarly, you can ensure that Homer doesn't have any permissions to access the data.

Chapter 2, "Understanding Identity and Access Management," covers these topics in more depth.

Steganography and Obfuscation

A third method you can use for confidentiality is **steganography**. Chapter 10 covers steganography in more depth, but as an introduction, it is the practice of hiding data within data. It obscures the data and can be used in a use case to support obfuscation.

Obfuscation methods attempt to make something unclear or difficult to understand. Within the context of information technology (IT) security, it's called security by obscurity or security through obscurity. It's worth noting that most security experts reject security through obscurity as a reliable method of maintaining security.

Many people refer to steganography as hiding data in plain sight. For example, you can embed a hidden message in an image by modifying certain bits within the file. If other people look at the file, they won't notice anything. However, if other people know what to look for, they will be able to retrieve the message.

As a simpler example, you can add a text file to an image file without the use of any special tools other than WinRAR and the Windows command line. If you're interested in seeing how to do this, check out the Steganography Lab in the online exercises for this book at *http://gcgapremium.com/501labs/*.

> **Remember this**
>
> Confidentiality ensures that data is only viewable by authorized users. The best way to protect the confidentiality of data is by encrypting it. This includes any type of data, such as PII, data in databases, and data on mobile devices. Access controls help protect confidentiality by restricting access. Steganography helps provide confidentiality by hiding data, such as hiding text files within an image file.

Provide Integrity

Another common use case is to support integrity. **Integrity** provides assurances that data has not changed. This includes ensuring that no one has modified, tampered with, or corrupted the data. Ideally, only authorized users modify data. However, there are times when unauthorized or unintended changes occur. This can be from unauthorized users, from malicious software (malware), and through system and human errors. When this occurs, the data has lost integrity.

Hashing

You can use hashing techniques to enforce integrity. Chapter 10 discusses the relevant hashing algorithms, such as Message Digest 5 (MD5), Secure Hash Algorithm (SHA), and Hash-based Message Authentication Code (HMAC). Briefly, a **hash** is simply a number created by executing a hashing algorithm against data, such as a file or message. If the data never changes, the resulting hash will always be the same. By comparing hashes created at two different times, you can determine if the original data is still the same. If the hashes are the same, the data is the same. If the hashes are different, the data has changed.

For example, imagine Homer is sending a message to Marge and they both want assurances that the message retained integrity. Homer's message is, "The price is $19.99." He creates a hash of this message. For simplicity's sake, imagine the hash is 123. He then sends both the message and the hash to Marge.

> ### *Acronyms*
>
> Don't you just love these acronyms? MD5, SHA, HMAC. There are actually three different meanings of MAC within the context of CompTIA Security+:
>
> 1. Media access control (MAC) addresses are the physical addresses assigned to network interface cards (NICs).
> 2. The mandatory access control (MAC) model is one of several access control models discussed in Chapter 2.
> 3. Message authentication code (MAC) provides integrity similar to how a hash is used.
>
> If you're having trouble keeping them all straight, don't feel alone. Appendix A, "Glossary," spells out—and lists brief descriptions—for relevant acronyms used in this book.

Marge receives both the message and the hash. She can calculate the hash on the received message and compare her hash with the hash that Homer sent. If the hash of the received message is 123 (the same as the hash of the sent message), she knows the message hasn't lost data integrity. However, if the hash of the received message is something different, such as 456, then she knows that the message she received is not the same as the message that Homer sent. Data integrity has been lost.

Hashing doesn't tell you what modified the message. It only tells you that the message has been modified. This implies that the information should not be trusted as valid.

You can use hashes with messages, such as email, and any other type of data files. Some email programs use a message authentication code (MAC) instead of a hash to verify integrity, but the underlying concept works the same way.

You can also use hashing techniques to verify that integrity is maintained when files are downloaded or transferred. Some programs can automatically check hashes and determine if a file loses even a single bit during the download process. The program performing the download will detect it by comparing the source hash with the destination hash. If a program detects that the hashes are different, it knows that integrity has been lost and reports the problem to the user.

As another example, a web site administrator can calculate and post the hash of a file on a web site. Users can manually calculate the hash of the file after downloading it and compare the calculated hash with the posted hash. If a virus infects a file on the web server, the hash of the infected file would be different from the hash of the original file (and the hash posted on the web site). You can use freeware such as *md5sum.exe* to calculate MD5 hashes. If you want to see this in action, check out the Creating and Comparing Hashes Lab in the online exercises for this book at *http://gcgapremium.com/501labs/*.

It's also possible to lose data integrity through human error. For example, if a database administrator needs to modify a significant amount of data in a database, the administrator can write a script to perform a bulk update. However, if the script is faulty, it can corrupt the database, resulting in a loss of integrity.

Two key concepts related to integrity are:

- **Integrity provides assurances that data has not been modified, tampered with, or corrupted.** Loss of integrity indicates the data is different. Unauthorized users can change data, or the changes can occur through system or human errors.

- **Hashing verifies integrity.** A hash is simply a numeric value created by executing a hashing algorithm against a message or file. Hashes are created at the source and destination or at two different times (such as on the first and fifteenth of the month). If the hashes are the same, integrity is maintained. If the two hashes are different, data integrity has been lost.

> ### Remember this
>
> Integrity verifies that data has not been modified. Loss of integrity can occur through unauthorized or unintended changes. Hashing algorithms, such as MD5, SHA-1, and HMAC, calculate hashes to verify integrity. A hash is simply a number created by applying the algorithm to a file or message at different times. By comparing the hashes, you can verify integrity has been maintained.

Digital Signatures, Certificates, and Non-Repudiation

You can also use digital signatures for integrity. Chapter 10 covers digital signatures in more depth, but as an introduction, a **digital signature** is similar in concept to a handwritten signature. Imagine you sign a one-page contract. Anyone can look at the contract later, see your signature, and know it is the same contract. It isn't possible for other people to modify the words in the contract unless they can reproduce your signature, which isn't easy to do.

It's common to use digital signatures with email. For example, imagine that Lisa wants to send an email to Bart. She can attach a digital signature to the email and when Bart receives it, the digital signature provides assurances to him that the email has not been modified.

A digital signature also provides authentication. In other words, if the digital signature arrives intact, it authenticates the sender. Bart knows that Lisa sent it.

Authentication from the digital signature prevents attackers from impersonating others and sending malicious emails. For example, an attacker could make an email look like it came from Lisa and include a link to a malicious web site urging Bart to click it. Without a digital signature, Bart might be fooled into thinking that Lisa sent it and click the link. This might result in Bart inadvertently downloading malware onto his system.

Digital signatures also provide **non-repudiation**. In other words, Lisa cannot later deny sending the email because the digital signature proves she did. Another way of thinking about non-repudiation is with credit cards. If you buy something with a credit card and sign the receipt, you can't later deny making the purchase. If you do, the store will use your signature to repudiate your claim. In other words, they use your signature for non-repudiation.

Security systems implement non-repudiation methods in other ways beyond digital signatures. Another example is with audit logs that record details such as who, what, when, and where. Imagine Bart logged on to a computer with his username and password, and then deleted several important files. If the audit log recorded these actions, it provides non-repudiation. Bart cannot believably deny he deleted the files.

Digital signatures require the use of certificates and a Public Key Infrastructure (PKI). Certificates include keys used for encryption and the PKI provides the means to create, manage, and distribute certificates. Obviously, there's much more to certificates and a PKI, but there isn't room in this chapter for more than an introduction. Feel free to jump ahead to Chapter 10 if you want to learn more right now.

> **Remember this**
>
> Digital signatures can verify the integrity of emails and files and they also provide authentication and non-repudiation. Digital signatures require certificates.

Increase Availability

Availability indicates that data and services are available when needed. For some organizations, this simply means that the data and services must be available between 8:00 a.m. and 5:00 p.m., Monday through Friday. For other organizations, this means they must be available 24 hours a day, 7 days a week, 365 days a year.

Organizations commonly implement redundancy and fault-tolerant methods to ensure high levels of availability for key systems. Additionally, organizations ensure systems stay up to date with current patches to ensure that software bugs don't affect their availability.

Redundancy and Fault Tolerance

Redundancy adds duplication to critical systems and provides fault tolerance. If a critical component has a fault, the duplication provided by the redundancy allows the service to continue without interruption. In other words, a system with fault tolerance can suffer a fault, but it can tolerate it and continue to operate.

A common goal of fault tolerance and redundancy techniques is to remove each single point of failure (SPOF). If an SPOF fails, the entire system can fail. For example, if a server has a single drive, the drive is an SPOF because its failure takes down the server.

Chapter 9, "Implementing Controls to Protect Assets," covers many fault-tolerance and redundancy techniques in more depth. As an introduction, here are some common examples:

- **Disk redundancies.** Fault-tolerant disks, such as RAID-1 (mirroring), RAID-5 (striping with parity), and RAID-10 (striping with a mirror), allow a system to continue to operate even if a disk fails.
- **Server redundancies.** Failover clusters include redundant servers and ensure a service will continue to operate, even if a server fails. In a failover cluster, the service switches from the failed server in a cluster to an operational server in the same cluster. Virtualization can also increase availability of servers by reducing unplanned downtime. The "Implementing Virtualization" section later in this chapter covers virtualization in more depth.
- **Load balancing.** Load balancing uses multiple servers to support a single service, such as a high-volume web site. It can increase the availability of web sites and web-based applications.
- **Site redundancies.** If a site can no longer function due to a disaster, such as a fire, flood, hurricane, or earthquake, the organization can move critical systems to an alternate site. The alternate site can be a hot site (ready and available 24/7), a cold site (a location where equipment, data, and personnel can be moved to when needed), or a warm site (a compromise between a hot site and cold site).
- **Backups.** If personnel back up important data, they can restore it if the original data is lost. Data can be lost due to corruption, deletion, application errors, human error, and even hungry gremlins that just randomly decide to eat your data. Without data backups, data is lost forever after any one of these incidents.

- **Alternate power.** Uninterruptible power supplies (UPSs) and power generators can provide power to key systems even if commercial power fails.
- **Cooling systems.** Heating, ventilation, and air conditioning (HVAC) systems improve the availability of systems by reducing outages from overheating.

> **Remember this**
>
> Availability ensures that systems are up and operational when needed and often addresses single points of failure. You can increase availability by adding fault tolerance and redundancies, such as RAID, failover clusters, backups, and generators. HVAC systems also increase availability.

Patching

Another method of ensuring systems stay available is with patching. Software bugs cause a wide range of problems, including security issues and even random crashes. When software vendors discover the bugs, they develop and release code that patches or resolves these problems. Organizations commonly implement patch management programs to ensure that systems stay up to date with current patches. Chapter 5, "Securing Hosts and Data," covers patching and patch management in greater depth.

Resource Versus Security Constraints

Organizations frequently need to balance resource availability with security constraints. Consider using encryption to maintain the confidentiality of data. If this is possible, why not just encrypt all the data? The reason is that encryption consumes resources.

As an example, the above paragraph is about 260 characters. Encrypted, it is about 360 characters. That's an increase of about 40 percent, which is typical with many encryption methods. If a company decides to encrypt all data, it means that it will need approximately 40 percent more disk space to store the data. Additionally, when processing the data, it consumes more memory. Last, it takes additional processing time and processing power to encrypt and decrypt the data.

Security experts might say the cost for additional resources is worth it, but executives looking to increase the value of the company don't. Instead, executives have a responsibility to minimize costs without sacrificing security. They do this by looking for the best balance between resource costs and security needs.

Introducing Basic Risk Concepts

One of the basic goals of implementing IT security is to reduce risk. Because risk is so important and so many chapters refer to elements of risk, it's worth providing a short introduction here.

Risk is the possibility or likelihood of a threat exploiting a vulnerability resulting in a loss. A *threat* is any circumstance or event that has the potential to compromise confidentiality, integrity, or availability. A *vulnerability* is a weakness. It can be a weakness in the hardware, the software, the configuration, or even the users operating the system.

If a threat (such as an attacker) exploits a vulnerability, it can result in a security incident. A *security incident* is an adverse event or series of events that can negatively affect the confidentiality, integrity, or availability of an organization's information technology (IT) systems and data. This includes intentional attacks, malicious software (malware) infections, accidental data loss, and much more.

Threats can come from inside an organization, such as from a disgruntled employee or a malicious insider. They can come from outside the organization, such as from an attacker anywhere in the world with access to the Internet. Threats can be natural, such as hurricanes, tsunamis, or tornadoes, or manmade, such as malware written by a criminal. Threats can be intentional, such as from attackers, or accidental, such as from employee mistakes or system errors.

Reducing risk is also known as risk mitigation. **Risk mitigation** reduces the chances that a threat will exploit a vulnerability. You reduce risks by implementing controls (also called countermeasures and safeguards), and many of the actions described throughout this book are different types of controls. You can't prevent most threats. For example, you can't stop a tornado or prevent a criminal from writing malware. However, you can reduce risk by reducing vulnerabilities to the threat, or by reducing the impact of the threat.

For example, access controls (starting with authentication) ensure that only authorized personnel have access to specific areas, systems, or data. If employees do become disgruntled and want to cause harm, access controls reduce the amount of potential harm by reducing what they can access. If a natural disaster hits, business continuity and disaster recovery plans help reduce the impact. Similarly, antivirus software prevents the impact of any malware by intercepting it before it causes any harm.

> ### Remember this
> Risk is the likelihood that a threat will exploit a vulnerability. Risk mitigation reduces the chances that a threat will exploit a vulnerability, or reduces the impact of the risk, by implementing security controls.

Understanding Control Types

There are hundreds, perhaps thousands, of security controls that organizations can implement to reduce risk. The good news is that you don't need to be an expert on all of the possible security controls to pass the CompTIA Security+ exam. However, you do need to have a basic understanding of control types.

CompTIA lists the following control types in the objectives:

- Technical controls use technology.
- Administrative controls use administrative or management methods.
- Physical controls refer to controls you can physically touch.
- Preventive controls attempt to prevent an incident from occurring.
- Detective controls attempt to detect incidents after they have occurred.
- Corrective controls attempt to reverse the impact of an incident.
- Deterrent controls attempt to discourage individuals from causing an incident.
- Compensating controls are alternative controls used when a primary control is not feasible.

The first three control types in the list (technical, administrative, and physical) refer to how the security controls are implemented. The remaining control types refer to the goals of the security control.

> ### Remember this
>
> Most security controls can be classified as technical (implemented with technology), administrative (implemented using administrative or management methods), or physical (items you can touch).

Technical Controls

Technical controls use technology to reduce vulnerabilities. An administrator installs and configures a technical control, and the technical control then provides the protection automatically. Throughout this book, you'll come across several examples of technical controls. The following list provides a few examples:

- **Encryption.** Encryption is a strong technical control used to protect the confidentiality of data. This includes data transferred over a network and data stored on devices, such as servers, desktop computers, and mobile devices.
- **Antivirus software.** Once installed, the antivirus software provides protection against malware infection. Chapter 6, "Comparing Threats, Vulnerabilities, and Common Attacks," covers malware and antivirus software in more depth.
- **Intrusion detection systems (IDSs) and intrusion prevention systems (IPSs).** IDSs and IPSs can monitor a network or host for intrusions and provide ongoing protection against various threats. Chapter 4, "Securing Your Network," covers different types of IDSs and IPSs.
- **Firewalls.** Network firewalls restrict network traffic going in and out of a network. Chapter 3, "Exploring Network Technologies and Tools," covers firewalls in more depth.
- **Least privilege.** The principle of least privilege specifies that individuals or processes are granted only the privileges they need to perform their assigned tasks or functions, but no more. Privileges are a combination of rights and permissions.

> ### Remember this
>
> Technical controls use technology to reduce vulnerabilities. Some examples include encryption, antivirus software, IDSs, IPSs, firewalls, and the principle of least privilege. Technical physical security and environmental controls include motion detectors and fire suppression systems.

Administrative Controls

Administrative controls use methods mandated by organizational policies or other guidelines. For example, management may require personnel to periodically complete assessments and tests to reduce and manage risk. Many of these assessments provide an ongoing review of an organization's risk management capabilities. Some common administrative controls are:

- **Risk assessments.** Risk assessments help quantify and qualify risks within an organization so that the organization can focus on the serious risks. For example, a quantitative risk assessment uses cost and asset values to quantify risks based on monetary values. A qualitative risk assessment uses judgments to categorize risks based on probability and impact.

- **Vulnerability assessments.** A vulnerability assessment attempts to discover current vulnerabilities or weaknesses. When necessary, an organization implements additional controls to reduce the risk from these vulnerabilities.
- **Penetration tests.** These go a step further than a vulnerability assessment by attempting to exploit vulnerabilities. For example, a vulnerability assessment might discover a server isn't kept up to date with current patches, making it vulnerable to some attacks. A penetration test would attempt to compromise the server by exploiting one or more of the unpatched vulnerabilities.

Chapter 8, "Using Risk Management Tools," covers these assessments and tests in more depth. Some administrative controls focus on physical security and the environment. For example, an access list identifies individuals allowed into a secured area. Guards then verify individuals are on the access list before allowing them in.

Many administrative controls are also known as operational or management controls. They help ensure that day-to-day operations of an organization comply with the organization's overall security plan. People (not technology) implement these controls. Operational controls include the following families:

- **Awareness and training.** The importance of training to reduce risks cannot be overstated. Training helps users maintain password security, follow a clean desk policy, understand threats such as phishing and malware, and much more.
- **Configuration and change management.** Configuration management often uses baselines to ensure that systems start in a secure, hardened state. Change management helps ensure that changes don't result in unintended configuration errors. Chapter 5 covers configuration and change management in more detail.
- **Contingency planning.** Chapter 9 presents several different methods that help an organization plan and prepare for potential system outages. The goal is to reduce the overall impact on the organization if an outage occurs.
- **Media protection.** Media includes physical media such as USB flash drives, external and internal drives, and backup tapes.
- **Physical and environmental protection.** This includes physical controls, such as cameras and door locks, and environmental controls, such as heating and ventilation systems.

Physical Controls

Physical controls are any controls that you can physically touch. Some examples include lighting, signs, fences, security guards, and more. CompTIA has placed a lot more emphasis on physical security controls, including environmental controls such as hot and cold aisles and fire suppression. You'll see these covered in more depth in Chapter 9.

However, it's important to realize that many of these are also technical controls. For example, a fire suppression system is a physical security control because you can touch it. However, it's also a technical control because it uses technologies to detect, suppress, or extinguish fires.

Control Goals

Technical and administrative controls categorize the controls based on how they are implemented. Another way of classifying security controls is based on their goals in relationship to security incidents. Some common classifications are preventive, detective, corrective, deterrent, and compensating. The following sections describe them in more depth.

NIST and SP 800 Documents

The National Institute of Standards and Technology (**NIST**) is a part of the U.S. Department of Commerce, and it includes a Computer Security Division hosting the Information Technology Laboratory (ITL). The ITL publishes Special Publications (SPs) in the 800 series that are of general interest to the computer security community.

Many IT security professionals use these documents as references to design secure IT systems and networks. Additionally, many security-related certifications (beyond the CompTIA Security+ certification) also reference the SP 800 documents both directly and indirectly.

SP 800-53 Revision 4, "Security and Privacy Controls for Federal Information Systems and Organizations," includes a wealth of information on security controls. It includes three relatively short chapters introducing security controls followed by multiple appendixes. Appendix F is a security control catalog that provides details on hundreds of individual security controls, divided into 21 different families.

Additionally, each of these 21 families includes multiple groups. As an example, the Access Control family (AC) includes 25 different groups (AC-1 through AC-25). The Account Management group (AC-2) describes 110 individual security controls related to account management.

It's worth noting that SP 800-53 Revision 3 attempted to identify every control as technical, management, or operational. However, many controls included characteristics from more than just one of these classifications. NIST removed these references in Revision 4.

If you're interested in pursuing other security-related certifications or making IT security a career, the SP 800 documents are well worth your time. You can download SP 800-53 Revision 4 and other SP 800 documents at *http://csrc.nist.gov/publications/PubsSPs.html*.

Preventive Controls

Ideally, an organization won't have any security incidents and that is the primary goal of *preventive controls*—to prevent security incidents. Some examples include:

- **Hardening.** Hardening is the practice of making a system or application more secure than its default configuration. This uses a defense-in-depth strategy with layered security. This includes disabling unnecessary ports and services, implementing secure protocols, using strong passwords along with a robust password policy, and disabling default and unnecessary accounts. These topics are covered in more depth in Chapter 5.
- **Security awareness and training.** Ensuring that users are aware of security vulnerabilities and threats helps prevent incidents. When users understand how social engineers operate, they are less likely to be tricked. For example, uneducated users might be tricked into giving a social engineer their passwords, but educated users will see through the tactics and keep their passwords secure.
- **Security guards.** Guards prevent and deter many attacks. For example, guards can prevent unauthorized access into secure areas of a building by first verifying user identities. Although a social engineer might attempt to fool a receptionist into letting him into a secure area, the presence of a guard will deter many social engineers from even trying these tactics.

- **Change management.** Change management ensures that changes don't result in unintended outages. In other words, instead of administrators making changes on the fly, they submit the change to a change management process. Notice that change management is an operational control, which attempts to prevent incidents. In other words, it's both an operational control and a preventive control.
- **Account disablement policy.** An account disablement policy ensures that user accounts are disabled when an employee leaves. This prevents anyone, including ex-employees, from continuing to use these accounts. Chapter 2 covers account disablement policies in more depth.

Remember this

Preventive controls attempt to prevent security incidents. Hardening systems increases their basic configuration to prevent incidents. Security guards can prevent unauthorized personnel from entering a secure area. Change management processes help prevent outages from configuration changes. An account disablement policy ensures that accounts are disabled when a user leaves the organization.

Detective Controls

Although preventive controls attempt to prevent security incidents, some will still occur. *Detective controls* attempt to detect when vulnerabilities have been exploited, resulting in a security incident. An important point is that detective controls discover the event after it's occurred. Some examples of detective controls are:

- **Log monitoring.** Several different logs record details of activity on systems and networks. For example, firewall logs record details of all traffic that the firewall blocked. By monitoring these logs, it's possible to detect incidents. Some automated methods of log monitoring automatically detect potential incidents and report them right after they've occurred.
- **Trend analysis.** In addition to monitoring logs to detect any single incident, you can also monitor logs to detect trends. For example, an intrusion detection system (IDS) attempts to detect attacks and raise alerts or alarms. By analyzing past alerts, you can identify trends, such as an increase of attacks on a specific system.
- **Security audit.** Security audits can examine the security posture of an organization. For example, a password audit can determine if the password policy is ensuring the use of strong passwords. Similarly, a periodic review of user rights can detect if users have more permissions than they should.
- **Video surveillance.** A closed-circuit television (CCTV) system can record activity and detect what occurred. It's worth noting that video surveillance can also be used as a deterrent control.
- **Motion detection.** Many alarm systems can detect motion from potential intruders and raise alarms.

Remember this

Detective controls attempt to detect when vulnerabilities have been exploited. Some examples include log monitoring, trend analysis, security audits, and CCTV systems.

Comparing Detection and Prevention Controls

It's worth stressing the differences between detection and prevention controls. A detective control can't predict when an incident will occur and it can't prevent it. In contrast, prevention controls stop the incident from occurring at all. Consider cameras and guards:

- **Video surveillance.** A simple camera without recording capabilities can prevent incidents because it acts as a deterrent. Compare this with a CCTV system with recording abilities. It includes cameras, which can prevent incidents. The full system is also a detection control because of the recording capabilities. Security professionals can review the recordings to detect incidents after they've occurred.
- **Guards.** Guards are primarily prevention controls. They will prevent many incidents just by their presence.

Corrective Controls

Corrective controls attempt to reverse the impact of an incident or problem after it has occurred. Some examples of corrective controls are:

- **IPS.** An intrusion prevention system (IPS) attempts to detect attacks and then modify the environment to block the attack from continuing. Chapter 4 covers IPSs in more depth.
- **Backups and system recovery.** Backups ensure that personnel can recover data if it is lost or corrupted. Similarly, system recovery procedures ensure administrators can recover a system after a failure. Chapter 9 covers backups and disaster recovery plans in more depth.

Deterrent Controls

Deterrent controls attempt to discourage a threat. Some deterrent controls attempt to discourage potential attackers from attacking, and others attempt to discourage employees from violating a security policy.

You can often describe many deterrent controls as preventive controls. For example, imagine an organization hires a security guard to control access to a restricted area of a building. This guard will deter most people from trying to sneak in simply by discouraging them from even trying. This deterrence prevents security incidents related to unauthorized access.

The following list identifies some physical security controls used to deter threats:

- **Cable locks.** Securing laptops to furniture with a cable lock deters thieves from stealing the laptops. Thieves can't easily steal a laptop secured this way. If they try to remove the lock, they will destroy it. Admittedly, a thief could cut the cable with a large cable cutter. However, someone walking around with a four-foot cable cutter looks suspicious. If you're not familiar with a cable lock, refer to the "Using Hardware Locks" section in Chapter 9.
- **Hardware locks.** Other locks such as locked doors securing a wiring closet or a server room also deter attacks. Many server bay cabinets also include locking cabinet doors.

Compensating Controls

Compensating controls are alternative controls used instead of a primary control. As an example, an organization might require employees to use smart cards when authenticating on a system. However, it might take time for new employees to receive their smart card. To allow new employees to access the network and still maintain a high level of security, the organization might choose to implement a Time-based One-Time Password (TOTP) as a compensating control. The compensating control still provides a strong authentication solution.

Combining Control Types and Goals

It's important to realize that the control types (technical, administrative, and physical) and control goals (preventive, detective, corrective, deterrent, and compensating) are not mutually exclusive. In other words, you can describe most controls using more than one category.

As an example, encryption is a preventive technical control. It helps prevent the loss of data confidentiality, so it is a preventive control. You implement it with technology, so it is a technical control. If you understand control categories, you shouldn't have any problems picking out the correct answers on the exam even if CompTIA combines them in a question, such as a preventive technical control.

Implementing Virtualization

Virtualization is a popular technology used within large data centers and can also be used on a regular personal computer (PC). It allows you to host one or more virtual systems, or virtual machines (VMs), on a single physical system. With today's technologies, you can host an entire virtual network within a single physical system and organizations are increasingly using virtualization to reduce costs.

When discussing VMs, you should understand the following terms:

- **Hypervisor.** The software that creates, runs, and manages the VMs is the hypervisor. Several virtualization technologies currently exist, including VMware products, Microsoft Hyper-V products, and Oracle VM VirtualBox. These applications have their own hypervisor software.
- **Host.** The physical system hosting the VMs is the host. It requires more resources than a typical system, such as multiple processors, massive amounts of RAM, fast and abundant hard drive space, and one or more fast network cards. Although these additional resources increase the cost of the host, it is still less expensive than paying for multiple physical systems. It also requires less electricity, less cooling, and less physical space.
- **Guest.** Operating systems running on the host system are guests or guest machines. Most hypervisors support several different operating systems, including various Microsoft operating systems and various Linux distributions. Additionally, most hypervisors support both 32-bit and 64-bit operating systems.
- **Host elasticity and scalability.** Elasticity and scalability refer to the ability to resize computing capacity based on the load. For example, imagine one VM has increased traffic. You can increase the amount of processing power and memory used by this server relatively easily. Similarly, it's relatively easy to decrease the resources when the load decreases.

Virtualization typically provides the best return on investment (ROI) when an organization has many underutilized servers. For example, imagine an organization has nine servers with each using only about 20 percent processing power, memory, and disk space. You could convert three physical servers to virtual hosts and run three guest servers on each physical server. Assuming all the servers are similar, this wouldn't cost any more money for the physical servers. Additionally, three physical servers consume less electricity and require less heating and ventilation to maintain.

In contrast, imagine the organization has nine servers with each using about 80 percent of their processing power, memory, and disk space. Although it is possible to convert them all to virtual servers, it requires the purchase of additional hardware. The savings from less electricity and less heating and ventilation is offset by the cost of the new servers.

Comparing Hypervisors

Hypervisor virtualization is divided into primarily two different types:

- **Type I.** *Type I hypervisors* run directly on the system hardware. They are often called bare-metal hypervisors because they don't need to run within an operating system. For example, VMware has a family of ESX/ESXi products that are Type I hypervisors.
- **Type II.** *Type II hypervisors* run as software within a host operating system. For example, the Microsoft Hyper-V hypervisor runs within a Microsoft operating system.

Figure 1.1 shows a single computer hosting three guest operating systems using Type II hypervisor-based virtualization. Notice that each guest has a full operating system, including its own *kernel*. Don't let the term kernel throw you. Generically, a kernel is just the central part or most important part of something. When referring to a computer, the kernel is the central part of the operating system.

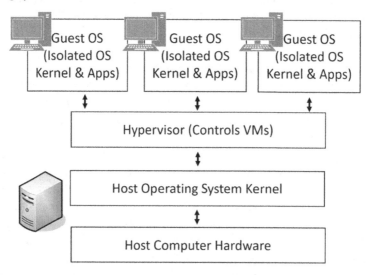

Figure 1.1: Type II hypervisor-based virtualization

When implementing virtualization on a PC, you will use Type II hypervisor-based virtualization. However, virtualization in large-scale data centers typically uses Type I virtualization.

Application Cell or Container Virtualization

Application cell virtualization or container virtualization runs services or applications within isolated application cells (or containers). For comparison, Figure 1.2 shows an example of container virtualization. Notice that the containers don't host an entire operating system. Instead, the host's operating system and kernel run the service or app within each of the containers. However, because they are running in separate containers, none of the services or apps can interfere with services and apps in other containers.

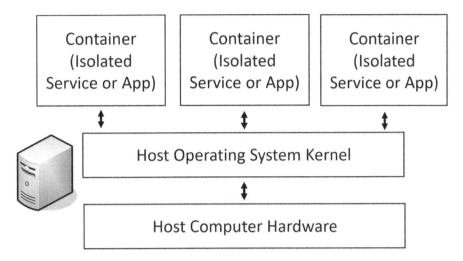

Figure 1.2: Container-based virtualization

A benefit of container virtualization is that it uses fewer resources and can be more efficient than a system using a traditional Type II hypervisor virtualization. Internet Service Providers (ISPs) often use it for customers who need specific applications. One drawback is that containers must use the operating system of the host. As an example, if the host is running Linux, all the containers must run Linux.

> **Remember this**
>
> Type I hypervisors run directly on bare-metal systems without an operating system. Type II hypervisors are software that run within an operating system. Container virtualization runs within isolated cells or containers and does not have its own kernel.

Secure Network Architecture

It is possible to use virtualization as part of an overall secure network architecture. One of the primary benefits is that VMs can provide segregation, segmentation, and isolation of individual systems. One way of doing so is to disable the network interface card (NIC) in the VM. This prevents it from transmitting any data in or out of the VM.

Snapshots

A *snapshot* provides you with a copy of the VM at a moment in time, which you can use as a backup. You are still able to use the VM just as you normally would. However, after taking a snapshot, the hypervisor keeps a record of all changes to the VM. If the VM develops a problem, you can revert the VM to the state it was in when you took the snapshot.

Administrators commonly take snapshots of systems prior to performing any risky operation. Risky operations include applying patches or updates, testing security controls, and installing new applications. Ideally, these operations do not cause any problems, but occasionally they do. By creating snapshots before these operations, administrators can easily revert or roll back the system to a known good state with a known good configuration.

> ### Remember this
>
> Virtualization allows multiple virtual servers to operate on a single physical server. It provides increased availability with lower operating costs. Additionally, virtualization provides a high level of flexibility when testing security controls, updates, and patches because they can easily be reverted using snapshots.

VDI/VDE and Non-Persistence

In addition to virtualization servers, it's also possible to virtualize desktops. In a virtual desktop infrastructure (VDI) or virtual desktop environment (VDE), a user's desktop operating system runs as a VM on a server.

One benefit of using a *VDI/VDE* is that user PCs can have limited hardware resources. If the PC can connect to a server over a network, it can run a full-featured desktop operating system from the server.

A primary consideration when running virtual desktops is whether they will support persistence or *non-persistence*. In a persistent virtual desktop, each user has a custom desktop image. Users can customize them and save their data within the desktop. A drawback is the amount of disk space required on the server to support unique desktop images for all users.

Virtual desktops that support non-persistence serve the same desktop for all users. When a user accesses the remote server, it provides a desktop operating system from a preconfigured snapshot. Although users can make changes to the desktop as they're using it, it reverts to a known state (the original snapshot) when they log off. Another way of viewing this is that it rolls back to a known configuration.

VMs as Files

It's worth pointing out that virtual machines are simply files. These files certainly have some complexity, but still, they are just files. If you do the labs to create VMs on your computer, you'll be asked where you want to store these files. If you have a Windows computer, you can use File Explorer to browse to that location and view the files.

Because the VM is just a group of files, it becomes relatively easy to move them from one physical server to another. For example, if one of your physical servers becomes overloaded, you can move virtual servers off the overloaded system to another physical server. Some virtual server management software makes this as simple as dragging and dropping the virtual servers from one host to another.

It's also easy to restore a failed virtual server. If you create a backup of the virtual server files and the original server fails, you simply restore the files. You can measure the amount of time it takes to restore a virtual server in minutes. In contrast, rebuilding a physical server can take hours.

Many virtualization products allow you to manage multiple virtual systems on a single server, even when the virtual servers are running on separate physical hosts. For example, you might have five physical servers hosting three virtual servers each, and you can manage all of them through a single management interface. This includes taking snapshots, reverting snapshots, and moving the virtual servers from one physical host to another.

Risks Associated with Virtualization

Despite the strengths of virtualization technologies, you should understand some weaknesses. Many people consider virtual machine escape (VM escape) to be the most serious threat to virtual system security. Loss of confidentiality and loss of availability can also be a concern.

VM Escape

VM escape is an attack that allows an attacker to access the host system from within the virtual system. As previously mentioned, the host system runs an application or process called a hypervisor to manage the virtual systems. In some situations, the attacker can run code on the virtual system and interact with the hypervisor.

Most virtual systems run on a physical server with elevated privileges, similar to administrator privileges. A successful VM escape attack often gives the attacker unlimited control over the host system and each virtual system within the host.

When vendors discover VM escape vulnerabilities, they write and release patches. Just as with any patches, it is important to test and install these patches as soon as possible. This includes keeping both the physical and the virtual servers patched.

VM Sprawl

VM sprawl occurs when an organization has many VMs that aren't managed properly. Most organizations have specific policies in place to ensure physical servers are kept up to date and personnel only make changes to these servers after going through a change management process. These same policies should also apply to virtual servers.

Consider this scenario. Bart creates a VM running a Microsoft Windows Server version to test a software application. After testing the application, he leaves the VM running. Later, Microsoft releases security patches for the server. The IT department tests these patches and applies them to all of the known servers that need them. However, because Bart didn't tell anyone he was creating the VM, it remains unpatched and vulnerable to attack.

Another challenge with VM sprawl is that each VM adds additional load onto a server. If unauthorized VMs are added to physical servers, they can consume system resources. The servers might become slower and potentially crash.

Loss of Confidentiality

As a reminder, each virtual system or virtual machine is just one or more files. Although this makes it easy to manage and move virtual machines, it also makes them easy to steal.

It's worth pointing out that many VMs include the operating system and data, just as a physical system would have both the operating system and data on its physical drives. For example, a virtual machine can include a database with credit card data, company financial records, or any type of proprietary data.

Imagine if an administrator became disgruntled. He has access to the systems and as a malicious insider, he can copy the virtual machine, take it home, and launch it on another physical server. At this point, he has access to the system and the data.

Running Kali Linux in a VM

Kali Linux is a free Linux distribution used by many security professionals for penetration testing and security auditing. Additionally, CompTIA listed Kali as one of the recommended software tools. The good news is that you can download Kali Linux for free and install it as a VM using one of the available free virtualization tools.

You can follow the online labs (*http://gcgapremium.com/501labs/*) to install Kali Linux within a VM. Note that you have some choices:

- **Hyper-V.** If you're running a version of Windows that supports Hyper-V, you can enable it on Windows and run VMs within it. One benefit of this is that in addition to creating a VM, you can also create a virtual switch.
- **VMware Workstation Player.** If your system doesn't support Hyper-V, you can run the free version of VMware Workstation Player. A drawback is that the free version of VMware Workstation Player doesn't support running multiple VMs within a single virtual environment. However, you can upgrade to the paid version of VMware Workstation Pro to gain this and multiple other features.
- **Oracle VM VirtualBox.** This has been my favorite in the past. However, when writing this chapter, Kali Linux wouldn't successfully install in Oracle VM VirtualBox on my Windows system. This might be due to technical issues that Microsoft or Oracle will resolve with updates. Give it a try if you like. It might work perfectly for you.

Once you have Kali Linux installed in a virtual environment, you'll also be able to run some of the command-line tools mentioned in the CompTIA objectives that only run within Linux.

Using Command-Line Tools

Command-line tools can be invaluable when troubleshooting or analyzing systems. If you know how to use them, they can make many tasks easier. Additionally, the CompTIA Security+ objectives list several command-line tools that you should know to help you assess the security posture of an organization. Some are specific to Windows systems and run through the Windows Command Prompt window. Others are specific to Linux systems and run through the Linux terminal (sometimes called the shell).

As you read through this section and learn about these tools, I strongly encourage you to run the commands. You will also find some basic commands that you can run through in the online labs at *http://gcgapremium.com/501labs/*.

A challenge many test takers have is that they don't have a Linux system to play around with these commands. If you can't enter them and see what they do, you might have trouble with even the easy questions. The online labs include labs you can use to create a virtual Linux environment on a Windows system.

Windows Command Line

Before you can use the command line in Windows, you first need to launch the Windows Command Prompt window. The simplest way to launch the Command Prompt window is to right-click the Start button and select Command Prompt, as shown in Figure 1.3. The Start button is at the lower left of your screen and clicking it displays the Start menu with links to many commonly used applications.

Figure 1.3: Launching the Windows Command Prompt window

In some situations, you need to start the Command Prompt window with elevated permissions as an administrator. To do this, right-click the Start button and select Command Prompt (Admin).

If you're using a different version of Windows (or Microsoft decides to modify the function of the Start button again), a quick search with your favorite search engine should help you identify how to open the Command Prompt window.

Linux Terminal

The terminal is where you run commands in a Linux system. There are different ways to access the terminal depending on the distribution you're using. If you're running Kali Linux (recommended while using this book), you can start it by simply clicking the terminal icon on the Kali menu.

Figure 1.4 shows an instance of Kali with the menu on the left. If you hover over the second icon, you'll see "Terminal" appear. Click it and it starts the terminal.

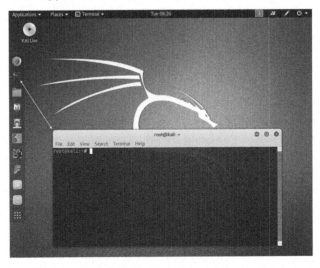

Figure 1.4: Launching the terminal in Kali Linux

For simplicity, instead of stating "Linux or Unix" throughout this book, I'm just stating it as Linux. Note that Linux is a version of Unix and commands that can be run in a Unix terminal can also be run in a Linux terminal.

Understanding Switches and Getting Help

Almost every command you'll run across has options available that you can invoke with a switch. A Windows command-line switch uses a forward slash (/) or a dash (-) after the command and includes an option that modifies the command to perform a different function.

Linux commands use switches too, but they typically only use a dash. If you use a forward slash, you will typically get unexpected results or an error.

The most used switch in Windows systems is the help switch identified with a question mark. For example, you can use the help switch to get help using these commands:

- ping /? or ping -?
- ipconfig /? or ipconfig -?
- netstat /? or netstat -?

Although Linux terminal commands use switches too, they don't use the question mark for help. Instead, if you want basic help on a command, you can often just type the command without any switch, or use the pipe symbol (|) and the word help:

- ping
- ping | help

Most Linux distributions include a built-in user manual that you can query. The manual is organized by man pages and you query them with the man command. For example, you can use the following command to get help on ping:

- man ping

Unfortunately, there isn't a consistent standard to get help for all commands in Linux. Sometimes, one method works, but another one doesn't. The key is to know the different methods so that you can use an alternate method if necessary.

Understanding Case

Most Windows commands are not case sensitive. In other words, you can type in a command using uppercase characters, lowercase characters, or any combination. For example, each of the following commands will ping the localhost IPv6 address (::1) and provide the same output:

- ping -6 localhost
- PiNg -6 localHOST
- PING -6 LocalHost

However, this is not true in the Linux terminal. Instead, commands are typically lowercase and if you use uppercase letters, you'll find that the command is not recognized. Of the three commands shown for the Windows command line, only ping -6 localhost will work within the Linux terminal.

As you go through these commands, note that many of them support both IPv4 addresses and IPv6 addresses. By querying help, you can see how to do each.

Ping

Ping is a basic command used to test connectivity for remote systems. You can also use it to verify a system can resolve valid host names to IP addresses, test the NIC, and check the security posture of a network.

The ping command checks connectivity by sending Internet Control Message Protocol (ICMP) echo request packets. Remote systems answer with ICMP echo reply packets and if you receive echo replies, you know that the remote system is operational. As a simple example, the following command verifies that your computer can connect with another computer on your network:

ping 192.168.1.1

On Windows systems, ping sends out four ICMP echo requests. Systems that receive the ICMP echo requests respond with ICMP echo replies. On Linux-based systems, ping continues until you press the Ctrl + C keys to stop it. You can mimic this behavior on Windows systems by using the -t switch like this:

ping -t 192.168.1.1

Similarly, you can mimic the behavior of a Windows ping on a Linux system using the -c switch (for count) like this:

ping -c 4 192.168.1.1

This example tested connectivity with an IP address in a local network, but you can just as easily test connectivity with any system. For example, if you knew the IP address of a system hosting a web site on the Internet, you could ping its IP address.

Using Ping to Check Name Resolution

The name resolution process resolves a host name (such as getcertifiedgetahead.com) to an IP address. There are several elements of name resolution. Typically, a computer will query a Domain Name System (DNS) with the host name and DNS will respond with an IP address.

Some malware attempts to break the name resolution process for specific hosts. For example, Windows systems get updates from a Windows Update server. In some cases, malware changes the name resolution process to prevent systems from reaching the Windows Update server and getting updates.

You can ping the host name of a remote system and verify that name resolution is working. As an example, the following command will resolve the host name (getcertifiedgetahead.com) to an IP address:

ping getcertifiedgetahead.com

Here's the result when the command is executed at the command prompt on a Windows 10 system. Notice that the first line shows that ping resolved the host name (getcertifiedgetahead.com) to its IP address (72.52.206.134):

```
Pinging getcertifiedgetahead.com [72.52.206.134] with 32 bytes of
data:
Reply from 72.52.206.134: bytes=32 time=45ms TTL=116
Reply from 72.52.206.134: bytes=32 time=45ms TTL=116
Reply from 72.52.206.134: bytes=32 time=48ms TTL=116
Reply from 72.52.206.134: bytes=32 time=45ms TTL=116
Ping statistics for 72.52.206.134:
Packets: Sent = 4, Received = 4, Lost = 0 (0% loss),
Approximate round trip times in milli-seconds:
Minimum = 45ms, Maximum = 48ms, Average = 45ms
```

Beware of Firewalls

If you receive replies from a system, it verifies the other system is operational and reachable. However, if the ping command fails, it doesn't necessarily mean that the remote system is operational or not reachable. Ping might show a "Reply Timed Out" error even if the remote system is functioning properly.

Many denial-of-service (DoS) attacks use ICMP to disrupt services on Internet-based systems. To protect systems, firewalls commonly block ICMP traffic to prevent these attacks from succeeding. In other words, a remote system might be operational, but a ping will fail because the firewall is blocking ICMP traffic.

As an example, you might be able to connect to the *http://blogs.getcertifiedgetahead.com* web site using a web browser, but ping might fail. This indicates that the web site is operational with Hypertext Transfer Protocol (HTTP), but a firewall is blocking ICMP traffic.

Using Ping to Check Security Posture

You can also use ping to check the security posture of a network. For example, if you've configured firewalls and routers to block ping traffic, you can verify the firewalls and routers are blocking the traffic by using ping to check it.

Chapter 4 covers intrusion prevention systems (IPSs) in more depth, but as an introduction, they can often detect attacks and block them automatically. For example, a simple distributed denial-of-service (DDoS) attack can send thousands of pings to a server and overload it. An IPS can detect the attack and automatically block ICMP traffic, effectively preventing any impact from the attack.

You can use ping to simulate an attack from a couple of computers to repeatedly send ping requests. If the IPS is working, it will block these attacks and the pings will stop receiving replies.

> **Remember this**
>
> Administrators use ping to check connectivity of remote systems and verify name resolution is working. They also use ping to check the security posture of systems and networks by verifying that routers, firewalls, and IPSs block ICMP traffic when configured to do so.

Ipconfig, ifconfig, and ip

The *ipconfig* command (short for Internet Protocol configuration) shows the Transmission Control Protocol/Internet Protocol (TCP/IP) configuration information for a system. This includes items such as the computer's IP address, subnet mask, default gateway, MAC address, and the address of a Domain Name System (DNS) server. The command shows the configuration information for all network interface cards (NICs) on a system, including both wired and wireless NICs. Technicians often use ipconfig as a first step when troubleshooting network problems.

Linux-based systems use *ifconfig* (short for interface configuration) instead of ipconfig. A benefit is that ifconfig has more capabilities than ipconfig, allowing you to use it to configure the NIC in addition to listing the properties of the NIC.

The following list shows some common commands:

- **ipconfig.** Entered by itself, the command provides basic information about the NIC, such as the IP address, subnet mask, and default gateway.

- **ipconfig /all.** This command shows a comprehensive listing of TCP/IP configuration information for each NIC. It includes the media access control (MAC) address, the address of assigned DNS servers, and the address of a Dynamic Host Configuration Protocol (DHCP) server if the system is a DHCP client. You can use ifconfig -a on Linux systems.
- **ipconfig /displaydns.** Each time a system queries DNS to resolve a host name to an IP address, it stores the result in the DNS cache and this command shows the contents of the DNS cache. It also shows any host name to IP address mappings included in the hosts file.
- **ipconfig /flushdns.** You can erase the contents of the DNS cache with this command. Use this when the cache has incorrect information and you want to ensure that DNS is queried for up-to-date information.

The following commands are unique to Linux systems:

- **ifconfig eth0.** This command shows the configuration of the first Ethernet interface (NIC) on a Linux system. If the system has multiple NICs, you can use eth1, eth2, and so on. You can also use wlan0 to view information on the first wireless interface.
- **ifconfig eth0 promisc.** This command enables promiscuous mode on the first Ethernet interface. Promiscuous mode allows a NIC to process all traffic it receives. Normally, a NIC is in non-promiscuous mode and it ignores all packets not addressed to it. You can disable promiscuous mode with this command: ifconfig eth0 -promisc.
- **ifconfig eth0 allmulti.** This command enables multicast mode on the NIC. This allows the NIC to process all multicast traffic received by the NIC. Normally, a NIC will only process multicast traffic for multicast groups that it has joined. You can disable multicast mode with this command: ifconfig eth0 -allmulti.

Normally, a NIC uses non-promiscuous mode and only processes packets addressed directly to its IP address. However, when you put it in promiscuous mode, it processes all packets regardless of the IP address. This allows the protocol analyzer to capture all packets that reach the NIC.

The ifconfig command was deprecated in 2009 in Debian distributions of Linux. Deprecated means that its use is discouraged but tolerated. The ifconfig command is part of the net-tools package and Linux Debian developers are no longer maintaining that package. However, you'll still see ifconfig and other tools in the net-tools package on most Linux systems, including Kali Linux.

Instead of using ifconfig, Linux developers recommend you use *ip* instead. Although the ip command can display information and configure network interfaces, it doesn't use the same commands or have the same abilities. For example, it doesn't have a command you can use to enable promiscuous mode on a NIC. Here are a few commands that you can use with ip:

- **ip link show.** Shows the interfaces along with some details on them
- **ip link set eth0 up.** Enables a network interface
- **ip -s link.** Shows statistics on the network interfaces

Remember this

Windows systems use ipconfig to view network interfaces. Linux systems use ifconfig, and ifconfig can also manipulate the settings on the network interfaces. You can enable promiscuous mode on a NIC with ifconfig. The ip command is similar to ifconfig and can be used to view and manipulate NIC settings.

Netstat

The *netstat* command (short for network statistics) allows you to view statistics for TCP/IP protocols on a system. It also gives you the ability to view active TCP/IP network connections. Many attacks establish connections from an infected computer to a remote computer. If you suspect this, you can often identify these connections with netstat.

Some of the common commands you can use with netstat are:

- **Netstat.** Displays a listing of all open TCP connections.
- **Netstat -a.** Displays a listing of all TCP and User Datagram Protocol (UDP) ports that a system is listening on, in addition to all open connections. This listing includes the IP address followed by a colon and the port number, and you can use the port number to identify protocols. As an example, if you see an IP address followed by :80, it indicates the system is listening on the default port of 80 for HTTP. This indicates this system is likely a web server.
- **Netstat –r.** Displays the routing table.
- **Netstat -e.** Displays details on network statistics, including how many bytes the system sent and received.
- **Netstat -s.** Displays statistics of packets sent or received for specific protocols, such as IP, ICMP, TCP, and UDP.
- **Netstat -n.** Displays addresses and port numbers in numerical order. This can be useful if you're looking for information related to a specific IP address or a specific port.
- **Netstat -p *protocol*.** Shows statistics on a specific protocol, such as TCP or UDP. For example, you could use netstat -p tcp to show only TCP statistics.

You can combine many of the netstat switches to show different types of information. For example, if you want to show a listing of ports that the system is listening on (-a), listed in numerical order (-n), for only the TCP protocol (-p tcp), you could use this command:

netstat -anp tcp

Netstat displays the state of a connection, such as ESTABLISHED to indicate an active connection. RFC 793 (*https://tools.ietf.org/rfc/rfc793.txt*) formally defines these states. Some of the common states are:

- **ESTABLISHED.** This is the normal state for the data transfer phase of a connection. It indicates an active open connection.
- **LISTEN.** This indicates the system is waiting for a connection request. The well-known port a system is listening on indicates the protocol.
- **CLOSE_WAIT.** This indicates the system is waiting for a connection termination request.
- **TIME_WAIT.** This indicates the system is waiting for enough time to pass to be sure the remote system received a TCP-based acknowledgment of the connection.
- **SYN_SENT.** This indicates the system sent a TCP SYN (synchronize) packet as the first part of the SYN, SYN-ACK (synchronize-acknowledge), ACK (acknowledge) handshake process and it is waiting for the SYN-ACK response.
- **SYN_RECEIVED.** This indicates the system sent a TCP SYN-ACK packet after receiving a SYN packet as the first part of the SYN, SYN-ACK, ACK handshake process. It is waiting for the ACK response to establish the connection. An excessive number of SYN_RECEIVED states indicate a SYN attack where an attacker is flooding a system with SYN packets but never finalizes the connection with ACK packets.

Tracert

The *tracert* command lists the routers between two systems. In this context, each router is referred to as a hop. Tracert identifies the IP address and sometimes the host name of each hop in addition to the round-trip times (RTTs) for each hop. Windows-based systems use tracert and Linux-based systems use traceroute, but they both function similarly. For simplicity, I'm using the command name tracert in this section, but this section applies to both equally.

Network administrators typically use tracert to identify faulty routers on the network. Ping tells them if they can reach a distant server. If the ping fails, they can use tracert to identify where the traffic stops. Some of the hops will succeed, but at some point, tracert will identify where packets are lost, giving them insight into where the problem has occurred. Other times, they will see where the RTTs increase as traffic is routed around a faulty router. Tracing a path is especially valuable when troubleshooting issues through a wide area network (WAN).

From a security perspective, you can use tracert to identify modified paths. As an example, consider Figure 1.5. Users within the internal network normally access the Internet directly through Router 1. However, what if an attacker installed an unauthorized router between Router 1 and the Internet?

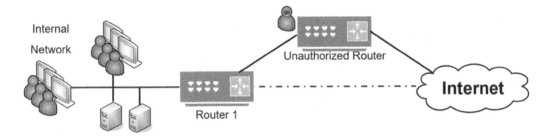

Figure 1.5: Tracing a path with tracert

Traffic will still go back and forth to the users. However, the attacker could capture the traffic with a protocol analyzer and view any data sent in cleartext. The attacker may also launch other attacks, such as some of the attacks discussed in Chapter 7.

From another perspective, you can identify if Internet paths have been modified. Imagine that you often connect to a server in New York from a New York location. Today, the connection seems abnormally slow. You could use tracert to verify the path. If you notice that traffic is now going through IP addresses in foreign countries, it indicates a problem.

Give it a try. Launch a command prompt and use the following commands to see some common uses and outputs from the tracert command:

- Type in **tracert blogs.getcertifiedgetahead.com** and press Enter. Identify how many hops are between your system and this web server. Identify if any RTTs are significantly longer than others.
- Type in **tracert –d blogs.getcertifiedgetahead.com** and press Enter. Notice that the -d switch forces tracert to not resolve IP addresses to host names, allowing the command to finish more quickly.

Arp

Arp is a command-line tool that is related to the Address Resolution Protocol (ARP); however, arp (the command) and ARP (the protocol) are not the same thing. Chapter 3 discusses ARP (the protocol), but as a short introduction, ARP resolves IP addresses to MAC addresses and stores the result in the ARP cache.

You can use the arp command to view and manipulate the ARP cache. Here are some sample commands:

- **arp.** Without a switch, shows help on Windows
- **arp.** Without a switch, shows the ARP cache on Linux
- **arp -a.** Shows the ARP cache on Windows
- **arp -a 192.168.1.1.** Displays the ARP cache entry for the specified IP address

You can also use arp to identify the MAC address of other systems on your local network. As an example, imagine you want to identify the MAC address of server1. You can ping server1 and ARP will identify server1's IP address. You can then use arp -a to show the ARP cache, which includes the MAC address for server1.

Chapter 7 covers several attacks, including ARP cache poisoning where attackers manipulate the ARP cache. If you suspect an ARP cache poisoning attack, you can use arp to check the cache.

Chapter 1 Exam Topic Review

When preparing for the exam, make sure you understand these key concepts covered in this chapter.

Understanding Core Security Goals

- A use case helps professionals identify and clarify requirements to achieve a goal.
- Confidentiality ensures that data is only viewable by authorized users. Encryption is the best choice to provide confidentiality. Access controls also protect the confidentiality of data.
- Steganography (hiding data inside other data) is one method of supporting obfuscation by making the hidden data harder to see.
- Integrity provides assurances that data has not been modified, tampered with, or corrupted through unauthorized or unintended changes. Data can be a message, a file, or data within a database. Hashing is a common method of ensuring integrity.
- Non-repudiation prevents entities from denying they took an action. Digital signatures and audit logs provide non-repudiation. Digital signatures also provide integrity for files and email.
- Availability ensures that data and services are available when needed. A common goal is to remove single points of failure. Methods used to increase or maintain availability include fault tolerance, failover clusters, load balancing, backups, virtualization, HVAC systems, and generators.

Introducing Basic Risk Concepts

- Risk is the possibility of a threat exploiting a vulnerability and resulting in a loss.
- A threat is any circumstance or event that has the potential to compromise confidentiality, integrity, or availability.
- A vulnerability is a weakness. It can be a weakness in the hardware, software, configuration, or users operating the system.

- Risk mitigation reduces risk by reducing the chances that a threat will exploit a vulnerability or by reducing the impact of the risk.
- Security controls reduce risks. For example, antivirus software is a security control that reduces the risk of virus infection.

Understanding Control Types

- The three primary security control types are technical (implemented with technology), administrative (using administrative or management methods), and physical (using controls that you can physically touch).
- A technical control is one that uses technology to reduce vulnerabilities. Encryption, antivirus software, IDSs, firewalls, and the principle of least privilege are technical controls.
- Administrative controls are primarily administrative and include items such as risk and vulnerability assessments. Some administrative controls help ensure that day-to-day operations of an organization comply with their overall security plan. Some examples include security awareness and training, configuration management, and change management.
- Preventive controls attempt to prevent security incidents. Examples include system hardening, user training, guards, change management, and account disablement policies.
- Detective controls attempt to detect when a vulnerability has been exploited. Examples include log monitoring, trend analysis, security audits (such as a periodic review of user rights), video surveillance systems, and motion detection systems.
- Corrective controls attempt to reverse the impact of an incident or problem after it has occurred. Examples include intrusion prevention systems (IPSs), backups, and system recovery plans.
- Deterrent controls attempt to prevent incidents by discouraging threats.
- Compensating controls are alternative controls used when it isn't feasible or possible to use the primary control.

Implementing Virtualization

- Virtualization allows multiple servers to operate on a single physical host. They provide increased availability with various tools such as snapshots and easy restoration.
- Type I hypervisors run directly on the system hardware. They are often called bare-metal hypervisors because they don't need to run within an operating system.
- Type II hypervisors run as software within a host operating system.
- Container virtualization is a specialized version of a Type II hypervisor. It allows services or applications to run within their own isolated cells or containers. Containers don't have a full operating system but instead use the kernel of the host.
- Snapshots capture the state of a VM at a moment in time. Administrators often take a snapshot before performing a risky operation. If necessary, they can revert the VM to the snapshot state.
- VM sprawl can occur if personnel within the organization don't manage the VMs.
- VM escape attacks allow an attacker to access the host system from the VM. The primary protection is to keep the host and guests up to date with current patches.

Using Command-Line Tools

- You run command-line tools in the Command Prompt window (in Windows) and the terminal (in Linux).

- The ping command can be used to check connectivity; check name resolution; and verify that routers, firewalls, and intrusion prevention systems block ICMP.
- The ipconfig command on Windows allows you to view the configuration of network interfaces.
- Linux uses ifconfig and/or ip to view and manipulate the configuration of network interfaces. You can enable promiscuous mode on a NIC with ifconfig.
- Netstat allows you to view statistics for TCP/IP protocols and view all active network connections. This can be useful if you suspect malware is causing a computer to connect with a remote computer.
- Tracert lists the routers (also called hops) between two systems. It can be used to verify a path has not changed.
- The arp command allows you to view and manipulate the ARP cache. This can be useful if you suspect a system's ARP cache has been modified during an attack.

Online References

- Remember, you can access online references such as labs and sample performance-based questions at *http://gcgapremium.com/501-extras*.

Chapter 1 Practice Questions

1. You need to transmit PII via email and you want to maintain its confidentiality. Which of the following choices is the BEST solution?
    A. Use hashes.
    B. Encrypt it before sending.
    C. Protect it with a digital signature.
    D. Use RAID.

2. Apu manages network devices in his store and maintains copies of the configuration files for all the managed routers and switches. On a weekly basis, he creates hashes for these files and compares them with hashes he created on the same files the previous week. Which of the following use cases is he MOST likely using?
    A. Supporting confidentiality
    B. Supporting integrity
    C. Supporting encryption
    D. Supporting availability

3. Louie hid several plaintext documents within an image file. He then sent the image file to Tony. Which of the following BEST describes the purpose of his actions?
    A. To support steganography
    B. To support integrity
    C. To support availability
    D. To support obfuscation

4. Management has mandated the use of digital signatures by all personnel within your organization. Which of the following use cases does this primarily support?
    A. Supporting confidentiality
    B. Supporting availability
    C. Supporting obfuscation
    D. Supporting non-repudiation

5. As the CTO, Marge is implementing a security program. She has included security controls to address confidentiality and availability. Of the following choices, what else should she include?
    A. Ensure critical systems provide uninterrupted service.
    B. Protect data-in-transit from unauthorized disclosure.
    C. Ensure systems are not susceptible to unauthorized changes.
    D. Secure data to prevent unauthorized disclosure.

6. Your organization wants to reduce the amount of money it is losing due to thefts. Which of the following is the BEST example of an equipment theft deterrent?
    A. Snapshots
    B. Cable locks
    C. Strong passwords
    D. Persistent VDI

7. Your organization is considering virtualization solutions. Management wants to ensure that any solution provides the best ROI. Which of the following situations indicates that virtualization would provide the best ROI?
    A. Most physical servers within the organization are currently utilized at close to 100 percent.
    B. The organization has many servers that do not require failover services.
    C. Most desktop PCs require fast processors and a high amount of memory.
    D. Most physical servers within the organization are currently underutilized.

8. You are preparing to deploy a new application on a virtual server. The virtual server hosts another server application that employees routinely access. Which of the following is the BEST method to use when deploying the new application?
    A. Take a snapshot of the VM before deploying the new application.
    B. Take a snapshot of the VM after deploying the new application.
    C. Ensure the server is configured for non-persistence.
    D. Back up the server after installing the new application.

9. Ned is not able to access any network resources from his Linux-based computer. Which of the following commands would he use to view the network configuration of his system?
    A. ifconfig
    B. ipconfig
    C. netstat
    D. tracert

10. Administrators frequently create VMs for testing. They sometimes leave these running without using them again after they complete their tests. Which of the following does this describe?
    A. VM escape
    B. VDI snapshot
    C. VM sprawl
    D. Type II hypervisor

11. Users within your organization access virtual desktops hosted on remote servers. This describes which of the following?
    A. VDE
    B. Snapshots for non-persistence
    C. Type I hypervisors
    D. VM sprawl

12. Your organization has implemented a VDI for most users. When a user logs off, the desktop reverts to its original state without saving any changes made by the user. Which of the following BEST describes this behavior?
    A. Container virtualization
    B. VM escape
    C. Non-persistence
    D. Elasticity

13. Which type of virtualization allows a computer's operating system kernel to run multiple isolated instances of a guest virtual machine, with each guest sharing the kernel?
    A. Container virtualization
    B. Type I hypervisor virtualization
    C. Type II hypervisor virtualization
    D. VDE

14. You are considering rebooting a database server and want to identify if it has any active network connections. Which of the following commands will list active network connections?
    A. arp
    B. ipconfig
    C. ping
    D. netstat

15. You have configured a firewall in your network to block ICMP traffic. You want to verify that it is blocking this traffic. Which of the following commands would you use?
    A. arp
    B. ipconfig
    C. netstat
    D. ping

Chapter 1 Practice Question Answers

1. **B.** You can maintain confidentiality of any data, including Personally Identifiable Information (PII) with encryption. Hashes provide integrity, not confidentiality. A digital signature provides authentication, non-repudiation, and integrity. A redundant array of inexpensive disks (RAID) provides higher availability for a disk subsystem.

2. **B.** He is most likely using a use case of supporting integrity. By verifying that the hashes are the same on the configuration files, he is verifying that the files have not changed. Confidentiality is enforced with encryption, access controls, and steganography. Encryption is a method of enforcing confidentiality and it doesn't use hashes. Availability ensures systems are up and operational when needed.

3. **D.** Hiding data within data is one way to support a use case of supporting obfuscation. In this scenario, Louie is using steganography to hide the files within the image, but that is the method, not the purpose. Hashing methods and digital signatures support integrity. Redundancy and fault-tolerance methods increase availability.

4. **D.** Digital signatures will support a use case of supporting non-repudiation. Digital signatures don't encrypt data, so they do not support a use case of supporting confidentiality. Redundancy and fault-tolerance solutions will increase availability. Steganography is one way of supporting obfuscation.

5. **C.** The chief technology officer (CTO) should ensure systems are not susceptible to unauthorized changes, which is an element of integrity. A security program should address the three core security principles of confidentiality, integrity, and availability (CIA). The system in the example is already addressing confidentiality and availability. Ensuring critical systems provide uninterrupted service addresses availability. Protecting data and securing data to prevent unauthorized disclosure addresses confidentiality.

6. **B.** Cable locks are effective equipment theft deterrents for laptops and other systems. Snapshots refer to digital snapshots that capture the state of a virtual machine at a moment in time. Passwords prevent unauthorized access to systems, but don't provide physical security. A virtual desktop infrastructure (VDI) allows users to access a desktop on a remote server. A persistent VDI saves the user changes on the desktop, but it does not deter thefts.

7. **D.** If most physical servers within the organization are currently underutilized, virtualization will provide a high return on investment (ROI). If the servers are currently utilized close to 100 percent, new servers will need to be purchased to virtualize them. It is possible to implement failover services on virtualized servers so there is little cost difference between physical and virtualized servers. The amount of processing power or memory requirements isn't relevant unless you know how much systems are currently utilizing.

8. **A.** Taking a snapshot of the virtual machine (VM) before deploying it ensures that the VM can be reverted to the original configuration if the new application causes problems. Taking a snapshot after the installation doesn't allow you to revert the image. Non-persistence is used in a virtual desktop infrastructure (VDI), where user changes to the desktop are not changed. It isn't appropriate to use non-persistence on a virtual server. Backing up the server might be appropriate before installing the new application but not after.

9. **A.** The ifconfig command displays network settings on a Linux computer. This includes the IP address, subnet mask, and default gateway assigned to the network interface card (NIC). The ipconfig command performs similar checks on Windows computers, but not on Linux systems. Netstat shows network statistics and active connections but not the network settings. The tracert command traces the route of data and can help determine which network devices are failing.

10. **C.** VM sprawl occurs when an organization has many VMs that aren't managed properly. Unmonitored VMs typically won't get updated and can be vulnerable to attacks. VM escape is an attack that allows an attacker to access the host system from within the

virtual system. A virtual desktop infrastructure (VDI) provides users with virtual desktops hosted on a server. A VDI snapshot is commonly used to provide users with the same non-persistent desktop that doesn't save changes. The VMs might be Type II hypervisors (running as software within a host operating system), but that isn't relevant to leaving them running and unmonitored.

11. **A.** In a virtual desktop environment (VDE), users access virtual desktops hosted on remote servers. VDE desktops can use snapshots for non-persistence, but it is also possible to allow users to have persistent unique desktops in a VDE. Type I hypervisors (bare-metal hypervisors) run directly on the system without an operating system and are not used for a VDE. VM sprawl describes a problem of many unmanaged VMs, but the scenario doesn't mention that the virtual desktops are not managed.

12. **C.** Non-persistence in a virtual desktop infrastructure (VDI) indicates that the desktop is the same for most (or all) users and when the user logs off, the desktop reverts to a known state or rolls back to a known configuration. With container virtualization, application cells run isolated services or applications within the host, using the host's kernel. Virtual machine (VM) escape is an attack where the attacker accesses the host system from within the VM. Elasticity refers to the ability to resize a VM in response to increased or decreased load.

13. **A.** Container-based virtualization (also called application cell virtualization) uses the same operating system kernel of the host computer. It is often used to run isolated applications or services within a virtual environment. Type I hypervisor virtualization runs directly on the system hardware. Type II hypervisor virtualization runs VMs that all include their own operating system, including their own kernel. A virtual desktop environment (VDE) provides a full desktop operating system to users.

14. **D.** The netstat command displays active connections on a system. Arp displays information related to media access control (MAC) addresses. Ipconfig displays TCP/IP configuration information for wired and wireless network interface cards. Ping checks connectivity with remote systems.

15. **D.** The ping command sends Internet Control Message Protocol (ICMP) echo requests and checks for ICMP echo replies. Arp resolves IP addresses to media access control (MAC) addresses and does not use echo commands. Ipconfig checks the configuration of a NIC. Netstat shows active connections and network statistics.

Chapter 2

Understanding Identity and Access Management

CompTIA Security+ objectives covered in this chapter:

1.6   Explain the impact associated with types of vulnerabilities.
- Improperly configured accounts

2.3   Given a scenario, troubleshoot common security issues.
- Unencrypted credentials/clear text, Authentication issues

2.6   Given a scenario, implement secure protocols.
- Protocols (LDAPS)

3.3   Given a scenario, implement secure systems design.
- Operating systems (Disable default accounts/passwords)

4.1   Compare and contrast identity and access management concepts.
- Identification, authentication, authorization and accounting (AAA), Multifactor authentication (Something you are, Something you have, Something you know, Somewhere you are, Something you do), Federation, Single sign-on, Transitive trust

4.2   Given a scenario, install and configure identity and access services.
- LDAP, Kerberos, SAML, OpenID Connect, OAUTH, Shibboleth, Secure token, NTLM

4.3   Given a scenario, implement identity and access management controls.
- Access control models (MAC, DAC, ABAC, Role-based access control, Rule-based access control), Biometric factors (Fingerprint scanner, Retinal scanner, Iris scanner, Voice recognition, Facial recognition, False acceptance rate, False rejection rate, Crossover error rate), Tokens (Hardware, Software, HOTP/TOTP), Certificate-based authentication (PIV/CAC/smart card)

4.4   Given a scenario, differentiate common account management practices.
- Account types (User account, Shared and generic accounts/credentials, Guest accounts, Service accounts, Privileged accounts)

- General Concepts (Least privilege, Time-of-day restrictions, Recertification, Standard naming convention, Account maintenance, Group-based access control, Location-based policies)
- Account policy enforcement (Credential management, Group policy, Password complexity, Expiration, Recovery, Disablement, Lockout, Password history, Password reuse, Password length)

6.1   Compare and contrast basic concepts of cryptography.
- Common use cases (Supporting authentication)

**

Domain 4.0 in the CompTIA Security+ objectives is Identity and Access Management, which admittedly is a mouthful. In simpler language, users claim an identity with a username and prove their identity by authenticating (such as with a password). They are then granted access to resources based on their proven identity. In this chapter, you'll learn about various authentication concepts and methods, along with some basic security principles used to manage accounts. This chapter closes with a comparison of some access control models.

Exploring Authentication Concepts

Authentication proves an identity with some type of credentials, such as a username and password. For example, *identification* occurs when users claim (or profess) their identity with identifiers such as usernames or email addresses. Users then prove their identity with *authentication*, such as with a password. In this context, a user's credentials refer to both a claimed identity and an authentication mechanism.

At least two entities know the credentials. One entity, such as a user, presents the credentials. The other entity is the authenticator that verifies the credentials. For example, Marge knows her username and password, and an authenticating server knows her username and password. Marge presents her credentials to the authenticating server, and the server authenticates her.

The importance of authentication cannot be understated. You can't have any type of access control if you can't identify a user. In other words, if everyone is anonymous, then everyone has the same access to all resources.

Also, authentication is not limited to users. Services, processes, workstations, servers, and network devices all use authentication to prove their identities. Many computers use mutual authentication, where both parties authenticate to each other.

Comparing Identification and AAA

Authentication, authorization, and accounting (*AAA*) work together with identification to provide a comprehensive access management system. If you understand identification (claiming an identity, such as with a username) and authentication (providing the identity, such as with a password), it's easier to add in the other two elements of AAA—authorization and accounting.

If users can prove their identity, that doesn't mean that they are automatically granted access to all resources within a system. Instead, users are granted *authorization* to access resources based on their proven identity. This can be as simple as granting a user permission to read data in a shared folder. Access control systems include multiple security controls to ensure that users can access resources they're authorized to use, but no more.

Accounting methods track user activity and record the activity in logs. As an example, audit logs track activity and administrators use these to create an audit trail. An *audit trail* allows security professionals to re-create the events that preceded a security incident.

Effective access control starts with strong authentication mechanisms, such as the use of robust passwords, smart cards, or biometrics. If users can bypass the authentication process, the authorization and accounting processes are ineffective.

> ### Remember this
>
> Identification occurs when a user claims an identity such as with a username or email address. Authentication occurs when the user proves the claimed identity (such as with a password) and the credentials are verified. Access control systems provide authorization by granting access to resources based on permissions granted to the proven identity. Logging provides accounting.

Comparing Authentication Factors

Authentication is often simplified as types, or factors, of authentication. A use case of supporting authentication may require administrators to implement one factor of authentication for basic authentication, two factors for more secure authentication, or more factors for higher security. As an introduction, the factors are:

- Something you know, such as a password or personal identification number (PIN)
- Something you have, such as a smart card or USB token
- Something you are, such as a fingerprint or other biometric identification
- Somewhere you are, such as your location using geolocation technologies
- Something you do, such as gestures on a touch screen

Something You Know

The *something you know* authentication factor typically refers to a shared secret, such as a password or even a PIN. This factor is the least secure form of authentication. However, you can increase the security of a password by following some simple guidelines. The following sections provide more details on important password security concepts.

Password Complexity

One method used to make passwords more secure is to require them to be complex and strong. A strong password is of sufficient length, doesn't include words found in a dictionary or any part of a user's name, and combines at least three of the four following character types:

- Uppercase characters (26 letters A–Z)
- Lowercase characters (26 letters a–z)
- Numbers (10 numbers 0–9)
- Special characters (32 printable characters, such as !, $, and *)

A complex password uses multiple character types, such as Ab0@. However, a complex password isn't necessarily strong. It also needs to be sufficiently long. It's worth noting that recommendations for the best length of a strong password vary depending on the type of account. As of January 2016, Microsoft began recommending a best practice of setting the minimum password length to at least 14 characters. Organizations often require administrators to create longer passwords. A key point is that longer passwords using more character types are more secure and short passwords of 4 or 5 characters are extremely weak.

The combination of different characters in a password makes up the key space, and you can calculate the key space with the following formula: C^N (C^N). C is the number of possible characters used, and N is the length of the password. The ^ character in C^N indicates that C is raised to the N power.

For example, a 6-character password using only lowercase letters (26 letters) is calculated as 26^6 (26^6), or about 308 million possibilities. Change this to a 10-character password and the value is 26^10 (26^{10}), or about 141 trillion possibilities. Although this looks like a high number of possibilities, there are password-cracking tools that can test more than 20 billion passwords per second on desktop computers with a high-end graphics processor. An attacker can crack a 10-character password using only lowercase characters (141 trillion possibilities) in less than two hours.

However, if you use all 94 printable characters (uppercase, lowercase, numbers, and special characters) with the same 6- and 10-character password lengths, the values change significantly: 94^6 (94^6) is about 689 billion possibilities, and 94^10 (94^{10}) is about 53 quintillion. That's 53 followed by 18 zeroes.

You probably don't come across quintillion very often. The order is million, billion, trillion, quadrillion, and then quintillion. The password-cracking tool that cracks a lowercase password in two hours will take years to crack a 10-character password using all four character types.

Security experts often mention that if you make a password too complex, you make it less secure.

Read that again. It is not a typo.

More complexity equates to less security. This is because users have problems remembering overly complex passwords such as 4%kiEINsB* and they are more likely to write them down. A password written on paper or stored in a file on a user's computer significantly reduces security.

Instead, users are encouraged to use passphrases. Instead of nonsensical strings of characters, a passphrase is a long string of characters that has meaning to the user. A few examples of strong passphrases are IL0veSecurity+, IL0veThi$B00k, and IWi11P@$$. Note that these examples include all four character types—uppercase letters, lowercase letters, one or more numbers, and one or more special characters. These passwords are also known as passphrases because they are a combination of words that are easier to remember than a nonsensical string of characters such as 4*eiRS@<].

Strong passwords never include words that can be easily guessed, such as a user's name, words in a dictionary (for any language), or common key combinations.

Remember this

Complex passwords use a mix of character types. Strong passwords use a mix of character types and have a minimum password length of at least 14 characters.

Training Users About Password Behaviors

Common user habits related to password behaviors have historically ignored security. Many users don't understand the value of their password, or the potential damage if they give it out. It's important for an organization to provide adequate training to users on password security if

Ashley Madison Passwords

You might think that users never use weak passwords anymore, but that simply isn't true. As an example, attackers hacked into the Ashley Madison site in 2015 and posted information on 36 million accounts. Ashley Madison is an online dating service marketed to people who are married or in committed relationships, but still want to date others. Users have a vested interest in keeping their information private, but many were still using weak passwords.

Here's a list of some of the passwords in the top 10 list that users had created for their accounts: 123456, 12345, password, DEFAULT, 123456789, qwerty, 12345678, abc123, and 1234567. Over 120,000 users had 123456 as their password.

they use passwords within the organization. This includes both the creation of strong passwords and the importance of never giving out their passwords.

For example, the password "123456" frequently appears on lists as the most common password in use. The users who are creating this password probably don't know that it's almost like using no password at all. Also, they probably don't realize that they can significantly increase the password strength by using a simple passphrase such as "ICanCountTo6." A little training can go a long way.

Check out the online lab Using John the Ripper available at *http://gcgapremium.com/501labs/*. It shows how easy it can be to crack weak passwords.

Password Expiration

In addition to using strong passwords, users should change their passwords regularly, such as every 45 or 90 days. In most systems, technical password policies require users to change their passwords regularly. When the password expires, users are no longer able to log on unless they first change their password.

I can tell you from experience that if users are not forced to change their passwords through technical means, they often simply don't. It doesn't matter how many reminders you give them. On the other hand, when a password policy locks out user accounts until they change their password, they will change it right away.

Password Recovery

It's not uncommon for users to occasionally forget their password. In many organizations, help-desk professionals or other administrators reset user passwords.

Before resetting the password, it's important to verify the user's identity. Imagine that Hacker Harry calls into the help desk claiming to be the CEO and asks for his password to be reset. If the help-desk professional does so, it locks the CEO out of the account. Worse, depending on the process, it might give Hacker Harry access to the CEO's account. Organizations use a variety of different methods of identification before resetting a user's account to prevent these vulnerabilities.

In some systems, help-desk professionals manually change the user's password. This causes a different problem. Imagine a user calls the help desk and asks for a password reset. The help-desk professional changes the password and lets the user know the new password. However, at this point, two people know the password. The help-desk professional could use the password and impersonate the user, or the user could blame the help-desk professional for impersonating the user.

Instead, the help-desk professional should set the password as a temporary password that expires upon first use. This requires the user to change the password immediately after logging on and it maintains password integrity.

Instead of an IT professional spending valuable time resetting passwords, a self-service password reset or password recovery system automates the process. For example, many online systems include a link, such as "Forgot Password." If you click on this link, the system might send you your password via email, or reset your password and send the new password via email.

Some systems invoke an identity-proofing system. The identity-proofing system asks you questions that you previously answered, such as the name of your first dog, the name of your first boss, and so on. Once you adequately prove your identity, the system gives you the opportunity to change your password.

Many password reset systems send you a code, such as a six-digit PIN, to your mobile phone or to an alternate email address that you've preconfigured. When you receive this PIN, you can enter it and then change your password.

Remember this

Before resetting passwords for users, it's important to verify the user's identity. When resetting passwords manually, it's best to create a temporary password that expires upon first use.

Password History and Password Reuse

Many users would prefer to use the same password forever simply because it's easier to remember. Even when technical password policies force users to change their passwords, many users simply change them back to the original password. Unfortunately, this significantly weakens password security.

A password history system remembers past passwords and prevents users from reusing passwords. It's common for password policy settings to remember the last 24 passwords and prevent users from reusing these until they've used 24 new passwords.

Group Policy

Windows domains use Group Policy to manage multiple users and computers in a domain. Group Policy allows an administrator to configure a setting once in a Group Policy Object (**GPO**) and apply this setting to many users and computers within the domain. Active Directory Domain Services (AD DS) is a directory service Microsoft developed for Windows domain networks. It is included in most Windows Server operating systems as a set of processes and services. Administrators implement domain Group Policy on domain controllers.

Although you can implement Group Policy on single, stand-alone Windows computers, the great strength of Group Policy comes when you implement it in a Microsoft domain. As an example, if you want to change the local Administrator password on all the computers in your domain, you can configure a GPO once, link the GPO to the domain, and it changes the local Administrator password for all the computers in the domain. The magic of Group Policy is that it doesn't matter if you have five systems or five thousand systems. The policy still only needs to be set once to apply to all systems in the domain.

Administrators also use Group Policy to target specific groups of users or computers. For example, in a Microsoft domain, administrators organize user accounts and computer accounts in organizational units (OUs). They can then create a GPO, link it to a specific OU, and the GPO settings only apply to the users and computers within the OU. These settings do not apply to users and computers in other OUs.

> ### Remember this
>
> Group Policy is implemented on a domain controller within a domain. Administrators use it to create password policies, implement security settings, configure host-based firewalls, and much more.

Using a Password Policy

A common group of settings that administrators configure in Group Policy is the Password Policy settings. Password policies typically start as a written document that identifies the organization's security goals related to passwords. For example, it might specify that passwords must be at least 14 characters long, complex, and users should change them every 45 days. Administrators then implement these requirements with a technical control such as a technical Password Policy within a GPO.

Figure 2.1 shows the Local Group Policy Editor with the Password Policy selected in the left pane. The right pane shows the password policy for a Windows system and the following text explains these settings:

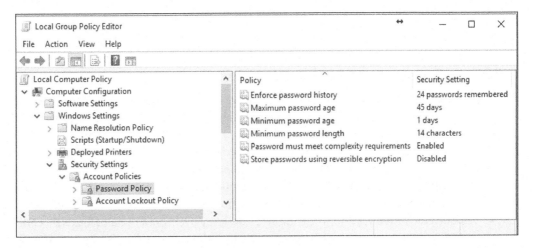

Figure 2.1: Password Policy in Windows

- **Enforce password history.** Some users will go back and forth between two passwords that they constantly use and reuse. However, password history remembers past passwords and prevents the user from reusing previously used passwords. For example, setting this to 24 prevents users from reusing passwords until they've used 24 new passwords.
- **Maximum password age.** This setting defines when users must change their password. For example, setting this to 45 days causes the password to expire after 45 days. This forces users to reset their password to a new password on the 46th day.
- **Minimum password age.** The minimum password age defines how long users must wait before changing their password again. If you set this to 1 day, it prevents users from

changing their passwords until 1 day has passed. This is useful with a password history to prevent users from changing their password multiple times until they get back to the original password. If the password history is set to 24 and the minimum password age is set to 1 day, it will take a user 25 days to get back to the original password. This is enough to discourage most users.

- **Minimum password length.** This setting enforces the character length of the password. It's common to require users to have passwords at least 14 characters long, but some organizations require administrators to have longer passwords.
- **Password must meet complexity requirements.** This setting requires users to have complex passwords that include at least three of the four character types (uppercase letters, lowercase letters, numbers, and special characters).
- **Store passwords using reversible encryption.** Reversible encryption stores the password in such a way that the original password can be discovered. This is rarely enabled.

Remember this

Password policies include several elements. The password history is used with the minimum password age to prevent users from changing their password to a previously used password. Maximum password age causes passwords to expire and requires users to change their passwords periodically. Minimum password length specifies the minimum number of characters in the password. Password complexity increases the key space, or complexity, of a password by requiring more character types.

Implementing Account Lockout Policies

Accounts will typically have lockout policies preventing users from guessing the password. If a user enters the wrong password too many times (such as three or five times), the system locks the user's account. Figure 2.1 shows the Password Policy settings. The Account Lockout Policy is right below it and allows administrators to use Group Policy to implement a lockout policy.

Two key phrases associated with account lockout policies are:

- **Account lockout threshold.** This is the maximum number of times a user can enter the wrong password. When the user exceeds the threshold, the system locks the account.
- **Account lockout duration.** This indicates how long an account remains locked. It could be set to 30, indicating that the system will lock the account for 30 minutes. After 30 minutes, the system automatically unlocks the account. If the duration is set to 0, the account remains locked until an administrator unlocks it.

Changing Default Passwords

Many systems and devices start with default passwords. A basic security practice is to change these defaults before putting a system into use. As an example, many wireless routers have default accounts named "admin" or "administrator" with a default password of "admin." If you don't change the password, anyone who knows the defaults can log on and take control of the router. In that case, the attacker can even go as far as locking you out of your own network.

Changing defaults also includes changing the default name of the Administrator account, if possible. In many systems, the Administrator account can't be locked out through regular lockout policies, so an attacker can continue to try to guess the password of the Administrator account without risking being locked out. Changing the name of the Administrator account to something else, such as Not4U2Know, reduces the chances of success for the attacker. The attacker needs to know the new administrator name before he can try to guess the password.

Some administrators go a step further and add a dummy user account named "administrator." This account has no permissions. If someone does try to guess the password of this account, the system will lock it out, alerting administrators of possible illicit activity.

> ### Remember this
>
> The first factor of authentication (something you know, such as a password or PIN) is the weakest factor. Passwords should be strong, changed regularly, never shared with another person, and stored in a safe if written down. Technical methods (such as a technical password policy) ensure that users regularly change their passwords and don't reuse the same passwords.

Something You Have

The *something you have* authentication factor refers to something you can physically hold. This section covers many of the common items in this factor, including smart cards, Common Access Cards, and hardware tokens. It also covers two open source protocols used with both hardware and software tokens.

Smart Cards

Smart cards are credit card-sized cards that have an embedded microchip and a certificate. Users insert the *smart card* into a smart card reader, similar to how someone would insert a credit card into a credit card reader. The smart card reader reads the information on the card, including the details from the certificate, which provides certificate-based authentication.

Chapter 10, "Understanding Cryptography and PKI," covers certificates in more detail, but as an introduction, they are digital files that support cryptography for increased security. The embedded certificate allows the use of a complex encryption key and provides much more secure authentication than is possible with a simple password. Additionally, the certificate can be used with digital signatures and data encryption. The smart card provides confidentiality, integrity, authentication, and non-repudiation.

Requirements for a smart card are:

- **Embedded certificate.** The embedded certificate holds a user's private key (which is only accessible to the user) and is matched with a public key (that is publicly available to others). The private key is used each time the user logs on to a network.
- **Public Key Infrastructure (PKI).** Chapter 10 covers PKI in more depth, but in short, the PKI supports issuing and managing certificates.

Smart cards are often used with another factor of authentication. For example, a user may also enter a PIN or password, in addition to using the smart card. Because the smart card is in the something you have factor and the PIN is in the something you know factor, this combination provides dual-factor authentication.

CACs and PIVs

A Common Access Card (*CAC*) is a specialized type of smart card used by the U.S. Department of Defense. In addition to including the capabilities of a smart card, it also includes a picture of the user and other readable information. Users can use the CAC as a form of photo identification to gain access into a secure location. For example, they can show their CAC to guards who are protecting access to secure areas. Once inside the secure area, users can use the CAC as a smart card to log on to computers.

Similarly, a Personal Identity Verification (*PIV*) card is a specialized type of smart card used by U.S. federal agencies. It also includes photo identification and provides confidentiality, integrity, authentication, and non-repudiation for the users, just as a CAC does.

CACs and PIVs both support dual-factor authentication (sometimes called two-factor authentication) because users generally log on with the smart card and by entering information they know such as a password. Additionally, just as with smart cards, these cards include embedded certificates used for digital signatures and encryption.

> ### Remember this
>
> Smart cards are often used with dual-factor authentication where users have something (the smart card) and know something (such as a password or PIN). Smart cards include embedded certificates used with digital signatures and encryption. CACs and PIVs are specialized smart cards that include photo identification. They are used to gain access into secure locations and to log on to computer systems.

Tokens or Key Fobs

A *token* or key fob (sometimes simply called a fob) is an electronic device about the size of a remote key for a car. You can easily carry them in a pocket or purse, or connect them to a key chain. They include a liquid crystal display (LCD) that displays a number, and this number changes periodically, such as every 60 seconds. They are sometimes called hardware tokens to differentiate them from logical, or software tokens.

The token is synced with a server that knows what the number is at any moment. For example, at 9:01, the number displayed on the token may be 135792 and the server knows the number is 135792. At 9:02, the displayed number changes to something else and the server also knows the new number.

This number is a one-time use, rolling password. It isn't useful to attackers for very long, even if they can discover it. For example, a shoulder surfing attacker might be able to look over someone's shoulder and read the number. However, the number expires within the next 60 seconds and is replaced by another one-time password.

Users often use tokens to authenticate via a web site. They enter the number displayed in the token along with their username and password. This provides dual-factor authentication because the users must have something (the token) and know something (their password).

RSA sells RSA Secure ID, a popular token used for authentication. You can Google "Secure ID image" to view many pictures of these tokens. Although RSA tokens are popular, other brands are available.

HOTP and TOTP

Hash-based Message Authentication Code (HMAC) uses a hash function and cryptographic key for many different cryptographic functions. Chapter 1, "Mastering Security Basics," introduced hashes. As a reminder, a hash is simply a number created with a hashing algorithm. HMAC-based One-Time Password (**HOTP**) is an open standard used for creating one-time passwords, similar to those used in tokens or key fobs. The algorithm combines a secret key and an incrementing counter, and uses HMAC to create a hash of the result. It then converts the result into an HOTP value of six to eight digits.

Imagine Bart needs to use HOTP for authentication. He requests a new HOTP number using a token or a software application. He can then use this number for authentication along with some other authentication method, such as a username and password. As soon as he uses it, the number expires. No one else is able to use it, and Bart cannot use it again either.

Here's an interesting twist, though. A password created with HOTP remains valid until it's used. Suppose Bart requested the HOTP number but then got distracted and never used it. What happens now? Theoretically, it remains usable forever. This presents a risk related to HOTP because other people can use the password if they discover it.

A Time-based One-Time Password (**TOTP**) is similar to HOTP, but it uses a timestamp instead of a counter. One-time passwords created with TOTP typically expire after 30 seconds.

One significant benefit of HOTP and TOTP is price. Hardware tokens that use these open source standards are significantly less expensive than tokens that use proprietary algorithms. Additionally, many software applications use these algorithms to create software tokens used within the application.

For example, Figure 2.2 shows the free VIP Access app created by Symantec and running on an iPad. It's also available for many other tablets and smartphones. Once you configure it to work with a compatible authentication server, it creates a steady stream of one-time use passwords. The six-digit security code is the password, and the counter lets you know how much more time you have before it changes again.

Figure 2.2: VIP Access app

Similar to a hardware token, the user enters a username and password as the something you know factor, and then enters the security code from the app as the something you have factor. This provides dual-factor authentication. Many public web sites like eBay and PayPal support it, allowing many end users to implement dual-factor authentication as long as they have a smartphone or tablet device.

> ### Remember this
>
> HOTP and TOTP are both open source standards used to create one-time use passwords. HOTP creates a one-time use password that does not expire. TOTP creates a one-time password that expires after 30 seconds. Both can be used as software tokens for authentication.

Something You Are

The *something you are* authentication factor uses biometrics for authentication. Biometric methods are the strongest form of authentication because they are the most difficult for an attacker to falsify. In comparison, passwords are the weakest form of authentication.

Biometric Methods

Biometrics use a physical characteristic, such as a fingerprint, for authentication. Biometric systems use a two-step process. In the first step, users register with the authentication system. For example, an authentication system first captures a user's fingerprint and associates it with the user's identity. Later, when users want to access the system, they use their fingerprints to prove their identity. There are multiple types of biometrics, including:

- **Fingerprint scanner.** Many laptop computers include *fingerprint scanners* or fingerprint readers, and they are also common on tablet devices and smartphones. Similarly, some USB flash drives include a fingerprint scanner. They can store multiple fingerprints of three or four people to share access to the same USB drive. Law enforcement agencies have used fingerprints for decades, but they use them for identification, not biometric authentication.

- **Retina scanner.** *Retina scanners* scan the retina of one or both eyes and use the pattern of blood vessels at the back of the eye for recognition. Some people object to the use of these scanners for authentication because they can identify medical issues, and because you typically need to have physical contact with the scanner.

- **Iris scanner.** *Iris scanners* use camera technologies to capture the patterns of the iris around the pupil for recognition. They are used in many passport-free border crossings around the world. They can take pictures from about 3 to 10 inches away, avoiding physical contact.

- **Voice recognition.** *Voice recognition* methods identify who is speaking using speech recognition methods to identify different acoustic features. One person's voice varies from another person's voice due to differences in their mouth and throat, and behavioral patterns that affect their speaking style. As an example, Apple's Siri supports voice recognition. After setting it up, Siri will only respond to the owner's voice. Unfortunately, that does prevent the old party trick of yelling out "Hey Siri" at a party where multiple people have iPhones.

- **Facial recognition.** *Facial recognition* systems identify people based on facial features. This includes the size of their face compared with the rest of their body, and the size, shape, and position of their eyes, nose, mouth, cheekbones, and jaw. A drawback with this is that it is sometimes negatively affected by changes in lighting. Microsoft Windows systems support Windows Hello facial recognition services. To avoid the challenges from normal lighting, it uses infrared (IR) and can operate in diverse lighting conditions.

Biometric Errors

Biometrics can be very exact when the technology is implemented accurately. However, it is possible for a biometric manufacturer to take shortcuts and not implement it correctly, resulting in false readings. Two biometric false readings are:

- **False acceptance.** This is when a biometric system incorrectly identifies an unauthorized user as an authorized user. The false acceptance rate (*FAR*, also known as a false match rate) identifies the percentage of times false acceptance occurs.

- **False rejection.** This is when a biometric system incorrectly rejects an authorized user. The false rejection rate (**FRR**, also known as a false nonmatch rate) identifies the percentage of times false rejections occur.

True readings occur when the biometric system accurately accepts or rejects a user. For example, true acceptance is when the biometric system accurately determines a positive match. In contrast, true rejection occurs when the biometric system accurately determines a nonmatch.

Biometric systems allow you to adjust the sensitivity or threshold level where errors occur. By increasing the sensitivity, it decreases the number of false matches and increases the number of false rejections. In contrast, decreasing the sensitivity increases the false matches and decreases the false rejections. By plotting the FAR and FRR rates using different sensitivities, you can determine the effectiveness of a biometric system.

Figure 2.3 shows the **crossover error rate** (CER) for two biometric systems. The CER is the point where the FAR crosses over with the FRR. A lower CER indicates that the biometric system is more accurate. For example, the system represented with the solid lines in the figure is more accurate than the system represented by the dotted lines.

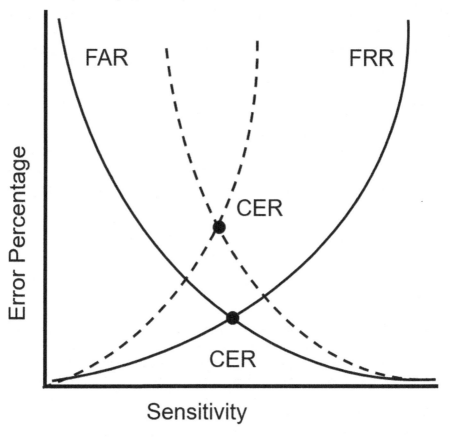

Figure 2.3: Crossover error rate

Somewhere You Are

The **somewhere you are** authentication factor identifies a user's location. Geolocation is a group of technologies used to identify a user's location and is the most common method used

> ### *Remember this*
>
> The third factor of authentication (something you are, defined with biometrics) is the strongest individual method of authentication because it is the most difficult for an attacker to falsify. Biometric methods include fingerprints, retina scans, iris scans, voice recognition, and facial recognition. Iris and retina scans are the strongest biometric methods mentioned in this section, though iris scans are used more than retina scans due to the privacy issues and the scanning requirements. Facial recognition is the most flexible and when using alternate lighting (such as infrared), they might become the most popular. The crossover error rate (CER) measures the accuracy of a system and lower CERs are better.

in this factor. Many authentication systems use the Internet Protocol (IP) address for geolocation. The IP address provides information on the country, region, state, city, and sometimes even the zip code.

As an example, I once hired a virtual assistant in India to do some data entry for me. I created an account for the assistant in an online application called Hootsuite and sent him the logon information. However, when he attempted to log on, Hootsuite recognized that his IP was in India but I always logged on from an IP in the United States. Hootsuite blocked his access and then sent me an email saying that someone from India was trying to log on. They also provided me directions on how to grant him access if he was a legitimate user, but it was comforting to know they detected and blocked this access automatically.

It's worth noting that using an IP address for geolocation isn't foolproof. There are many virtual private network (VPN) IP address changers available online. For example, a user in Russia can use one of these services in the United States to access a web site. The web site will recognize the IP address of the VPN service, but won't see the IP address of the user in Russia.

Within an organization, it's possible to use the computer name or the media access control (MAC) address of a system for the somewhere you are factor. For example, in a Microsoft Active Directory domain, you can configure accounts so that users can only log on to the network through one specific computer. If they aren't at that computer, the system blocks them from logging on at all.

Something You Do

The *something you do* authentication factor refers to actions you can take such as gestures on a touch screen. As an example, Microsoft Windows 10 supports picture passwords. Users first select a picture, and then they can add three gestures as their picture password. Gestures include tapping in specific places on the picture, drawing lines between items with a finger, or drawing a circle around an item such as someone's head. After registering the picture and their gestures, users repeat these gestures to log on again later.

Other examples of something you do include how you write or how you type. For example, keystroke dynamics measure the pattern and rhythm as a user types on a keyboard. It measures details such as speed, dwell time, and flight time. Dwell time is the time a key is pressed, and flight time is the time between releasing one key and pressing the next key. Many security professionals refer to this as behavioral biometrics because it identifies behavioral traits of an individual. However, some people put these actions into the something you do authentication factor.

Dual-Factor and Multifactor Authentication

Dual-factor authentication (sometimes called two-factor authentication) uses two different factors of authentication, such as something you have and something you know. Dual-factor authentication often uses a smart card and a PIN, a USB token and a PIN, or combines a smart card or hardware token with a password. In each of these cases, the user must have something and know something.

Multifactor authentication uses two or more factors of authentication. For example, you can combine the something you are factor with one or more other factors of authentication.

Note that technically you can call an authentication system using two different factors either dual-factor authentication or multifactor authentication. Multifactor authentication indicates multiple factors and multiple is simply more than one.

It's worth noting that using two methods of authentication in the same factor is not dual-factor authentication. For example, requiring users to enter a password and a PIN (both in the something you know factor) is single-factor authentication, not dual-factor authentication. Similarly, using a thumbprint and a retina scan is not dual-factor authentication because both methods are in the something you are factor.

> ### Remember this
>
> Using two or more methods in the same factor of authentication (such as a PIN and a password) is single-factor authentication. Dual-factor (or two-factor) authentication uses two different factors, such as using a hardware token and a PIN. Multifactor authentication uses two or more factors.

Summarizing Identification Methods

So far, this chapter has presented several different identification methods and because identification is so important, it's worthwhile to summarize them. They are usernames, photo identification cards, and biometrics.

The most commonly used identification method is a username. This can be a traditional username, such as DarrilGibson, or it can be an email address, such as Darril@gcgapremium.com, depending on how the system is configured. Many other identification methods can be used for both identification and authentication.

CACs and PIVs include a picture and other information about the owner, so owners often use them for identification. They also function as smart cards in the something you have authentication factor.

The "Something You Are" section focused on using biometrics for authentication, but several entities also use biometric methods for identification. For example, law enforcement agencies have used fingerprints to identify individuals at crime scenes for decades. Similarly, retina and palm scanners can identify individuals with a high degree of accuracy.

Troubleshooting Authentication Issues

Some common authentication issues that can cause security problems have been mentioned in this section. As a summary, they are:

- **Weak passwords.** If users aren't forced to use strong, complex passwords, they probably won't and their accounts will be vulnerable to attacks. A technical password policy ensures users implement strong passwords, don't reuse them, and change them regularly.
- **Forgotten passwords.** An organization needs to have a password recovery procedure in place to help users recover their passwords. If passwords are manually reset without verifying the identity of the user, it's possible for an attacker to trick someone into resetting the password.
- **Biometric errors.** Weak biometric systems with a high crossover error rate may have a high false match rate (also called a false acceptance rate) or a low nonmatch rate (also called a false rejection rate).

Comparing Authentication Services

Several other authentication services are available that fall outside the scope of the previously described factors of authentication. A common goal they have is to ensure that unencrypted credentials are not sent across a network. In other words, they ensure that credentials are not sent in cleartext. If credentials are sent in cleartext, attackers can use tools such as a protocol analyzer to capture and view them. The following sections describe many of these services.

Kerberos

Kerberos is a network authentication mechanism used within Windows Active Directory domains and some Unix environments known as realms. It was originally developed at MIT (the Massachusetts Institute of Technology) for Unix systems and later released as a request for comments (RFC). Kerberos provides mutual authentication that can help prevent man-in-the-middle attacks and uses tickets to help prevent replay attacks. Chapter 7, "Protecting Against Advanced Attacks," covers these attacks in more depth.

Kerberos includes several requirements for it to work properly. They are:

- **A method of issuing tickets used for authentication.** The Key Distribution Center (**KDC**) uses a complex process of issuing ticket-granting tickets (TGTs) and other tickets. The KDC (or TGT server) packages user credentials within a ticket. Tickets provide authentication for users when they access resources such as files on a file server. These tickets are sometimes referred to as tokens, but they are logical tokens, not a key fob type of token discussed earlier in the "Something You Have" section.
- **Time synchronization.** Kerberos version 5 requires all systems to be synchronized and within five minutes of each other. The clock that provides the time synchronization is used to timestamp tickets, ensuring they expire correctly. This helps prevent replay attacks. In a replay attack, a third party attempts to impersonate a client after intercepting data captured in a session. However, if an attacker intercepts a ticket, the timestamp limits the amount of time an attacker can use the ticket.
- **A database of subjects or users.** In a Microsoft environment, this is Active Directory, but it could be any database of users.

When a user logs on with Kerberos, the KDC issues the user a ticket-granting ticket, which typically has a lifetime of 10 hours to be useful for a single workday. When the user tries to access a resource, the ticket-granting ticket is presented as authentication, and the user is issued a ticket for the resource. However, the ticket expires if users stay logged on for an extended period, such as longer than 10 hours. This prevents them from accessing network resources. In this case, users may be prompted to provide a password to renew the ticket-granting ticket, or they might need to log off and back on to generate a new ticket-granting ticket.

> ### Remember this
>
> Kerberos is a network authentication protocol within a Microsoft Windows Active Directory domain or a Unix realm. It uses a database of objects such as Active Directory and a KDC (or TGT server) to issue timestamped tickets that expire after a certain time period.
>
> Additionally, Kerberos uses symmetric-key cryptography to prevent unauthorized disclosure and to ensure confidentiality. Chapter 10 explains algorithms in more depth, but in short, symmetric-key cryptography uses a single key for both encryption and decryption of the same data.

NTLM

New Technology LAN Manager (**NTLM**) is a suite of protocols that provide authentication, integrity, and confidentiality within Windows systems. At their most basic, they use a Message Digest hashing algorithm to challenge users and check their credentials. There are three versions of NTLM:

- NTLM is a simple MD4 hash of a user's password. MD4 has been cracked and neither NTLM nor MD4 are recommended for use today.
- NTLMv2 is a challenge-response authentication protocol. When a user attempts to log on, NTMLv2 creates an HMAC-MD5 hash composed of a combination of the username, the logon domain name (or computer name), the user's password, the current time, and more. To create an HMAC-MD5 message, authentication code starts as the MD5 hash of a user's password, which is then encrypted.
- NTLM2 Session improves NTLMv2 by adding in mutual authentication. In other words, the client authenticates with the server, and the server also authenticates with the client.

So, which protocol should you select? Actually, Microsoft specifically recommends that developers don't select one of these protocols. Instead, developers should use the Negotiate security package within their applications. This security package selects the most secure security protocols available between the systems. It first tries to use Kerberos if it is available. If not, it uses either NTLMv2 or NLTM2 Session depending on the capabilities of the systems involved in the session.

LDAP and LDAPS

Lightweight Directory Access Protocol (**LDAP**) specifies formats and methods to query directories. In this context, a directory is a database of objects that provides a central access point to manage users, computers, and other directory objects. LDAP is an extension of the X.500 standard that Novell and early Microsoft Exchange Server versions used extensively.

Windows domains use Active Directory, which is based on LDAP. Active Directory is a directory of objects (such as users, computers, and groups), and it provides a single location for object management. Queries to Active Directory use the LDAP format. Similarly, Unix realms use LDAP to identify objects.

Administrators often use LDAP in scripts, but they need to have a basic understanding of how to identify objects. For example, a user named Homer in the Users container within the GetCertifiedGetAhead.com domain is identified with the following LDAP string: LDAP://CN=Homer,CN=Users,DC=GetCertifiedGetAhead,DC=com

- **CN=Homer.** CN is short for common name.
- **CN=Users.** CN is sometimes referred to as container in this context.
- **DC=GetCertifiedGetAhead.** DC is short for domain component.
- **DC=com.** This is the second domain component in the domain name.

LDAP Secure (LDAPS) uses encryption to protect LDAP transmissions. When a client connects with a server using LDAPS, the two systems establish a Transport Layer Security (TLS) session before transmitting any data. TLS encrypts the data before transmission.

> ### Remember this
>
> LDAP is based on an earlier version of X.500. Windows Active Directory domains and Unix realms use LDAP to identify objects in query strings with codes such as CN=Users and DC=GetCertifiedGetAhead. LDAPS encrypts transmissions with TLS.

Single Sign-On

Single sign-on (**SSO**) refers to the ability of a user to log on or access multiple systems by providing credentials only once. SSO increases security because the user only needs to remember one set of credentials and is less likely to write them down. It's also much more convenient for users to access network resources if they only have to log on one time.

As an example, consider a user who needs to access multiple servers within a network to perform normal work. Without SSO, the user would need to know one set of credentials to log on locally, and additional credentials for each of the servers. Many users would write these credentials down to remember them.

Alternatively, in a network with SSO capabilities, the user only needs to log on to the network once. The SSO system typically creates some type of SSO secure token used during the entire logon session. Each time the user accesses a network resource, the SSO system uses this secure token for authentication. Kerberos and LDAP both include SSO capabilities.

SSO requires strong authentication to be effective. If users create weak passwords, attackers might be able to guess them, giving them access to multiple systems. Some people debate that SSO adds in risks because if an attacker can gain the user's credentials, it gives the attacker access to multiple systems.

> ### Remember this
>
> Single sign-on enhances security by requiring users to use and remember only one set of credentials for authentication. Once signed on using SSO, this one set of credentials is used throughout a user's entire session. SSO can provide central authentication against a federated database for different operating systems. SSO systems depend on strong authentication.
>
> Same sign-on is not the same as SSO. In a same sign-on system, users reenter their credentials each time they access another system. However, they use the same credentials.

SSO and Transitive Trusts

A **transitive trust** creates an indirect trust relationship. As an example, imagine a transitive trust relationship exists between Homer, Moe, and Fat Tony:

- Homer trusts Moe.
- Moe trusts Fat Tony.
- Because of the transitive trust relationship, Homer trusts Fat Tony.

Of course, this isn't always true with people and Homer might be a little upset with Moe if Moe shares Homer's secrets with Fat Tony. However, it reduces network administration in a domain.

Within an LDAP-based network, domains use transitive trusts for SSO. Figure 2.4 shows a common configuration with three domains in the same network. The parent domain is GetCertifiedGetAhead.com and the configuration includes two child domains—Training and Blogs.

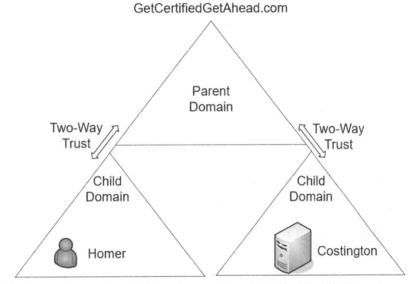

Figure 2.4: An LDAP transitive trust used for SSO

In this example, there is a two-way trust between the parent domain (GetCertifiedGetAhead.com) and the child domain (Training.GetCertifiedGetAhead.com). The parent trusts the child, and the child trusts the parent. Similarly, there is a two-way trust between the parent domain and the Blogs child domain. There isn't a direct trust between the two child domains. However, the transitive relationship creates a two-way trust between them.

All of these domains contain objects, such as users, computers, and groups. Homer's user account is in the Training domain, and a server named Costington is in the Blogs domain. With the transitive trust, it's possible to grant Homer access to the Costington server without creating another trust relationship directly between the Training and Blogs domains.

Without a trust relationship, you'd have to create another account for Homer in the Blogs domain before you could grant him access. Additionally, Homer would need to manage the second account's password separately. However, with the transitive trust relationships, the network supports SSO, so Homer only needs a single account.

SSO and SAML

Security Assertion Markup Language (**SAML**) is an Extensible Markup Language (**XML**)–based data format used for SSO on web browsers. Imagine two web sites hosted by two different organizations. Normally, a user would have to provide different credentials to access either web site. However, if the organizations trust each other, they can use SAML as a federated identity management system. Users authenticate with one web site and are not required to authenticate again when accessing the second web site.

Many web-based portals use SAML for SSO. The user logs on to the portal once, and the portal then passes proof of the user's authentication to back-end systems. As long as one organization has authenticated users, they are not required to authenticate again to access other sites within the portal.

SAML defines three roles:

- **Principal.** This is typically a user. The user logs on once. If necessary, the principal requests an identity from the identity provider.
- **Identity provider.** An identity provider creates, maintains, and manages identity information for principals.
- **Service provider.** A service provider is an entity that provides services to principals. For example, a service provider could host one or more web sites accessible through a web-based portal. When a principal tries to access a resource, the service provider redirects the principal to obtain an identity first.

This process sends several XML-based messages between the systems. However, it is usually transparent to the user.

SAML and Authorization

It's important to realize that the primary purpose of SSO is for identification and authentication of users. Users claim an identity and prove that identity with credentials. SSO does not provide authorization. For example, if the power plant and the school system create a federation using SAML, this doesn't automatically grant everyone in the school system full access to the nuclear power plant resources. Authorization is completely separate.

However, many federation SSO systems, including SAML, include the ability to transfer authorization data between their systems. In other words, it's possible to use SAML for single sign-on authentication and for authorization.

> **Remember this**
>
> SAML is an XML-based standard used to exchange authentication and authorization information between different parties. SAML provides SSO for web-based applications.

SSO and a Federation

Some SSO systems can connect authentication mechanisms from different environments, such as different operating systems or different networks. One common method is with a federated identity management system, often integrated as a federated database. This federated database provides central authentication in a nonhomogeneous environment.

As an example, imagine that the Springfield Nuclear Power Plant established a relationship with the Springfield school system, allowing the power plant employees to access school resources. It's not feasible or desirable to join these two networks into one. However, you can create a federation of the two networks. Once it's established, the power plant employees will log on using their power plant account, and then access the shared school resources without logging on again.

A *federation* requires a federated identity management system that all members of the federation use. In the previous example, the members of the federation are the power plant and the school system. Members of the federation agree on a standard for federated identities and then exchange the information based on the standard. A federated identity links a user's credentials from different networks or operating systems, but the federation treats it as one identity.

Shibboleth is one of the federated identity solutions mentioned specifically in the CompTIA Security+ exam objectives. It is open source and freely available, making it a more affordable solution than some of the commercially available federated identity solutions. It also includes Open SAML libraries written in C++ and Java, making it easier for developers to expand its usefulness.

OAuth and OpenID Connect

OAuth is an open standard for authorization many companies use to provide secure access to protected resources. Instead of creating a different account for each web site you access, you can often use the same account that you've created with Google, Facebook, PayPal, Microsoft, or Twitter.

As an example, imagine that the Try-N-Save Department Store decides to sell some of its products online and management has decided to allow customers to make purchases through PayPal. Developers configure their web site to exchange application programming interface (API) calls between it and PayPal servers. Now, when customers make a purchase, they log on with their PayPal account and make their purchase through PayPal. OAuth transfers data between PayPal and the Try-N-Save site so that the department store receives the money and knows what to ship to the customer. A benefit for the customers is that they don't have to create another account for Try-N-Save.

OpenID Connect works with OAuth 2.0 and it allows clients to verify the identity of end users without managing their credentials. In this context, the client is typically a web site or application that needs to authenticate users. OpenID Connect provides identification services, without requiring the application to handle the credentials. It also streamlines the user experience for users. For example, Skyscanner is an application for finding flights, hotels, and car rentals. It allows users to sign in using their Facebook credentials. After doing so, Skyscanner provides a more personalized experience for the users.

Managing Accounts

Account management is concerned with the creation, management, disablement, and termination of accounts. When the account is active, access control methods are used to control what the user can do. Additionally, administrators use access controls to control when and where users can log on. The following sections cover common account management practices, along with some basic principles used with account management. Improperly configured accounts don't follow these principles, increasing risks.

Least Privilege

The principle of **least privilege** is an example of a technical control implemented with access controls. Privileges are the rights and permissions assigned to authorized users. Least privilege specifies that individuals and processes are granted only the rights and permissions needed to perform assigned tasks or functions, but no more. For example, if Lisa needs read access to a folder on a server, you should grant her read access to that folder, but nothing else.

A primary goal of implementing least privilege is to reduce risks. As an example, imagine that Carl works at the Nuclear Power Plant, but administrators have improperly configured accounts ignoring the principle of least privilege. In other words, Carl has access to all available data within the Nuclear Power Plant, not just the limited amount of data he needs to perform his job. Later, Lenny gets into trouble and needs money, so he convinces Carl to steal data from the power plant so that they can sell it. In this scenario, Carl can steal and sell all the data at the plant, which can result in serious losses.

In contrast, if administrators applied the principle of least privilege, Carl would only have access to a limited amount of data. Even if Lenny convinces him to steal the data, Carl wouldn't be able to steal very much simply because he doesn't have access to it. This limits the potential losses for the power plant.

This principle applies to regular users and administrators. As an example, if Marge administers all the computers in a training lab, it's appropriate to give her administrative control over all these computers. However, her privileges don't need to extend to the domain, so she wouldn't have administrative control over all the computers in a network. Additionally, she wouldn't have the privileges required to add these computers to the domain, unless that was a requirement in the training lab. Similarly, if a network administrator needs to review logs and update specific network devices, it's appropriate to give the administrator access to these logs and devices, but no more.

Many services and applications run under the context of a user account. These services have the privileges of this user account, so it's important to ensure that these accounts are only granted the privileges needed by the service or the application. In the past, many administrators configured these service and application accounts with full administrative privileges. When attackers compromised a service or application configured this way, they gained administrative privileges and wreaked havoc on the network.

> ### Remember this
>
> Least privilege is a technical control. It specifies that individuals or processes are granted only those rights and permissions needed to perform their assigned tasks or functions.

Need to Know

The principle of need to know is similar to the principle of least privilege in that users are granted access only to the data and information that they need to know for their job. Notice that need to know is focused on data and information, which is typically protected with permissions. In contrast, the principle of least privilege includes both rights and permissions.

Rights refer to actions and include actions such as the right to change the system time, the right to install an application, or the right to join a computer to a domain. Permissions typically refer to permissions on files, such as read, write, modify, read & execute, and full control.

Account Types

When managing accounts, it's important to recognize the common types of accounts used within a network. They are:

- **End user accounts.** Most accounts are for regular users. Administrators create these accounts and then assign appropriate privileges based on the user's job responsibilities. Microsoft refers to this as a Standard user account.
- **Privileged accounts.** A *privileged account* has additional rights and privileges beyond what a regular user has. As an example, someone with administrator privileges on a Windows computer has full and complete control over the Windows computer.
- **Guest accounts.** Windows operating systems include a *Guest account*. These are useful if you want to grant someone limited access to a computer or network without creating a new account. For example, imagine an organization contracts with a temp agency to have someone do data entry. It's possible that the agency sends a different person every day. Enabling the Guest account for this person would be simpler than creating a new account every day. Administrators commonly disable the Guest account and only enable it in special situations.
- **Service accounts.** Some applications and services need to run under the context of an account and a *service account* fills this need. As an example, SQL Server is a database application that runs on a server and it needs access to resources on the server and the network. Administrators create a regular user account, name it something like sqlservice, assign it appropriate privileges, and configure SQL Server to use this account. Note that this is like a regular end-user account. The only difference is that it's only used by the service or application, not an end user.

One of the challenges with service accounts is that they often aren't managed. For example, imagine a regular user account that has a password that expires after 45 days. The user is notified to change the password and the user does so. A service account might send a notification to the application to change the password, but the notification is ignored. When the password expires, the account is locked. Suddenly, the application (or service) stops working and administrators have to troubleshoot the issue to figure out why.

A solution is to configure the service account so that it doesn't have to comply with the password policy. However, this allows the service account to ignore other policy requirements such as using a strong, complex password. It's important that developers using these types of accounts take steps to ensure their accounts follow existing policies.

Require Administrators to Use Two Accounts

It's common to require administrators to have two accounts. They use one account for regular day-to-day work. It has the same limited privileges as a regular end user. The other account has elevated privileges required to perform administrative work, and they use this only when performing administrative work. The benefit of this practice is that it reduces the exposure of the administrative account to an attack.

For example, when malware infects a system, it often attempts to gain additional rights and permissions using privilege escalation techniques. It may exploit a bug or flaw in an application or operating system. Or, it may simply assume the rights and permissions of the logged-on user.

If an administrator logs on with an administrative account, the malware can assume these elevated privileges. In contrast, if the administrator is logged on with a regular standard user account, the malware must take additional steps to escalate its privileges.

This also reduces the risk to the administrative account for day-to-day work. Imagine Homer is an administrator and he's called away to a crisis. It is very possible for him to walk away without locking his computer. If he was logged on with his administrator account, an attacker walking by can access the system and have administrative privileges. Although systems often have password-protected screen savers, these usually don't start until about 10 minutes or longer after a user walks away.

Standard Naming Convention

It's common for an organization to adopt a standard naming convention to ensure user account names and email addresses are created similarly. For example, one convention uses the first name, a dot, and the last name. This creates accounts like homer.simpson and bart.simpson. If the organization hires a second person with the same name, such as a second Bart Simpson, the naming convention might specify adding a number to the name, such as bart.simpson2.

You probably won't need to design a naming convention. However, if you start with a different organization and you need to create accounts, you should understand that the organization probably has a naming convention in place. You should follow the convention for any accounts you create.

Prohibiting Shared and Generic Accounts

Account management policies often dictate that personnel should not use shared or generic accounts. Instead, each user has at least one account, which is only accessible to that user. If multiple users share a single account, you cannot implement basic authorization controls. As a reminder, four key concepts are:

- **Identification.** Users claim an identity with an identifier such as a username.
- **Authentication.** Users prove their identity using an authentication method such as a password.
- **Authorization.** Users are authorized access to resources, based on their proven identity.
- **Accounting.** Logs record activity using the users' claimed identity.

Imagine that Bart, Maggie, and Lisa all used a Guest account. If you want to give Lisa access to certain files, you'd grant access to the Guest account, but Bart and Maggie would have the same access. If Bart deleted the files, logs would indicate the Guest account deleted the files, but you wouldn't know who actually deleted them. In contrast, if users have unique user accounts, you can give them access to resources individually. Additionally, logs would indicate exactly who took an action.

Note that having a single, temporary user log on with the Guest account does support identification, authentication, authorization, and accounting. It is only when multiple users are sharing the same account that you lose these controls. Still, some organizations prohibit the use of the Guest account for any purposes.

> ### Remember this
>
> Requiring administrators to use two accounts, one with administrator privileges and another with regular user privileges, helps prevent privilege escalation attacks. Users should not use shared accounts.

Disablement Policies

Many organizations have a ***disablement policy*** that specifies how to manage accounts in different situations. For example, most organizations require administrators to disable user accounts as soon as possible when employees leave the organization. Additionally, it's common to disable default accounts (such as the Guest account mentioned previously) to prevent them from being used.

Disabling is preferred over deleting the account, at least initially. If administrators delete the account, they also delete any encryption and security keys associated with the account. However, these keys are retained when the account is disabled. As an example, imagine that an employee encrypted files with his account. The operating system uses cryptography keys to encrypt and decrypt these files. If administrators deleted this account, these files may remain encrypted forever unless the organization has a key escrow or recovery agent that can access the files.

Some contents of an account disablement policy include:

- **Terminated employee.** An account disablement policy specifies that accounts for ex-employees are disabled as soon as possible. This ensures a terminated employee doesn't become a disgruntled ex-employee who wreaks havoc on the network. Note that "terminated" refers to both employees who resign and employees who are fired.
- **Leave of absence.** If an employee will be absent for an extended period, the account should be disabled while the employee is away. Organizations define extended period differently, with some organizations defining it as only two weeks, whereas other organizations extend it out to as long as two months.
- **Delete account.** When the organization determines the account is no longer needed, administrators delete it. For example, the policy may direct administrators to delete accounts that have been inactive for 60 or 90 days.

Remember this

An account disablement policy identifies what to do with accounts for employees who leave permanently or on a leave of absence. Most policies require administrators to disable the account as soon as possible, so that ex-employees cannot use the account. Disabling the account ensures that data associated with it remains available. Security keys associated with an account remain available when the account is disabled, but are no longer accessible if the account is deleted.

Recovering Accounts

In some situations, administrators need to recover accounts. The two primary account recovery scenarios are:

- **Enable a disabled account.** Administrators can reset the user's password and take control of the account. Similarly, they pass control of the account to someone else, such as a supervisor or manager of an ex-employee. Administrators reset the user's password, set it to expire on first use, and then give the password to the other person.
- **Recover a deleted account.** It is also possible to recover a deleted account. This is more complex than simply creating another account with the same name. Instead, administrators follow detailed procedures to recover the account.

Time-of-Day Restrictions

Time-of-day restrictions specify when users can log on to a computer. If a user tries to log on to the network outside the restricted time, the system denies access to the user.

As an example, imagine a company operates between 8:00 a.m. and 5:00 p.m. on a daily basis. Managers decide they don't want regular users logging on to the network except between 6:00 a.m. and 8:00 p.m., Monday through Friday. You could set time-of-day restrictions for user accounts, as shown in Figure 2.5. If a user tries to log on outside the restricted time (such as during the weekend), the system prevents the user from logging on.

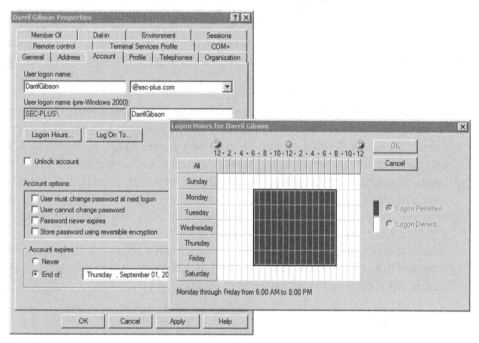

Figure 2.5: User account properties with time restrictions

If users are working overtime on a project, the system doesn't log them off when the restricted time arrives. For example, if Maggie is working late on a Wednesday night, the system doesn't log her off at 8:00 p.m. (assuming the time restrictions are set as shown in Figure 2.5). However, the system will prevent her from creating any new network connections.

Location-Based Policies

Location-based policies restrict access based on the location of the user. The "Somewhere You Are" section earlier in this chapter discussed common methods used to enforce this. For example, geolocation technologies can often detect a location using the IP address, and block any traffic from unacceptable addresses, such as from foreign countries. It's also possible to identify a set of IP addresses as the only addresses that are acceptable. This is often referred to as whitelisting the IP addresses.

Within a network, it's possible to restrict access based on computer names or MAC addresses. For example, imagine Bart has been logging on to multiple computers with his account. It is possible to restrict his account to only his computer. When he tries to log on to his account, he is successful. If he tries to log on to another computer, the location-based policy blocks him.

> ### Remember this
>
> Time-of-day restrictions prevent users from logging on during restricted times. They also prevent logged-on users from accessing resources during certain times. Location-based policies restrict access based on the location of the user.

Expiring Accounts and Recertification

It's possible to set user accounts to expire automatically. When the account expires, the system disables it, and the user is no longer able to log on using the account.

If you look back at Figure 2.5, it shows the properties of an account. The Account Expires section is at the bottom of the page, and the account is set to expire on September 1. When September 1 arrives, the account is automatically disabled and the user will no longer be able to log on.

It's common to configure temporary accounts to expire. For example, an organization may hire contractors for a 90-day period to perform a specific job. An administrator creates accounts for the contractors and sets them to expire in 90 days. This automatically disables the accounts at the end of the contract.

If the organization extends the contract, it's a simple matter to recertify the account. Administrators verify that the contract has been extended, change the expiration date, and enable the account.

> ### Remember this
>
> Account expiration dates automatically disable accounts on the expiration date. This is useful for temporary accounts such as temporary contractors.

Account Maintenance

Administrators routinely perform account maintenance. This is often done with scripts to automate the processes.

As an example, it's relatively simple to create and run a script listing all enabled accounts that haven't been used in the last 30 days in a Microsoft AD DS domain. This provides a list of inactive accounts. Often, these are accounts of ex-employees or temporary employees who are no longer at the organization. Ideally, an account disablement policy would ensure that the accounts are disabled as soon as the employee leaves. The scripts provide an additional check to ensure inactive accounts are disabled.

Additionally, account maintenance includes deleting accounts that are no longer needed. For example, if an organization has a policy of disabling accounts when employees leave, but deleting them 60 days later, account maintenance procedures ensure the accounts are deleted.

Credential Management

A credential is a collection of information that provides an identity (such as a username) and proves that identity (such as with a password). Over time, users often have multiple credentials that they need to remember, especially when they access many web sites. Credential management systems help users store these credentials securely. The goal is to simplify credential management for users, while also ensuring that unauthorized personnel do not have access to the users' credentials.

As an example of a credential management system, Windows 10 includes the Credential Manager, accessible from Control Panel. Users are able to add credentials into the Credential Manager, which stores them securely in special folders called vaults. Then, when users access web sites needing credentials, the system automatically retrieves the credentials from the vault and submits them to the web site.

Similarly, web browsers such as Google Chrome use a credential management system to remember passwords. When you access a web site that needs your password, Chrome prompts you asking if you'd like Chrome to remember it. Later, when you visit the same web site, Chrome fills in the credentials for you.

Comparing Access Control Models

Access control ensures that only authenticated and authorized entities can access resources. For example, it ensures that only authenticated users who have been granted appropriate permissions can access files on a server. This starts by ensuring that users are accurately identified and authenticated. Then, you grant access using one of several different models. The models covered in this section are:

- Role-based access control (role-BAC)
- Rule-based access control (rule-BAC)
- Discretionary access control (DAC)
- Mandatory access control (MAC)
- Attribute-based access control (ABAC)

You might notice that CompTIA uses the acronym RBAC for both rule-based access control and role-based access control. For clarity, this book uses role-BAC or rule-BAC instead of the ambiguous RBAC.

By understanding a little more of the underlying design principles, you'll understand why some of the rules are important, and you'll be better prepared to ensure that security principles are followed.

Often, when using any of the models, you'll run across the following terms:

- **Subjects.** Subjects are typically users or groups that access an object. Occasionally, the subject may be a service that is using a service account to access an object.
- **Objects.** Objects are items such as files, folders, shares, and printers that subjects access. For example, users access files and printers. The access control helps determine how a system grants authorization to objects. Or, said another way, the access control model determines how a system grants users access to files and other resources.

Role-Based Access Control

Role-based access control (***role-BAC***) uses roles to manage rights and permissions for users. This is useful for users within a specific department who perform the same job functions. An administrator creates the roles and then assigns specific rights and permissions to the roles (instead of to the users). When an administrator adds a user to a role, the user has all the rights and permissions of that role.

Using Roles Based on Jobs and Functions

Imagine your organization has several departments, such as Accounting, Sales, and IT, and each department has a separate server hosting its files. You can create roles of Accounting, Sales, and IT and assign these roles to users based on the department where they work. Next, you'd grant these roles access to the appropriate server. For example, you'd grant the Accounting role to the Accounting server, grant the Sales role to the Sales server, and so on.

Another example of the role-BAC model is Microsoft Project Server. The Project Server can host multiple projects managed by different project managers. It includes the following roles:

- **Administrators.** Administrators have complete access and control over everything on the server, including all of the projects managed on the server.
- **Executives.** Executives can access data from any project held on the server, but do not have access to modify system settings on the server.
- **Project Managers.** Project managers have full control over their own projects, but do not have any control over projects owned by other project managers.
- **Team Members.** Team members can typically report on work that project managers assign to them, but they have little access outside the scope of their assignments.

Microsoft Project Server includes more roles, but you can see the point with these four. Each of these roles has rights and permissions assigned to it, and to give someone the associated privileges, you'd simply add the user's account to the role.

Documenting Roles with a Matrix

Think about the developers of Microsoft Project Server. They didn't just start creating roles. Instead, they did some planning and identified the roles they envisioned in the application. Next, they identified the privileges each of these roles required. It's common to document role-based permissions with a matrix listing all of the job titles and the privileges for each role, as shown in Table 2.1.

Role	Server Privileges	Project Privileges
Administrators	All	All
Executives	None	All
Project Managers	None	All on assigned projects No access on unassigned projects
Team Members	None	Access for assigned tasks Limited views within scope of their assigned tasks No views outside the scope of their assigned tasks

Table 2.1: Role-BAC matrix for Project Server

Role-BAC is also called hierarchy-based or job-based:

- **Hierarchy-based.** In the Project Server example, you can see how top-level roles, such as the Administrators role, have significantly more permissions than lower-level roles, such as the Team Members role. Roles may mimic the hierarchy of an organization.
- **Job-, task-, or function-based.** The Project Server example also shows how the roles are centered on jobs or functions that users need to perform.

> **Remember this**
>
> A role-BAC model uses roles based on jobs and functions. A matrix is a planning document that matches the roles with the required privileges.

Establishing Access with Group-Based Privileges

Administrators commonly grant access in the role-BAC model using roles, and they often implement roles as groups. Windows systems refer to these as security groups. They assign rights and permissions (privileges) to groups and then add user accounts to the appropriate group. This type of **group-based access control**, where access is based on roles or groups, simplifies user administration.

One implementation of the role-BAC model is the Microsoft built-in security groups and specially created security groups that administrators create on workstations, servers, and within domains.

The Administrators group is an example of a built-in security group. For example, the Administrators group on a local computer includes all of the rights and permissions on that computer. If you want to grant Marge full and complete control to a computer, you could add Marge's user account to the Administrators group on that computer. Once Marge is a member of the Administrators group, she has all the rights and permissions of the group.

Similarly, you can grant other users the ability to back up and restore data by adding their user accounts to the Backup Operators group. Although the built-in groups are very useful, they don't meet all the requirements in most organizations. For example, if your organization wants to separate backup and restore responsibilities, you can create one group that can only back up data and another group that can only restore data.

In Windows domains, administrators often create groups that correspond to the departments of an organization. For example, imagine that Homer, Marge, and Bart work in the Sales department and need to access data stored in a shared folder named Sales on a network server. An administrator would simplify administration with the following steps, as shown in Figure 2.6:

1. Create a Sales group and add each of the user accounts to the Sales group.
2. Add the Sales group to the Sales folder.
3. Assign appropriate permissions to the Sales group for the Sales folder.

If the company adds new salespeople, the administrator creates accounts for them and places their accounts into the Sales group. These new salespeople now have access to everything assigned to this group. If any users change jobs within the company and leave the Sales department, the administrator removes them from the Sales group. This automatically prevents them from accessing any resources granted to the Sales group. This example shows how to use a group for the Sales department, but you can apply the same steps to any department or group of users.

Without groups, you would use user-assigned privileges. In other words, you would assign all the specific rights and permissions for every user individually. This might work for one or two users, but quickly becomes unmanageable with more users.

As an example, imagine that people within the Sales department need access to 10 different resources (such as files, folders, and printers) within a network. When the company hires a new salesperson, you'd need to assign permissions to these 10 different resources manually, requiring

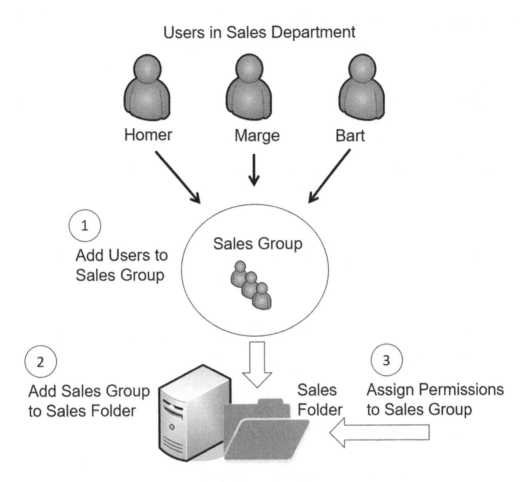

Figure 2.6: Establishing access with groups as roles

10 different administrative tasks. If you assign the permissions to the Sales group, you only need to add the new user to one group and you're done.

Groups provide another security benefit. Imagine that a user is promoted out of the Sales department and now works in Marketing. If you have a Marketing group, you can place this user account into the Marketing group and remove the account from the Sales group. Removing the user from the Sales group instantly removes all the user rights and permissions applied from that group. However, if you're not using groups and assign permissions to users directly, you probably won't remember which resources were assigned to the user as a member of the Sales department. Instead, the user will continue to have access to this sales data, violating the principle of least privilege.

> **Remember this**
>
> Group-based privileges reduce the administrative workload of access management. Administrators put user accounts into security groups, and assign privileges to the groups. Users within a group automatically inherit the privileges assigned to the group.

Rule-Based Access Control

Rule-based access control (**rule-BAC**) uses rules. The most common example is with rules in routers or firewalls. However, more advanced implementations cause rules to trigger within applications, too.

Routers and firewalls use rules within access control lists (ACLs). These rules define the traffic that the devices allow into the network, such as allowing Hypertext Transfer Protocol (HTTP) traffic for web browsers. These rules are typically static. In other words, administrators create the rules and the rules stay the same unless an administrator changes them again.

However, some rules are dynamic. For example, intrusion prevention systems can detect attacks, and then modify rules to block traffic from an attacker. In this case, the attack triggers a change in the rules.

As another example, it's possible to configure user applications with rules. For example, imagine you want to give Homer additional permissions to a database if Marge is absent. You can configure a database rule to trigger a change to these permissions when the system recognizes that Marge is absent.

> **Remember this**
>
> Rule-based access control is based on a set of approved instructions, such as an access control list. Some rule-BAC systems use rules that trigger in response to an event, such as modifying ACLs after detecting an attack or granting additional permissions to a user in certain situations.

Discretionary Access Control

In the discretionary access control (**DAC**) model, every object (such as files and folders) has an owner, and the owner establishes access for the objects. Many operating systems, such as Windows and most Unix-based systems, use the DAC model.

A common example of the DAC model is the New Technology File System (NTFS) used in Windows. NTFS provides security by allowing users and administrators to restrict access to files and folders with permissions. NTFS is based on the DAC model and the following section explains how it uses the DAC model.

SIDs and DACLs

Microsoft systems identify users with security identifiers (SIDs), though you will rarely see a SID. A SID is a long string of characters that is meaningless to most people and may look like this: S-1-5-21-3991871189-223218. Instead of the system displaying the SID, it looks up the name associated with the SID and displays the name. Similarly, Microsoft systems identify groups with a SID.

Every object (such as a file or folder) includes a discretionary access control list (DACL) that identifies who can access it in a system using the DAC model. The DACL is a list of Access Control Entries (ACEs). Each ACE is composed of a SID and the permission(s) granted to the SID. As an example, a folder named Study Notes might have the following permissions assigned:

- Lisa: Full Control
- Bart: Read
- Maggie: Modify

Each of these entries is an ACE and combined they are a DACL. The Viewing a DACL Lab shows how to view the DACL for a folder. You can access the online exercises for this book at *http://gcgapremium.com/501labs/*.

The Owner Establishes Access

If users create a file, they are designated as the owner and have explicit control over the file. As the owner, users can modify the permissions on the object by adding user or group accounts to the DACL and assigning the desired permissions.

The DAC model is significantly more flexible than the MAC model described in the next section. MAC has predefined access privileges, and the administrator is required to make the changes. With DAC, if you want to grant another user access to a file you own, you simply make the change, and that user has access.

Remember this

The DAC model specifies that every object has an owner, and the owner has full, explicit control of the object. Microsoft NTFS uses the DAC model.

Beware of Trojans

An inherent flaw associated with the DAC model is the susceptibility to Trojan horses. Chapter 6, "Comparing Threats, Vulnerabilities, and Common Attacks," presents malware in much more depth, but for this discussion, you should understand some basics related to Trojan horses.

Trojan horses are executable files. They masquerade as something useful, but they include malware. For example, Bart might decide to download and install a program that a friend raved about. After installation, he decides it's not so great and forgets about it. However, the damage is done.

What really happened? When Bart installed the program, it also installed malware. Moreover, if Bart was logged on with administrative privileges when he installed it, the Trojan is able to run with these administrative privileges.

Many organizations require administrators to have two accounts to mitigate the risks associated with Trojans. Most of the time, administrators log on with a regular user account. If the system is infected with malware, the malware has limited permissions assigned to the regular user account. In contrast, if the system is infected with malware while the administrator is logged on with an administrative account, the malware has the elevated permissions of an administrator.

Mandatory Access Control

The mandatory access control (*MAC*) model uses labels (sometimes referred to as sensitivity labels or security labels) to determine access. Security administrators assign labels to both subjects (users) and objects (files or folders). When the labels match, the system can grant a subject access to an object. When the labels don't match, the access model blocks access.

Military units make wide use of this model to protect data. You might have seen movies where they show a folder with a big red and black cover page labeled "Top Secret." The cover page identifies the sensitivity label for the data contained within the folder. Users with a Top Secret label (a Top Secret clearance) and a need to know can access the data within the Top Secret folder.

Need to know is an important concept to understand. Just because individuals have a Top Secret clearance doesn't mean they should automatically have access to all Top Secret data. Instead, access is restricted based on a need to know.

Security-enhanced Linux (SELinux) is one of the few operating systems using the mandatory access control model. SELinux was specifically created to demonstrate how mandatory access controls can be added to an operating system. In contrast, Windows operating systems use the discretionary access control model.

Labels and Lattice

The MAC model uses different levels of security to classify both the users and the data. These levels are defined in a lattice. The lattice can be a complex relationship between different ordered sets of labels. These labels define the boundaries for the security levels.

Figure 2.7 shows how the MAC model uses a lattice to divide access into separate compartments based on a need to know. The lattice starts by defining different levels of Top Secret, Secret, Confidential, and For Official Use. Each of these labels defines specific security boundaries. Within these levels, the lattice defines specific compartments. For example, the Top Secret level includes compartments labeled Nuclear Power Plant, 007, and Happy Sumo.

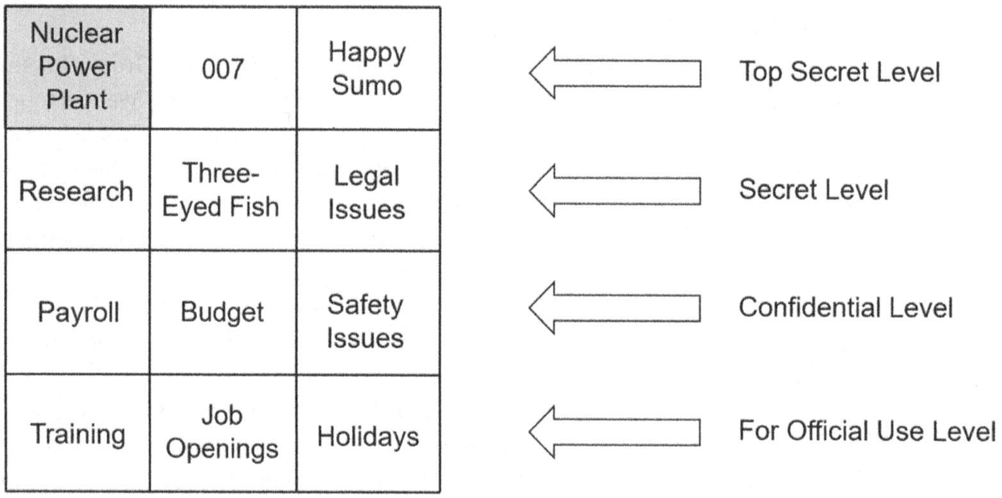

Nuclear Power Plant	007	Happy Sumo	⇐ Top Secret Level
Research	Three-Eyed Fish	Legal Issues	⇐ Secret Level
Payroll	Budget	Safety Issues	⇐ Confidential Level
Training	Job Openings	Holidays	⇐ For Official Use Level

Figure 2.7: MAC model lattice

Imagine that Homer has a Top Secret clearance with a Nuclear Power Plant label. This gives him access to data within the Nuclear Power Plant compartment. However, he does not have access to data in the 007 or Happy Sumo compartment unless he also has those clearances (and associated labels).

Higher-level clearances include lower-level clearances. For example, because Homer has a Top Secret clearance, he can be granted access to Secret and lower-level data. Again though, he will only be able to access data on these lower levels based on his need to know.

As another example, imagine that Lisa has a Secret level clearance. Administrators can grant her access to data on the Secret level and lower levels, based on her need to know. For example, they might grant her access to the Research data by assigning the Research label to her, but not necessarily grant her access to Three-eyed Fish or Legal Issues data. However, they cannot grant her access to any data on the Top Secret level.

> **Remember this**
>
> The MAC model uses sensitivity labels for users and data. It is commonly used when access needs to be restricted based on a need to know. Sensitivity labels often reflect classification levels of data and clearances granted to individuals.

Establishing Access

An administrator is responsible for establishing access, but only someone at a higher authority can define the access for subjects and objects.

Typically, a security professional identifies the specific access individuals are authorized to access. This person can also upgrade or downgrade the individuals' access, when necessary. Note that the security professional does all this via paperwork and does not assign the rights and permissions on computer systems. Instead, the administrator assigns the rights based on the direction of the security professional.

Multiple approval levels are usually involved in the decision-making process to determine what a user can access. For example, in the military an officer working in the security professional role would coordinate with higher-level government entities to upgrade or downgrade clearances. These higher-level entities approve or disapprove clearance requests.

Once an individual is formally granted access, a network administrator would be responsible for establishing access based on the clearances identified by the security professional. From the IT administrator's point of view, all the permissions and access privileges are predefined.

If someone needed different access, the administrator would forward the request to the security professional, who may approve or disapprove the request. On the other hand, the security professional may forward the request to higher entities based on established procedures. This process takes time and results in limited flexibility.

Attribute-Based Access Control

An attribute-based access control (**ABAC**) evaluates attributes and grants access based on the value of these attributes. Attributes can be almost any characteristic of a user, the environment, or the resource. ABAC uses policies to evaluate attributes and grant access when the system detects a match in the policy.

As a simple example, Homer is a Nuclear Safety Inspector at the Springfield Nuclear Power Plant. His user account may be defined with the following attributes: employee, inspector, and nuclear aware. A file server at the plant includes a share called Inspector and it holds documents commonly used by nuclear safety inspectors. An ABAC policy for the share might grant access to the share for any subjects that have the attributes of employee, inspector, and nuclear aware.

Many software defined networks (SDNs) use ABAC models. Instead of rules on physical routers, policies in the ABAC system control the traffic. These policies typically use plain language statements. For example, an ABAC policy rule for a company that employs researchers might be "Allow logged-on researchers to access research sites via the main network."

Policy statements typically include four elements:

- **Subject.** This is typically a user. You can use any user property as an attribute such as employment status, group memberships, job roles, logged-on status, and more. In the example, the subject is identified as being logged on and a member of a researchers group.

- **Object.** This is the resource (such as a file, database, or application) that the user is trying to access. In the example, the object is research sites. The research sites object would include Internet access via a proxy server along with a specific list of URLs of research sites.
- **Action.** The action is what the user is attempting to do, such as reading or modifying a file, accessing specific web sites, and accessing web site applications. The example allows access to specific web sites.
- **Environment.** The environment includes everything outside of the subject and object attributes. This is often referred to as the context of the access request. It can include the time, location, protocols, encryption, devices, and communication method. In the example, it specifies the main network as an environmental attribute.

An ABAC system has a lot of flexibility and can enforce both a DAC and a MAC model. There are also many similarities between the ABAC model and the DAC and MAC models. In the DAC model, owners have control over the access and in an ABAC model, owners can create policies to grant access. The MAC model uses labels assigned to both subjects and objects and grants access when the labels match. The ABAC model uses attributes that identify both subjects and objects, and grants access when a policy identifies a match.

> ### Remember this
>
> The ABAC model uses attributes defined in policies to grant access to resources. It's commonly used in software defined networks (SDNs).

If you want to dig into the ABAC model a little more, check out NIST SP 800-162, "Guide to Attribute Based Access Control (ABAC) Definition and Considerations."

Chapter 2 Exam Topic Review

When preparing for the exam, make sure you understand these key concepts covered in this chapter.

Exploring Authentication Concepts

- Authentication allows entities to prove their identity by using credentials known to another entity.
- Identification occurs when a user claims or professes an identity, such as with a username, an email address, a PIV card, or by using biometrics.
- Authentication occurs when an entity provides proof of an identity (such as a password). A second identity is the authenticator and it verifies the authentication.
- Authorization provides access to resources based on a proven identity.
- Accounting methods track user activity and record the activity in logs.
- Five factors of authentication are:
    o Something you know, such as a username and password
    o Something you have, such as a smart card, CAC, PIV, or token
    o Something you are, using biometrics, such as fingerprints or retina scans
    o Somewhere you are, using geolocation, a computer name, or a MAC address
    o Something you do, such as gestures on a touch screen
- The something you know factor typically refers to a shared secret, such as a password or

a PIN. This is the least secure form of authentication.

- Passwords should be strong and changed often. Complex passwords include multiple character types. Strong passwords are complex and at least 14 characters long.
- Administrators should verify a user's identity before resetting the user's password. When resetting passwords manually, administrators should configure them as temporary passwords that expire after the first use, requiring users to create a new password the first time they log on. Self-service password systems automate password recovery.
- Password policies provide a technical means to ensure users employ secure password practices.
- Password length specifies the minimum number of characters in the password.
- Password complexity ensures passwords are complex and include at least three of the four character types, such as special characters.
- Password history remembers past passwords and prevents users from reusing passwords.
- Minimum password age is used with password history to prevent users from changing their password repeatedly to get back to the original password.
- Maximum password age or password expiration forces users to change their password periodically. When administrators reset user passwords, the password should expire upon first use.
- Password policies should apply to any entity using a password. This includes user accounts and accounts used by services and applications. Applications with internally created passwords should still adhere to the organization's password policy.
- Account lockout policies lock out an account after a user enters an incorrect password too many times.
- Smart cards are credit card-sized cards that have embedded certificates used for authentication. They require a PKI to issue certificates.
- Common Access Cards (CACs) and Personal Identity Verification (PIV) cards can be used as photo IDs and as smart cards (both identification and authentication).
- Tokens (or key fobs) display numbers in an LCD. These numbers provide rolling, one-time use passwords and are synchronized with a server. USB tokens include an embedded chip and a USB connection. Generically, these are called hardware tokens.
- HOTP and TOTP are open source standards used to create one-time-use passwords. HOTP creates a one-time-use password that does not expire and TOTP creates a one-time password that expires after 30 seconds.
- Biometric methods are the most difficult to falsify. Physical methods include voice and facial recognition, fingerprints, retina scans, iris scans, and palm scans. Biometric methods can also be used for identification.
- The false acceptance rate (FAR), or false match rate, identifies the percentage of times false acceptance occurs. The false rejection rate (FRR), or false nonmatch rate, identifies the percentage of times false rejections occur. The crossover error rate (CER) indicates the quality of the biometric system. Lower CERs are better.
- Single-factor authentication includes one or more authentication methods in the same factor, such as a PIN and a password. Dual-factor (or two-factor) authentication uses two factors of authentication, such as a USB token and a PIN. Multifactor authentication uses two or more factors. Multifactor authentication is stronger than any form of single-factor authentication.

- Authentication methods using two or more methods in the same factor are single-factor authentication. For example, a password and a PIN are both in the something you know factor, so they only provide single-factor authentication.

Comparing Authentication Services

- Kerberos is a network authentication protocol using tickets issued by a KDC or TGT server. If a ticket-granting ticket expires, the user might not be able to access resources. Microsoft Active Directory domains and Unix realms use Kerberos for authentication.
- LDAP specifies formats and methods to query directories. It provides a single point of management for objects, such as users and computers, in an Active Directory domain or Unix realm. The following is an example of an LDAP string: LDAP:// CN=Homer,CN=Users,DC=GetCertifiedGetAhead,DC=com
- LDAP Secure (LDAPS) encrypts transmissions with SSL or TLS.
- Single sign-on (SSO) allows users to authenticate with a single user account and access multiple resources on a network without authenticating again.
- SSO can be used to provide central authentication with a federated database and use this authentication in an environment with different operating systems (nonhomogeneous environment).
- SAML is an XML-based standard used to exchange authentication and authorization information between different parties. SAML is used with web-based applications.
- A federated identity links a user's credentials from different networks or operating systems, but the federation treats it as one identity.
- Shibboleth is an open source federated identity solution that includes Open SAML libraries.
- OAuth and OpenID Connect are used by many web sites to streamline the authentication process for users. They allow users to log on to many web sites with another account, such as one they've created with Google, Facebook, PayPal, Microsoft, or Twitter.

Managing Accounts

- The principle of least privilege is a technical control that uses access controls. It specifies that individuals or processes are granted only the rights and permissions needed to perform assigned tasks or functions, but no more.
- Users should not share accounts. It prevents effective identification, authentication, authorization, and accounting. Most organizations ensure the Guest account is disabled.
- Account policies often require administrators to have two accounts (an administrator account and a standard user account) to prevent privilege escalation and other attacks.
- An account disablement policy ensures that inactive accounts are disabled. Accounts for employees who either resign or are terminated should be disabled as soon as possible. Configuring expiration dates on temporary accounts ensures they are disabled automatically.
- Time restrictions can prevent users from logging on or accessing network resources during specific hours. Location-based policies prevent users from logging on from certain locations.
- Accounts should be recertified to verify they are still required. For example, if the organization extends a contract, it's a simple matter to recertify the account. Administrators verify that the contract has been extended, change the expiration date,

and enable the account.

- Administrators routinely perform account maintenance. This is often done with scripts to automate the processes and includes deleting accounts that are no longer needed.
- Credential management systems store and simplify the use of credentials for users. When users access web sites needing credentials, the system automatically retrieves the stored credentials and submits them to the web site.

Comparing Access Control Models

- The role-based access control (role-BAC) model uses roles to grant access by placing users into roles based on their assigned jobs, functions, or tasks. A matrix matching job titles with required privileges is useful as a planning document when using role-BAC.
- Group-based privileges are a form of role-BAC. Administrators create groups, add users to the groups, and then assign permissions to the groups. This simplifies administration because administrators do not have to assign permissions to users individually.
- The rule-based access control (rule-BAC) model is based on a set of approved instructions, such as ACL rules in a firewall. Some rule-BAC implementations use rules that trigger in response to an event, such as modifying ACLs after detecting an attack.
- In the discretionary access control (DAC) model, every object has an owner. The owner has explicit access and establishes access for any other user. Microsoft NTFS uses the DAC model, with every object having a discretionary access control list (DACL). The DACL identifies who has access and what access they are granted. A major flaw of the DAC model is its susceptibility to Trojan horses.
- Mandatory access control (MAC) uses security or sensitivity labels to identify objects (what you'll secure) and subjects (users). It is often used when access needs to be restricted based on a need to know. The administrator establishes access based on predefined security labels. These labels are often defined with a lattice to specify the upper and lower security boundaries.
- An attribute-based access control (ABAC) evaluates attributes and grants access based on the value of these attributes. It is used in many software defined networks (SDNs).

Online References

- Have you looked at the online content recently? You can view labs and additional sample questions at *http://gcgapremium.com/501-extras*.

Chapter 2 Practice Questions

1. Developers in your organization have created an application designed for the sales team. Salespeople can log on to the application using a simple password of 1234. However, this password does not meet the organization's password policy. Which of the following is the BEST response by the security administrator after learning about this?

   A. Nothing. Strong passwords aren't required in applications.

   B. Modify the security policy to accept this password.

   C. Document this as an exception in the application's documentation.

   D. Direct the application team manager to ensure the application adheres to the organization's password policy.

2. Ned is reviewing password security for employees of The Leftorium. The password policy has the following settings:
    -   The password maximum age is 30 days.
    -   The password minimum length is 14 characters.
    -   Passwords cannot be reused until five other passwords have been used.
    -   Passwords must include at least one of each of the following four character types: uppercase letters, lowercase letters, numbers, and special characters.

    Ned discovers that despite having this password policy in place, users are still using the same password that they were using more than a month ago. Which of the following actions will resolve this issue?
    A. Create a rule in the password policy for the password minimum age to be 7 days.
    B. Change the password history to 10.
    C. Require the use of complex passwords.
    D. Change the maximum age setting to 60 days.

3. Your organization is planning to implement remote access capabilities. Management wants strong authentication and wants to ensure that passwords expire after a predefined time interval. Which of the following choices BEST meets this requirement?
    A. HOTP
    B. TOTP
    C. CAC
    D. Kerberos

4. Your organization has decided to implement a biometric solution for authentication. One of the goals is to ensure that the biometric system is highly accurate. Which of the following provides the BEST indication of accuracy with the biometric system?
    A. The lowest possible FRR
    B. The highest possible FAR
    C. The lowest possible CER
    D. The highest possible CER

5. Your organization recently updated an online application employees use to log on when working from home. Employees enter their username and password into the application from their smartphone and the application logs their location using GPS. Which type of authentication is being used?
    A. One-factor
    B. Dual-factor
    C. Something you are
    D. Somewhere you are

6. A network includes a ticket-granting ticket server used for authentication. Which authentication service does this network use?
    A. Shibboleth
    B. SAML
    C. LDAP
    D. Kerberos

7. Lisa is a training instructor and she maintains a training lab with 18 computers. She has enough rights and permissions on these machines so that she can configure them as needed for classes. However, she does not have the rights to add them to the organization's domain. Which of the following choices BEST describes this example?

    A. Least privilege

    B. Need to know

    C. Group-based privileges

    D. Location-based policies

8. Marge is reviewing an organization's account management processes. She wants to ensure that security log entries accurately report the identity of personnel taking specific actions. Which of the following steps would BEST meet this requirement?

    A. Update ACLs for all files and folders.

    B. Implement role-based privileges.

    C. Use an SSO solution.

    D. Remove all shared accounts.

9. A recent security audit discovered several apparently dormant user accounts. Although users could log on to the accounts, no one had logged on to them for more than 60 days. You later discovered that these accounts are for contractors who work approximately one week every quarter. Which of the following is the BEST response to this situation?

    A. Remove the account expiration from the accounts.

    B. Delete the accounts.

    C. Reset the accounts.

    D. Disable the accounts.

10. Members of a project team chose to meet at a local library to complete some work on a key project. All of them are authorized to work from home using a VPN connection and have connected from home successfully. However, they found that they were unable to connect to the network using the VPN from the library and they could not access any of the project data. Which of the following choices is the MOST likely reason why they can't access this data?

    A. Role-based access control

    B. Time-of-day access control

    C. Location-based policy

    D. Discretionary access control

11. You need to create an account for a contractor who will be working at your company for 60 days. Which of the following is the BEST security step to take when creating this account?

    A. Configure history on the account.

    B. Configure a password expiration date on the account.

    C. Configure an expiration date on the account.

    D. Configure complexity.

12. A company recently hired you as a security administrator. You notice that some former accounts used by temporary employees are currently enabled. Which of the following choices is the BEST response?
   A. Disable all the temporary accounts.
   B. Disable the temporary accounts you've noticed are enabled.
   C. Craft a script to identify inactive accounts based on the last time they logged on.
   D. Set account expiration dates for all accounts when creating them.

13. Developers are planning to develop an application using role-based access control. Which of the following would they MOST likely include in their planning?
   A. A listing of labels reflecting classification levels
   B. A requirements list identifying need to know
   C. A listing of owners
   D. A matrix of functions matched with their required privileges

14. A security administrator needs to implement an access control system that will protect data based on the following matrix.

Document Type	Security Level	Security Label
Employment documents	Private	Employee
Salary and compensation documents	Private	Payroll
Internal phone listing documents	Private	Employee

(Note that this matrix only represents a subset of the overall requirements.)

Which of the following models is the administrator implementing?
   A. DAC
   B. MAC
   C. Role-BAC
   D. ABAC

15. Your organization is implementing an SDN. Management wants to use an access control model that controls access based on attributes. Which of the following is the BEST solution?
   A. DAC
   B. MAC
   C. Role-BAC
   D. ABAC

Chapter 2 Practice Question Answers

1. **D.** The application should be recoded to adhere to the company's password policy, so the best response is to direct the application team manager to do so. Application passwords should be strong and should adhere to an organization's security policy. It is not appropriate to weaken a security policy to match a weakness in an application. Nor is it appropriate to simply document that the application uses a weak password.

2. **A.** The best solution is to create a rule in the password policy for the password minimum age. Currently, users can change their passwords five more times in just a couple of minutes,

changing it back to their original password on the sixth change. None of the other settings prevent the users from doing this. A password history of 10 forces the users to take a couple more minutes to get back to the original password. The password policy currently requires complex passwords. A maximum age of 60 days increases how long a user can keep the same password.

3. **B.** A Time-based One-Time Password (TOTP) meets this requirement. Passwords created with TOTP expire after 30 seconds. An HMAC-based One-Time Password (HOTP) creates passwords that do not expire. A Common Access Card (CAC) is a type of smart card, but it does not create passwords. Kerberos uses tickets instead of passwords.

4. **C.** A lower crossover error rate (CER) indicates a more accurate biometric system. The false acceptance rate (FAR) and the false rejection rate (FRR) vary based on the sensitivity of the biometric system and don't indicate accuracy by themselves. A higher CER indicates a less accurate biometric system.

5. **A.** This is using one-factor authentication—something you know. The application uses the username for identification and the password for authentication. Note that even though the application is logging the location using Global Positioning System (GPS), there isn't any indication that it is using this information for authentication. Dual-factor authentication requires another factor of authentication. If the application verified you were logging on from a specific GPS location as part of the authentication, it would be dual-factor authentication (something you know and somewhere you are). Something you are refers to biometric authentication methods. The somewhere you are authentication method verifies you are somewhere, such as in a specific GPS location, but this isn't being used for authentication in this scenario.

6. **D.** Kerberos uses a ticket-granting ticket (TGT) server, which creates tickets for authentication. Shibboleth is a federated identity solution used in some single sign-on (SSO) solutions. Security Assertion Markup Language (SAML) is an Extensible Markup Language (XML) used for some SSO solutions. Lightweight Directory Access Protocol (LDAP) is an X.500-based authentication service used to identify objects.

7. **A.** When following the principle of least privilege, individuals have only enough rights and permissions to perform their job, and this is exactly what is described in this scenario. Need to know typically refers to data and information rather than the privileges required to perform an action, such as adding computers to a domain. Group-based privileges refer to giving permissions to groups, and then adding the users to the groups to give them appropriate privileges. A location-based policy allows or blocks access based on location, but the scenario doesn't indicate the location is being checked.

8. **D.** Removing all shared accounts is the best answer of the available choices. If two employees are using the same account, and one employee maliciously deletes data in a database, it isn't possible to identify which employee deleted the data. File and folder access control lists (ACLs) identify permissions for users, but don't control the user identity. Role-based (or group-based) privileges assign the same permissions to all members of a group, which simplifies administration. A single sign-on (SSO) solution allows a user to log on once and access multiple resources.

9. **D.** The best response is to disable the accounts and then enable them when needed by the contractors. Ideally, the accounts would include an expiration date so that they would automatically expire when no longer needed, but the scenario doesn't indicate the accounts have an expiration date. Because the contractors need to access the accounts periodically, it's better to disable them rather than delete them. Reset the accounts implies you are changing the password, but this isn't needed.

10. **C.** A location-based policy restricts access based on location, such as with an IP address, and this is the best possible answer of those given. The scenario indicates they could use the virtual private network (VPN) connection from home, but it was blocked when they tried to access it from the library. A time-of-day access control restricts access based on the time of day, but the scenario doesn't indicate the time. Neither a discretionary access control model nor a role-based access control model restricts access based on location.

11. **C.** When creating temporary accounts, it's best to configure expiration dates so that the system will automatically disable the accounts on the specified date. History, password expiration, and complexity all refer to password policy settings. However, it's rare to configure a specific password policy on a single account.

12. **C.** Running a last logon script allows you to identify inactive accounts, such as accounts that haven't been logged on to in the last 30 days. It's appropriate to disable unused accounts, but it isn't necessarily appropriate to disable all temporary accounts, because some might still be in use. If you disable the accounts you notice, you might disable accounts that some employees are still using, and you might miss some accounts that should be disabled. Setting expiration dates for newly created accounts is a good step, but it doesn't address previously created accounts.

13. **D.** A matrix of functions, roles, or job titles matched with the required access privileges for each of the functions, roles, or job titles is a common planning document for a role-based access control (role-BAC) model. The mandatory access control (MAC) model uses sensitivity labels and classification levels. MAC is effective at restricting access based on a need to know. The discretionary access control (DAC) model specifies that every object has an owner and it might identify owners in a list.

14. **B.** This is a mandatory access control (MAC) model. You can tell because it is using security labels. None of the other models listed use labels. A discretionary access control (DAC) model has an owner, and the owner establishes access for the objects. A role-based access control (role-BAC) model uses roles or groups to assign rights and permissions. An attribute-based access control (ABAC) model uses attributes assigned to subjects and objects within a policy to grant access.

15. **D.** A software defined network (SDN) typically uses an attribute-based access control (ABAC) model, which is based on attributes that identify subjects and objects within a policy. A discretionary access control (DAC) model has an owner, and the owner establishes access for the objects. A mandatory access control (MAC) model uses labels assigned to subjects and objects. A role-based access control (role-BAC) model uses roles or groups to assign rights and permissions.

Chapter 3

Exploring Network Technologies and Tools

CompTIA Security+ objectives covered in this chapter:

1.2   Compare and contrast types of attacks.
- Application/service attacks (ARP poisoning, DNS poisoning)

2.1   Install and configure network components, both hardware- and software-based, to support organizational security.
- Firewall (ACL, Application-based vs. network-based, Stateful vs. stateless, Implicit deny), Router (ACLs, Antispoofing), Switch (Port security, Layer 2 vs. Layer 3, Loop prevention, Flood guard), Proxy (Forward and reverse proxy, Transparent, Application/multipurpose), Mail gateway (Spam filter, DLP, Encryption), Bridge, Media gateway

2.2   Given a scenario, use appropriate software tools to assess the security posture of an organization.
- Command line tools (nslookup/dig)

2.3   Given a scenario, troubleshoot common security issues.
- Misconfigured devices (Firewall, Content filter)

2.4   Given a scenario, analyze and interpret output from security technologies.
- Host-based firewall, UTM, Web application firewall

2.6   Given a scenario, implement secure protocols.
- Protocols (DNSSEC, SSH, SRTP, FTPS, SFTP, SNMPv3, SSL/TLS, HTTPS, Secure POP/IMAP)
- Use cases (Voice and video, Time synchronization, Email and web, File transfer, Directory services, Remote access, Domain name resolution, Routing and switching, Network address allocation, Subscription services)

3.2   Given a scenario, implement secure network architecture concepts.
- Zones/topologies (DMZ, Extranet, Intranet, NAT), Segregation/segmentation/isolation (Physical, Logical (VLAN), Air gaps), Security device/technology placement (Filters, Proxies, Firewalls, Load balancers, DDoS mitigator, Aggregation switches)

1.3   Given a scenario, implement secure systems design.
- Operating systems (Disabling unnecessary ports and services)
**

CompTIA expects prospective CompTIA Security+ exam takers to have at least two years of networking experience. However, even with that amount of experience, there are often gaps in an information technology (IT) professional's or security professional's knowledge. For example, you may have spent a lot of time troubleshooting connectivity but rarely manipulated access control lists (ACLs) on a router or modified firewall rules. This chapter reviews some basic networking concepts, devices, and network topologies used within secure networks. When appropriate, it digs into these topics a little deeper with a focus on security.

Reviewing Basic Networking Concepts

Before you can tackle any of the relevant security issues on a network, you'll need a basic understanding of networking. As a reminder, CompTIA expects you to have a minimum of two years of experience in IT administration. Further, CompTIA recommends obtaining the Network+ certification before taking the Security+ exam. Although the Network+ certification isn't required, the knowledge goes a long way in helping you pass the networking portion of the Security+ exam.

This section includes a very brief review of many of the different protocols and networking concepts that are relevant to security. If any of these concepts are completely unfamiliar to you, you might need to pick up a networking book to review them.

This section also mentions some of the common attacks used against the protocols, or that the protocols help protect against. The following bullets introduce some of these attacks and Chapter 7, "Protecting Against Advanced Attacks," covers these attacks in more depth:

- **Sniffing attack.** Attackers often use a protocol analyzer to capture data sent over a network. After capturing the data, attackers can easily read the data within the protocol analyzer when it has been sent in cleartext. Chapter 8, "Using Risk Management Tools," covers protocol analyzers in more depth.
- **DoS and DDoS.** A denial-of-service (*DoS*) attack is a service attack from a single source that attempts to disrupt the services provided by another system. A distributed DoS (*DDoS*) attack includes multiple computers attacking a single target.
- **Poisoning attack.** Many protocols store data in cache for temporary access. Poisoning attacks attempt to corrupt the cache with different data.

Basic Networking Protocols

Networking protocols provide the rules needed for computers to communicate with each other on a network. Some of the Transmission Control Protocol/Internet Protocol (TCP/IP) protocols, such as TCP and IP, provide basic connectivity. Other protocols, such as Hypertext Transfer Protocol (HTTP) and Simple Mail Transfer Protocol (SMTP), support specific types of traffic. This section includes information on common protocols that you'll need to understand for the CompTIA Security+ exam.

TCP/IP isn't a single protocol, but a full suite of protocols. Obviously, there isn't room in this book to teach the details of all the TCP/IP protocols. Instead, the purpose of this section is to remind you of some of the commonly used protocols. Additionally, many of these protocols meet specific use cases and this section describes these protocols within the context of use cases.

CompTIA has historically placed a lot of emphasis on well-known ports used by protocols. For example, the default port for HTTP is 80 and CompTIA Security+ test takers needed to know that. The current objectives have deemphasized the importance of ports. However, you still need to know them when implementing access control lists (ACLs) in routers and stateless firewalls, and when disabling unnecessary ports and services. With that in mind, I've included the well-known ports for many of the protocols in this chapter.

The following list describes some basic networking protocols:

- **TCP.** Transmission Control Protocol (TCP) provides connection-oriented traffic (guaranteed delivery). TCP uses a three-way handshake and Figure 3.1 shows the TCP handshake process. To start a TCP session, the client sends a SYN (synchronize) packet. The server responds with a SYN/ACK (synchronize/acknowledge) packet, and the client completes the third part of the handshake with an ACK packet to establish the connection.

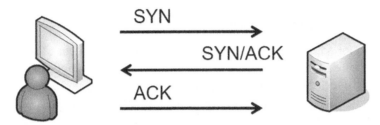

Figure 3.1: TCP handshake process

- **UDP.** User Datagram Protocol (UDP) provides connectionless sessions (without a three-way handshake). While TCP traffic provides guaranteed delivery, UDP makes a best effort to deliver traffic without using extra traffic to ensure delivery. ICMP traffic such as the ping command and audio/video streaming use UDP. Many network-based denial-of-service (DoS) attacks use UDP. TCP/IP traffic is either connection-oriented TCP traffic or connectionless UDP.
- **IP.** The Internet Protocol (IP) identifies hosts in a TCP/IP network and delivers traffic from one host to another using IP addresses. IPv4 uses 32-bit addresses represented in dotted decimal format, such as 192.168.1.100. IPv6 uses 128-bit addresses using hexadecimal code, such as FE80:0000:0000:0000:20D4:3FF7:003F:DE62.
- **ICMP.** Internet Control Message Protocol (ICMP) is used for testing basic connectivity and includes tools such as ping, pathping, and tracert. As an example, ping can check for basic connectivity between two systems, as discussed in Chapter 1, "Mastering Security Basics." Many DoS attacks use ICMP. Because of how often ICMP is used in attacks, it has become common to block ICMP at firewalls and routers, which disables a ping response. Blocking ICMP prevents attackers from discovering devices in a network. For example, a scan can send a ping to every IP address in a subnet. The devices that reply verify that they are on and have an IP address.
- **ARP.** Address Resolution Protocol (ARP) resolves IPv4 addresses to media access control (**MAC**) addresses. MACs are also called physical addresses, or hardware addresses. TCP/IP uses the IP address to get a packet to a destination network, but once it arrives on the destination network, it uses the MAC address to get it to the correct host. In other words, ARP is required once the packet reaches the destination subnet. **ARP poisoning** attacks

use ARP packets to give clients false hardware address updates and attackers use it to redirect or interrupt network traffic.

- **NDP.** Neighbor Discovery Protocol (NDP) performs several functions on IPv6. For example, it performs functions similar to IPv4's ARP. It also performs autoconfiguration of device IPv6 addresses and discovers other IPv6 devices on the network such as the address of the default gateway.

Implementing Protocols for Use Cases

Networks don't automatically support all the available protocols. Instead, IT professionals identify a need based on an organizational goal and enable the best protocol to meet that need. Chapter 1 discusses use cases. As a reminder, a *use case* typically describes an organizational goal. Many protocols mentioned in the CompTIA Security+ objectives support specific use cases and are discussed in this section.

Voice and Video Use Case

It's common for an organization to transport voice and video over a network and some protocols work better with voice and video than others. As mentioned previously, UDP is commonly used instead of TCP as the underlying protocol with voice and video streaming.

The Real-time Transport Protocol (RTP) delivers audio and video over IP networks. This includes Voice over Internet Protocol (VoIP) communications, streaming media, video teleconferencing applications, and devices using web-based push-to-talk features. However, organizations often want to secure these transmissions. The Secure Real-time Transport Protocol (*SRTP*) provides encryption, message authentication, and integrity for RTP.

SRTP helps protect the confidentiality of data from these attacks while also ensuring the integrity of the data transmissions. This provides protection against replay attacks. In a replay attack, an attacker captures data sent between two entities, modifies it, and then attempts to impersonate one of the parties by replaying the data. SRTP can be used for both unicast transmissions (such as one person calling another) and multicast transmissions where one person sends traffic to multiple recipients.

File Transfer Use Case

Data-in-transit is any traffic sent over a network. When data is sent in cleartext, attackers can use a protocol analyzer to capture and read it. You can protect the confidentiality of Personally Identifiable Information (PII) and any other sensitive data-in-transit by encrypting it. Note that you can also encrypt data-at-rest, which is data stored on any type of medium. Chapter 10, "Understanding Cryptography and PKI," covers several specific encryption algorithms in more depth.

Some common use cases related to transferring files are transmit data over the network, ensure confidentiality when transmitting data over a network, and ensure administrators connect to servers using secure connections. The following list identifies basic protocols used to transfer data over a network:

- **FTP.** File Transfer Protocol (FTP) uploads and downloads large files to and from an FTP server. By default, FTP transmits data in cleartext, making it easy for an attacker to capture and read FTP data with a protocol analyzer. FTP active mode uses TCP port 21 for control signals and TCP port 20 for data. FTP passive mode (also known as PASV) uses

TCP port 21 for control signals, but it uses a random TCP port for data. If FTP traffic is going through a firewall, this random port is often blocked, so it is best to disable PASV in FTP clients.

- **TFTP.** Trivial File Transfer Protocol (TFTP) uses UDP port 69 and is used to transfer smaller amounts of data, such as when communicating with network devices. Many attacks have used TFTP, but it is not an essential protocol on most networks. Because of this, administrators commonly disable it.

The following list identifies several encryption protocols used to encrypt data-in-transit. They can be used for various use cases related to secure file transfer:

- **SSH.** Secure Shell (**SSH**) encrypts traffic in transit and can be used to encrypt other protocols such as FTP. Linux administrators often used Telnet when remotely administering systems, but this is not recommended because Telnet sends traffic over the network in cleartext. Instead, administrators commonly use SSH to remotely administer systems. Secure Copy (SCP) is based on SSH and is used to copy encrypted files over a network. SSH can also encrypt TCP Wrappers, a type of access control list used on Linux systems to filter traffic. When SSH encrypts traffic, it uses TCP port 22.

- **SSL.** The Secure Sockets Layer (**SSL**) protocol was the primary method used to secure HTTP traffic as Hypertext Transfer Protocol Secure (HTTPS). SSL can also encrypt other types of traffic, such as SMTP and Lightweight Directory Access Protocol (LDAP). However, it has been compromised and is not recommended for use.

- **TLS.** The Transport Layer Security (**TLS**) protocol is the designated replacement for SSL and should be used instead of SSL. Additionally, many protocols that support TLS use **STARTTLS**. STARTTLS looks like an acronym, but it isn't. Instead, it is a command used to upgrade an unencrypted connection to an encrypted connection on the same port.

- **IPsec.** Internet Protocol security (**IPsec**) is used to encrypt IP traffic. It is native to IPv6 but also works with IPv4. IPsec encapsulates and encrypts IP packet payloads and uses Tunnel mode to protect virtual private network (VPN) traffic. IPsec includes two main components: Authentication Header (AH) identified by protocol ID number 51 and Encapsulating Security Payload (ESP) identified by protocol ID number 50. It uses the Internet Key Exchange (IKE) over UDP port 500 to create a security association for the VPN. Chapter 4, "Securing Your Network," covers IPsec in more depth.

- **SFTP.** Secure File Transfer Protocol (**SFTP**) is a secure implementation of FTP. It is an extension of Secure Shell (SSH) using SSH to transmit the files in an encrypted format. SFTP transmits data using TCP port 22.

- **FTPS.** File Transfer Protocol Secure (**FTPS**) is an extension of FTP and uses TLS to encrypt FTP traffic. Some implementations of FTPS use TCP ports 989 and 990. However, TLS can also encrypt the traffic over the ports used by FTP (20 and 21). Notice that the difference between SFTP and FTPS is that SFTP uses SSH and FTPS uses TLS.

Remember this

Secure Shell (SSH) encrypts traffic over TCP port 22. Transport Layer Security (TLS) is a replacement for SSL and is used to encrypt many different protocols. Secure FTP (SFTP) uses SSH to encrypt traffic. FTP Secure (FTPS) uses TLS to encrypt traffic.

SSL Versus TLS

SSL has been compromised and is not recommended for use. In September 2014, a team at Google discovered a serious vulnerability with SSL that they nicknamed the POODLE attack. Poodle is short for Padding Oracle on Downgraded Legacy Encryption. The SSL protocol is not maintained or patched, so this vulnerability remains.

This is one of the reasons that the U. S. government and many other organizations prohibit the use of SSL to protect any sensitive data. For example, National Institute of Standards and Technology (NIST) Special Publication (SP) 800-52 "Guidelines for the Selection, Configuration, and Use of Transport Layer Security (TLS) Implementations" specifically states that federal agencies should not use SSL.

TLS is the recommended replacement. While TLS can be used in almost any implementation that previously used SSL, the two aren't the same protocol. Still, you will often see both SSL and TLS mentioned as if they are the same. Even the CompTIA objectives for the Security+ exam use "SSL/TLS" as if they are the same protocol.

The reason seems to be simply that people understand SSL. By lumping the topics together as SSL/TLS, many people understand the general purpose.

From a generic perspective, using the term SSL/TLS is effective at helping people understand the similarities. However, from a technical perspective, it's important to realize that SSL is compromised and TLS should be used instead.

Email and Web Use Cases

Some common use cases related to email are send and receive email, send and receive secure email, and manage email folders. For the web, common use cases for internal employees are to provide access to the Internet and provide secure access to the Internet. Many organizations host web servers and common use cases for these web servers are to provide access to web servers by external clients.

Many of these protocols support the use of STARTTLS. Instead of using one port to transmit data in cleartext and a second port to transmit data in ciphertext, the STARTTLS command allows the protocol to use the same port for both. Some common protocols used for email and the web include:

- **SMTP.** Simple Mail Transfer Protocol (SMTP) transfers email between clients and SMTP servers. SMTP uses TCP port 25. SMTP unofficially used port 465 with SSL and port 587 with TLS. However, it is now recommended that SMTP use STARTTLS to initialize a secure connection.
- **POP3 and Secure POP.** Post Office Protocol v3 (*POP3*) transfers emails from servers down to clients. POP3 uses TCP port 110. Secure POP3 encrypts the transmission with SSL or TLS and can use TCP port 995. However, STARTTLS is now recommended to create a secure connection on port 110.
- **IMAP4 and Secure IMAP.** Internet Message Access Protocol version 4 (*IMAP4*) is used to store email on an email server. IMAP4 allows a user to organize and manage email in folders on the server. As an example, Google Mail uses IMAP4. IMAP4 uses TCP port 143. IMAP4 with SSL or TLS can use TCP port 993, but STARTTLS is recommended using the same TCP port 143.

- **HTTP.** Hypertext Transfer Protocol (HTTP) transmits web traffic on the Internet and in intranets. Web servers use HTTP to transmit web pages to clients' web browsers. Hypertext Markup Language (HTML) is the common language used to display the web pages. HTTP uses TCP port 80.
- **HTTPS.** Hypertext Transfer Protocol Secure (*HTTPS*) encrypts web traffic to ensure it is secure while in transit. Web browsers commonly indicate that a secure session is using HTTPS by displaying a lock icon and by including HTTPS in the Uniform Resource Locator (URL) field. HTTPS is encrypted with either SSL or TLS and it uses TCP port 443.

> ### Remember this
>
> SMTP sends email on TCP port 25, POP3 receives email on port 110, and IMAP4 uses port 143. STARTTLS allows an encrypted version of the protocol to use the same port as the unencrypted version. HTTP and HTTPS use ports 80 and 443 and transmit data over the Internet in unencrypted and encrypted formats, respectively.

Directory Services Use Case

Network operating systems commonly use a directory service to streamline management and implement security. A common use case is to provide secure access to the network. As an example, many organizations use Microsoft Active Directory Domain Services (AD DS). AD DS provides the means for administrators to create user objects for each authorized user and computer objects for each authorized computer. Administrators then use various methods within the directory service to enforce identification, authentication, and authorization methods.

Chapter 2, "Understanding Identity and Access Management," covers three relevant topics that help support this use case:

- **Kerberos.** Kerberos is the authentication protocol used in Windows domains and some Unix environments. It uses a Key Distribution Center (KDC) to issue timestamped tickets. Kerberos uses UDP port 88.
- **LDAP.** Lightweight Directory Access Protocol (*LDAP*) is the protocol used to communicate with directories such as AD DS. LDAP provides a clear syntax for object identification and management. LDAP uses TCP port 389. LDAP Secure (*LDAPS*) encrypts data with TLS using TCP port 636.
- **Group Policy.** Administrators use Group Policy Objects (*GPOs*) to configure settings. They can then apply these GPOs to users and computers within the domain.

Remote Access Use Cases

There are many situations where personnel need to access systems from remote locations. Some common use cases are remotely administer systems and remotely access desktops. For example, imagine a server room hosts hundreds of servers, including domain controllers for a Microsoft domain. If administrators need to create a user account or implement a change in a GPO, they would rarely go to the server room. Instead, they access the server remotely and make the change from their desk computer.

Administrators often implement SSH (discussed in the "File Transfer Use Case" section) to meet a use case of supporting remote access. As an example, many Linux administrators use Netcat when connecting to remote systems for administration, and secure the Netcat transmissions with SSH. Chapter 8 covers Netcat in more depth, but you can check out the Chapter 3 labs for an introduction to Netcat.

Administrators and clients often use Remote Desktop Protocol (RDP) to connect to other systems from remote locations. Microsoft uses RDP in different solutions such as Remote Desktop Services and Remote Assistance. RDP uses either port TCP 3389 or UDP 3389, though TCP port 3389 is more common. A common reason why users are unable to connect to systems with RDP is that port 3389 is blocked on a host-based or network firewall. Another method of supporting remote access use cases is with a virtual private network (VPN). Chapter 4 discusses VPNs in more depth.

> ### Remember this
>
> Administrators connect to servers remotely using protocols such as Secure Shell (SSH) and the Remote Desktop Protocol (RDP). In some cases, administrators use virtual private networks to connect to remote systems.

Time Synchronization Use Case

There are many instances when systems need to be using the same time (or at least a time that is reasonably close). A common use case is to ensure systems have the accurate time. As an example, Kerberos requires all systems to be synchronized and be within five minutes of each other.

Within a Microsoft domain, one domain controller periodically uses the Windows Time service to locate a reliable Internet server running the Network Time Protocol (NTP). NTP is the most commonly used protocol for time synchronization, allowing systems to synchronize their time to within tens of milliseconds. Other domain controllers within the network periodically synchronize their time with the first domain controller. Last, all computers in the domain synchronize their time with one of these domain controllers. This process ensures all the computers have the accurate time.

The Simple NTP (SNTP) protocol can also be used for time synchronization. However, NTP uses complex algorithms and queries multiple time servers to identify the most accurate time. SNTP does not use these algorithms, so it might not be as accurate as the result from NTP.

Network Address Allocation Use Case

Network address allocation refers to allocating IP addresses to hosts within your network. You can do so manually, but most networks use Dynamic Host Configuration Protocol (DHCP) to dynamically assign IP addresses to hosts. DHCP also assigns other TCP/IP information, such as subnet masks, default gateways, DNS server addresses, and much more. The following sections provide a review of some basic networking concepts.

IPv4

IPv4 uses 32-bit IP addresses expressed in dotted decimal format. For example, the IPv4 IP address of 192.168.1.5 is four decimals separated by periods or dots. You can also express the address in binary form with 32 bits.

All Internet IP addresses are public IP addresses, and internal networks use private IP addresses. Public IP addresses are tightly controlled. You can't just use any public IP address.

Instead, you must either purchase or rent it. Internet Service Providers (ISPs) purchase entire ranges of IP addresses and issue them to customers. If you access the Internet from home, you are very likely receiving a public IP address from an ISP.

Routers on the Internet include rules to drop any traffic that is coming from or going to a private IP address, so you cannot allocate private IP addresses on the Internet. RFC 1918 specifies the following private address ranges:

- **10.x.y.z.** 10.0.0.0 through 10.255.255.255
- **172.16.y.z–172.31.y.z.** 172.16.0.0 through 172.31.255.255
- **192.168.y.z.** 192.168.0.0 through 192.168.255.255

These are the only three IPv4 address ranges that you should allocate within a private network.

> ### Remember this
>
> Private networks should only have private IP addresses. These are formally defined in RFC 1918.

IPv6

Although the number of IP addresses at first seemed inexhaustible, the Internet Assigned Numbers Authority (IANA) assigned the last block of IPv4 addresses in February 2011. To prepare, the Internet Engineering Task Force (IETF) created IPv6, which provides a significantly larger address space than IPv4.

IPv6 uses 128-bit IP addresses expressed in hexadecimal format. For example, the IPv6 IP address of fe80:0000:0000:0000:02d4:3ff7:003f:de62 includes eight groups of four hexadecimal characters, separated by colons. Each hexadecimal character is composed of 4 bits.

Instead of private IP addresses, IPv6 uses unique local addresses. They are only allocated within private networks and not assigned to systems on the Internet. Unique local addresses start with the prefix of fc00.

Domain Name Resolution Use Case

The primary purpose of Domain Name System (**DNS**) is for domain name resolution. DNS resolves host names to IP addresses. Systems are constantly querying DNS, though it is usually transparent to users. Imagine that you want to visit *http://getcertifiedgetahead.com/*. You enter the URL into your web browser or click a link on a page and your system queries a DNS server for the site's IP address. Figure 3.2 shows what is occurring between your system and DNS. DNS uses UDP port 53 for these types of queries.

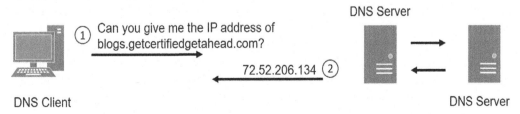

Figure 3.2: A basic DNS query

Sometimes, the DNS server you query knows the answer and just gives the response. Other times, it queries one or more other DNS servers to get the answer. When the DNS server queries other DNS servers, it puts the answer in its cache so that it doesn't have to do the same query again. Similarly, when clients receive answers from DNS servers, they store the answer in their cache so that they don't have to repeat the query.

DNS servers host data in zones, which you can think of as databases. Zones include multiple records, such as the following:

- **A.** Also called a host record. This record holds the host name and IPv4 address and is the most commonly used record in a DNS server. A DNS client queries DNS with the name using a forward lookup request, and DNS responds with the IPv4 address from this record.
- **AAAA.** This record holds the host name and IPv6 address. It's similar to an A record except that it is for IPv6.
- **PTR.** Also called a pointer record. It is the opposite of an A record. Instead of a DNS client querying DNS with the name, the DNS client queries DNS with the IP address. When configured to do so, the DNS server responds with the name. PTR records are optional, so these reverse lookups do not always work.
- **MX.** Also called mail exchange or mail exchanger. An MX record identifies a mail server used for email. The MX record is linked to the A record or AAAA record of a mail server.
- **CNAME.** A canonical name, or alias, allows a single system to have multiple names associated with a single IP address. For example, a server named Server1 in the domain *getcertifiedgetahead.com* might have an alias of FileServer1 in the same domain.
- **SOA.** The start of authority (SOA) record includes information about the DNS zone and some of its settings. For example, it includes the TTL (Time to Live) settings for DNS records. DNS clients use the TTL setting to determine how long to cache DNS results. TTL times are in seconds and lower times cause clients to renew the records more often.

Most DNS servers on the Internet run Berkeley Internet Name Domain (BIND) software and run on Unix or Linux servers. Internal networks can use BIND, but in Microsoft networks, DNS servers commonly use the Microsoft DNS software.

Occasionally, DNS servers share information with each other in a process known as a zone transfer. In most cases, a zone transfer only includes a small number of updated records. However, some transfers include all the records in the zone. DNS servers use TCP port 53 for zone transfers. In contrast, name resolution queries use UDP port 53.

DNSSEC

One risk with DNS is **DNS poisoning**, also known as DNS cache poisoning. When successful, attackers modify the DNS cache with a bogus IP address. For example, imagine an attacker wants to send users to a malicious web site each time they want to go to *msn.com*. One way is to modify the A or AAAA record in the DNS cache for msn.com. Instead of sending users to the IP address used by msn.com, it will send users to the IP address of the malicious web site.

One of the primary methods of preventing DNS cache poisoning is with Domain Name System Security Extensions (**DNSSEC**). DNSSEC is a suite of extensions to DNS that provides validation for DNS responses. It adds a digital signature to each record that provides data integrity. If a DNS server receives a DNSSEC-enabled response with digitally signed records, the DNS server knows that the response is valid.

> ### Remember this
>
> DNS zones include records such as A records for IPv4 addresses and AAAA records for IPv6 addresses. DNS uses TCP port 53 for zone transfers and UDP port 53 for DNS client queries. Most Internet-based DNS servers run BIND software on Unix or Linux servers, and it's common to configure DNS servers to only use secure zone transfers. DNSSEC helps prevent DNS poisoning attacks. Nslookup and dig are two command-line tools used to test DNS. Microsoft systems include nslookup; Linux systems include dig.

Nslookup and Dig

Technicians use the ***nslookup*** command (short for name server lookup) to troubleshoot problems related to DNS. For example, you can use nslookup to verify that a DNS server can resolve specific host names or fully qualified domain names (FQDNs) to IP addresses. A fully qualified domain name includes the host name and the domain name.

The ***dig*** command-line tool has replaced the nslookup tool on Linux systems. It is sometimes referred to as domain information groper. You can use dig to query DNS servers to verify that the DNS server is reachable and to verify that a DNS server can resolve names to IP addresses. For example, these tools can verify that a DNS server has a host record that maps a host name to an IP address for a web server (or any host). Dig verifies DNS functionality by querying DNS, verifying a record exists, and verifying that the DNS server responds.

Some versions of both commands support the @ symbol to identify a specific DNS server you want to query. This is useful if you want to pull all the records from a DNS zone. When doing this, you would use the any switch (indicating all records) or the axfr switch (short for all transfer). However, most DNS servers are configured to block these queries.

Check out the online resources for labs that show how to use these tools at *http://gcgapremium.com/501labs/*.

Subscription Services Use Case

Subscription services refer to a subscription-based business model. For example, instead of selling software applications to users, many vendors have moved to a subscription model where users pay over time.

As an example, years ago, it was common for people to purchase Microsoft Office for access to applications such as Microsoft Word, Microsoft Excel, Microsoft Outlook, and others. Today, organizations often pay monthly or annually for access to Office 365. This gives them the most current version of Microsoft Office products, along with additional features such as cloud storage.

The protocols used for subscription services use cases vary widely depending on the actual service. However, it's common for these to use HTTPS connections for security. Database servers maintain databases of customers, along with the products they're renting. The connections between web servers and database servers should be secure and might use HTTPS or TLS. When the subscription is nearing an end, systems send automated emails to customers using SMTP.

Understanding and Identifying Ports

Ports are logical numbers used by TCP/IP to identify what service or application should handle data received by a system. Both TCP and UDP use ports with a total of 65,536 TCP ports (0 to 65,535) and 65,536 UDP ports (0 to 65,535). Administrators open ports on firewalls and routers to allow the associated protocol into or out of a network. For example, HTTP uses port 80, and an administrator allows HTTP traffic by opening port 80.

Additionally, administrators disable unnecessary ports and services as part of a basic security practice. These ports and services are associated with specific protocols and if they are disabled, it blocks any attacks on these ports, services, and protocols.

The Internet Assigned Numbers Authority (IANA) maintains a list of official port assignments that you can view at *http://www.iana.org/assignments/port-numbers*. IANA divided the ports into three ranges, as follows:

- **Well-known ports: 0–1023.** IANA assigns port numbers to commonly used protocols in the well-known ports range.
- **Registered ports: 1024–49,151.** IANA registers these ports for companies as a convenience to the IT community. A single company may register a port for a proprietary use, or multiple companies may use the same port for a specific standard. As an example, Microsoft SQL Server uses port 1433 for database servers, Layer 2 Tunneling Protocol (L2TP) uses port 1701, and Point-to-Point Tunneling Protocol (PPTP) uses port 1723.
- **Dynamic and private ports: 49,152–65,535.** These ports are available for use by any application. Applications commonly use these ports to temporarily map an application to a port. These temporary port mappings are often called ephemeral ports, indicating that they are short lived.

Although virtually all the ports are subject to attack, most port attacks are against the well-known ports. Port scanners often simply check to see if a well-known port is open. For example, SMTP uses the well-known port 25, so if port 25 is open, the system is likely running SMTP.

Network administrators who regularly work with routers and firewalls can easily tell you which protocol is associated with which well-known port, such as 20, 21, 22, 23, 25, 80, or 443. The reason is that they use these ports to allow or block traffic.

For example, an administrator can close port 25 to block all SMTP traffic into a network. The router then ignores traffic on port 25 instead of forwarding it. Similarly, an administrator can close port 1433 to block database traffic to a Microsoft SQL server. On the other hand, the administrator can open port 25 to allow SMTP traffic.

Although ports are second nature to router and firewall administrators, they might not be so familiar to you. If you don't work with the ports often, you'll need to spend some extra time studying to ensure you're ready for the exam.

Combining the IP Address and the Port

At any moment, a computer could be receiving dozens of packets. Each of these packets includes a destination IP address and a destination port. TCP/IP uses the IP address to get the packet to the computer. The computer then uses the port number to get the packet to the correct service, protocol, or application that can process it.

For example, if the packet has a destination port of 80 (the well-known port for HTTP), the system passes the packet to the process handling HTTP. It wouldn't do much good to pass an SMTP email packet to the HTTP service or send an HTTP request packet to the SMTP service.

IP Address Used to Locate Hosts

Imagine that the IP address of *GetCertifiedGetAhead.com* is 72.52.206.134, and the address assigned to your computer from your ISP is 70.150.56.80. TCP/IP uses these IP addresses to get the packets from your computer to the web server and the web server's answer back to your computer.

There's a lot more that occurs under the hood with TCP/IP (such as DNS, NAT, and ARP), but the main point is that the server's IP address is used to get the requesting packet from your computer to the server. The server gets the response packets back to your computer using your IP address (or the IP address of your NAT server).

Server Ports

Different protocols are enabled and running on a server. These protocols have well-known or registered port numbers, such as port 22 for SSH, 25 for SMTP, 80 for HTTP, 443 for HTTPS, and so on. When the system receives traffic with a destination of port 80, the system knows to send it to the service handling HTTP.

Any web browser knows that the well-known port for HTTP is 80. Even though you don't see port 80 in the URL, it is implied as *http://GetCertifiedGetAhead.com:**80***. If you omit the port number, HTTP uses the well-known port number of 80 by default.

Popular web servers on the Internet include Apache and Internet Information Services (IIS). Apache is free and runs on Unix or Linux systems. Apache can also run on other platforms, such as Microsoft systems. IIS is included in Microsoft Server products. These web servers use port 80 for HTTP. When the server receives a packet with a destination port of 80, the server sends the packet to the web server application (Apache or IIS) that processes it and sends back a response.

Client Ports

TCP/IP works with the client operating system to maintain a table of client-side ports. This table associates port numbers with different applications that are expecting return traffic. Client-side ports start at port 49,152 and increment up to 65,535. If the system uses all the ports between 49,152 and 65,535 before being rebooted, it'll start over at 49,152.

When you use your web browser to request a page from a site, your system will record an unused client port number such as 49,152 in an internal table to handle the return traffic. When the web server returns the web page, it includes the client port as a destination port. When the client receives web page packets with a destination port of 49,152, it sends these packets to the web browser application. The browser processes the packets and displays the page.

Putting It All Together

The previous section described the different pieces, but it's useful to put this together into a single description. Imagine that you decide to visit the web site *http://GetCertifiedGetAhead.com* using your web browser so you type the URL into the browser, and the web page appears. Here are the details of what is happening. Figure 3.3 provides an overview of how this will look and the following text explains the process.

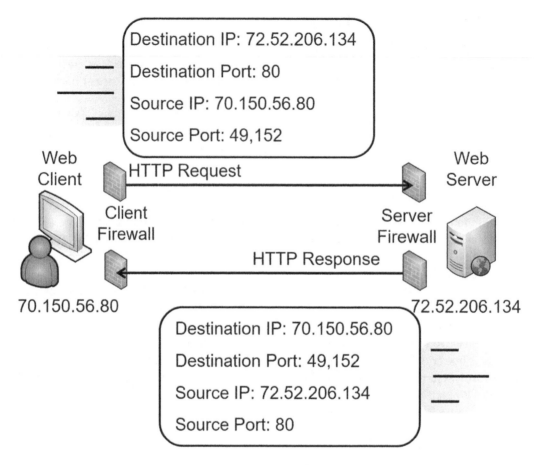

Figure 3.3: Using source and destination ports

Your computer creates a packet with source and destination IP addresses and source and destination ports. It queries a DNS server for the IP address of *GetCertifiedGetAhead.com* and learns that the IP address is 72.52.206.134. Additionally, your computer will use its IP address as the source IP address. For this example, imagine your computer's IP address is 70.150.56.80.

Because the web server is serving web pages using HTTP and the well-known port is used, the destination port is 80. Your computer will identify an unused port in the dynamic and private ports range (a port number between 49,152 and 65,535) and map that port to the web browser. For this example, imagine it assigns 49,152 to the web browser. It uses this as the source port.

At this point, the packet has both destination and source data as follows:
- Destination IP address: 72.52.206.134 (the web server)
- Destination port: 80
- Source IP address: 70.150.56.80 (your computer)
- Source port: 49,152

TCP/IP uses the IP address (72.52.206.134) to get the packet to the *GetCertifiedGetAhead* web server. When it reaches the web server, the server looks at the destination port (80) and determines that the packet needs to go to the web server program servicing HTTP. The web server creates the page and puts the data into one or more return packets. At this point, the source and destinations are swapped because the packet is coming from the server back to you:

Comparing Ports and Protocol Numbers

Ports and protocol numbers are not the same thing, though they are often confused. Well-known ports identify many services or protocols, as discussed previously.

However, many protocols aren't identified by the port, but instead by the protocol numbers. For example, within IPsec, protocol number 50 indicates the packet is an Encapsulating Security Payload (ESP) packet, and protocol number 51 indicates it's an Authentication Header (AH) packet. Similarly, ICMP has a protocol number of 1, TCP is 6, and UDP is 17.

You can use a protocol number to block or allow traffic on routers and firewalls just as you can block or allow traffic based on the port. Note that it is not accurate to say that you can allow IPsec ESP traffic by opening *port* 50. IANA lists port 50 as a Remote Mail Checking Protocol. However, you can allow IPsec traffic by allowing traffic using protocol number 50.

Protocol analyzers can capture and examine IP headers to determine the protocol number and the port, as well as read any unencrypted data. Note that you might see the protocol number listed as the protocol ID or a protocol identifier. Chapter 8 covers protocol analyzers in more depth.

- Destination IP address: 70.150.56.80 (your computer)
- Destination port: 49,152
- Source IP address: 72.52.206.134 (the web server)
- Source port: 80

Again, TCP/IP uses the IP address to get the packets to the destination, which is your computer at this point. Once the packets reach your system, it sees that port 49,152 is the destination port. Because your system mapped this port to your web browser, it sends the packets to the web browser, which displays the web page.

The Importance of Ports in Security

Routers, and the routing component of firewalls, filter packets based on IP addresses, ports, and some protocols such as ICMP or IPsec. Because many protocols use well-known ports, you can control protocol traffic by allowing or blocking traffic based on the port.

In the previous example, the client firewall must allow outgoing traffic on port 80. Firewalls automatically determine the client ports used for return traffic, and if they allow the outgoing traffic, they allow the return traffic. In other words, because the firewall allows the packet going to the web server on the destination port 80, it also allows the web page returning on the dynamic source port of 49,152.

Note that the client firewall doesn't need to allow incoming traffic on port 80 for this to work. The web client isn't hosting a web server with HTTP, so the client firewall would block incoming traffic on port 80. However, the firewall that is filtering traffic to the web server needs to allow incoming traffic on port 80.

You can apply this same principle for any protocol and port. For example, if you want to allow SMTP traffic, you create a rule on the firewall to allow traffic on port 25. IT professionals modifying access control lists (ACLs) on routers and firewalls commonly refer to this as opening a port to allow traffic or closing a port to block traffic.

Understanding Basic Network Devices

Networks connect computing devices together so that users can share resources, such as data, printers, and other devices. Any device with an IP address is a host, but you'll often see them referred to as clients or nodes.

A common use case for a switch is to connect hosts together within a network. A common use case for a router is to connect multiple networks together to create larger and larger networks.

When discussing the different network devices, it's important to remember the primary methods IPv4 uses when addressing TCP/IP traffic:

- **Unicast.** One-to-one traffic. One host sends traffic to another host, using a destination IP address. The host with the destination IP address will process the packet. Most other hosts will see the packet, but because it isn't addressed to them, they will not process it.
- **Broadcast.** One-to-all traffic. One host sends traffic to all other hosts on the subnet, using a broadcast address such as 255.255.255.255. Every host that receives broadcast traffic will process it. Switches pass broadcast traffic between their ports, but routers do not pass broadcast traffic.

Switches

A *switch* can learn which computers are attached to each of its physical ports. It then uses this knowledge to create internal switched connections when two computers communicate with each other.

Consider Figure 3.4. When the switch turns on, it starts out without any knowledge other than knowing it has four physical ports. Imagine that the first traffic is the beginning of a TCP/IP conversation between Lisa's computer and Homer's computer.

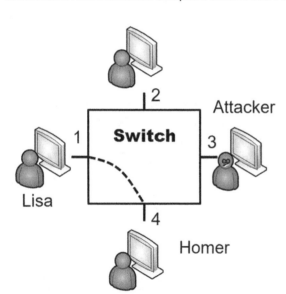

Figure 3.4: Switch

When Lisa's computer sends the first packet, it includes the MAC address of the destination computer. However, because the switch doesn't know which port Homer's computer is connected to, it forwards this first packet to all the ports on the switch.

Included in that first packet is the MAC address of Lisa's computer. The switch logs this information into an internal table. It then directs any future traffic addressed to Lisa's MAC address to port 1, and port 1 only.

When Homer's computer receives the packet, it responds. Embedded in this return packet is the MAC address of Homer's computer. The switch captures Homer's MAC address and logs it with port 4 in the internal table. From here on, any unicast traffic between Lisa's and Homer's computers is internally switched between only ports 1 and 4. Switches will internally switch unicast traffic. However, they pass broadcast traffic to all ports.

Security Benefit of a Switch

Most of the previous discussion is basic networking, but what you really need to know is why it's relevant in security. If an attacker installed a protocol analyzer on a computer attached to another port (such as port 3 in Figure 3.4), the protocol analyzer would not capture unicast traffic going through the switch to other ports. If Lisa and Homer are exchanging data on ports 1 and 4, none of the traffic reaches port 3. The protocol analyzer can't capture traffic that doesn't reach the port.

In contrast, if the computers were connected with a simple hub, the attacker could capture it because unicast traffic goes to all ports on a hub. This is the main security reason why organizations replace hubs with switches. The switch reduces the risk of an attacker capturing data with a protocol analyzer. Of course, switches also increase the efficiency of a network.

Port Security

Port security limits the computers that can connect to physical ports on a switch. At the most basic level, administrators disable unused ports. For example, individual RJ-45 wall jacks in an office lead to specific physical ports on a switch. If the wall jack is not being used, administrators can disable the switch port. This prevents someone from plugging in a laptop or other computer into the wall jack and connecting to the network.

MAC address filtering is another example of port security. In a simple implementation, the switch remembers the first one or two MAC addresses that connect to a port. It then blocks access to systems using any other MAC addresses. You can also manually configure each port to accept traffic only from a specific MAC address. This limits each port's connectivity to a specific device using this MAC address. This can be very labor intensive, but it provides a higher level of security.

> ### Remember this
>
> Port security includes disabling unused ports and limiting the number of MAC addresses per port. A more advanced implementation is to restrict each physical port to only a single specific MAC address.

Physical Security of a Switch

Many switches have a console port that administrators can use to monitor all traffic. Unlike the normal ports that only see traffic specifically addressed to the port, the monitoring port will see all traffic in or out of the switch. This includes any unicast traffic the switch is internally switching between two regular ports. The monitoring port is useful for legitimate troubleshooting, but if the switch isn't protected with physical security, it can also be useful to an attacker.

Physical security protects a switch by keeping it in a secure area such as in a locked wiring closet. Physical security ensures that attackers don't have physical access to the switch and other network devices.

Loop Prevention

In some situations, a network can develop a switching loop or bridge loop problem. The effect is similar to a broadcast storm and it can effectively disable a switch. For example, if a user connects two ports of a switch together with a cable, it creates a switching loop where the switch continuously sends and resends unicast transmissions through the switch. In addition to disabling the switch, it also degrades performance of the overall network.

This is trivial for many network administrators, because most current switches have Spanning Tree Protocol (**STP**) or the newer Rapid STP (**RSTP**) installed and enabled for **loop prevention**. However, if these protocols are disabled, the switch is susceptible to loop problems. The simple solution is to ensure that switches include loop protection such as STP or RSTP.

Spanning Tree Protocol also protects the network against potential attackers. For example, imagine an attacker visits a conference room and has access to RJ-45 wall jacks. If loop protection isn't enabled, he can connect two jacks together with a cable, slowing network performance down to a crawl.

Remember this

Loop protection such as STP or RSTP is necessary to protect against switching loop problems, such as those caused when two ports of a switch are connected together.

Flood Attacks and Flood Guards

A MAC flood attack attempts to overload a switch with different MAC addresses associated with each physical port. You typically have only one device connected to any physical port. During normal operation, the switch's internal table stores the MAC address associated with this device and maps it to the port. In a MAC flood attack, an attacker sends a large amount of traffic with spoofed MAC addresses to the same port.

At some point in a MAC flood attack, the switch runs out of memory to store all the MAC addresses and enters a fail-open state. Instead of working as a switch, it begins operating as a simple hub. Traffic sent to any port of the switch is now sent to all other switch ports. At this point, the attacker can connect a protocol analyzer to any port and collect all the traffic sent through the switch.

Many switches include a **flood guard** to protect against MAC flood attacks. When enabled, the switch will limit the amount of memory used to store MAC addresses for each port. For example, the switch might limit the number of entries for any port to 132 entries. This is much more than you need for normal operation. If the switch detects an attempt to store more than 132 entries, it raises an alert.

The flood guard typically sends a Simple Network Management Protocol (SNMP) trap or error message in response to the alert. Additionally, it can either disable the port or restrict updates for the port. By disabling the port, it effectively blocks all traffic through the port until an administrator intervenes. If it restricts updates, the switch will use currently logged entries for the port, but ignore attempts to update it. All other ports will continue to operate normally.

Another flood guard supported by some switches is a setting for the maximum number of MACs supported by a port. Most ports will typically have this set to 1 to support only a single MAC address. However, consider a virtual machine (VM) running within a physical host. If the VM is set to bridged, it can access the network using the physical host's NIC, but with the MAC address of the VM. In this scenario, the Maximum MAC setting should be set to 2.

> ## Comparing Ports and Ports
>
> Note that a physical port used by a network device, such as a switch or a router, is completely different from the logical ports discussed previously. You plug a cable into a physical port. A logical port is a number embedded in a packet and identifies services and protocols.
>
> This is like minute (60 seconds) and minute (tiny), or like the old joke about the meaning of *secure*. The Secretary of Defense directed members of different services to "secure that building." Navy personnel turned off the lights and locked the doors. The Army occupied the building and ensured no one could enter. The Marines attacked it, captured it, and set up defenses to hold it. The Air Force secured a two-year lease with an option to buy.

Routers

A **router** connects multiple network segments together into a single network and routes traffic between the segments. As an example, the Internet is effectively a single network hosting billions of computers. Routers route the traffic from segment to segment.

Because routers don't pass broadcasts, they effectively reduce traffic on any single segment. Segments separated by routers are sometimes referred to as broadcast domains. If a network has too many computers on a single segment, broadcasts can result in excessive collisions and reduce network performance. Moving computers to a different segment separated by a router can significantly improve overall performance. Similarly, subnetting networks creates separate broadcast domains.

Cisco routers are popular, but many other brands exist. Most routers are physical devices, and physical routers are the most efficient. However, it's also possible to add routing software to computers with more than one NIC. For example, Windows Server products can function as routers by adding additional services to the server.

Routers and ACLs

Access control lists (**ACLs**) are rules implemented on a router (and on firewalls) to identify what traffic is allowed and what traffic is denied. Rules within an ACL provide rule-based management for the router and control inbound and outbound traffic.

Router ACLs provide basic packet filtering. They filter packets based on IP addresses, ports, and some protocols, such as ICMP or IPsec, based on the protocol identifiers:

- **IP addresses and networks.** You can add a rule in the ACL to block access from any single computer based on the IP address. If you want to block traffic from one subnet to another, you can use a rule to block traffic using the subnet IDs. For example, the Sales department may be in the 192.168.1.0/24 network and the Accounting department may be in the 192.168.5.0/24 network. You can ensure traffic from these two departments stays separate with an ACL on a router.
- **Ports.** You can filter traffic based on logical ports. For example, if you want to block HTTP traffic, you can create a rule to block traffic on port 80. Note that you can choose to block incoming traffic, outgoing traffic, or both. In other words, it's possible to allow outgoing HTTP traffic while blocking incoming HTTP traffic.
- **Protocol numbers.** Many protocols are identified by their protocol numbers. For

example, ICMP uses a protocol number of 1 and many DoS attacks use ICMP. You can block all ICMP traffic (and the attacks that use it) by blocking traffic using this protocol number. Many automated intrusion prevention systems (IPSs) dynamically block ICMP traffic in response to attacks. Similarly, you can restrict traffic to only packets encrypted with IPsec ESP using a rule that allows traffic using protocol number 50, but blocks all other traffic. PPTP uses protocol number 47 and can be allowed by allowing traffic using protocol ID 47.

Implicit Deny

Implicit deny is an important concept to understand, especially in the context of ACLs. It indicates that all traffic that isn't explicitly allowed is implicitly denied. For example, imagine you configure a router to allow Hypertext Transfer Protocol (HTTP) to a web server. The router now has an explicit rule defined to allow this traffic to the server. If you don't define any other rules, the implicit deny rule blocks all other traffic. Firewalls (discussed later in this chapter) also use an implicit deny rule.

The implicit deny rule is the last rule in an ACL. Some devices automatically apply the implicit deny rule as the last rule. Other devices require an administrator to place the rule at the end of the ACL manually. Syntax of an implicit deny rule varies on different systems, but it might be something like DENY ANY ANY, or DENY ALL ALL, where both ANY and ALL refer to any type of traffic.

Antispoofing

Attackers often use spoofing to impersonate or masquerade as someone or something else. In the context of routers, an attacker will spoof the source IP address by replacing the actual source IP address with a different one. This is often done to hide the actual source of the packet.

You can implement *antispoofing* on a router by modifying the access list to allow or block IP addresses. As an example, private IP addresses (listed earlier in this chapter) should only be used in private networks. Any traffic coming from the Internet using a private IP address as the source IP address is obviously an attempt to spoof the source IP address. The following three rules would be implemented on a router (though the syntax may be different on various routers for antispoofing):

- deny ip 10.0.0.0 0.255.255.255 any
- deny ip 172.16.0.0 0.15.255.255 any
- deny ip 192.168.0.0 0.0.255.255 any

Notice that the subnet mask portion of these rules is shown a little differently, but this is common syntax for many router rules. For example, 10.0.0.0 0.255.255.255 covers all the IP addresses in the range of 10.0.0.0 through 10.255.255.255.

> ## Remember this
>
> Routers and stateless firewalls (or packet-filtering firewalls) perform basic filtering with an access control list (ACL). ACLs identify what traffic is allowed and what traffic is blocked. An ACL can control traffic based on networks, subnets, IP addresses, ports, and some protocols. Implicit deny blocks all access that has not been explicitly granted. Routers and firewalls use implicit deny as the last rule in the access control list. Antispoofing methods block traffic using ACL rules.

Bridge

A network **bridge** connects multiple networks together and can be used instead of a router in some situations. As discussed previously, a router directs network traffic based on the destination IP address and a switch directs traffic to specific ports based on the destination MAC address. Similarly, a bridge directs traffic based on the destination MAC address. Figure 3.5 shows all three devices in a simplified network diagram.

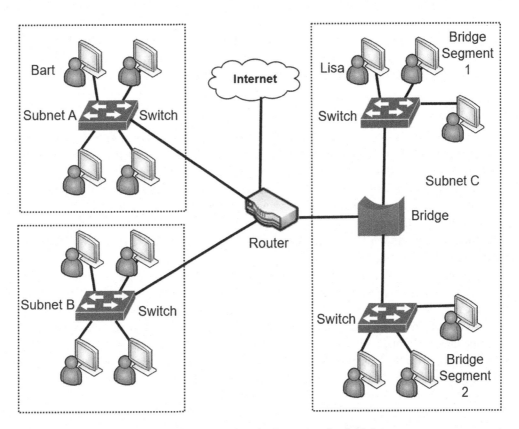

Figure 3.5: Network with a router, switches, and a bridge

Notice that there are three subnets (Subnet A, Subnet B, and Subnet C). The router directs traffic to each of these subnets. Subnet C has two segments separated by a bridge. The bridge sends traffic to the appropriate segment in Subnet C based on the MAC address.

A bridge typically learns MAC addresses in different bridge networks by analyzing traffic. This is similar to how a switch learns which MAC addresses are associated with each physical port. Imagine that Bart (in Subnet A) sends traffic to Lisa (in Subnet C). When the bridge receives the traffic, it doesn't know if Lisa's MAC address is in Bridge Segment 1 or Bridge Segment 2, so it sends the traffic to both bridge networks. When Lisa's computer replies, the bridge identifies her MAC address as being in Bridge Network 1 and stores this information in an internal table. When Bart sends other traffic to Lisa, the bridge forwards it to Bridge Segment 1 only.

A hardware bridge using this learning method is relatively easy to install. Connect the wires, turn it on, and it will begin learning.

Aggregation Switch

An *aggregation switch* connects multiple switches together in a network. Aggregate simply means that you are creating something larger from smaller elements. As an example, look back at Figure 3.5. If you replace the bridge with a switch, the switch is an aggregation switch.

Similarly, you can use an aggregation switch to connect Subnet A and Subnet B. The switches in Subnet A and Subnet B connect to the aggregation switch instead of connecting to the router. The aggregation switch connects to the router. This reduces the number of ports used in the router.

It's common to place an aggregation switch in the same location as you'd place routers. For example, large organizations locate network devices in the data center while smaller organizations locate them in a wiring closet. Both are secured using physical security.

Firewalls

A *firewall* filters incoming and outgoing traffic for a single host or between networks. In other words, a firewall can ensure only specific types of traffic are allowed into a network or host, and only specific types of traffic are allowed out of a network or host.

The purpose of a firewall in a network is similar to a firewall in a car. The firewall in a car is located between the engine and passenger compartment. If a fire starts in the engine compartment, the firewall provides a layer of protection for passengers in the passenger compartment. Similarly, a firewall in a network will try to keep the bad traffic (often in the form of attackers) out of the network.

Of course, an engine has a lot of moving parts that can do damage to people if they accidentally reach into it while it's running. The firewall in a car protects passengers from touching any of those moving parts. Similarly, a network can also block users from going to places that an administrator deems dangerous. For example, uneducated users could inadvertently download damaging files, but many firewalls can block potentially malicious downloads.

Firewalls start with a basic routing capability for packet filtering as described in the "Routers and ACLs" section, including the use of an implicit deny rule. More advanced firewalls go beyond simple packet filtering and include advanced content filtering.

Host-Based Firewalls

A host-based firewall monitors traffic going in and out of a single host, such as a server or a workstation. It monitors traffic passing through the NIC and can prevent intrusions into the computer via the NIC. Many operating systems include software-based firewalls used as host-based firewalls. For example, Microsoft has included a host-based firewall on operating systems since Windows XP. Additionally, many third-party host-based firewalls are available.

Figure 3.6 shows the host-based Windows Firewall on Windows 10. Notice that you can configure inbound rules to allow or restrict inbound traffic and outbound rules to allow or restrict outbound traffic. The connection security rules provide additional capabilities, such as configuring an IPsec connection in Tunnel or Transport mode to encrypt the traffic.

Linux systems support iptables and many additions to iptables, such as ipv6tables, arptables, and so on. Generically, administrators commonly refer to these as xtables. You can configure rules within different tables. Combined, these rules work just like an ACL.

Personal firewalls provide valuable protection for systems against unwanted intrusions.

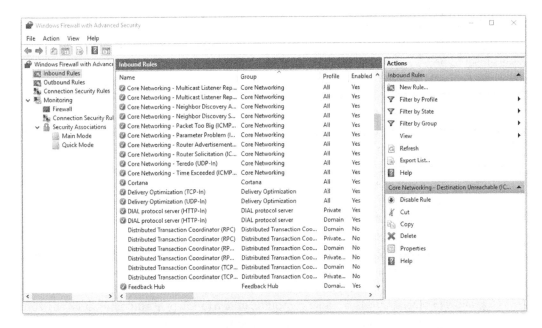

Figure 3.6: Windows Firewall with Advanced Security on Windows 10

Many organizations use personal firewalls on each system in addition to network firewalls as part of an overall defense-in-depth strategy.

It's especially important to use personal firewalls when accessing the Internet in a public place. Free Wi-Fi Internet access is often available in public places, such as airports, hotels, and many fast-food establishments, such as Starbucks and McDonald's. However, connecting to a public Wi-Fi hot spot without the personal firewall enabled is risky, and never recommended.

> **Remember this**
>
> Host-based firewalls provide protection for individual hosts, such as servers or workstations. A host-based firewall provides intrusion protection for the host. Linux systems support xtables for firewall capabilities. Network-based firewalls are often dedicated servers or appliances and provide protection for the network.

Application-Based Versus Network-Based Firewalls

An application-based firewall is typically software running on a system. For example, host-based firewalls are commonly application-based. A network-based firewall is usually a dedicated system with additional software installed to monitor, filter, and log traffic. For example, Cisco makes a variety of different network-based firewalls. Many of them are dedicated servers with proprietary firewall software installed.

A network-based firewall would have two or more network interface cards (NICs) and all traffic passes through the firewall. The firewall controls traffic going in and out of a network. It does this by filtering traffic based on firewall rules and allows only authorized traffic to pass through it. Most organizations include at least one network-based firewall at the border, between their intranet (or internal network) and the Internet.

Stateless Firewall Rules

Stateless firewalls use rules implemented as ACLs to identify allowed and blocked traffic. This is similar to how a router uses rules. Firewalls use an implicit deny strategy to block all traffic that is not explicitly allowed. Although rules within ACLs look a little different depending on what hardware you're using, they generally take the following format:

Permission   Protocol   Source   Destination   Port

- **Permission.** You'll typically see this as PERMIT or ALLOW allowing the traffic. Most systems use DENY to block the traffic.
- **Protocol.** Typically, you'll see TCP or UDP here, especially when blocking specific TCP or UDP ports. If you want to block both TCP and UDP traffic using the same port, you can use IP instead. Using ICMP here blocks ICMP traffic, effectively blocking ping and some other diagnostics that use ICMP.
- **Source.** Traffic comes from a source IP address. You identify an IP address to allow or block traffic from a single computer, or from a range of IP addresses, such as from a single subnet. Wildcards such as any or all include all IP addresses.
- **Destination.** Traffic is addressed to a destination IP address. You identify an IP address to allow or block traffic to a single computer, or to a range of IP addresses, such as to an entire subnet. Wildcards such as any or all include all IP addresses.
- **Port or protocol.** Typically, you'll see the well-known port such as port 80 for HTTP. However, some devices support codes such as www for HTTP traffic. Some systems support the use of keywords such as eq for equal, lt for less than, and gt for greater than. For example, instead of just using port 80, it might indicate eq 80.

Some firewalls require you to include a subnet mask in the rule. For example, if you want to block all SMTP traffic to the 192.168.1.0/24 network, you would use an IP address of 192.168.1.0 and a subnet mask of 255.255.255.0. However, if you only wanted to allow SMTP traffic to a single computer with the IP address of 192.168.1.20/24, you would use an IP address of 192.168.1.20 and a subnet mask of 255.255.255.255.

> **Remember this**
>
> Firewalls use a deny any any, deny any, or a drop all statement at the end of the ACL to enforce an implicit deny strategy. The statement forces the firewall to block any traffic that wasn't previously allowed in the ACL. The implicit deny strategy provides a secure starting point for a firewall.

Stateful Versus Stateless

A stateful firewall inspects traffic and makes decisions based on the context, or state, of the traffic. It keeps track of established sessions and inspects traffic based on its state within a session. It blocks traffic that isn't part of an established session. As an example, a TCP session starts with a three-way handshake. If a stateful firewall detects TCP traffic without a corresponding three-way handshake, it recognizes this as suspicious traffic and can block it.

A common security issue with stateless firewalls is misconfigured ACLs. For example, if the ACL doesn't include an implicit deny rule, it can allow almost all traffic into the network.

Web Application Firewall

A *web application firewall (WAF)* is a firewall specifically designed to protect a web application, which is commonly hosted on a web server. In other words, it's placed between a server hosting a web application and a client. It can be a stand-alone appliance, or software added to another device.

As an example, an organization may host an e-commerce web site to generate revenue. The web server will be placed within a demilitarized zone (DMZ) (discussed later in this chapter), but due to the data that the web server handles, it needs more protection. A successful attack may be able to take the web server down, and allow an attacker to access or manipulate data.

Note that you wouldn't use a WAF in place of a network-based firewall. Instead, it provides an added layer of protection for the web application in addition to a network-based firewall.

Remember this

A stateless firewall blocks traffic using an ACL. A stateful firewall blocks traffic based on the state of the packet within a session. Web application firewalls provide strong protection for web servers. They protect against several different types of attacks, with a focus on web application attacks and can include load-balancing features.

Implementing a Secure Network

There are several elements of a secure network, including the implementation of different zones and topologies, segmenting and isolating some elements, and using various network devices. This section covers these topics in more depth.

Zones and Topologies

Most networks have Internet connectivity, but it's rare to connect a network directly to the Internet. Instead, it's common to divide the network into different zones, using different topologies. Two terms that are relevant here are:

- **Intranet.** An *intranet* is an internal network. People use the intranet to communicate and share content with each other. While it's common for an intranet to include web servers, this isn't a requirement.
- **Extranet.** An *extranet* is part of a network that can be accessed by authorized entities from outside of the network. For example, it's common for organizations to provide access to authorized business partners, customers, vendors, or others.

The network perimeter provides a boundary between the intranet and the Internet. Boundary protection includes multiple methods to protect the network perimeter.

DMZ

The demilitarized zone (*DMZ*) is a buffered zone between a private network and the Internet. Attackers seek out servers on the Internet, so any server placed directly on the Internet has the highest amount of risk. However, the DMZ provides a layer of protection for these Internet-facing servers, while also allowing clients to connect to them.

As an example, Figure 3.7 shows a common network configuration with a DMZ. The DMZ is the area between the two firewalls (FW1 and FW2) and hosts several Internet-facing servers. Many DMZs have two firewalls, creating a buffer zone between the Internet and the internal network, as shown in Figure 3.7, though other DMZ configurations are possible.

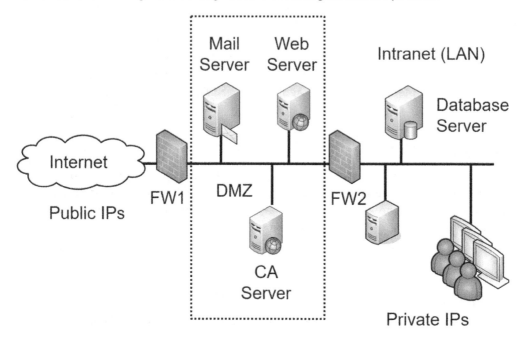

Figure 3.7: Network with DMZ

In this configuration, one firewall separates the DMZ from the Internet. The second firewall separates the DMZ from the internal network. Each firewall includes detailed rules designed to filter traffic and protect both the internal network and the public servers. One way of saying this is that the DMZ provides access to the services hosted in the DMZ, while segmenting access to the internal network.

For example, FW1 can have rules to allow traffic to the servers in the DMZ, but block unsolicited traffic to FW2. The mail server would send and receive email to other email servers on the Internet through port 25 of FW1, and also send and receive email to internal clients through port 25 on FW2. The web server hosts web pages to any Internet users through ports 80 and 443 on FW1, but FW2 blocks incoming traffic using these ports. The Certificate Authority (CA) server validates certificates for Internet clients by answering through FW1.

Notice in Figure 3.7 that the intranet includes a database server. The web server may use this to create web pages for an e-commerce site. It could hold product data, customer data, and much more. FW2 allows traffic between the web server (and only the web server) and the database server on port 1433. FW2 would block all other Internet traffic to the database server.

It's also possible for the web server and the database server to be part of an extranet. For example, imagine that the web server hosts a site that business partners can use to place orders. The web server would first authenticate them before granting them full access. After users log on, the web site connects to the back-end database server, allowing them to browse the inventory and place orders. Because this site is only for authorized business partners, it is an extranet.

The DMZ can host any Internet-facing server, not just those shown in the figure. Other examples include FTP servers used for uploading and downloading files and virtual private network (VPN) servers used for providing remote access.

Remember this

A DMZ is a buffer zone between the Internet and an internal network. It allows access to services while segmenting access to the internal network. In other words, Internet clients can access the services hosted on servers in the DMZ, but the DMZ provides a layer of protection for the intranet (internal network).

Understanding NAT and PAT

Network Address Translation (**NAT**) is a protocol that translates public IP addresses to private IP addresses and private addresses back to public. You'll often see NAT enabled on an Internet-facing firewall. A commonly used form of NAT is network address and port translation, commonly called Port Address Translation (PAT).

If you run a network at your home (such as a wireless network), the router that connects to the Internet is very likely running NAT. Some of the benefits of NAT include:

- **Public IP addresses don't need to be purchased for all clients.** A home or company network can include multiple computers that can access the Internet through one router running NAT. Larger companies requiring more bandwidth may use more than one public IP address.
- **NAT hides internal computers from the Internet.** Computers with private IP addresses are isolated and hidden from the Internet. NAT provides a layer of protection to these private computers because they aren't as easy to attack and exploit from the Internet.

One of the drawbacks to NAT is that it is not compatible with IPsec. You can use IPsec to create VPN tunnels and use it with L2TP to encrypt VPN traffic. Although there are ways of getting around NAT's incompatibility with IPsec, if your design includes IPsec going through NAT, you'll need to look at it closely.

NAT can be either static NAT or dynamic NAT:

- **Static NAT.** Static NAT uses a single public IP address in a one-to-one mapping. It maps a private IP address with a single public IP address.
- **Dynamic NAT.** Dynamic NAT uses multiple public IP addresses in a one-to-many mapping. Dynamic NAT decides which public IP address to use based on load. For example, if several users are connected to the Internet on one public IP address, NAT maps the next request to a less-used public IP address.

Remember this

NAT translates public IP addresses to private IP addresses, and private IP addresses back to public. A common form of NAT is Port Address Translation. Dynamic NAT uses multiple public IP addresses while static NAT uses a single public IP address.

Network Separation

A common network security practice is to use different components to provide network separation. The CompTIA objectives list these as segregation, segmentation, and isolation. Segregation provides basic separation, segmentation refers to putting traffic on different segments, and isolation indicates the systems are completely separate. Chapter 1 covers virtualization concepts in depth and virtualization can be used to provide isolation. For example, some antivirus experts use virtual machines to analyze malware. This section covers physical security and logical security methods used for isolation.

Physical Isolation and Airgaps

Physical isolation ensures that a network isn't connected to any other network. As an example, consider supervisory control and data acquisition (SCADA) systems. These are typically industrial control systems within large facilities such as power plants or water treatment facilities. While SCADA systems operate within their own network, it's common to ensure that they are isolated from any other network.

This physical isolation significantly reduces risks to the SCADA system. If an attacker can't reach it from the Internet, it is much more difficult to attack it. However, if the system is connected to the internal network, it's possible for an attacker to gain access to internal computers, and then access any resource on the internal network.

An *airgap* is a metaphor for physical isolation, indicating that there is a gap of air between an isolated system and other systems. When considered literally, an air-gapped system is not connected to any other systems. As an example, many organizations use both classified (red) and unclassified (black) networks. Strict rules ensure that these two systems are not connected to each other. Some rules require that any cable from a red network must be physically separated from black network cables.

Logical Separation and Segmentation

As mentioned previously in this chapter, routers and firewalls provide a basic level of separation and segmentation. Routers segment traffic between networks using rules within ACLs. Administrators use subnetting to divide larger IP address ranges into smaller ranges. They then implement rules within ACLs to allow or block traffic. Firewalls separate network traffic using basic packet-filtering rules and can also use more sophisticated methods to block undesirable traffic.

It's also possible to segment traffic between logical groups of users or computers with a virtual local area network (VLAN). This provides logical separation.

Comparing a Layer 2 Versus Layer 3 Switch

A traditional switch operates on Layer 2 of the Open Systems Interconnection (OSI) model. As discussed previously, a traditional switch (a Layer 2 switch) uses the destination MAC address within packets to determine the destination port. Additionally, a Layer 2 switch forwards broadcast traffic to all ports on the switch.

Routers operate on Layer 3 of the OSI model. They forward traffic based on the destination IP address within a packet, and they block broadcast traffic. A Layer 3 switch mimics the behavior of a router and allows network administrators to create virtual local area networks (VLANs). Because a Layer 3 switch forwards traffic based on the destination IP address instead of the MAC address, it is not susceptible to ARP-based attacks.

Isolating Traffic with a VLAN

A virtual local area network (**VLAN**) uses a switch to group several different computers into a virtual network. You can group the computers together based on departments, job function, or any other administrative need. This provides security because you're able to isolate the traffic between the computers in the VLAN.

Normally, a router would group different computers onto different subnets, based on physical locations. All the computers in a routed segment are typically located in the same physical location, such as on a specific floor or wing of a building.

However, a single Layer 3 switch can create multiple VLANs to separate the computers based on logical needs rather than physical location. Additionally, administrators can easily reconfigure the switch to add or subtract computers from any VLAN if the need arises.

For example, a group of users who normally work in separate departments may begin work on a project that requires them to be on the same subnet. You can configure a Layer 3 switch to logically group these workers together, even if the computers are physically located on different floors or different wings of the building. When the project is over, you can simply reconfigure the switch to return the network to its original configuration.

As another example, VoIP streaming traffic can consume quite a bit of bandwidth. One way to increase the availability and reliability of systems using this voice traffic is to put them on a dedicated VLAN. Other systems transferring traditional data traffic can be placed on a separate VLAN. This separates the voice and data traffic within the VLAN.

Similarly, you can use a single switch with multiple VLANs to separate user traffic. For example, if you want to separate the traffic between the HR department and the IT department, you can use a single switch with two VLANs. The VLANs logically separate all the computers between the two different departments, even if the computers are located close to each other.

> **Remember this**
>
> Virtual local area networks (VLANs) separate or segment traffic on physical networks and you can create multiple VLANs with a single Layer 3 switch. A VLAN can logically group several different computers together, or logically separate computers, without regard to their physical location. VLANs are also used to separate traffic types, such as voice traffic on VLAN and data traffic on a separate VLAN.

Media Gateway

A media gateway is a device that converts data from the format used on one network to the format used on another network. As an example, a VoIP gateway converts telephony traffic between traditional phone lines and an IP-based network. This allows users to make and receive phone calls using VoIP equipment and the gateway can translate the traffic and transmit the calls over a traditional phone line.

Proxy Servers

Many networks use *proxy* servers (or forward proxy servers) to forward requests for services (such as HTTP or HTTPS) from clients. They can improve performance by caching content and some proxy servers can restrict users' access to inappropriate web sites by filtering content. A proxy server is located on the edge of the network bordering the Internet and the intranet, as shown in Figure 3.8.

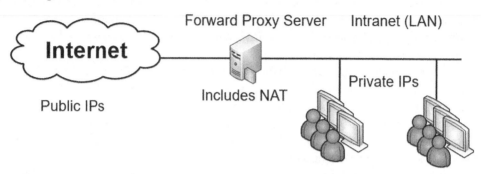

Figure 3.8: Proxy server

Administrators configure internal clients to use the proxy server for specific protocols. The proxy accepts their requests, retrieves the content from the Internet, and then returns the data to the client. Most proxy servers only act as a proxy for HTTP and HTTPS. However, proxy servers can also proxy other Internet protocols, such as FTP.

Caching Content for Performance

The proxy server increases the performance of Internet requests by caching each result received from the Internet. Any data that is in the proxy server's cache doesn't need to be retrieved from the Internet again to fulfill another client's request. In this context, *cache* simply means "temporary storage." Cache could be a dedicated area of RAM, or, in some situations, it could also be an area on a high-performance disk subsystem.

As an example, if Lisa retrieves a web page from *GetCertifiedGetAhead.com*, the proxy server would store the result in cache. If Homer later requests the same page, the proxy server retrieves the page from cache and sends it to Homer. This reduces the amount of Internet bandwidth used for web browsing because the page doesn't need to be retrieved again.

Transparent Proxy Versus Nontransparent Proxy

A transparent proxy will accept and forward requests without modifying them. It is the simplest to set up and use and it provides caching.

In contrast, a nontransparent proxy server can modify or filter requests. Organizations often use nontransparent proxy servers to restrict what users can access with the use of URL filters. A URL filter examines the requested URL and chooses to allow the request or deny the request.

Many third-party companies sell subscription lists for URL filtering. These sites scour the Internet for web sites and categorize the sites based on what companies typically want to block. Categories may include anonymizers, pornography, gambling, web-based email, and warez sites. Anonymizers are sites that give the illusion of privacy on the Internet. Employees sometimes try to use anonymizers to bypass proxy servers, but a proxy server usually detects, blocks, and logs these attempts. Web-based email bypasses the security controls on internal email servers, so many organizations block them. Warez sites often host pirated software, movies, MP3 files, and hacking tools.

The subscription list can be loaded into the proxy server, and whenever a user attempts to access a site on the URL filter block list, the proxy blocks the request. Often, the proxy server presents users with a warning page when they try to access a restricted page. Many organizations use this page to remind users of a corporate acceptable usage policy, and some provide reminders that the proxy server is monitoring their online activity.

Proxy servers include logs that record each site visited by users. These logs can be helpful to identify frequently visited sites and to monitor user web browsing activities.

> ### Remember this
>
> A proxy server forwards requests for services from a client. It provides caching to improve performance and reduce Internet bandwidth usage. Transparent proxy servers use URL filters to restrict access to certain sites, and can log user activity.

Reverse Proxy

A reverse proxy accepts requests from the Internet, typically for a single web server. It appears to clients as a web server, but is forwarding the requests to the web server and serving the pages returned by the web server. Figure 3.9 shows how a reverse proxy server is configured to protect a web server. Note that this configuration allows the web server to be located in the private network behind a second firewall.

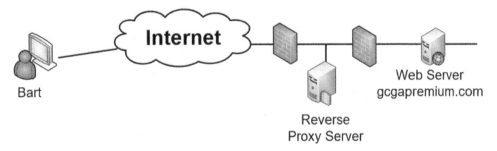

Figure 3.9: Reverse proxy server

Imagine that Bart wants to access *http://gcgapremium.com*. He types the URL into his browser and it connects to the reverse proxy server. The reverse proxy server connects to the web server and retrieves the web page. It then sends the web page to Bart. A reverse proxy server caches the web pages just as a forward proxy server does, so it can improve the overall web site performance.

The reverse proxy server can be used for a single web server or a web farm of multiple servers. When used with a web farm, it can act as a *load balancer*. You would place the load balancer in the DMZ to accept the requests and it then forwards the requests to different servers in the web farm using a load-balancing algorithm. Chapter 9, "Implementing Controls to Protect Assets," covers load balancing in more depth.

Application Proxy

An application proxy is used for specific applications. It accepts requests, forwards the requests to the appropriate server, and then sends the response to the original requestor. A forward proxy used for HTTP is a basic application proxy. However, most application proxies are multipurpose proxy servers supporting multiple protocols such as HTTP and HTTPS.

As a more advanced example, imagine you buy a book from Amazon and Amazon ships it via United Parcel Service (UPS). Later, you check your account to see the status of the shipment. The Amazon web site sends a query to a UPS application proxy for the status. The UPS application proxy provides the status in a response. Internet applications exchange data this way using application programming interfaces (APIs). For example, UPS specifies the format of the request in an API. If the application proxy receives a properly formatted and valid request, it provides an answer.

Unified Threat Management

Unified threat management (**UTM**) is a single solution that combines multiple security controls. The overall goal of UTMs is to provide better security, while also simplifying management requirements. In many cases, a UTM device will reduce the workload of administrators without sacrificing security.

As IT-based threats first began appearing, security experts created various solutions to deal with each of them. When attackers began releasing malware to infect computers, vendors created antivirus software. Attackers started attacking networks, and in response, security experts developed and steadily improved firewalls. When organizations recognized a need to control what sites users can visit, organizations implemented proxies with URL filters.

Although these solutions are effective, they are also complex. Administrators often find it challenging to manage each of these solutions separately. Because of this, UTM security appliances have become quite popular.

UTM security appliances combine the features of multiple security solutions into a single appliance. For example, a UTM security appliance might include a firewall, antivirus protection, anti-spam protection, URL filtering, and content filtering.

In general, a computer appliance is a hardware device designed to provide a specific solution. For example, spam appliances scan all incoming email and strip off spam. The intent of the word *appliance* is to evoke a sense of simplicity. For example, you don't have to know the details of how a toaster works to make toast. Similarly, you don't have to know the details of how a computer appliance operates to use it.

UTM security appliances include multiple capabilities, including:

- **URL filtering.** URL filters within a UTM security appliance perform the same job as a proxy server. They block access to sites based on the URL. It's common to subscribe to a service and select categories to block access to groups of sites. Administrators can also configure URL filters manually to allow or block access to specific web sites. As an example, if an administrator realizes that users are routinely connecting to a peer-to-peer (P2P) file sharing site, the administrator can add the URL to the filter, and block access to that site.
- **Malware inspection.** Malware often comes into a network via spam, or malicious web pages. The malware inspection component of a UTM appliance screens incoming data for known malware and blocks it. Organizations often scan for malware at email servers and at individual systems as part of a layered security or defense-in-depth solution.
- **Content inspection.** Content inspection includes a combination of different content filters. It monitors incoming data streams and attempts to block any malicious content. It can include a spam filter to inspect incoming email and reject spam. It can also block specific types of transmissions, such as streaming audio and video, and specific types of files such as Zip files.

- **DDoS mitigator.** A DDoS mitigator attempts to detect DDoS attacks and block them. This is similar to how intrusion prevention systems (IPSs) block attacks. Chapter 4 covers IPSs in more depth.

The output of the UTM varies depending on the device and what it sees. For example, if it detects malware, it will typically raise an alert and send it to administrators.

A common security issue with UTMs is a misconfigured content filter. For example, if the spam filter is misconfigured, it can block valid mail or allow too much spam into the network. Administrators adjust the sensitivity of the spam filter to meet the needs of the organization. For example, one organization might find it unacceptable to block emails from customers or potential customers. Administrators would adjust the sensitivity allowing more spam into the network to meet this need.

It's common to place UTM appliances at the network border, between the Internet and the intranet (or the private network). This allows it to intercept and analyze all traffic to and from the Internet. However, the placement is dependent on how the UTM appliance is being used. As an example, if it is being used as a proxy server, it can be placed within the DMZ. Administrators would configure the clients to use the UTM appliance for proxy servers ensuring that all relevant traffic goes through it.

> **Remember this**
>
> A unified threat management (UTM) appliance combines multiple security controls into a single appliance. They can inspect data streams and often include URL filtering, malware inspection, and contention inspection components. Many UTMs include a DDoS mitigator to block DDoS attacks.

Mail Gateways

A *mail gateway* is a server that examines all incoming and outgoing email and attempts to reduce risks associated with email. Many vendors sell appliances that perform all the desired services of a mail gateway. Administrators locate it between the email server and the Internet and configure it for their purposes. All mail goes to the gateway before it goes to the email server. Additionally, many vendors include a mail gateway within a UTM appliance. The mail gateway is just another security feature within the UTM appliance.

Spam is unsolicited email and attackers commonly use spam to launch attacks. For example, spam can include malware as an attachment or it might include a link to a malicious web site. A spam filter within a mail gateway filters out spam from incoming email. By filtering out spam, it helps block attacks.

Mail gateways often include data loss prevention (*DLP*) capabilities. They examine outgoing email looking for confidential or sensitive information and block them. As an example, imagine an organization is working on a secret project with a codeword of "DOH." All documents associated with this project have the keyword within them. The mail gateway includes this keyword in its searches and when it detects the keyword within an email or an attachment, it blocks the email. Administrators have the choice of configuring the gateway to notify security personnel, the user who sent the email, or both when it blocks an email. Chapter 5, "Securing Hosts and Data," discusses DLP in more depth.

Many mail gateways also support encryption. They can encrypt all outgoing email to ensure confidentiality for the data-in-transit, or only encrypt certain data based on policies. For example, if an organization is working on a project with another organization, administrators can configure the gateway to encrypt all traffic sent to the other organization. The method of encryption varies from vendor to vendor. For example, some vendors use certificate-based encryption. Others use password-based encryption. Chapter 10 discusses encryption in more depth.

Summarizing Routing and Switching Use Cases

Several use cases were covered earlier in this chapter. While they could be covered independently, it was important to have a basic understanding of routers and switches before connecting them with routing and switching use cases. This section summarizes some of the routing and switching topics.

The following bullets identify some use cases that you can implement with switches:

- **Prevent switching loops.** You do this by implementing STP or RSTP on switches.
- **Block flood attacks.** Flood guards block MAC flood attacks.
- **Prevent unauthorized users from connecting to unused ports.** Port security methods, such as disabling unused ports, prevent these unauthorized connections.
- **Provide increased segmentation of user computers.** VLANs provide increased segmentation. They are implemented on Layer 3 switches.

Simple Network Management Protocol version 3 (**SNMPv3**) monitors and manages network devices, such as routers or switches. This includes using SNMPv3 to modify the configuration of the devices or have network devices report status back to a central network management system. SNMPv3 agents installed on devices send information to an SNMP manager via notifications known as traps (sometimes called device traps).

The first version of SNMP had vulnerabilities, such as passing passwords across the network in cleartext. SNMPv2 and SNMPv3 are much more secure and they provide strong authentication mechanisms. SNMPv3 uses UDP port 161. It sends traps (error messages and notifications) on UDP port 162.

The following bullets identify some use cases that you can implement with routers:

- **Prevent IP address spoofing.** Antispoofing methods prevent IP address spoofing. These are implemented with rules in ACLs.
- **Provide secure management of routers.** SNMPv3 is used to securely manage network devices such as routers.

> ## Remember this
>
> Administrators use SNMPv3 to manage and monitor network devices and SNMP uses UDP ports 161 and 162. It includes strong authentication mechanisms and is more secure than earlier versions.

Chapter 3 Exam Topic Review

When preparing for the exam, make sure you understand these key concepts covered in this chapter.

Reviewing Basic Networking Concepts

- A use case typically describes an organizational goal and administrators enable specific protocols to meet organizational goals.
- Protocols used for voice and video include Real-time Transport Protocol (RTP) and Secure Real-time Transport Protocol (SRTP). SRTP provides encryption, message authentication, and integrity for RTP.
- File Transfer Protocol (FTP) is commonly used to transfer files over networks, but FTP does not encrypt the transmission.
- Several encryption protocols encrypt data-in-transit to protect its confidentiality. They include File Transfer Protocol Secure (FTPS), Secure File Transfer Protocol (SFTP), Secure Shell (SSH), Secure Sockets Layer (SSL), and Transport Layer Security (TLS).
- SMTP sends email using TCP port 25. POP3 receives email using TCP port 110. IMAP4 uses TCP port 143. Secure POP uses TLS on port 995 (legacy) or with STARTTLS on port 110. Secure IMAP uses TLS on port 993 (legacy) or with STARTTLS on port 143.
- HTTP uses port 80 for web traffic. HTTPS encrypts HTTP traffic in transit and uses port 443.
- Directory services solutions implement Kerberos as the authentication protocol. They also use Lightweight Directory Access Protocol (LDAP) over TCP port 389 and LDAP Secure (LDAPS) over TCP port 636.
- Administrators commonly connect to remote systems using SSH instead of Telnet because SSH encrypts the connection. Administrators also use Remote Desktop Protocol (RDP) to connect to remote systems using TCP port 3389.
- The Network Time Protocol (NTP) provides time synchronization services.
- Domain Name System (DNS) provides domain name resolution. DNS zones include A records for IPv4 addresses and AAAA records for IPv6 addresses. Zone data is updated with zone transfers and secure zone transfers help prevent unauthorized access to zone data. DNS uses TCP port 53 for zone transfers and UDP port 53 for DNS client queries.
- Domain Name System Security Extensions (DNSSEC) provides validation for DNS responses and helps prevent DNS poisoning attacks.
- Two command-line tools used to query DNS are nslookup and dig. Both support the axfr switch, allowing them to download all zone data from a DNS server, unless the DNS server blocks the attempt.

Understanding Basic Network Devices

- Switches are used for network connectivity and they map media access control (MAC) addresses to physical ports.
- Port security limits access to switch ports. It includes limiting the number of MAC addresses per port and disabling unused ports. You can also manually map each port to a specific MAC address or group of addresses.

- An aggregation switch connects multiple switches together in a network.
- Routers connect networks and direct traffic based on the destination IP address. Routers (and firewalls) use rules within access control lists (ACLs) to allow or block traffic.
- Implicit deny indicates that unless something is explicitly allowed, it is denied. It is the last rule in an ACL.
- Host-based firewalls (sometimes called application-based) filter traffic in and out of individual hosts. Some Linux systems use iptables or xtables for firewall capabilities.
- Network-based firewalls filter traffic in and out of a network. They are placed on the border of the network, such as between the Internet and an internal network.
- A stateless firewall controls traffic between networks using rules within an ACL. The ACL can block traffic based on ports, IP addresses, subnets, and some protocols. Stateful firewalls filter traffic based on the state of a packet within a session.
- A web application firewall (WAF) protects a web server against web application attacks. It is typically placed in the demilitarized zone (DMZ) and will alert administrators of suspicious events.

Implementing a Secure Network

- A DMZ provides a layer of protection for servers that are accessible from the Internet.
- An intranet is an internal network. People use the intranet to communicate and share content with each other. An extranet is part of a network that can be accessed by authorized entities from outside of the network.
- NAT translates public IP addresses to private IP addresses, private back to public, and hides IP addresses on the internal network from users on the Internet.
- Networks use various methods to provide network segregation, segmentation, and isolation.
- An airgap is a metaphor for physical isolation, indicating a system or network is completely isolated from another system or network.
- Routers provide logical separation and segmentation using ACLs to control traffic.
- Forward proxy servers forward requests for services from a client. It can cache content and record users' Internet activity. A transparent proxy accepts and forwards requests without modifying them. A nontransparent proxy can modify or filter requests, such as filtering traffic based on destination URLs.
- Reverse proxy servers accept traffic from the Internet and forward it to one or more internal web servers. The reverse proxy server is placed in the DMZ and the web servers can be in the internal network.
- A unified threat management (UTM) security appliance includes multiple layers of protection, such as URL filters, content inspection, malware inspection, and a distributed denial-of-service (DDoS) mitigator. UTMs typically raise alerts and send them to administrators to interpret.
- Mail gateways are logically placed between an email server and the Internet. They examine and analyze all traffic and can block unsolicited email with a spam filter. Many include data loss prevention (DLP) and encryption capabilities.

Summarizing Routing and Switching Use Cases

- Loop protection protects against switching loop problems, such as when a user connects two switch ports together with a cable. Spanning Tree Protocols protect against switching loops.

- Flood guards prevent MAC flood attacks on switches.
- VLANs can logically separate computers or logically group computers regardless of their physical location. You create them with Layer 3 switches.
- Routers use rules within ACLs as an antispoofing method. Border firewalls block all traffic coming from private IP addresses.
- SNMPv3 is used to monitor and configure network devices and uses notification messages known as traps. It uses strong authentication mechanisms and is preferred over earlier versions. SNMP uses UDP ports 161 and 162.

Online References

- Remember, the online content includes some extras, such as labs, performance-based question examples, and more. Check it out at *http://gcgapremium.com/501-extras.*

Chapter 3 Practice Questions

1. Your organization's security policy requires that PII data-in-transit must be encrypted. Which of the following protocols would BEST meet this requirement?
    A. FTP
    B. SSH
    C. SMTP
    D. HTTP

2. Marge needs to collect network device configuration information and network statistics from devices on the network. She wants to protect the confidentiality of credentials used to connect to these devices. Which of the following protocols would BEST meet this need?
    A. SSH
    B. FTPS
    C. SNMPv3
    D. TLS

3. Lisa is enabling NTP on some servers within the DMZ. Which of the following use cases is she MOST likely supporting with this action?
    A. Support voice and video transmissions
    B. Provide time synchronization
    C. Enable email usage
    D. Encrypt data-in-transit

4. Your organization wants to increase security for VoIP and video teleconferencing applications used within the network. Which of the following protocols will BEST support this goal?
    A. SMTP
    B. TLS
    C. SFTP
    D. SRTP

5. Management within your organization wants to ensure that switches are not susceptible to switching loop problems. Which of the following protocols is the BEST choice to meet this need?

    A. Flood guard

    B. SNMPv3

    C. SRTP

    D. RSTP

6. A network technician incorrectly wired switch connections in your organization's network. It effectively disabled the switch as though it was a victim of a denial-of-service attack. Which of the following should be done to prevent this situation in the future?

    A. Install an IDS.

    B. Only use Layer 2 switches.

    C. Install SNMPv3 on the switches.

    D. Implement STP or RSTP.

7. Developers recently configured a new service on ServerA. ServerA is in a DMZ and accessed by internal users and via the Internet. Network administrators modified firewall rules to access the service. Testing shows the service works when accessed from internal systems. However, it does not work when accessed from the Internet. Which of the following is MOST likely configured incorrectly?

    A. The new service

    B. An ACL

    C. ServerA

    D. The VLAN

8. You manage a Linux computer used for security within your network. You plan to use it to inspect and handle network-based traffic using iptables. Which of the following network devices can this replace?

    A. Wireless access point

    B. Firewall

    C. Layer 2 switch

    D. Bridge

9. You need to implement antispoofing on a border router. Which one of the following choices will BEST meet this goal?

    A. Create rules to block all outgoing traffic from a private IP address.

    B. Implement a flood guard on switches.

    C. Add a web application firewall.

    D. Create rules to block all incoming traffic from a private IP address.

10. An organization has recently had several attacks against servers within a DMZ. Security administrators discovered that many of these attacks are using TCP, but they did not start with a three-way handshake. Which of the following devices provides the BEST solution?

    A. Stateless firewall

    B. Stateful firewall

    C. Network firewall

    D. Application-based firewall

11. Which type of device would have the following entries used to define its operation?
    permit IP any any eq 80
    permit IP any any eq 443
    deny IP any any
    - A. Firewall
    - B. Layer 2 switch
    - C. Proxy server
    - D. Web server

12. Your organization hosts a web server and wants to increase its security. You need to separate all web-facing traffic from internal network traffic. Which of the following provides the BEST solution?
    - A. DMZ
    - B. VLAN
    - C. Firewall
    - D. WAF

13. Management at your organization wants to prevent employees from accessing social media sites using company-owned computers. Which of the following devices would you implement?
    - A. Transparent proxy
    - B. Reverse proxy
    - C. Nontransparent proxy
    - D. Caching proxy

14. You need to configure a UTM security appliance to restrict traffic going to social media sites. Which of the following are you MOST likely to configure?
    - A. Content inspection
    - B. Malware inspection
    - C. URL filter
    - D. DDoS mitigator

15. Your organization recently purchased a sophisticated security appliance that includes a DDoS mitigator. Where should you place this device?
    - A. Within the DMZ
    - B. At the border of the network, between the intranet and the DMZ
    - C. At the border of the network, between the private network and the Internet
    - D. In the internal network

Chapter 3 Practice Question Answers

1. **B.** You can use Secure Shell (SSH) to encrypt Personally Identifiable Information (PII) data when transmitting it over the network (data-in-transit). Secure File Transfer Protocol (SFTP) uses SSH to encrypt File Transfer Protocol (FTP) traffic. FTP, Simple Mail Transfer Protocol (SMTP), and Hypertext Transfer Protocol (HTTP) transmit data in cleartext unless they are combined with an encryption protocol.

2. **C.** Simple Network Management Protocol version 3 (SNMPv3) is a secure protocol that can monitor and collect information from network devices. It includes strong authentication mechanisms to protect the confidentiality of credentials. None of the other protocols listed are used to monitor network devices. Secure Shell (SSH) provides a secure method of connecting to devices, but does not monitor them. File Transfer Protocol Secure (FTPS) is useful for encrypting large files in transit, using Transport Layer Security (TLS). TLS is commonly used to secure transmissions, but doesn't include methods to monitor devices.

3. **B.** The Network Time Protocol (NTP) provides time synchronization services, so enabling NTP on servers would meet this use case. The Real-time Transport Protocol (RTP) delivers audio and video over IP networks, and Secure RTP (SRTP) provides encryption, message authentication, and integrity for RTP. Protocols such as Simple Mail Transfer Protocol (SMTP), Post Office Protocol v3 (POP3), and Internet Message Access Protocol version 4 (IMAP4) are used for email. Encrypting data isn't relevant to time synchronization services provided by NTP.

4. **D.** The Secure Real-time Transport Protocol (SRTP) provides encryption, message authentication, and integrity for Voice over Internet Protocol (VoIP), video teleconferencing, and other streaming media applications. None of the other answers are directly related to VoIP or video teleconferencing. Simple Mail Transfer Protocol (SMTP) transfers email. The Transport Layer Security (TLS) protocol is used to encrypt data-in-transit, but isn't the best choice for streaming media. Secure File Transfer Protocol (SFTP) is a secure implementation of FTP to transfer files.

5. **D.** Rapid STP (RSTP) prevents switching loop problems and should be enabled on the switches to meet this need. A flood guard on a switch helps prevent a media access control (MAC) flood attack. Simple Network Management Protocol version 3 (SNMPv3) is used to manage and monitor network devices. The Secure Real-time Transport Protocol (SRTP) provides encryption, message authentication, and integrity for video and voice data.

6. **D.** Spanning Tree Protocol (STP) and Rapid STP (RSTP) both prevent switching loop problems. It's rare for a wiring error to take down a switch. However, if two ports on a switch are connected to each other, it creates a switching loop and effectively disables the switch. An intrusion detection system (IDS) will not prevent a switching loop. Layer 2 switches are susceptible to this problem. Administrators use Simple Network Management Protocol version 3 (SNMPv3) to manage and monitor devices, but it doesn't prevent switching loops.

7. **B.** The most likely problem of the available choices is that an access control list (ACL) is configured incorrectly. The server is in a demilitarized zone (DMZ) and the most likely problem is an incorrectly configured ACL on the border firewall. The service is operating when accessed from internal clients, so it isn't likely that it is the problem. Also, the server works for internal systems indicating it is working correctly. There isn't any indication a virtual local area network (VLAN) is in use.

8. **B.** Iptables include settings used by the Linux Kernel firewall and can be used to replace a

firewall. While it's possible to implement iptables on a wireless access point (assuming it is Linux-based), iptables still function as a firewall, not a wireless access point. A Layer 2 switch routes traffic based on the destination media access control (MAC) address, but iptables focus on IP addresses. A network bridge connects multiple networks together.

9. **D.** You would create rules to block all incoming traffic from private IP addresses. The border router is between the internal network and the Internet and any traffic coming from the Internet with a private IP address is a spoofed source IP address. All outgoing traffic will typically use a private IP address, so you shouldn't block this outgoing traffic. A flood guard on a switch protects against media access control (MAC) flood attacks and is unrelated to this question. A web application firewall protects a web application and is unrelated to antispoofing.

10. **B.** A stateful firewall filters traffic based on the state of the packet within a session. It would filter a packet that isn't part of a TCP three-way handshake. A stateless firewall filters traffic based on the IP address, port, or protocol ID. While it's appropriate to place a network firewall in a demilitarized zone (DMZ), a network firewall could be either a stateless firewall or a stateful firewall. An application-based firewall is typically only protecting a host, not a network.

11. **A.** These are rules in an access control list (ACL) for a firewall. The first two rules indicate that traffic from any IP address, to any IP address, using ports 80 or 443 is permitted or allowed. The final rule is also known as an implicit deny rule and is placed last in the ACL. It ensures that all traffic that hasn't been previously allowed is denied. Layer 2 switches do not use ACLs. A proxy server would not use an ACL, although it would use ports 80 and 443 for Hypertext Transfer Protocol (HTTP) and HTTP Secure (HTTPS), respectively. A web server wouldn't use an ACL, although it would also use ports 80 and 443.

12. **A.** A demilitarized zone (DMZ) is a buffered zone between a private network and the Internet, and it will separate the web server's web-facing traffic from the internal network. You can use a virtual local area network (VLAN) to group computers together based on job function or some other administrative need, but it is created on switches in the internal network. A firewall does provide protection for the web server, but doesn't necessarily separate the web-facing traffic from the internal network. A web application firewall (WAF) protects a web server from incoming attacks, but it does not necessarily separate Internet and internal network traffic.

13. **C.** A nontransparent proxy includes the ability to filter traffic based on the URL and is the best choice. A transparent proxy doesn't modify or filter requests. A reverse proxy is used for incoming traffic to an internal firewall, not traffic going out of the network. Proxy servers are caching proxy servers, but won't block outgoing traffic.

14. **C.** You would most likely configure the Uniform Resource Locator (URL) filter on the unified threat management (UTM) security appliance. This would block access to the peer-to-peer sites based on their URL. Content inspection and malware inspection focus on inspecting the data as it passes through the UTM, but they do not block access to sites. A distributed denial-of-service (DDoS) mitigator will attempt to block incoming DDoS attack traffic.

15. **C.** A distributed denial-of-service (DDoS) mitigator attempts to block DDoS attacks and should be placed at the border of the network, between the private network and the Internet. If the network includes a demilitarized zone (DMZ), the appliance should be placed at the border of the DMZ and the Internet. Placing it in the DMZ or the internal network doesn't ensure it will block incoming traffic.

Chapter 4

Securing Your Network

CompTIA Security+ objectives covered in this chapter:

1.2 Compare and contrast types of attacks.
- Wireless attacks (Replay, IV, Evil twin, Rogue AP, Jamming, WPS, Bluejacking, Bluesnarfing, RFID, NFC, Disassociation)

2.1 Install and configure network components, both hardware- and software-based, to support organizational security.
- VPN concentrator (Remote access vs. site-to-site, IPSec [Tunnel mode, Transport mode, AH, ESP], Split tunnel vs. full tunnel, TLS, Always-on VPN), NIPS/NIDS (Signature-based, Heuristic/behavioral, Anomaly, Inline vs. passive, In-band vs. out-of-band, Rules, Analytics [False positive, False negative]), Access point (SSID, MAC filtering, Signal strength, Band selection/width, Antenna types and placement, Fat vs. thin, Controller-based vs. standalone), NAC (Dissolvable vs. permanent, Host health checks, Agent vs. agentless), SSL/TLS accelerators, SSL decryptors

2.2 Given a scenario, use appropriate software tools to assess the security posture of an organization.
- Honeypot

2.3 Given a scenario, troubleshoot common security issues.
- Misconfigured devices (Access points)

2.4 Given a scenario, analyze and interpret output from security technologies.
- HIDS/HIPS

2.6 Given a scenario, implement secure protocols.
- Use cases (Remote access)

3.2 Given a scenario, implement secure network architecture concepts.
- Zones/topologies (Wireless, Guest, Honeynets, Ad hoc), Tunneling/VPN (Site-to-site, Remote access), Security device/technology placement (Sensors, Collectors, VPN concentrators, SSL accelerators, Taps and port mirror), SDN

4.2   Given a scenario, install and configure identity and access services.
  - TACACS+, CHAP, PAP, MSCHAP, RADIUS

4.3   Given a scenario, implement identity and access management controls.
  - Certificate-based authentication (IEEE 802.1x)

6.3   Given a scenario, install and configure wireless security settings.
  - Cryptographic protocols (WPA, WPA2, CCMP, TKIP), Authentication protocols (EAP, PEAP, EAP-FAST, EAP-TLS, EAP-TTLS, IEEE 802.1x, RADIUS Federation), Methods (PSK vs. Enterprise vs. Open, WPS, Captive portals)

**
In this chapter, you'll learn about some of the more advanced network security concepts. Topics include intrusion detection systems (IDSs) and intrusion prevention systems (IPSs), methods used to secure wireless networks, and virtual private network (VPN) technologies.

Exploring Advanced Security Devices

Chapter 3, "Exploring Network Technologies and Tools," discusses basic network technologies and protocols. This section explores many of the more advanced security devices used to secure networks.

Understanding IDSs and IPSs

Intrusion detection systems (IDSs) monitor a network and send alerts when they detect suspicious events on a system or network. Intrusion prevention systems (IPSs) react to attacks in progress and prevent them from reaching systems and networks.

Chapter 8, "Using Risk Management Tools," discusses protocol analyzers, or sniffers, in more depth, but as an introduction, administrators use them to capture and analyze network traffic sent between hosts. IDSs and IPSs have the same capability. They capture the traffic and analyze it to detect potential attacks or anomalies.

Both IDSs and IPSs have the ability of detecting attacks using similar detection methods. The biggest difference is in their responses to an attack. This section presents IDSs first, and then wraps up with some information on IPSs and compares the two. However, as you go through this section, it's worth remembering that IDSs and IPSs can implement the same monitoring and detection methods.

HIDS

A host-based intrusion detection system (**HIDS**) is additional software installed on a system such as a workstation or server. It provides protection to the individual host and can detect potential attacks and protect critical operating system files. The primary goal of any IDS is to monitor traffic. For a HIDS, this traffic passes through the network interface card (NIC).

Many host-based IDSs have expanded to monitor application activity on the system. As one example, you can install a HIDS on different Internet-facing servers, such as web servers, mail servers, and database servers. In addition to monitoring the network traffic reaching the servers, the HIDS can also monitor the server applications.

It's worth stressing that a HIDS can help detect malicious software (malware) that traditional antivirus software might miss. Because of this, many organizations install a HIDS on every workstation as an extra layer of protection in addition to traditional antivirus software. Just as the HIDS on a server is used primarily to monitor network traffic, a workstation HIDS is primarily used to monitor network traffic reaching the workstation. However, a HIDS can also monitor some applications and can protect local resources such as operating system files.

In other organizations, administrators only install a HIDS when there's a perceived need. For example, if an administrator is concerned that a specific server with proprietary data is at increased risk of an attack, the administrator might choose to install a HIDS on this system as an extra layer of protection.

NIDS

A network-based intrusion detection system (**NIDS**) monitors activity on the network. An administrator installs NIDS sensors or collectors on network devices such as routers and firewalls. These sensors gather information and report to a central monitoring server hosting a NIDS console.

A NIDS is not able to detect anomalies on individual systems or workstations unless the anomaly causes a significant difference in network traffic. Additionally, a NIDS is unable to decrypt encrypted traffic. In other words, it can only monitor and assess threats on the network from traffic sent in plaintext or nonencrypted traffic.

Figure 4.1 shows an example of a NIDS configuration. In the figure, sensors are located before the firewall, after the firewall, and on routers. These sensors collect and monitor network traffic on subnets within the network and report to the NIDS console. The NIDS provides overall monitoring and analysis and can detect attacks on the network.

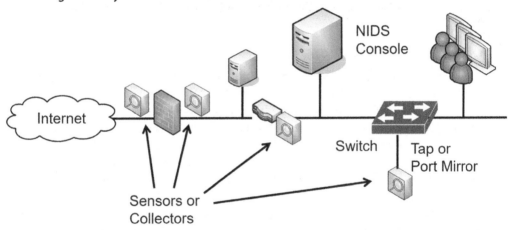

Figure 4.1: NIDS sensors

Figure 4.1 also shows a tap or **port mirror** on the internal switch. Most switches support port mirroring, allowing administrators to configure the switch to send all traffic received by the switch to a single port. After configuring a port mirror, you can use it as a tap to send all switch data to a sensor or collector, and forward this to a NIDS. Similarly, it's possible to configure **taps** on routers to capture all traffic sent through the switch and send it to the IDS.

Sensor and Collector Placement

The decision on where you want to place the sensors depends on what you want to measure. For example, the sensor on the Internet side of the firewall will see all the traffic. However, the sensor on the internal side of the firewall will only see traffic that passes through the firewall. In other words, the firewall will filter some attacks, and the internal sensor won't see them.

If you want to see all attacks on your network, put a sensor on the Internet side. If you only want to see what gets through, put sensors internally only. If you want to see both, put sensors in both places.

> **Remember this**
>
> A HIDS can monitor all traffic on a single host system such as a server or a workstation. In some cases, it can detect malicious activity missed by antivirus software. A NIDS is installed on network devices, such as routers or firewalls, to monitor network traffic and detect network-based attacks. It can also use taps or port mirrors to capture traffic. A NIDS cannot monitor encrypted traffic and cannot monitor traffic on individual hosts.

Detection Methods

An IDS can only detect an attack. It cannot prevent attacks. In contrast, an IPS prevents attacks by detecting them and stopping them before they reach the target. An attack is any attempt to compromise confidentiality, integrity, or availability.

The two primary methods of detection are signature-based and heuristic- or behavioral-based (also called anomaly-based). Any type of IDS can detect attacks based on signatures, anomalies, or both. The HIDS monitors the network traffic reaching its NIC and the NIDS monitors the traffic on the network.

Signature-Based Detection

Signature-based IDSs (also called definition-based) use a database of known vulnerabilities or known attack patterns. For example, tools are available for an attacker to launch a SYN flood attack on a server by simply entering the IP address of the system to attack. The attack tool then floods the target system with synchronize (SYN) packets, but never completes the three-way Transmission Control Protocol (TCP) handshake with the final acknowledge (ACK) packet. If the attack isn't blocked, it can consume resources on a system and ultimately cause it to crash.

However, this is a known attack with a specific pattern of successive SYN packets from one IP to another IP. The IDS can detect these patterns when the signature database includes the attack definitions. The process is very similar to what antivirus software uses to detect malware. You need to update both IDS signatures and antivirus definitions from the vendor on a regular basis to protect against current threats.

Heuristic/Behavioral Detection

Heuristic/behavioral-based detection (also called *anomaly*-based detection) starts by identifying normal operation or normal behavior of the network. It does this by creating a performance baseline under normal operating conditions.

The IDS provides continuous monitoring by constantly comparing current network behavior against the baseline. When the IDS detects abnormal activity (outside normal boundaries as identified in the baseline), it gives an alert indicating a potential attack.

Heuristic-based detection is similar to how heuristic-based antivirus software works. Although the internal methods are different, both examine activity and detect abnormal activity that is beyond the capability of signature-based detection.

SYN Flood Attack

The SYN flood attack is a common denial-of-service (DoS) attack. Chapter 3 describes the three-way handshake to establish a session. As a reminder, one system sends a SYN packet, the second system responds with a SYN/ACK packet, and the first system then completes the handshake with an ACK packet. However, in a SYN flood attack, the attacker sends multiple SYN packets but never completes the third part of the TCP handshake with the last ACK packet.

This is like a friend extending his hand to shake hands with you, you extending your hand in response, and then, at the last instant, the friend pulls his hand away. Although you or I would probably stop extending our hand back to someone doing this, the server doesn't know any better and keeps answering every SYN packet with a SYN/ACK packet.

Each uncompleted session consumes resources on the server, and if the SYN flood attack continues, it can crash the server. Some servers reserve a certain number of resources for connections, and once the attack consumes these resources, the system blocks additional connections. Instead of crashing the server, the attack prevents legitimate users from connecting to the server.

IDSs and IPSs can detect a SYN flood attack and IPSs can prevent the attack. Additionally, many firewalls include a SYN flood guard that can detect SYN flood attacks and take steps to close the open sessions. This is different than a flood guard on a switch designed to stop MAC flood attacks, as discussed in Chapter 3.

This can be effective at discovering zero-day exploits. A zero-day vulnerability is usually defined as one that is unknown to the vendor. However, in some usage, administrators define a zero-day exploit as one where the vendor has not released a patch. In other words, the vendor might know about the vulnerability but has not written, tested, and released a patch to close the vulnerability yet.

In both cases, the vulnerability exists and systems are unprotected. If attackers discover the vulnerabilities, they try to exploit them. However, the attack has the potential to create abnormal traffic allowing an anomaly-based system to detect it.

Any time administrators make any significant changes to a system or network that cause the normal behavior to change, they should re-create the baseline. Otherwise, the IDS will constantly alert on what is now normal behavior.

Remember this

Signature-based detection identifies issues based on known attacks or vulnerabilities. Signature-based detection systems can detect known anomalies. Heuristic or behavior-based IDSs (also called anomaly-based) can detect unknown anomalies. They start with a performance baseline of normal behavior and then compare network traffic against this baseline. When traffic differs significantly from the baseline, the IDS sends an alert.

Data Sources and Trends

Any type of IDS will use various raw data sources to collect information on activity. This includes a wide variety of logs, such as firewall logs, system logs, and application logs. These logs can be analyzed to provide insight on trends. These trends can detect a pattern of attacks and provide insight into how to better protect a network.

Many IDSs have the capability to monitor logs in real time. Each time a system records a log entry, the IDS examines the log to determine if it is an item of interest or not. Other IDSs will periodically poll relevant logs and scan new entries looking for items of interest.

Reporting Based on Rules

IDSs report on events of interest based on rules configured within the IDS. All events aren't attacks or actual issues, but instead, they provide a report indicating an event might be an alert or an alarm. Administrators investigate to determine if it is valid. Some systems consider an alarm and an alert as the same thing. Other systems use an alarm for a potentially serious issue, and an alert as a relatively minor issue. The goal in these latter systems is to encourage administrators to give a higher precedence to alarms than alerts.

The actual reporting mechanism varies from system to system and in different organizations. For example, one IDS might write the event into a log as an alarm or alert, and then send an email to an administrator account. In a large network operations center (NOC), the IDS might send an alert to a monitor easily viewable by all personnel in the NOC. The point is that administrators configure the rules within the IDS based on the needs of the organization.

False Positives Versus False Negatives

While IDSs use advanced analytics to examine traffic, they are susceptible to both false positives and false negatives. A *false positive* is an alert or alarm on an event that is nonthreatening, benign, or harmless. A *false negative* is when an attacker is actively attacking the network, but the system does not detect it. Neither is desirable, but it's impossible to eliminate both. Most IDSs trigger an alert or alarm when an event exceeds a threshold.

Consider the classic SYN flood attack, where the attacker withholds the third part of the TCP handshake. A host will send a SYN packet and a server will respond with a SYN/ACK packet. However, instead of completing the handshake with an ACK packet, the attacking host never sends the ACK, but continues to send more SYN packets. This leaves the server with open connections that can ultimately disrupt services.

If a system receives 1 SYN packet without the accompanying ACK packet, is it an attack? Probably not. This can happen during normal operations. If a system receives over 1,000 SYN packets from a single IP address in less than 60 seconds, without the accompanying ACK packet, is it an attack? Absolutely.

Administrators configure rules within the IDS and set the threshold to a number between 1 and 1,000 to indicate an attack. If administrators set it too low, they will have too many false positives and a high workload as they spend their time chasing ghosts. If they set the threshold too high, actual attacks will get through without administrators knowing about them. Similarly, they can configure many settings based on the analytics and capabilities of the IDS.

Most administrators want to know if their system is under attack. That's the primary purpose of the IDS. However, an IDS that constantly cries "Wolf!" will be ignored when the real wolf attacks. It's important to set the threshold high enough to reduce the number of false positives, but low enough to alert on any actual attacks.

There is no perfect number for the threshold. Administrators adjust thresholds in different networks based on the network's activity level and their personal preferences.

> ### Remember this
>
> A false positive incorrectly indicates an attack is occurring when an attack is not active. A high incidence of false positives increases the administrator's workload. A false negative is when an attack is occurring, but the system doesn't detect and report it. Administrators often set the IDS threshold high enough that it minimizes false positives but low enough that it does not allow false negatives.

IPS Versus IDS—Inline Versus Passive

Intrusion prevention systems (IPSs) are an extension of IDSs. Just as you can have both a HIDS and a NIDS, you can also have a HIPS and a NIPS, but a network-based IPS (**NIPS**) is more common. There are some primary distinctions of an IPS when compared with an IDS:

- An IPS can detect, react, and prevent attacks.
- In contrast, an IDS monitors and will respond after detecting an attack, but it doesn't prevent them.
- An IPS is **inline** with the traffic. In other words, all traffic passes through the IPS and the IPS can block malicious traffic. This is sometimes referred to as in-band.
- In contrast, an IDS is **out-of-band**. It monitors the network traffic, but the traffic doesn't go through the IDS. This is sometimes referred to as passive.

Most IDSs will only respond by raising alerts. For example, an IDS will log the attack and send a notification. The notification can come in many forms, including an email to a group of administrators, a text message, a pop-up window, or a notification on a central monitor. Some IDSs have additional capabilities allowing them to change the environment in addition to sending a notification.

For example, an IDS might be able to modify access control lists (ACLs) on firewalls to block offending traffic, close processes on a system that were caused by the attack, or divert the attack to a safe environment, such as a honeypot or honeynet (discussed later in this chapter). While this is sometimes referred to as an active IDS, this phrase can be misleading.

Specifically, the CompTIA Security+ objectives use the terms inline and in-band for an IPS and passive and out-of-band for an IDS.

> ### Remember this
>
> An IPS can detect, react, and prevent attacks. It is placed inline with the traffic (also known as in-band). An IDS monitors and responds to an attack. It is not inline but instead collects data passively (also known as out-of-band).

As a reminder from the introduction of this section, both IDSs and IPSs have protocol analyzer capabilities. This allows them to monitor data streams looking for malicious behavior. An IPS can inspect packets within these data streams and block malicious packets before they enter the network.

In contrast, a NIDS has sensors or data collectors that monitor and report the traffic. An active NIDS can take steps to block an attack, but only after the attack has started. The inline configuration of the IPS allows an IPS to prevent attacks from reaching the internal network.

As an example, Figure 4.2 shows the location of two network-based IPSs (NIPS 1 and NIPS 2). All Internet traffic flows through NIPS 1, giving it an opportunity to inspect incoming traffic. NIPS 1 protects the internal network by detecting malicious traffic and preventing attacks from reaching the internal network.

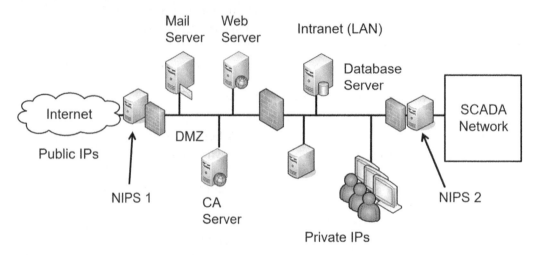

Figure 4.2: NIPS used to detect and prevent attacks

NIPS 2 is protecting an internal private network. As an example, imagine that Homer needs to manage some equipment within a supervisory control and data acquisition (SCADA) network in the nuclear power plant. The SCADA equipment is in the private network. The firewall next to NIPS 2 can have rules that allow traffic from Homer's computer into the network, but block all other traffic. NIPS 2 will then inspect all the incoming traffic and block malicious traffic.

This might seem like overkill, but many advanced persistent threats (APTs) have successfully installed remote access Trojans (RATs) onto internal systems through phishing or malware attacks. Once the **RAT** is installed, attackers can now attack from within. If an attacker began launching attacks on the private network from Homer's system, the firewall wouldn't block it. However, the NIPS will prevent this attack from reaching the private network.

Notice that each IPS is placed on the edge of the protected network. NIPS 1 is placed on the edge of the network between the Internet and the demilitarized zone (DMZ). NIPS 2 is on the edge of the SCADA network between it and the intranet. This placement ensures that the NIPS can inspect all traffic going into the network.

> **Remember this**
>
> An intrusion prevention system (IPS) is a preventive control. It is placed inline with traffic. An IPS can actively monitor data streams, detect malicious content, and stop attacks in progress. It can also be used internally to protect private networks.

SSL/TLS Accelerators

SSL/TLS accelerators refer to hardware devices focused on handling Transport Layer Security (TLS) traffic. As mentioned previously in this book, TLS is the designated replacement for Secure Sockets Layer (SSL), but many people are familiar with SSL terminology so you'll continue to see it, even if the only protocol it's using is TLS.

TLS provides encryption for many different protocols, including Hypertext Transfer Protocol Secure (HTTPS). HTTPS uses a certificate and asymmetric encryption, both described in more depth in Chapter 10, "Understanding Cryptography and PKI." The process of establishing the HTTPS session, negotiating the best security supported by both the client and the server, sharing encryption keys, and encrypting session data all take a lot of time and resources. By off-loading this to another hardware device, it frees up the primary computer's resources, such as CPU power and RAM.

When using an SSL accelerator, it's best to place it as close as possible to related devices. For example, if you're using an SSL accelerator to off-load HTTPS sessions for a web server, place the SSL accelerator close to the web server.

SSL Decryptors

Some organizations use **SSL decryptors** to combat many threats. For example, attackers are often using encryption to prevent inspection methods from detecting malware coming into a network.

As an example, imagine Homer innocently goes to a malicious web site. The web site establishes a secure HTTPS connection, and then downloads malware to Homer's computer. Because the site is using HTTPS, the malware is encrypted while in transit. Even if an organization had the best content inspection methods and malware detection software, it wouldn't detect the malware while it's encrypted.

An SSL decryptor solves this problem. You would place it in the DMZ, and redirect all traffic to and from the Internet through it. Unencrypted data goes through the device without any modification. However, any attempts to establish an encrypted session prompt the SSL decryptor to create a separate SSL (or TLS) session.

When Homer innocently goes to a malicious web site, the traffic goes though the SSL decryptor. The SSL decryptor establishes an HTTPS session between it and Homer's computer. It also establishes an HTTPS session between it and the web site. All data-in-transit is encrypted. However, the SSL decryptor can view the unencrypted data and inspect it.

SSL decryptors are often used with a NIPS. The NIPS is inline but malicious traffic can get through if it's encrypted. The SSL decryptor allows the NIPS to inspect unencrypted traffic and prevent attacks.

SDN

A software defined network (**SDN**) uses virtualization technologies to route traffic instead of using hardware routers and switches. More specifically, an SDN separates the data planes and control planes within a network. Another way of thinking of this is that an SDN separates the logic used to forward or block traffic (the data plane) and the logic used to identify the path to take (the control plane).

Hardware routers use rules within an ACL to identify whether a router will forward or block traffic on the data plane. This is always proprietary because it's implemented on specific hardware routers. However, an SDN implements the data plane with software and virtualization technologies, allowing an organization to move away from proprietary hardware.

Routing protocols such as Open Shortest Path First (OSPF) and Border Gateway Protocol (BGP) help routers determine the best path to route traffic on the control plane. Routers use these protocols to share information with each other, creating a map of the known network. An SDN can still use these routing protocols, but without the hardware routers.

Chapter 2, "Understanding Identity and Access Management," discusses the attribute-based access control (**ABAC**), which is commonly used in SDNs. Instead of rules within ACLs, ABAC models allow administrators to create data plane policies to route traffic. A huge benefit of these policies is that they typically use plain language statements instead of complex rules within an ACL.

Honeypots

A *honeypot* is a sweet-looking server—at least it's intended to look sweet to the attacker, similar to how honey looks sweet to a bear. It's a server that is left open or appears to have been sloppily locked down, allowing an attacker relatively easy access. The intent is for the server to look like an easy target so that the attacker spends his time in the honeypot instead of in a live network. In short, the honeypot diverts the attacker away from the live network.

As an example, a honeypot could be a web server designed to look like a live web server. It would have bogus data such as files and folders containing fabricated credit card transaction data. If an organization suspects it has a problem with a malicious insider, it can create an internal honeypot with bogus information on proprietary projects.

Honeypots typically have minimal protection that an attacker can easily bypass. If administrators don't use any security, the honeypot might look suspicious to experienced attackers and they might simply avoid it.

Security personnel often use honeypots as a tool to gather intelligence on the attacker. Attackers are constantly modifying their methods to take advantage of different types of attacks. Some sophisticated attackers discover vulnerabilities before a patch is released (also known as a zero-day exploit, or zero-day vulnerability). In some cases, security professionals observe attackers launching zero-day vulnerability attacks against a honeypot.

Honeypots never hold any data that is valuable to the organization. The data may appear to be valuable to an attacker, but its disclosure is harmless. Honeypots have two primary goals:

- **Divert attackers from the live network.** If an attacker is spending time in the honeypot, he is not attacking live resources.
- **Allow observation of an attacker.** While an attacker is in the honeypot, security professionals can observe the attack and learn from the attacker's methodologies. Honeypots can also help security professionals learn about zero-day exploits, or previously unknown attacks.

Honeynets

A *honeynet* is a group of honeypots within a separate network or zone, but accessible from an organization's primary network. Security professionals often create honeynets using multiple virtual servers contained within a single physical server. The servers within this network are honeypots and the honeynet mimics the functionality of a live network.

As an example, you can use a single powerful server with a significant amount of RAM and processing power. This server could host multiple virtual servers, where each virtual server is running an operating system and applications. A physical server hosting six virtual servers will appear as seven systems on a subnet. An attacker looking in will not be able to easily determine if the servers are physical or virtual.

The purpose of this virtual network is to attract the attention of an attacker, just as a single honeypot tries to attract the attention of an attacker. If the attacker is in the honeynet, the live network isn't being attacked, and administrators can observe the attacker's actions.

Sun Tzu famously wrote in *The Art of War*, "All warfare is based on deception," and "Know your enemies." Cyberwarfare is occurring daily and security professionals on the front lines of network and system attacks recognize that these attacks mimic warfare in many ways. Honeypots and honeynets provide these professionals with some additional tools to use in this war.

Remember this

Honeypots and honeynets attempt to divert attackers from live networks. They give security personnel an opportunity to observe current methodologies used in attacks and gather intelligence on these attacks.

IEEE 802.1x Security

Chapter 3 discusses port security by disabling unused ports or using MAC address filtering. Another method of port security is to use *IEEE 802.1x*, a port-based authentication protocol. It requires users or devices to authenticate when they connect to a specific wireless access point, or a specific physical port, and it can be implemented in both wireless and wired networks.

It secures the authentication process prior to a client gaining access to a network and blocks network access if the client cannot authenticate. 802.1x can use simple usernames and passwords for authentication, or certificates for certificate-based authentication.

The 802.1x server prevents rogue devices from connecting to a network. Consider open RJ-45 wall jacks. Although disabling them is a good port security practice, you can also configure an 802.1x server to require authentication for these ports. If clients cannot authenticate, the 802.1x server blocks or restricts access to the network.

It's possible to combine an 802.1x server with other network elements such as a virtual local area network (VLAN). For example, imagine you want to provide visitors with Internet access, but prevent them from accessing internal network resources. You can configure the 802.1x server to grant full access to authorized clients, but redirect unauthorized clients to a guest area of the network via a VLAN.

You can implement 802.1x as a Remote Authentication Dial-In User Service (RADIUS) or Diameter server, as discussed later in this chapter. This helps authenticate virtual private network (VPN) clients before they connect. You can also implement 802.1x in wireless networks to force wireless clients to authenticate before they connect.

Remember this

An 802.1x server provides port-based authentication, ensuring that only authorized clients can connect to a network. It prevents rogue devices from connecting.

Securing Wireless Networks

Wireless local area networks (WLANs) have become quite popular in recent years, in both home and business networks. A wireless network is easy to set up and can quickly connect several computers without the need to run cables, which significantly reduces costs.

The significant challenge with wireless networks is security. Wireless security has improved over the years, but wireless networks are still susceptible to vulnerabilities and many users just don't understand how to lock down a wireless network adequately.

Reviewing Wireless Basics

Before digging into wireless security, you need to understand some basic concepts related to wireless devices and networks. If you've recently passed the CompTIA Network+ exam, these topics will likely be very familiar to you, but they are still worth looking at to ensure you understand them from the perspective of the CompTIA Security+ exam.

A wireless *access point (AP)* connects wireless clients to a wired network. However, many APs also have routing capabilities. Vendors commonly market APs with routing capabilities as wireless routers so that's how you'll typically see them advertised. Two distinctions are:

- **All wireless routers are APs.** These are APs with an extra capability—routing.
- **Not all APs are wireless routers.** Many APs do not have any additional capabilities. They provide connectivity for wireless clients to a wired network, but do not have routing capabilities.

Figure 4.3 shows a diagram of a wireless router providing connectivity to multiple systems. Notice that the wireless router has both a switch component and a router component, and the drawing at the bottom of Figure 4.3 shows the logical configuration of the network. The devices connect to the switch component and the router component provides connectivity to the Internet through a broadband modem or similar device depending on the Internet Service Provider (ISP) requirements.

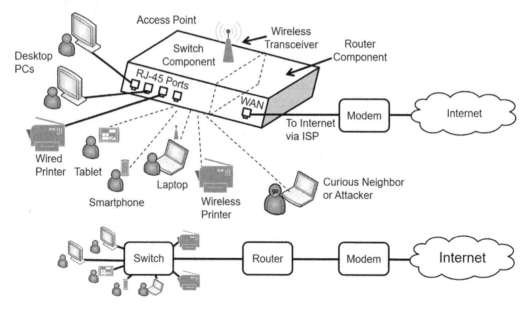

Figure 4.3: Wireless access point with routing capabilities (wireless router)

Most APs include physical ports for wired access (labeled as "RJ-45 Ports" in the diagram) and a wireless transceiver for wireless clients. In other words, some users can connect with regular twisted-pair cable, and other users can connect using wireless transmissions. The wired ports and wireless connections all connect through the switch component of the wireless router. Many vendors label the Internet connection WAN for wide area network, but some vendors label this port as "Internet."

When used as shown in Figure 4.3, the AP also includes extra services and capabilities, such as routing, Network Address Translation (NAT), Dynamic Host Configuration Protocol (DHCP), and more. These extra services reduce the setup time required for the WLAN.

Because wireless networks broadcast on known frequency bands, other wireless users can often see them. This includes authorized users, curious neighbors, and attackers.

Fat Versus Thin Access Points

A *fat AP*, also known as a stand-alone, intelligent, or autonomous AP, includes everything needed to connect wireless clients to a wireless network. It typically includes features such as a routing component, NAT, DHCP, wireless security options, access control lists (ACLs), and more. If you're running a wireless network at your home or in a small office network, you are probably using a fat access point. Fat APs must be configured separately from each other, which isn't really a problem if you're only configuring a single AP.

Consider a network that has a dozen APs spread around the organization. If these were all fat APs, administrators would need to configure each one separately, which is highly inefficient. Enter the *thin AP*. A thin AP is a *controller-based AP*, meaning that it isn't a stand-alone AP, but rather an AP managed by a controller. Administrators use a wireless controller to configure and manage thin-based APs. This streamlines the administration by consolidating it in one place.

Thin APs are also making their way into small office and home networks. For example, NETGEAR's Orbi wireless router includes one fat AP and one or more thin satellite APs. You configure the single AP and it then configures the satellite APs.

> ### Remember this
>
> A fat AP is also known as a stand-alone AP and is managed independently. A thin AP is also known as a controller-based AP and is managed by a wireless controller. The wireless controller configures the thin AP.

Band Selection and Channel Widths

Wireless networks use two primary radio bands: 2.4 GHz and 5 GHz. However, wireless devices don't transmit exactly on 2.4 GHz or 5 GHz. Instead, the two bands have multiple channels starting at about 2.4 GHz and 5 GHz. There isn't a single standard that applies to every country, so you'll find that the number of channels within each band varies from country to country.

The Institute of Electrical and Electronics Engineers (IEEE) defines many standards, including the IEEE 802.11 group of wireless network protocols. Table 4.1 shows some common wireless standards along with the frequency band (or bands) they support. It also shows the channel widths supported by each. However, the channel widths are somewhat misleading. For example, 802.11n supports channel widths of both 20 MHz and 40 MHz. However, a 40 MHz channel is two combined 20 MHz channels.

IEEE Standard	Frequency Band	Channel Width
802.11b	2.4 GHz	22 MHz
802.11g	2.4 GHz	20 MHz
802.11n	2.4 GHz and 5 GHz	20 MHz and 40 MHz
802.11ac	5 GHz	20 MHZ, 40 MHz, 80 MHz, and 160 MHz

Table 4.1: Common wireless standards, frequencies, and channel widths

Theoretically, wider channels allow you to transfer more data through the channel. Unfortunately, there are two challenges. First, when you increase the channel width, you decrease the distance of the radio transmissions. A device that connects with a 20 MHz channel at a specific distance away might not be able to connect at 40 MHz from the same location. Second, you increase the possibility of interference. Wider channels are more likely to overlap with other wireless devices and this interference affects overall performance.

These challenges are much more prevalent in the 2.4 GHz band because there are more technologies operating in this band. For example, Bluetooth devices, microwave ovens, and cordless phones operate in this range. Additionally, the 2.4 GHz range has only three nonoverlapping channels. APs typically allow you to choose the frequency band (2.4 GHz and/or 5 GHz). Additionally, most APs allow you to manually select a channel or allow the AP to pick the best channel. The "PSK, Enterprise, and Open Modes" section (found later in this chapter) shows a screenshot of an AP with some of these selections.

Access Point SSID

Wireless networks are identified by a service set identifier (*SSID*), which is simply the name of the wireless network. Some APs still come with default SSIDs, though most vendors have moved away from this practice. For example, the default SSID of some older Linksys APs is "Linksys." Some newer APs force you to enter a name for the SSID when you first install it and do not include a default. From a defense-in-depth perspective, it's a good idea to change the name of the SSID if a default is used. It simply gives attackers less information.

For example, if an attacker sees a wireless network with an SSID of Linksys, the attacker has a good idea that the network is using a Linksys AP. If the attacker knows about specific weaknesses with this AP, he can start exploiting these weaknesses. On the other hand, an AP with an SSID of "Success" doesn't give the attacker any clues about the AP.

Disable SSID Broadcasting or Not

One of the goals of 802.11 wireless networks is ease of use. The designers wanted wireless computers to be able to easily find each other and work together. They were successful with this goal. Unfortunately, attackers can also easily find your networks. By default, APs broadcast the SSID in cleartext, making it easy to locate wireless networks.

At some point years ago, someone stated that the SSID was a password (not true!), and many information technology (IT) professionals latched onto the idea that you can increase security by disabling the SSID broadcast. Others say that the SSID has nothing to do with security and disabling the broadcast reduces usability but does not increase security.

As background, APs must regularly send out a beacon frame to ensure interoperability with other devices in the wireless network. This beacon frame includes the SSID, and if the SSID broadcast is disabled, the SSID entry is blank. However, even if the SSID broadcast is disabled, the AP includes the SSID in Probe responses sent in response to Probe requests from authorized wireless clients. Because of this, it's easy for an attacker with a wireless protocol analyzer to listen for the Probe responses and detect the SSID.

In other words, disabling the SSID makes it a little more difficult for attackers to find your network, but not much. It's almost like locking the front door of your house, but leaving the key in the lock.

Steve Riley wrote in a security blog titled "Myth vs. Reality: Wireless SSIDs" that disabling the SSID for security "is a myth that needs to be forcibly dragged out behind the woodshed, strangled until it wheezes its last labored breath, then shot several times for good measure." In case it isn't clear, Mr. Riley is in the camp that says you should not disable the SSID for security. For the record, I agree with him.

For the CompTIA Security+ exam, you should know that it is possible to disable the SSID broadcast and hide the network from casual users. However, an attacker with a wireless protocol analyzer can easily discover the SSID even if SSID broadcast is disabled.

> **Remember this**
>
> The service set identifier (SSID) identifies the name of the wireless network. You should change the SSID from the default name. Disabling SSID broadcast can hide the network from casual users, but an attacker can easily discover it with a wireless sniffer.

Enable MAC Filtering

Enabling media access control (MAC) filtering provides a small measure of security to a wireless network. As a reminder from your networking studies, the MAC address (also called a physical address or hardware address) is a 48-bit address used to identify network interface cards (NICs). You will usually see the MAC address displayed as six pairs of hexadecimal characters such as 00-16-EA-DD-A6-60. Every NIC, including wireless NICs, has a MAC address.

MAC filtering is a form of network access control. It's used with port security on switches (covered in Chapter 3) and you can use it to restrict access to wireless networks.

For example, Figure 4.4 shows the MAC filter on a NETGEAR Orbi AP. In the figure, you can see that the system is set to Permit PCs Listed Below to Access the Wireless Network. The MAC Address column shows the MAC addresses of the allowed devices. The Status column shows that each of these devices is set to Allows, granting them access. The Block all new devices from connecting setting prevents any other devices from connecting. It's also possible to select the check box for any device, and click on Block to change its status to Blocked.

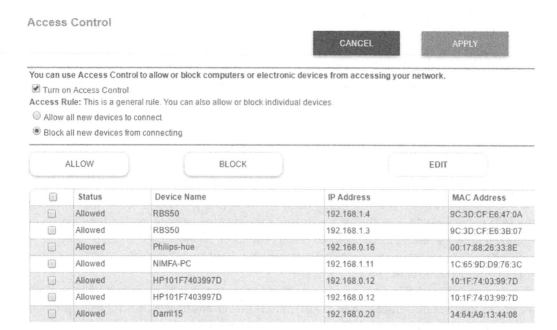

Figure 4.4: MAC filter on an AP

Theoretically, MAC addresses are unique. The MAC filter in Figure 4.4 limits access to only the devices with these MAC addresses. This might sound secure, but an attacker with a wireless sniffer can easily identify the MAC addresses allowed in a wireless network. Additionally, it's very easy to change a MAC address. An attacker can launch a spoofing attack by changing the MAC address on his laptop to impersonate one of the allowed MAC addresses.

Many operating systems include built-in functionality to change a NIC's MAC address. For example, in Windows 10 you can access the NIC's properties from Device Manager, click the Advanced tab, and configure the Network Address setting with a new MAC.

> **Remember this**
>
> MAC filtering can restrict access to a wireless network to specific clients. However, an attacker can use a sniffer to discover allowed MAC addresses and circumvent this form of network access control. It's relatively simple for an attacker to spoof a MAC address.

Antenna Types and Placement

The most commonly used wireless antenna on both APs and wireless devices is an omnidirectional (or omni) antenna. Omnidirectional antennas transmit and receive signals in all directions at the same time. This allows wireless devices to connect to an AP from any direction.

Another type of antenna is a directional antenna. A directional antenna transmits in a single direction and receives signals back from the same direction. Because the power of the antenna is focused in a single direction, the directional antenna has greater gain than an omni antenna, and it can transmit and receive signals over greater distances. The directional antenna also has a very narrow radiation pattern, focusing the signal in a specific area.

When considering antenna placement, you should also configure the antenna orientation. Many APs have adjustable antennas. Should you orient them vertically, pointed straight up? Or, should you orient them horizontally, pointed straight out, even with the floor? It depends. Reception is maximized when your AP's antenna orientation matches the orientation used by your wireless devices. However, you'll find that antenna orientation isn't consistent in all devices. Some place them horizontally and others place them vertically. If your AP has two antennas, some experts recommend orienting one of them horizontally and one of them vertically.

Administrators often perform a site survey while planning and deploying a wireless network. The site survey examines the wireless environment to identify potential issues, such as areas with noise or other devices operating on the same frequency bands. Administrators and security personnel periodically repeat the site survey to verify the environment hasn't changed and to detect potential security issues.

One method of performing a site survey is to configure an AP and position the antenna within the organization. Administrators then measure the power levels of the AP from different areas to determine if it provides the desired coverage. If the AP doesn't provide adequate coverage, administrators might try to modify the placement of the AP and/or its antenna, or add additional APs.

Antenna Power and Signal Strength

You cannot modify the gain of an antenna without changing its physical properties. However, many wireless access points include a power setting that you can manipulate to increase or decrease the transmit power. Administrators sometimes reduce the power level to restrict access to a small area such as a conference room, or to prevent wireless users from connecting from the parking lot or somewhere else outside the building. Similarly, administrators sometimes increase the power level to increase the range of the AP.

Figure 4.5 shows several APs in two buildings. The dotted circles around APs 1 through 6 show their range. They are each using omnidirectional antennas. AP 4 has a larger circle than the others, indicating the power level is the highest in this AP. The two APs labeled A and B are using directional antennas. Organizations sometimes use this configuration to connect networks between two buildings.

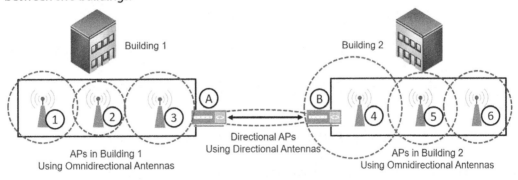

Figure 4.5: Omnidirectional and directional APs

Remember this

You can limit the range of an AP to a room or building by reducing the AP's power level. This prevents people from connecting because they will be out of the AP's range.

Network Architecture Zones

Chapter 3 introduces several zones and topologies used within a network. These commonly provide separation for networks based on usage. Some additional zones and topologies are:

- **Wireless.** Many organizations provide wireless networks for both employees and guests. Wireless networks for employees provide a bridge to a wired network, allowing employees access to all network resources just as if they were connected from a wired PC at their desk.
- **Guest.** A guest network is typically a wireless network used to provide guests with Internet access. The guest network rarely gives guests access to network resources, but instead gives them a simple way to check their email or access web sites.
- **Ad hoc.** In *ad hoc* mode, wireless devices connect to each other without an AP. For example, if you and another user have wireless laptops, you can create an ad hoc wireless network to connect your two computers. Ad hoc is Latin for "as needed," which is a good way to think about an ad hoc wireless network. You create it as needed. In contrast, when you connect to a wireless network via an AP, you are using infrastructure mode.

Wireless Cryptographic Protocols

Because wireless networks broadcast over the air, anyone who has a wireless transceiver can intercept the transmissions. You can secure wireless networks with several different steps, but the most important step is to implement a strong security protocol, such as Wi-Fi Protected Access II (WPA2). The following sections describe the primary security protocols available for wireless networks.

WPA

Wi-Fi Protected Access (*WPA*) was an interim replacement for Wired Equivalent Privacy (WEP). WEP has known vulnerabilities and should not be used. WPA provided an immediate solution to the weaknesses of WEP without requiring users to upgrade their hardware. Even when WPA replaced WEP, its developers recognized that WPA wasn't solid enough to last for an extended period. Instead, WPA improved wireless security by giving users an alternative to WEP with existing hardware while the developers worked on creating the stronger WPA2 protocol.

WPA is susceptible to password-cracking attacks, especially when the AP has a weak passphrase. The attacker uses a wireless protocol analyzer to capture the authentication traffic and then uses an offline brute force attack to discover the passphrase. Attackers often use a disassociation attack (discussed later in this chapter) to force the user to reauthenticate.

WPA2

Wi-Fi Protected Access II (*WPA2*) is the permanent replacement for WPA. WPA2 (also known as IEEE 802.11i) uses stronger cryptography than WPA. The Wi-Fi Alliance requires all devices carrying its WI-FI CERTIFIED logo to meet WPA2 standards, including the use of the Counter Mode with Cipher Block Chaining Message Authentication Code Protocol (*CCMP*).

Although WPA2 provides significant security improvements over previous wireless encryption techniques, some enterprises need stronger security. Another step you can take is to enable authentication with Enterprise mode, described later in this chapter.

TKIP Versus CCMP

Temporal Key Integrity Protocol (*TKIP*) is an older encryption protocol used with WPA, and CCMP is a newer encryption protocol used with WPA2. IEEE has deprecated WPA and TKIP due to various security issues, but many wireless networks are still using these older protocols. IEEE recommends using WPA2 with CCMP because it provides significantly more security.

A benefit of TKIP is that it didn't require new hardware. WEP users could upgrade software and/or firmware and implement WPA with TKIP without the need to replace the hardware. Newer hardware supports WPA2, so the usage of WPA and TKIP is waning. However, you might still see some legacy hardware using WPA and TKIP.

Later implementations of WPA support Advanced Encryption Standard (*AES*) instead of TKIP. Chapter 10 presents AES in more depth, but, in short, it is a very strong and efficient encryption algorithm. Many applications beyond WPA/WPA2 use AES to provide secure encryption and ensure confidentiality. Several people have been successful at cracking WPA with TKIP, so whenever possible, it's best to upgrade WPA to WPA2, or at least upgrade TKIP to use AES.

WPA2 supports CCMP, which is based on AES and is much stronger than WPA using TKIP. WPA2 also employs much more secure methods of managing the encryption keys than WPA.

> ### Remember this
> WPA provided an immediate replacement for WEP and originally used TKIP, which was compatible with older hardware. Later implementations support the stronger AES encryption algorithm. WPA2 is the permanent replacement for WEP and WPA. WPA2 supports CCMP (based on AES), which is much stronger than the older TKIP protocol and CCMP should be used instead of TKIP.

PSK, Enterprise, and Open Modes

Both WPA and WPA2 can operate in either pre-shared key (PSK) or Enterprise modes. When using *PSK* mode, users access the wireless network anonymously with a PSK or passphrase. This doesn't provide authentication. As a reminder, authentication proves a user's identity with the use of credentials such as a username and password. Users claim an identity with a username and prove their identity with a password. Just a passphrase without a username provides authorization without authentication.

In contrast, *Enterprise* mode forces users to authenticate with unique credentials before granting them access to the wireless network. Enterprise mode uses an 802.1x server, often implemented as a RADIUS server, which accesses a database of accounts. If users don't have the proper credentials, Enterprise mode (using an 802.1x server) blocks their access. Also, an 802.1x server can provide certificate-based authentication to increase the security of the authentication process. The authentication protocol (discussed later in this chapter) determines if the 802.1x server will use a certificate or not.

Figure 4.6 shows a screenshot of a NETGEAR Orbi router web page. The Wireless Network section shows the SSID (Success) and selections for 2.4 GHz and 5 GHz channels. The Auto selection for 2.4 GHz allows the AP to automatically select the best channel to use. The 5 GHz Channel selection indicates the device will pick from 48 available channels in this band.

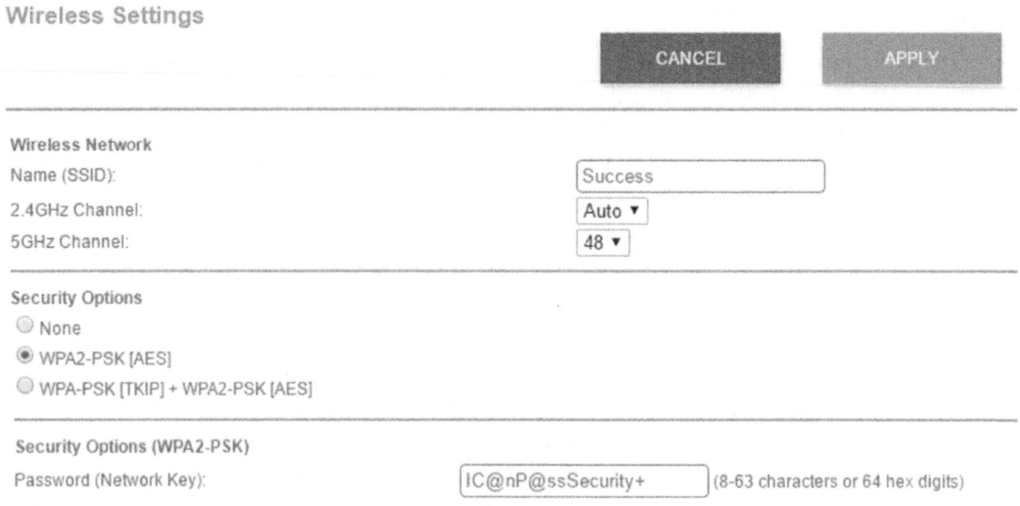

Wireless Settings

	CANCEL	APPLY

Wireless Network

Name (SSID): `Success`

2.4GHz Channel: `Auto ▼`

5GHz Channel: `48 ▼`

Security Options

○ None

◉ WPA2-PSK [AES]

○ WPA-PSK [TKIP] + WPA2-PSK [AES]

Security Options (WPA2-PSK)

Password (Network Key): `IC@nP@ssSecurity+`   (8-63 characters or 64 hex digits)

Figure 4.6: Configuring wireless security

The Security Options section shows that it's selected to use WPA2-PSK with AES and the password (the passphrase or PSK) is IC@nP@ssSecurity+. It can be as many as 63 characters long and the passphrase you enter here is the same passphrase you would enter on all the wireless devices. Many security experts recommend using a passphrase at least 20 characters long, with a mix of uppercase, lowercase, numbers, and special characters. This device also supports the use of WPA for backward compatibility.

Note that the Security Options section also includes a choice of None. If you select None, the AP will operate in *Open* mode, meaning that it doesn't have any security.

Some APs support Enterprise mode, but the one shown in Figure 4.6 doesn't. If it did, it would include a check box to implement WPA2 Enterprise. When you select Enterprise mode, you'll need to enter three pieces of information:

- **RADIUS Server.** You enter the IP address assigned to the 802.1x server, which is often a RADIUS server. This is sometimes referred to as an AAA server.
- **RADIUS port.** You enter the port used by the RADIUS server. The official default port for RADIUS is 1812. However, some vendors have used other ports such as 1645. The key is that you must enter the same port here that the server is using.
- **Shared Secret.** The shared secret is similar to a password and you must enter it here exactly as it is entered on the RADIUS server.

Check out the online labs for this chapter to see how to configure a wireless router using WPA2 Enterprise mode. You can access them at *http://gcgapremium.com/501labs/*.

After configuring WPA2 Enterprise on an AP, it redirects all attempts to connect to the RADIUS server to authenticate. After users authenticate, the RADIUS server tells the AP to grant them access.

Wireless authentication systems using an 802.1x server are more advanced than most home networks need, but many larger organizations use them. In other words, most home networks use Personal mode, but organizations that want to increase wireless security use Enterprise mode. A combination of both a security protocol such as WPA2 and an 802.1x authentication server significantly reduces the chance of a successful access attack against a wireless system.

> **Remember this**
>
> PSK mode (or WPA-PSK and WPA2-PSK) uses a pre-shared key and does not provide individual authentication. Open mode doesn't use any security and allows all users to access the AP. Enterprise mode is more secure than Personal mode, and it provides strong authentication. Enterprise mode uses an 802.1x server (implemented as a RADIUS server) to add authentication.

Authentication Protocols

Wireless networks support several different authentication protocols. Many are built on the Extensible Authentication Protocol (EAP), an authentication framework that provides general guidance for authentication methods. IEEE 802.1x servers typically use one of these methods to increase the level of security during the authentication process. Additionally, while they are often used in wireless networks, they can also be used anywhere an 802.1x server is implemented.

A key point to remember for each of these methods is if they support or require certificates. Some methods are:

- **EAP.** *EAP* provides a method for two systems to create a secure encryption key, also known as a Pairwise Master Key (PMK). Systems then use this key to encrypt all data transmitted between the devices. Both TKIP and AES-based CCMP use this key, though CCMP is much more secure.
- **EAP-Flexible Authentication via Secure Tunneling (EAP-FAST).** Cisco designed *EAP-FAST* as a secure replacement for Lightweight EAP (LEAP) that Cisco also designed. EAP-FAST supports certificates, but they are optional.
- **Protected EAP (PEAP).** *PEAP* provides an extra layer of protection for EAP. The EAP designers assumed that EAP would be used with adequate physical security to ensure the communication channel was secure. In practice, that wasn't always the case, but PEAP protects the channel. PEAP encapsulates and encrypts the EAP conversation in a Transport Layer Security (TLS) tunnel. PEAP requires a certificate on the server, but not the clients. A common implementation is with Microsoft Challenge Handshake Authentication Protocol version 2 (MS-CHAPv2).
- **EAP-Tunneled TLS (EAP-TTLS).** This is an extension of PEAP, allowing systems to use some older authentication methods such as Password Authentication Protocol (PAP) within a TLS tunnel. *EAP-TTLS* requires a certificate on the 802.1x server but not the clients.
- **EAP-TLS.** This is one of the most secure EAP standards and is widely implemented. The primary difference between PEAP and *EAP-TLS* is that it requires certificates on the 802.1x server and on each of the wireless clients.
- **RADIUS Federation.** Chapter 2 covers federations used for single sign-on (SSO). As a reminder, a federation includes two or more entities (such as companies) that share the same identity management system. Users can log on once and access shared resources with the other entity without logging on again. Similarly, it's possible to create a federation using 802.1x and RADIUS servers.

Note that EAP-FAST supports digital certificates, but they are optional. PEAP and EAP-TTLS require a certificate on the server, but not the clients. EAP-TLS requires certificates on both the servers and the clients. Chapter 10 digs into certificates much deeper, but as an introduction, certificates help provide strong authentication and encryption services. However, a Certificate Authority (CA) must issue certificates, so an organization must either purchase certificates from a public CA, or implement a private CA within the network.

> **Remember this**
>
> Enterprise mode requires an 802.1x server. EAP-FAST supports certificates. PEAP and EAP-TTLS require a certificate on the 802.1x server. EAP-TLS also uses TLS, but it requires certificates on both the 802.1x server and each of the clients.

Captive Portals

A **captive portal** is a technical solution that forces clients using web browsers to complete a specific process before it allows them access to the network. Organizations commonly use it as a hot spot that requires users to log on or agree to specific terms before they can access the Internet. Here are three common examples:

- **Free Internet access.** Many hospitals and other medical facilities provide free Internet access to patients and visitors. The captive portal requires users to acknowledge and agree to abide by an acceptable use policy (AUP). Free captive portals rarely require users to log on, but instead just require them to check a box indicating they agree, and then click a button to continue.
- **Paid Internet access.** Many hotels, resorts, cruise ships, and airlines provide Internet access to customers, but on a pay-as-you-go basis. When users attempt to access the Internet, they are redirected to the captive portal and must successfully log on with a pre-created account or enter credit card information to pay for access.
- **Alternative to IEEE 802.1x.** Adding an 802.1x server can be expensive and is sometimes not a feasible option. Organizations can use captive portals as an alternative. It requires users to authenticate before granting them access.

Understanding Wireless Attacks

There are several known attacks against wireless networks. Most can be avoided by using strong security protocols such as WPA2 with CCMP. In contrast, WPA is vulnerable to many attacks, especially if it is using TKIP.

Disassociation Attacks

A **disassociation attack** effectively removes a wireless client from a wireless network. To understand the attack, it's valuable to first understand the normal operation.

After a wireless client authenticates with a wireless AP, the two devices exchange frames, causing the client to be associated with the AP. At any point, a wireless device can send a disassociation frame to the AP to terminate the connection. This frame includes the wireless client's MAC address. When the AP receives the disassociation frame, it deallocates all the memory it was using for the connection.

In a disassociation attack, attackers send a disassociation frame to the AP with a spoofed MAC address of the victim. The AP receives the frame and shuts down the connection. The victim is now disconnected from the AP and must go through the authentication process again to reconnect.

Interestingly, many hotels were using this attack to prevent guests from using their own personal wireless networks. For example, if you have an iPhone with cellular access to the Internet, you can enable the Personal Hotspot feature. This lets you share the connection with other devices, such as a laptop. Some hotels looked for these personal wireless networks, and launched disassociation attacks against them. Customers were then forced to pay for the hotel's wireless services. As an example, the Federal Communications Commission (FCC) fined Marriott Hotel Services $600,000 for launching attacks on its customers that prevented them from using their personal wireless networks.

Remember this

A disassociation attack effectively removes a wireless client from a wireless network, forcing it to reauthenticate. WPS allows users to easily configure a wireless device by entering an eight-digit PIN. A WPS attack guesses all possible PINs until it finds the correct one. It will typically discover the PIN within hours and use it to discover the passphrase.

WPS and WPS Attacks

Wi-Fi Protected Setup (**WPS**) allows users to configure wireless devices without typing in the passphrase. Instead, users can configure devices by pressing buttons or by entering a short eight-digit personal identification number (PIN).

For example, a user can configure a new wireless device by pressing a button on the AP and on the wireless device. It will automatically configure the device within about 30 seconds with no other actions needed. These buttons can be physical buttons on the devices, or virtual buttons that the user clicks via an application or web page. When using the PIN method, users first identify the eight-digit PIN on the AP and then enter the PIN on the new wireless device.

Unfortunately, WPS is susceptible to brute force attacks. A **WPS attack** keeps trying different PINs until it succeeds. As an example, Reaver is an open source tool freely available that allows attackers to discover the PIN within 10 hours, and often much quicker. Once it discovers the PIN, it can then discover the passphrase in both WPA and WPA2 wireless networks.

Security experts recommend disabling WPS on all devices. This is typically possible via the AP configuration page. Even if you choose to enable WPS to easily connect some devices, you should immediately turn it off once you're done.

Rogue AP

A rogue access point (**rogue AP**) is an AP placed within a network without official authorization. It might be an employee who is bypassing security or installed by an attacker. If an employee installs a rogue AP, the chances are higher that this AP will not be managed properly, increasing vulnerabilities to the network.

Generically, you can think of a rogue as a scoundrel, a crook, or a villain. Clearly, if a rogue is a crook or villain, then rogue access points are not an administrator's friend. You might also see them called counterfeit access points, which is also a clear indication they aren't legitimate.

Attackers may connect a rogue access point to network devices in wireless closets that lack adequate physical security. This access point acts as a sniffer to capture traffic passing through the wired network device, and then broadcasts the traffic using the wireless capability of the AP. The attacker can then capture the exfiltrated data files while sitting in the parking lot. Data exfiltration is the unauthorized transfer of data from an organization to a location controlled by an attacker.

Additionally, attackers may be able to use the rogue access point to connect into the wired network. This works the same way that regular users can connect to a wired network via a wireless network. The difference is that the attacker configures all the security for the counterfeit access point and can use it for malicious purposes.

If you discover an unauthorized AP, you should disconnect it as quickly as possible. A basic first step to take when you discover any attack is to contain or isolate the threat. By simply unplugging the Ethernet cable, you can stop the unauthorized AP from capturing network traffic.

Evil Twin

An **evil twin** is a rogue access point with the same SSID as a legitimate access point. For example, many public places such as coffee shops, hotels, and airports include free Wi-Fi as a service. An attacker can set up an AP using the same SSID as the public Wi-Fi network, and many unsuspecting users will connect to this evil twin.

Once a user connects to an evil twin, wireless traffic goes through the evil twin instead of the legitimate AP. Often, the attacker presents bogus logon pages to users to capture usernames and passwords. Other times, they simply capture traffic from the connection, such as email or text typed into web page text boxes, and analyze it to detect sensitive information they can exploit.

Although it might sound complex to set up an evil twin, it's rather easy. Attackers can configure a laptop that has a wireless access card as an AP. With it running, the attackers look just like any other user in a coffee shop or airport waiting area. They'll have their laptop open and appear to be working (just like you perhaps), and you'll have no idea they are trying to steal your credentials or other personal data that you send over the Internet via the evil twin. Similarly, attackers can set one up in a parking lot or another location close to an organization and try to trick employees or visitors.

Often, administrators will use wireless scanners to perform site surveys. In addition to detecting noise on frequency bands, they can also detect rogue APs, including evil twins. The site survey can help them identify the physical location of access points because the signal will get stronger as the administrator gets closer.

> ## Remember this
>
> Rogue access points are often used to capture and exfiltrate data. An evil twin is a rogue access point using the same SSID as a legitimate access point. A secure AP blocks unauthorized users, but a rogue access point provides access to unauthorized users.

Jamming Attacks

Attackers can transmit noise or another radio signal on the same frequency used by a wireless network. This interferes with the wireless transmissions and can seriously degrade performance. This type of denial-of-service attack is commonly called **jamming** and it usually prevents all users from connecting to a wireless network. In some cases, users have intermittent connectivity because the interference causes them to lose their association with the AP and forces them to try to reconnect.

In some cases, you can increase the power levels of the AP to overcome the attack. Another method of overcoming the attack is to use different wireless channels. Each wireless standard has several channels you can use, and if one channel is too noisy, you can use another one. Although this is useful to overcome interference in home networks, it won't be as effective to combat an interference attack. If you switch channels, the attacker can also switch channels.

IV Attacks

A wireless initialization vector (IV) attack attempts to discover the pre-shared key from the IV. The IV is simply a number. Some wireless protocols use an IV by combining it with the pre-shared key to encrypt data-in-transit. An *IV attack* is successful when an encryption system reuses the same IV. Unfortunately, WEP uses a relatively small 24-bit number for the IV. This small IV results in wireless networks reusing keys.

In many IV attacks, the attacker uses packet injection techniques to add additional packets into the data stream. The AP responds with more packets, increasing the probability that it will reuse a key. An IV attack using packet injection decreases the time it takes to crack a WEP key to a very short time, sometimes less than a minute. It's worth repeating that WEP has been deprecated and should not be used.

NFC Attacks

Near field communication (NFC) is a group of standards used on mobile devices that allow them to communicate with other mobile devices when they are close to them. For example, you can share pictures, contacts, and other data with friends. One person shares the data, and after placing the smartphones close to each other, the other person selects it to download.

During an *NFC attack*, an attacker uses an NFC reader to capture data from another NFC device. One method is an eavesdropping attack. The NFC reader uses an antenna to boost its range, and intercepts the data transfer between two other devices.

A more advanced attack was discovered by security researchers in 2012. They designed Trojan malware and installed it on an Android-based smartphone. They used the Trojan to initiate a payment. The NFC reader was then able to capture the payment data and use it in a live payment transaction. Google quickly modified Google Wallet to prevent this type of attack.

Bluetooth Attacks

Bluetooth is a short-range wireless system used in personal area networks (PANs) and within networks. A PAN is a network of devices close to a single person. Bluetooth devices include smartphones, headsets, and computer devices.

The range of Bluetooth was originally designed for about three meters (about 10 feet), but the range is often farther, and ultimately extends beyond a person's personal space. Attackers have discovered methods of exploiting these networks. Some common attacks are bluejacking, bluesnarfing, and bluebugging:

- **Bluejacking** is the practice of sending unsolicited messages to nearby Bluetooth devices. Bluejacking messages are typically text, but can also be images or sounds. Bluejacking is relatively harmless, but does cause some confusion when users start receiving messages.

- **Bluesnarfing** refers to the unauthorized access to, or theft of information from, a Bluetooth device. A bluesnarfing attack can access information, such as email, contact lists, calendars, and text messages. Attackers use tools such as hcitool and obexftp.
- Bluebugging is like bluesnarfing, but it goes a step further. In addition to gaining full access to the phone, the attacker installs a backdoor. The attacker can have the phone call the attacker at any time, allowing the attacker to listen in on conversations within a room. Attackers can also listen in on phone conversations, enable call forwarding, send messages, and more.

When Bluetooth devices are first configured, they are configured in Discovery mode. Bluetooth devices use MAC addresses, and in Discovery mode the Bluetooth device broadcasts its MAC address, allowing other devices to see it and connect to it. This is required when pairing Bluetooth devices.

In earlier versions of Bluetooth, this pairing process could happen any time a device is in Discovery mode. However, most software vendors have rewritten their software to prevent this. Today, users typically manually pair the device. If a user doesn't acknowledge an attempted pairing, it fails. As a result, Bluetooth attacks are rare today. However, if a device doesn't require a user to manually pair a device, it is still susceptible to these attacks.

> **Remember this**
>
> Bluejacking is the unauthorized sending of text messages to a nearby Bluetooth device. Bluesnarfing is the unauthorized access to, or theft of information from, a Bluetooth device. Ensuring devices cannot be paired without manual user intervention prevents these attacks.

Wireless Replay Attacks

In a **replay attack**, an attacker captures data sent between two entities, modifies it, and then attempts to impersonate one of the parties by replaying the data. WPA2 using CCMP and AES is not vulnerable to replay attacks. However, WPA using TKIP is vulnerable to replay attacks.

WPA uses a sequence counter to number the packets and an access point will reject packets received out of order. Additionally, TKIP uses a 64-bit Message Integrity Check (MIC) to verify the integrity of the packets. While this sounds secure, security experts identified a method to discover the MIC key. After discovering the key, an attacker can transmit and decrypt packets. Later, other security experts improved this attack allowing them to launch a replay attack. This is one of the reasons that TKIP was deprecated in 2012 and should not be used.

RFID Attacks

Radio-frequency identification (RFID) systems include an RFID reader and RFID tags placed on objects. They are used to track and manage inventory, and any type of valuable assets, including objects and animals.

There's an almost endless assortment of tags available for multiple purposes. This includes tags implanted into animals, packaging for any type of product (such as computers), pharmaceuticals, transportation systems (such as shipping containers, railcars, and busses), and controlled substances (such as pharmaceutical containers). Some tags are only slightly larger than a grain of rice.

Tags do not have a power source. Instead, they include electronics that allow them to collect and use power to transmit data stored on the device. This is similar to how a proximity card (described in Chapter 9, "Implementing Controls to Protect Assets") receives a charge from a proximity card reader and then transmits data to the reader. One difference is that RFID transmitters can transmit to and from tags from a much greater distance than proximity readers.

Some of the common **RFID attacks** are:

- **Sniffing or eavesdropping.** Because RFID transmits data over the air, it's possible for an attacker to collect it by listening. A key requirement is to know the frequency used by the RFID system and have a receiver that can be tuned to that frequency. The attacker also needs to know the protocols used by the RFID system to interpret the data.
- **Replay.** Successful eavesdropping attacks allow the attacker to perform a replay attack. For example, an attacker can configure a bogus tag to mimic the tag attached to a valuable object. The attacker can then steal the valuable object without the theft being easily detected.
- **DoS.** A denial-of-service (DoS) attack attempts to disrupt services. If an attacker knows the frequency used by the RFID system, it's possible to launch a jamming or interference attack, flooding the frequency with noise. This prevents the RFID system from operating normally.

> ### Remember this
>
> WPA2 using CCMP and AES prevents wireless replay attacks. TKIP is vulnerable and should not be used. Radio-frequency identification (RFID) attacks include eavesdropping, replay, and DoS.

Misconfigured Access Points

One of the primary reasons that wireless attacks are successful is because APs are misconfigured. For example, if an AP is not using WPA2 with AES and CCMP, it is susceptible to many attacks. Similarly, if WPS is enabled on an AP, a WPS attack can discover the PIN in a few hours simply by guessing. After it discovers the PIN, it can discover the passphrase.

The Configuring a Wireless Router Lab shows how to configure several security settings on a wireless router. Although your wireless router might be a little different, you'll still be able to see many of the typical configuration settings. You can access this lab and other online exercises for this book at *http://gcgapremium.com/501labs/*.

Using VPNs for Remote Access

Chapter 3 covers several use cases for remote access, including the use of Secure Shell (SSH) and Remote Desktop Protocol (RDP). A virtual private network (**VPN**) is another method used for remote access. VPNs allow users to access private networks via a public network. The public network is most commonly the Internet, but it can also be a semiprivate leased line from a telecommunications company. Because the telecommunications company will often lease access to one physical line to several companies, the leased line is not truly private.

Access over a public network is a core security concern with VPNs. Different tunneling protocols encapsulate and encrypt the traffic to protect the data from unauthorized disclosure. The tunnel prevents anyone from reading the data transferred through it.

VPNs and VPN Concentrators

It's possible to create a VPN by enabling services on a server. For example, if you have a Windows server, you can enable the Direct Access VPN role and configure the Routing and Remote Access console. The only additional hardware requirement is that the server has two network interface cards (NICs). One NIC is accessible from the Internet, and the second NIC provides access to the private network. If you are only supporting a few VPN clients, this might be the perfect solution.

Larger organizations often use a VPN concentrator, which is a dedicated device used for VPNs. A VPN concentrator includes all the services needed to create a VPN, including strong encryption and authentication techniques, and it supports many clients.

When using a VPN concentrator, you would typically place it in the DMZ. The firewall between the Internet and the DMZ would forward VPN traffic to the VPN concentrator. The concentrator would route all private VPN traffic to the firewall between the DMZ and the intranet.

Remember this

A virtual private network (VPN) provides remote access to a private network via a public network. VPN concentrators are dedicated devices used for VPNS. They include all the services needed to create a secure VPN supporting many clients.

Remote Access VPN

Figure 4.7 shows an example of how users can connect to internal networks from remote locations. The VPN client first connects to the Internet using a broadband connection to an Internet Service Provider (ISP). After connecting to the Internet, the VPN client can then initiate the VPN connection.

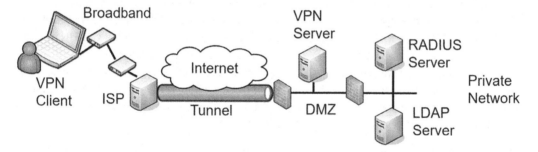

Figure 4.7: Connecting to a VPN server

The VPN server is in the DMZ and reachable through a public IP address. This makes it accessible from any other host on the Internet. A VPN server needs to authenticate clients. A common method is to use an internal Remote Authentication Dial-in User Service (RADIUS) server. When a user logs on, the VPN server sends the user's credentials to the RADIUS server.

While the RADIUS server might have a database of users and passwords, it's more common for it to pass the credentials on to another server to validate them. For example, the RADIUS server can pass the credentials on to a Lightweight Directory Access Protocol (LDAP) server during the authentication process. In a Microsoft domain, the LDAP server is a domain controller.

IPsec as a Tunneling Protocol

Chapter 3 introduces Internet Protocol security (*IPsec*) as a method of encrypting data-in-transit. IPsec supports both Tunnel mode and Transport mode.

Tunnel mode encrypts the entire IP packet used in the internal network, and is the mode used with VPNs transmitted over the Internet. The benefit is that the IP addressing used within the internal network is encrypted and not visible to anyone who intercepts the traffic. If someone does intercept the traffic, he can see the source IP address from the client and the destination address to the VPN server, but the internal IP address information remains hidden.

Transport mode only encrypts the payload and is commonly used in private networks, but not with VPNs. If traffic is transmitted and used only within a private network, there isn't any need to hide the IP addresses by encrypting them.

IPsec provides security in two ways:

- **Authentication.** IPsec includes an Authentication Header (*AH*) to allow each of the hosts in the IPsec conversation to authenticate with each other before exchanging data. AH provides authentication and integrity. AH uses protocol number 51.
- **Encryption.** IPsec includes Encapsulating Security Payload (*ESP*) to encrypt the data and provide confidentiality. ESP includes AH so it provides confidentiality, authentication, and integrity. ESP uses protocol number 50.

The term protocol number might look like a typo, but it isn't. AH and ESP are identified with protocol numbers, not port numbers. Chapter 3 discusses routers and firewalls. You may remember from Chapter 3 that a basic packet-filtering firewall can filter packets based on IP addresses, ports, and some protocols, such as Internet Control Message Protocol (ICMP) and IPsec. Packet filters use the protocol numbers to identify AH and ESP traffic.

IPsec uses Internet Key Exchange (IKE) over port 500 to authenticate clients in the IPsec conversation. IKE creates security associations (SAs) for the VPN and uses these to set up a secure channel between the client and the VPN server.

TLS as a Tunneling Protocol

Some tunneling protocols use Transport Layer Security (TLS) to secure the VPN channel. As an example, Secure Socket Tunneling Protocol (SSTP) encrypts VPN traffic using TLS over port 443. Using port 443 provides a lot of flexibility for many administrators and rarely requires opening additional firewall ports. It is a useful alternative when the VPN tunnel must go through a device using NAT, and IPsec is not feasible. OpenVPN and OpenConnect are two open source applications that can use TLS to create a secure channel. While this can also use Secure Sockets Layer (SSL), SSL has known weaknesses and TLS is the designated replacement.

Split Tunnel Versus Full Tunnel

Imagine that Lisa connects to a company VPN server using IPsec from her home computer. The VPN is using ESP so all traffic in the tunnel is encrypted. Now, Lisa wants to do an Internet search on saxophones. Will her computer connect directly to the Internet for her search? Or will her computer make a connection through the VPN server first? It depends on how the VPN is configured.

In a *split tunnel*, a VPN administrator determines what traffic should use the encrypted tunnel. For example, it's possible to configure the tunnel to only encrypt traffic going to private

IP addresses used within the private network. If Lisa did an Internet search with the VPN server configured in a split tunnel configuration, her Internet search traffic will not go through the encrypted tunnel. Instead, her search will go directly to Internet sites via her ISP.

In a **full tunnel**, all traffic goes through the encrypted tunnel while the user is connected to the VPN. If Lisa was connected to the VPN and then tried to connect to a public web site, the traffic would first go through the encrypted tunnel and then out to the public web site from within the private network. If the private network routed Internet traffic through a unified threat management (**UTM**) device, Lisa's traffic would go through the UTM device. The web site would send web pages back to the UTM device and the VPN server would encrypt it and send it back to Lisa via the encrypted tunnel.

Chapter 3 discusses UTM devices. As a reminder, a UTM device can perform URL filtering, malware inspection, and content inspection of all traffic sent through it. This is one of the reasons why an organization may choose to use a full tunnel for users connected to a VPN server. A disadvantage is that it can be slow. Not only is the Internet traffic taking an indirect route through the VPN server, but it's also being encrypted and decrypted a couple of times.

> ### Remember this
>
> IPsec is a secure encryption protocol used with VPNs. Encapsulating Security Payload (ESP) provides confidentiality, integrity, and authentication for VPN traffic. IPsec uses Tunnel mode for VPN traffic and can be identified with protocol ID 50 for ESP. It uses IKE over port 500. A full tunnel encrypts all traffic after a user has connected to a VPN. A split tunnel only encrypts traffic destined for the VPN's private network.

Site-to-Site VPNs

A site-to-site VPN includes two VPN servers that act as gateways for two networks separated geographically. For example, an organization can have two locations. One is its headquarters and the other is a remote office. It can use two VPN servers to act as gateways to connect the networks at the two locations together, as shown in Figure 4.8.

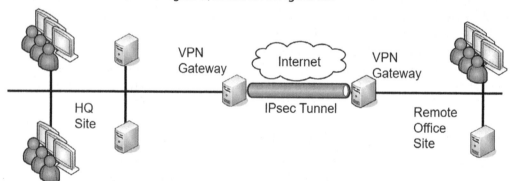

Figure 4.8: Site-to-site VPN

A benefit of the site-to-site model is that it connects both networks without requiring additional steps on the part of the user. Users in the remote office can connect to servers in the headquarters location as easily as if the servers were in the remote office. Connecting to the remote server might be slower than connecting to a local server, but, otherwise, it's transparent to end users.

In contrast, in a traditional remote access VPN (also called a host-to-gateway model), the end user makes the direct connection to the VPN server and is very much aware of the process.

Always-On VPN

Some VPNs are always-on VPNs. They can be used with both site-to-site VPNs and remote access VPNs. When used with a site-to-site VPN, the two VPN gateways maintain the VPN connection. In contrast, some site-to-site VPNs use an on-demand connection. The VPN connection is only established when a user connects to a remote system.

Several vendors have always-on VPNs for remote access VPNs. They attempt to create the VPN connection as soon as the user's device connects to the Internet. For a home user, this might be right after the user turns on a desktop PC or laptop computer.

When configured on mobile devices, such as cell phones, the device will connect to the always-on VPN anytime the device connects to an Internet connection. As an example, if a user visits a coffee shop that has free Internet access and the user connects to the network, the device will automatically connect to the always-on VPN.

Network Access Control

Allowing remote access to your private network can expose your network to a significant number of risks from the clients. If a user logs on to a VPN with a malware-infected computer, this computer can then infect other computers on the internal network. Network access control (**NAC**) methods provide continuous security monitoring by inspecting computers and preventing them from accessing the network if they don't pass the inspection.

Most administrators have complete control over computers in their network. For example, they can ensure the clients have up-to-date antivirus software installed, operating systems have current patches applied, and their firewalls are enabled. However, administrators don't have complete control of computers employees use at home or on the road.

NAC provides a measure of control for these other computers. It ensures that clients meet predetermined characteristics prior to accessing a network. NAC systems often use *health* as a metaphor, indicating that a client meets these predetermined characteristics. Just as doctors can quarantine patients with certain illnesses, NAC can quarantine or isolate unhealthy clients that don't meet the predefined NAC conditions.

Host Health Checks

Administrators set predefined conditions for healthy clients and those that meet these preset conditions can access the network. The NAC system isolates computers that don't meet the conditions. Common health conditions checked by a NAC are:

- Up-to-date antivirus software, including updated signature definitions
- Up-to-date operating system, including current patches and fixes
- Firewall enabled on the client

NAC systems use authentication agents (sometimes called health agents) to inspect NAC clients. These agents are applications or services that check different conditions on the computer and document the status in a statement of health. When a client connects to a NAC-controlled network, the agent reports the health status of the NAC client.

Consider Figure 4.9. When a VPN client accesses the network, the VPN server queries the NAC health server to determine required health conditions. The VPN server also queries the client for a statement of the client's health. If the client meets all health requirements, the NAC system allows the client to access the network.

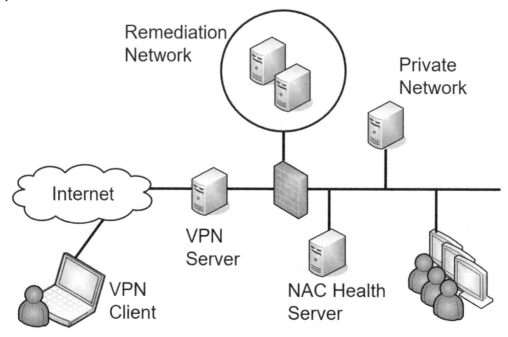

Figure 4.9: Using network access control

However, if a client doesn't meet the health conditions mandated by the NAC server, the VPN server redirects the client to a remediation network (also called a quarantine network). The remediation network includes resources the client can use to get healthy. For example, it would include current approved patches, antivirus software, and updated virus signatures. The client can use these resources to improve its health and then try to access the network again.

While NAC can inspect the health of VPN clients, you can also use it to inspect the health of internal clients. For example, internal computers may occasionally miss patches and be vulnerable. NAC will detect the unpatched system and quarantine it. If you use this feature, it's important that the detection is accurate. A false positive by the NAC system can quarantine a healthy client, and prevent it from accessing the network.

Similarly, your organization may allow visitors or employees to plug in their mobile computers to live wall jacks for connectivity, or connect to a wireless network. NAC inspects the clients, and if they don't meet health conditions, they may be granted Internet access through the network but remain isolated from any other network activity.

Permanent Versus Dissolvable

Agents on clients can be either dissolvable or permanent. A ***permanent agent*** (sometimes called a persistent NAC agent) is installed on the client and stays on the client. NAC uses the agent when the client attempts to log on remotely. This is the most common implementation for corporate-owned devices, and for approved laptops and PCs that employees use to connect remotely.

A *dissolvable agent* is downloaded and run on the client when the client logs on remotely. It collects the information it needs, identifies the client as healthy or not healthy, and reports the status back to the NAC system. Some dissolvable NAC agents remove themselves immediately after they report back to the NAC system. Others remove themselves after the remote session ends.

Dissolvable agents are often used on mobile devices when an organization has implemented a bring your own device (BYOD) policy. Employee-owned devices are inspected for health, but the organization doesn't require users to install extra software on their devices. However, these dissolvable agents can detect vulnerabilities on mobile devices, such as a jail-broken or rooted device. A jail-broken Apple device removes software restrictions, such as the ability to install software from sources other than the Apple store. A rooted Android device has been modified, allowing root-level access to, and the ability to modify, the Android operating system.

Many NAC vendors refer to dissolvable agents as an agentless capability, though this is somewhat of a misnomer. The NAC is still using an agent to inspect the client, but it is not installing the agent on the client.

> ### Remember this
>
> Network access control (NAC) includes methods to inspect clients for health, such as having up-to-date antivirus software. NAC can restrict access of unhealthy clients to a remediation network. You can use NAC for VPN clients and for internal clients. Permanent agents are installed on the clients. Dissolvable agents (sometimes called agentless) are not installed on the clients and are often used to inspect employee-owned mobile devices.

Identity and Access Services

An important step when implementing a VPN is to ensure only authorized entities can access it. Authorization begins with authentication, and VPNs support multiple methods of authentication. The following sections describe the different remote access authentication mechanisms in more depth, but here's a quick introduction:

- **Password Authentication Protocol (PAP).** PAP sends passwords in cleartext so PAP is used only as a last resort.
- **Challenge Handshake Authentication Protocol (CHAP).** CHAP uses a handshake process where the server challenges the client. The client then responds with appropriate authentication information.
- **Microsoft CHAP (MS-CHAP).** This is the Microsoft implementation of CHAP, which is used only by Microsoft clients.
- **MS-CHAPv2.** MS-CHAP is deprecated in favor of MS-CHAPv2. It includes several improvements, including the ability to perform mutual authentication.
- **Remote Authentication Dial-In User Service (RADIUS).** RADIUS provides a centralized method of authentication for multiple remote access servers. RADIUS encrypts the password packets, but not the entire authentication process.
- **Diameter.** Diameter was created to overcome some of the limitations of RADIUS and is often used instead of RADIUS.
- **Terminal Access Controller Access-Control System Plus (TACACS+).** TACACS+ is an alternative to RADIUS, but it is proprietary to Cisco systems. A benefit of TACACS+ is that

it can interact with Kerberos, allowing it to work with a broader range of environments, including Microsoft domains using Kerberos. Additionally, TACACS+ encrypts the entire authentication process, whereas RADIUS encrypts only the password.

PAP

Password Authentication Protocol (**PAP**) is used with Point-to-Point Protocol (PPP) to authenticate clients. A significant weakness of PAP is that it sends passwords over a network in cleartext, representing a significant security risk.

PPP was primarily used with dial-up connections. Believe it or not, there was a time when the thought of someone wiretapping a phone was rather remote. Because of this, security was an afterthought with PPP. Today, PPP is only used as a last resort due to passwords being passed in cleartext, or it is used with another protocol that provides encryption.

CHAP

Challenge Handshake Authentication Protocol (**CHAP**) also uses PPP and authenticates remote users, but it is more secure than PAP. The goal of CHAP is to allow the client to pass credentials over a public network (such as a phone or the Internet) without allowing attackers to intercept the data and later use it in an attack.

The client and server both know a shared secret (similar to a password) used in the authentication process. However, the client doesn't send the shared secret over the network in plaintext as PAP does. Instead, the client hashes it after combining it with a nonce (number used once) provided by the server. This handshake process is used when the client initially tries to connect to the server, and at different times during the connection.

> **Remember this**
>
> PAP authentication uses a password or a PIN. A significant weakness is that PAP sends the information across a network in cleartext, making it susceptible to sniffing attacks. CHAP is more secure than PAP because passwords are not sent over the network in cleartext.

MS-CHAP and MS-CHAPv2

Microsoft introduced Microsoft Challenge Handshake Authentication Protocol (MS-CHAP) as an improvement over CHAP for Microsoft clients. MS-CHAP supported clients as old as Windows 95. Later, Microsoft improved MS-CHAP with MS-CHAPv2.

A significant improvement of **MS-CHAPv2** over MS-CHAP is the ability to perform mutual authentication. Not only does the client authenticate to the server, but the server also authenticates to the client. Chapter 7, "Protecting Against Advanced Attacks," covers different types of attacks, including attacks in which an attacker may try to impersonate a server. Mutual authentication provides assurances of the server's identity before the client transmits data, which reduces the risk of a client sending sensitive data to a rogue server.

RADIUS

Remote Authentication Dial-In User Service (**RADIUS**) is a centralized authentication service. Instead of each individual VPN server needing a separate database to identify who can authenticate, the VPN servers forward the authentication requests to a central RADIUS server. RADIUS can also be used as an 802.1x server with WPA2 Enterprise mode (described earlier in this chapter).

Imagine your company has locations in Virginia Beach, Atlanta, and Chicago. Each location has a VPN server that users can access. Bart is a traveling salesman, and he can connect to any of these VPN servers. When entering sales data, he connects to the Atlanta VPN. When using the company-sponsored always-on VPN for his mobile devices, he connects to the Virginia Beach VPN server. Bart has one account for all company access and today he was prompted to change his password.

If each VPN server has a separate database with Bart's username and password, each of these databases must be updated. This can be labor intensive and result in needless errors.

However, the company could use a centralized RADIUS server, as shown in Figure 4.10, instead. Each VPN server is configured with a shared secret (similar to a password) and the RADIUS server is configured with a matching shared secret for each of the VPN servers.

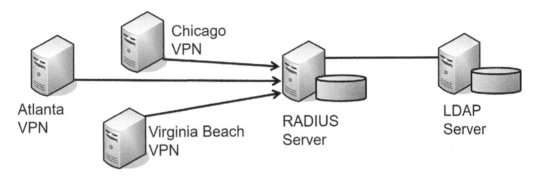

Figure 4.10: RADIUS configuration

This centralized RADIUS server could hold a centralized database of user accounts. However, it is more common for the RADIUS server to access an LDAP server that holds the accounts. For example, in a Microsoft domain, the RADIUS server would pass the credentials to a domain controller. A significant benefit is that there is only one account for the user. If Bart changes his password, the domain controller knows the new password.

RADIUS uses the User Datagram Protocol (UDP), which provides a best-effort delivery mechanism. As a result, RADIUS includes logic to detect communication problems. In contrast, RADIUS alternatives use TCP, which provides guaranteed delivery. These alternatives allow TCP to detect and handle communication issues. Also, RADIUS only encrypts the password, while alternatives encrypt the entire authentication process.

Even though RADIUS was created before Extensible Authentication Protocol (EAP) was developed, RADIUS does work with EAP. RFC 3579 "RADIUS Support for EAP" is an informational RFC and describes how to do so. However, alternatives make it easier to extend the use of EAP.

TACACS+

Terminal Access Controller Access-Control System Plus (**TACACS+**) is the Cisco alternative to RADIUS. It provides two important security benefits over RADIUS. First, it encrypts the entire authentication process, whereas RADIUS encrypts only the password. Second, TACACS+ uses multiple challenges and responses between the client and the server.

Although TACACS+ is proprietary to Cisco, it can interact with Kerberos. This allows a Cisco VPN concentrator to interact in a Microsoft Active Directory environment. As a reminder, Microsoft Active Directory uses Kerberos for authentication.

Organizations also use TACACS+ as an authentication service for network devices. In other words, you can use it to authenticate users before they are able to access a configuration page for a router or a switch. The network devices must be TACACS+ enabled, and a TACACS+ server provides the authentication services.

Diameter

Diameter is an extension of RADIUS and many organizations have switched to it due to its extra capabilities. Diameter adds several other commands beyond the capabilities of RADIUS, along with adding new commands that can be used with EAP. Diameter uses TCP instead of UDP used by RADIUS. A key benefit is that it is backwards compatible with RADIUS and provides an upgrade path from RADIUS to Diameter.

In geometry, the diameter of a circle is a straight line between the two edges of a circle, whereas the radius is a straight line from the center to an edge. In other words, the diameter of a circle is twice as long as the radius. The designers considered this when naming Diameter to indicate indirectly that it is twice as good as RADIUS.

> **Remember this**
>
> RADIUS, TACACS+, and Diameter all provide centralized authentication. TACACS+ is proprietary to Cisco, but can be used with Kerberos. Diameter is an improvement over RADIUS, and it supports many additional capabilities, including securing transmissions with EAP.

AAA Protocols

AAA protocols provide authentication, authorization, and accounting. Authentication verifies a user's identification. Authorization determines if a user should have access. Accounting tracks user access with logs.

As an example, RADIUS, TACACS+, and Diameter are considered AAA protocols because they provide all three services. They authenticate users who attempt remote access, determine if the user is authorized for remote access by checking a database, and then record the user's activity. TACACS+ uses multiple challenges and responses during a session. Kerberos is sometimes referred to as an AAA protocol, but it does not provide any accounting services.

Chapter 4 Exam Topic Review

When preparing for the exam, make sure you understand these key concepts covered in this chapter.

Exploring Advanced Security Devices

- Intrusion detection systems (IDSs) and intrusion prevention systems (IPSs) inspect traffic using the same functionality as a protocol analyzer.
- A host-based IDS (HIDS) can detect attacks on local systems such as workstations and servers. The HIDS protects local resources on the host and can detect some malware

that isn't detected by traditional antivirus software. A network-based IDS (NIDS) detects attacks on networks.

- A signature-based IDS or IPS uses signatures to detect known attacks or vulnerabilities.
- Heuristic-based or behavioral-based IDSs (also called anomaly-based IDSs) require a baseline and detect attacks based on anomalies or when traffic is outside expected boundaries.
- A false positive incorrectly raises an alert indicating an attack when an attack is not active. False positives increase the workload of administrators. A false negative is when an attack is active, but not reported.
- An IPS is similar to an active IDS except that it's placed inline with the traffic (sometimes called in-band) and can stop attacks before they reach the internal network. An IPS can actively monitor data streams, detect malicious content, and prevent it from reaching a network. In contrast, an IDS is out-of-band.
- IDSs and IPSs can also protect internal private networks, such as private supervisory control and data acquisition (SCADA) networks.
- SSL/TLS accelerators are dedicated hardware devices that handle Transport Layer Security (TLS) traffic. Other devices, such as a web server, can off-load TLS traffic handling to the accelerator.
- SSL decryptors allow an organization to inspect traffic, even when traffic is using SSL or TLS.
- A software defined network (SDN) uses virtualization technologies to route traffic instead of using hardware routers and switches. It separates the data and control planes.
- Honeypots and honeynets appear to have valuable data and attempt to divert attackers away from live networks. Security personnel use them to observe current attack methodologies and gather intelligence on attacks.
- An 802.1x server provides strong port security using port-based authentication. It prevents rogue devices from connecting to a network by ensuring that only authorized clients can connect.

Securing Wireless Networks

- Wireless access points (APs) connect wireless clients to a wired network.
- A fat AP, also known as a stand-alone AP, includes everything needed to connect wireless clients to a wireless network.
- Thin APs are controller-based APs. A controller configures and manages a thin AP.
- The service set identifier (SSID) is the name of the wireless network. Disabling the SSID broadcast hides a wireless network from casual users.
- You can restrict access to wireless networks with media access control (MAC) filtering. However, attackers can discover authorized MACs and spoof an authorized MAC address.
- Most WAPs have omnidirectional antennas. Directional antennas have narrower beams and longer ranges.
- An ad hoc wireless network is two or more devices connected together without an AP.
- Wi-Fi Protected Access (WPA) can use Temporal Key Integrity Protocol (TKIP) or Counter Mode Cipher Block Chaining Message Authentication Code Protocol (CCMP). Both WPA and TKIP have been deprecated.
- Personal mode uses a pre-shared key (PSK). It is easy to implement and is used in many smaller wireless networks.

- Enterprise mode is more secure than Personal mode because it adds authentication. It uses an 802.1x authentication server implemented as a RADIUS server.
- Open mode doesn't use a PSK or an 802.1x server. Many hot spots use Open mode when providing free wireless access to customers.
- 802.1x servers use one of the Extensible Authentication Protocol (EAP) versions, such as Protected EAP (PEAP), EAP-Tunneled TLS (EAP-TTLS), EAP-TLS, or EAP-Flexible Authentication via Secure Tunneling (EAP-FAST).
- The most secure EAP method is EAP-TLS, and it requires a certificate on the server and on each of the wireless clients. PEAP and EAP-TTLS require a certificate on the server, but not the client. PEAP is often implemented with Microsoft Challenge Handshake Authentication Protocol version 2 (MS-CHAPv2). LEAP is proprietary to Cisco and does not require a certificate. Cisco designed EAP-FAST to replace Lightweight EAP (LEAP).
- A captive portal forces wireless clients to complete a process, such as acknowledging a policy or paying for access, before it grants them access to the network.

Understanding Wireless Attacks

- A disassociation attack effectively removes a wireless client from a wireless network, forcing it to reauthenticate.
- Wi-Fi Protected Setup (WPS) allows users to easily configure a wireless device by pressing a button or entering a short PIN. WPS is not secure. A WPS attack can discover the PIN within hours. It then uses the PIN to discover the passphrase.
- A rogue access point (rogue AP) is an AP placed within a network without official authorization. An evil twin is a rogue access point with the same SSID as a legitimate access point.
- A jamming attack floods a wireless frequency with noise, blocking wireless traffic.
- An initialization vector (IV) attack attempts to discover the IV and uses it to discover the passphrase.
- Near field communication (NFC) attacks use an NFC reader to read data from mobile devices.
- Bluejacking is the practice of sending unsolicited messages to a phone. Bluesnarfing is the unauthorized access to, or theft of information from, a Bluetooth device.
- In a wireless replay attack, an attacker captures data sent between two entities, modifies it, and then impersonates one of the parties by replaying the data. WPA2 using CCMP and AES prevents wireless replay attacks.
- Radio-frequency identification (RFID) attacks include eavesdropping, replay, and DoS.

Using VPNs for Remote Access

- A virtual private network (VPN) provides access to private networks via a public network, such as the Internet. VPN concentrators are dedicated devices that provide secure remote access to remote users.
- IPsec is a common tunneling protocol used with VPNs. It secures traffic within a tunnel. IPsec provides authentication with an Authentication Header (AH). Encapsulating Security Payload (ESP) encrypts VPN traffic and provides confidentiality, integrity, and authentication.
- IPsec Tunnel mode encrypts the entire IP packet used in the internal network. IPsec Transport mode only encrypts the payload and is commonly used in private networks, but not with VPNs.

- Some VPNs use TLS to encrypt traffic within the VPN tunnel.
- A full tunnel encrypts all traffic after a user has connected to a VPN. A split tunnel only encrypts traffic destined for the VPN's private network.
- Site-to-site VPNs provide secure access between two networks. These can be on-demand VPNs or always-on VPNs.
- Mobile devices can also use always-on VPNs to protect traffic when users connect to public hot spots.
- Network access control (NAC) inspects clients for specific health conditions such as up-to-date antivirus software, and can redirect unhealthy clients to a remediation network.
- A permanent NAC agent (sometimes called a persistent NAC agent) is installed on the client and stays on the client. A dissolvable NAC agent (sometimes called agentless) is downloaded and run on the client when the client logs on, and deleted after the session ends. Dissolvable agents are commonly used for employee-owned mobile devices.
- Remote access authentication is used when a user accesses a private network from a remote location, such as with a VPN connection.
- Password Authentication Protocol (PAP) uses a password or PIN for authentication. A significant weakness is that PAP sends passwords across a network in cleartext.
- Challenge Handshake Authentication Protocol (CHAP) is more secure than PAP and uses a handshake process when authenticating clients.
- MS-CHAP and MS-CHAPv2 are the Microsoft improvement over CHAP. MS-CHAPv2 provides mutual authentication.
- RADIUS provides central authentication for multiple remote access services. RADIUS relies on the use of shared secrets and only encrypts the password during the authentication process. It uses UDP.
- TACACS+ is used by some Cisco systems as an alternative to RADIUS. TACACS+ uses TCP, encrypts the entire authentication process, and supports multiple challenges and responses.
- Diameter is an improvement over RADIUS. Diameter uses TCP, encrypts the entire authentication process, and supports many additional capabilities.
- RADIUS, TACACS+, and Diameter are all authentication, authorization, and accounting (AAA) protocols.

Online References

- Have you done any of the online labs at *http://gcgapremium.com/501-extras*? Online resources also include sample practice test questions, including performance-based questions.

Chapter 4 Practice Questions

1. You are preparing to deploy a heuristic-based detection system to monitor network activity. Which of the following would you create first?
   A. Flood guards
   B. Signatures
   C. Baseline
   D. Honeypot

2. Attackers have recently launched several attacks against servers in your organization's DMZ. You are tasked with identifying a solution that will have the best chance at preventing these attacks in the future. Which of the following is the BEST choice?
    A. An out-of-band IPS
    B. An in-band IPS
    C. A passive IDS
    D. An out-of-band IDS

3. Lisa oversees and monitors processes at a water treatment plant using SCADA systems. Administrators recently discovered malware on her system that was connecting to the SCADA systems. Although they removed the malware, management is still concerned. Lisa needs to continue using her system and it's not possible to update the SCADA systems. Which of the following can mitigate this risk?
    A. Install HIPS on the SCADA systems.
    B. Install a firewall on the border of the SCADA network.
    C. Install a NIPS on the border of the SCADA network.
    D. Install a honeypot on the SCADA network.

4. Which of the following BEST describes a false negative?
    A. An IDS falsely indicates a buffer overflow attack occurred.
    B. Antivirus software reports that a valid application is malware.
    C. A heuristic-based IDS detects a previously unknown attack.
    D. An IDS does not detect a buffer overflow attack.

5. Your wireless network includes one centralized AP that you configure. This AP forwards the configuration to other APs in your wireless network. Which of the following BEST describes these APs?
    A. The centralized AP is a stand-alone AP and it configures fat APs in your network.
    B. The centralized AP is a thin AP and it configures fat APs in your network.
    C. The centralized AP is a controller-based AP and it configures stand-alone APs in your network.
    D. The centralized AP is a fat AP and it configures thin APs in your network.

6. You need to provide connectivity between two buildings without running any cables. You decide to use two 802.11ac APs to provide wireless connectivity between the buildings. Which of the following is the BEST choice to support this need?
    A. Use omnidirectional antennas on both APs.
    B. Use wide channels.
    C. Use the 2.4 GHz frequency band.
    D. Use directional antennas on both APs.

7. You want to implement the STRONGEST level of security on a wireless network. Which of the following supports this goal?
    A. Implementing WPA with TKIP
    B. Disabling SSID broadcast
    C. Enabling MAC filtering
    D. Implementing WPA2 with CCMP

8. Your organization is planning to implement a wireless network using WPA2 Enterprise. Of the following choices, what is required?

    A. An authentication server with a digital certificate installed on the authentication server

    B. An authentication server with DHCP installed on the authentication server

    C. An authentication server with DNS installed on the authentication server

    D. An authentication server with WEP running on the access point

9. A security administrator is testing the security of an AP. The AP is using WPA2. She ran an automated program for several hours and discovered the AP's passphrase. Which of the following methods was she MOST likely using?

    A. IV attack

    B. Disassociation attack

    C. WPS attack

    D. Evil twin attack

10. Your wireless network name is myoffice. You disabled the SSID broadcast several days ago. Today, you notice that a wireless network named myoffice is available to wireless users. You verified that SSID broadcast is still disabled. Which of the following is the MOST likely reason for this behavior?

    A. Evil twin attack

    B. Disassociation attack

    C. WPS attack

    D. Jamming attack

11. Mobile users in your network report that they frequently lose connectivity with the wireless network on some days, but on other days they don't have any problems. You suspect this is due to an attack. Which of the following attacks is MOST likely causing this problem?

    A. Wireless jamming

    B. IV

    C. Replay

    D. Bluesnarfing

12. Management within your organization wants some users to be able to access internal network resources from remote locations. Which of the following is the BEST choice to meet this need?

    A. NAC

    B. VPN

    C. IDS

    D. IPS

13. Your organization is planning to implement a VPN. They want to ensure that after a VPN client connects to the VPN server, all traffic from the VPN client is encrypted. Which of the following would BEST meet this goal?

    A. Split tunnel

    B. Full tunnel

    C. IPsec using Tunnel mode

    D. IPsec using Transport mode

14. You are tasked with configuring authentication services settings on computers in your network. You are entering shared secrets on different servers. Which of the following services are you MOST likely configuring? (Select TWO.)

    A. RADIUS
    B. Kerberos
    C. LDAP
    D. EAP-TLS

15. Your organization recently implemented a BYOD policy. However, management wants to ensure that mobile devices meet minimum standards for security before they can access any network resources. Which of the following agents would the NAC MOST likely have?

    A. Permanent
    B. Health
    C. RADIUS
    D. Dissolvable

Chapter 4 Practice Question Answers

1. **C.** A heuristic-based (also called anomaly-based or behavior-based) detection system compares current activity with a previously created baseline to detect any anomalies or changes. Flood guards help protect against flood attacks (such as a SYN flood attack). Signature-based systems (also called definition-based) use signatures of known attack patterns to detect attacks. A honeypot is a server designed to look valuable to an attacker and can divert attacks.

2. **B.** The best solution of the given choices is an in-band intrusion prevention system (IPS). Traffic goes through the IPS and the IPS has the best chance of preventing attacks from reaching internal systems. An IPS is in-band not out-of-band. An intrusion detection system (IDS) is passive and not in-band, so it can only detect and react to the attacks, not block them.

3. **C.** A network intrusion prevention system (NIPS) installed on the supervisory control and data acquisition (SCADA) network can intercept malicious traffic coming into the network and is the best choice of those given. The scenario states you cannot update the SCADA systems, so you cannot install a host-based IPS (HIPS) on any of them. A firewall provides a level of protection. However, it wouldn't be able to differentiate between valid traffic sent by Lisa and malicious traffic sent by malware from Lisa's system. A honeypot might be useful to observe malicious traffic, but wouldn't prevent it.

4. **D.** If an intrusion detection system (IDS) does not detect and report a buffer overflow attack, it is a false negative. It is a false positive if the IDS falsely (incorrectly) indicates an attack occurred. If antivirus software indicates a valid application is malware, it is also a false positive. If a heuristic-based IDS accurately detects a previously unknown attack, it is working correctly.

5. **D.** The centralized access point (AP) is a fat AP and it configures thin APs in the network. The fat AP could also be called a stand-alone, intelligent, or autonomous AP and it is used to

configure thin APs, not fat APs. Thin APs do not configure other APs. Stand-alone APs are not configured by other APs.

6. **D.** Using directional antennas on both access points (APs) is the best choice to meet this need because they have high gain with a very narrow radiation pattern. Omnidirectional antennas transmit the signal in all directions at the same time and are not a good choice when connecting networks between two buildings. Wider channels reduce the range of wireless transmissions and aren't a good choice here. Because 802.11ac uses only the 5 GHz frequency band, you can't use 2.4 GHz.

7. **D.** Wi-Fi Protected Access II (WPA2) with Counter Mode with Cipher Block Chaining Message Authentication Code Protocol (CCMP) provides the strongest level of security of the given choices. Temporal Key Integrity Protocol (TKIP) is an older encryption protocol used with WPA and it isn't as strong as CCMP. Disabling service set identifier (SSID) broadcast hides the network from casual users, but attackers can still discover it because the SSID is still included in some packets in plaintext. Attackers can bypass media access control (MAC) address filtering by spoofing authorized MAC addresses.

8. **A.** WPA2 Enterprise requires an 802.1x authentication server and most implementations require a digital certificate installed on the server. The network will likely have Dynamic Host Configuration Protocol (DHCP) and Domain Name System (DNS) services, but it isn't necessary to install them on the authentication server. Wired Equivalent Privacy (WEP) provides poor security and is not compatible with WPA2 Enterprise.

9. **C.** This is most likely a Wi-Fi Protected Setup (WPS) attack. Reaver is an automated program that will discover the WPS PIN and after it discovers the PIN, it can discover the passphrase or secret key used by the access point (AP). While an initialization vector (IV) attack can discover the passphrase in legacy wireless security protocols, Wi-Fi Protected Access II (WPA2) isn't susceptible to an IV attack. A disassociation attack effectively removes a wireless client from a wireless network, but it doesn't discover the passphrase. An evil twin attack uses a separate AP with the same name as an existing AP with the goal of tricking users into connecting to it.

10. **A.** The scenario indicates an evil twin attack is in progress. An attacker can easily discover the service set identifier (SSID) even with SSID broadcast disabled and can then create another access point with the same SSID. A disassociation attack disconnects wireless clients from the wireless network. A Wi-Fi Protected Setup (WPS) attack discovers the eight-digit PIN and then uses it to discover the passphrase. A jamming attack floods the frequency channel with noise to prevent connections.

11. **A.** A wireless jamming attack is a type of denial-of-service (DoS) attack that can cause wireless devices to lose their association with access points and disconnect them from the network. None of the other attacks are DoS attacks. An initialization vector (IV) attack attempts to discover the passphrase. A replay attack captures traffic with the goal of replaying it later to impersonate one of the parties in the original transmission. Bluesnarfing is a Bluetooth attack that attempts to access information on Bluetooth devices.

12. **B.** A virtual private network (VPN) provides access to a private network over a public network such as the Internet via remote locations and is the best choice. Network access control (NAC) methods can check VPN clients for health before allowing them access to the network, but it doesn't directly provide the access. Intrusion detection systems (IDSs) and intrusion prevention systems (IPSs) protect networks, but do not control remote access.

13. **B.** A full tunnel encrypts all traffic after a user has connected to a VPN using a tunnel. A split tunnel only encrypts traffic destined for the VPN's private network. Traffic from the client directly to another Internet site is not encrypted. Internet Protocol security (IPsec) Tunnel mode encrypts the entire IP packet used in the internal network. It encrypts all traffic used within the VPN's private network, but not all traffic from the VPN client. IPsec Transport mode only encrypts the payload and is used within private networks, not for VPN traffic.

14. **A, C.** Remote Authentication Dial-in User Service (RADIUS) servers use shared secrets. You can configure them to interact with Lightweight Directory Access Protocol (LDAP)–based systems by entering the same shared secret on both a RADIUS server and an LDAP server. A shared secret is basically just an identical password on both systems. Kerberos uses tickets for authentication, not shared secrets. Extensible Authentication Protocol-Transport Layer Security (EAP-TLS) is an authentication protocol that requires the use of certificates on both clients and servers, not shared secrets.

15. **D.** A dissolvable agent is often used on employee-owned devices and would be appropriate if an organization implemented a bring your own device (BYOD) policy. A permanent network access control (NAC) agent is installed on the device permanently, but this might cause problems for employee-owned devices. Any NAC agent is a health agent. Remote Authentication Dial-In User Service (RADIUS) is used for authentication, not to inspect clients.

Chapter 5

Securing Hosts and Data

CompTIA Security+ objectives covered in this chapter:

1.6   Explain the impact associated with types of vulnerabilities.
- Vulnerabilities due to: (End-of-life systems, Embedded systems, Lack of vendor support), Misconfiguration/weak configuration

2.1   Install and configure network components, both hardware- and software-based, to support organizational security.
- DLP (USB blocking, Cloud-based, Email), Hardware security module

2.3   Given a scenario, troubleshoot common security issues.
- Permission issues, Access violations, Data exfiltration, Weak security configurations, Unauthorized software, Baseline deviation, License compliance violation (availability/integrity)

2.4   Given a scenario, analyze and interpret output from security technologies.
- Application whitelisting, Removable media control, Patch management tools, DLP

2.5   Given a scenario, deploy mobile devices securely.
- Connection methods (Cellular, WiFi, SATCOM, Bluetooth, NFC, ANT, Infrared, USB), Mobile device management concepts (Application management, Content management, Remote wipe, Geofencing, Geolocation, Screen locks, Push notification services, Passwords and pins, Biometrics, Context-aware authentication, Containerization, Storage segmentation, Full device encryption), Enforcement and monitoring for: (Third-party app stores, Rooting/jailbreaking, Sideloading, Custom firmware, Carrier unlocking, Firmware OTA updates, Camera use, SMS/MMS, External media, USB OTG, Recording microphone, GPS tagging, WiFi direct/ad hoc, Tethering, Payment methods), Deployment models (BYOD, COPE, CYOD, Corporate-owned, VDI)

3.3   Given a scenario, implement secure systems design.
- Hardware/firmware security (FDE/SED, TPM, HSM, UEFI/BIOS, Secure boot and attestation, Supply chain, Hardware root of trust, EMI/EMP), Operating systems (Types, Network, Server, Workstation, Appliance, Kiosk, Mobile OS, Patch management, Least functionality,

Secure configurations, Trusted operating system, Application whitelisting/
blacklisting), Peripherals (Wireless keyboards, Wireless mice, Displays, WiFi-enabled
MicroSD cards, Printers/MFDs, External storage devices, Digital cameras)

3.4   Explain the importance of secure staging deployment concepts.
  - Sandboxing, Environment (Development, Test, Staging, Production), Secure baseline,
    Integrity measurement

3.5   Explain the security implications of embedded systems.
  - SCADA/ICS, Smart devices/IoT (Wearable technology, Home automation), HVAC, SoC,
    RTOS, Printers/MFDs, Camera systems, Special purpose (Medical devices, Vehicles,
    Aircraft/UAV)

3.7   Summarize cloud and virtualization concepts.
  - Cloud storage, Cloud deployment models (SaaS, PaaS, IaaS, Private, Public, Hybrid,
    Community), On-premise vs. hosted vs. cloud, Cloud access security broker, Security
    as a Service

3.8   Explain how resiliency and automation strategies reduce risk.
  - Automation/scripting (Automated courses of action), Templates, Master image,
    Non-persistence (Live boot media)

4.3   Given a scenario, implement identity and access management controls.
  - File system security, Database security

5.3   Explain risk management processes and concepts.
  - Change management

**

In this chapter, you'll learn about different methods used to implement a secure systems
design. This includes the use of different operating systems, peripherals, and hardware and
firmware security. More and more organizations are using cloud resources and this chapter
summarizes the important cloud concepts. Additionally, the use of mobile devices has exploded
in the last few years with more and more organizations allowing employees to connect mobile
devices to the network. This results in many challenges for an organization, but mobile device
management tools help administrators handle these challenges. This chapter also covers the
security implications of embedded systems that are now in printers, vehicles, smart devices, and
more. Last, you'll learn many different methods used to protect data.

Implementing Secure Systems

Secure systems design concepts help ensure that computing systems are deployed and
maintained in a secure state. In this context, a system is any host such as a server, workstation,
laptop, network device, or mobile device. In an ideal world, systems start in a secure state.
Unfortunately, it's not an ideal world, and administrators need to be proactive to secure systems
before deployment and keep them secure after deployment. This section outlines several steps
used to secure hosts.

Hardening is the practice of making an operating system (OS) or application more secure
from its default installation. It helps eliminate vulnerabilities from default configurations,
misconfigurations, and weak configurations.

A core principle associated with secure systems design is *least functionality*. Systems
should be deployed with only the applications, services, and protocols they need to meet their
purpose. If a service or protocol is not running on a system, attackers cannot attack it. As a simple

example, a system is not vulnerable to any File Transfer Protocol (FTP) attacks if FTP is not running and available on the system.

In addition to disabling unnecessary services to reduce vulnerabilities, it's important to uninstall unneeded software. Software frequently has bugs and vulnerabilities. Although patching software frequently closes these vulnerabilities, you can eliminate these vulnerabilities by simply eliminating unneeded applications.

Years ago, I was working at a small training company. One of the servers had a default configuration for Windows that resulted in a significant vulnerability. We were using the server as a file server, but because it wasn't hardened from the default configuration, it was also running Internet Information Services (IIS), the Microsoft web server.

At some point, attackers released the Nimda virus, which exploited a vulnerability with IIS. Microsoft released a patch for IIS, but because IIS was installed by default and we weren't using it, we also weren't managing it. Ultimately, the Nimda virus found our server, and the worm component of Nimda quickly infected our network. If the IIS software hadn't been installed, the server would not have been vulnerable to the attack.

It's also important to disable unnecessary accounts. For example, the Guest account is disabled by default in current Windows systems and it should remain disabled unless there is a specific need for it.

Some applications also include backdoor accounts. A backdoor is an access point to an application or service that bypasses normal security mechanisms. Developers use backdoors for legitimate purposes to view the internal workings of an application or for ease of administration. However, the use of backdoors is strongly discouraged in the final released version. If a backdoor exists, you can expect attackers to locate and exploit it. Similarly, if a system or application has a default account with a default password, the password should be changed.

Remember this

Least functionality is a core security principle stating that systems should be deployed with the least amount of applications, services, and protocols.

Operating Systems

There are three primary types of computer operating systems (OSs): Windows, Apple's operating systems, and Linux- or Unix-based systems. Chapter 1, "Mastering Security Basics," introduces Linux and Unix. For simplicity, instead of stating "Linux or Unix" throughout this book, I'm just stating it as Linux.

Within these types, there are many different versions. For example, the Windows operating system includes versions for desktop workstations (including laptops) and other versions for servers. Additionally, these versions are regularly updated such as Windows 8 and Windows 10, and Windows Server 2012 and Windows Server 2016. Windows operating systems are closed source software, meaning that the underlying code is not freely available to the public. Microsoft developed these OSs and updates them.

Apple also uses closed source OSs—macOS for its Macintosh computers and iOS as a mobile OS for mobile devices such as iPhones and iPads. Because they are closed source, only Apple updates or modifies these OSs.

Linux is derived from Unix and is open source, meaning that it is freely available to anyone. Developers have access to the code and can modify, improve, and, at times, freely redistribute it. Because of this, there is an almost endless assortment of Linux versions. As an example, the Android OS is open source software, and it was derived from the open source Linux OS. Additionally, many mobile device manufacturers modify the Android OS and use it as a mobile OS for their devices. It's worth noting that the use of Linux in many systems has steadily increased. More, CompTIA has been adding additional Linux-based objectives in their exams, including the Security+ exam.

While you primarily see OSs operating on desktops, laptops, and servers, they are also operating in other locations, including:

- **Kiosks.** A kiosk is a small structure in an open area used to sell something, provide information, or display advertisements. For example, an organization can create a touch-screen application installed on a computer and place it in a kiosk. This could be in a mall or store (designed to advertise something), in a medical center (designed to share information), or anywhere an organization thinks it might be useful.
- **Network.** Many network devices such as switches, routers, and firewalls include an operating system used to manage the device. These are often a version of Linux. Some Cisco network devices use the Cisco IOS (originally called the Internetwork Operating System).
- **Appliance.** A network appliance is a dedicated hardware device that bundles several features within it. As an example, Chapter 3, "Exploring Network Technologies and Tools," discusses a unified threat management (UTM) device that includes multiple layers of protection. Many appliances run on a Linux version.

It's also possible to use live boot media to create a non-persistent operating system on a computer. As an example, the Defense Information Systems Agency (DISA) uses Bootable Media (BootMe), which is a CD that authorized Department of Defense (DoD) users can use to run an operating system on almost any computer. It provides users with an operating system to perform specific functions, such as accessing DoD resources via remote access. It's called a non-persistent operating system because it disappears when users turn off the computer.

Secure Operating System Configurations

Most operating systems aren't secure out of the box. Instead, administrators must take specific steps to secure them. A common method of deploying systems is to create a master image with a secure configuration, and then deploy the image to multiple systems.

A **trusted operating system** meets a set of predetermined requirements with a heavy emphasis on authentication and authorization. The overall goal of a trusted operating system is to ensure that only authorized personnel can access data based on their permissions. Additionally, a trusted operating system prevents any modifications or movement of data by unauthorized entities. A trusted OS helps prevent malicious software (malware) infections because it prevents malicious or suspicious code from executing.

A trusted OS meets a high level of security requirements imposed by a third party. For example, the Common Criteria for Information Technology Security Evaluation (or simply Common Criteria) includes requirements for a trusted OS. Operating systems that meet these requirements can be certified as trusted operating systems. Also, a trusted OS typically uses the mandatory access control (MAC) model, discussed in Chapter 2, "Understanding Identity and Access Management."

> ### Remember this
>
> A trusted operating system meets a set of predetermined requirements, such as those identified in the Common Criteria. It uses the mandatory access control (MAC) model.

Using Master Images

One of the most common methods of deploying systems is with images starting with a master image. An image is a snapshot of a single system that administrators deploy to multiple other systems. Imaging has become an important practice for many organizations because it streamlines deployments while also ensuring they are deployed in a secure manner. Figure 5.1 and the following text identify the overall process of capturing and deploying an image:

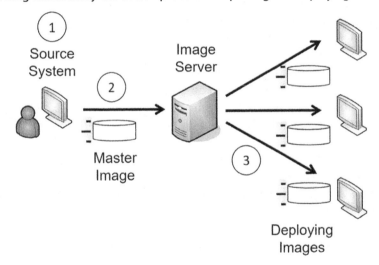

Figure 5.1: Capturing and deploying images

1. Administrators start with a blank source system. They install and configure the operating system, install and configure any desired applications, and modify security settings. Administrators perform extensive testing to ensure the system works as desired and that it is secure before going to the next step.
2. Next, administrators capture the image, which becomes their master image. Symantec Ghost is a popular imaging application, and Windows Server versions include free tools many organizations use to capture and deploy images. The captured image is simply a file that can be stored on a server or copied to external media, such as a DVD or external USB drive.
3. In step 3, administrators deploy the image to multiple systems. When used within a network, administrators can deploy the same image to dozens of systems during an initial deployment, or to just a single system to rebuild it. The image installs the same configuration on the target systems as the original source system created in step 1.

Administrators will often take a significant amount of time to configure and test the source system. They follow the same hardening practices discussed earlier and often use security and configuration baselines. If they're deploying the image to just a few systems such as in a classroom setting, they may create the image in just a few hours. However, if they're deploying it to thousands of systems within an organization, they may take weeks or months to create and test the image. Once they've created the image, they can deploy it relatively quickly with very little administrative effort.

Imaging provides two important benefits:

- **Secure starting point.** The image includes mandated security configurations for the system. Personnel who deploy the system don't need to remember or follow extensive checklists to ensure that new systems are set up with all the detailed configuration and security settings. The deployed image retains all the settings of the original image. Administrators will still configure some settings, such as the computer name, after deploying the image.
- **Reduced costs.** Deploying imaged systems reduces the overall maintenance costs and improves reliability. Support personnel don't need to learn several different end-user system environments to assist end users. Instead, they learn just one. When troubleshooting, support personnel spend their time focused on helping the end user rather than trying to learn the system configuration. Managers understand this as reducing the total cost of ownership (TCO) for systems.

Many virtualization tools include the ability to convert an image to a virtual system. In other words, once you create the image, you can deploy it to either a physical system or a virtual system. From a security perspective, there is no difference how you deploy it. If you've locked down the image for deployment to a physical system, you've locked it down for deployment to a virtual system.

Imaging isn't limited to only desktop computers. You can image any system, including servers. For example, consider an organization that maintains 50 database servers in a large data center. The organization can use imaging to deploy new servers or as part of its disaster recovery plan to restore failed servers. It is much quicker to deploy an image to rebuild a failed server than it is to rebuild a server from scratch. If administrators keep the images up to date, this also helps ensure the recovered server starts in a secure state.

Resiliency and Automation Strategies

Resiliency and automation strategies include automation, scripting, and templates and they can help deploy systems securely, and keep them in a secure state. As an example, administrators often use Group Policy in Microsoft domains to automatically check and configure systems. Chapter 2 discusses the use of Group Policy in more depth. It provides automated courses of action by applying security and other settings.

Additionally, Microsoft has created several security templates with various levels of security. Administrators can modify these templates to fit their needs, import them into a Group Policy Object (GPO), and then apply them to systems within the domain. Some organizations deploy a master image to all systems, and then use the security templates to automatically apply different security settings to different groups of systems based on their security needs.

Secure Baseline and Integrity Measurements

A baseline is a known starting point and organizations commonly use secure baselines to provide known starting points for systems. One of the primary benefits of secure baselines is that they improve the overall security posture of systems. Weak security configuration is a common security issue, but secure baselines help eliminate this.

The use of baselines works in three steps:

1. **Initial baseline configuration.** Administrators use various tools to deploy systems consistently in a secure state.
2. **Integrity measurements for baseline deviation.** Automated tools monitor the systems for any baseline changes, which is a common security issue. Some tools such as vulnerability scanners monitor the systems and report any changes they detect. Other tools such as Group Policy automatically reconfigure the systems to the baseline settings when they detect changes.
3. **Remediation.** Chapter 4, "Securing Your Network," covers network access control (NAC). NAC methods can detect some changes to baseline settings and automatically isolate or quarantine systems in a remediation network. Typically, administrators need to correct the problems in these systems manually.

> ### Remember this
>
> A master image provides a secure starting point for systems. Administrators sometimes create them with templates or with other tools to create a secure baseline. They then use integrity measurements to discover when a system deviates from the baseline.

Patch Management

Software is not secure. There. I said it. As someone who has written a few programs over the years, that's not easy to say. In a perfect world, extensive testing would discover all the bugs, exploits, and vulnerabilities that cause so many problems.

However, because operating systems and applications include millions of lines of code, testing simply doesn't find all the problems. Instead, most companies make a best effort to test software before releasing it. Later, as problems crop up, companies write and release patches or updates. Administrators must apply these patches to keep their systems up to date and protected against known vulnerabilities.

Patch management ensures that systems and applications stay up to date with current patches. This is one of the most efficient ways to reduce operating system and application vulnerabilities because it protects systems from known vulnerabilities. Patch management includes a group of methodologies and includes the process of identifying, downloading, testing, deploying, and verifying patches.

After testing the patches, administrators deploy them. They don't deploy the patches manually though. Instead, they use systems management tools to deploy the patches in a controlled manner. For example, Microsoft System Center Configuration Manager (SCCM, also known as ConfigMgr) is a systems management tool used for many purposes, including patch management.

In addition to deploying patches, systems management tools also include a verification component that verifies patch deployment. They periodically query the systems and retrieve a list of installed patches and updates. They then compare the retrieved list with the list of deployed patches and updates, providing reports for any discrepancies. In some networks, administrators combine this with network access control (NAC) technologies and isolate unpatched systems in quarantined networks until they are patched.

> ## WannaCry Ransomware Attacked Unpatched Systems
>
> In May 2017, attackers launched an attack infecting more than 200,000 computers in over 150 countries in just a few days. When users logged on, they saw the WannaCry ransomware message: "Ooops, your files have been encrypted!" The message demanded a payment of $300 within three days, doubled the ransom after six days, and threatened to delete the files after seven days if users didn't pay.
>
> However, this was 100 percent preventable if users followed one simple security practice—keep systems up to date with current patches. The WannaCry ransomware exploited a known vulnerability in Microsoft Windows systems, but Microsoft released an update to this vulnerability two months before the attack. Patched systems were not vulnerable to the attack. Unpatched systems were vulnerable.

Change Management Policy

The worst enemies of many networks have been unrestrained administrators. A well-meaning administrator can make what appears to be a minor change to fix one problem, only to cause a major problem somewhere else. A misconfiguration can take down a server, disable a network, stop email communications, and even stop all network traffic for an entire enterprise.

For example, I once saw a major outage occur when an administrator was troubleshooting a printer problem. After modifying the printer's Internet Protocol (IP) address, the printer began to work. Sounds like a success, doesn't it? Unfortunately, the new IP address was the same IP address assigned to a Domain Name System (DNS) server, and it created an IP address conflict. The conflict prevented the DNS server from resolving names to IP addresses. This resulted in a major network outage until another administrator discovered and corrected the problem.

These self-inflicted disasters were relatively common in the early days of IT. They still occur today, but organizations with mature change management processes in place have fewer of these problems. *Change management* defines the process for any type of system modifications or upgrades, including changes to applications. It provides two key goals:

- To ensure changes to IT systems do not result in unintended outages
- To provide an accounting structure or method to document all changes

When a change management program is in place, administrators are discouraged from making configuration changes without submitting the change for review and approval. In other words, they don't immediately make a change as soon as they identify a potential need for the change. This includes making any type of configuration changes to systems, applications, patches, or any other change. Instead, they follow the change management process before making a change.

Experts from different areas of an organization examine change requests and can either approve or postpone them. The process usually approves simple changes quickly. A formal change review board regularly reviews postponed requests and can approve, modify, or reject the change.

This entire process provides documentation for approved changes. For example, some automated change management systems create accounting logs for all change requests. The system tracks the request from its beginning until implementation. Administrators use this documentation for configuration management and disaster recovery. If a modified system fails, change and configuration management documentation identifies how to return the system to its prefailure state.

> ### *Remember this*
>
> Patch management procedures ensure that operating systems and applications are up to date with current patches. This protects systems against known vulnerabilities. Change management defines the process and accounting structure for handling modifications and upgrades. The goals are to reduce risks related to unintended outages and provide documentation for all changes.

Unauthorized Software and Compliance Violations

A common security issue is the use of unauthorized software, which can cause many different problems. The most common problem is that unauthorized software often includes malware. When users install the software, they are also installing malware.

Another problem is related to support. Users who install unauthorized software typically want the IT department to help them with it when they have problems. However, the IT department personnel can't be experts on everything, so this takes them away from other tasks.

Another common security issue related to the use of unauthorized software is license compliance violations. As an example, imagine an organization purchases 10 licenses for an application. Nine users have this installed and have activated it on their systems. Bart discovers the key and decides to install the software on his computer, even though he doesn't need it for his job.

Later, the organization hires Maggie. IT personnel set her up with a new computer and try to activate the application, but it fails because the tenth license is already in use. This results in a loss of availability of the application for Maggie.

Some applications verify the key is valid, but they don't necessarily check to see if the key is already in use. If IT personnel successfully install and activate the software on Maggie's computer, it results in a loss of integrity for the organization's license compliance. The organization can be susceptible to fines and penalties if the application developer discovers that the organization is violating the license requirements.

Application Whitelisting and Blacklisting

Whitelisting and blacklisting are two additional methods used to protect hosts, including workstations, servers, and mobile devices. An *application whitelist* is a list of applications authorized to run on a system. An *application blacklist* is a list of applications the system blocks.

You can use Software Restriction Policies in Microsoft Group Policy for both whitelisting and blacklisting for computers within a domain. For a whitelist, you identify the applications that can run on the system, and Group Policy blocks all other applications. For a blacklist, you identify the applications that cannot run on the system, and Group Policy allows any other applications.

Similarly, many mobile device management (MDM) applications use application whitelists and blacklists to allow or block applications on mobile devices. MDM applications are discussed later in this chapter.

Messages that users see when they can't install an application due to whitelisting or blacklisting are sometimes cryptic. When users try to install an application that isn't on the whitelist, it will often report a permission issue or sometimes just fail with a vague error. However, application logs will typically include details on why the installation failed.

> **Remember this**
>
> An application whitelist is a list of authorized software and it prevents users from installing or running software that isn't on the list. An application blacklist is a list of unauthorized software and prevents users from installing or running software on the list.

Secure Staging and Deployment

Another concept within secure systems design is secure staging and deployment concepts. These include sandboxing, controlling the environment, using secure baselines, and performing integrity measurements.

Sandboxing with VMs

Sandboxing is the use of an isolated area on a system and it is often used for testing. Chapter 1 covers the use of virtual machines (VMs) and you can create them so that they are isolated in a sandbox environment. Chapter 7, "Protecting Against Advanced Attacks," discusses how sandboxing is often used for testing applications.

Administrators and security professionals also use sandboxing to test various security controls before deploying them to a live production network. Virtualization provides a high level of flexibility when testing security controls because the environments are easy to re-create. For example, they can test the effectiveness of antivirus software to detect malware released within a sandbox. If the antivirus software doesn't detect the malware and the malware causes problems, it is easy to revert the system to a previous state. Also, the isolation within the sandbox prevents the malware from spreading.

Similarly, virtualized sandboxes are useful for testing patches. For example, software vendors typically develop software updates and patches, but they need to test them in various environments before releasing them. They could create VMs for multiple operating systems. When they're ready to test, they turn on one of the VMs, take a snapshot, and then apply and test the patch. If the patch causes a problem, they can easily revert the VM.

Sandboxing with Chroot

Another method of sandboxing is with the Linux-based **chroot** command. It is used to change the root directory for an application, effectively isolating it. Normally, the root of Linux is designated as / and all other directories can be accessed from here. Users often have their own home directories within the /home directory. For example, Lisa's root directory on a Linux system might be /home/lisa. Regular users won't have access to the root directory, but only to files within their directory. In contrast, a root user (or administrator) has root access and can access all files and folders on the drive.

Imagine Lisa is a root user and wants to test an application within an isolated area. She could create a directory named testing in her environment. It would be /home/lisa/testing. She would copy her application files and copy any other required directories such as the /bin and /lib directories into the sandbox directory. She would then use chroot to create the isolated sandbox in the testing directory. This sandbox is often referred to as a chroot jail.

At this point, any commands she enters can only access files within the /home/lisa/testing directory. Additionally, her application can only access files with the same path. If the application is malicious or buggy, it cannot access any system files.

Secure Staging Environment

A secure staging environment includes multiple environments, and typically includes different systems used for each stage. As an example, imagine a software development team is creating an application that will be used to sell products via the Internet. The different environments are:

- **Development.** Software developers use a development environment to create the application. This typically includes version control and change management controls to track the application development.
- **Test.** Testers put the application through its paces and attempt to discover any bugs or errors. The testing environment typically doesn't simulate a full production environment, but instead includes enough hardware and software to test software modules.
- **Staging.** The staging environment simulates the production environment and is used for late stage testing. It provides a complete but independent copy of the production environment.
- **Production.** The production environment is the final product. It includes everything needed to support the application and allow customers and others to use it. In this example, it would include the live web server, possibly a back-end database server, and Internet access.

> ### Remember this
>
> Sandboxing is the use of an isolated area and it is often used for testing. You can create a sandbox with a virtual machine (VM) and on Linux systems with the chroot command. A secure deployment environment includes development, testing, staging, and production elements.

Secure systems design includes secure staging and deployment.

Peripherals

When implementing secure systems design, organizations should consider the use of various computer peripherals, including the following:

- **Wireless keyboards and wireless mice.** Wireless transmissions can sometimes be intercepted. If these devices are used with systems processing sensitive data, it might be prudent to use wired devices instead.
- **Displays.** If displays show sensitive or private data, their view should be limited. For example, they shouldn't be viewable from windows. Additionally, privacy screens can be placed over displays to limit the view of the information unless someone is looking straight at the display.
- **External storage devices.** External storage devices include any external device that has memory capabilities. It typically refers to external USB drives, but also includes other devices such as smartphones, tablets, MP3 players, and digital cameras. Users can plug them into a system and easily copy data to and from a system. They can transport malware without the user's knowledge and can be a source of data leakage. Malicious users can copy and steal a significant amount of information using an easily concealable thumb drive. Also, users can misplace these drives and the data can easily fall into the

wrong hands. Many organizations block the use of any external devices using technical policies.

- **Digital cameras.** Digital cameras typically include built-in storage and support additional storage by plugging in a memory card. These include the same risks as any external storage device.
- **Wi-Fi-enabled MicroSD cards.** Traditional Micro Secure Digital (SD) cards need to be plugged into a port to read the data. They are typically used in digital cameras. However, newer MicroSD cards include wireless capabilities. As with any wireless devices, the risk is that wireless transmissions can be intercepted, so if these are necessary, they should be configured with strong wireless security.
- **Printers and other multi-function devices (MFDs).** *MFDs* often have extra features that should be considered when purchasing them, especially if they will process sensitive information. These typically have embedded systems with their own risks discussed later in this chapter. Additionally, they often have internal storage that might retain documents that they process. For example, if the device is used to copy or scan a document, a copy of the document might remain in the system's internal memory.

Hardware and Firmware Security

When implementing secure systems design, it's also important to evaluate several hardware elements, including those covered in this section. Additionally, an organization should evaluate the supply chain. A supply chain includes all the elements required to produce a product. In secure systems design, the product is a secure system.

There have been many incidents where new computers were shipped with malware. As an example, Microsoft researchers purchased several new computers in China and found them infected with the Nitol virus. These computers were also running counterfeit versions of Windows. This helps illustrate the importance of purchasing computers from reputable sources.

EMI and EMP

When designing systems, it's important to consider electromagnetic interference (EMI) and electromagnetic pulse (EMP). *EMI* comes from sources such as motors, power lines, and fluorescent lights and it can interfere with signals transmitted over wires. Chapter 9, "Implementing Controls to Protect Assets," discusses shielding that helps prevent EMI from causing problems. It's easier to include shielding during the design process rather than add shielding later.

EMP is a short burst of electromagnetic energy. EMP can come from a wide assortment of sources and some sources can cause damage to computing equipment. Some sources include:

- **Electrostatic discharge (ESD).** Basic ESD prevention practices, such as using ESD wrist straps, help prevent ESD damage.
- **Lightning.** Lightning pulses can go through electrical wires and damage unprotected systems. Surge protection methods, such as surge protection strips, protect electrical systems.
- **Military weapons.** Nuclear explosions create a large EMP that can damage electronic equipment (including embedded systems) over a large area. Some non-nuclear weapons have been designed to mimic the nuclear EMP, but without the nuclear explosion. Non-nuclear EMP has a smaller range than nuclear EMP, but can still damage equipment. The best publicly known protection is to turn equipment off, but you're unlikely to know when one of these explosions will occur.

> ### *Remember this*
>
> Secure systems design considers electromagnetic interference (EMI) and electromagnetic pulse (EMP). EMI comes from sources such as motors, power lines, and fluorescent lights and can be prevented with shielding. Systems can be protected from mild forms of EMP (a short burst of electromagnetic energy) such as electrostatic discharge and lightning.

FDE and SED

Full disk encryption (*FDE*) encrypts an entire disk. Several applications are available to do this. For example, VeraCrypt is an open source utility that can encrypt partitions or the entire storage device.

Many hardware vendors now manufacture hardware-based FDE drives. These are sometimes referred to as self-encrypting drives (SEDs). An *SED* includes the hardware and software to encrypt all data on the drive and securely store the encryption keys. These typically allow users to enter credentials when they set up the drive. When users power up the system, they enter their credentials again to decrypt the drive and boot the system.

UEFI and BIOS

The Basic Input/Output System (*BIOS*) includes software that provides a computer with basic instructions on how to start. It runs some basic checks, locates the operating system, and starts. The BIOS is often referred to as firmware. It is a hardware chip that you can physically see and touch and it includes software that executes code on the computer. The combination of hardware and software is firmware.

Newer systems use Unified Extensible Firmware Interface (*UEFI*) instead of BIOS. UEFI performs many of the same functions as BIOS, but provides some enhancements. As an example, it can boot from larger disks and it is designed to be CPU-independent.

Both BIOS and UEFI can be upgraded using a process called flashing. Flashing overwrites the software within the chip with newer software.

Trusted Platform Module

A Trusted Platform Module (*TPM*) is a hardware chip on the computer's motherboard that stores cryptographic keys used for encryption. Many laptop computers include a TPM and you may see them on many mobile devices, too. However, if the system doesn't include a TPM, it is not feasible to add one. Once enabled, the TPM provides full disk encryption capabilities. It keeps hard drives locked, or sealed, until the system completes a system verification and authentication process.

A TPM supports secure boot and attestation processes. When the TPM is configured, it captures signatures of key files used to boot the computer and stores a report of the signatures securely within the TPM. When the system boots, the *secure boot* process checks the files against the stored signatures to ensure they haven't changed. If it detects that the files have been modified, such as from malware, it blocks the boot process to protect the data on the drive.

A remote *attestation* process works like the secure boot process. However, instead of checking the boot files against the report stored in the TPM, it uses a separate system. Again, when the TPM is configured, it captures the signatures of key files, but sends this report to a remote system. When the system boots, it checks the files and sends a current report to the remote system. The remote system verifies the files are the same and attests, or confirms, that the system is safe.

The TPM ships with a unique Rivest, Shamir, Adleman (RSA) private key burned into it, which is used for asymmetric encryption. This private key is matched with a public key and provides a **hardware root of trust**, or a known secure starting point. The private key remains private and is matched with a public key. Additionally, the TPM can generate, store, and protect other keys used for encrypting and decrypting disks. Chapter 10, "Understanding Cryptography and PKI," discusses asymmetric encryption and public and private keys in more depth.

If the system includes a TPM, you use an application within the operating system to enable it. For example, many Microsoft systems include BitLocker, which you can enable for systems that include the TPM.

BitLocker uses the TPM to detect tampering of any critical operating system files or processes as part of a platform verification process. Additionally, users provide authentication, such as with a smart card, a password, or a personal identification number (PIN). The drive remains locked until the platform verification and user authentication processes are complete.

If a thief steals the system, the drive remains locked and protected. An attacker wouldn't have authentication credentials, so he can't access the drive using a normal boot process. If the attacker tries to modify the operating system to bypass security controls, the TPM detects the tampering and keeps the drive locked. If a thief moves the drive to another system, the drive remains locked because the TPM isn't available.

> ### Remember this
>
> A Trusted Platform Module (TPM) is a hardware chip included on many laptops and mobile devices. It provides full disk encryption and supports a secure boot process and remote attestation. A TPM includes a unique RSA asymmetric key burned into the chip that provides a hardware root of trust.

Hardware Security Module

A hardware security module (**HSM**) is a security device you can add to a system to manage, generate, and securely store cryptographic keys. High-performance HSMs are external devices connected to a network using TCP/IP. Smaller HSMs come as expansion cards you install within a server, or as devices you plug into computer ports.

HSMs support the security methods as a TPM. They provide a hardware root of trust, secure boot, and can be configured for remote attestation.

One of the noteworthy differences between an HSM and a TPM is that HSMs are removable or external devices. In comparison, a TPM is a chip embedded into the motherboard. You can easily add an HSM to a system or a network, but if a system didn't ship with a TPM, it's not feasible to add one later. Both HSMs and TPMs provide secure encryption capabilities by storing and using RSA keys. Many high-performance servers use HSMs to store and protect keys.

> ### Remember this
>
> A hardware security module (HSM) is a removable or external device that can generate, store, and manage RSA keys used in asymmetric encryption. Many server-based applications use an HSM to protect keys.

Additional Vulnerabilities

Two issues that organizations need to avoid are vulnerabilities associated with end-of-life systems and a lack of vendor support. When systems reach the end of their life, you need to ensure that they don't have any valuable data on them before disposing of them. Chapter 11, "Implementing Policies to Mitigate Risks," discusses several methods of sanitization.

Also, when a vendor stops supporting a system, an operating system, or an application, it is time to start using something else. As an example, consider Windows XP. It was a solid operating system for 12 years and it probably still runs fine on many computers. However, Microsoft stopped supporting it on April 8, 2014. This means that they no longer provide security updates or technical support for it. Any new vulnerabilities discovered after April 8, 2014, remain unpatched.

Summarizing Cloud Concepts

Cloud computing refers to accessing computing resources via a different location than your local computer. In most scenarios, you're accessing these resources through the Internet.

As an example, if you use web-based email such as Gmail, you're using cloud computing. More specifically, the web-based mail is a Software as a Service cloud computing service. You know that you're accessing your email via the Internet, but you really don't know where the physical server hosting your account is located. It could be in a data center in the middle of Virginia, tucked away in Utah, or just about anywhere else in the world.

Cloud storage has become very popular for both individuals and organizations. For example, Apple offers iCloud storage, Microsoft offers OneDrive, and Google offers Google Drive. You can typically get some storage for free or pay nominal fees for more storage. Their prices continue to drop as they continue to offer more storage space.

Heavily utilized systems and networks often depend on cloud computing resources to handle increased loads. As an example, consider the biggest shopping day in the United States—Black Friday, the day after Thanksgiving, when retailers hope to go into the black. Several years ago, Amazon.com had so much traffic during the Thanksgiving weekend that its servers could barely handle it. The company learned its lesson, though. The next year, it used cloud computing to rent access to servers specifically for the Thanksgiving weekend, and, despite increased sales, it didn't have any problems.

As many great innovators do, Amazon didn't look on this situation as a problem, but rather an opportunity. If it needed cloud computing for its heavily utilized system, other companies probably had the same need. Amazon now hosts cloud services to other organizations via its Amazon Elastic Compute Cloud (Amazon EC2) service. Amazon EC2 combines virtualization with cloud computing and they currently provide a wide variety of services via Amazon EC2.

As a comparison, organizations can also use on-premise or hosted services:

- **On-premise.** All resources are owned, operated, and maintained within the organization's building or buildings.
- **Hosted.** Organizations can rent access to resources from a specific organization. Note that the line is blurred between hosted and cloud services. In some cases, you know exactly where the services are hosted. However, in most cases, hosted services are somewhere within the cloud.

Software as a Service

Software as a Service (**SaaS**) includes any software or application provided to users over a network such as the Internet. Internet users access the SaaS applications with a web browser. It usually doesn't matter which web browser or operating system a SaaS customer uses. They could be using Microsoft Edge, Chrome, Firefox, or just about any web browser.

As mentioned previously, web-based email is an example of SaaS. This includes Gmail, Yahoo! Mail, and others. The service provides all the components of email to users via a simple web browser.

If you have a Gmail account, you can also use Google Docs, another example of SaaS. Google Docs provides access to several SaaS applications, allowing users to open text documents, spreadsheets, presentations, drawings, and PDF files through a web browser.

A talented developer and I teamed up to work on a project a while ago. He's an Apple guy running a macOS while I'm a Microsoft guy running Windows, and we live in different states. However, we post and share documents through Google Docs and despite different locations and different applications running on our individual systems, we're able to easily collaborate. One risk is that our data is hosted on Google Docs, and if attackers hack into Google Docs, our data may be compromised.

Platform as a Service

Platform as a Service (**PaaS**) provides customers with a preconfigured computing platform they can use as needed. It provides the customer with an easy-to-configure operating system, combined with appropriate applications and on-demand computing.

Many cloud providers refer to this as a managed hardware solution. For example, I host *http://gcgapremium.com/* on a virtual server through Liquid Web (*http://www.liquidweb.com/*) using one of their "Fully Managed" offerings.

Liquid Web provides several features in their fully managed solutions, including an installed operating system, a core software package used for web servers, Apache as a web server, antivirus software, spam protection, and more. Additionally, they keep the operating system up to date with relevant updates and patches. I manage the software used for the web site, including software changes and updates. However, I don't need to worry about managing the server itself. The couple of times when the server developed a problem, they fixed it before I was even aware of the problem.

Infrastructure as a Service

Infrastructure as a Service (**IaaS**) allows an organization to outsource its equipment requirements, including the hardware and all support operations. The IaaS service provider owns the equipment, houses it in its data center, and performs all the required hardware maintenance. The customer essentially rents access to the equipment and often pays on a per-use basis.

Many cloud providers refer to this as a self-managed solution. They provide access to a server with a default operating system installation, but customers must configure it and install additional software based on their needs. Additionally, customers are responsible for all operating system updates and patches.

IaaS can also be useful if an organization is finding it difficult to manage and maintain servers in its own data center. By outsourcing its requirements, the company limits its hardware footprint. It can do this instead of, or in addition to, virtualizing some of its servers. With IaaS, it needs fewer servers in its data center and fewer resources, such as power, HVAC, and personnel to manage the servers.

> **Remember this**
>
> Applications such as web-based email provided over the Internet are Software as a Service (SaaS) cloud-based technologies. Platform as a Service (PaaS) provides customers with a fully managed platform, which the vendor keeps up to date with current patches. Infrastructure as a Service (IaaS) provides customers with access to hardware in a self-managed platform.

Security Responsibilities with Cloud Models

One important consideration with cloud service models is the difference in security responsibilities assigned to the cloud service provider (CSP) and the customer. Figure 5.2 (derived from Figure 1 in the U.S. Department of Defense (DoD) "Cloud Computing Security Requirements Guide") shows the difference in the amount of responsibilities for a SaaS, PaaS, and IaaS. This includes both maintenance responsibilities and security responsibilities.

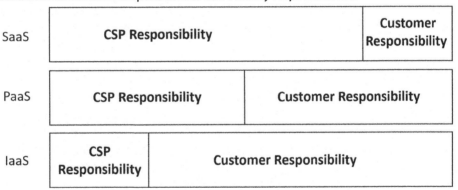

Figure 5.2: Security responsibilities with cloud models

As an example, for SaaS, consider Gmail. Google has the primary responsibility for maintaining the app and ensuring it is available. Additionally, Google has the primary responsibility of ensuring the security for Gmail. If you use it, you still have some responsibility, such as ensuring you use a strong password that is different from other online accounts.

With a PaaS solution, the CSP has the responsibility to provide you with the platform and ensure it remains available. Many CSPs provide additional security protection, such as firewalls, malware content filters, and intrusion detection systems. Still, the customer has a much greater responsibility for the operation, configuration, and security of the platform.

The CSP has the least responsibility for an IaaS solution and the customer has the most responsibility when compared with both PaaS and SaaS.

Security as a Service

Another entry into cloud computing is Security as a Service. It includes any services provided via the cloud that provide security services, and is commonly viewed as a subset of the Software as a Service (SaaS) model.

A common example of a Security as a Service application is antivirus software. Imagine radio station W-KOMA decides to purchase antivirus software for its eight employees. They purchase licenses to access the software from an antivirus company. Each employee then configures their system to use the software with their individual licenses. Once installed, the software automatically downloads virus definitions keeping each user's system up to date without relying on the user to do so.

A key benefit of Security as a Service is that it outsources the administrative tasks associated with implementing the service. Additionally, professionals are focused on the specific security services offered, eliminating the need for employees to be experts on everything.

Organizations that use cloud resources often add a *cloud access security broker (CASB)* for additional security. This is a software tool or service deployed between an organization's network and the cloud provider. It monitors all network traffic and can enforce security policies. As an example, it can ensure that all data stored in the cloud is encrypted.

Cloud Deployment Models

There are four categories of *cloud deployment models*: public, private, community, and hybrid. These identify who has access to the cloud infrastructure.

Public cloud services are available from third-party companies, such as Amazon, Google, Microsoft, and Apple. They provide similar services to anyone willing to pay for them.

A private cloud is set up for specific organizations. For example, the Shelbyville Nuclear Power Plant might decide it wants to store data in the cloud, but does not want to use a third-party vendor. Instead, the plant chooses to host its own servers and make these servers available to internal employees through the Internet.

Communities with shared concerns (such as goals, security requirements, or compliance considerations) can share cloud resources within a community cloud. As an example, imagine that the Shelbyville Nuclear Power Plant and several schools within Springfield decided to share educational resources within a cloud. They could each provide resources for the cloud and only organizations within the community would have access to the resources.

Not all cloud implementations fit exactly into these definitions, though. A hybrid cloud is a combination of two or more clouds. They can be private, public, community, or a combination. These retain separate identities to help protect resources in private clouds. However, they are bridged together, often in such a way that it is transparent to the users.

Remember this

A cloud access security broker (CASB) is a software tool or service deployed between an organization's network and the cloud provider. It provides Security as a Service by monitoring traffic and enforcing security policies. Private clouds are only available for one organization. Public cloud services are provided by third-party companies and available to anyone. A community cloud is shared by multiple organizations. A hybrid cloud is a combination of two or more clouds.

Deploying Mobile Devices Securely

Mobile devices represent significant challenges for organizations today. Organizations need to determine if employees can connect mobile devices to the network. If so, organizations need to identify methods to manage the security related to the devices, and how to monitor the devices and enforce security policies.

What is a mobile device? Within the context of the CompTIA Security+ exam, you can think of a mobile device as a smartphone or tablet. Further, NIST SP 800-124, "Guidelines for Managing the Security of Mobile Devices in the Enterprise," mentions that mobile devices have additional characteristics, such as at least one wireless network interface, local data storage, an operating system (that isn't a full-fledged desktop or laptop operating system), and the ability to install additional applications.

Mobile devices typically have other optional features. This includes other networking options such as Bluetooth, near field communication, cellular access for voice communications, and Global Positioning System (GPS) services. They typically include a digital camera, a video recorder, a microphone, and the ability to transfer data to another system such as a traditional computer or to other mobile devices.

The NIST definition excludes many devices. For example, a laptop is not considered a mobile device within this definition. Laptops have full operating systems and there are many security controls available for them, which aren't available in smartphones and tablets. Additionally, basic cell phones and digital cameras are not included in this definition because they cannot access networks and aren't susceptible to the same risks associated with smartphones and tablets.

Deployment Models

Any device connected to an organization's network represents a potential risk. As a simple example, if someone connects an infected device to a network, it might be able to infect other devices on the network. To limit this risk, organizations take steps to monitor and manage mobile devices.

If the organization owns all the devices connected to the network, it's a simple matter to monitor and manage them. However, if employees own these devices (such as their own smartphone), monitoring and managing the devices becomes more challenging. As an example, employees want to access the network resources with their own device, but they are sometimes resistant to allowing the organization to monitor and manage their personal device.

The following list identifies some common deployment models for mobile devices. Notice that in some models, the organization owns the device, but in other models, employees own the device:

- **Corporate-owned.** In this traditional deployment model, the organization purchases devices and issues them to employees.
- **COPE (corporate-owned, personally enabled).** *COPE* is similar to the traditional corporate-owned model, but the primary difference is that the employees are free to use the device as if it was their personally owned device. This allows employees to use the devices for personal activities in addition to connecting them to the organization's network. Because the organization owns the devices, it makes it easier to manage them.
- **BYOD (bring your own device).** Some organizations allow employees to bring their own mobile devices to work and attach them to the network. Employees are responsible for

selecting and supporting the device and they typically must comply with a **BYOD** policy when connecting their device to the network. While this is simple for the employees, it is sometimes referred to as *bring your own disaster* among IT professionals. Because employees can have any possible device, the IT department is now responsible for supporting, monitoring, and managing any possible device owned by employees.

- **CYOD (choose your own device).** To avoid some of the challenges related to supporting any possible mobile devices, some organizations create a list of acceptable devices along with a **CYOD** policy. Employees can purchase devices on the list and bring them to work. This gives the IT department a specific list of devices that they need to support, monitor, and manage.

- **VDI (virtual desktop infrastructure).** Chapter 1 discusses VDIs, which host a user's desktop operating system on a server. While these are typically accessed by traditional computers within a network, it's also possible to deploy a **VDI** that users can access with their mobile device. This allows users to access any applications installed on their desktop. When the organization hosts a remote access solution such as a virtual private network (VPN), users can access the mobile VDI from anywhere if they have Internet access.

> ### Remember this
>
> Corporate-owned, personally enabled (COPE) devices are owned by the organization, but employees can use them for personal reasons. A bring your own device (BYOD) policy allows employees to connect their own personal devices to the corporate network. A choose your own device (CYOD) policy includes a list of approved devices. Employees with a device on the list can connect them to the network. A virtual desktop infrastructure (VDI) is a virtual desktop and these can be created so that users can access them from a mobile device.

Connection Methods

There are several methods that mobile devices can use to connect to networks and other devices. They include:

- **Cellular.** Smartphones (and many tablets) include the ability to connect to a cellular network, such as a third generation (3G), long-term-evolution (LTE), fourth generation (4G), or 4G LTE network. The type of network you connect with is dependent on your cellular provider. Newer generations typically provide increased speed for digital transfers and improved voice communications.

- **Wi-Fi.** Mobile devices almost always have a wireless network interface that you can configure to connect to a wireless network. Chapter 4 discusses common wireless security methods and wireless protocols. Typical wireless networks require you to enter or select the service set identifier (**SSID**) and enter the pre-shared key or password to access the network. More secure networks use **Enterprise mode** with an 802.1x server.

- **SATCOM.** Some mobile devices support connections to networks using satellite communications (**SATCOM**). The most common usage of SATCOM is in mobile phones rather than tablets. However, you can purchase satellite hot spots. You can connect mobile devices to the hot spot, and the hot spot provides Internet and voice access via a satellite connection. Additionally, some vehicles include satellite communication technologies that can be used for phone calls and sometimes for shared Internet access.

- **Bluetooth.** Most mobile devices include Bluetooth support. Bluetooth is a wireless protocol commonly used with personal area networks. For example, most smartphones support the use of a Bluetooth headset for hands-free use of the phone. Additionally, some technologies use Bluetooth to connect two smartphones. For example, Apple's AirDrop uses Bluetooth to create a peer-to-peer network. This makes it easy to exchange files such as photos or videos between two phones.
- **NFC (near field communication).** NFC is most commonly used as a payment gateway allowing you to make payments simply by waving your phone in front of an NFC reader at a retailer. You can also create a peer-to-peer network between two devices with NFC. For example, Android Beam allows two users with Android devices to share data displayed on the screen by placing two devices back to back. Some applications use NFC to enable Bluetooth on the two devices, send the shared data via Bluetooth, and then disable Bluetooth.
- **ANT.** *ANT* and ANT+ are proprietary wireless protocols used by some mobile devices. While it looks like an acronym, it isn't spelled out on the ANT Wireless web site (*https://www.thisisant.com/*). Many sports and fitness sensors (such as Fitbit) collect data on users (such as heart rate, steps taken, and so on) and use ANT to send the data to a mobile device application.
- **Infrared.** Infrared is a line-of-sight wireless technology used by some mobile devices. This is the same technology used by most remote controls for TVs and other audiovisual equipment. Many people add apps to their smartphones and use them as a universal remote for their equipment. It's also possible to transfer files between smartphones using infrared, as long as both smartphones support infrared.
- **USB (Universal Serial Bus).** Mobile devices can typically be connected to a desktop PC or laptop via a USB cable. Most Apple devices have a Lightning port and can connect to PCs via a Lightning to USB cable. Many Android devices have a mini-USB cable and can connect to PCs via a mini-USB to standard USB cable.

Mobile Device Management

Mobile device management (*MDM*) includes the technologies to manage mobile devices. The goal is to ensure these devices have security controls in place to keep them secure.

System management tools, such as Microsoft System Center Configuration Manager (SCCM, also known as ConfigMgr), ensure systems are kept up to date with current patches, have antivirus software installed with up-to-date definitions, and are secured using standard security practices. While these tools originally focused on desktop PCs and laptops, they have expanded to include many mobile devices. As an example, ConfigMgr includes support for many mobile devices, including Apple iOS-based devices and Android-based devices.

MDM applications help administrators manage mobile devices. The following bullets describe many of the MDM concepts that apply to mobile devices:

- **Application management.** MDM tools can restrict what applications can run on mobile devices. They often use application whitelists to control the applications and prevent unapproved applications from being installed.
- **Full device encryption.** Encryption protects against loss of confidentiality on multiple platforms, including workstations, servers, mobile devices, and data transmissions. Encryption methods such as full device encryption provide device security, application security, and data security. While an organization can ensure corporate-owned devices

use full device encryption, this isn't always possible when employees use their own devices.

- **Storage segmentation.** In some mobile devices, it's possible to use *storage segmentation* to isolate data. For example, users might be required to use external storage for any corporate data to reduce the risk of data loss if the device is lost or stolen. It's also possible to create separate segments within the device. Users would store corporate data within an encrypted segment and personal data elsewhere on the device.

- **Content management.** After creating segmented storage spaces, it's important to ensure that appropriate content is stored there. An MDM system can ensure that all content retrieved from an organization source (such as a server) is stored in an encrypted segment. Also, content management can force the user to authenticate again when accessing data within this encrypted segment.

- **Containerization.** Chapter 1 discusses the use of application cell virtualization (also known as container virtualization). *Containerization* can also be implemented in mobile devices. By running an application in a container, it isolates and protects the application, including any of its data. This is very useful when an organization allows employees to use their own devices. It's possible to encrypt the container to protect it without encrypting the entire device.

- **Passwords and PINs.** Mobile devices commonly support the use of passwords or personal identification numbers (PINs). MDM systems typically support password policies, similar to the password policies used in desktop systems. The only limitation is that some mobile devices only support PINs, while others support either passwords or PINs.

- **Biometrics.** Chapter 2 discusses biometrics as one of the authentication factors (something you are). Many mobile devices now support biometrics for authentication. For example, you can teach the device your fingerprint and then use your fingerprint to authenticate instead of entering a password or PIN.

> ### Remember this
>
> Mobile device management (MDM) tools help enforce security policies on mobile devices. This includes the use of storage segmentation, containerization, and full device encryption to protect data. They also include enforcing strong authentication methods to prevent unauthorized access.

- **Screen locks.** Most devices support the use of a passcode or password to lock the device. This is like a password-protected screen saver on desktop systems that automatically locks the device after a period of time. It prevents someone from easily accessing the device and the data it contains. This is often combined with an erase function. For example, if someone steals the phone and enters the incorrect passcode ten times, the smartphone will automatically erase all data on the phone.

- **Remote wipe.** *Remote wipe* capabilities are useful if the phone is lost. It sends a remote signal to the device to wipe or erase all the data. The owner can send a remote wipe signal to the phone to delete all the data on the phone. This also deletes any cached data, such as cached online banking passwords, and provides a complete sanitization of the device by removing all valuable data.

- **Geolocation.** Mobile devices commonly include Global Positioning System (**GPS**) capabilities that can be used for **geolocation**. Applications commonly use GPS to identify the location of the device. This can also be used to locate a lost device.
- **Geofencing.** Organizations sometimes use GPS to create a virtual fence or geographic boundary using **geofencing** technologies. Apps can respond when the device is within the virtual fence. As an example, an organization can configure mobile apps so that they will only run when the device is within the virtual fence. Similarly, an organization can configure a wireless network to only operate for mobile devices within the defined boundary.
- **GPS tagging.** *GPS tagging* (also called geotagging) adds geographical information to files such as pictures when posting them to social media web sites. For example, when you take a picture with a smartphone that has GPS features enabled, the picture application adds latitude and longitude coordinates to the picture. Thinking of friends and family, this is a neat feature. However, thinking of thieves and criminals, they can exploit this data. For example, if Lisa frequently posts pictures of friends and family at her house, these pictures identify her address. If she later starts posting pictures from a vacation location, thieves can realize she's gone and burglarize her home.
- **Context-aware authentication.** *Context-aware authentication* uses multiple elements to authenticate a user and a mobile device. It can include the user's identity, geolocation, verification that the device is within a geofence, time of day, and type of device. Combined, these elements help prevent unauthorized users from accessing apps or data.
- **Push notification services.** *Push notification services* send messages to mobile devices from apps. As an example, if Lisa installs the Facebook app on her smartphone and enables notifications, the Facebook app will send her notifications. Software developers can configure the notifications to appear even if the device is in screen lock mode and even if the app is not running. MDM apps can send notifications to remind users of security settings, or to let them know if their device is complying with security policy requirements.

Remember this

Remote wipe sends a signal to a lost or stolen device to erase all data. Geolocation uses Global Positioning System (GPS) and can help locate a lost or stolen device. Geofencing creates a virtual fence or geographic boundary and can be used to detect when a device is within an organization's property. GPS tagging adds geographical data to files such as pictures. Context-aware authentication uses multiple elements to authenticate a user and a mobile device.

Mobile Device Enforcement and Monitoring

MDM tools often manage devices differently depending on who owns them. If the organization owns the device, the MDM tool will typically download and install all required applications, and ensure they are kept up to date.

If the device is employee-owned, MDM tools will monitor them for compliance and block access to the network if the device doesn't meet minimum requirements. For example, if the device isn't patched or doesn't have up-to-date antivirus software, the MDM software works with network access control (NAC) technologies to prevent the device from connecting to the network. The following paragraphs identify many common issues that an MDM can monitor and/or enforce.

Unauthorized Software

Organizations typically want users to only install apps obtained from approved sources. For example, all iPhone and iPad devices would only obtain apps from Apple's App Store. Apple is aggressive in testing these apps for malware and any developer who attempts to distribute malware through the Apple store is often banned. Similarly, Google maintains the Google Play site for Android devices.

A *third-party app store* is something other than Apple's App Store or Google Play. Apps obtained from these third-party app stores don't undergo the same level of scrutiny as apps on the App Store or Google Play and represent a higher risk. Apple makes it very difficult to obtain apps from a third-party app store, but it is relatively easy to obtain apps from third-party stores for Android devices.

Jailbreaking refers to removing all software restrictions from an Apple device. After jailbreaking a device, users can install software from any third-party source. *Rooting* is the process of modifying an Android device to give the user root-level (or full administrator) access to the device. Both rooting and jailbreaking introduce risks and vulnerabilities to the device, so it's common for an MDM to block all access to a network if it detects a device has either been rooted or jailbroken.

Mobile devices typically have the operating system stored in onboard memory such as flash memory, which retains data even without power. Because the operating system is the software and the memory is hardware, this is commonly called firmware. Updates to the operating system overwrite the firmware using over-the-air (OTA) techniques. *Firmware OTA updates* keep the device up to date.

It's also possible to overwrite the firmware with *custom firmware*. Some people do this as another method of rooting Android devices. The process is typically complex and fraught with risks. However, some people find downloadable images and copy them onto their devices to overwrite the firmware.

It's also possible to install applications on Android devices by *sideloading* them. Sideloading is the process of copying an application package in the Application Packet Kit (APK) format to the device and then activating it. The device must be set to allow apps from Unknown Sources, which can significantly weaken security. Sideloading is useful for developers testing apps, but considered risky when installing apps from third parties.

> ## Remember this
>
> Jailbreaking removes all software restrictions from an Apple device. Rooting modifies an Android device, giving users root-level access to the device. Overwriting the firmware on an Android device with custom firmware is another way to root an Android device. Sideloading is the process of installing software on an Android device from a source other than an authorized store.

Many people use text messaging services such as Short Message Service (**SMS**) and Multimedia Messaging Service (**MMS**). SMS is a basic text messaging service supported on many telephone and mobile devices. MMS is an extension of SMS that allows users to include multimedia content such as a picture, a short video, audio, or even a slideshow of multiple images.

There are two primary risks with text messaging. First, both send text in plaintext, allowing the information to be intercepted and read by others. However, many apps such as iMessage offer encryption capabilities.

The second risk only applies to MMS because it can send media. Attackers have discovered ways to send an MMS message to a phone number and gain remote code execution privileges on the user's phone. For example, security researchers identified a vulnerability in Stagefright, a media library within the Android operating system that is susceptible to attacks. In 2015, experts indicated that 95 percent of Android devices were vulnerable. At this point, the vulnerability is patched on most devices.

Most smartphones can store credit card data and be used for payments. For example, NFC (described earlier in this chapter) is often used as a payment gateway with some mobile devices. When issuing phones to users, organizations need to consider if they want to put their own payment methods on the phone for some payments. If so, this typically needs to be monitored closely.

Hardware Control

An organization might want to control the use of some of the hardware on mobile devices and MDM tools can help. Mobile devices commonly include a camera and a recording microphone. These are useful for regular users, but can present significant risks for employees within an organization.

As an example, attackers have successfully inserted malicious code into some apps available on some third-party sites. When users install the apps, it allows an attacker to remotely connect to the phone, snap pictures, record audio, and much more.

To eliminate the risk, an organization can configure the MDM software to disable the camera and recording microphone. Ideally, the MDM tool will only disable the camera and microphone when it detects the device is within a previously configured geofence. Unfortunately, all MDM tools don't support disabling hardware based on geolocation. If the MDM tool doesn't support this feature, the organization may prohibit the possession of smartphones in certain areas.

MDM tools can also prevent the use of external media and Universal Serial Bus On-The-Go (**USB OTG**) cables. Mobile devices commonly have one or more ports where you can plug in a cable. Apple devices have a Lightning port and Android devices typically have a micro-USB or mini-USB. In some cases, it's possible to connect external media (such as an external drive) to the device. Organizations might want to prevent this because the media presents additional risks. It could contain malware. It might also allow a malicious insider to copy a massive amount of data.

USB OTG cables allow you to connect just about any device to your mobile device, including another mobile device. This includes a mouse, keyboard, Musical Instrument Digital Interface (MIDI) keyboard, and external media. Many people find this very useful to transfer photos from digital cameras to their mobile device. Again, though, because this allows connections to external media, an organization might choose to disable the feature using MDM tools.

Unauthorized Connections

Management within an organization might want to limit a mobile device's connection. For example, if the mobile device can connect to the primary network, management might want to ensure that the mobile device cannot access the Internet using another connection. This section identifies other connections that can be modified and blocked with an MDM tool.

Most smartphones support **tethering**, which allows you to share one device's Internet connection with other devices. As an example, you can connect your smartphone to the Internet and then use this Internet connection with a laptop, a tablet, or any device that has a wireless connection. If employees use tethering within the organization, it allows them to bypass security such as firewalls and proxy servers. Imagine Bart wants to visit a not safe for work (NSFW) site with his work laptop. The proxy server blocks his access. However, he can tether his laptop to his smartphone and visit the site. This direct connection will also bypass any content filters in the network, and possibly allow malware onto his laptop.

Many mobile devices also support **Wi-Fi Direct**, which is a standard that allows devices to connect without a wireless access point, or wireless router. This is similar to a wireless **ad hoc** network, which allows devices to connect together without a wireless access point or wireless router. The difference is that Wi-Fi Direct uses single radio hop communication. In other words, none of the devices in a Wi-Fi Direct network can share an Internet connection. However, systems in a wireless ad hoc network use multihop wireless communications and can share an Internet connection.

Smartphones are typically locked into a specific carrier such as Verizon or AT&T. A subscriber identification module (SIM) card identifies what countries and/or networks the phone will use. In other words, if Lisa has a smartphone and a Verizon plan, the SIM card in her phone will connect her to a Verizon network instead of an AT&T network.

If Lisa purchased her phone under a two-year contract and fulfilled all the terms of her plan, she can unlock her phone (also called **carrier unlocking**) and use it with another carrier. An organization might want to block this capability for all COPE devices.

> **Remember this**
>
> Tethering is the process of sharing a mobile device's Internet connection with other devices. Wi-Fi Direct is a standard that allows devices to connect without a wireless access point, or wireless router. MDM tools can block access to devices using tethering or Wi-Fi Direct to access the Internet.

Exploring Embedded Systems

An **embedded system** is any device that has a dedicated function and uses a computer system to perform that function. Desktop PCs, laptops, and servers all use central processing units (CPUs), operating systems, and applications to perform various functions. Similarly, embedded systems use CPUs, operating systems, and one or more applications to perform various functions.

As a simple example, a wireless multi-function printer typically includes an embedded system. It runs a web site that you can access wirelessly to configure the printer. Of course, you can also send print jobs to it, scan documents, and copy documents with the printer. Many include faxing capabilities and sending documents via email.

Person of Interest

Person of Interest, a science fiction TV show that includes a mix of fiction and facts, does give some realistic insight into how mobile devices can be compromised and used by attackers.

Some scenarios showed John Reese (and others on the show) using Bluetooth to pair with a device or send a message to a phone and then install malware. Once installed, Reese and others on the show have almost unlimited access to the phone. Some of their capabilities include:

- Monitoring all text messages
- Tracking the phone's location
- Turning on the microphone to listen in on conversations
- Monitoring and recording all phone calls (including phone numbers)

While there aren't any known ways to do this on current phones, these capabilities have existed in the past. For example, forced Bluetooth pairing was frequently possible in the early 2000s, but security measures have closed this security hole for most, if not all, smartphones today. Similarly, MMS vulnerabilities on Android smartphones allowed attackers to take over a phone just by sending an MMS message to it. Once an attacker takes over the phone, the other capabilities become almost trivial.

Other systems that include embedded systems are camera systems, medical devices, smart televisions, automobiles, and household appliances like refrigerators, microwave ovens, and burglar alarm systems. Each device can use a different CPU, operating system, and application depending on its function.

Security Implications and Vulnerabilities

The challenge with embedded systems is keeping them up to date with security fixes. Exploits are regularly discovered for desktop PC and server operating systems and applications. When vendors discover them, they release patches. When you apply the patch, the system is no longer vulnerable to the exploit. In contrast, vendors of embedded systems are not as aggressive in identifying vulnerabilities and creating patches to fix them.

Also, patch management is a routine function for IT administrators in most organizations. They regularly review patches, test them, and apply them when necessary. In contrast, how often does a regular user think about checking or applying patches to his refrigerator?

Another significant security concern is when embedded systems are deployed with default configurations. For example, imagine Homer creates a home security system using Internet-accessible security cameras, deployed with default username and passwords. If attackers discover the cameras, they can access them over the Internet.

Worse, if attackers discover a vulnerability within the cameras' embedded systems, they can exploit them. This is exactly what attackers did in the 2016 Dyn cyberattack that took down the Internet. Chapter 7 discusses this attack within the "DNS Attacks" section. Attackers infected cameras and other Internet-connected devices and joined them to a botnet. They then used these devices to launch attacks.

Comparing Embedded Systems

The CompTIA Security+ objectives include a long list of embedded systems. Some of these might be familiar to you, but others use acronyms that aren't familiar to many people. The following section describes many common embedded systems.

A smart television (TV) is one of many smart devices that you might have in your home. You can easily connect it to your home's wired or wireless network and use it to access the Internet. Many people use it to stream TV shows and movies to their TV. This is possible because these smart TVs have embedded systems giving them additional capabilities.

Other smart devices include wearable technology and home automation systems. Combined, these smart devices are often referred to as the Internet of things (*IoT*).

Wearable technology has exploded in recent years. It includes any device you can wear or have implanted. These devices can then be used to interact with other devices, such as a smartphone. As an example, Fitbit has manufactured a range of products that you can wear to monitor your health and fitness. Combined with an app on their smartphone, people can gain insight into how well they're doing on their goals.

Most veterinarians recommend implanting microchips in pets. Animal shelters routinely look for these and if found, they can help return the pets to their owners. Some can even be used to open some pet doors. The company Dangerous Things sells a similar device for people that can reportedly be injected into your hand at the tattoo parlor. Once injected, you can program it to open some smart locks or control your cell phone. Be careful, though. Dangerous Things warns "Use of this device is strictly at your own risk."

Home automation includes Internet-connected devices, such as wireless thermostats, lighting, coffee makers, and more. These devices typically connect to the home's network, which gives them Internet access. This allows people to access or control these devices from the Internet, even when they aren't home.

Camera systems often include Internet-connected cameras. These cameras can be within a home automation system or supporting physical security goals for an organization.

A system on a chip (*SoC*) is an integrated circuit that includes all the functionality of a computing system within the hardware. It typically includes an application contained within onboard memory, such as read-only memory (ROM), electrically erasable programmable ROM (EEPROM), or flash memory. Many mobile computing devices include an SoC.

> ### Remember this
>
> An embedded system is any device that has a dedicated function and uses a computer system to perform that function. It includes any devices in the Internet of things (IoT) category, such as wearable technology and home automation systems. Some embedded systems use a system on a chip (SoC).

An industrial control system (*ICS*) typically refers to systems within large facilities such as power plants or water treatment facilities. An ICS is controlled by a supervisory control and data acquisition (*SCADA*) system. Ideally, these systems are contained within isolated networks, such as within a virtual local area network (VLAN), that do not have access to the Internet. If they are connected to the corporate network, they are often protected by a network intrusion prevention system (NIPS) to block unwanted traffic. Chapter 3 discusses VLANs and Chapter 4 discusses NIPS.

Understanding Stuxnet

Stuxnet provides a great example of the need to protect embedded systems, such as SCADA systems. Stuxnet is a computer worm designed to attack a specific embedded system used in one of Iran's nuclear enrichment facilities. It caused centrifuges to spin fast enough to tear themselves apart and some reports indicated it destroyed as many as 20 percent of these centrifuges.

Security expert Roel Schouwenberg completed extensive research on Stuxnet and identified how it operated in six major steps:

1. **Infection.** Stuxnet first infected Windows systems through infected USB drives after someone plugged one into the system. One of the architects of Stuxnet reportedly said "...there is always an idiot around who doesn't think much about the thumb drive in their hand." Indeed, USB sticks have been the source of many infections.

2. **Search.** Stuxnet checks the network of the infected system looking for the targeted system.

3. **Update.** If it finds the targeted system, it downloads an updated version of the worm.

4. **Compromise.** It then attempts to compromise the targeted system. When first released, Stuxnet took advantage of four zero-day vulnerabilities. Zero-day vulnerabilities are either unknown to the vendor, or the vendor hasn't released a patch for them yet.

5. **Control.** It then sends signals to the systems. A late version of Stuxnet told the systems to spin the centrifuges uncontrollably.

6. **Deceive and destroy.** While it was causing the centrifuges to spin out of control, it was sending false data to engineers monitoring the system. Monitoring systems indicated everything was fine.

A real-time operating system (**RTOS**) is an operating system that reacts to input within a specific time. If it can't respond within the specified time, it doesn't process the data and typically reports an error. As an example, imagine an automated assembly line used to create donuts. Each location on the line receives materials from the previous location, adds additional materials or somehow processes the materials (such as mixing them), and passes the result to the next location. Each of these locations could include an embedded system with an RTOS to ensure it receives and processes the materials within a specified time. If it doesn't, it can raise an error or alert and stop the assembly line.

Admittedly, an RTOS is probably overkill for a donut assembly line. There are simpler ways. However, some assembly lines are much quicker and require response times for each location in the millisecond or nanosecond range. An RTOS can be used reliably in these systems.

Heating, ventilation, and air conditioning (**HVAC**) systems keep computing systems at the proper temperature and with the proper humidity. Most have embedded systems to control them. If attackers can access these systems, they may be able to remotely turn off the HVAC system or trick it into keeping the temperature at 95 degrees within a data center. The resulting damage to systems within this data center could be catastrophic.

You can also find many embedded systems in special-purpose devices, such as medical devices, automotive vehicles, and unmanned aerial vehicles. Some control dedicated tasks, such as ensuring each engine cylinder fires at exactly the right time. Others control much more complex tasks, such as automatically parallel parking a car. Select the option and take your hands off the wheel. The car will park itself, within the space, and without hitting anything.

While these systems aren't necessarily accessible via the Internet, many autos now include Internet access via satellite communications. Manufacturers could decide to integrate all the embedded systems in an automobile, making them all accessible via the Internet.

Aircraft and unmanned aerial vehicles (*UAVs*) include embedded systems. Hobbyists use small UAVs to take pictures remotely. Other organizations such as the military include sophisticated embedded systems for reconnaissance and to deliver weapons.

> ### Remember this
>
> A supervisory control and data acquisition (SCADA) system has embedded systems that control an industrial control system (ICS), such as one used in a power plant or water treatment facility. Embedded systems are also used for many special purposes, such as medical devices, automotive vehicles, aircraft, and unmanned aerial vehicles (UAVs).

Protecting Data

Data is one of the most valuable resources any organization manages, second only to its people. If you ever tune into the news, you've likely heard about data breaches at organizations such as Arby's, Edmodo, OkCupid, St. Mark's Surgery Center, Uber, Verizon, Washington State University, and Yahoo!. Unfortunately, data breaches are frequent and they affect millions of people. In the worst-case scenarios, thieves use the stolen data to empty bank accounts, rack up fraudulent charges on credit cards, and steal individuals' identities.

Losing control of data directly affects the reputation, and often the bottom line, of an organization. The importance of taking steps to protect valuable data cannot be overstated.

Chapter 11 covers security policies that an organization can implement to protect data. The security policy helps an organization classify and label its data. This section presents many of the security controls an organization can use to protect data based on the requirements set within a data security policy.

Confidentiality is primarily protected through encryption and strong access controls. Chapter 2 focuses on access controls starting with strong authentication methods. This chapter discusses software-based and hardware-based encryption methods, and Chapter 10 covers specific encryption algorithms used to protect data.

Protecting Confidentiality with Encryption

As mentioned in Chapter 1, one of the primary ways you can prevent the loss of confidentiality is by encrypting data. This includes encrypting data-at-rest no matter what type of device it is stored on and encrypting data-in-transit no matter what type of transmission media is used. It is much more difficult for an attacker to view encrypted data than it is to view unencrypted data.

You can use other tools to restrict access to data, but this isn't always effective. For example, consider the Microsoft New Technology File System (NTFS), which allows you to configure permissions within access control lists (ACLs). You can use NTFS to set permissions on files and folders to restrict access. However, if a thief steals a laptop with NTFS-protected files, it's a simple matter to access them. The thief simply moves the drive to another system as an extra drive, logs on as the administrator, and takes ownership of the files. Encryption isn't as easy to bypass.

Database Security

Another form of software-based encryption is with databases. For example, many database applications such as Oracle Database or Microsoft SQL Server include the ability to encrypt data held within a database. Although it's possible to encrypt the entire database, it's more common to encrypt specific data elements.

As an example, imagine a database includes a table named Customers. Each record within the table has multiple columns, including customer number, last name, first name, credit card number, and security code. Instead of encrypting the entire table, administrators can choose to encrypt only the credit card number and security code fields within each record. This protects the sensitive data, but doesn't waste valuable processing power encrypting data that isn't sensitive.

> **Remember this**
>
> The primary methods of protecting the confidentiality of data are with encryption and strong access controls. Database column encryption protects individual fields within a database.

File System Security

Many operating systems support file- and folder-level encryption. Linux systems support GNU Privacy Guard (GnuPG or GPG), which is a command-line tool used to encrypt and decrypt files with a password. Microsoft NTFS includes the Encrypting File System (EFS), available in most Windows operating systems. An attacker will have a more difficult time accessing these encrypted files.

A benefit of file- and folder-level encryption is that you can encrypt individual files without encrypting an entire disk. For example, a server may store files accessed by users throughout the company. Access controls provide a first level of protection for these files, but administrators may be able to bypass the access controls. Imagine that a company stores payroll data on the server and wants to ensure that a malicious insider with administrative privileges can't access the data. Using file encryption provides an additional level of protection.

Permission Issues and Access Violations

A common security issue with permissions is giving users more permissions than they need. The principle of least privilege is a core security principle and mentioned several times in this book. In short, it means that users are given only the rights and permissions they need to do their job, and no more. When users have more permissions than they need, they can accidentally, or maliciously, cause problems.

An access violation occurs if users access materials that they shouldn't. As an example, imagine that Bart is a help-desk technician. During a review of logs, security administrators discover that Bart has accessed payroll data though he has no business looking at this data. This is an access violation and should be investigated. A primary objective of security investigators is to discover how Bart accessed the materials.

Linux Permissions

CompTIA has been increasingly adding questions about Linux so you should understand some basics about Linux permissions. There are three primary entities that you can assign permissions to within Linux. They are:

- **Owner.** This is a user who owns the file or directory and the owner is typically granted all permissions for the file or directory.
- **Group.** The file can also be owned by a named group. Members of this group are granted specific permissions for the file or directory. These permissions are typically less than the permissions applied to the owner.
- **Others.** You can think of this as everyone else. Permissions applied here do not override the Owner or Group permissions.

In addition to understanding who you can assign permissions to, it's also important to understand the basic Linux permissions. These may be represented as letters (*r*, *w*, and *x*) or as numbers. They are:

- **Read (r).** This allows you to view the file and is represented with the number **4**.
- **Write (w).** This allows you to modify the file and is represented with the number **2**.
- **Execute (x).** This allows you to run the file (assuming it is an application) and is represented with the number **1**.

If a permission is not assigned, you'll see it represented as a dash. It's also possible to assign multiple permissions, such as Read and Execute; Read and Write; and Read, Write, and Execute. The following bullets show the numbers used to represent combined permissions:

- **5** indicates Read (4) + Execute (1)
- **6** indicates Read (4) + Write (2)
- **7** indicates Read (4) + Write (2) + Execute (1)

Table 5.1 shows how these Linux permission types are often displayed in a file access control list (FACL). Each line represents the FACL for a different file.

File Name	Owner	Group	All Other Users
Success.exe	rwx	rw-	- - -
Study.docx	rwx	rw-	r- -
UCanPass.exe	rwx	r-x	r-x

Table 5.1: Linux permissions

Looking at Table 5.1, you can see that the following permissions will be assigned to the different entities:

- **Success.exe.** Owner has read, write, and execute permissions (rwx), Group has read and write permissions (rw-), and other users have zero permissions (- - -).
- **Study.docx.** Owner has read, write, and execute permissions (rwx), Group has read and write permissions (rw-), and other users have read permissions (r- -).
- **UCanPass.exe.** Owner has read, write, and execute permissions (rwx), Group has read and execute permissions (r-x), and other users have read and execute permissions (r-x).

Table 5.2 shows these same permissions represented as numbers.

File Name	Number	Owner	Group	All Other Users
Success.exe	760	111	110	000
Study.docx	764	111	110	100
UCanPass.exe	755	111	101	101

Table 5.2: Linux permissions in octal notation

Administrators typically use the chmod command (short for change mode) to change permissions for files. As an example, imagine that a file named *Success.exe* currently has the permissions set as 760 (rwx rw- - - -), but you want to change the permissions to 755 (rwx r-x r-x). You could use the following command:

chmod 755 success.exe

Remember this

File- and folder-level protection protects individual files. Full disk encryption protects entire disks, including USB flash drives and drives on mobile devices. The chmod command changes permissions on Linux systems.

Windows Permissions

Windows file and folder permissions are a little easier to understand because they are assigned by just pointing and clicking. For example, to modify the permissions for a file or folder, an administrator would right-click the file within File Explorer, select the Security tab, and modify the permissions. The following list shows the basic Windows permissions:

- **Read.** Users granted read permission can view the contents of a file or folder.
- **Read & Execute.** Users granted the Read & Execute permission have Read permission and they can also run or execute programs.
- **Write.** Users can create new files and folders, and they can also make changes to existing files and folders. This would typically be assigned with Read permission.
- **Modify.** When granted the Modify permission to a file or a folder, a user can read, execute, write, and delete files and folders. The primary addition is the ability to delete files and folders.

Data Loss Prevention

Organizations often use data loss prevention (**DLP**) techniques and technologies to prevent data loss. They can block the use of USB flash drives and control the use of removable media. They can also examine outgoing data and detect many types of unauthorized data transfers.

Removable Media

Removable media refers to any storage system that you can attach to a computer and easily copy data. It primarily refers to USB hard drives and USB flash drives, but many personal music devices, such as MP3 players, use the same type of flash drive memory as a USB flash drive. Users can plug them into a system and easily copy data to and from a system. Additionally, many of today's smartphones include storage capabilities using the same type of memory.

It's common for an organization to include security policy statements to prohibit the use of USB flash drives and other removable media. Some technical policies block use of USB drives completely.

A DLP solution is more selective and it can prevent a user from copying or printing files with specific content. For example, it's possible to configure a DLP solution to prevent users from copying or printing any classified documents marked with a label of Confidential. The DLP software scans all documents sent to the printer, and if it contains the label, the DLP software blocks it from reaching the printer.

In addition to blocking the transfer, a DLP solution will typically log these events. Some DLP solutions will also alert security administrators of the event. Depending on the organization's policy, personnel may be disciplined for unauthorized attempts to copy or print files.

Data Exfiltration

Data exfiltration is the unauthorized transfer of data outside an organization and is a significant concern. In some cases, attackers take control of systems and transfer data outside an organization using malware. It's also possible for malicious insiders to transfer data.

Chapter 3 discusses different types of content filters used in unified threat management (UTM) devices. These devices monitor incoming data streams looking for malicious code. In contrast, a network-based DLP monitors outgoing data looking for sensitive data, specified by an administrator.

DLP systems can scan the text of all emails and the content of any attached files, including documents, spreadsheets, presentations, and databases. Even if a user compresses a file as a zipped file before sending it, the DLP examines the contents by simply unzipping it.

As an example, I know of one organization that routinely scans all outgoing emails looking for Personally Identifiable Information (PII), such as Social Security numbers. The network-based DLP includes a mask to identify Social Security numbers as a string of numbers in the following format: ###-##-####. If an email or an attachment includes this string of numbers, the DLP detects it, blocks the email, and sends an alert to a security administrator.

Many organizations classify and label data using terms such as Confidential, Private, and Proprietary. It is easy to include these search terms in the DLP application, or any other terms considered important by the organization.

Network-based DLP systems are not limited to scanning only email. Many can scan the content of other traffic, such as FTP and HTTP traffic. Sophisticated data exfiltration attacks often encrypt data before sending it out, making it more difficult for a DLP system to inspect the data. However, a DLP system can typically be configured to look for outgoing encrypted data and alert security administrators when it is detected.

Cloud-Based DLP

It's common for personnel within organizations to store data in the cloud. This makes it easier to access the data from any location and from almost any device. Cloud-based DLP solutions allow an organization to implement policies for data stored in the cloud.

As an example, an organization can implement policies to detect Personally Identifiable Information (PII) or Protected Health Information (PHI) stored in the cloud. After detecting the data, a DLP policy can be configured to take one or more actions such as sending an alert to a security administrator, blocking any attempts to save the data in the cloud, and quarantining the data.

> ### *Remember this*
>
> Data exfiltration is the unauthorized transfer of data out of a network. Data loss prevention (DLP) techniques and technologies can block the use of USB devices to prevent data loss and monitor outgoing email traffic for unauthorized data transfers. A cloud-based DLP can enforce security policies for data stored in the cloud, such as ensuring that Personally Identifiable Information (PII) is encrypted.

Chapter 5 Exam Topic Review

When preparing for the exam, make sure you understand these key concepts covered in this chapter.

Implementing Secure Systems

- Least functionality is a core secure system design principle. It states that systems should be deployed with only the applications, services, and protocols they need to function.
- A trusted operating system meets a set of predetermined requirements such as those defined in the Common Criteria. It typically uses the mandatory access control (MAC) model.
- A master image provides a secure starting point for systems. Master images are typically created with templates or other baselines to provide a secure starting point for systems. Integrity measurement tools detect when a system deviates from the baseline.
- Patch management procedures ensure operating systems and applications are kept up to date with current patches. This ensures they are protected against known vulnerabilities.
- Change management policies define the process for making changes and help reduce unintended outages from changes.
- Application whitelisting allows authorized software to run, but blocks all other software. Application blacklisting blocks unauthorized software, but allows other software to run.
- Sandboxing provides a high level of flexibility for testing security controls and testing patches. You can create sandboxes in virtual machines (VMs) and with the chroot command on Linux systems.
- Electromagnetic interference (EMI) comes from sources such as motors, power lines, and fluorescent lights and can be prevented with shielding.
- Electromagnetic pulse (EMP) is a short burst of electromagnetic energy. Mild forms such as electrostatic discharge and lightning can be prevented but EMP damage from military weapons may not be preventable.
- Full disk encryption (FDE) encrypts an entire disk. A self-encrypting drive (SED) includes the hardware and software necessary to automatically encrypt a drive.
- A Trusted Platform Module (TPM) is a chip included with many laptops and some mobile devices and it provides full disk encryption, a secure boot process, and supports remote attestation. TPMs have an encryption key burned into them that provides a hardware root of trust.
- A hardware security module (HSM) is a removable or external device used for encryption. An HSM generates and stores RSA encryption keys and can be integrated with servers to provide hardware-based encryption.

Summarizing Cloud Concepts

- Cloud computing provides an organization with additional resources. Most cloud services are provided via the Internet or a hosting provider. On-premise clouds are owned and maintained by an organization.
- Software as a Service (SaaS) includes web-based applications such as web-based email.
- Infrastructure as a Service (IaaS) provides hardware resources via the cloud. It can help an organization limit the size of their hardware footprint and reduce personnel costs.
- Platform as a Service (PaaS) provides an easy-to-configure operating system and on-demand computing for customers.
- A cloud access security broker (CASB) is a software tool or service deployed between an organization's network and the cloud provider. It monitors all network traffic and can enforce security policies acting as Security as a Service.
- Private clouds are only available for a specific organization. Public cloud services are provided by third-party companies and available to anyone. A community cloud is shared by multiple organizations. A hybrid cloud is a combination of two or more clouds.

Deploying Mobile Devices Securely

- Mobile devices include smartphones and tablets and run a mobile operating system.
- Corporate-owned, personally enabled (COPE) mobile devices are owned by the organization, but employees can use them for personal reasons.
- Bring your own device (BYOD) policies allow employees to connect their mobile device to the organization's network. Choose your own device (CYOD) policies include a list of acceptable devices and allow employees with one of these devices to connect them to the network.
- A virtual desktop infrastructure (VDI) is a virtual desktop and these can be created so that users can access them from a mobile device.
- Mobile devices can connect to the Internet, networks, and other devices using cellular, wireless, satellite, Bluetooth, near field communication (NFC), ANT, infrared, and USB connections.
- Mobile device management (MDM) tools help ensure that devices meet minimum security requirements. They can monitor devices, enforce security policies, and block network access if devices do not meet these requirements.
- MDM tools can restrict applications on devices, segment and encrypt data, enforce strong authentication methods, and implement security methods such as screen locks and remote wipe.
- A screen lock is like a password-protected screen saver on desktop systems that automatically locks the device after a period of time. A remote wipe signal removes all the data from a lost phone.
- Geolocation uses Global Positioning System (GPS) to identify a device's location. Geofencing uses GPS to create a virtual fence or geographic boundary. Organizations use geofencing to enable access to services or devices when they are within the boundary, and block access when they are outside of the boundary.
- Geotagging uses GPS to add geographical information to files (such as pictures) when posting them on social media sites.

- A third-party app store is something other than the primary store for a mobile device. Apple's App Store is the primary store for Apple devices. Google Play is a primary store for Android devices.
- Jailbreaking removes all software restrictions on Apple devices. Rooting provides users with root-level access to an Android device. Custom firmware can also root an Android device. MDM tools block network access for jailbroken or rooted devices.
- Sideloading is the process of copying an application to an Android device instead of installing it from an online store.
- A Universal Serial Bus On-The-Go (USB OTG) cable allows you to connect mobile devices.
- Tethering allows one mobile device to share its Internet connection with other devices. Wi-Fi Direct allows you to connect devices together without a wireless router.

Exploring Embedded Systems

- An embedded system is any device that has a dedicated function and uses a computer system to perform that function. A security challenge with embedded systems is keeping them up to date.
- Embedded systems include smart devices sometimes called the Internet of things (IoT), such as wearable technology and home automation devices.
- A system on a chip (SoC) is an integrated circuit that includes a full computing system.
- A supervisory control and data acquisition (SCADA) system controls an industrial control system (ICS). The ICS is used in large facilities such as power plants or water treatment facilities. SCADA and ICS systems are typically in isolated networks without access to the Internet, and are sometimes protected by network intrusion prevention systems (NIPSs).
- A real-time operating system (RTOS) is an operating system that reacts to input within a specific time.
- Embedded systems are found in many common and special-purpose devices. This includes multi-function devices (MFDs), such as printers; heating, ventilation, and air conditioning (HVAC) systems; medical devices; automotive vehicles; aircraft; and unmanned aerial vehicles (UAVs).

Protecting Data

- The primary method of protecting the confidentiality of data is with encryption and strong access controls. File system security includes the use of encryption to encrypt files and folders.
- You can encrypt individual columns in a database (such as credit card numbers), entire databases, individual files, entire disks, and removable media.
- Users should be given only the permissions they need. When they have too much access, it can result in access violations or the unauthorized access of data.
- You can use the chmod command to change permissions on a Linux system.
- Data exfiltration is the unauthorized transfer of data outside an organization.
- Data loss prevention (DLP) techniques and technologies help prevent data loss. They can block transfer of data to USB devices and analyze outgoing data via email to detect unauthorized transfers. Cloud-based DLP systems can enforce security policies for any data stored in the cloud.

Online References

- Are you ready for performance-based questions? Don't forget to check out the online content at *http://gcgapremium.com/501-extras*.

Chapter 5 Practice Questions

1. Attackers recently attacked a web server hosted by your organization. Management has tasked administrators with configuring the servers following the principle of least functionality. Which of the following will meet this goal?
   - A. Disabling unnecessary services
   - B. Installing and updating antivirus software
   - C. Identifying the baseline
   - D. Installing a NIDS

2. Network administrators have identified what appears to be malicious traffic coming from an internal computer, but only when no one is logged on to the computer. You suspect the system is infected with malware. It periodically runs an application that attempts to connect to web sites over port 80 with Telnet. After comparing the computer with a list of applications from the master image, you verify this application is very likely the problem. What allowed you to make this determination?
   - A. Least functionality
   - B. Sandbox
   - C. Blacklist
   - D. Integrity measurements

3. Security experts want to reduce risks associated with updating critical operating systems. Which of the following will BEST meet this goal?
   - A. Implement patches when they are released.
   - B. Implement a change management policy.
   - C. Use only trusted operating systems.
   - D. Implement operating systems with secure configurations.

4. Your organization wants to ensure that employees do not install any unauthorized software on their computers. Which of the following is the BEST choice to prevent this?
   - A. Master image
   - B. Application whitelisting
   - C. Anti-malware software
   - D. Antivirus software

5. A software vendor recently developed a patch for one of its applications. Before releasing the patch to customers, the vendor needs to test it in different environments. Which of the following solutions provides the BEST method to test the patch in different environments?
   - A. Baseline image
   - B. BYOD
   - C. Sandbox
   - D. Change management

6. Managers within your organization want to implement a secure boot process for some key computers. During the boot process, each computer should send data to a remote system to check the computer's configuration. Which of the following will meet this goal?
   A. Trusted Platform Module
   B. Hardware root of trust
   C. Remote attestation
   D. Trusted operating system

7. The Springfield Nuclear Power Plant has created an online application teaching nuclear physics. Only students and teachers in the Springfield Elementary school can access this application via the cloud. What type of cloud service model is this?
   A. IaaS
   B. PaaS
   C. SaaS
   D. Public

8. An organization has a critical SCADA network it is using to manage a water treatment plant for a large city. Availability of this system is important. Which of the following security controls would be MOST relevant to protect this system?
   A. DLP
   B. TPM
   C. EMP
   D. NIPS

9. Bizzfad is planning to implement a CYOD deployment model. You're asked to provide input for the new policy. Which of the following concepts are appropriate for this policy?
   A. SCADA access
   B. Storage segmentation
   C. Database security
   D. Embedded RTOS

10. A new mobile device security policy has authorized the use of employee-owned devices, but mandates additional security controls to protect them if they are lost or stolen. Which of the following meets this goal?
    A. Screen locks and GPS tagging
    B. Patch management and change management
    C. Screen locks and device encryption
    D. Full device encryption and IaaS

11. Management within your company wants to restrict access to the Bizz app from mobile devices. If users are within the company's property, they should be granted access. If they are not within the company's property, their access should be blocked. Which of the following answers provides the BEST solution to meet this goal?
    A. Geofencing
    B. Geolocation
    C. GPS tagging
    D. Containerization

12. Management within your company wants to implement a method that will authorize employees based on several elements, including the employee's identity, location, time of day, and type of device used by the employee. Which of the following will meet this need?
    A. Geofence
    B. Containerization
    C. Tethering
    D. Context-aware authentication

13. Lisa does not have access to the *project.doc* file, but she needs access to this file for her job. Homer is the system administrator and he has identified the following permissions for the file:

    rwx rw- ---

    What should Homer use to grant Lisa read access to the file?
    A. The chmod command
    B. A remote wipe
    C. Push notification
    D. The chroot command

14. Management within your organization wants to prevent users from copying documents to USB flash drives. Which of the following can be used to meet this goal?
    A. DLP
    B. HSM
    C. COPE
    D. SED

15. Your organization hosts a web site with a back-end database. The database stores customer data, including credit card numbers. Which of the following is the BEST way to protect the credit card data?
    A. Full database encryption
    B. Whole disk encryption
    C. Database column encryption
    D. File-level encryption

Chapter 5 Practice Question Answers

1. **A.** Disabling unnecessary services is one of the elements of the principle of least functionality. Other elements include deploying the server with only the applications and protocols they need to meet their purpose. Installing up-to-date antivirus software is a valid preventive control, but it isn't related to least functionality. Identifying the baseline should be done after disabling unnecessary services. A network-based intrusion detection system (NIDS) helps protect the server, but it doesn't implement least functionality.

2. **D.** The master image is the baseline and the administrators performed integrity measurements to identify baseline deviations. By comparing the list of applications in the baseline with the applications running on the suspect computer, you can identify unauthorized applications. None of the other answers include the troubleshooting steps

necessary to discover the problem. The master image would include only the applications, services, and protocols needed to meet the principle of least functionality. A sandbox is an isolated area of a system, typically used to test applications. A blacklist is a list of prohibited applications.

3. **B.** A change management policy helps reduce risk associated with making any changes to systems, including updating them. Patches should be tested and evaluated before implementing them and implementing them when they are released sometimes causes unintended consequences. The use of a trusted operating system or operating systems with secure configurations doesn't address how they are updated.

4. **B.** Application whitelisting identifies authorized applications and prevents users from installing unauthorized software. Alternately, you can use a blacklist to identify specific applications that cannot be installed or run on a system. A master image provides a secure baseline, but it doesn't prevent users from installing additional applications. Anti-malware software and antivirus software can detect and block malware, but they don't prevent users from installing unauthorized software.

5. **C.** A sandbox provides a simple method of testing patches and would be used with snapshots so that the virtual machine (VM) can easily be reverted to the original state. A baseline image is a starting point of a single environment. Bring your own device (BYOD) refers to allowing employee-owned mobile devices in a network, and is not related to this question. Change management practices ensure changes are not applied until they are approved and documented.

6. **C.** A remote attestation process checks a computer during the boot cycle and sends a report to a remote system. The remote system attests, or confirms, that the computer is secure. None of the other answers sends data to a remote system. A Trusted Platform Module (TPM) is a hardware chip on a motherboard and provides a local secure boot process. A TPM includes an encryption key burned into the CPU, which provides a hardware root of trust. A trusted operating system meets a set of predetermined requirements typically enforced with the mandatory access control (MAC) model.

7. **C.** This is a Software as a Service (SaaS) model. The software is the online application and the cloud provider (the Springfield Nuclear Power Plant in this example) maintains it. Infrastructure as a Service (IaaS) provides customers with the hardware via the cloud. Customers are responsible for installing the operating system and any applications. Platform as a Service (PaaS) is a computing platform. For example, a cloud provider can provide a server with a preconfigured operating system. Anyone can access a public cloud. However, the question states that only students and teachers can access it.

8. **D.** A network intrusion prevention system (NIPS) is the most relevant security control of those listed to ensure availability of the supervisory control and data acquisition (SCADA) system. A data loss prevention (DLP) system helps prevent loss of data, but wouldn't protect a SCADA system from potential attacks. A Trusted Platform Module (TPM) is a hardware chip on a computer's motherboard that stores cryptographic keys used for encryption. An electromagnetic pulse (EMP) is a short burst of electromagnetic energy and unrelated to a SCADA system.

9. **B.** Storage segmentation creates separate storage areas in mobile devices and can be used with a choose your own device (CYOD) mobile device deployment model. None of the other answers are directly related to mobile devices. A supervisory control and data acquisition (SCADA) system controls an industrial control system (ICS), such as those used in nuclear power plants or water treatment facilities, and it should be isolated. Database security includes the use of permissions and encryption to protect data in a database. Some embedded systems use a real-time operating system (RTOS) when the system must react within a specific time.

10. **C.** Screen locks provide protection for lost devices by making it more difficult for someone to access the device. Device encryption protects the confidentiality of the data. Global Positioning System (GPS) tagging includes location information on pictures and other files but won't help protect a lost or stolen device. Patch management keeps devices up to date and change management helps prevent outages from unauthorized changes. Infrastructure as a Service (IaaS) is a cloud computing option.

11. **A.** Geofencing can be used to create a virtual fence or geographic boundary, outlining the company's property. Geofencing will use geolocation to identify the mobile device's location, but geolocation without geofencing won't detect if a user is on the company's property. Global Positioning System (GPS) tagging adds geographic data (such as latitude and longitude data) to files and is unrelated to this question. Containerization runs applications in a container to isolate them.

12. **D.** Context-aware authentication can authenticate a user and a mobile device using multiple elements, including identity, geolocation, time of day, and type of device. None of the other answers meets all the requirements of the question. A geofence creates a virtual fence, or geographic boundary, and can be used with context-aware authentication. Containerization isolates an application, protecting it and its data. Tethering allows one device to share its Internet connection with other devices.

13. **A.** The system administrator should modify permissions with the chmod (short for change mode) command. Remote wipe sends a remote signal to a mobile device to wipe or erase all the data and is unrelated to this question. Push notification services send messages to users but don't change permissions. The chroot command is used to create a sandbox for testing an application.

14. **A.** A data loss prevention (DLP) solution can prevent users from copying documents to a USB drive. None of the other answers control USB drives. A hardware security module (HSM) is an external security device used to manage, generate, and securely store cryptographic keys. COPE (corporate-owned, personally enabled) is a mobile device deployment model. A self-encrypting drive (SED) includes the hardware and software to encrypt all data on the drive and securely store the encryption keys.

15. **C.** Database column (or field) encryption is the best choice because it can be used to encrypt the fields holding credit card data, but not fields that don't need to be encrypted. Full database encryption and whole disk encryption aren't appropriate because everything doesn't need to be encrypted to protect the credit card data. File-level encryption isn't appropriate on a database and will often make it inaccessible to the database application.

Chapter 6

Comparing Threats, Vulnerabilities, and Common Attacks

CompTIA Security+ objectives covered in this chapter:

1.1 Given a scenario, analyze indicators of compromise and determine the type of malware.
- Viruses, Crypto-malware, Ransomware, Worm, Trojan, Rootkit, Keylogger, Adware, Spyware, Bots, RAT, Logic bomb, Backdoor

1.2 Compare and contrast types of attacks.
- Social engineering (Phishing, Spear phishing, Whaling, Vishing, Impersonation, Dumpster diving, Shoulder surfing, Hoax, Watering hole attack), Principles (reasons for effectiveness), (Authority, Intimidation, Consensus, Scarcity, Familiarity, Trust, Urgency), Application/service attacks (DoS, DDoS)

1.3 Explain threat actor types and attributes.
- Types of actors (Script kiddies, Hacktivist, Organized crime, Nation states/APT, Insiders, Competitors), Attributes of actors (Internal/external, Level of sophistication, Resources/funding, Intent/motivation), Use of open-source intelligence

1.6 Explain the impact associated with types of vulnerabilities.
- Resource exhaustion, Untrained users

2.1 Install and configure network components, both hardware- and software-based, to support organizational security.
- Mail gateway (Spam filter)

2.3 Given a scenario, troubleshoot common security issues.
- Personnel issues (Insider threat, Social engineering, Social media)

2.4 Given a scenario, analyze and interpret output from security technologies.
- Antivirus, File integrity check, Advanced malware tools, Data execution prevention

3.9 Explain the importance of physical security controls.
- Screen filters

**

Organizations need to understand and protect themselves from many different types of threat actors, so it's valuable to know a little about them, their attributes, and the types of attacks they are likely to launch. Malicious software (malware) and social engineering are two common attack categories that any organization will face, but there are some complexities to each category. Attackers are becoming more and more sophisticated with these attacks, so it's important to know how to reduce the success of attackers.

Understanding Threat Actors

When considering attacks, it's important to realize that there are several different types of threat actors, and they each have different attributes. Don't let the phrase threat actors confuse you. It's just a fancier name given to attackers—anyone who launches a cyberattack on others.

One common method that attackers often use before launching an attack is to gather information from **open-source intelligence**. This includes any information that is available via web sites and social media. For example, if attackers want to get the name of the chief executive officer (CEO) of a company, they can probably find it on the company's web site. Similarly, many organizations post information on social media sites such as Facebook and Twitter.

A **script kiddie** is an attacker who uses existing computer scripts or code to launch attacks. Script kiddies typically have very little expertise or sophistication, and very little funding. Many people joke about the bored teenager as the script kiddie, attacking sites or organizations for the fun of it. However, there isn't any age limit for a script kiddie. More important, they can still get their hands on powerful scripts and launch dangerous attacks. Their motivations vary, but they are typically launching attacks out of boredom, or just to see what they can do.

A **hacktivist** launches attacks as part of an activist movement or to further a cause. Hacktivists typically aren't launching these attacks for their own benefit, but instead to increase awareness about a cause. As an example, Deric Lostutter (known online as KYAnonymous) was upset about the rape of a Steubenville, Ohio, high school girl, and what he perceived as a lack of justice. He later admitted to participating in several efforts to raise awareness of the case, including targeting a web site ran by one of the high school's football players. Eventually, two high school football players were convicted of the rape. One was sentenced to a year in juvenile detention and served about 10 months. The other one was sentenced to two years and served about 20 months. Lostutter was ultimately sentenced to two years in federal prison.

An **insider** is anyone who has legitimate access to an organization's internal resources. Common security issues caused by insider threats include loss of confidentiality, integrity, and availability of the organization's assets. The extent of the threat depends on how much access the insider has. For example, an administrator would have access to many more IT systems than a regular user.

Malicious insiders have a diverse set of motivations. For example, some malicious insiders are driven by greed and simply want to enhance their finances, while others want to exact revenge on the organization. They may steal files that include valuable data, install or run malicious scripts, or redirect funds to their personal accounts.

Remember this

A script kiddie is an attacker who uses existing computer scripts or code to launch attacks. Script kiddies typically have very little expertise, sophistication, and funding. A hacktivist launches attacks as part of an activist movement or to further a cause. An insider is anyone who has legitimate access to an organization's internal resources, such as an employee of a company.

Competitors can also engage in attacks. Their motivation is typically to gain proprietary information about another company. Although it's legal to gather information using open-source intelligence, greed sometimes causes competitors to cross the line into illegal activity. This can be as simple as rummaging through a competitor's trash bin, which is known as dumpster diving. In some cases, competitors hire employees from other companies and then get these new employees to provide proprietary information about their previous employer.

Organized crime is an enterprise that employs a group of individuals working together in criminal activities. This group is organized with a hierarchy with a leader and workers, like a normal business. Depending on how large the enterprise is, it can have several layers of management. However, unlike a legitimate business, the enterprise is focused on criminal activity. As an example, Symantec reported on Butterfly, a group of well-organized and highly capable attackers who steal market-sensitive information on companies and sell that information to the highest bidder. They have compromised some large U.S. companies, including Apple, Microsoft, and Facebook. Additionally, they have steadily increased their targets to include pharmaceutical and commodities-based organizations.

The primary motivation of criminals in organized crime is money. Almost all their efforts can be traced back to greed with the goal of getting more money, regardless of how they get it. However, because there isn't a defined size for organized crime, their sophistication, resources, and motivations can vary widely. Imagine a group of 10 individuals decides to target a single company. They will probably have significantly less sophistication and resources than the criminals within Butterfly.

Some attackers are organized and sponsored by a nation-state or government. An advanced persistent threat (*APT*) is a targeted attack against a network. The attacks are typically launched by a group that has both the capability and intent to launch sophisticated and targeted attacks. They often have a significant amount of resources and funding. Additionally, individuals within an APT group typically have very specific targets, such as a specific company, organization, or government agency. Successful attacks often allow unauthorized access for long periods of time, allowing attacks to exfiltrate a significant amount of data.

Remember this

Organized crime elements are typically motivated by greed and money but often use sophisticated techniques. Advanced persistent threats (APTs) are sponsored by governments and they launch sophisticated, targeted attacks.

As an example, Mandiant concluded that the group they named APT1 operates as Unit 61398 of the People's Liberation Army (PLA) inside China. Mandiant estimates that APT1 includes over 1,000 servers and between dozens and hundreds of individual operators and has:

- Released at least 40 different families of malware
- Stolen hundreds of terabytes of data from at least 141 organizations
- Maintained access to some victim networks for over four years before being detected
- Established footholds within many networks after email recipients opened malicious files that installed backdoors, allowing attackers remote access

Chinese officials have denied these claims.

More recently, the U.S. Department of Homeland Security (DHS) and the Federal Bureau of Investigation (FBI) released a joint analysis report (JAR-16-20296A), named GRIZZLY STEPPE, that provides detailed information on these APTs. They are nicknamed Fancy Bear (APT 28) and Cozy Bear (APT 29). The joint report states that these groups have targeted many government organizations, think tanks, universities, and corporations around the world. GRIZZLY STEPPE also indicates these two APTs compromised and exploited networks associated with the 2016 U.S. presidential election.

Cybersecurity firms such as CrowdStrike, SecureWorks, ThreatConnect, and FireEye's Mandiant have all indicated that APT 28 is sponsored by the Russian government and has probably been operating since the mid-2000s. Similarly, CrowdStrike has suggested that APT 29 is associated with Russian agencies. Symantec believes the organization has been attacking government and diplomatic organizations since at least 2010.

Russian officials have denied these claims.

Chapter 7, "Protecting Against Advanced Attacks," discusses many different types of attacks in detail. Two generic types of attacks are denial-of-service (**DoS**) attacks and distributed denial-of-service (**DDoS**) attacks. A DoS attack is from one attacker against one target. A DDoS attack is an attack from two or more computers against a single target. DDoS attacks often include sustained, abnormally high network traffic on the network interface card of the attacked computer.

DoS and DDoS attacks often attempt to overload an application or service on a computer. As an example, a web server responds to Hypertext Transfer Protocol (HTTP) requests to serve web pages. A DDoS attack can overload the web server by sending thousands of HTTP requests to the server a second. These requests overload the resources (such as the processor and memory) and lead to **resource exhaustion**. At some point, the attacked computer is no longer able to keep up with the requests. The attacked computer typically slows down significantly, preventing legitimate users from viewing web pages. In extreme cases of resource exhaustion, the attacked computer might crash.

> **Remember this**
>
> A denial-of-service (DoS) attack is an attack from a single source that attempts to disrupt the services provided by another system. A distributed denial-of-service (DDoS) attack includes multiple computers attacking a single target. DDoS attacks typically include sustained, abnormally high network traffic.

Determining Malware Types

Malware (malicious software) includes a wide range of software that has malicious intent. Malware is not software that you would knowingly purchase or download and install. Instead, it is installed onto your system through devious means. Infected systems give various symptoms, such as running slower, starting unknown processes, sending out email without user action, rebooting randomly, and more.

You might hear people use the term virus to describe all types of malware, but that isn't accurate. A virus is a specific type of malware, and malware includes many other types of malicious software, including worms, logic bombs, Trojans, ransomware, rootkits, spyware, and more.

It's also worth stressing that malware continues to evolve. In its 2017 report, "Cybersecurity Predictions 2017," Panda Security wrote that PandaLabs detected over 200,000 new malware samples a day in 2016. Most of these aren't completely new. Instead, they are slightly modified versions of existing malware.

Viruses

A *virus* is malicious code that attaches itself to a host application. The host application must be executed to run, and the malicious code executes when the host application is executed. The virus tries to replicate by finding other host applications to infect with the malicious code. At some point, the virus activates and delivers its payload.

Typically, the payload of a virus is damaging. It may delete files, cause random reboots, join the computer to a botnet, or enable backdoors that attackers can use to access systems remotely. Some older viruses merely displayed a message at some point, such as "Legalize Marijuana!" Most viruses won't cause damage immediately. Instead, they give the virus time to replicate first.

A user will often execute the virus (though unknowingly), but other times, an operating system will automatically execute it after user interaction. For example, when a user plugs in an infected USB drive, the system might automatically execute the virus, infecting the system.

Worms

A *worm* is self-replicating malware that travels throughout a network without the assistance of a host application or user interaction. A worm resides in memory and can use different transport protocols to travel over the network.

One of the significant problems caused by worms is that they consume network bandwidth. Worms can replicate themselves hundreds of times and spread to all the systems in the network. Each infected system tries to locate and infect other systems on the network, and network performance can slow to a crawl.

> **Remember this**
>
> Malware includes a wide variety of malicious code, including viruses, worms, Trojans, ransomware, and more. A virus is malicious code that attaches itself to an application and runs when the application is started. A worm is self-replicating and doesn't need user interaction to run.

Logic Bombs

A *logic bomb* is a string of code embedded into an application or script that will execute in response to an event. The event might be a specific date or time, or a user action such as when a user launches a specific program.

There's an often-repeated story about a company that decided it had to lay off an engineer due to an economic downturn. His bosses didn't see him doing much, so they thought they could do without him. Within a couple of weeks after he left, they started having all sorts of computer problems they just couldn't resolve.

They called him back, and within a couple of weeks, everything was fine. A few months later, they determined they had to lay him off again. You guessed it. Within a couple of weeks, things went haywire again.

The engineer had programmed a logic bomb that executed when the payroll program ran. It checked for his name on the payroll, and when it was there, things were fine, but when his name wasn't there, ka-boom—the logic bomb exploded.

> **Remember this**
>
> A logic bomb executes in response to an event, such as when a specific application is executed or a specific time arrives.

Backdoors

A **backdoor** provides another way of accessing a system, similar to how a backdoor in a house provides another method of entry. Malware often installs backdoors on systems to bypass normal authentication methods.

While application developers often code backdoors into applications, this practice is not recommended. For example, an application developer might create a backdoor within an application intended for maintenance purposes. However, if attackers discover the backdoor, they can use it to access the application.

Effective account management policies help prevent ex-employees from creating backdoors after they are fired. For example, if an employee loses network access immediately after being fired, the employee cannot create a backdoor account. In contrast, if an administrator retains network access, he might create another administrative account. IT personnel might disable his account after they learn he has been fired, but he can still use this new backdoor account. That's exactly what a Fannie Mae Unix engineer did after being told he was fired.

Fannie Mae's account management policy did not revoke his elevated system privileges right away, giving him time to create a backdoor account. After going home, he accessed the system remotely and installed a logic bomb script scheduled to run at 9:00 a.m. on January 31. If another administrator hadn't discovered the logic bomb, it would have deleted data and backups for about four thousand servers, changed their passwords, and shut them down.

> **Remember this**
>
> A backdoor provides another way to access a system. Many types of malware create backdoors, allowing attackers to access systems from remote locations. Employees have also created backdoors in applications and systems.

Trojans

A **Trojan**, also called a Trojan horse, looks like something beneficial, but it's actually something malicious. Trojan horses are named after the infamous horse from the Trojan War. In Greek mythology, the Achaeans tried to sack the city of Troy for several years, but they simply couldn't penetrate the city's defenses. At some point, someone got the idea of building a huge wooden horse and convincing the people of Troy that it was a gift from the gods. Warriors hid inside, and the horse was rolled up to the gates.

The people of Troy partied all day and all night celebrating their good fortune, but when the city slept, the warriors climbed down from inside the horse and opened the gates. The rest of the warriors flooded in. What the Greek warriors couldn't do for years, the Trojan horse helped them do in a single day.

In computers, a Trojan horse can come as pirated software, a useful utility, a game, or something else that users might be enticed to download and try. Attackers are increasingly using drive-by downloads to deliver Trojans. In a drive-by download, web servers include malicious code that attempts to download and install itself on user computers after the user visits. Here are the typical steps involved in a drive-by download:

1. Attackers compromise a web site to gain control of it.
2. Attackers install a Trojan embedded in the web site's code.
3. Attackers attempt to trick users into visiting the site. Sometimes, they simply send the link to thousands of users via email hoping that some of them click the link.
4. When users visit, the web site attempts to download the Trojan onto the users' systems.

Another Trojan method that has become popular in recent years is rogueware, also known as scareware. Rogueware masquerades as a free antivirus program. When a user visits a site, a message on the web page or a pop-up appears indicating it detected malware on the user's system. The user is encouraged to download and install free antivirus software.

On the surface, this free antivirus software looks useful. However, it isn't. If a user installs and runs it on a system, it appears to do a system scan. After the scan completes, it reports finding multiple issues, such as infections by dozens of viruses. The report isn't true. The application reports these issues even on a freshly installed operating system with zero infections.

It then encourages the user to resolve these issues immediately. If the user tries to resolve the issues, the program informs the user that this is only the trial version, and the trial version won't resolve these issues. However, for the small fee of $79.95, users can unlock the full version to remove the threats. Some rogueware installs additional malicious components. For example, it might allow the attacker to take remote control of the infected system.

Many web browser extensions include malicious Trojans. As an example, I once added an extension into my Google Chrome browser so that I could download videos and view them offline. Unfortunately, it modified the browser's behavior. When I went to a page from a Google search and then right-clicked on the page, it took to me to a malicious web site encouraging me to install malware disguised as a Windows Repair tool. At one point after right-clicking, it indicated my Chrome browser was out of date and encouraged me to download and install an update. However, using Chrome's tools, I verified that Chrome was up to date. When I clicked on Extensions to remove it, it redirected me to a malicious web site. I ultimately reset Chrome to the default settings, disabling all the extensions, and deleted the malicious extension.

> ### Remember this
>
> A Trojan appears to be something useful but includes a malicious component, such as installing a backdoor on a user's system. Many Trojans are delivered via drive-by downloads. They can also infect systems from fake antivirus software, pirated software, games, or infected USB drives.

RAT

A remote access Trojan (**RAT**) is a type of malware that allows attackers to take control of systems from remote locations. It is often delivered via drive-by downloads. Once installed on a system, attackers can then access the infected computer at any time, and install additional malware if desired.

Some RATs automatically collect and log keystrokes, usernames and passwords, incoming and outgoing email, chat sessions, and browser history as well as take screenshots. The RAT can then automatically send the data to the attackers at predetermined times.

Additionally, attackers can explore the network using the credentials of the user or the user's computer. Attackers often do this to discover, and exploit, additional vulnerabilities within the network. It's common for attackers to exploit this one infected system and quickly infect the entire network with additional malware, including installing RATs on other systems.

Ransomware

A specific type of Trojan is **ransomware**. Attackers encrypt the user's data or take control of the computer and lock out the user. Then, they demand that the user pay a ransom to regain access to the data or computer. Criminals often deliver ransomware via drive-by downloads or embedded in other software delivered via email. Attackers originally targeted individuals with ransomware. However, they have increasingly been targeting organizations demanding larger and larger ransoms.

Many organizations indicate that ransomware attacks continue to grow and are becoming one of the greatest cyber threats:

- Symantec reported that ransomware attacks grew by 35 percent in 2015 (compared with 2014).
- The Cyber Threat Alliance (CTA) reported that CryptoWall 3, a specific version of ransomware, resulted in $325 million in losses in 2015 alone. It's difficult to know how much money has been lost by all versions of ransomware.
- In a public service announcement (Alert Number I-091516-PSA), the FBI reported that a single variant of ransomware infected as many as 100,000 computers a day in the first quarter of 2016.
- In their 2017 Annual Threat Report, SonicWall reported that the number of ransomware attacks observed by the SonicWall GRID Threat Network increased from 4 million in 2015 to 638 million in 2016.

Ransomware types continue to evolve. In early versions, they sometimes just locked the user out of the system. However, this is rarely done anymore. Instead, attackers typically encrypt the user's data to ensure that users can't retrieve it. Ransomware that encrypts the user's data is sometimes called **crypto-malware**.

Some ransomware has added in a new blackmail technique called doxing. If the user doesn't pay the ransom to decrypt the files, the attacker threatens to publish the files along with the victim's credentials. Malware that uses doxing is sometimes called doxingware.

> **Remember this**
>
> Ransomware is a type of malware that takes control of a user's system or data. Criminals then attempt to extort payment from the victim. Ransomware often includes threats of damaging a user's system or data if the victim does not pay the ransom. Ransomware that encrypts the user's data is sometimes called crypto-malware.

Keylogger

A *keylogger* attempts to capture a user's keystrokes. The keystrokes are stored in a file, and are either sent to an attacker automatically, or the attacker may manually retrieve the file.

While a keylogger is typically software, it can also be hardware. For example, you can purchase a USB keylogger, plug it into the computer, and plug the keyboard into the USB keylogger. This hardware keylogger will record all keystrokes and store them within memory on the USB device.

Spyware

Spyware is software installed on users' systems without their awareness or consent. Its purpose is often to monitor the user's computer and the user's activity. Spyware takes some level of control over the user's computer to learn information and sends this information to a third party. If spyware can access a user's private data, it results in a loss of confidentiality.

Some examples of spyware activity are changing a user's home page, redirecting web browsers, and installing additional software within the browser. In some situations, these changes can slow a system down, resulting in poorer performance. These examples are rather harmless compared with what more malicious spyware (called privacy-invasive software) might do.

Privacy-invasive software tries to separate users from their money using data-harvesting techniques. It attempts to gather information to impersonate users, empty bank accounts, and steal identities. For example, some spyware includes keyloggers. The spyware periodically reads the data stored by the keylogger, and sends it to the attacker. In some instances, the spyware allows the attacker to take control of the user's system remotely.

Spyware is often included with other software like a Trojan. The user installs one application but unknowingly gets some extras. Spyware can also infect a system in a drive-by download. The user simply visits a malicious web site that includes code to automatically download and install the spyware onto the user's system.

> **Remember this**
>
> Keyloggers capture a user's keystrokes and store them in a file. This file can be automatically sent to an attacker or manually retrieved depending on the keylogger. Spyware monitors a user's computer and often includes a keylogger.

Adware

When adware first emerged, its intent was primarily to learn a user's habits for the purpose of targeted advertising. As the practice of gathering information on users became more malicious, more people began to call it spyware. However, some traditional adware still exists. Internet marketers have become very sophisticated and use a combination of web analytics with behavioral analytics to track user activity. They then provide targeted ads based on past user activity.

The term adware also applies to software that is free but includes advertisements. The user understands that the software will show advertisements and has the option to purchase a version of the software that does not include the ads. All of this is aboveboard without any intention of misleading the user.

Bots and Botnets

Generically, **bots** are software robots. For example, Google uses bots as search engine spiders to crawl through the Internet looking for web pages. However, attackers also use bots for malicious purposes. A botnet combines the words *robot* and *network*. It includes multiple computers that act as software robots (bots) and function together in a network (such as the Internet), often for malicious purposes. The bots in a botnet are often called zombies and they will do the bidding of whoever controls the botnet.

Bot herders are criminals who manage botnets. They attempt to infect as many computers as possible and control them through one or more servers running command-and-control software. The infected computers periodically check in with the command-and-control servers, receive direction, and then go to work. The user is often unaware of the activity.

Most computers join a botnet through malware infection. For example, a user could download pirated software with a Trojan or click a malicious link, resulting in a drive-by download. The malware then joins the system to a botnet.

Bot herders have been using Mirai to create large botnets. Mirai infects Linux systems that are running out-of-date versions of Linux and join them to a botnet. This includes Linux software running on Internet of things (IoT) devices such as digital cameras connected to the Internet. Infected devices search for other IoT devices on the Internet and infect them. Attackers have published the source code for Mirai in public forums, making it easily accessible by many attackers.

A Mirai botnet launched an attack in October 2016 against Domain Name System (DNS) servers. It included about 100,000 simple devices such as digital cameras and printers that were connected to the Internet. The bot herders directed the devices to repeatedly query DNS servers in a protracted distributed denial-of-service (DDoS) attack. This attack overwhelmed the DNS servers and prevented users in the United States and Europe from accessing many common web sites, such as Amazon, Second Life, Twitter, CNN, BBC, Fox News, Tumblr, Reddit, and many more.

Similarly, Wordfence discovered attacks coming from a botnet of approximately 10,000 separate IP addresses in April 2017. After investigating the attacks, they learned that the attacking systems were typically home routers that had a known vulnerability, named the Misfortune Cookie by Checkpoint Software Technologies. Interestingly, Checkpoint reported the vulnerability in 2005. However, this attack showed that a specific Internet Service Provider (ISP) in Algeria was issuing these unpatched routers to its customers.

Botnet herders sometimes maintain complete control over their botnets. Other times, they rent access out to others to use as desired. Some of the instructions sent by the command-and-control servers include:

- Send spam.
- Launch a distributed denial-of-service attack.
- Download additional malware, adware, or spyware such as keyloggers.

Rootkits

A *rootkit* is a group of programs (or, in rare instances, a single program) that hides the fact that the system has been infected or compromised by malicious code. A user might suspect something is wrong, but antivirus scans and other checks indicate everything is fine because the rootkit hides its running processes to avoid detection.

In addition to modifying the internal operating system processes, rootkits often modify system files such as the Registry. In some cases, the rootkit modifies system access, such as removing users' administrative access.

Rootkits have system-level access to systems. This is sometimes called root-level access, or kernel-level access, indicating that they have the same level of access as the operating system. Rootkits use hooked processes, or hooking techniques, to intercept calls to the operating system. In this context, *hooking* refers to intercepting system-level function calls, events, or messages. The rootkit installs the hooks into memory and uses them to control the system's behavior.

Antivirus software often makes calls to the operating system that could detect malware, but the rootkit prevents the antivirus software from making these calls. This is why antivirus software will sometimes report everything is OK, even if the system is infected with a rootkit. However, antivirus software can often detect the hooked processes by examining the contents of the system's random access memory (RAM).

Another method used to detect rootkits is to boot into safe mode, or have the system scanned before it boots, but this isn't always successful. It's important to remember that rootkits are very difficult to detect because they can hide so much of their activity. A clean bill of health by a malware scanner may not be valid.

It's important to remember that behind any type of malware, you'll likely find an attacker involved in criminal activity. Attackers who have successfully installed a rootkit on a user's system might log on to the user's computer remotely, using a backdoor installed by the rootkit. Similarly, attackers might direct the computer to connect to computers on the Internet and send data. Data can include anything collected from a keylogger, collected passwords, or specific files or file types stored on the user's computer.

> ## Remember this
>
> Rootkits have system-level or kernel access and can modify system files and system access. Rootkits hide their running processes to avoid detection with hooking techniques. Tools that can inspect RAM can discover these hidden hooked processes.

Recognizing Common Attacks

In addition to malware, it's important to understand some other common attacks. Social engineering includes several techniques attackers use to trick users. Additionally, many attackers use email, instant messaging, and the phone to deliver attacks.

Social Engineering

Social engineering is the practice of using social tactics to gain information. It's often low-tech and encourages individuals to do something they wouldn't normally do, or cause them to reveal some piece of information, such as user credentials. Some of the individual methods and techniques include:

- Using flattery and conning
- Assuming a position of authority
- Encouraging someone to perform a risky action
- Encouraging someone to reveal sensitive information
- Impersonating someone, such as an authorized technician
- Tailgating or closely following authorized personnel without providing credentials

In the movie *Catch Me If You Can*, Leonardo DiCaprio played Frank Abagnale Jr., an effective con artist. He learned some deep secrets about different professions by conning and flattering people into telling him. He then combined all he learned to impersonate pilots and doctors and perform some sophisticated forgery.

Social engineers con people in person, as Frank Abagnale Jr. did, and they use other methods as well. They may use the phone, send email with phishing tactics, and even use some trickery on web sites, such as fooling someone into installing malware.

As an example of a social engineer using the phone, consider this scenario. Maggie is busy working and receives a call from Hacker Herman, who identifies himself as a member of the IT department.

Hacker Herman: "Hi, Maggie. I just wanted to remind you, we'll be taking your computer down for the upgrade today, and it'll be down for a few hours."

Maggie: "Wait. I didn't hear anything about this. I need my computer to finish a project today."

Hacker Herman: "You should have gotten the email. I'm sorry, but I have to get the last few computers updated today."

Maggie: "Isn't there any other way? I really need my computer."

Hacker Herman: "Well…it is possible to upgrade it over the network while you're still working. We don't normally do it that way because we need the user's password to do it."

Maggie: "If I can still work on my computer, please do it that way."

Hacker Herman: "OK, Maggie. Don't tell anyone I'm doing this for you, but if you give me your username and password, I'll do this over the network."

This is certainly a realistic scenario, and many end users will give out their passwords unless security-related awareness and training programs consistently repeat the mantra: "Never give out your password."

Attackers aren't always so blatant though. Many times, instead of asking you for your password outright, they ask questions they can use in a password reset system to reset your password. A skilled con man can ask these questions as though he's generally interested in you. Before you know it, you've told him the name of your first dog, your childhood best friend, the name of your first boss, and more. When people post this information in social media, attackers don't even need to ask.

The following sections describe many common security issues related to social engineering.

> **Remember this**
>
> Social engineering uses social tactics to trick users into giving up information or performing actions they wouldn't normally take. Social engineering attacks can occur in person, over the phone, while surfing the Internet, and via email.

Impersonation

Some social engineers often attempt to impersonate others. The goal is to convince an authorized user to provide some information, or help the attacker defeat a security control.

As an example, an attacker can impersonate a repair technician to gain access to a server room or telecommunications closet. After gaining access, the attacker can install hardware such as a rogue access point to capture data and send it wirelessly to an outside collection point. Similarly, attackers impersonate legitimate organizations over the phone and try to gain information. Identity verification methods are useful to prevent the success of impersonation attacks.

Shoulder Surfing

Shoulder surfing is simply looking over the shoulder of someone to gain information. The goal is to gain unauthorized information by casual observation, and it's likely to occur within an office environment. This can be to learn credentials, such as a username and password, or a PIN used for a smart card or debit card. Recently, attackers have been using cameras to monitor locations where users enter PINs, such as at automatic teller machines (ATMs).

A simple way to prevent shoulder surfing is to position monitors and other types of screens so that unauthorized personnel cannot see them. This includes ensuring people can't view them by looking through a window or from reception areas.

Another method used to reduce shoulder surfing is to use a *screen filter* placed over the monitor. This restricts the visibility of the screen for anyone who isn't looking directly at the monitor.

> **Remember this**
>
> A social engineer can gain unauthorized information just by looking over someone's shoulder. This might be in person, such as when a user is at a computer, or remotely using a camera. Screen filters help prevent shoulder surfing by obscuring the view for people unless they are directly in front of the monitor.

Tricking Users with Hoaxes

A *hoax* is a message, often circulated through email, that tells of impending doom from a virus or other security threat that simply doesn't exist. Users may be encouraged to delete files or change their system configuration.

An older example is the teddy bear virus (*jdbgmgr.exe*), which was not a virus at all. Victims received an email saying this virus lies in a sleeping state for 14 days and then it will destroy the user's system. It then told users that they can protect their system by deleting the file (which has an icon of a little bear), and provided instructions on how to do so. Users who deleted the file lost some system capability.

More serious virus hoaxes have the potential to be as damaging as a real virus. If users are convinced to delete important files, they may make their systems unusable. Additionally, they waste help-desk personnel's time due to needless calls about the hoax or support calls if users damaged their systems in response to the hoax.

Tailgating and Mantraps

Tailgating is the practice of one person following closely behind another without showing credentials. For example, if Homer uses a badge to gain access to a secure building and Francesca follows closely behind Homer without using a badge, Francesca is tailgating.

Employees often do this as a matter of convenience and courtesy. Instead of shutting the door on the person following closely behind, they often hold the door open for the person. However, this bypasses the access control, and if employees tailgate, it's very easy for a nonemployee to slip in behind someone else. Often, all it takes is a friendly smile from someone like Francesca to encourage Homer to keep the door open for her.

Chapter 9, "Implementing Controls to Protect Assets," discusses physical security controls such as mantraps and security guards. A simple *mantrap* can be a turnstile like those used in subways or bus stations. Imagine two men trying to go through a turnstile like this together. It's just not likely. Security guards can check the credentials of each person, and they won't be fooled by a smile as easily as Homer.

Dumpster Diving

Dumpster diving is the practice of searching through trash or recycling containers to gain information from discarded documents. Many organizations either shred or burn paper instead of throwing it away.

For example, old copies of company directories can be valuable to attackers. They may identify the names, phone numbers, and titles of key people within the organization. Attackers may be able to use this information in a whaling attack against executives or social engineering attacks against anyone in the organization. An attacker can exploit any document that contains detailed employee or customer information, and can often find value in seemingly useless printouts and notes.

On a personal basis, preapproved credit applications or blank checks issued by credit card companies can be quite valuable to someone attempting to gain money or steal identities. Documentation with any type of Personally Identifiable Information (PII) or Protected Health Information (PHI) should be shredded or burned.

> **Remember this**
>
> Dumpster divers search through trash looking for information. Shredding or burning papers instead of throwing them away mitigates this threat.

Watering Hole Attacks

A *watering hole attack* attempts to discover which web sites a group of people are likely to visit and then infects those web sites with malware that can infect the visitors. The attacker's goal is to infect a web site that users trust already, making them more likely to download infected files.

As an example, an attack discovered in late 2016 initially targeted Polish banks. The attack was discovered by a single Polish bank that discovered previously unknown malware on internal computers. Symantec reported the source of the attack was servers at the Polish Financial Supervision Authority. This is a well-trusted institution by Polish bank employees, and they are likely to visit the organization's web sites often.

This isn't an isolated incident though. Symantec reported over 100 similar attacks located in over 30 countries.

Attacks via Email and Phone

Attackers have been increasingly using email to launch attacks. One of the reasons is because they've been so successful. Many people don't understand how dangerous a simple email can be for the entire organization. Without understanding the danger, they often click a link within a malicious email, which gives attackers access to an entire network. Email attacks include spam, phishing, spear phishing, and whaling.

Spam

Spam is unwanted or unsolicited email. Depending on which study you quote, between 80 percent and 92 percent of all Internet email is spam. Some spam is harmless advertisements, while much more is malicious. Spam can include malicious links, malicious code, or malicious attachments. Even when it's not malicious, when only 1 of 10 emails is valid, it can waste a lot of your time.

In some cases, legitimate companies encourage users to opt in to their email lists and then send them email about their products. When users opt in to a mailing list, they agree to the terms. On the surface, you'd think that this means that you agree to receive email from the company and that's true. However, terms often include agreeing to allow their partners to send you email, which means the original company can share your email address with others.

Legitimate companies don't send you malicious spam, but they might send you more email than you want. Laws require them to include the ability to opt out, indicating you don't want to receive any more emails from them. Once you opt out, you shouldn't receive any more emails from that company.

Criminals use a variety of methods to collect email addresses. They buy lists from other criminals and harvest them from web sites. Some malware scans address books of infected computers to collect email. Because they are criminals, they don't care about laws, but they might include opt-out instructions in spam they send. However, instead of using this to remove you from their email list, attackers use this as confirmation that your email address is valid. The result is more spam.

Phishing

Phishing is the practice of sending email to users with the purpose of tricking them into revealing personal information or clicking on a link. A phishing attack often sends the user to a malicious web site that appears to the user as a legitimate site.

The classic example is where a user receives an email that looks like it came from eBay, PayPal, a bank, or some other well-known company. The "phisher" doesn't know if the recipient has an account at the company, just as a fisherman doesn't know if any fish are in the water

Malspam

In late 2016, some bad actors launched three malicious spam (malspam) campaigns that attempted to install the Cerber ransomware onto victims' computers. Each campaign followed a similar pattern, with each wave targeting domain administrators:

- The subject line included **Domain Abuse Notice** for the targeted domain.
- The body indicated that the targeted domain had been repeatedly used to send spam and spread malware.
- In some emails, it indicated this was a final notice and the domain would be suspended after 24 hours if it wasn't resolved.
- The body included at least one link labeled Click Here or Click Here to Download your Report.

The links were malicious and attempted to download Cerber ransomware. Some linked to a malicious JavaScript file (such as *Domain_Abuse_Report_Viewer.js*) and others linked to an infected Word document (such as *Invoice_349KL.doc*) with a malicious macro. These malicious documents were hosted on different servers for each wave.

where he casts his line. However, if the attacker sends out enough emails, the odds are good that someone who receives the email has an account.

The email may look like this:

> "We have noticed suspicious activity on your account. To protect your privacy, we will suspend your account unless you are able to log in and validate your credentials. Click here to validate your account and prevent it from being locked out."

The email often includes the same graphics that you would find on the vendor's web site or an actual email from the vendor. Although it might look genuine, it isn't. Legitimate companies do not ask you to revalidate your credentials via email. If you go directly to the actual site, you might be asked to provide additional information to prove your identity beyond your credentials, but legitimate companies don't send emails asking you to follow a link and input your credentials to validate them.

Remember this

Spam is unwanted email. Phishing is malicious spam. Attackers attempt to trick users into revealing sensitive or personal information or clicking on a link. Links within email can also lead unsuspecting users to install malware.

Beware of Email from Friends

Criminals have become adept at impersonating your friends. They scan social media sites and identify your friends and family. They then send emails to you that look like they are from your friends or family members, but they really aren't. This has become a common security issue related to social media.

As an example, imagine you are friends with Lisa Simpson and her email address is lisa@

simpsons.com. You might receive an email that includes "Lisa Simpson" in the From block. However, if you look at the actual email address, you'd find it is something different, such as homer@moes.com. The underlying email address might belong to someone, but the forgery doesn't mean that they sent the email. To identify the actual sender, you often need to look at the full header of the email address.

I see emails such as this quite often lately. They seem to be related to comments or Likes that I make on Facebook. For example, after Liking a Facebook post on Lisa Simpson's Facebook page, I later receive an email with Lisa Simpson in the From block and a forged email address. These emails typically include a single line such as "I thought you might like this" and a malicious link. Clicking the link often takes the user to a server that attempts a drive-by download. This is a common way users inadvertently install ransomware on their systems.

Another possible scenario is that an attacker has joined your friend's computer to a botnet. A bot herder is now using your friend's computer to send out phishing emails.

Phishing to Install Malware

One phishing email looked like it was from a news organization with headlines of recent news events. If the user clicked anywhere in the email, it showed a dialog box indicating that the user's version of Adobe Flash was too old to view the story. It then asked, "Would you like to upgrade your version of Adobe Flash?" If the user clicked Yes, it downloaded and installed malware.

Another email had the subject line "We have hijacked your baby" and the following content:

> "You must pay once to us $50,000. The details we will
> send later. We have attached photo of your family."

The English seems off, and the receiver might not even have a baby, making this look bogus right away. However, the attackers are only trying to pique your curiosity. The attached file isn't a photo. Instead, it's malware. If a user clicks on the photo to look at it, it installs malware on the user's system.

Phishing to Validate Email Addresses

A simple method used to validate email addresses is the use of beacons. A beacon is a link included in the email that links to an image stored on an Internet server. The link includes unique code that identifies the receiver's email address.

For the email application to display the image, it must retrieve the image from the Internet server. When the server hosting the image receives the request, it logs the user's email address, indicating it's valid. This is one of the reasons that most email programs won't display images by default.

Phishing to Get Money

The classic Nigerian scam (also called a 419 scam) continues to thrive. You receive an email from someone claiming a relative or someone else has millions of dollars. Unfortunately, the sender can't get the money without your help. The email says that if you help retrieve the money, you'll get a substantial portion of the money for your troubles.

This scam often requires the victim to pay a small sum of money with the promise of a large sum of money. However, the large sum never appears. Instead, the attackers come up with reasons why they need just a little more money. In many cases, the scammers request access to your bank account to deposit your share, but instead they use it to empty your bank account.

There are countless variations on this scam. Lottery scams inform email recipients they won. Victims sometimes have to pay small fees to release the funds or provide bank information to get the money deposited. They soon learn there is no prize.

Spear Phishing

Spear phishing is a targeted form of phishing. Instead of sending the email out to everyone indiscriminately, a spear phishing attack attempts to target specific groups of users, or even a single user. Spear phishing attacks may target employees within a company or customers of a company.

As an example, an attacker might try to impersonate the CEO of an organization in an email. It's relatively simple to change the header of an email so that the From field includes anything, including the CEO's name and title. Attackers can send an email to all employees requesting that they reply with their password. Because the email looks like it's coming from the CEO, these types of phishing emails fool uneducated users.

One solution that deters the success of these types of spear phishing attacks is to use digital signatures. The CEO and anyone else in the company can sign their emails with a digital signature. This provides a high level of certainty to personnel on who sent the email. Chapter 10, "Understanding Cryptography and PKI," covers digital signatures in great depth.

Whaling

Whaling is a form of spear phishing that attempts to target high-level executives. Las Vegas casinos refer to the big spenders as whales, and casino managers are willing to spend extra time and effort to bring them into their casinos. Similarly, attackers consider high-level executives the whales, and attackers are willing to put in some extra effort to catch a whale because the payoff can be so great. When successful, attackers gain confidential company information that they might not be able to get anywhere else.

As an example, attackers singled out as many as 20,000 senior corporate executives in a fine-tuned phishing attack. The emails looked like official subpoenas requiring the recipient to appear before a federal grand jury and included the executive's full name and other details, such as their company name and phone number. The emails also included a link for more details about the subpoena. If the executives clicked the link, it took them to a web site that indicated they needed a browser add-on to read the document. If they approved this install, they actually installed a keylogger and malware. The keylogger recorded all their keystrokes to a file, and the malware gave the attackers remote access to the executives' systems.

Similar whaling attacks have masqueraded as complaints from the Better Business Bureau or the Justice Department. Executives are sensitive to issues that may affect the company's profit, and these attacks get their attention. Although not as common, some whaling attacks attempt to reach the executive via phone to get the data. However, many executives have assistants who screen calls to prevent attackers from reaching the executive via phone.

> **Remember this**
>
> A spear phishing attack targets specific groups of users. It could target employees within a company or customers of a company. Digital signatures provide assurances to recipients about who sent an email, and can reduce the success of spear phishing. Whaling targets high-level executives.

Vishing

Vishing attacks use the phone system to trick users into giving up personal and financial information. It often uses Voice over IP (VoIP) technology and tries to trick the user similar to other phishing attacks. When the attack uses VoIP, it can spoof caller ID, making it appear as though the call came from a real company.

In one form, a machine leaves a phone message saying that you need to return the call concerning one of your credit cards. In another form, you receive an email with the same information. If you call, you'll hear an automated recording giving some vague excuse about a policy and prompting you to verify your identity. One by one, the recording prompts you for more information, such as your name, birthday, Social Security number, credit card number, expiration date, and so on. Sometimes, the recording asks for usernames and passwords. If you give all the requested information, the recording indicates they have verified your account. In reality, you just gave up valuable information on yourself.

Another example of vishing is just a regular phone call from a criminal. A popular ploy is a call from a company claiming to be "Credit Services" and offering to give you lower credit card rates. They play around with caller ID and have it display anything they want. A common ploy is to display a number similar to yours, making them appear local. They often announce, "This is your second and final notice," trying to evoke a sense of urgency.

If you answer, the automated system forwards you to a live person who begins asking a series of "qualifying" questions, such as how much credit card debt you have and what your interest rates are. They then promise that they can help you lower your debt and get you a better rate. Next, they start asking some personal questions. They might ask for the last four digits of your Social Security number so they can "verify your account is in good standing." They might ask you for the code on your credit card "to verify you still have it."

Eventually, they hope to get your credit card number, expiration date, and code so that they can use it to post fraudulent charges. Some people have reported similar callers trying to get their bank information so that they can transfer money out of the accounts.

They hang up right away if you ask them to take you off their list, or stop calling. Similarly, they hang up when they hear words such as *criminal*, *thief*, and other words I'll leave out of this book. Some even reply with insults. They've called me so often, I've played along a few times. I love it when they ask for information on my credit card. I respond by saying, "Can you hold on so I can get it?" I then put the phone in a drawer and go back to work. Once, they stayed on the line for more than three hours waiting for me.

Remember this

Vishing is a form of phishing that uses the phone system or VoIP. Some vishing attempts are fully automated. Others start automated but an attacker takes over at some point during the call.

One Click Lets Them In

It's worth stressing that it only takes one click by an uneducated user to give an attacker almost unlimited access to an organization's network. Consider Figure 6.1. It outlines the process APTs have used to launch attacks.

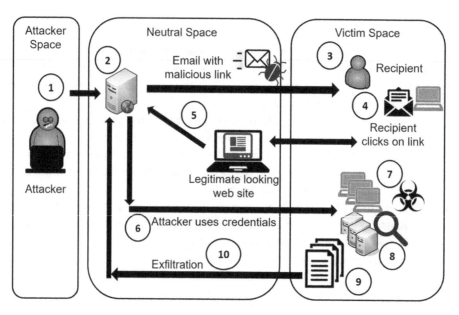

Figure 6.1: Steps in an attack

Note that the attacker (located in the attacker space) can be located anywhere in the world, and only needs access to the Internet. The neutral space might be servers owned and operated by the attackers. They might be in the same country as attackers, or they might be in another country. In some cases, the attackers use servers owned by others, but controlled by the attackers, such as servers in a botnet. The victim space is the internal network of the target. Refer to Figure 6.1 as you read the following steps in an attack:

1. The attacker uses open-source intelligence to identify a target. Some typical sources are social media sites and news outlets. Other times, attackers use social engineering tactics via phone calls and emails to get information on the organization or individuals employed by the organization.

2. Next, the attacker crafts a spear phishing email with a malicious link. The email might include links to malware hosted on another site and encourage the user to click the link. In some cases, this link can activate a drive-by download that installs itself on the user's computer without the user's knowledge. Cozy Bear (APT 29) used this technique and at least one targeted individual clicked the link. Similarly, criminals commonly use this technique to download ransomware onto a user's computer. In other cases, the email might indicate that the user's password has expired and the user needs to change the password or all access will be suspended. Fancy Bear (APT 28) used a similar technique.

3. The attacker sends the spear phishing email to the recipient from a server in the neutral space. This email includes a malicious link and uses words designed to trick the user into clicking it.

4. If the user clicks on the link, it takes the user to a web site that looks legitimate. This web site might attempt a drive-by download, or it might mimic a legitimate web site and encourage the user to enter a username and password.

5. If the malicious link tricked the user into entering credentials, the web site sends

the information back to the attacker. If the malicious link installed malware on the user's system, such as a RAT, the attacker uses it to collect information on the user's computer (including the user's credentials, once discovered) and sends it back to the attacker.

6. The attacker uses the credentials to access targeted systems. In many cases, the attacker uses the infected computer to scan the network for vulnerabilities.
7. The attacker installs malware on the targeted systems.
8. This malware examines all the available data on these systems, such as emails and files on computers and servers.
9. The malware gathers all data of interest and typically divides it into encrypted chunks.
10. These encrypted chunks are exfiltrated out of the network and back to the attacker.

Privilege escalation occurs when a user or process accesses elevated rights and permissions. Combined, rights and permissions are privileges. When attackers first compromise a system, they often have minimal privileges. However, privilege escalation tactics allow them to get more and more privileges. The recipient shown in Figure 6.1 might have minimal privileges, but malware will use various privilege escalation techniques to gain more and more privileges on the user's computer and within the user's network.

If users are logged on with administrative privileges, it makes it much easier for the malware to gain control of the user's system and within the network. This is one of the reasons organizations require administrators to have two accounts. Administrators use one account for regular use and one for administrative use. The only time they would log on with the administrator account is when they are performing administrative work. This reduces the time the administrative account is in use, and makes it more difficult for the malware to use privilege escalation techniques.

Blocking Malware and Other Attacks

The previous sections described several different methods attackers and criminals use to launch new attacks. However, organizations and individuals can prevent many of these attacks from succeeding with just a few steps. These steps include using anti-malware software and educating users.

Protecting Systems from Malware

Malware is a significant threat for any organization. Administrators commonly implement layered security, or a defense-in-depth plan, to protect against malware. The following bullets list some common security controls used to protect against malware:

- **Spam filter on mail gateways.** Phishing attacks are delivered as malicious spam. Spam filters on mail gateways (email servers) detect and filter spam before it ever gets to users. Some networks route email through another device first to filter out spam. If users never receive a malicious email, there isn't any chance of them clicking on a malicious link in that email.
- **Anti-malware software on mail gateways.** Malicious email often includes malware as attachments. Anti-malware software on the mail server can detect and block it. The software strips potentially malicious attachments off the email, and typically sends a notification to the user explaining what was removed and why.

- **All systems.** All workstations and servers have anti-malware software installed. Servers may have additional, specialized anti-malware software installed depending on the applications running on the servers.
- **Boundaries or firewalls.** Many networks include detection tools that monitor network traffic through the firewall. For example, unified threat management (UTM) inspects network traffic to reduce the risk of malware entering the network. Chapter 3, "Exploring Network Technologies and Tools," covers UTM systems.

Antivirus and Anti-Malware Software

Anti-malware software provides protection against many types of malware. You'll often hear the term *antivirus* software indicating it only protects against viruses. However, the lines have blurred. Viruses aren't the only threats. Attackers have changed their methodologies using different types of malware, and antivirus software vendors have adapted by including methods to detect and block these new threats. Most antivirus software detects, blocks, and removes several different types of malware, such as viruses, Trojans, worms, rootkits, spyware, and adware.

Antivirus software provides real-time protection and can perform both scheduled and manual scans. The real-time protection continuously monitors the system. For example, when a user visits a web site, antivirus software scans the downloaded web site files and attempts to block malicious code. Similarly, when a user downloads or opens a file, antivirus software scans it before opening it. Scheduled scans occur regularly, such as once a week. If users or technicians detect suspicious activity, they can perform manual scans to check the system.

If the antivirus software detects malware, it will typically quarantine it and notify the user. However, the exact way antivirus software does so varies from one vendor to another. The key to analyzing and interpreting the output from the antivirus software is to recognize the alert and read it. Some people just click OK without paying attention to alerts and can inadvertently override the antivirus software.

Antivirus software detects viruses using either signature-based detection or heuristic-based detection.

Signature-Based Detection

Viruses and other malware have known patterns. Signature files (also called data definition files) define the patterns, and the antivirus software scans files for matching patterns. When the software identifies a matching pattern, it reports it as an infection and takes action, such as deleting or quarantining the file.

A quarantined virus is not harmful to the system while it is in quarantine, but it's still available for analysis. As an example, a security professional could release a quarantined virus into an unprotected but isolated virtual machine environment for research and study.

Malware developers constantly release new viruses, so it's important to update signature definition files regularly. Most antivirus software includes the ability to automate the process of checking and downloading updated signature definition files. They typically check for updates several times a day.

It's also possible to download and install signature files manually. Administrators do this when updating systems that do not have Internet access. When doing so, it's important for administrators to ensure the signature file has not lost data integrity by comparing the hash of the signature file posted on the antivirus vendor's web site with the hash of the downloaded file.

Heuristic-Based Detection

Some antivirus software includes heuristic-based detection. Heuristic-based detection attempts to detect viruses that were previously unknown and do not have signatures. This includes zero-day exploits, mentioned later in this chapter.

Heuristic-based analysis runs questionable code in a sandbox or virtualized environment specifically designed to protect the live environment, while it observes the code's behavior. Most viruses engage in viral activities—actions that can be harmful, but are rarely performed by legitimate programs. The heuristic-based analysis detects these viral activities.

As an example, polymorphic malware adds variations to files when it creates copies. It's highly unusual for any application to add variations in files like this, and heuristic methods are often successful at detecting polymorphic malware.

> **Remember this**
>
> Antivirus software detects and removes malware, such as viruses, Trojans, and worms. Signature-based antivirus software detects known malware based on signature definitions. Heuristic-based software detects previously unknown malware based on behavior.

Checking File Integrity

Some antivirus scanners use file integrity checkers to detect modified system files. A file integrity checker calculates hashes on system files as a baseline. It then periodically recalculates the hashes on these files and compares them with the hashes in the baseline. If the hashes are ever different, it indicates the system files have been modified. When an antivirus scanner detects a modified file, it sends an alert. Many times, these alerts can detect rootkit infections.

It's also possible to check file integrity with command-line tools. For example, the Microsoft File Checksum Integrity Verifier (*fciv.exe*) tool can verify the integrity of all files within a folder, or a group of nested folders. Check out the lab Using the File Checksum Integrity Verifier in the labs for this chapter at *http://gcgapremium.com/501labs/*.

The *fciv.exe* allows you to create a data file listing all the hashes for files within a directory. You can then run the command later to verify the hashes are the same. Normally, you'll see the following message indicating the files haven't lost integrity: "All files verified successfully." However, if the application detects a file has a different hash, you'll see a message similar to this:

List of modified files:

----

exefiles\md5Sum.exe
    Hash is: 08ab4b9b40448d77079f61751f989702bbebe2ed
    It should be: 7648ec1a2d8c8b65a024973d30b4b2dc48ad0cec

In this example, it indicates that the file *md5sum.exe* has been modified. Because executable files aren't normally modified, this indicates the file has likely been infected with malware and it shouldn't be used.

Data Execution Prevention

Data execution prevention (DEP) is a security feature that prevents code from executing in memory regions marked as nonexecutable. It helps prevent an application or service from executing code from a nonexecutable memory region. The primary purpose of DEP is to protect a system from malware.

DEP is enforced by both hardware and software. Advanced Micro Devices (AMD) implement DEP using the no-execute page-protection (NX) feature. Intel implements DEP using the Execute Disable Bit (XD) feature. Both are enabled in the Basic Input/Output System (BIOS) or Unified Extensible Firmware Interface (UEFI). Within Windows, DEP is enabled in the System Properties – Performance Settings.

If DEP is not enabled in the BIOS or UEFI, but you try to install Windows, you will typically see an error message such as "Your PC's CPU isn't compatible with Windows." The solution is to enable DEP in BIOS or the UEFI.

Advanced Malware Tools

Many vendors have begun developing advanced malware tools. These go beyond just examining files to determine if they are malware. As an example, Cisco's Advanced Malware Protection (AMP) combines multiple technologies to protect a network before an attack, during an attack, and after an attack.

AMP analyzes a network to prevent attacks using threat intelligence and analytics. It collects worldwide threat intelligence from Cisco's Security Intelligence organization, Talos Security Intelligence and Research Group, and Threat Grid intelligence feeds. This information helps it detect and alert on malware similar to any antivirus software.

During an attack, AMP uses a variety of techniques to detect and block emerging threats before they infiltrate a network, or contain and remediate malware that gets into a network. AMP uses continuous analysis to detect suspicious file and network activity within a network, which helps it detect malware operating within the network.

Security administrators view logs and alerts to analyze and interpret the output from advanced malware tools such as AMP. For example, administrators might see an alert indicating that encrypted data is being sent out of the network. This is a serious red flag and indicates malware is collecting data and sending it to an attacker.

Spam Filters

Organizations often implement a multipronged approach to block spam. For example, many UTM systems include spam filters to detect and block spam. The output of the UTM goes to an email server. Email servers also have methods of detecting and blocking spam. The email server sends all email to the users, except for what it detects as spam. User systems also have anti-spam filters, or junk mail options, as a final check.

The challenge with any *spam filter* is to only filter out spam, and never filter out actual email. For example, a company wouldn't want a spam filter to filter out an email from a customer trying to buy something. Because of this, most spam filters err on the side of caution, allowing spam through rather than potentially marking valid email as spam. Although the science behind spam filtering continues to improve, criminals have also continued to adapt.

Spam filters typically allow you to identify email addresses as safe, or to be blocked. You can add these as individual addresses or entire domains. For example, if you want to ensure you get email from Homer when he sends email from *springfield.com*, you can identify *homer@ springfield.com* as a safe email address. If you want to ensure you get all email from *springfield.com*, you can designate *springfield.com* as a safe domain. Similarly, you can block either the single email address *homer@springfield.com* or the entire domain *springfield.com*.

Educating Users

Untrained users provide a significant risk to any organization and are often one of the largest vulnerabilities. They don't need to be malicious insiders. They can simply be unaware of the risks. Think back to the Fancy Bear and Cozy Bear APT attacks mentioned in this chapter. No matter how much money an organization is spending on technology, it can all be bypassed by a single user clicking on a malicious link in an email. The impact can be the infection of an entire network.

The single best protection against many attacks, such as social engineering and phishing attacks, is to train and raise the security awareness of users. Many users simply aren't aware of the attackers' methods. However, once they understand the risks and methods used by social engineers and other attackers, they are less likely to fall prey to these attacks. Similarly, raising users' security awareness helps them recognize and respond appropriately to new threats and security trends.

Security-related awareness and training programs take many forms. Some common methods include formal classes, short informal live training sessions, online courses, posters, newsletters, logon banners, and periodic emails. These programs often keep users aware of new threats and new security trends and alerts, such as new malware, current phishing attacks, and zero-day exploits.

New Viruses

Criminals are constantly releasing new viruses and some prove to be exceptionally damaging. Many of these require administrators to take quick action to mitigate the threat. For example, when vendors discover a vulnerability that attackers can exploit, they release patches and updates to remove the vulnerability. Administrators then need to evaluate, test, and implement the patches or upgrades to servers. Similarly, home users should keep their systems and applications up to date.

Phishing Attacks

In addition to releasing new viruses regularly, criminals are also launching new phishing attacks. Some new attempts are tricky and fool many people. The best way to prevent successful attacks is to educate people about what the criminals are doing now.

As an example, criminals crafted a sophisticated attack on Gmail users that fooled even tech-savvy users. Once they had captured the Gmail credentials of one user, they quickly logged on to that user's account and scoured it for sent emails, attachments, and subject lines.

They then used this account to send emails to people this person previously emailed, often using similar subject lines. Additionally, they often include what looks like a thumbnail of a document. Typically, clicking the thumbnail provides a preview of the document. However, this instead opened up another tab within the browser with a URL like this: *data:text/html,https://accounts.google.com/ServiceLogin?service=mail...*

When users see *accounts.google.com*, it looks legitimate. Additionally, the page shows a sign-in page that looks exactly like the Google sign-in page. It isn't, though. Users who were tricked into "logging on" on this bogus but perfectly created web page were compromised. Attackers quickly logged on to this account and started the process all over again, hoping to snare other unsuspecting users.

In one publicized example, the attackers used a compromised account to resend a team practice schedule to all the members of the team. It included a similar subject line and screenshot of the original attachment. Some recipients who received the email clicked the thumbnail and were taken to the same URL with *accounts.google.com* in it. Some were tricked and entered their credentials to apparently log on to Google. Attackers quickly logged on to the newly compromised accounts and started the process again.

Zero-Day Exploits

Chapter 4, "Securing Your Network," discusses zero-day vulnerabilities and zero-day exploits. As a reminder, a ***zero-day vulnerability*** is a vulnerability or bug that is unknown to trusted sources, such as operating system and antivirus vendors. Operating system vendors write and release patches once they know about them, but until the vendors know about them, the vulnerability remains. As an example, the Heartbleed vulnerability existed for a couple of years before it was widely published. Up until the time that OpenSSL developers released a fix, everyone using it was vulnerable.

Users might adopt the idea that up-to-date antivirus software will protect them from all malware. This simply isn't true. No matter how great an antivirus company is at identifying new malware, there is always going to be a lag between the time when criminals release the malware and the antivirus company releases new signatures to discover it. This is especially true when attackers are releasing more than 200,000 new variants of malware daily. This includes malware designed to take advantage of zero-day vulnerabilities.

Remember this

Educating users about new viruses, phishing attacks, and zero-day exploits helps prevent incidents. Zero-day exploits take advantage of vulnerabilities that aren't known by trusted sources, such as operating system vendors and antivirus vendors.

With this in mind, users need to practice safe computing habits. They can't depend on the antivirus software and other technical controls to protect them. Some basic guidelines are:
- Don't click on links within emails from unknown sources (no matter how curious you might be).
- Don't open attachments from unknown sources. Malware can be embedded into many different files, such as Portable Document Format (PDF) files, Word documents, Zipped (compressed) files, and more.
- Be wary of free downloads from the Internet. (Trojans entice you with something free, but they include malware.)
- Limit information you post on social media sites. (Criminals use this to answer password reset questions.)
- Back up your data regularly (unless you're willing to see it disappear forever).
- Keep your computer up to date with current patches (but beware of zero-day exploits).
- Keep antivirus software up to date (but don't depend on it to catch everything).

Why Social Engineering Works

Social engineers typically use one or more psychology-based principles to increase the effectiveness of their attacks. In addition to teaching users about the different social engineering tactics, it's also useful to teach them about these underlying principles. The following sections introduce these topics.

Authority

Many people have grown up to respect authority and are more likely to comply when a person of authority says to do so. As an example, volunteers participating in the Milgram experiment continued to send shocks to unseen subjects even though they could hear them scream in pain, simply because a man in a lab coat told them to continue. They weren't actually sending shocks and the screams were fake, but everything seemed real to the volunteers. Psychologists have repeated these experiments and have seen similar results. Using authority is most effective with impersonation, whaling, and vishing attacks:

- **Impersonation.** Some social engineers impersonate others to get people to do something. For example, many have called users on the phone claiming they work for Microsoft. The Police Virus (a form of ransomware) attempts to impersonate a law enforcement agency. Other times, social engineers attempt to impersonate a person of authority, such as an executive within a company, or a technician.
- **Whaling.** Executives respect authorities such as legal entities. As an example, the "Whaling" section mentioned how many executives were tricked into opening infected PDF files that looked like official subpoenas.
- **Vishing.** Some attackers use the phone to impersonate authority figures.

Intimidation

In some cases, the attacker attempts to intimidate the victim into taking action. Intimidation might be through bullying tactics, and it is often combined with impersonating someone else. Using intimidation is most effective with impersonation and vishing attacks.

For example, a social engineer might call an executive's receptionist with this request: "Mr. Simpson is about to give a huge presentation to potential customers, but his files are corrupt. He told me to call you and get you to send the files to me immediately so that I can get him set up for his talk." If the receptionist declines, the social engineer can use intimidation tactics by saying something like: "Look, if you want to be responsible for this million-dollar sale falling through, that's fine. I'll tell him you don't want to help."

Note that this tactic can use multiple principles at the same time. In this example, the attacker is combining intimidation with urgency. The receptionist doesn't have much time to respond.

Consensus

People are often more willing to like something that other people like. Some attackers take advantage of this by creating web sites with fake testimonials that promote a product. For example, criminals have set up some web sites with dozens of testimonials listing all the benefits of their fake antivirus software. If users search the Internet before downloading the fake antivirus software, they will come across these web sites, and might believe that other real people are vouching for the product.

Using consensus, sometimes called social proof, is most effective with Trojans and hoaxes. Victims are more likely to install a Trojan if everyone seems to indicate it's safe. Similarly, if a person suspects a virus notice is just a hoax, but everyone seems to be saying it's real, the victim is more likely to be tricked.

Scarcity

People are often encouraged to take action when they think there is a limited quantity. As an example of scarcity, think of Apple iPhones. When Apple first releases a new version, they typically sell out quickly. A phishing email can take advantage of this and encourage users to click a link for exclusive access to a new product. If the users click, they'll end up at a malicious web site. Scarcity is often effective with phishing and Trojan attacks. People make quick decisions without thinking them through.

Urgency

Some attacks use urgency as a technique to encourage people to take action now. As an example, the ransomware uses the scarcity principle with a countdown timer. Victims typically have 72 hours to pay up before they lose all their data. Each time they look at their computer, they'll see the timer counting down.

Using urgency is most effective with ransomware, phishing, vishing, whaling, and hoaxes. For example, phishing emails with malicious links might indicate that there are a limited number of products at a certain price, so the user should "Click Now." Executives might be tricked into thinking a subpoena requires immediate action. Many virus hoaxes have a deadline such as at 4:00 p.m. when the hoax claims the virus will cause the damage.

> **Remember this**
>
> Many of the reasons that social engineers are effective are because they use psychology-based techniques to overcome users' objections. Scarcity and urgency are two techniques that encourage immediate action.

Familiarity

If you like someone, you are more likely to do what the person asks. This is why so many big companies hire well-liked celebrities. And, it's also why they fire them when they become embroiled in a scandal that affects their credibility.

Some social engineers attempt to build rapport with the victim to build a relationship before launching the attack. This principle is most effective with shoulder surfing and tailgating attacks:

- **Shoulder surfing.** People are more likely to accept someone looking over their shoulder when they are familiar with the other person, or they like them. In contrast, if you don't know or don't like someone, you are more likely to recognize a shoulder surfing attack and stop it immediately.
- **Tailgating.** People are much more likely to allow someone to tailgate behind them if they know the person or like the person. Some social engineers use a simple, disarming smile to get the other person to like them.

Trust

In addition to familiarity, some social engineers attempt to build a trusting relationship between them and the victim. This often takes a little time, but the reward for the criminal can be worth it. Vishing attacks often use this method.

As an example, someone identifying himself as a security expert once called me. He said he was working for some company with "Secure" in its name, and they noticed that my computer was sending out errors. He stressed a couple of times that they deploy and support Windows systems. The company name and their experience was an attempt to start building trust.

He then guided me through the process of opening Event Viewer and viewing some errors on my system. He asked me to describe what I saw and eventually said, "Oh my God!" with the voice of a well-seasoned actor. He explained that this indicated my computer was seriously infected. In reality, the errors were trivial.

After seriously explaining how much trouble I was in with my computer, he then added a smile to his voice and said, "But this is your lucky day. I'm going to help you." He offered to guide me through the process of fixing my computer before the malware damaged it permanently.

All of this was to build trust. At this point, he went in for the kill. He had me open up the Run window and type in a web site address and asked me to click OK. This is where I stopped. I didn't click OK.

I tried to get him to answer some questions, but he was evasive. Eventually, I heard a click. My "lucky day" experience with this social engineering criminal was over.

The link probably would have taken me to a malicious web site ready with a drive-by download. Possibly the attacker was going to guide me through the process of installing malware on my system. If my system objected with an error, I'm betting he would have been ready with a soothing voice saying "That's normal. Just click OK. Trust me." He spent a lot of time with me. I suspect that they've been quite successful with this ruse with many other people.

Chapter 6 Exam Topic Review

When preparing for the exam, make sure you understand these key concepts covered in this chapter.

Understanding Threat Actors

- Script kiddies use existing computer scripts or code to launch attacks. They typically have very little expertise or sophistication, and very little funding.
- A hacktivist launches attacks as part of an activist movement or to further a cause.
- Insiders (such as employees of a company) have legitimate access to an organization's internal resources. They sometimes become malicious insiders out of greed or revenge.
- Competitors sometimes engage in attacks to gain proprietary information about another company.
- Organized crime is an enterprise that employs a group of individuals working together in criminal activities. Their primary motivation is money.
- Some attackers are organized and sponsored by a nation-state or government.
- An advanced persistent threat (APT) is a targeted attack against a network. An APT group has both the capability and intent to launch sophisticated and targeted attacks. They are sponsored by a nation-state and often have a significant amount of resources and funding.
- A common method attackers often use before launching an attack is to gather

information from open-source intelligence, including any information available via web sites and social media.

Determining Malware Types

- Malware includes several different types of malicious code, including viruses, worms, logic bombs, backdoors, Trojans, ransomware, rootkits, and more.
- A virus is malicious code that attaches itself to a host application. The code runs when the application is launched.
- A worm is self-replicating malware that travels throughout a network without user intervention.
- A logic bomb executes in response to an event, such as a day, time, or condition. Malicious insiders have planted logic bombs into existing systems, and these logic bombs have delivered their payload after the employee left the company.
- Backdoors provide another way of accessing a system. Malware often inserts backdoors into systems, giving attackers remote access to systems.
- A Trojan appears to be one thing, such as pirated software or free antivirus software, but is something malicious. A remote access Trojan (RAT) is a type of malware that allows attackers to take control of systems from remote locations.
- Drive-by downloads often attempt to infect systems with Trojans.
- Ransomware is a type of malware that takes control of a user's system or data. Criminals attempt to extort payment as ransom combined to return control to the user. Crypto-malware is ransomware that encrypts the user's data. Attackers demand payment to decrypt the data.
- Spyware is software installed on user systems without the user's knowledge or consent and it monitors the user's activities. It sometimes includes a keylogger that records user keystrokes.
- A botnet is a group of computers called zombies controlled through a command-and-control server. Attackers use malware to join computers to botnets. Bot herders launch attacks through botnets.
- Rootkits take root-level or kernel-level control of a system. They hide their processes to avoid detection. They can remove user privileges and modify system files.

Recognizing Common Attacks

- Social engineering is the practice of using social tactics to gain information or trick users into performing an action they wouldn't normally take.
- Social engineering attacks can occur in person, over the phone, while surfing the Internet, and via email. Many social engineers attempt to impersonate others.
- Shoulder surfing is an attempt to gain unauthorized information through casual observation, such as looking over someone's shoulder, or monitoring screens with a camera. Screen filters can thwart shoulder surfing attempts.
- A hoax is a message, often circulated through email, that tells of impending doom from a virus or other security threat that simply doesn't exist.
- Tailgating is the practice of one person following closely behind another without showing credentials. Mantraps help prevent tailgating.
- Dumpster divers search through trash looking for information. Shredding or burning documents reduces the risk of dumpster diving.

- Watering hole attacks discover sites that a targeted group visits and trusts. Attackers then modify these sites to download malware. When the targeted group visits the modified site, they are more likely to download and install infected files.
- Spam is unwanted or unsolicited email. Attackers often use spam in different types of attacks.
- Phishing is the practice of sending email to users with the purpose of tricking them into revealing sensitive information, installing malware, or clicking on a link.
- Spear phishing and whaling are types of phishing. Spear phishing targets specific groups of users and whaling targets high-level executives.
- Vishing is a form of phishing that uses voice over the telephone and often uses Voice over IP (VoIP). Some vishing attacks start with a recorded voice and then switch over to a live person.

Blocking Malware and Other Attacks

- Antivirus software can detect and block different types of malware, such as worms, viruses, and Trojans. Antivirus software uses signatures to detect known malware.
- When downloading signatures manually, hashes can verify the integrity of signature files.
- Antivirus software typically includes a file integrity checker to detect files modified by a rootkit.
- Data execution prevention (DEP) prevents code from executing in memory locations marked as nonexecutable. The primary purpose of DEP is to protect a system from malware.
- Advanced malware tools monitor files and activity within the network.
- Anti-spam software attempts to block unsolicited email. You can configure a spam filter to block individual email addresses and email domains.
- Security-related awareness and training programs help users learn about new threats and security trends, such as new viruses, new phishing attacks, and zero-day exploits. Zero-day exploits take advantage of vulnerabilities that are not known by trusted sources.
- Social engineers and other criminals employ several psychology-based principles to help increase the effectiveness of their attacks. They are authority, intimidation, consensus, scarcity, urgency, familiarity, and trust.

Online References

- Have you done the online labs? They might help you understand some key content. Check out the online content to view some extra materials at *http://gcgapremium.com/501-extras*.

Chapter 6 Practice Questions

1. The Marvin Monroe Memorial Hospital recently suffered a serious attack. The attackers notified management personnel that they encrypted a significant amount of data on the hospital's servers and it would remain encrypted until the management paid a hefty sum to the attackers. Which of the following identifies the MOST likely threat actor in this attack?

    A. Organized crime
    B. Ransomware
    C. Competitors
    D. Hacktivist

2. Dr. Terwilliger installed code designed to enable his account automatically if he ever lost his job as a sidekick on a television show. The code was designed to reenable his account three days after it is disabled. Which of the following does this describe?
   A. Logic bomb
   B. Rootkit
   C. Spyware
   D. Ransomware

3. Lisa recently developed an application for the Human Resources department. Personnel use this application to store and manage employee data, including PII. She programmed in the ability to access this application with a username and password that only she knows, so that she can perform remote maintenance on the application if necessary. Which of the following does this describe?
   A. Virus
   B. Worm
   C. Backdoor
   D. Trojan

4. Dr. Terwilliger installed code designed to run if he ever lost his job as a sidekick on a television show. The code will create a new account with credentials that only he knows three days after his original account is deleted. Which type of account does this code create?
   A. Backdoor
   B. Logic bomb
   C. Rootkit
   D. Ransomware

5. Security administrators recently discovered suspicious activity within your network. After investigating the activity, they discovered malicious traffic from outside your network connecting to a server within your network. They determined that a malicious threat actor used this connection to install malware on the server and the malware is collecting data and sending it out of the network. Which of the following BEST describes the type of malware used by the threat actor?
   A. APT
   B. Organized crime
   C. RAT
   D. Crypto-malware

6. A security administrator recently noticed abnormal activity on a workstation. It is connecting to systems outside the organization's internal network using uncommon ports. The administrator discovered the computer is also running several hidden processes. Which of the following choices BEST describes this activity?
   A. Rootkit
   B. Backdoor
   C. Spam
   D. Trojan

7. Lisa is a database administrator and received a phone call from someone identifying himself as a technician working with a known hardware vendor. The technician said he's aware of a problem with database servers they've sold, but it only affects certain operating system versions. He asks Lisa what operating system the company is running on their database servers. Which of the following choices is the BEST response from Lisa?

   A. Let the caller know what operating system and versions are running on the database servers to determine if any further action is needed.

   B. Thank the caller and end the call, report the call to her supervisor, and independently check the vendor for issues.

   C. Ask the caller for his phone number so that she can call him back after checking the servers.

   D. Contact law enforcement personnel.

8. Bart is in a break area outside the office. He told Lisa that he forgot his badge inside and asked Lisa to let him follow her when she goes back inside. Which of the following does this describe?

   A. Spear phishing

   B. Whaling

   C. Mantrap

   D. Tailgating

9. While cleaning out his desk, Bart threw several papers containing PII into the recycle bin. Which type of attack can exploit this action?

   A. Vishing

   B. Dumpster diving

   C. Shoulder surfing

   D. Tailgating

10. Your organization recently suffered a loss from malware that wasn't previously known by any trusted sources. Which of the following BEST describes this attack?

    A. Phishing

    B. Zero-day

    C. Open-source intelligence

    D. Hoax

11. A recent change in an organization's security policy states that monitors need to be positioned so that they cannot be viewed from outside any windows. Additionally, users are directed to place screen filters over the monitor. What is the purpose of this policy?

    A. Reduce success of phishing

    B. Reduce success of shoulder surfing

    C. Reduce success of dumpster diving

    D. Reduce success of impersonation

12. Attackers recently sent some malicious emails to the CFO within your organization. These emails have forged From blocks and look like they are coming from the CEO of the organization. They include a PDF file that is described as a funding document for an upcoming project. However, the PDF is infected with malware. Which of the following BEST describes the attack type in this scenario?
    A. Phishing
    B. Spam
    C. Trojan
    D. Whaling

13. A recent spear phishing attack that appeared to come from your organization's CEO resulted in several employees revealing their passwords to attackers. Management wants to implement a security control to provide assurances to employees that email that appears to come from the CEO actually came from the CEO. Which of the following should be implemented?
    A. Digital signatures
    B. Spam filter
    C. Training
    D. Heuristic-based detection

14. A recent attack on your organization's network resulted in the encryption of a significant amount of data. Later, an attacker demanded that your organization pay a large sum of money to decrypt the data. Security investigators later determined that this was the result of a new employee within your company clicking on a malicious link he received in an email. Which of the following BEST describes the vulnerability in this scenario?
    A. Ransomware
    B. Untrained user
    C. Resource exhaustion
    D. Insider threat

15. The CEO of a company recently received an email. The email indicates that her company is being sued and names her specifically as a defendant in the lawsuit. It includes an attachment and the email describes the attachment as a subpoena. Which of the following BEST describes the social engineering principle used by the sender in this scenario?
    A. Whaling
    B. Phishing
    C. Consensus
    D. Authority

Chapter 6 Practice Question Answers

1. **A.** This attack was most likely launched by an organized crime group because their motivation is primarily money. While the scenario describes ransomware, ransomware is the malware, not the threat actor. Competitors often want to obtain proprietary information and it would be very rare for a hospital competitor to extort money from another hospital. A hacktivist typically launches attacks to further a cause, not to extort money.

2. **A.** A logic bomb is code that executes in response to an event. In this scenario, the logic bomb executes when it discovers the account is disabled (indicating Dr. Bob Terwilliger is no longer employed at the company). In this scenario, the logic bomb is creating a backdoor. A rootkit includes hidden processes, but it does not activate in response to an event. Spyware is software installed on user systems without their awareness or consent. Its purpose is often to monitor the user's computer and the user's activity. Ransomware demands payment as ransom.

3. **C.** A backdoor provides someone an alternative way of accessing a system or application, which is exactly what Lisa created in this scenario. It might seem as though she's doing so with good intentions, but if attackers discover a backdoor, they can exploit it. A virus is malicious code that attaches itself to an application and executes when the application runs, not code that is purposely written into the application. A worm is self-replicating malware that travels throughout a network without the assistance of a host application or user interaction. A Trojan is software that looks like it has a beneficial purpose but includes a malicious component.

4. **A.** The code is creating a new account that Dr. Terwilliger can use to access as a backdoor. He is creating this with a logic bomb, but a logic bomb is the malware type, not the type of account that he created. Rootkits include hidden processes, but they do not activate in response to events. Ransomware demands payment to release a user's computer or data.

5. **C.** The scenario describes a remote access Trojan (RAT), which is a type of malware that allows attackers to take control of systems from remote locations. While the threat actor may be a member of an advanced persistent threat (APT) or an organized crime group, these are threat actor types, not types of malware. Crypto-malware is a type of ransomware that encrypts data, but there isn't indication that the data is being encrypted in this scenario.

6. **A.** A rootkit typically runs processes that are hidden and it also attempts to connect to computers via the Internet. Although an attacker might have used a backdoor to gain access to the user's computer and install the rootkit, backdoors don't run hidden processes. Spam is unwanted email and is unrelated to this question. A Trojan is malware that looks like it's beneficial, but is malicious.

7. **B.** This sounds like a social engineering attack where the caller is attempting to get information on the servers, so it's appropriate to end the call, report the call to a supervisor, and independently check the vendor for potential issues. It is not appropriate to give external personnel information on internal systems from a single phone call. It isn't necessary to ask for a phone number because you wouldn't call back and give information on the servers. The caller has not committed a crime by asking questions, so it is not appropriate to contact law enforcement personnel.

8. **D.** Tailgating is the practice of following closely behind someone else without using credentials. In this scenario, Bart might be an employee who forgot his badge, or he might be a social engineer trying to get in by tailgating. Spear phishing and whaling are two types of phishing with email. Mantraps prevent tailgating.

9. **B.** Dumpster divers look through trash or recycling containers for valuable paperwork, such as documents that include Personally Identifiable Information (PII). Instead, paperwork should be shredded or incinerated. Vishing is a form of phishing that uses the phone. Shoulder surfers attempt to view monitors or screens, not papers thrown into the trash or recycling containers. Tailgating is the practice of following closely behind someone else, without using proper credentials.

10. **B.** A zero-day exploit is one that isn't known by trusted sources such as antivirus vendors or operating system vendors. Phishing is malicious spam and it can include malware, but there isn't indication this loss was from an email. Attackers use open-source intelligence to identify a target. Some typical sources are social media sites and news outlets. A hoax is not a specific attack. It is a message, often circulated through email, that tells of impending doom from a virus or other security threat that simply doesn't exist.

11. **B.** Shoulder surfing is the practice of viewing data by looking over someone's shoulder and it includes looking at computer monitors. Positioning monitors so that they cannot be viewed through a window and/or placing screen filters over the monitors reduces this threat. Phishing is an email attack. Dumpster diving is the practice of looking through dumpsters. Social engineers often try to impersonate others to trick them.

12. **D.** Whaling is a type of phishing that targets high-level executives, such as chief financial officers (CFOs) or chief executive officers (CEOs) and this scenario describes an attack targeting the CFO. Because whaling is more specific than phishing, phishing isn't the best answer. Spam is unwanted email, but spam isn't necessarily malicious. While the infected Portable Document File (PDF) might include a Trojan, the scenario doesn't describe the type of malware within the PDF.

13. **A.** A digital signature provides assurances of who sent an email and meets the goal of this scenario. Although a spam filter might filter a spear phishing attack, it does not provide assurances about who sent an email. A training program would help educate employees about attacks and would help prevent the success of these attacks, but it doesn't provide assurances about who sent an email. Some antivirus software includes heuristic-based detection. Heuristic-based detection attempts to detect viruses that were previously unknown and do not have virus signatures.

14. **B.** Of the given choices, an untrained user is the most likely vulnerability in this scenario. A trained user would be less likely to click on a malicious link received in an email. While the attack describes ransomware, ransomware isn't a vulnerability. A denial-of-service (DoS) or distributed denial-of-service (DDoS) attack often results in resource exhaustion, but that is the result of an attack, not a vulnerability. An insider threat implies a malicious insider, but there isn't any indication that the new employee was malicious.

15. **D.** The sender is using the social engineering principle of authority in this scenario. A chief executive officer (CEO) would respect legal authorities and might be more inclined to open an attachment from such an authority. While the scenario describes whaling, a specific type of phishing attack, whaling and phishing are attacks, not social engineering principles. The social engineering principle of consensus attempts to show that other people like a product, but this is unrelated to this scenario.

Chapter 7

Protecting Against Advanced Attacks

CompTIA Security+ objectives covered in this chapter:

1.2 Compare and contrast types of attacks.

- Application/service attacks (DoS, DDoS, Man-in-the-middle, Buffer overflow, Injection, Cross-site scripting, Cross-site request forgery, Privilege escalation, ARP poisoning, Amplification, DNS poisoning, Domain hijacking, Man-in-the-browser, Zero day, Replay, Pass the hash, Hijacking and related attacks [Clickjacking, Session hijacking, URL hijacking, Typo squatting], Driver manipulation [Shimming, Refactoring], MAC spoofing, IP spoofing), Cryptographic attacks (Birthday, Known plain text/cipher text, Rainbow tables, Dictionary, Brute force [Online vs. offline], Collision, Replay)

1.6 Explain the impact associated with types of vulnerabilities.

- Race conditions, Improper input handling, Improper error handling, Memory/buffer vulnerability (Memory leak, Integer overflow, Buffer overflow, Pointer dereference, DLL injection), New threats/zero day

3.1 Explain use cases and purpose for frameworks, best practices and secure configuration guides.

- Industry-standard frameworks and reference architectures (Regulatory, Non-regulatory, National vs. international, Industry-specific frameworks), Benchmarks/secure configuration guides (Platform/vendor-specific guides [Web server, Operating system, Application server, Network infrastructure devices], General purpose guides)

3.6 Summarize secure application development and deployment concepts.

- Development life-cycle models (Waterfall vs. Agile), Secure DevOps (Security automation, Continuous integration, Baselining, Immutable systems, Infrastructure as code), Version control and change management, Provisioning and deprovisioning, Secure coding techniques (Proper error handling, Proper input validation, Normalization, Stored procedures, Code signing, Encryption, Obfuscation/camouflage, Code reuse/dead code, Server-side vs. client-side execution and validation, Memory management, Use of third-party libraries and SDKs, Data exposure), Code quality and testing (Static code analyzers, Dynamic analysis (e.g., fuzzing), Stress testing, Sandboxing, Model verification), Compiled vs. runtime code

6.1   Compare and contrast basic concepts of cryptography.
- Collision
**

If there's one thing that's abundant in the IT world, it is attacks and attackers. Attackers lurk almost everywhere. If you have computer systems, you can't escape them. However, you can be proactive in identifying the different types of attacks and take steps to prevent them, or at least prevent their effectiveness. This chapter covers a wide assortment of attacks from different sources and provides some insight into preventing many of them.

Comparing Common Attacks

This section summarizes many common and advanced types of attacks launched against systems and networks. It's important to realize that effective countermeasures exist for all of the attacks listed in this book. However, attackers are actively working on beating the countermeasures. As they do, security professionals create additional countermeasures and the attackers try to beat them. The battle continues daily.

The goal in this section is to become aware of many of the well-known attacks. By understanding these, you'll be better prepared to comprehend the improved attacks as they emerge and the improved countermeasures.

DoS Versus DDoS

A denial-of-service (**DoS**) attack is an attack from one attacker against one target. A distributed denial-of-service (**DDoS**) attack is an attack from two or more computers against a single target. DDoS attacks often include sustained, abnormally high network traffic on the network interface card of the attacked computer. Other system resource usage (such as the processor and memory usage) will also be abnormally high. The goal of both is to perform a service attack and prevent legitimate users from accessing services on the target computer.

> **Remember this**
>
> A denial-of-service (DoS) attack is an attack from a single source that attempts to disrupt the services provided by another system. A distributed denial-of-service (DDoS) attack includes multiple computers attacking a single target. DDoS attacks typically include sustained, abnormally high network traffic.

Privilege Escalation

Chapter 6, "Comparing Threats, Vulnerabilities, and Common Attacks," discusses **privilege escalation** tactics that attackers often use. For example, attackers often use remote access Trojans (RATs) to gain access to a single system. They typically have limited privileges (a combination of rights and permissions) when they first exploit a system. However, they use various privilege escalation techniques to gain more and more privileges.

Most of the attacks in this chapter also use privilege escalation techniques for the same reason—to gain more and more access to a system or a network.

Spoofing

Spoofing occurs when one person or entity impersonates or masquerades as someone or something else. Two common spoofing attacks mentioned specifically in the CompTIA objectives are media access control (MAC) address spoofing and Internet Protocol (IP) address spoofing.

Host systems on a network have a media access control (MAC) address assigned to the network interface card (NIC). These are hard-coded into the NIC. However, it's possible to use software methods to associate a different MAC address to the NIC in a **MAC spoofing** attack. For example, Chapter 3, "Exploring Network Technologies and Tools," discusses a MAC flood attack where an attacker overwhelms a switch with spoofed MAC addresses. Flood guards prevent these types of attacks. Chapter 4, "Securing Your Network," discusses how wireless attackers can bypass MAC address filtering by spoofing the MAC address of authorized systems.

In an **IP spoofing** attack, the attacker changes the source address so that it looks like the IP packet originated from a different source. This can allow an attacker to launch an attack from a single system, while it appears that the attack is coming from different IP addresses.

Remember this

Spoofing attacks typically change data to impersonate another system or person. MAC spoofing attacks change the source MAC address and IP spoofing attacks change the source IP address.

SYN Flood Attacks

The SYN flood attack is a common attack used against servers on the Internet. They are easy for attackers to launch, difficult to stop, and can cause significant problems. The SYN flood attack disrupts the TCP handshake process and can prevent legitimate clients from connecting.

Chapter 3 explains how TCP sessions use a three-way handshake when establishing a session. As a reminder, two systems normally start a TCP session by exchanging three packets in a TCP handshake. For example, when a client establishes a session with a server, it takes the following steps:

1. The client sends a SYN (synchronize) packet to the server.
2. The server responds with a SYN/ACK (synchronize/acknowledge) packet.
3. The client completes the handshake by sending an ACK (acknowledge) packet. After establishing the session, the two systems exchange data.

However, in a SYN flood attack, the attacker never completes the handshake by sending the ACK packet. Additionally, the attacker sends a barrage of SYN packets, leaving the server with multiple half-open connections. Figure 7.1 compares a normal TCP handshake with the start of a SYN flood attack.

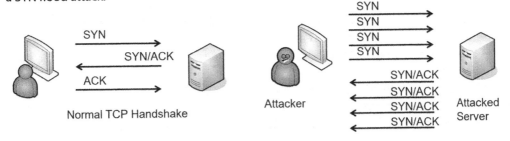

Figure 7.1: TCP handshake and SYN flood attack

In some cases, these half-open connections can consume a server's resources while it is waiting for the third packet, and it can actually crash. More often, though, the server limits the number of these half-open connections. Once the limit is reached, the server won't accept any new connections, blocking connections from legitimate users. For example, Linux systems support an iptables command that can set a threshold for SYN packets, blocking them after the threshold is set. Although this prevents the SYN flood attack from crashing the system, it also denies service to legitimate clients.

Attackers can launch SYN flood attacks from a single system in a DoS attack. They will often spoof the source IP address when doing so. Attackers can also coordinate an attack from multiple systems using a DDoS attack.

Man-in-the-Middle Attacks

A *man-in-the-middle (MITM)* attack is a form of active interception or active eavesdropping. It uses a separate computer that accepts traffic from each party in a conversation and forwards the traffic between the two. The two computers are unaware of the MITM computer, and it can interrupt the traffic at will or insert malicious code.

For example, imagine that Maggie and Bart are exchanging information with their two computers over a network. If Hacker Harry can launch an MITM attack from a third computer, he will be able to intercept all traffic. Maggie and Bart still receive all the information, so they are unaware of the attack. However, Hacker Harry also receives all the information. Because the MITM computer can control the entire conversation, it is easy to insert malicious code and send it to the computers. Address Resolution Protocol (ARP) poisoning is one way that an attacker can launch an MITM attack.

Kerberos helps prevent man-in-the-middle attacks with mutual authentication. It doesn't allow a malicious system to insert itself in the middle of the conversation without the knowledge of the other two systems.

ARP Poisoning Attacks

ARP poisoning is an attack that misleads computers or switches about the actual MAC address of a system. The MAC address is the physical address, or hardware address, assigned to the NIC. ARP resolves the IP addresses of systems to their hardware address and stores the result in an area of memory known as the ARP cache.

TCP/IP uses the IP address to get a packet to a destination network. Once the packet arrives on the destination network, it uses the MAC address to get it to the correct host. ARP uses two primary messages:

- **ARP request.** The ARP request broadcasts the IP address and essentially asks, "Who has this IP address?"
- **ARP reply.** The computer with the IP address in the ARP request responds with its MAC address. The computer that sent the ARP request caches the MAC address for the IP. In many operating systems, all computers that hear the ARP reply also cache the MAC address.

A vulnerability with ARP is that it is very trusting. It will believe any ARP reply packet. Attackers can easily create ARP reply packets with spoofed or bogus MAC addresses, and poison the ARP cache on systems in the network. Two possible attacks from ARP poisoning are a man-in-the-middle attack and a DoS attack.

ARP Man-in-the-Middle Attacks

In a man-in-the-middle attack, an attacker can redirect network traffic and, in some cases, insert malicious code. Consider Figure 7.2. Normally, traffic from the user to the Internet will go through the switch directly to the router, as shown in the top of Figure 7.2. However, after poisoning the ARP cache of the victim, traffic is redirected to the attacker.

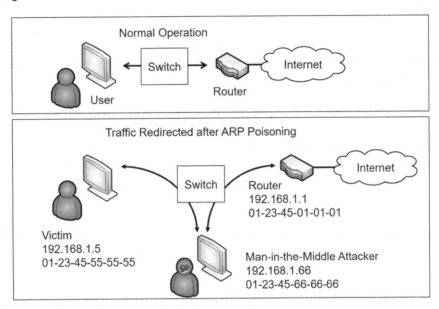

Figure 7.2: ARP poisoning used to redirect traffic

The victim's ARP cache should include this entry to send data to the router:
192.168.1.1, 01-23-45-01-01-01
However, after poisoning the ARP cache, it includes this entry:
192.168.1.1, 01-23-45-66-66-66
The victim now sends all traffic destined for the router to the attacker. The attacker captures the data for analysis later. It also uses another method such as IP forwarding to send the traffic to the router so that the victim is unaware of the attack.

> **Remember this**
>
> ARP poisoning attacks attempt to mislead systems about the actual MAC address of a system. ARP poisoning is sometimes used in man-in-the-middle attacks.

ARP DoS Attacks

An attacker can also use ARP poisoning in a DoS attack. For example, an attacker can send an ARP reply with a bogus MAC address for the default gateway. The default gateway is the IP address of a router connection that provides a path out of the network. If all the computers cache a bogus MAC address for the default gateway, none of them can reach it, and it stops all traffic out of the network.

DNS Attacks

Chapter 3 covers Domain Name System (DNS) in much more depth, but as a reminder, DNS resolves host names to IP addresses. This eliminates the need for you and me to have to remember the IP address for web sites. Instead, we simply type the name into the browser, and it connects. For example, if you type in *gcgapremium.com* as the Uniform Resource Locator (URL) in your web browser, your system queries a DNS server for the IP address. DNS responds with the correct IP address and your system connects to the web site using the IP address.

DNS also provides reverse lookups. In a reverse lookup, a client sends an IP address to a DNS server with a request to resolve it to a name. Some applications use this as a rudimentary security mechanism to detect spoofing. For example, an attacker may try to spoof the computer's identity by using a different name during a session. However, the Transmission Control Protocol/ Internet Protocol (TCP/IP) packets in the session include the IP address of the masquerading system and a reverse lookup shows the system's actual name. If the names are different, it shows suspicious activity. Reverse lookups are not 100 percent reliable because reverse lookup records are optional on DNS servers. However, they are useful when they're available.

Three attacks against DNS services are DNS poisoning, pharming, and DDoS.

DNS Poisoning Attacks

A **DNS poisoning** attack attempts to modify or corrupt DNS results. For example, a successful DNS poisoning attack can modify the IP address associated with *google.com* and replace it with the IP address of a malicious web site. Each time a user queries DNS for the IP address of *google.com*, the DNS server responds with the IP address of the malicious web site.

There have been several successful DNS poisoning attacks over the years. Many current DNS servers use Domain Name System Security Extensions (**DNSSEC**) to protect the DNS records and prevent DNS poisoning attacks. Chapter 3 covers DNSSEC in more depth.

Pharming Attacks

A pharming attack is another type of attack that manipulates the DNS name resolution process. It either tries to corrupt the DNS server or the DNS client. Just as a DNS poisoning attack can redirect users to different web sites, a successful pharming attack redirects a user to a different web site.

Pharming attacks on the client computer modify the hosts file used on Windows systems. This file is in the *C:\Windows\System32\drivers\etc* folder and can include IP addresses along with host name mappings. By default, it doesn't have anything other than comments on current Windows computers. However, a mapping might look like this:

```
127.0.0.1        localhost
13.207.21.200    google.com
```

The first entry maps the name localhost to the loopback IP address of 127.0.0.1. The second entry maps the name google.com to the IP address of bing.com (13.207.21.200). If a user enters google.com into the address bar of a browser, the browser will instead go to bing.com. Practical jokers might do this to a friend's computer and it isn't malicious. However, if the IP address points to a malicious server, this might cause the system to download malware.

DDoS DNS Attacks

It's difficult to take down the Internet. However, a cyberattack in October 2016 effectively did so for millions of users in North America and Europe. Specifically, on October 21, attackers launched three DDoS attacks during the day at 7:00 a.m., at 11:52 a.m., and at 4:00 p.m. These attacks prevented users from accessing a multitude of sites, such as Amazon, CNN, Fox News, Netflix, PayPal, Reddit, Spotify, Twitter, Xbox Live, and more.

Attackers infected many Internet-connected devices, such as video cameras, video recorders, printers, and baby monitors, with malware called Mirai. Mirai forces individual systems to become bots within large botnets. Chapter 6 covers bots and botnets in more depth. On October 21, they sent commands to millions of infected devices directing them to repeatedly send queries to DNS servers. These queries overwhelmed the DNS servers and prevented regular users from accessing dozens of web sites.

These three attacks were launched against DNS servers maintained by Dyn, Inc., an Internet performance management company. They clearly demonstrated that it is possible to seriously disrupt DNS services, causing Internet access problems for millions of people.

Amplification Attacks

An *amplification attack* is a type of DDoS attack. It typically uses a method that significantly increases the amount of traffic sent to, or requested from, a victim. As an example, a smurf attack spoofs the source address of a directed broadcast ping packet to flood a victim with ping replies. It's worthwhile to break this down:

- **A ping is normally unicast—one computer to one computer.** A ping sends ICMP echo requests to one computer, and the receiving computer responds with ICMP echo responses.
- **The smurf attack sends the ping out as a broadcast.** In a broadcast, one computer sends the packet to all other computers in the subnet.
- **The smurf attack spoofs the source IP.** If the source IP address isn't changed, the computer sending out the broadcast ping will get flooded with the ICMP replies. Instead, the smurf attack substitutes the source IP with the IP address of the victim, and the victim gets flooded with these ICMP replies.

DNS amplification attacks send DNS requests to DNS servers spoofing the IP address of the victim. Instead of just asking for a single record, these attacks tell the DNS servers to send as much zone data as possible, amplifying the data sent to the victim. Repeating this process from multiple attackers can overload the victim system.

An example of a Network Time Protocol (NTP) amplification attack uses the monlist command. When used normally, it sends a list of the last 600 hosts that connected to the NTP server. In an NTP amplification attack with monlist, the attacker spoofs the source IP address when sending the command. The NTP server then floods the victim with details of the last 600 systems that requested the time from the NTP server.

> **Remember this**
>
> DNS poisoning attacks attempt to corrupt DNS data. Amplification attacks increase the amount of traffic sent to or requested from a victim and can be used against a wide variety of systems, including individual hosts, DNS servers, and NTP servers.

Password Attacks

Password attacks attempt to discover or bypass passwords used for authentication on systems and networks, and for different types of files. Some password attacks are sophisticated cryptographic attacks, while others are rather simple brute force attacks. The following sections cover some common password attacks.

Brute Force Attacks

A *brute force* attack attempts to guess all possible character combinations. The two types of brute force attacks are online and offline.

An online password attack attempts to discover a password from an online system. For example, an attacker can try to log on to an account by repeatedly guessing the username and password. Many tools are available that attackers can use to automate the process. For example, ncrack is a free tool that can be used to run online brute force password attacks.

Chapter 2, "Understanding Identity and Access Management," discusses account lockout policies used in Windows systems. They are effective against online brute force password attacks. An account lockout setting locks an account after the user enters the incorrect password a preset number of times. Individual services often have their own settings to prevent brute force attacks. For example, Secure Shell (SSH) can disconnect an attacker if he hasn't logged on within 60 seconds and limit the number of authentication attempts per connection. These settings often thwart brute force attacks against these services.

Offline password attacks attempt to discover passwords from a captured database or captured packet scan. For example, when attackers hack into a system or network causing a data breach, they can download entire databases. They then perform offline attacks to discover the passwords contained within the databases.

One of the first steps to thwart offline brute force attacks is to use complex passwords and to store the passwords in an encrypted or hashed format. Complex passwords include a mix of uppercase letters, lowercase letters, numbers, and special characters. Additionally, longer passwords are much more difficult to crack than shorter passwords.

Dictionary Attacks

A *dictionary* attack is one of the original password attacks. It uses a dictionary of words and attempts every word in the dictionary to see if it works. A dictionary in this context is simply a list of words and character combinations.

Dictionaries used in these attacks have evolved over time to reflect user behavior. Today, they include many of the common passwords that uneducated users configure for their accounts. For example, even though 12345 isn't a dictionary word, many people use it as a password, so character sets such as these have been added to many dictionaries used by dictionary attack tools.

These attacks are thwarted by using complex passwords. A complex password will not include words in a dictionary.

> ## Remember this
>
> Brute force attacks attempt to guess passwords. Online attacks guess the password of an online system. Offline attacks guess the password stored within a file, such as a database. Dictionary attacks use a file of words and common passwords to guess a password. Account lockout policies help protect against brute force attacks and complex passwords thwart dictionary attacks.

Password Hashes

Most systems don't store the actual password for an account. Instead, they store a hash of the password. Hash attacks attack the hash of a password instead of the password. Chapter 1, "Mastering Security Basics," introduces hashing and Chapter 10, "Understanding Cryptography and PKI," discusses hashing in much more depth. A *hash* is simply a number created with a hashing algorithm such as Message Digest 5 (**MD5**) or Secure Hash Algorithm 3 (**SHA-3**). A system can use a hashing algorithm such as MD5 to create a hash of a password.

As an example, if a user's password is IC@nP@$$S3curity+, the system calculates the hash and stores it instead. In this example, the MD5 hash is 75c8ac11c86ca966b58166187589cc15. Later, a user authenticates with a username and password. The system then calculates the hash of the password that the user entered, and compares the calculated hash against the stored hash. If they match, it indicates the user entered the correct password.

Unfortunately, tools are available to discover many hashed passwords. For example, MD5 Online (*http://www.md5online.org/*) allows you to enter a hash and it gives you the text of the password. If the password is 12345, the hash is 827ccb0eea8a706c4c34a16891f84e7b. If you enter that hash into MD5 Online, it returns the password of 12345 in less than a second. MD5 Online uses a database of hashed words from a dictionary. If the hash matches a database entry, the site returns the password.

The password is rarely sent across the network in cleartext. Chapter 8, "Using Risk Management Tools," discusses protocol analyzers and shows how an attacker can capture and view a password if it is sent across a network in cleartext. To prevent this, a protocol can calculate the hash of the password on the user's system and then send the hash across the network instead of the password. Unfortunately, if the hash is passed across the network in an unencrypted format, the attacker may be able to capture the hash and use it to log on to a system. Instead, most authentication protocols encrypt the password or the hash before sending it across the network.

Pass the Hash Attacks

In a *pass the hash* attack, the attacker discovers the hash of the user's password and then uses it to log on to the system as the user. Any authentication protocol that passes the hash over the network in an unencrypted format is susceptible to this attack. However, it is most associated with Microsoft LAN Manager (LM) and NT LAN Manager (NTLM), two older security protocols used to authenticate Microsoft clients. They are both susceptible to pass the hash attacks.

Any system using LM or NTLM is susceptible to a pass the hash attack. The simple solution (and the recommended solution) is to use NTLMv2 or Kerberos instead. NTLMv2 uses a number used once (nonce) on both the client and the authenticating server. The authentication process uses both the client nonce and the server nonce in a challenge/response process. Chapter 2 discusses Kerberos.

Unfortunately, many existing applications still use NTLM, so it can still be enabled on many Windows systems for backward compatibility. However, Microsoft recommends configuring clients to only send NTLMv2 responses and configuring authenticating servers to refuse any use of LM or NTLM. This is relatively easy to do via a Group Policy setting.

Birthday Attacks

A *birthday* attack is named after the birthday paradox in mathematical probability theory. The birthday paradox states that for any random group of 23 people, there is a 50 percent chance that 2 of them have the same birthday. This is not the same year, but instead one of the 365 days in any year.

In a birthday attack, an attacker is able to create a password that produces the same hash as the user's actual password. This is also known as a hash collision.

A hash **collision** occurs when the hashing algorithm creates the same hash from different passwords. This is not desirable. As an example, imagine a simple hashing algorithm creates three-digit hashes. The password "success" might create a hash of 123 and the password "passed" might create the same hash of 123. In this scenario, an attacker could use either "success" or "passed" as the password and both would work.

Birthday attacks on hashes are thwarted by increasing the number of bits used in the hash to increase the number of possible hashes. For example, the MD5 algorithm uses 128 bits and is susceptible to birthday attacks. SHA-3 can use as many as 512 bits and it is not susceptible to birthday attacks.

Rainbow Table Attacks

Rainbow table attacks are a type of attack that attempts to discover the password from the hash. A rainbow table is a huge database of precomputed hashes. It helps to look at the process of how some password cracker applications discover passwords without a rainbow table. Assume that an attacker has the hash of a password. The application can use the following steps to crack it:

1. The application guesses a password (or uses a password from a dictionary).
2. The application hashes the guessed password.
3. The application compares the original password hash with the guessed password hash. If they are the same, the application now knows the password.
4. If they aren't the same, the application repeats steps 1 through 3 until finding a match.

From a computing perspective, the most time-consuming part of these steps is hashing the guessed password in step 2. However, by using rainbow tables, applications eliminate this step. Rainbow tables are huge databases of passwords and their calculated hashes. Some rainbow tables are as large as 160 GB in size, and they include hashes for every possible combination of characters up to eight characters in length. Larger rainbow tables are also available using more characters.

In a rainbow table attack, the application simply compares the hash of the original password against hashes stored in the rainbow table. When the application finds a match, it identifies the password used to create the hash (or at least text that can reproduce the hash of the original password). Admittedly, this is a simplistic explanation of a rainbow table attack, but it is adequate unless you plan on writing an algorithm to create your own rainbow table attack software.

Salting passwords is a common method of preventing rainbow table attacks, along with other password attacks such as dictionary attacks. A **salt** is a set of random data such as two additional characters. Password salting adds these additional characters to a password before hashing it. These additional characters add complexity to the password, and also result in a different hash than the system would create using only the original password. This causes password attacks that compare hashes to fail.

Chapter 10 covers bcrypt and Password-Based Key Derivation Function 2 (PBKDF2). Both use salting techniques to increase the complexity of passwords and thwart brute force and rainbow table attacks.

> ### Remember this
>
> Passwords are typically stored as hashes. A pass the hash attack attempts to use an intercepted hash to access an account. Salting adds random text to passwords before hashing them and thwarts many password attacks, including rainbow table attacks. A hash collision occurs when the hashing algorithm creates the same hash from different passwords. Birthday attacks exploit collisions in hashing algorithms.

Replay Attacks

A *replay attack* is one where an attacker replays data that was already part of a communication session. In a replay attack, a third party attempts to impersonate a client that is involved in the original session. Replay attacks can occur on both wired and wireless networks.

As an example, Maggie and Bart may initiate a session with each other. During the communication, each client authenticates with the other by passing authentication credentials to the other system. Hacker Harry intercepts all the data, including the credentials, and later initiates a conversation with Maggie pretending to be Bart. When Maggie challenges Hacker Harry, he sends Bart's credentials.

Many protocols use timestamps and sequence numbers to thwart replay attacks. For example, Kerberos, covered in Chapter 2, helps prevent replay attacks with timestamped tickets.

> ### Remember this
>
> Replay attacks capture data in a session with the intent of later impersonating one of the parties in the session. Timestamps and sequence numbers are effective countermeasures against replay attacks.

Known Plaintext Attacks

Many cryptographic attacks attempt to decrypt encrypted data. Chapter 10 covers encryption and decryption in more depth, but two relevant terms in this section are plaintext and ciphertext. Plaintext is human-readable data. An encryption algorithm scrambles the data, creating ciphertext.

An attacker can launch a *known plaintext* attack if he has samples of both the plaintext and the ciphertext. As an example, if an attacker captures an encrypted message (the ciphertext) and knows the plaintext of the message, he can use both sets of data to discover the encryption and decryption method. If successful, he can use the same decryption method on other ciphertext.

A chosen plaintext attack is similar, but the attacker doesn't have access to all the plaintext. As an example, imagine a company includes the following sentences at the end of every email:

"The information contained in this email and any accompanying attachments may contain proprietary information about the Pay & Park & Pay parking garage. If you are not the intended recipient of this information, any use of this information is prohibited."

If the entire message is encrypted, the attacker can try various methods to decrypt the chosen plaintext (the last two sentences included in every email). When he's successful, he can use the same method to decrypt the entire message.

In a ciphertext only attack, the attacker doesn't have any information on the plaintext. Known plaintext and chosen plaintext attacks are almost always successful if an attacker has the resources and time. However, ciphertext only attacks are typically only successful on weak encryption algorithms. They can be thwarted by not using legacy and deprecated encryption algorithms.

Hijacking and Related Attacks

Typo squatting (also called **URL hijacking**) occurs when someone buys a domain name that is close to a legitimate domain name. People often do so for malicious purposes. As an example, CompTIA hosts the comptia.org web site. If an attacker purchases the name compt**ai**.org with a slight misspelling at the end of comptia, some users might inadvertently go to the attacker's web site instead of the legitimate web site.

Attackers might buy a similar domain for a variety of reasons, including:

- **Hosting a malicious web site.** The malicious web site might try to install drive-by malware on users' systems when they visit.
- **Earning ad revenue.** The attacker can host pay-per-click ads. When visitors go to the site and click on the ads, advertisers pay revenue to the attacker.
- **Reselling the domain.** Attackers can buy domain names relatively cheaply, but resell them to the owner of the original site for a hefty profit.

Clickjacking tricks users into clicking something other than what they think they're clicking. As a simple example, imagine Bart is browsing Facebook. He sees a comment labeled Chalkboard Sayings, so he clicks it. He's taken to a page with a heading of "Human Test" and directions to "Find the blue button to continue." This looks like a Completely Automated Public Turing test to tell Computers and Humans Apart (CAPTCHA), but it isn't. When he clicks the blue button, he is actually clicking on a Facebook share button, causing him to share the original comment labeled Chalkboard Sayings with his Facebook friends.

While it's rarely apparent to the user, most clickjacking attacks use Hypertext Markup Language (HTML) frames. A frame allows one web page to display another web page within an area defined as a frame or iframe.

Attackers continue to find new ways to launch clickjacking attacks. As they appear, web developers implement new standards to defeat them. Most methods focus on breaking or disabling frames. This ensures that attackers cannot display your web page within a frame on their web page. For example, the Facebook share example is thwarted by Facebook web developers adding code to their web pages preventing the use of frames.

Session hijacking takes advantage of session IDs stored in cookies. When a user logs on to a web site, the web site often returns a small text file (called a cookie) with a session ID. In many cases, this cookie is stored on the user's system and remains active until the user logs off. If the user closes the session and returns to the web site, the web site reads the cookie and automatically logs the user on. This is convenient for the user, but can be exploited by an attacker.

In a session hijacking attack, the attacker utilizes the user's session ID to impersonate the user. The web server doesn't know the difference between the original user and the attacker because it is only identifying the user based on the session ID.

Attackers can read cookies installed on systems through several methods, such as through cross-site scripting attacks (described later in this chapter). Once they have the session ID, they can insert it into the HTTP header and send it to the web site. If the web server uses this session ID to log the user on automatically, it gives the attacker access to the user's account.

Domain Hijacking

In a *domain hijacking* attack, an attacker changes the registration of a domain name without permission from the owner. Attackers often do so with social engineering techniques to gain unauthorized access to the domain owner's email account.

As an example, imagine that Homer sets up a domain named homersimpson.com. He uses his Gmail account as the email address when he registers it, though he rarely checks his Gmail account anymore.

Attackers watch his Facebook page and notice that he often adds simple comments like "Doh!" Later, they try to log on to his Gmail account with a brute force attempt. They try the password of Doh!Doh! and get in. They then go to the domain name registrar, and use the Forgot Password feature. It sends a link to Homer's Gmail account to reset the password. After resetting the password at the domain name registrar site, the attackers change the domain ownership. They also delete all the emails tracking what they did. Later, Homer notices his web site is completely changed and he no longer has access to it.

> ## Remember this
>
> Attackers purchase similar domain names in typo squatting (also called URL hijacking) attacks. Users visit the typo squatting domain when they enter the URL incorrectly with a common typo. In a session hijacking attack, the attacker utilizes the user's session ID to impersonate the user. In a domain hijacking attack, an attacker changes the registration of a domain name without permission from the owner.

Man-in-the-Browser

A *man-in-the-browser* is a type of proxy Trojan horse that infects vulnerable web browsers. Successful man-in-the-browser attacks can capture browser session data. This includes keyloggers to capture keystrokes, along with all data sent to and from the web browser.

As an example, Zeus is a Trojan horse that has used man-in-the-browser techniques after infecting systems. Zeus includes keystroke logging and form grabbing. Once the attackers collect logon information for a user's bank, they use it to log on and transfer money to offshore accounts.

Driver Manipulation

Operating systems use drivers to interact with hardware devices or software components. For example, when you print a page using Microsoft Word, Word accesses the appropriate print driver via the Windows operating system. Similarly, if you access encrypted data on your system, the operating system typically accesses a software driver to decrypt the data so that you can view it.

Occasionally, an application needs to support an older driver. For example, Windows 10 needed to be compatible with drivers used in Windows 8, but all the drivers weren't compatible at first. *Shimming* provides the solution that makes it appear that the older drivers are compatible.

A driver shim is additional code that can be run instead of the original driver. When an application attempts to call an older driver, the operating system intercepts the call and redirects it to run the shim code instead. *Refactoring* code is the process of rewriting the internal processing of the code, without changing its external behavior. It is usually done to correct problems related to software design.

Developers have a choice when a driver is no longer compatible. They can write a shim to provide compatibility or they can completely rewrite the driver to refactor the relevant code. If the code is clunky, it's appropriate to rewrite the driver.

Attackers with strong programming skills can use their knowledge to manipulate drivers by either creating shims, or by rewriting the internal code. If the attackers can fool the operating system into using a manipulated driver, they can cause it to run malicious code contained within the manipulated driver.

Zero-Day Attacks

A *zero-day vulnerability* is a weakness or bug that is unknown to trusted sources, such as operating system and antivirus vendors. A zero-day attack exploits an undocumented vulnerability. Many times, the vendor isn't aware of the issue. At some point, the vendor learns of the vulnerability and begins to write and test a patch to eliminate it. However, until the vendor releases the patch, the vulnerability is still a zero-day vulnerability.

In most cases, a zero-day vulnerability is a new threat. However, there have been zero-day vulnerabilities that have existed for years.

As an example, a bug existed in the virtual DOS machine (VDM) that shipped with every version of 32-bit Windows systems from 1993 to 2010. The bug allowed attackers to escalate their privileges to full system level, effectively allowing them to take over the system. Google researcher Tavis Ormandy stated that he reported the bug to Microsoft in mid-2009. At this point, Microsoft (the vendor) knew about the bug, but didn't release a work-around until January 2010 and a patch until February 2010. Because the bug wasn't known publicly until January 2010, it remained a zero-day vulnerability until then.

Both attackers and security experts are constantly looking for new threats, such as zero-day vulnerabilities. Attackers want to learn about them so that they can exploit them. Most security experts want to know about them so that they can help ensure that vendors patch them before causing damage to users.

> ### Remember this
> Zero-day exploits are undocumented and unknown to the public. The vendor might know about it, but has not yet released a patch to address it.

Memory Buffer Vulnerabilities

Many application attacks take advantage of vulnerabilities in a system's memory or buffers. Because of this, it's important for developers to use secure memory management techniques within their code. For example, poor memory management techniques can result in a memory leak, or allow various overflow issues. The following sections describe some common memory issues related to applications.

Memory Leak

A *memory leak* is a bug in a computer application that causes the application to consume more and more memory the longer it runs. In extreme cases, the application can consume so much memory that the operating system crashes.

Memory leaks are typically caused by an application that reserves memory for short-term use, but never releases it. As an example, imagine a web application collects user profile data to personalize the browsing experience for users. However, it collects this data every time a user accesses a web page and it never releases the memory used to store the data. Over time, the web server will run slower and slower and eventually need to be rebooted.

Integer Overflow

An ***integer overflow*** attack attempts to use or create a numeric value that is too big for an application to handle. The result is that the application gives inaccurate results. As an example, if an application reserves 8 bits to store a number, it can store any value between 0 and 255. If the application attempts to multiply two values such as 95 × 59, the result is 5,605. This number cannot be stored in the 8 bits, so it causes an integer overflow error. It's a good practice to double-check the size of buffers to ensure they can handle any data generated by the applications.

In some situations, an integer overflow error occurs if an application expects a positive number, but receives a negative number instead. If the application doesn't have adequate error- and exception-handling routines, this might cause a buffer overflow error. Input handling and error handling are discussed later in this chapter.

Buffer Overflows and Buffer Overflow Attacks

A ***buffer overflow*** occurs when an application receives more input, or different input, than it expects. The result is an error that exposes system memory that would otherwise be protected and inaccessible. Normally, an application will have access only to a specific area of memory, called a buffer. The buffer overflow allows access to memory locations beyond the application's buffer, enabling an attacker to write malicious code into this area of memory.

As an example, an application may be expecting to receive a string of 15 characters for a username. If it receives more than 15 characters, it can cause a buffer overflow and expose system memory. The following HTTP GET command shows an example of sending a long string to the system to create a buffer overflow:

GET /index.php?username=ZZZZZZZZZZZZZZZZZZZZZZZZZZZZZZZZZZZZZZZZZZZZZZZZ

The buffer overflow exposes a vulnerability, but it doesn't necessarily cause damage by itself. However, once attackers discover the vulnerability, they exploit it and overwrite memory locations with their own code. If the attacker uses the buffer overflow to crash the system or disrupt its services, it is a DoS attack.

More often, the attacker's goal is to insert malicious code in a memory location that the system will execute. It's not easy for an attacker to know the exact memory location where the malicious code is stored, making it difficult to get the computer to execute it. However, an attacker can make educated guesses to get close.

A popular method that makes guessing easier is with no operation (NOP, pronounced as "no-op") commands, written as a NOP slide or NOP sled. Many Intel processors use hexadecimal 90 (often written as x90) as a NOP command, so a string of x90 characters is a NOP sled. The attacker writes a long string of x90 instructions into memory, followed by malicious code. When a computer is executing code from memory and it comes to a NOP, it just goes to the next memory location. With a long string of NOPs, the computer simply slides through all of them until it gets to the last one and then executes the code in the next instruction. If the attacker can get the computer to execute code from a memory location anywhere in the NOP slide, the system will execute the attacker's malicious code.

The malicious code varies. In some instances, the attackers write code to spread a worm through the web server's network. In other cases, the code modifies the web application so that the web application tries to infect every user who visits the web site with other malware. The attack possibilities are almost endless.

A buffer overflow attack includes several different elements, but they happen all at once. The attacker sends a single string of data to the application. The first part of the string causes the buffer overflow. The next part of the string is a long string of NOPs followed by the attacker's malicious code, stored in the attacked system's memory. Last, the malicious code goes to work.

In some cases, an attacker writes a malicious script to discover buffer overflow vulnerabilities. For example, the attacker could use JavaScript to send random data to another service on the same system.

Although error-handling routines and input validation go a long way to prevent buffer overflows, they don't prevent them all. Attackers occasionally discover a bug allowing them to send a specific string of data to an application, causing a buffer overflow. When vendors discover buffer overflow vulnerabilities, they are usually quick to release a patch or hotfix. From an administrator's perspective, the solution is easy: Keep the systems up to date with current patches.

> **Remember this**
>
> Buffer overflows occur when an application receives more data than it can handle, or receives unexpected data that exposes system memory. Buffer overflow attacks often include NOP instructions (such as x90) followed by malicious code. When successful, the attack causes the system to execute the malicious code. Input validation helps prevent buffer overflow attacks.

Pointer Dereference

Programming languages such as C, C++, and Pascal commonly use pointers, which simply store a reference to something. Some languages such as Java call them references.

As an example, imagine an application has multiple modules. When a new customer starts an order, the application invokes the CustomerData module. This module needs to populate the city and state in a form after the user enters a zip code.

How does the module get this array? One way is to pass the entire array to the module when invoking it. However, this consumes a lot of memory.

The second method is to pass a reference to the data array, which is simply a pointer to it. This consumes very little memory and is the preferred method. This method uses a ***pointer dereference***.

Dereferencing is the process of using the pointer to access the data array. Imagine the pointer is named ptrZip and the name of the full data array is named arrZip. The value within ptrZip is arrZip, which references the array. What is this thing that the pointer points to? There isn't a standard name, but some developers refer to it as a pointee.

Ah, I hear your question. What's the point?

A failed dereference operation can cause an application to crash. In some programming languages, it can subtly corrupt memory, which can be even worse than a crash. The subtle, random changes result in the application using incorrect data. This can often be difficult to troubleshoot and correct.

The cause of a failed dereference operation is a pointer that references a nonexistent pointee. If we continue with the previous example, imagine that the ptrZip pointer contains the value of arrayZip. This points to a nonexistent pointee because the array is named arrZip.

Admittedly, this programming error (using arrayZip instead of arrZip) would be quickly discovered because the CustomerData module wouldn't correctly populate the city and state. However, other pointer dereferencing problems aren't so easy to discover.

DLL Injection

Applications commonly use a Dynamic Link Library (DLL) or multiple DLLs. A DLL is a compiled set of code that an application can use without re-creating the code. As an example, most programming languages include math-based DLLs. Instead of writing the code to discover the square root of a number, a developer can include the appropriate DLL and access the square root function within it.

DLL injection is an attack that injects a DLL into a system's memory and causes it to run. For example, imagine an attacker creates a DLL named *malware.dll* that includes several malicious functions. In a successful DLL injection attack, the attacker attaches to a running process, allocates memory within the running process, connects the malicious DLL within the allocated memory, and then executes functions within the DLL.

Summarizing Secure Coding Concepts

Secure application development and deployment concepts are important for application developers to understand. Additionally, IT security managers who manage development projects should understand these concepts, too, even if they aren't writing the code.

Applications often provide an avenue for attackers to generate attacks unless developers create them using secure coding concepts. This section covers common methods used to create secure applications.

Compiled Versus Runtime Code

Compiled code has been optimized by an application (called a compiler) and converted into an executable file. The compiler checks the program for errors and provides a report of items developers might like to check. Some commonly used compiled programming languages are C, C++, Visual Basic, and Pascal.

Runtime code is code that is evaluated, interpreted, and executed when the code is run. As an example, HTML is the standard used to create web pages. It includes specific tags that are interpreted by the browser, when it renders the web page. HTML-based web pages are interpreted at runtime.

Many languages use a cross between compiled and runtime code. For example, Python is an interpreted language widely used to create sophisticated web sites. However, when it is first run, the Python interpreter compiles it. The server will then use the compiled version each time it runs. If the system detects a change in the Python source code, it will recompile it.

Proper Input Validation

One of the most important security steps that developers should take is to include *input validation*. Input validation is the practice of checking data for validity before using it. Input validation prevents an attacker from sending malicious code that an application will use by either sanitizing the input to remove malicious code or rejecting the input.

Improper input handling (or the lack of input validation) is one of the most common security issues on web-based applications. It allows many different types of attacks, such as buffer overflow attacks, SQL injection, command injection, and cross-site scripting attacks. Each of these attacks is covered within this chapter.

Consider a web form that includes a text box for a first name. You can logically expect a valid first name to have only letters, and no more than 25 letters. The developer uses input validation techniques to ensure that the name entered by the user meets this validity check. If a user enters other data, such as numbers, semicolons, or HTML code, it fails the validity check. Instead of using the data, the application rejects it and provides an error to the user.

You've probably seen input validation checks and error-handling routines in use if you've ever filled out a form on a web page. If you didn't fill out all the required text boxes, or if you entered invalid data into one or more of the boxes, the web site didn't crash. Instead, it redisplayed the page and showed an error. Web sites often use a red asterisk next to text boxes with missing or invalid data.

Some common checks performed by input validation include:

- **Verifying proper characters.** Some fields such as a zip code use only numbers, whereas other fields such as state names use only letters. Other fields are a hybrid. For example, a phone number uses only numbers and dashes. Developers can configure input validation code to check for specific character types, and even verify that characters are entered in the correct order. For example, a telephone number mask of ###-###-#### accepts only three numbers, a dash, three numbers, a dash, and four numbers.
- **Implementing boundary or range checking.** These checks ensure that values are within expected boundaries or ranges. For example, if the maximum purchase for a product is three, a range check verifies the quantity is three or less. The validation check identifies data outside the range as invalid and the application does not use it.
- **Blocking HTML code.** Some malicious attacks embed HTML code within the input as part of an attack. These can be blocked by preventing the user from entering the HTML code, such as the < and > characters.
- **Preventing the use of certain characters.** Some attacks, such as SQL injection attacks, use specific characters such as the dash (-), apostrophe ('), and equal sign (=). Blocking these characters helps to prevent these attacks.

Client-Side and Server-Side Input Validation

It's possible to perform input validation at the client and the server. Client-side execution indicates that the code runs on the client's system, such as a user's web browser. Server-side execution indicates that the code runs on the server, such as on a web server.

Client-side input validation is quicker, but is vulnerable to attacks. Server-side input validation takes longer, but is secure because it ensures the application doesn't receive invalid data. Many applications use both. Imagine Homer is using a web browser to purchase the newest version of Scrabbleships through the Duff web site. Customers cannot purchase more than three at a time.

In client-side input validation, the validation code is included in the HTML page sent to Homer. If he enters a quantity of four or more, the HTML code gives him an error message, and doesn't submit the page to the server until Homer enters the correct data.

Unfortunately, it's possible to bypass client-side validation techniques. Many web browsers allow users to disable JavaScript in the web browser, which bypasses client-side validation.

It's also possible to use a web proxy to capture the data sent from the client in the HTTP POST command and modify it before forwarding to the server.

Server-side input validation checks the inputted values when it reaches the server. This ensures that the user hasn't bypassed the client-side checks.

Using both client-side and server-side validation provides speed and security. The client-side validation checks prevent round-trips to the server until the user has entered the correct data. The server-side validation is a final check before the server uses the data.

> ### Remember this
>
> The lack of input validation is one of the most common security issues on web-based applications. Input validation verifies the validity of inputted data before using it, and server-side validation is more secure than client-side validation. Input validation protects against many attacks, such as buffer overflow, SQL injection, command injection, and cross-site scripting attacks.

Other Input Validation Techniques

Other input validation techniques attempt to sanitize HTML code before sending it to a web browser. These methods are sometimes referred to as escaping the HTML code or encoding the HTML code. As a simple example, the greater than symbol (>) can be encoded with the ASCII replacement characters (>). Doing so, along with following specific guidelines related to not inserting untrusted data into web pages, helps prevent many web application attacks.

Most languages include libraries that developers can use to sanitize the HTML code. As an example, the Open Web Application Security Project (OWASP) Enterprise Security API (ESAPI) is a free, open source library available for many programming languages. It includes a rich set of security-based tools, including many used for input validation.

Avoiding Race Conditions

When two or more modules of an application, or two or more applications, attempt to access a resource at the same time, it can cause a conflict known as a **race condition**. Most application developers are aware of race conditions and include methods to avoid them when writing code. However, when new developers aren't aware of race conditions, or they ignore them, a race condition can cause significant problems.

As a simple example of a potential problem, imagine you are buying a plane ticket online and use the web application to pick your seat. You find a window seat and select it. However, at the same time you're selecting this window seat, someone else is, too. You both make the purchase at the same time and you both have tickets with the same seat number. You arrive after the other person and he's unwilling to move, showing his ticket with the seat number. A flight attendant ultimately helps you find a seat. Unfortunately, it's between two burly gentlemen who have been on an all-cabbage diet for the last week. You probably wouldn't be too happy.

Online ticketing applications for planes, concerts, and other events avoid this type of race condition. In some cases, they lock the selection before offering it to a customer. In other cases, they double-check for a conflict later in the process. Most database applications have internal concurrency control processes to prevent two entities from modifying a value at the same time. However, inexperienced web application developers often overlook race conditions.

Proper Error Handling

Error-handling and exception-handling routines ensure that an application can handle an error gracefully. They catch errors and provide user-friendly feedback to the user. When an application doesn't catch an error, it can cause the application to fail. In the worst-case scenario, improper error-handling techniques within an application can cause the operating system to crash. Using effective error- and exception-handling routines protects the integrity of the underlying operating system.

Improper error handling can often give attackers information about an application. When an application doesn't catch an error, it often provides debugging information that attackers can use against the application. In contrast, when an application catches the error, it can control what information it shows to the user. There are two important points about error reporting:

- **Errors to users should be general.** Detailed errors provide information that attackers can use against the system, so the errors should be general. Attackers can analyze the errors to determine details about the system. For example, if an application is unable to connect with a database, a detailed error can let the attacker know exactly what type of database the system is using. This indirectly lets the attacker know what types of commands the system will accept. Also, detailed errors confuse most users.
- **Detailed information should be logged.** Detailed information on the errors typically includes debugging information. By logging this information, it makes it easier for developers to identify what caused the error and how to resolve it.

> **Remember this**
>
> Error and exception handling helps protect the integrity of the operating system and controls the errors shown to users. Applications should show generic error messages to users but log detailed information.

Cryptographic Techniques

Chapter 10 discusses various cryptographic techniques used for **encryption** and **authentication**. Some of these techniques can also be used when applying secure coding techniques.

In general, sensitive data is often encrypted to prevent the unauthorized disclosure of data. If an application is accessing any sensitive data, developers need to ensure that this access doesn't result in inadvertent data exposure. For example, if an application accesses encrypted data on a different server, the application needs to ensure that the data is encrypted while in transit.

Applications need to decrypt data before processing it. When done processing the data, applications need to encrypt the data before storing it. Additionally, applications need to ensure that all remnants of the data are flushed from memory.

Certificates are used for various purposes such as authenticating users and computers. They can also be used to authenticate and validate software code. As an example, developers can purchase a certificate and associate it with an application or code. This **code signing** process provides a digital signature for the code and the certificate includes a hash of the code. This provides two benefits. First, the certificate identifies the author. Second, the hash verifies the code has not been modified. If malware changes the code, the hash no longer matches, alerting the user that the code has been modified.

Code Reuse and SDKs

Developers are encouraged to reuse code whenever possible. As an example, imagine a developer created code for a web application to create, modify, and authenticate users and this code has been in use for a year. The code has gone through internal testing and has survived the use within the application. Instead of creating brand-new code for a new application, it's best to use this tested code. Code reuse saves time and helps prevent the introduction of new bugs.

However, when reusing code, developers should ensure that they are using all the code that they copy into another application. As an example, imagine a developer has created a module that has three purposes: create users, modify users, and authenticate users. While working on a new application, he realizes he needs a module that will authenticate users. If he simply copies the entire module into the new application, it creates dead code. **Dead code** is code that is never executed or used. In this example, the copied code to create and modify users isn't used in the new application, so it is dead code.

Logic errors can also create dead code. For example, imagine a function tests the value of a variable called Donuts. If Donuts has a value (such as 12), it squares it. If Donuts is null (a value of nothing), it returns an error and exits the function.

Next, the function checks to see if Donuts is null and if so, it prints a message in an error log. Do you see the error? The code to print to an error log never executes. If Donuts is null, the previous check exited the function, so the second check never occurs. This logic error creates the dead code.

Another popular method of code reuse is the use of third-party libraries. As an example, JavaScript is a rich, interpreted language used by many web applications. Netscape originally developed it and it was ultimately standardized as an open source language.

Software development kits (SDKs) are like third-party libraries, but they are typically tied to a single vendor. For example, if you're creating an Android app, you can use the Android SDK. It includes software tools that will help you create apps for Android-based devices.

Code Obfuscation

Developers often spend a lot of time developing code. If it is JavaScript, it is rather easy for other developers to just copy the code and use it. One way to slow this down is with an **obfuscation**/camouflage method.

Obfuscation attempts to make something unclear or difficult to understand. Code obfuscation (or code camouflage) attempts to make the code unreadable. It does things like rename variables, replace numbers with expressions, replace strings of characters with hexadecimal codes, and remove comments. For example, a meaningful variable of strFirstName might be renamed to 94mdiwl, and the number 11 might be changed to 0xF01B – 0x73 – 0xEF9D (which still results in the decimal number 11).

It's worth noting that most security experts reject security through obscurity as a reliable method of maintaining security. Similarly, code obfuscation might make the code difficult to understand by most people. However, it's still possible for someone with skills to dissect the code.

Code Quality and Testing

Many organizations that create applications also employ testers to verify the quality of the code. Testers use a variety of different methods to put the code through its paces. Ideally, they will detect problems with the code before it goes live. Some of the common methods of testing code include:

- **Static code analyzers.** Static code analysis examines the code without executing it. Automated tools can analyze code and mark potential defects. Some tools work as the developer creates the code, similar to a spell checker. Other tools can examine the code once it is semifinalized.
- **Dynamic analysis.** Dynamic analysis checks the code as it is running. A common method is to use fuzzing. Fuzzing uses a computer program to send random data to an application. In some cases, the random data can crash the program or create unexpected results, indicating a vulnerability. Problems discovered during a dynamic analysis can be fixed before releasing the application.
- **Stress testing.** Stress testing methods attempt to simulate a live environment and determine how effective or efficient an application operates with a load. As an example, a web application is susceptible to a DDoS attack. A stress test can simulate a DDoS attack and determine its impact on the web application.
- **Sandboxing.** A sandbox is an isolated area used for testing programs. The term comes from a sandbox in a playground. Children can play in the sandbox where they are relatively safe (and parents can easily keep their eyes on them). Similarly, application developers can test applications in a sandbox, knowing that any changes they make will not affect anything outside the sandbox. Virtual machines (VMs) are often used for sandboxing. For example, Java virtual machines include a sandbox to restrict untrusted applications.
- **Model verification.** Testing helps identify and remove bugs. However, it's also important that the software does what it's meant to do. Model verification is the process of ensuring that software meets specifications and fulfills its intended purpose.

> ### Remember this
>
> Static code analysis examines the code without running it and dynamic analysis checks the code while it is running. Fuzzing techniques send random strings of data to applications looking for vulnerabilities. Stress testing verifies an application can handle a load. Sandboxing runs an application within an isolated environment to test it. Model verification ensures that the application meets all specifications and fulfills its intended purpose.

Development Life-Cycle Models

Software development life cycle (SDLC) models attempt to give structure to software development projects.

Two popular models are waterfall and agile.

The *waterfall* model includes multiple stages going from top to bottom. Each stage feeds the next stage, so when you finish one stage, you move on to the next stage. When following the waterfall model strictly, you don't go back to a stage after finishing it. There are multiple variations of the waterfall model, but they all use stages. However, the names of these stages vary from one model to another. Some typical stages used with the waterfall model include:

- **Requirements.** The developers work with the customer to understand the requirements. The output of this stage is a requirements document, which provides clear guidance on what the application will do.
- **Design.** Developers begin to design the software architecture in this stage. This is similar to creating the blueprints for a building. The design stage doesn't include any detailed coding, but instead focuses on the overall structure of the project.
- **Implementation.** Developers write the code at this stage, based on the requirements and design.
- **Verification.** The verification stage ensures the code meets the requirements.
- **Maintenance.** The maintenance stage implements changes and updates as desired.

A challenge with the waterfall model is that it lacks flexibility. It is difficult to revise anything from previous stages. For example, if a customer realizes a change in the requirements is needed, it isn't possible to implement this change until the maintenance stage.

The *agile* model uses a set of principles shared by cross-functional teams. These principles stress interaction, creating a working application, collaborating with the customer, and responding to change.

Instead of strict phases, the agile model uses iterative cycles. Each cycle creates a working, if not complete, product. Testers verify the product works with the current features and then developers move on to the next cycle. The next cycle adds additional features, often adding small, incremental changes from the previous cycle.

A key difference of the agile model (compared with the waterfall model) is that it emphasizes interaction between customers, developers, and testers during each cycle. In contrast, the waterfall model encourages interaction with customers during the requirements stage, but not during the design and implementation stages.

The agile model can be very effective if the customer has a clear idea of the requirements. If not, the customer might ask for changes during each cycle, extending the project's timeline.

Secure DevOps

DevOps combines the words development and operations and it is an agile-aligned software development methodology. *Secure DevOps* is a software development process that includes extensive communication between software developers and operations personnel. It also includes security considerations throughout the project. When applied to a software development project, it can allow developers to push out multiple updates a day in response to changing business needs.

Some of the concepts included within a secure DevOps project are summarized in the following bullets:

- **Security automation** uses automated tests to check code. When modifying code, it's important to test it and ensure that the code doesn't introduce software bugs or security flaws. It's common to include a mirror image of the production environment and run automated tests on each update to ensure it is error free.
- **Continuous integration** refers to the process of merging code changes into a central repository. Software is then built and tested from this central repository. The central repository includes a version control system, and the version control system typically supports rolling back code changes when they cause a problem.
- **Baselining** refers to applying changes to the baseline code every day and building

the code from these changes. For example, imagine five developers are working on different elements of the same project. Each of them have modified and verified some code on their computers. At the end of the day, each of these five developers uploads and commits their changes. Someone then builds the code with these changes and then automation techniques check the code. The benefit is that bugs are identified and corrected quicker. In contrast, if all the developers applied their changes once a week, the bugs can multiply and be harder to correct.

- **Immutable systems** cannot be changed. Within the context of secure DevOps, it's possible to create and test systems in a controlled environment. Once they are created, they can be deployed into a production environment. As an example, it's possible to create a secure image of a server for a specific purpose. This image can be deployed as an immutable system to ensure it stays secure.
- **Infrastructure as code** refers to managing and provisioning data centers with code that defines virtual machines (VMs). Chapter 1 introduces virtualization concepts and many VMs are created with scripts. Once the script is created, new VMs can be created just by running the script.

Remember this

SDLC models provide structure for software development projects. Waterfall uses multiple stages going from top to bottom, with each stage feeding the next stage. Agile is a flexible model that emphasizes interaction with all players in a project. Secure DevOps is an agile-aligned methodology that stresses security throughout the lifetime of the project.

Version Control and Change Management

Chapter 5, "Securing Hosts and Data," covers change management policies for IT systems. The primary purpose is to ensure that changes to systems do not cause unintended outages. Secure coding practices use version control and change management practices for the same reason—to prevent unintended outages.

Change management helps ensure that developers do not make unauthorized changes. As an example, if a customer wants a change or addition to the application, a developer doesn't just implement it, no matter how easy it might be to do so. Instead, any changes to the application go through a specific, predefined process.

The change management process allows several people to examine the change to ensure it won't cause unintended consequences. Also, any change to the application becomes an added responsibility. If the customer discovers a bug due to this change after it's delivered, the developer may be responsible for fixing it, even if it wasn't authorized.

In addition to preventing unauthorized changes and related problems, a change management process also provides an accounting structure to document the changes. Once a change is authorized and implemented, the change is documented in a version control document.

Version control tracks the versions of software as it is updated, including who made the update and when. Many advanced software development tools include sophisticated version control systems. Developers check out the code to work on it and check it back into the system when they're done. The version control system can then document every single change made by the developer. Even better, this version control process typically allows developers to roll back changes to a previous version when necessary.

Provisioning and Deprovisioning

Provisioning and deprovisioning typically refers to user accounts. For example, when an employee starts working at an organization, administrators create the account and give the account appropriate privileges. This way, the user can use the account as authorization to access various resources. Deprovisioning an account refers to removing access to these resources and can be as simple as disabling the account.

Within the context of secure application development and deployment concepts, these terms apply to an application. Provisioning an application refers to preparing and configuring the application to launch on different devices and to use different application services.

As an example, developers who create iOS apps (running on Apple devices) provision the apps based on the devices they'll run on. Apps can run on iPhones, iPads, and Macs. Additionally, these apps can use different services, such as an accelerometer and gyroscope to detect movement. The app needs to be properly provisioned with the appropriate code on the target device to use these services.

Deprovisioning an app refers to removing it from a device. For example, if a user decides to delete the app, the app should be able to remove it completely. Leaving remnants of the app consumes resources on the device.

Identifying Application Attacks

Many attacks target server applications such as those hosted on web servers. Web servers are highly susceptible to several types of attacks, such as buffer overflow attacks and SQL injection attacks, because they commonly accept data from users. Other servers are susceptible to some types of command injection attacks. This section covers many of the common attacks related to different types of servers.

Web Servers

Web servers most commonly host web sites accessible on the Internet, but they can also serve pages within an internal network. Organizations place web servers within a demilitarized zone (DMZ) to provide a layer of protection.

The two primary applications used for web servers are:

- **Apache.** Apache is the most popular web server used on the Internet. It's free and can run on Unix, Linux, and Windows systems.
- **Internet Information Services (IIS).** IIS is a Microsoft web server, and it's included free with any Windows Server product.

Establishing a web presence is almost a requirement for organizations today, and users expect fancy web sites with dynamic pages that are easy to use. Although many applications make it easy to create web sites, they don't always include security. This often results in many web sites being highly susceptible to attacks. The following sections identify many common attacks on web sites.

Database Concepts

Several of the secure coding techniques and attacks apply directly to databases, so they're organized in this section. SQL (pronounced as "sequel" or "es-que-el") is a Structured Query Language used to communicate with databases. SQL statements read, insert, update, and delete data to and from a database. Many web sites use SQL statements to interact with a database, providing users with dynamic content.

A database is a structured set of data. It typically includes multiple tables and each table holds multiple columns and rows. As an example, consider Figure 7.3. It shows the database schema for a database intended to hold information about books and their authors. It includes two incorrect entries, which are described in the "Normalization" section.

Figure 7.3: Database schema

The Book table (on the left) identifies the column names for the table. Each of these columns has a name and identifies the data type or attribute type allowed in the column. For example, INT represents integer, VARCHAR represents a variable number of alphanumeric characters, TEXT is used for paragraphs, and decimal can store monetary values.

The Author table holds information on authors, such as their names and addresses. The BookAuthor table creates a relationship between the Book table and the Author table. The Publisher column should not be there, but it helps describe normalization in the next section.

Figure 7.4 shows three rows of the Author table. It also shows the difference between columns and rows. Because the column identifies the data type, columns are sometimes referred to as attributes. Also, because each row represents a record, rows are sometimes called records or tuples.

Column
↓

AuthorID	FirstName	LastName	StreetAddress	City	State	
1	Lisa	Simpson	742 Evergreen Terrace	Springfield	IDK	← Row
2	Moe	Szylak	1313 Walnut Street	Springfield	IDK	← Row
3	Ned	Flanders	744 Evergreen Terrace	Springfield	IDK	← Row

Figure 7.4: Database table

Individual elements within a database are called fields. For example, the field in the second row of the FirstName column is a field holding the value of Moe.

Normalization

Normalization of a database refers to organizing the tables and columns to reduce redundant data and improve overall database performance. Although there are several normal forms, the first three are the most important.

First Normal Form

A database is in first normal form (1NF) if it meets the following three criteria:

- **Each row within a table is unique and identified with a primary key.** For example, the Author table has a primary key of AuthorID and each row within the table has a different and unique AuthorID, or a different primary key. Primary keys are shown in Figure 7.3 as small key icons. The primary key in the Book table is BookID. The BookAuthor has a composite primary key using two values: Book_BookID and Author_AuthorID.
- **Related data is contained in a separate table.** The author information is contained in a different table. While it's possible to create one single table to hold all the information, this creates multiple problems. First, you'd have to create several extra columns such as FirstName, LastName, and so on every time you added a book. Imagine Lisa Simpson writes five books. Each of her books in the book table would then need to include all of Lisa's information. Entering the same information multiple times increases the chance for errors. If she moves to a new address, you need to change the address five times.
- **None of the columns include repeating groups.** As an example, the Author table includes FirstName for the first name and LastName for the last name. If you combine these into a single column of name, it violates this rule. It also makes it more difficult to access only one part of the repeating group, such as the first name or the last name.

Second Normal Form

Second normal form (2NF) only applies to tables that have a composite primary key, where two or more columns make up the full primary key. The BookAuthor table has a composite key that includes the Book_BookID column and the Author_AuthorID column. A database is in 2NF if it meets the following criteria:

- It is in 1NF.
- Non-primary key attributes are completely dependent on the composite primary key. If any column is dependent on only one column of the composite key, it is not in 2NF.

The BookAuthor table shown in Figure 7.3 violates this with the Publisher column. A book has a unique publisher so the publisher is related to the Book_BookID column. However, an author can publish books through multiple publishers, so the publisher value is not dependent on the Author_AuthorID column.

Notice that the Book table correctly has the Publisher column, so the easy fix to have this database in 2NF is to delete the Publisher column in the BookAuthor table.

Third Normal Form

Third normal form (3NF) helps eliminate unnecessary redundancies within a database. A database is in 3NF if it meets the following criteria:

- It is in 2NF. This implies it is also in 1NF.
- All columns that aren't primary keys are only dependent on the primary key. In other words, none of the columns in the table are dependent on non-primary key attributes.

The Book table violates the second rule of 3NF with the PublisherCity column. The city where the publisher is located is dependent on the publisher, not the book. Imagine this table had 100 book entries from the same publisher located in Virginia Beach. When entering the data, you'd need to repeatedly enter Virginia Beach for this publisher.

There are two ways to fix this. First, ask if the city is needed. If not, delete the column and the database is now in 3NF. If the city is needed, you can create another table with publisher data.

You would then relate the Publisher table with the Book table.

> **Remember this**
>
> Normalization is a process used to optimize databases. While there are several normal forms available, a database is considered normalized when it conforms to the first three normal forms.

SQL Queries

One of the vulnerabilities related to databases is SQL injection attacks. The following sections identify how SQL queries work, how attackers launch a SQL injection attack, and how to protect against SQL injection attacks.

As a simple example of a web site that uses SQL queries, think of Amazon.com. When you enter a search term and click Go (as shown in Figure 7.5), the web application creates a SQL query, sends it to a database server, and formats the results into a web page that it sends back to you.

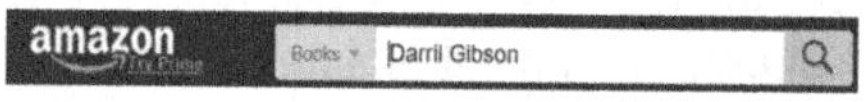

Figure 7.5: Web page querying a database with SQL

In the example, I selected the Books category and entered **Darril Gibson**. The result shows a list of books authored by Darril Gibson available for sale on Amazon. The query sent to the database from the Amazon web application might look like this:

SELECT * FROM Books WHERE Author = 'Darril Gibson'

The * is a wildcard and returns all columns in a table. Notice that the query includes the search term entered into the web page form (Darril Gibson) and encloses the search term in single quotes. If the web site simply plugs the search term into the SELECT statement, surrounded by single quotes, it will work, but it's also highly susceptible to SQL injection attacks.

SQL Injection Attacks

In a SQL injection attack, the attacker enters additional data into the web page form to generate different SQL statements. SQL query languages use a semicolon (;) to indicate the end of the SQL line and use two dashes (--) as an ignored comment. With this knowledge, the attacker could enter different information into the web form like this:

Darril Gibson'; SELECT * FROM Customers;--

If the web application plugged this string of data directly into the SELECT statement surrounded by the same single quotes, it would look like this:

SELECT * FROM Books WHERE Author = 'Darril Gibson';
SELECT * FROM Customers;
--'

The first line retrieves data from the database, just as before. However, the semicolon signals the end of the line and the database will accept another command. The next line reads all the data in the Customers table, which can give the attacker access to names, credit card data, and more. The last line comments out the second single quote to prevent a SQL error.

If the application doesn't include error-handling routines, these errors provide details about the type of database the application is using, such as an Oracle, Microsoft SQL Server, or MySQL database. Different databases format SQL statements slightly differently, but once the attacker learns the database brand, it's a simple matter to format the SQL statements required by that brand. The attacker then follows with SQL statements to access the database and may allow the attacker to read, modify, delete, and/or corrupt data.

This attack won't work against Amazon (please don't try it) because Amazon is using secure coding principles. I don't have access to its code, but I'd bet the developers are using input validation and SQL-based stored procedures (described in the next section).

Many SQL injection attacks use a phrase of **or '1' = '1'** to create a true condition. For example, if an online database allows you to search a Customers table looking for a specific record, it might expect you to enter a name. If you entered **Homer Simpson**, it would create a query like this:

SELECT * FROM Customers WHERE name = 'Homer Simpson'

This query will retrieve a single record for Homer Simpson. However, if the attacker enters **' or '1'='1' --** instead of Homer Simpson, it will create a query like this:

SELECT * FROM Customers WHERE name = '' or '1'='1' --'

Although this is a single SELECT statement, the **or** clause causes it to behave as two separate SELECT statements:

SELECT * FROM Customers WHERE name = ''
SELECT * FROM Customers WHERE '1'='1'

The first clause will likely not return any records because the table is unlikely to have any records with the name field empty. However, because the number 1 always equals the number 1, the WHERE clause in the second statement always equates to True, so the SELECT statement retrieves all records from the Customers table.

In many cases, a SQL injection attack starts by sending improperly formatted SQL statements to the system to generate errors. Proper error handling prevents the attacker from gaining information from these errors, though. Instead of showing the errors to the user, many web sites simply present a generic error web page that doesn't provide any details.

Remember this

Attackers use SQL injection attacks to pass queries to back-end databases through web servers. Many SQL injection attacks use the phrase **' or '1'='1' --** to trick the database server into providing information.

Input validation and stored procedures reduce the risk of SQL injection attacks.

Protecting Against SQL Injection Attacks

As mentioned previously, input validation provides strong protection against SQL injection attacks. Before using the data entered into a web form, the web application verifies that the data is valid.

Additionally, database developers often use *stored procedures* with dynamic web pages. A stored procedure is a group of SQL statements that execute as a whole, similar to a mini-program. A parameterized stored procedure accepts data as an input called a parameter. Instead of copying the user's input directly into a SELECT statement, the input is passed to the stored procedure as a parameter. The stored procedure performs data validation, but it also handles the parameter (the inputted data) differently and prevents a SQL injection attack.

Consider the previous example searching for a book by an author where an attacker entered the following text: **Darril Gibson'; SELECT * From Customers;--**. The web application passes this search string to a stored procedure. The stored procedure then uses the entire search string in a SELECT statement like this:

SELECT * From Books Where Author = "Darril Gibson'; SELECT * From Customers;-- "

In this case, the text entered by the user is interpreted as harmless text rather than malicious SQL statements. It will look for books with an author name using all of this text: Darril Gibson'; SELECT * From Customers;--. Books don't have names with SELECT statements embedded in them, so the query comes back empty.

Depending on how well the database server is locked down (or not), SQL injection attacks may allow the attacker to access the structure of the database, all the data, and even modify data. In some cases, attackers have modified the price of products from several hundred dollars to just a few dollars, purchased several of them, and then returned the price to normal.

Injection Attacks

There are multiple types of injection attacks beyond DLL injection and SQL injection attacks discussed previously in this chapter. Another type of *injection attack* is a command injection attack.

In some cases, attackers can inject operating system commands into an application using web page forms or text boxes. Any web page that accepts input from users is a potential threat. Directory traversal is a specific type of command injection attack that attempts to access a file by including the full directory path, or traversing the directory structure.

For example, in Unix systems, the passwd file includes user logon information, and it is stored in the /etc directory with a full directory path of /etc/passwd. Attackers can use commands such as **../../etc/passwd** or **/etc/passwd** to read the file. Similarly, they could use a remove directory command (such as **rm -rf**) to delete a directory, including all files and subdirectories. Input validation can prevent these types of attacks.

Cross-Site Scripting

Cross-site scripting (XSS) is another web application vulnerability that can be prevented with input validation techniques. Attackers embed malicious HTML or JavaScript code into a web site's code. The code executes when the user visits the site.

You may be wondering why the acronym isn't CSS instead of XSS. The reason is that web sites use Cascading Style Sheets identified as CSS and CSS files are not malicious.

The primary protection against XSS attacks is at the web application with sophisticated input validation techniques. Developers should avoid any methods that allow the web page to display untrusted data. Additionally, OWASP strongly recommends the use of a security encoding library. When implemented, an encoding library will sanitize HTML code and prevent XSS attacks. OWASP includes more than 10 rules that developers can follow to prevent XSS attacks.

It's also important to educate users about the dangers of clicking links. Some XSS attacks send emails with malicious links within them. The XSS attack fails if users do not click the link.

Remember this

Cross-site scripting (XSS) attacks allow attackers to capture user information such as cookies. Input validation techniques at the server help prevent XSS attacks.

Cross-Site Request Forgery

Cross-site request forgery (*XSRF* or CSRF) is an attack where an attacker tricks a user into performing an action on a web site. The attacker creates a specially crafted HTML link and the user performs the action without realizing it.

As an innocent example of how HTML links create action, consider this HTML link: *http://www.google.com/search?q=Success*. If users click this link, it works just as if the user browsed to Google and entered Success as a search term. The *?q=Success* part of the query causes the action.

Many web sites use the same type of HTML queries to perform actions. For example, imagine a web site that supports user profiles. If users wanted to change profile information, they could log on to the site, make the change, and click a button. The web site may use a link like this to perform the action:

http://getcertifiedgetahead.com/edit?action=set&key=email&value=you@home.com

Attackers use this knowledge to create a malicious link. For example, the following link could change the email address in the user profile, redirecting the user's email to the attacker:

http://getcertifiedgetahead.com/edit?action=set&key=email&value=hacker@hackersrs.com

Although this shows one possibility, there are many more. If a web site supports any action via an HTML link, an attack is possible. This includes making purchases, changing passwords, transferring money, and much more.

Web sites typically won't allow these actions without users first logging on. However, if users have logged on before, authentication information is stored on their system either in a cookie or in the web browser's cache. Some web sites automatically use this information to log users on as soon as they visit. In some cases, the XSRF attack allows the attacker to access the user's password.

Users should be educated on the risks related to links from sources they don't recognize. Phishing emails (covered in Chapter 6) often include malicious links that look innocent enough to users, but can cause significant harm. If users don't click the link, they don't launch the XSRF attack.

However, just as with cross-site scripting, the primary burden of protection from XSRF falls on the web site developers. Developers need to be aware of XSRF attacks and the different methods used to protect against them. One method is to use dual authentication and force the user to manually enter credentials prior to performing actions. Another method is to expire the cookie after a short period, such as after 10 minutes, preventing automatic logon for the user.

Many programming languages support XSRF tokens. For example, Python and Django, two popular web development languages, require the use of an XSRF token in any page that includes a form, though these languages call them CSRF tokens. This token is a large random number generated each time the form is displayed. When a user submits the form, the web page includes the token along with other form data. The web application then verifies that the token in the HTML request is the same as the token included in the web form.

The HTML request might look something like this:

getcertifiedgetahead.com/edit?action=set&key=email&value=you@home.com&token=1357924

The token is typically much longer. If the website receives a query with an incorrect error, it typically raises a 403 Forbidden error. Attackers can't guess the token, so they can't craft malicious links that will work against the site.

> **Remember this**
>
> Cross-site request forgery (XSRF) scripting causes users to perform actions on web sites, such as making purchases, without their knowledge. In some cases, it allows an attacker to steal cookies and harvest passwords.

Understanding Frameworks and Guides

Within the context of cybersecurity, there are multiple references available that describe best practices and provide instructions on how to secure systems. Some of these are industry-standard frameworks, while others are platform- or vendor-specific guides.

A *framework* is a structure used to provide a foundation. Cybersecurity frameworks typically use a structure of basic concepts and they provide guidance to professionals on how to implement security in various systems. Chapter 8 discusses various exploitation frameworks often used by penetration testers. Some generic categories of frameworks are:

- **Regulatory.** Regulatory frameworks are based on relevant laws and regulations. As an example, the Health Insurance Portability and Accountability Act (HIPAA) mandates specific protections of all health-related data. The Office of the National Coordinator for Health Information Technology (ONC) and the HHS Office for Civil Rights (OCR) created the HIPAA Security Risk Assessment (SRA) Tool. This tool provides a framework that organizations can use to help ensure compliance with HIPAA.

- **Non-regulatory.** A non-regulatory framework is not required by any law. Instead, it typically identifies common standards and best practices that organizations can follow. As an example, COBIT (Control Objectives for Information and Related Technologies) is a framework that many organizations use to ensure that business goals and IT security goals are linked together.

- **National versus international.** Some frameworks are used within a single country (and referred to as national frameworks), while others are used internationally. As an example, NIST created the Cybersecurity Framework, which focuses on cybersecurity activities and risks within the United States. In contrast, the International Organization for Standardization (ISO) and the International Electrotechnical Commission (IEC) create and publish international standards. For example, ISO/IEC 27002 provides a framework for IT security.

- **Industry-specific.** Some frameworks only apply to certain industries. As an example, organizations that handle credit cards typically comply with the Payment Card Industry Data Security Standard (PCI DSS). PCI DSS includes 12 requirements and over 220 subrequirements that organizations follow to protect credit card data.

In addition to frameworks, you can also use various guides to increase security. This includes benchmarks or secure configuration guides, platform- or vendor-specific guides, and general-purpose guides. On the surface, this is quite simple. When configuring Windows systems, use a Windows guide to identify secure settings. When configuring Linux systems, use a Linux guide.

Additionally, when configuring a system for a specific role (such as a web server, application server, or network infrastructure device), follow the appropriate guide for that role. As an example, a web server would need ports 80 and 443 open for HTTP and HTTPS, respectively. However, a database application server would not typically need these ports open, so they should be closed on a database application server. The individual guides for each of the roles provide this information.

Chapter 7 Exam Topic Review

When preparing for the exam, make sure you understand the key concepts covered in this chapter.

Comparing Common Attacks

- A DoS attack is an attack launched from a single system and attempts to disrupt services.
- DDoS attacks are DoS attacks from multiple computers. DDoS attacks typically include sustained, abnormally high network traffic.
- Spoofing attacks attempt to impersonate another system. MAC address spoofing changes the source MAC address and IP spoofing changes the source IP address.
- ARP poisoning attacks attempt to mislead computers or switches about the actual MAC address of a system. They can be used to launch a man-in-the-middle attack.
- DNS poisoning attacks modify DNS data and can redirect users to malicious sites. Many DNS servers use DNSSEC to protect DNS records and prevent DNS poisoning attacks.
- Amplification attacks send increased traffic to, or request additional traffic from, a victim.
- Password attacks attempt to discover passwords. A brute force attack attempts to guess all possible character combinations and a dictionary attack uses all the words and character combinations stored in a file. Account lockout policies thwart online brute force attacks and complex passwords thwart offline password attacks.
- Passwords are often stored as a hash. Weak hashing algorithms are susceptible to collisions, which allow different passwords to create the same hash.
- In a pass the hash attack, the attacker discovers the hash of the user's password and then uses it to log on to the system as the user.
- In a birthday attack, an attacker is able to create a password that produces the same hash as the user's actual password. This is also known as a hash collision.
- A hash collision occurs when the hashing algorithm creates the same hash from different passwords.
- Password salting adds additional characters to passwords before hashing them and prevents many types of attacks, including dictionary, brute force, and rainbow table attacks.
- Replay attacks capture data in a session with the intent of using information to impersonate one of the parties. Timestamps and sequence numbers thwart replay attacks.
- A known plaintext attack is possible if an attacker has both the plaintext and the ciphertext created by encrypting the plaintext. It makes it easier to decrypt other data using a similar method.
- Attackers buy domain names with minor typographical errors in typo squatting (also called URL hijacking) attacks. The goal is to attract traffic when users enter incorrect URLs. Attackers can configure the sites with malware to infect visitors or configure the site to generate ad revenue for the attacker.
- Clickjacking tricks users into clicking something other than what they think they're clicking.
- Attackers utilize the user's session ID to impersonate the user in a session ID attack.
- Domain hijacking attacks allow an attacker to change the registration of a domain name without permission from the owner.
- A man-in-the-browser is a proxy Trojan horse that exploits vulnerable web browsers.

When successful, it allows attacks to capture keystrokes and all data sent to and from the browser.

- A driver shim is additional code that can be run instead of the original driver.
- Attackers exploiting unknown or undocumented vulnerabilities are taking advantage of zero-day vulnerabilities. The vulnerability is no longer a zero-day vulnerability after the vendor releases a patch to fix it.
- Buffer overflows occur when an application receives more data, or unexpected data, than it can handle and exposes access to system memory. Integer overflow attacks attempt to use or create a numeric value bigger than the application can handle.
- Buffer overflow attacks exploit buffer overflow vulnerabilities. A common method uses NOP instructions or NOP sleds such as a string of x90 commands. Two primary protection methods against buffer overflow attacks are input validation and keeping a system up to date.

Summarizing Secure Coding Concepts

- Compiled code has been optimized by an application and converted into an executable file. Runtime code is code that is evaluated, interpreted, and executed when the code is run.
- A common coding error in web-based applications is the lack of input validation.
- Input validation checks the data before passing it to the application and prevents many types of attacks, including buffer overflow, SQL injection, command injection, and cross-site scripting attacks.
- Server-side input validation is the most secure. Attackers can bypass client-side input validation, but not server-side input validation.
- Race conditions allow two processes to access the same data at the same time, causing inconsistent results. Problems can be avoided by locking data before accessing it.
- Error-handling routines within applications can prevent application failures and protect the integrity of the operating systems. Error messages shown to users should be generic, but the application should log detailed information on the error.
- Code signing uses a digital signature within a certificate to authenticate and validate software code.
- Code quality and testing techniques include static code analysis, dynamic analysis (such as fuzzing), stress testing, sandboxing, and model verification.
- Software development life cycle (SDLC) models provide structure for software development projects. Waterfall uses multiple stages with each stage feeding the next stage. Agile is a more flexible model and it emphasizes interaction with all players in a project.
- Secure DevOps is an agile-aligned methodology. It stresses security throughout the lifetime of the project.

Identifying Application Attacks

- Common web servers are Apache (running on Linux) and Internet Information Services (running on Microsoft servers).
- Databases are optimized using a process called normalization. A database is considered normalized when it conforms to the first three normal forms.
- SQL injection attacks provide information about a database and can allow an attacker to read and modify data within a database. Input validation and stored procedures provide

the best protection against SQL injection attacks.
- Cross-site scripting (XSS) allows an attacker to redirect users to malicious web sites and steal cookies. It uses HTML and JavaScript tags with < and > characters.
- Cross-site request forgery (XSRF) causes users to perform actions on web sites without their knowledge and allows attackers to steal cookies and harvest passwords.
- XSS and XSRF attacks are mitigated with input validation techniques.

Understanding Frameworks and Guides

- Frameworks are references that provide a foundation. Cybersecurity frameworks typically use a structure of basic concepts and provide guidance on how to implement security.
- Regulatory frameworks are based on relevant laws and regulations. A non-regulatory framework is not required by any law.
- Some frameworks are used within a single country (and referred to as national frameworks), while others are used internationally.
- Some frameworks only apply to certain industries. As an example, organizations that handle credit cards typically comply with the Payment Card Industry Data Security Standard (PCI DSS).
- Vendor-specific guides should be used when configuring specific systems.

Online References

- Remember, you have additional resources available online. Check them out at *http://gcgapremium.com/501-extras*.

Chapter 7 Practice Questions

1. Attackers have launched an attack using multiple systems against a single target. Which type of attack is this?
    A. DoS
    B. DDoS
    C. SYN flood
    D. Buffer overflow

2. An attacker has captured a database filled with hashes of randomly generated passwords. Which of the following attacks is MOST likely to crack the largest number of passwords in this database?
    A. Dictionary attack
    B. Birthday attack
    C. Brute force attack
    D. Rainbow tables

3. An application stores user passwords in a hashed format. Which of the following can decrease the likelihood that attackers can discover these passwords?
    A. Rainbow tables
    B. MD5
    C. Salt
    D. Input validation

4. An attacker has been analyzing encrypted data that he intercepted. He knows that the end of the data includes a template sent with all similar messages. He uses this knowledge to decrypt the message. Which of the following types of attacks BEST describes this attack?
   A. Known ciphertext
   B. Known plaintext
   C. Brute force
   D. Rainbow table

5. An attacker is attempting to write more data into a web application's memory than it can handle. Which type of attack is this?
   A. XSRF
   B. DLL injection
   C. Pass the hash
   D. Buffer overflow

6. Management at your organization is planning to hire a development firm to create a sophisticated web application. One of their primary goals is to ensure that personnel involved with the project frequently collaborate with each other throughout the project. Which of the following is an appropriate model for this project?
   A. Waterfall
   B. SDLC
   C. Agile
   D. Secure DevOps

7. A web developer is adding input validation techniques to a web site application. Which of the following should the developer implement during this process?
   A. Perform the validation on the server side.
   B. Perform the validation on the client side.
   C. Prevent boundary checks.
   D. Implement pointer dereference techniques.

8. Developers have created an application that users can download and install on their computers. Management wants to provide users with a reliable method of verifying that the application has not been modified. Which of the following methods provides the BEST solution?
   A. Code signing
   B. Input validation
   C. Code obfuscation
   D. Stored procedures

9. Your organization is preparing to deploy a web-based application, which will accept user input. Which of the following will BEST test the reliability of this application to maintain availability and data integrity?
   A. Model verification
   B. Input validation
   C. Error handling
   D. Dynamic analysis

10. You are overseeing a large software development project. Ideally, developers will not add any unauthorized changes to the code. If they do, you want to ensure that it is easy to identify the developer who made the change. Which of the following provides the BEST solution for this need?
    A. Agile SDLC
    B. Version control
    C. Secure DevOps
    D. Static code analysis

11. Database administrators have created a database used by a web application. However, testing shows that the application is taking a significant amount of time accessing data within the database. Which of the following actions is MOST likely to improve the overall performance of a database?
    A. Normalization
    B. Client-side input validation
    C. Server-side input validation
    D. Obfuscation

12. Looking at logs for an online web application, you see that someone has entered the following phrase into several queries:
    ' or '1'='1' --

    Which of the following is the MOST likely explanation for this?
    A. A buffer overflow attack
    B. An XSS attack
    C. A SQL injection attack
    D. A DLL injection attack

13. While creating a web application, a developer adds code to limit data provided by users. The code prevents users from entering special characters. Which of the following attacks will this code MOST likely prevent?
    A. Man-in-the-browser
    B. Amplification
    C. XSS
    D. Domain hijacking

14. Homer recently received an email thanking him for a purchase that he did not make. He asked an administrator about it and the administrator noticed a pop-up window, which included the following code:

    <body onload="document.getElementByID('myform').submit()">

    <form id="myForm" action="gcgapremium.com/purchase.php" method="post"

    <input name="Buy Now" value="Buy Now" />

    </form>

    </body>

Which of the following is the MOST likely explanation?
- A. XSRF
- B. Buffer overflow
- C. SQL injection
- D. Dead code

15. Your organization recently purchased a new hardware-based firewall. Administrators need to install it as part of a DMZ within the network. Which of the following references will provide them with the MOST appropriate instructions to install the firewall?
- A. A regulatory framework
- B. A non-regulatory framework
- C. A general-purpose firewall guide
- D. A vendor-specific guide

Chapter 7 Practice Question Answers

1. **B.** A distributed denial-of-service (DDoS) attack includes attacks from multiple systems with the goal of depleting the target's resources. A DoS attack comes from a single system and a SYN flood is an example of a DoS attack. A buffer overflow is a type of DoS attack that attempts to write data into an application's memory.

2. **D.** A rainbow table attack attempts to discover the password from the hash. However, they use rainbow tables, which are huge databases of precomputed hashes. A dictionary attack compares passwords against words in a dictionary of words, but a dictionary of words wouldn't include randomly generated passwords. A birthday attack relies on hash collisions. However, it wouldn't necessarily be effective depending on what hashing algorithm is used. A brute force attack attempts to guess all possible character combinations but is very time-consuming for each password.

3. **C.** A password salt is additional random characters added to a password before hashing the password, and it decreases the success of password attacks. Rainbow tables are used by attackers and contain precomputed hashes. Message Digest 5 (MD5) is a hashing algorithm that creates hashes, but the scenario already states that passwords are hashed. Input validation techniques verify data is valid before using it and they are unrelated to protecting hashed passwords.

4. **B.** This describes a known plaintext attack because the attacker knows some of the plaintext data used to create the encrypted data. More specifically, this is a chosen plaintext attack (but that wasn't available as an answer) because the attacker knew a portion of the plaintext. In a known ciphertext attack, the attacker doesn't have any information on the plaintext. A brute force attack attempts to guess a password. A rainbow table attack uses a table of hashes to identify a password from a matched hash.

5. **D.** One type of buffer overflow attack attempts to write more data into an application's memory than it can handle. None of the other answers are directly related to overloading the application's memory. A cross-site request forgery (XSRF) attack attempts to launch attacks with HTML code. A Dynamic Link Library (DLL) injection attack injects a DLL into memory and causes it to run. A pass the hash attack attempts to discover a password.

6. **C.** The agile software development model is flexible, ensures that personnel interact with each other throughout a project, and is the best of the available choices. The waterfall model isn't as flexible and focuses instead on completing the project in stages. Both agile and waterfall are software development life cycle (SDLC) models, which is a generic concept designed to provide structure for software development projects. Secure DevOps is an agile-aligned development methodology that focuses on security considerations throughout a project.

7. **A.** Input validation should be performed on the server side. Client-side validation can be combined with server-side validation, but it can be bypassed, so it should not be used alone. Boundary or limit checks are an important part of input validation. Pointer dereference techniques use references to point to values and are unrelated to input validation techniques.

8. **A.** Code signing provides a digital signature for the code and verifies the publisher of the code and verifies that it hasn't been modified since the publisher released it. None of the other answers verify the application hasn't been modified. Input validation verifies data is valid before using it. Code obfuscation makes the code more difficult to read. Stored procedures are used with SQL databases and can be used for input validation.

9. **D.** Dynamic analysis techniques (such as fuzzing) can test the application's ability to maintain availability and data integrity for some scenarios. Fuzzing sends random data to an application to verify the random data doesn't crash the application or expose the system to a data breach. Model verification ensures that the software meets specifications and fulfills its intended purpose, but it doesn't focus on reliability or integrity. Input validation and error-handling techniques protect applications, but do not test them.

10. **B.** A version control system will track all changes to a system, including who made the change and when. Change management processes (not available as a possible answer) typically provide the same solution. An agile software development life cycle (SDLC) model focuses on interaction from all players in a project, but doesn't necessarily include a version control system. Secure DevOps is an agile-aligned software development methodology that focuses on security throughout the process. Static code analysis examines the code without executing it as a method of code testing.

11. **A.** Normalization techniques organize tables and columns in a database and improve overall database performance. None of the other answers improve the database performance. Input validation techniques help prevent many types of attacks, and server-side input validation techniques are preferred over client-side techniques. Obfuscation techniques make the code more difficult to read.

12. **C.** Attackers use the phrase (' or '1'='1'--) in SQL injection attacks to query or modify databases. A buffer overflow attack sends more data or unexpected data to an application with the goal of accessing system memory. A cross-site scripting (XSS) attack attempts to insert HTML or JavaScript code into a web site or email. A Dynamic Link Library (DLL) injection attack attempts to inject DLLs into memory, causing DLL commands to run.

13. **C.** A cross-site scripting (XSS) attack can be blocked by using input validation techniques to filter special characters such as the < and > characters used in HTML code. None of the other listed attacks require the use of special characters. A man-in-the-browser attack exploits vulnerabilities in browsers to capture user data entries. An amplification attack increases the amount of data sent to a victim to overwhelm it. A domain hijacking attack changes the domain registration of a domain name without permission of the owner.

14. **A.** A cross-site request forgery (XSRF) attack causes users to perform actions without their knowledge. This scenario indicates the user visited a web site, most likely through a malicious link, and the link initiated a purchase. None of the other attacks cause unsuspecting users to make purchases. A buffer overflow attacks a web site and attempts to access system memory. A SQL injection attack attempts to access data on a database server. Dead code is code that never executes and is unrelated to this scenario.

15. **D.** A vendor-specific guide for the new hardware-based firewall will have the most appropriate instructions for installing it. Frameworks (regulatory or non-regulatory) provide structures that can be followed for different purposes, but they wouldn't be available for a specific firewall. A general-purpose guide will provide general instructions, but not instructions for a specific vendor's firewall.

Chapter 8

Using Risk Management Tools

CompTIA Security+ objectives covered in this chapter:

1.4   Explain penetration testing concepts.
- Active reconnaissance, Passive reconnaissance, Pivot, Initial exploitation, Persistence, Escalation of privilege, Black box, White box, Gray box, Penetration testing vs. vulnerability scanning

1.5   Explain vulnerability scanning concepts.
- Passively test security controls, Identify vulnerability, Identify lack of security controls, Identify common misconfigurations, Intrusive vs. non-intrusive, Credentialed vs. non-credentialed, False positive

2.1   Install and configure network components, both hardware- and software-based, to support organizational security.
- SIEM (Aggregation, Correlation, Automated alerting and triggers, Time synchronization, Event deduplication, Logs/WORM)

2.2   Given a scenario, use appropriate software tools to assess the security posture of an organization.
- Protocol analyzer, Network scanners (Rogue system detection, Network mapping), Wireless scanners/cracker, Password cracker, Vulnerability scanner, Configuration compliance scanner, Exploitation frameworks, Banner grabbing, Passive vs. active, Command line tools (Tcpdump, nmap, netcat)

2.3   Given a scenario, troubleshoot common security issues.
- Unencrypted credentials/clear text, Logs and events anomalies

3.2   Given a scenario, implement secure network architecture concepts.
- Security device/technology placement
  - Correlation engines

3.8   Explain how resiliency and automation strategies reduce risk.
- Automation/scripting (Continuous monitoring, Configuration validation)

4.4   Given a scenario, differentiate common account management practices.
- General Concepts (Permission auditing and review, Usage auditing and review)

5.3   Explain risk management processes and concepts.
- Threat assessment (Environmental, Manmade, Internal vs. external), Risk assessment (SLE, ALE, ARO, Asset value, Risk register, Likelihood of occurrence, Supply chain assessment, Impact, Quantitative, Qualitative), Testing (Penetration testing authorization, Vulnerability testing authorization), Risk response techniques (Accept, Transfer, Avoid, Mitigate)

**
As a security professional, you need to be aware of the different security issues associated with threats, vulnerabilities, and risks, and the tools available to combat them. This chapter digs into risk management concepts, including risk assessment methods. You'll learn about vulnerability scanners and penetration testers, including key differences between them. This chapter also covers some specific tools used to assess networks and manage risks.

Understanding Risk Management

Risk is the likelihood that a threat will exploit a vulnerability. A vulnerability is a weakness, and a threat is a potential danger. The result is a negative impact on the organization. Impact refers to the magnitude of harm that can be caused if a threat exercises a vulnerability.

For example, a system without up-to-date antivirus software is vulnerable to malware. Malware written by malicious attackers is the threat. The likelihood that the malware will reach a vulnerable system represents the risk. Depending on what the malware does, the impact may be an unbootable computer, loss of data, or a remote-controlled computer that has joined a botnet.

However, the likelihood of a risk occurring isn't 100 percent. An isolated system without Internet access, network connectivity, or USB ports has a very low likelihood of malware infection. The likelihood significantly increases for an Internet-connected system, and it increases even more if a user visits risky web sites and downloads and installs unverified files.

It's important to realize that you can't eliminate risk. Sure, you can avoid information technology (IT) risks completely by unplugging your computer and burying it. However, that wouldn't be very useful. Instead, users and organizations practice risk management to reduce the risks.

You probably practice risk management every day. Driving or walking down roads and streets can be a very dangerous activity. Car-sized bullets are speeding back and forth, representing significant risks to anyone else on the road. However, you mitigate these risks with caution and vigilance. The same occurs with computers and networks. An organization mitigates risks using different types of security controls.

Threats and Threat Assessments

A *threat* is a potential danger. Within the context of risk management, a threat is any circumstance or event that can compromise the confidentiality, integrity, or availability of data or a system. Threats come in different forms, including the following:
- **Malicious human threats.** Chapter 6, "Comparing Threats, Vulnerabilities, and Common Attacks," discusses various types of threat actors. They include relatively inexperienced script kiddies, dedicated criminals working within an organized crime group, and sophisticated advanced persistent threats (APTs) sponsored by a government. These are

all malicious human threats. Malicious human threats regularly launch different types of attacks, including network attacks, system attacks, and the release of malware.

- **Accidental human threats.** Users can accidentally delete or corrupt data, or accidentally access data that they shouldn't be able to access. Even administrators can unintentionally cause system outages. The common cause is by a well-meaning administrator making a configuration change to fix one problem but inadvertently causing another one.
- **Environmental threats.** This includes long-term power failure, which could lead to chemical spills, pollution, or other possible threats to the environment. It also includes natural threats such as hurricanes, floods, tornadoes, earthquakes, landsides, electrical storms, and other similar events.

A *threat assessment* helps an organization identify and categorize threats. It attempts to predict the threats against an organization's assets, along with the likelihood the threat will occur. Threat assessments also attempt to identify the potential impact from these threats. Once the organization identifies and prioritizes threats, it identifies security controls to protect against the most serious threats.

Organizations have limited resources, so it's not possible to protect against all threats. However, threat assessments improve the security posture of any system or application by ensuring that the resources aren't squandered on low-priority threats. Some common types of threat assessments are:

- **Environmental.** An environmental threat assessment evaluates the likelihood of an environmental threat occurring. For example, I live in Virginia Beach, Virginia, and while we're concerned about the natural threat of hurricanes during the hurricane season, we aren't very concerned about earthquakes. My sister is a business continuity expert and she lives near San Francisco and works in Silicon Valley. She helps companies prepare for risks associated with earthquakes there, but she spends very little time or energy considering the risk of a hurricane hitting San Francisco.
- **Manmade.** A manmade threat assessment evaluates all threats from humans. These include both malicious human threats and accidental human threats. A malicious human threat refers to any potential attack from a person or group of people. An accidental human threat refers to any potential loss caused by a person or group accidentally.
- **Internal.** An internal threat assessment evaluates threats from within an organization. This includes threats from malicious employees and threats from accidents. It also includes threats related to hardware failure.
- **External.** An external threat assessment evaluates threats from outside an organization. This includes any threats from external attackers. It also includes any natural threats, such as hurricanes, earthquakes, and tornadoes.

Remember this

A threat is a potential danger and a threat assessment evaluates potential threats. Environmental threats include natural threats such as weather events. Manmade threats are any potential dangers from people and can be either malicious or accidental. Internal threats typically refer to employees within an organization, while external threats can come from any source outside the organization.

Vulnerabilities

A *vulnerability* is a flaw or weakness in software or hardware, or a weakness in a process that a threat could exploit, resulting in a security breach. Examples of vulnerabilities include:

- **Lack of updates.** If systems aren't kept up to date with patches, hotfixes, and service packs, they are vulnerable to bugs and flaws in the software.
- **Default configurations.** Hardening a system includes changing systems from their default hardware and software configurations, including changing default usernames and passwords. If systems aren't hardened, they are more susceptible to attacks. Chapter 5, "Securing Hosts and Data," covers hardening systems in more depth.
- **Lack of malware protection or updated definitions.** Antivirus and anti-spyware methods protect systems from malware, but if they aren't used and kept up to date, systems are vulnerable to malware attacks. Chapter 6 covers malware types and methods used to protect systems from malware attacks.
- **Lack of firewalls.** If personal and network firewalls aren't enabled or configured properly, systems are more vulnerable to network and Internet-based attacks.
- **Lack of organizational policies.** If job separation, mandatory vacations, and job rotation policies aren't implemented, an organization may be more susceptible to fraud and collusion from employees.

Not all vulnerabilities are exploited. For example, a user may install a wireless router using the defaults. It is highly vulnerable to an attack, but that doesn't mean that an attacker will discover it and attack. In other words, just because the wireless router has never been attacked, it doesn't mean that it isn't vulnerable. At any moment, a war driving attacker can drive by and exploit the vulnerability.

Risk Management

Risk management is the practice of identifying, monitoring, and limiting risks to a manageable level. It doesn't eliminate risks, but instead identifies methods to limit or mitigate them. The amount of risk that remains after managing risk is residual risk.

The primary goal of risk management is to reduce risk to a level that the organization will accept. Senior management is ultimately responsible for residual risk. Management must choose a level of acceptable risk based on their organizational goals. They decide what resources (such as money, hardware, and time) to dedicate to mitigate the risk.

There are multiple *risk response techniques*, or risk management methods, available to an organization. They include:

- **Avoid.** An organization can avoid a risk by not providing a service or not participating in a risky activity. For example, an organization may evaluate an application that requires multiple open ports on the firewall that it considers too risky. It can avoid the risk by purchasing a different application that doesn't require opening any additional firewall ports.
- **Transfer.** The organization transfers the risk to another entity, or at least shares the risk with another entity. The most common method is by purchasing insurance. Another method is by outsourcing, or contracting a third party.
- **Mitigate.** The organization implements controls to reduce risks. These controls either reduce the vulnerabilities or reduce the impact of the threat. For example, up-to-date antivirus software mitigates the risks of malware. Similarly, a security guard can reduce

the risk of an attacker accessing a secure area.

- **Accept.** When the cost of a control outweighs a risk, an organization will often accept the risk. For example, spending $100 in hardware locks to secure a $15 mouse doesn't make sense. Instead, the organization accepts the risk of someone stealing a mouse. Similarly, even after implementing controls, residual risk remains and the organization accepts this residual risk.

> ## Remember this
>
> It is not possible to eliminate risk, but you can take steps to manage it. An organization can avoid a risk by not providing a service or not participating in a risky activity. Insurance transfers the risk to another entity. You can mitigate risk by implementing controls, but when the cost of the controls exceeds the cost of the risk, an organization accepts the remaining, or residual, risk.

Risk Assessment

A *risk assessment*, or risk analysis, is an important task in risk management. It quantifies or qualifies risks based on different values or judgments. A risk assessment starts by first identifying assets and asset values.

An asset includes any product, system, resource, or process that an organization values. The *asset value* identifies the worth of the asset to the organization. It can be a specific monetary value or subjective value, such as Low, Medium, and High. The asset value helps an organization focus on the high-value assets and avoid wasting time on low-value assets.

After identifying asset values, the risk assessment then identifies threats and vulnerabilities and determines the likelihood a threat will attempt to exploit a vulnerability. A risk assessment attempts to identify the impact of potential threats and identify the potential harm, and prioritizes risks based on the likelihood of occurrence and impact. Last, a risk assessment includes recommendations on what controls to implement to mitigate risks.

A risk assessment is a point-in-time assessment, or a snapshot. In other words, it assesses the risks based on current conditions, such as current threats, vulnerabilities, and existing controls. For example, consider a library computer that has up-to-date antivirus protection and cannot access the Internet. Based on these conditions, the risks are low. However, if administrators connect the system to the Internet, or fail to keep the antivirus software up to date, the risk increases.

It's common to perform risk assessments on new systems or applications. For example, if an organization is considering adding a new service or application that can increase revenue, it will often perform a risk assessment. This helps it determine if the potential risks may offset the potential gains.

Risk assessments use quantitative measurements or qualitative measurements. Quantitative measurements use numbers, such as a monetary figure representing cost and asset values. Qualitative measurements use judgments. Both methods have the same core goal of helping management make educated decisions based on priorities.

Quantitative Risk Assessment

A *quantitative risk assessment* measures the risk using a specific monetary amount. This monetary amount makes it easier to prioritize risks. For example, a risk with a potential loss of $30,000 is much more important than a risk with a potential loss of $1,000.

The asset value is an important element in a quantitative risk assessment. It may include the revenue value or replacement value of an asset. A web server may generate $10,000 in revenue per hour. If the web server fails, the company will lose $10,000 in direct sales each hour it's down, plus the cost to repair it. It can also result in the loss of future business if customers take their business elsewhere. In contrast, the failure of a library workstation may cost a maximum of $1,000 to replace it.

One commonly used quantitative model uses the following values to determine risks:

- **Single loss expectancy (SLE).** The **SLE** is the cost of any single loss.
- **Annual rate of occurrence (ARO).** The **ARO** indicates how many times the loss will occur in a year. If the ARO is less than 1, the ARO is represented as a percentage. For example, if you anticipate the occurrence once every two years, the ARO is 50 percent or .5.
- **Annual loss expectancy (ALE).** The **ALE** is the value of SLE × ARO.

Imagine that employees at your company lose, on average, one laptop a month. Thieves have stolen them when employees left them in conference rooms during lunch, while they were on-site at customer locations, and from training rooms.

Someone suggested purchasing hardware locks to secure these laptops for a total of $1,000. These locks work similar to bicycle locks and allow employees to wrap the cable around a piece of furniture and connect into the laptop. A thief needs to either destroy the laptop to remove the lock or take the furniture with him when stealing the laptop. Should your company purchase them? With a little analysis, the decision is easy.

You have identified the average cost of these laptops, including the hardware, software, and data, is $2,000 each. This assumes employees do not store entire databases of customer information or other sensitive data on the systems, which can easily result in much higher costs. You can now calculate the SLE, ARO, and ALE as follows:

- **SLE.** The value of each laptop is $2,000, so the SLE is $2,000.
- **ARO.** Employees lose about one laptop a month, so the ARO is 12.
- **ALE.** You calculate the ALE as SLE × ARO, so $2,000 × 12 = $24,000.

Security experts estimate that these locks will reduce the number of lost or stolen laptops from 12 a year to only 2 a year. This changes the ALE from $24,000 to only $4,000 (saving $20,000 a year). In other words, the organization can spend $1,000 to save $20,000. It doesn't take a rocket scientist to see that this is a good fiscal decision, saving a net of $19,000. Buy them.

Managers use these two simple guidelines for most of these decisions:

- If the cost of the control is less than the savings, purchase it.
- If the cost of the control is greater than the savings, accept the risk.

The organization might be considering other controls, such as a combination of hardware locks, biometric authentication, LoJack for Laptops, and more. The final cost of all of these controls is $30,000 per year. Even if a laptop is never stolen again, the company is spending $30,000 to save $24,000, resulting in a higher net loss—they're losing $6,000 more a year.

Admittedly, a company could choose to factor in other values, such as the sensitivity of data on the laptops, and make a judgment to purchase these additional controls. However, if they're using a quantitative risk assessment, these values would need to be expressed in monetary terms.

Although you would normally know the SLE and ARO and use these to calculate the ALE, you might occasionally have the SLE and ALE, but not know the ARO. Using basic algebra, you can reformat the formula. Any of these are valid:

- ALE = SLE × ARO
- ARO = ALE / SLE
- SLE = ALE / ARO

Remember this

A quantitative risk assessment uses specific monetary amounts to identify cost and asset values. The SLE identifies the amount of each loss, the ARO identifies the number of failures in a year, and the ALE identifies the expected annual loss. You calculate the ALE as SLE × ARO. A qualitative risk assessment uses judgment to categorize risks based on likelihood of occurrence and impact.

Qualitative Risk Assessment

A *qualitative risk assessment* uses judgment to categorize risks based on *likelihood of occurrence* (or probability) and impact. The likelihood of occurrence is the probability that an event will occur, such as the likelihood that a threat will attempt to exploit a vulnerability. *Impact* is the magnitude of harm resulting from a risk. It includes the negative results of an event, such as the loss of confidentiality, integrity, or availability of a system or data.

Notice that this is much different from the exact numbers provided by a quantitative assessment that uses monetary figures. You can think of quantitative as using a quantity or a number, whereas qualitative is related to quality, which is often a matter of judgment.

Some qualitative risk assessments use surveys or focus groups. They canvass experts to provide their best judgments and then tabulate the results. For example, a survey may ask the experts to rate the probability and impact of risks associated with a web server selling products on the Internet and a library workstation without Internet access. The experts would use words such as low, medium, and high to rate them.

They could rate the probability of a web server being attacked as high, and if the attack takes the web server out of service, the impact is also high. On the other hand, the probability of a library workstation being attacked is low, and, even though a library patron may be inconvenienced, the impact is also low.

It's common to assign numbers to these judgments. For example, you can use terms such as low, medium, and high, and assign values of 1, 5, and 10, respectively. The experts assign a probability and impact of each risk using low, medium, and high, and when tabulating the results, you change the words to numbers. This makes it a little easier to calculate the results.

In the web server and library computer examples, you can calculate the risk by multiplying the probability and the impact:

- **Web server.** High probability and high impact: 10 × 10 = 100
- **Library computer.** Low probability and low impact: 1 × 1 = 1

Management can look at these numbers and easily determine how to allocate resources to protect against the risks. They would allocate more resources to protect the web server than the library computer.

One of the challenges with a qualitative risk assessment is gaining consensus on the probability and impact. Unlike monetary values that you can validate with facts, probability and impact are often subject to debate.

Documenting the Assessment

The final phase of the risk assessment is the report. This identifies the risks discovered during the assessment and the recommended controls. As a simple example, a risk assessment on a database-enabled web application may discover that it's susceptible to SQL injection attacks. The risk assessment will then recommend rewriting the web application with input validation techniques or stored procedures to protect the database.

Management uses this to decide which controls to implement and which controls to accept. In many cases, a final report documents the managerial decisions. Of course, management can decide not to implement a control, but instead accept a risk.

Think how valuable this report will be for an attacker. They won't need to dig to identify vulnerabilities or controls. Instead, the report lists all the details. Even when management approves controls to correct the vulnerabilities, it may take some time to implement them. Because of this, the results of a risk assessment are highly protected. Normally, only executive management and security professionals will have access to these reports.

Risk Registers

Some risk assessments use a ***risk register***. There are different definitions for a risk register, depending on which standard you're following. For example, ISO 73:2009 defines it as a "record of information about identified risks." Projects IN Controlled Environments (PRINCE2), a detailed project management method, defines a risk register as a "repository for all risks identified and includes additional information about each risk."

An easy way to create a risk register is in a table format. As an example, imagine you are evaluating risks related to a new e-commerce web site that accesses a back-end database. Your risk register might include the following columns:

- **Category.** Risk categories could include downtime due to hardware failures, outages from an attack, downtime to database server failure, data breaches, and more.
- **Specific risk.** One of the risks related to hardware failures could be hard drive failure. Of course, there are other potential hardware failures, but the remaining columns for this risk will focus on hard drive failure. For this example, imagine that one drive holds the operating system and applications. A second drive holds data.
- **Likelihood of occurrence.** Medium. This assumes that the installed hard drives are not currently using a redundant array of inexpensive disks (RAID) disk subsystem.
- **Impact.** High. If a hard drive fails, it will probably disable the entire web site.
- **Risk score.** 50 (out of 100). This assumes a score of Medium has a value of 5 and a score of High has a value of 10 ($5 \times 10 = 50$). Note that organizations can assign any desired values to the likelihood of occurrence and impact. The values used here are simply an example.
- **Security controls or mitigation steps.** Implement a RAID-1 to protect the hard drive hosting the operating system. Implement a RAID-6 to protect the data.
- **Contingencies.** Ensure backups exist and are kept up to date.
- **Risk score with security controls.** 10 (out of 100). With the RAID-1 and RAID-6 in place, the likelihood of occurrence is now Low, but the impact remains High. The new score assumes a score of Low has a value of 1 and a score of High has a value of 10 ($1 \times 10 = 10$).
- **Action assigned to.** A risk register may document who has responsibility for implementing the security control.
- **Action deadline.** The deadline identifies when the security control should be implemented.

Organizations might use columns such as these or modify them as they see fit. The key is that the risk register documents relevant risks based on the needs of the organization.

Supply Chain Assessment

A supply chain includes all the elements required to produce and sell a product. As a simple example, consider the Lard Lad Donuts store. They require a steady supply of flour, sugar, eggs, milk, oil, and other ingredients. They also require equipment such as refrigerators to store raw materials, space to manufacture the donuts, and fryers to cook them. Last, they need a method to sell the donuts to customers. If any of these items fail, the company won't be able to make and sell donuts.

It's important to realize that the supply chain isn't only the supply of raw materials. It also includes all the processes required to create and distribute a finished product.

A *supply chain assessment* evaluates these elements—the raw materials supply sources and all the processes required to create, sell, and distribute the product. In some cases, the assessment focuses on identifying risks. For example, are there any raw materials that come from only a single source? It would also examine processes and identify any tasks or steps that represent a single point of failure. If the donut store has only one fryer, it is a single point of failure. If it breaks, all sales stop.

Many organizations have mature supply chains. In other words, they have multiple sources in place for all raw materials. The failure of any single supply source will not affect the organization's ability to create and sell its products. Similarly, they have built-in redundancies in their processes. If any internal processes fail, they have alternative methods ready to implement and keep the organization operating.

Organizations with mature supply chains still perform supply chain assessments. The goal of these assessments is to look for methods to improve the supply chain.

> ### Remember this
>
> A risk register is a comprehensive document listing known information about risks. It typically includes risk scores along with recommended security controls to reduce the risk scores. A supply chain assessment evaluates everything needed to produce and sell a product. It includes all the raw materials and processes required to create and distribute a finished product.

Comparing Scanning and Testing Tools

Security administrators use tools to test their networks. Two common categories of tools are vulnerability scanners, which check for weaknesses and penetration tests, which attempt to exploit the vulnerabilities. This section covers vulnerability scanners and penetration tests in more depth.

Checking for Vulnerabilities

Vulnerabilities are weaknesses, and by reducing vulnerabilities, you can reduce risks. That sounds simple enough. However, how do you identify the vulnerabilities that present the greatest risks? Common methods are vulnerability assessments and various scans such as network scans and vulnerability scans.

The overall goal of a vulnerability assessment is to assess the security posture of systems and networks. They identify vulnerabilities, or weaknesses, within systems, networks, and organizations, and are part of an overall risk management plan.

Vulnerability assessments can include information from a wide variety of sources. This includes reviewing security policies and logs, interviewing personnel, and testing systems. Assessments often use a variety of scans and penetration tests, all discussed in this section. A vulnerability assessment typically includes the following high-level steps:

- Identify assets and capabilities.
- Prioritize assets based on value.
- Identify vulnerabilities and prioritize them.
- Recommend controls to mitigate serious vulnerabilities.

Many organizations perform vulnerability assessments internally. Organizations also hire external security professionals to complete external assessments. The following sections discuss many of the common tools used for vulnerability assessments and vulnerability scans.

Password Crackers

A *password cracker* attempts to discover a password. Passwords are typically encrypted or hashed so that they aren't easily readable. Chapter 10, "Understanding Cryptography and PKI," covers both encryption and hashing methods. Some methods are stronger than others. If passwords are protected with weak methods, a password cracker can discover the password.

As an example, Message Digest 5 (MD5) is a hashing algorithm. When executed against a password of P@ssw0rd, it creates the following MD5 hash: 161ebd7d45089b3446ee4e0d86dbcf92. A password cracker can analyze the MD5 hash of 161ebd7d45089b3446ee4e0d86dbcf92 and discover the actual password of P@ssw0rd. Chapter 7, "Protecting Against Advanced Attacks," discusses many of the common methods used to crack passwords. The point here is that password crackers are one of the tools security administrators use during a vulnerability assessment.

There are two categories of password crackers—offline and online:

- An offline password cracker attempts to discover passwords by analyzing a database or file containing passwords. For example, attackers often obtain large volumes of data during a data breach. This includes files that include hashed or encrypted passwords. They can then analyze the protected passwords to discover the actual passwords. A key benefit of an offline password cracking attack is that attackers have unlimited time to analyze the passwords.
- An online password cracker attempts to discover passwords by guessing them in a brute force attack. For example, some online password crackers attempt to discover the passwords for specific accounts by trying to log on to the accounts remotely. Other online password crackers collect network traffic and attempt to crack any passwords sent over the network.

Network Scanners

A *network scanner* uses various techniques to gather information about hosts within a network. As an example, Nmap (covered in more depth later in this chapter) is a popular network scanning tool that can give you a lot of information about hosts within a network. Other popular network scanning tools are Netcat and Nessus. Network scanners typically use the following methods:

- **Ping scan.** A ping scan (sometimes called a ping sweep) sends an Internet Control Message Protocol (ICMP) ping to a range of IP addresses in a network. If the host responds, the network scanner knows there is a host operational with that IP address. A problem with ping scans is that firewalls often block ICMP, so it can give inconsistent results.

- **Arp ping scan.** Chapter 1, "Mastering Security Basics," discusses the Address Resolution Protocol (ARP) and how systems use it to resolve IP addresses to media access control (MAC) addresses. Any host that receives an ARP packet with its IP address responds with its MAC address. If the host responds, the network scanner knows that a host is operational with that IP address.

- **Syn stealth scan.** Chapter 3, "Exploring Network Technologies and Tools," discusses the Transmission Control Protocol (TCP) three-way handshake. As a reminder, one host sends out a SYN (synchronize) packet to initiate a TCP session. The other host responds with a SYN/ACK (synchronize/acknowledge) packet. The first host then completes the handshake with an ACK packet to establish the connection. A syn stealth scan sends a single SYN packet to each IP address in the scan range. If a host responds, the scanner knows that a host is operational with that IP address. However, instead of responding with an ACK packet, a scanner typically sends an RST (reset) response to close the connection.

- **Port scan.** A port scan checks for open ports on a system. Each open port indicates the underlying protocol is running on the system. For example, if port 80 is open, it indicates the host is running HTTP and it is likely running a web server. A port scan typically uses the ports identified as well-known ports by the Internet Assigned Numbers Authority (IANA).

- **Service scan.** A service scan is like a port scan, but it goes a step further. A port scan identifies open ports and gives hints about what protocols or services might be running. The service scan verifies the protocol or service. For example, if a port scan identifies port 80 is open, a service scan will send an HTTP command, such as "Get /." If HTTP is running on port 80, it will respond to the Get command providing verification that it is a web server.

- **OS detection.** Operating system (OS) detection techniques analyze packets from an IP address to identify the OS. This is often referred to as TCP/IP fingerprinting. As a simple example, the TCP window size (the size of the receive window in the first packet of a TCP session) is not fixed. Different operating systems use different sizes. Some Linux versions use a size of 5,840 bytes, Cisco routers use a size of 4,128 bytes, and some different Windows versions use sizes of 8,192 and 65,535. OS detection techniques don't rely on a single value but typically evaluate multiple values included in responses from systems.

Figure 8.1 shows the result of a scan using Zenmap (the graphical version of Nmap). After starting it, I entered 192.168.0.0/24 as the Target. Nmap then scanned all the IP addresses from 192.168.0.1 to 192.168.0.254. After the scan completed, I selected the host with the IP address of 192.168.0.12 and selected the Ports/Hosts tab. Nmap discovered that this is a printer, the name and serial number of the printer, and that the printer is hosting an embedded web site running on port 80.

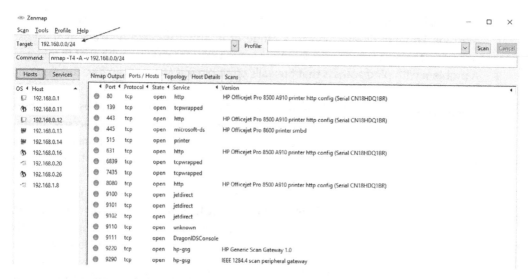

Figure 8.1: Zenmap scan

> ## Remember this
>
> Password crackers attempt to discover passwords and can identify weak passwords, or poorly protected passwords. Network scanners can detect all the hosts on a network, including the operating system and services or protocols running on each host.

Network Mapping

Network mapping discovers devices on the network and how they are connected with each other. It is often done as part of a network scan, but it only focuses on connectivity. In contrast, a full network scan also includes additional scans to identify open ports, running services, and OS details.

Some tools, such as Zenmap, provide you with a graphical representation of the network. To see how this looks, look at the Nmap and Zenmap labs available at *http://gcgapremium.com/501labs/.*

Wireless Scanners/Cracker

Chapter 4, "Securing Your Network," discusses how administrators often perform site surveys while planning and deploying a wireless network. Security personnel periodically repeat the site survey to verify the environment hasn't changed.

Wireless scanners can typically use both passive and active scans. When using a passive scan, a scanner just listens to all the traffic being broadcast on known channels within the 2.4 GHz and 5 GHz frequency ranges.

Figure 8.2 shows a screenshot from Acrylic Wi-Fi Professional, a wireless scanner with many capabilities. As with many scanners, it can collect and report quite a bit of information on local APs.

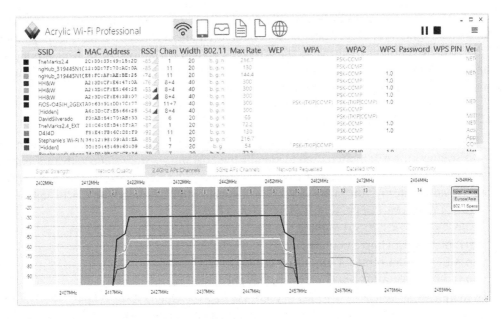

Figure 8.2: Acrylic Wi-Fi Professional

The following bullets describe some of the columns in Figure 8.2:

- **SSIDs.** A scanner will detect the service set identifier (**SSID**) of all access points within range of the scanner.
- **MAC addresses.** It shows the MAC, or hardware address of the AP.
- **Signal strength.** The signal strength typically identifies how near (or how far away) the AP is in relation to the computer performing the scan.
- **Channels.** This helps administrators determine if nearby APs are broadcasting on the same channel, causing interference.
- **Channel widths.** A channel is typically 20 MHz wide, but when an AP is using two channels, it is 40 MHz. The scanner will show this information.
- **Security.** The scanner will show if the AP is in Open mode or using one of the other wireless cryptographic protocols: Wi-Fi Protected Access (**WPA**) or Wi-Fi Protected Access II (**WPA2**). Chapter 4 discusses these modes in more depth.

When using an active scan, a wireless scanner acts like a scanner/cracker and can gain more information about an AP by sending queries to it. As an example, Chapter 4 discusses various attacks, including Wi-Fi Protected Setup (**WPS**) attacks. A WPS attack keeps guessing PINs until it discovers the eight-digit PIN used by an AP. It can then use this to discover the pre-shared key (PSK) used by the AP. Various wireless scanners have other capabilities, including password crackers using other methods.

Rogue System Detection

Chapter 4 discusses rogue APs, which are APs placed into service without authorization. As long as an administrator knows what APs are authorized, it's easy to discover rogue APs with a wireless scan. Administrators often perform site surveys while planning and deploying a wireless network. As an example, Figure 8.2 (the screenshot from Acrylic Wi-Fi Professional in the previous section) shows all the SSIDs it has detected.

Administrators can investigate any unknown SSIDs. The received signal strength indicator (RSSI) shows the strength of the signal. A lower negative number (closer to zero) is stronger than a higher negative number. By installing the wireless scanner on a laptop and walking around an organization, you can locate rogue APs. As you move closer to a rogue AP, the signal becomes stronger. As you move farther away from it, the signal becomes weaker.

Banner Grabbing

Banner grabbing is a technique used to gain information about remote systems and many network scanners use it. It is often used to identify the operating system along with information about some applications. If successful, the server returns a Hypertext Markup Language (HTML) banner providing information on the server. The banner might look something like the following:

```
<!DOCTYPE HTML PUBLIC "-//IETF//DTD HTML 2.0//EN">
<html><head><title>501 Method Not Implemented</title></head><body>
<h1>Method Not Implemented</h1>
<p>GET to /index.html not supported.<br /></p>
<p>Additionally, a 404 Not Found error was encountered.</p><hr>
<address>Apache/2.2.25    (Unix)    mod_ssl/2.2.25    OpenSSL/1.0.0-fips    mod_auth_
passthrough/2.1 mod_bwlimited/1.4 FrontPage/5.0.2.2635 Server at 72.52.230.233 Port 80</
address>
</body></html>
```

Most of this is formatting. However, the information in the address section provides a lot of information on the web server. It shows this is a Unix server running the Apache web server software along with additional information. The command-line tool Netcat can be used for banner grabbing, as shown later in this chapter. You can also check out the Banner Grabbing Lab in the online exercises for this book at *http://gcgapremium.com/501labs/*.

> ## Remember this
>
> Wireless scanners can detect rogue access points on a network and sometimes crack passwords used by access points. Netcat can be used for banner grabbing to identify the operating system and some applications and services on remote servers.

Vulnerability Scanning

A key part of a vulnerability assessment is a vulnerability scan. Security administrators often use a **vulnerability scanner** to identify which systems are susceptible to attacks. Vulnerability scanners identify a wide range of weaknesses and known security issues that attackers can exploit. Most vulnerability scanners combine multiple features into a single package. A vulnerability scan often includes the following actions:

- Identify vulnerabilities
- Identify misconfigurations
- Passively test security controls
- Identify lack of security controls

Identifying Vulnerabilities and Misconfigurations

Vulnerability scanners utilize a database or dictionary of known vulnerabilities and test systems against this database. For example, the MITRE Corporation maintains the Common

Vulnerabilities and Exposures (CVE) list, which is a dictionary of publicly known security vulnerabilities and exposures. This is similar to how antivirus software detects malware using virus signatures. The difference is that the CVE is one public list funded by the U.S. government, whereas antivirus vendors maintain proprietary signature files.

Other standards used by vulnerability scanners include the Security Content Automation Protocol (SCAP). SCAP utilizes the National Vulnerability Database (NVD), which includes lists of common misconfigurations, security-related software flaws, and impact ratings or risk scores. The risk scores quantify risks, allowing security experts to prioritize vulnerabilities. The SCAP also includes risk scores for items in the CVE.

Additionally, attackers often look for systems that are misconfigured and vulnerability scanners can detect some common misconfiguration settings. Some of the vulnerabilities and common misconfigurations discovered by a vulnerability scanner include:

- **Open ports.** Open ports can signal a vulnerability, especially if administrators aren't actively managing the services associated with these ports. For example, all web servers do not use File Transfer Protocol (FTP), so if TCP ports 20 and 21 are open, it indicates a potential vulnerability related to FTP. Similarly, Telnet uses port 23, so if this port is open, an attacker can try to connect to the server using Telnet.
- **Weak passwords.** Many scanners include a password cracker that can discover weak passwords or verify that users are creating strong passwords in compliance with an organization's policy. It is more efficient to use a technical password policy to require and enforce the use of strong passwords. However, if this isn't possible, administrators use a separate password cracker to discover weak passwords.
- **Default accounts and passwords.** Operating systems and applications can have default usernames and passwords. Basic operating system and application hardening steps should remove the defaults, and a scan can discover the weaknesses if operating systems and applications aren't secured properly. For example, some SQL database systems allow the sa (system administrator) account to be enabled with a blank password. Scanners such as Nessus will detect this.
- **Sensitive data.** Some scanners include data loss prevention (DLP) techniques to detect sensitive data sent over the network. For example, a DLP system can scan data looking for patterns such as Social Security numbers or key words that identify classified or proprietary data.
- **Security and configuration errors.** Vulnerability scans can also check the system against a configuration or security baseline to identify unauthorized changes.

Administrators can scan specific systems or an entire network. For example, many organizations perform periodic scans on the entire network to detect vulnerabilities. If an administrator makes an unauthorized change resulting in a vulnerability, the scan can detect it. Similarly, if a rebuilt system is missing some key security settings, the scan will detect them. It's also possible to scan a new system before or right after it's deployed.

Passively Testing Security Controls

An important point about a vulnerability scan is that it does not attempt to exploit any vulnerabilities. Instead, a vulnerability scan is a passive attempt to identify weaknesses. This ensures that the testing does not interfere with normal operations. Security administrators then assess the vulnerabilities to determine which ones to mitigate. In contrast, a penetration test (covered later in this chapter) is an active test that attempts to exploit vulnerabilities.

Identifying Lack of Security Controls

Vulnerability scanners can also identify missing security controls, such as the lack of up-to-date patches or the lack of antivirus software. Although many patch management tools include the ability to verify systems are up to date with current patches, vulnerability scanners provide an additional check to detect unpatched systems.

> **Remember this**
>
> A vulnerability scanner can identify vulnerabilities, misconfigured systems, and the lack of security controls such as up-to-date patches. Vulnerability scans are passive and have little impact on a system during a test. In contrast, a penetration test is intrusive and can potentially compromise a system.

False Positive

Unfortunately, vulnerability scanners aren't perfect. Occasionally, they report a vulnerability when it doesn't actually exist. In other words, the scan indicates a system has a known vulnerability, but the report is false. As an example, a vulnerability scan on a server might report that the server is missing patches related to a database application, but the server doesn't have a database application installed.

This is similar to false positives in an intrusion detection system (IDS) where the IDS alerts on an event, but the event isn't an actual intrusion. Similarly, an antivirus scanner can identify a useful application as malware, even though the application does not have any malicious code. False positives can result in higher administrative overhead because administrators have to investigate them.

Credentialed Versus Non-Credentialed

Vulnerability scanners can run as a credentialed scan using the credentials of an account, or as non-credentialed without any user credentials. Attackers typically do not have credentials of an internal account, so when they run scans against systems, they run non-credentialed scans.

Security administrators often run credentialed scans with the privileges of an administrator account. This allows the scan to check security issues at a much deeper level than a non-credentialed scan. Additionally, because the credentialed scan has easier access to internal workings of systems, it results in a lower impact on the tested systems, along with more accurate test results and fewer false positives.

It's worth mentioning that attackers typically start without any credentials but use privilege escalation techniques to gain administrative access. This allows them to run a credentialed scan against a network if desired. Similarly, even though a credentialed scan is typically more accurate, administrators often run non-credentialed scans to see what an attacker without credentials would see.

> **Remember this**
>
> A false positive from a vulnerability scan indicates the scan detected a vulnerability, but the vulnerability doesn't exist. Credentialed scans run under the context of a valid account and are typically more accurate than non-credentialed scans.

Configuration Compliance Scanner

A *configuration compliance scanner* verifies that systems are configured correctly. They will often use a file that identifies the proper configuration for systems. When running the scan, the scanner will verify that systems have the same configuration defined in the configuration file. This is also known as configuration validation. Security administrators often configure these tools to use automation or scripting methods so that they automatically run on a set schedule.

As an example, Nessus, a vulnerability scanner developed by Tenable Network Security, uses plug-ins to perform configuration compliance scans. They currently have plug-ins used to perform against both Windows and Unix systems. Administrators can also create custom audit files to perform custom compliance configuration scans on Windows and Unix systems. AutoNessus is a free tool that can be used to automate Nessus scans.

Configuration compliance scans typically need to be run as credentialed scans. This helps ensure they can accurately read the configuration of systems during the scan.

Obtaining Authorization

It's important to obtain vulnerability testing authorization and penetration testing authorization before performing any vulnerability testing or penetration testing. In most cases, this consent is in writing. If it isn't in writing, many security professionals won't perform the test. A penetration test without consent is an attack. An organization may perceive a well-meaning administrator doing an unauthorized penetration test as a black hat or gray hat attacker. The administrator might be updating his résumé after running an unauthorized scan or penetration test.

Many organizations use a written rules-of-engagement document when hiring outside security professionals to perform the test. The rules-of-engagement document identifies the boundaries of the penetration test. If testing does result in an outage even though the testers followed the rules of engagement, repercussions are less likely.

Penetration Testing

Penetration testing actively assesses deployed security controls within a system or network. It starts with passive reconnaissance, such as a vulnerability scan, but takes it a step further and tries to exploit vulnerabilities by simulating or performing an attack.

Security testers typically perform a penetration test to demonstrate the actual security vulnerabilities within a system. This can help the organization determine the impact of a threat against a system. In other words, it helps an organization determine the extent of damage that an attacker could inflict by exploiting a vulnerability.

Although it's not as common, it's also possible to perform a penetration test to determine how an organization will respond to a compromised system. This allows an organization to demonstrate security vulnerabilities and flaws in policy implementation. For example, many organizations may have perfect policies on paper. However, if employees aren't consistently following the policies, a penetration test can accurately demonstrate the flaws.

Because a penetration test can exploit vulnerabilities, it has the potential to disrupt actual operations and cause system instability. Because of this, it's important to strictly define boundaries for a test. Ideally, the penetration test will stop right before performing an exploit that can cause damage or result in an outage. However, some tests cause unexpected results.

Testers sometimes perform penetration tests on test systems rather than the live production systems. For example, an organization may be hosting a web application accessible on the Internet. Instead of performing the test on the live server and affecting customers, penetration testers or administrators configure another server with the same web application. If a penetration test cripples the test server, it accurately demonstrates security vulnerabilities, but it doesn't affect customers.

Many penetration tests include the following activities:

- Passive reconnaissance
- Active reconnaissance
- Initial exploitation
- Escalation of privilege
- Pivot
- Persistence

Remember this

A penetration test is an active test that can assess deployed security controls and determine the impact of a threat. It starts with a vulnerability scan and then tries to exploit vulnerabilities by actually attacking or simulating an attack.

Passive Reconnaissance

Passive reconnaissance collects information about a targeted system, network, or organization using open-source intelligence. This includes viewing social media sources about the target, news reports, and even the organization's web site. If the organization has wireless networks, it could include passively collecting information from the network such as network SSIDs. Note that because passive reconnaissance doesn't engage a target, it isn't illegal.

Passive reconnaissance does not include using any tools to send information to targets and analyze the responses. However, passive reconnaissance can include using tools to gather information from systems other than the target. For example, you can sometimes gain information about a domain name holder using the Whois lookup site (*https://www.whois.com*). Other times, you can gain information by querying Domain Name System (DNS) servers.

Active Reconnaissance

Active reconnaissance includes using tools to send data to systems and analyzing the responses. It typically starts by using various scanning tools such as network scanners and vulnerability scanners. It's important to realize that active reconnaissance does engage targets and is almost always illegal. It should never be started without first getting explicit authorization to do so.

The "Network Scanners" section earlier in this chapter discussed how tools such as Nmap and Nessus can gather a significant amount of information about networks and individual systems. This includes identifying all IP addresses active in a network, the ports and services active on individual systems, and the operating system running on individual systems.

> **Remember this**
>
> Penetration tests include both passive and active reconnaissance. Passive reconnaissance uses open-source intelligence methods, such as social media and an organization's web site. Active reconnaissance methods use tools such as network scanners to gain information on the target.

Initial Exploitation

After scanning the target, testers discover vulnerabilities. They then take it a step further and look for a vulnerability that they can exploit. For example, a vulnerability scan may discover that a system doesn't have a patch installed for a known vulnerability. The vulnerability allows attackers (and testers) to remotely access the system and install malware on it.

With this knowledge, the testers can use known methods to exploit this vulnerability. This gives the testers full access to the system. They can then install additional software on the exploited system.

Escalation of Privilege

In many penetration tests, the tester first gains access to a low-level system or low-level account. For example, a tester might gain access to Homer's computer using Homer's user account. Homer has access to the network, but doesn't have any administrative privileges. However, testers use various techniques to gain more and more privileges on Homer's computer and his network.

Chapter 6 discusses privilege escalation tactics that attackers often use. The "One Click Lets Them In" section discusses how advanced persistent threats (APTs) often use remote access Trojans (RATs) to gain access to a single system. Attackers trick a user into clicking a malicious link, which gives them access to a single computer. Attackers then use various scripts to scan the network looking for vulnerabilities. By exploiting these vulnerabilities, the attackers gain more and more privileges on the network.

Penetration testers typically use similar tactics. Depending on how much they are authorized to do, testers can use other methods to gain more and more access to a network.

Pivot

Pivoting is the process of using various tools to gain additional information. For example, imagine a tester gains access to Homer's computer within a company's network. The tester can then *pivot* and use Homer's computer to gather information on other computers. Homer might have access to network shares filled with files on nuclear power plant operations. The tester can use Homer's computer to collect this data and then send it back out of the network from Homer's computer.

Testers (and attackers) can use pivoting techniques to gather a wide variety of information. Many times, the tester must first use escalation of privilege techniques to gain more privileges. However, after doing so, it's possible that the tester can access databases (such as user accounts and password databases), email, and any other type of data stored within a network.

Persistence

Attackers often use various threats that allow them to stay within a network for weeks, months, or even years without being detected. Penetration testing techniques use similar techniques to maintain persistence within the network.

A common technique used to maintain persistence is to create a backdoor back into the network. For example, a tester may be able to create alternate accounts that can be accessed remotely. In some cases, it's also possible to install or modify services to connect back into a system. For example, a tester may be able to enable Secure Shell (SSH) and then create a method used to log on to a system using SSH.

White, Gray, and Black Box Testing

It's common to identify testing based on the level of knowledge the testers have prior to starting the test. These testers could be internal employees or external security professionals working for a third-party organization hired to perform the test. The three types of testing are:

- **Black box testing.** Testers have zero knowledge of the environment prior to starting a *black box test*. Instead, they approach the test with the same knowledge as an attacker. When testing new applications, black box testers wouldn't have any prior experience with the application. When testing networks, they aren't provided any information or documentation on the network before the test. Black box testers often use fuzzing to check for application vulnerabilities.
- **White box testing.** Testers have full knowledge of the environment before starting a *white box test*. For example, they would have access to product documentation, source code, and possibly even logon details.
- **Gray box testing.** Testers have some knowledge of the environment prior to starting a *gray box test*. For example, they might have access to some network documentation, but not know the full network layout.

You may also come across the terms black hat, white hat, and gray hat. These aren't referring to testers but instead to different types of attackers. They are reminiscent of the Wild West, where you could easily identify the good guys and the bad guys by the color of their hat. Black hat identifies a malicious attacker performing criminal activities. White hat identifies a security professional working within the law. Gray hat identifies individuals who may have good intentions, but their activities may cross ethical lines. For example, an activist, sometimes called a hacktivist, may use attack methods to further a cause, but not for personal gain.

Hackers and crackers are terms you may also come across. Originally, a hacker indicated someone proficient with computers who wanted to share knowledge with others. They weren't malicious. In contrast, a cracker was a proficient hacker who used the knowledge for malicious purposes. However, English is a living language that continues to evolve and the media consistently uses the term hacker to identify malicious attackers. This book often uses the term attacker to identify an individual attacking a system for malicious purposes.

Intrusive Versus Non-Intrusive Testing

Scans can be either intrusive or non-intrusive. You can also think of these terms as invasive and non-invasive, respectively. Tools using intrusive methods can potentially disrupt the operations of a system. In contrast, tools using non-intrusive methods will not compromise a system. These terms also apply to penetration testing (intrusive) and vulnerability scanning (non-intrusive).

When comparing penetration testing and vulnerability scanning, it's important to remember that penetration tests are intrusive and more invasive than vulnerability scans. They involve probing a system and attempting to exploit any vulnerabilities they discover. If they successfully exploit a vulnerability, a penetration test can potentially disrupt services and even take a system down.

Vulnerability scans are generally non-intrusive and less invasive than penetration tests. They never attempt to exploit a vulnerability. Because of this, a vulnerability scan is much safer to run on a system or network because it is significantly less likely that it will affect services.

Passive Versus Active Tools

In the context of tools used to discover security threats and vulnerabilities, it's important to understand the difference between passive tools and active tools. A passive tool tests systems in a non-intrusive manner and has little possibility of compromising a system. An active tool uses intrusive and invasive methods and can potentially affect the operations of a system.

The "Vulnerability Scanning" section earlier in this chapter mentioned that vulnerability scanning is passive, and penetration testing is active. In this context, passive doesn't mean that a vulnerability scanner isn't doing anything. It certainly is probing systems to identify vulnerabilities and other problems. However, it does not take any action to exploit these vulnerabilities.

That doesn't mean that you can feel free to run a vulnerability scanner on any network simply because it is passive and non-intrusive. If your actions are discovered, you might be identified as an attacker and face legal action.

> **Remember this**
>
> A vulnerability scanner is passive and non-intrusive and has little impact on a system during a test. In contrast, a penetration test is active and intrusive, and can potentially compromise a system. A penetration test is more invasive than a vulnerability scan.

Exploitation Frameworks

An exploitation framework is a tool used to store information about security vulnerabilities. It is often used by penetration testers (and attackers) to detect and exploit software. *Exploitation frameworks* typically include tools used to check for vulnerabilities and execute exploits on any discovered vulnerabilities. Chapter 4 discusses intrusion detection systems (IDSs) and many IDSs use information from an existing framework to detect attacks. Some commonly used exploitation frameworks are:

- **Metasploit Framework.** Metasploit is an open source project that runs on Linux systems. It has data on over 1,600 exploits and includes methods to develop, test, and use exploit code. Rapid7 acquired Metasploit in 2009. While the framework is still free and open source, there are more advanced editions available for purchase.
- **BeEF (Browser Exploitation Framework).** BeEF is an open source web browser exploitation framework. It focuses on identifying web browser vulnerabilities. Successful attacks allow testers (and attackers) to launch attacks from within an exploited web browser.
- **w3af (Web Application Attack and Audit Framework).** This open source framework focuses on web application vulnerabilities. The stated goal is to find and exploit all web application vulnerabilities and make this information known to others. Web application developers can then ensure their web applications are not vulnerable to the exploits.

Using Security Tools

Several tools are available for use by security professionals and attackers alike. Vulnerability scanners were discussed at length earlier in this chapter, including their use as ping scanners and port scanners. However, other tools are available. This section discusses tools such as protocol analyzers, command-line tools, logs, and audits.

Sniffing with a Protocol Analyzer

A *protocol analyzer* can capture and analyze packets on a network. The process of using a protocol analyzer is sometimes referred to as sniffing or using a sniffer. Both administrators and attackers can use a protocol analyzer to view IP headers and examine packets. For example, administrators can use a protocol analyzer to troubleshoot communication issues between network systems, or identify potential attacks using manipulated or fragmented packets.

Attackers can use a protocol analyzer to capture data sent across a network in cleartext. For example, unencrypted credentials are usernames and passwords sent across a network in cleartext. One of the ways attackers can view this data is by connecting an unauthorized switch within a network to capture traffic and forward it to a system running a protocol analyzer. If cabling isn't protected, they might be able to simply connect a switch above a drop-down ceiling.

Wireshark is a free protocol analyzer that you can download from the Wireshark site: *http://www.wireshark.org/*. Figure 8.3 shows Wireshark after it captured packets transmitted over the network. It includes about 150 packets and has packet 121 selected in the top pane. The top pane shows the source and destination IP addresses and the Server Message Block (SMB) protocol. Many networks use SMB to send files over the network, and this packet includes the contents of that file. The middle pane shows details from this packet with the Internet Protocol version 4 header information partially expanded. The bottom pane shows the entire contents of the packet (including the unencrypted credentials) displayed in hexadecimal and ASCII characters.

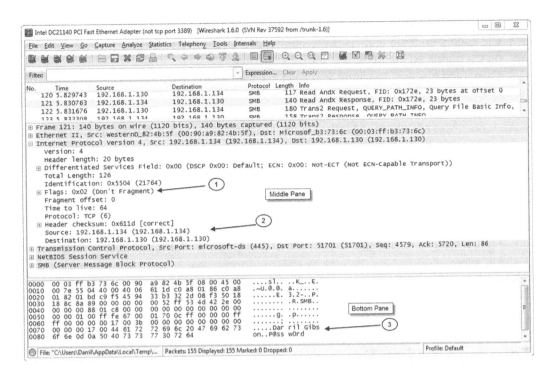

Figure 8.3: Wireshark capture

Although it can be tedious to analyze a packet capture, there is a lot of information in it for anyone willing to take the time to do so. Occasionally, attackers manipulate flags (arrow 1) within the headers for different types of attacks, and the protocol analyzer allows you to verify header manipulation attacks. You can also see the source and destination IP addresses (arrow 2) within the IP header field. You can expand the Ethernet II section to show the media access control (MAC) addresses of the source and destination computers.

Notice that you can view the unencrypted credentials—username (Darril) and password (P@ssw0rd)—in the bottom pane (arrow 3) because SMB sends it in cleartext. However, if an application encrypted the data before sending it across the network, it would not be readable.

Although this packet capture only includes about 150 packets, a packet capture can easily include thousands of packets. Wireshark includes filters that administrators use to focus on specific types of traffic. These filters also allow them to quantify the traffic. For example, they can determine the percentage of SMTP traffic or HTTP traffic on the network.

In addition to seeing a capture using the Wireshark graphical interface, you can also view them as text files. The information in the text file is usually limited using filters, but normally includes the time, source information labeled as src, destination information labeled as dst, and sometimes protocol information. Here's an example:

22:33:44, src 192.168.5.55:3389, dst 192.168.7.17:8080, syn/ack

The time is shown in a 24-hour clock as 10:33 p.m. and 44 seconds. Notice the source and destination includes an IP address and a port number. This reiterates the importance of knowing commonly used ports mentioned in Chapter 3. It also shows you how you can identify the source of traffic. For example, if an attacker is manipulating or fragmenting packets as part of an attack, you can use the src IP address to identify the potential source of the attack.

It's worth noting that the source IP address doesn't always identify the actual attacker. For example, attackers often take control of other computers and launch attacks from them without the knowledge of the owner. Similarly, Port Address Translation (PAT) translates public and private IP addresses. If the traffic goes through a device using PAT, the protocol analyzer only captures the translated IP address, not the original IP address.

When using a protocol analyzer, you need to configure the network interface card (NIC) on the system to use promiscuous mode. Normally, a NIC uses non-promiscuous mode and only processes packets addressed directly to its IP address. However, when you put it in promiscuous mode, it processes all packets regardless of the IP address. This allows the protocol analyzer to capture all packets that reach the NIC.

> ### Remember this
>
> Administrators use a protocol analyzer to capture, display, and analyze packets sent over a network. It is useful when troubleshooting communications problems between systems. It is also useful to detect attacks that manipulate or fragment packets. A capture shows information such as the type of traffic (protocol), flags, source and destination IP addresses, and source and destination MAC addresses. The NIC must be configured to use promiscuous mode to capture all traffic.

Command-Line Tools

Chapter 1 introduces some command-line tools available on Windows and Linux systems. Some tools are useful when performing vulnerability scans and penetration tests. Three tools discussed in this section are tcpdump, Nmap, and Netcat.

As with any command-line tools, it's best to dig in and give them a try. I strongly encourage you to check out the free online labs at *http://gcgapremium.com/501labs/* and do each of them.

Tcpdump

Tcpdump is a command-line packet analyzer (or protocol analyzer). It allows you to capture packets like you can with Wireshark (mentioned in the "Sniffing with a Protocol Analyzer" section). The difference is that Wireshark is a Windows-based tool and tcpdump is executed from the command line. Many administrators use tcpdump to capture the packets and later use Wireshark to analyze the packet capture. One of the online labs for this chapter shows how to do this.

Kali Linux includes tcpdump, but you won't find it on Windows systems. As with most Linux command-line tools, tcpdump is case sensitive. You need to enter tcpdump in all lowercase. Additionally, the switches must be entered with the proper case. For example, -c (lowercase c) represents count and indicates the capture should stop after receiving the specified number of packets. However, -C (uppercase C) represents file size and indicates the maximum size (in millions of bytes) of a packet capture. When the file reaches this size, tcpdump closes it and starts storing packets in a new file.

Nmap

Nmap is a network scanner and was discussed earlier in the "Network Scanners" section. The graphical side of Nmap is Zenmap, and Figure 8.1 showed a screenshot from Zenmap. Additionally, online labs show you how to install and use Nmap and Zenmap.

It includes many capabilities, including identifying all the active hosts and their IP addresses in a network, the protocols and services running on each of these hosts, and the operating system of the host. When running the command, you include the scan type(s), optional options, and target specifications. As an example, consider the following command:

nmap -T4 -A -v 192.168.0.0/24

Notice that it has three switches, -T4, -A, and -v:

- **T4.** T4 refers to the speed of the scan. Valid switches are T0 through T5 with T0 being the slowest and T5 being the fastest. Faster scans are likely to be detected, while slower scans may not be detected.
- **A.** The -A switch indicates the scan should include OS detection, version detection, script scanning, and traceroute.
- **-v.** The -v switch indicates the verbosity level. You can get more data output by using -vv or -vvv.

Netcat

Chapter 3 discusses **Netcat** and how administrators often use it for remotely accessing Linux systems. It doesn't include native encryption so it's common to use SSH to secure the session. Additionally, the "Banner Grabbing" section earlier in this chapter mentioned that Netcat can easily be used for banner grabbing. The following is a sample command used for banner grabbing:

echo "" | nc -vv -n -w1 72.52.206.134 80

It uses the netcat command (nc) along with some switches: -vv for a verbose output, -n to not resolve host names, -w1 to wait no more than 1 second for a reply. The command connects to port 80 of the system with an IP address of 72.52.206.134. The echo "" sends a blank command to the server and the pipe symbol (|) tells Netcat to send the command after establishing the connection.

Some other uses of Netcat include:

- **Transferring files.** One of the online labs for Chapter 3 shows how to create a chat session between two systems. Once this session is open, you can use the connection to copy files between the systems.
- **Port scanner.** You can use Netcat to run a port scan against a single IP address. It allows you to specify the range of ports, such as 10 through 1024 and randomize the ports scanned to evade detection. It also supports waiting longer periods of time between port checks, again, to evade detection.

> **Remember this**
>
> Tcpdump is a command-line protocol analyzer. It can create packet captures that can then be viewed in Wireshark. Nmap is a sophisticated network scanner that runs from the command line. Netcat can be used to remotely administer systems and also gather information on remote systems.

Monitoring Logs for Event Anomalies

Logs have the capability to record what happened, when it happened, where it happened, and who did it. One of the primary purposes of logging is to allow someone, such as an administrator or security professional, to identify exactly what happened and when.

Many times, security administrators are searching the logs looking for event anomalies. As a simple example, attackers sometimes try to log on to accounts by guessing passwords. Security logs will record these attempts as failed logons, which is an event anomaly. After investigating the failed logons, administrators can determine if the failed logons were part of normal operation, or a security incident.

It's tempting to set up logging to record every event and provide as much detail as possible—most logs support a verbose mode that will log additional details. However, a limiting factor is the amount of disk space available. Additionally, when logging is enabled, there is an implied responsibility to review the logs. The more you choose to log, the more you may have to review. The goal is to strike a balance between what is needed and the amount of available space for storage. The following sections cover some commonly used logs.

Operating System Event Logs

Operating systems have basic logs that record events. For example, Windows systems have several common logs that record what happened on a Windows computer system. These logs are viewable using the Windows Event Viewer. One of the primary logs in a Windows system is the Security log and it functions as a security log, an audit log, and an access log.

The Security log records auditable events, such as when a user logs on or off, or when a user accesses a resource. Some auditing is enabled by default in some systems, but administrators can add additional auditing. The Security log records audited events as successes or failures. Success indicates an audited event completed successfully, such as a user successfully logging on or successfully deleting a file. Failure indicates that a user tried to perform an action but failed, such as failing to log on or trying to delete a file but receiving a permission error instead. Some additional logs in a Windows system include:

- **Application.** The Application log records events recorded by applications or programs running on the system. Any application has the capability of recording errors in the Application log.
- **System.** The operating system uses the System log to record events related to the functioning of the operating system. This can include when it starts, when it shuts down, information on services starting and stopping, drivers loading or failing, or any other system component event deemed important by the system developers.

If a system is attacked, you may be able to learn details of the attack by reviewing the operating system logs. Depending on the type of attack, any of the operating system logs may be useful.

Firewall and Router Access Logs

You can typically manipulate firewalls and routers to log specific information, such as logging all traffic that the device passes, all traffic that the device blocks, or both. These logs are useful when troubleshooting connectivity issues and when identifying potential intrusions or attacks.

Firewall and router logs include information on where the packet came from (the source) and where it is going (the destination). This includes IP addresses, MAC addresses, and ports.

Linux Logs

The CompTIA Security+ exam includes several Linux-based commands. Understanding this, it's valuable to know about some common Linux logs. You can view logs using the System Log Viewer on Linux systems or by using the cat command from the terminal. For example, to view the authentication log (auth.log), you can use the following command:

cat /var/log/auth.log

Some of the Linux logs administrators often look at include:

- **var/log/messages.** This log contains a wide variety of general system messages. It includes some messages logged during startup, some messages related to mail, the kernel, and messages related to authentication. It stores general system activity log entries.
- **var/log/boot.log.** Log entries created when the system boots are contained here.
- **var/log/auth.log.** The authentication log contains information related to successful and unsuccessful logins.
- **var/log/faillog.** This log contains information on failed login attempts. It can be viewed using the faillog command.
- **/var/log/kern.log.** The kernel log contains information logged by the system kernel, which is the central part of the Linux operating system.
- **/var/log/httpd/.** If the system is configured as an Apache web server, you can view access and error logs with this directory.

Some Linux distributions include the utmp, wtmp, and btmp files (or the utmpx, wtmpx, and btmpx variants). They are created so that administrators can answer questions such as who is currently logged in, who has logged in recently, and what accounts have failed login attempts. They are typically within the /var/log folder but might be elsewhere. The following bullets describe these files:

- The utmp file maintains information on the current status of the system, including who is currently logged in. The who command queries this file to display a list of users currently logged in.
- The wtmp file is an archive of the utmp file. Depending on how it is implemented, it can be a circular file, overwriting itself when it reaches a predetermined size. The last command queries this file to show the last logged-in users.
- The btmp file records failed login attempts. The lastb command shows the last failed login attempts.

Other Logs

In addition to the basic operating system logs and firewall and router access logs, administrators use other logs when maintaining systems and networks. These include:

- **Antivirus logs.** Antivirus logs log all antivirus activity, including when scans were run and if any malware was detected. These logs also identify if malware was removed or quarantined.
- **Application logs.** Many server applications include logging capabilities within the application. For example, database applications such as Microsoft SQL Server or Oracle Database include logs to record performance and user activity.
- **Performance logs.** Performance logs can monitor system performance and give an alert when preset performance thresholds are exceeded.

> **Remember this**
>
> Logs record what happened, when it happened, where it happened, and who did it. By monitoring logs, administrators can detect event anomalies. Additionally, by reviewing logs, security personnel can create an audit trail.

SIEM

A security information and event management (**SIEM**) system provides a centralized solution for collecting, analyzing, and managing data from multiple sources. They combine the services of security event management (SEM) and security information management (SIM) solutions. A SEM provides real-time monitoring, analysis, and notification of security events, such as suspected security incidents. A SIM provides long-term storage of data, along with methods of analyzing the data looking for trends, or creating reports needed to verify compliance of laws or regulations.

SIEMs are very useful in large enterprises that have massive amounts of data and activity to monitor. Consider an organization with over 1,000 servers. When an incident occurs on just one of those servers, administrators need to know about it as quickly as possible. The SIEM provides continuous monitoring and provides real-time reporting. For example, in a large network operations center (NOC), the SIEM might display alerts on a large heads-up display. A benefit is that the monitoring and reporting is automated with scripts with the SIEM.

Vendors sell SIEMs as applications that can be installed on systems, and as dedicated hardware appliances. However, no matter how a vendor bundles it, it will typically have common capabilities. This starts with a database that can be easily searched and analyzed. The SIEM collects log data from devices throughout the network and stores these logs in the database.

The following bullets outline some additional capabilities shared by most SIEMs:

- **Aggregation.** Aggregation refers to combining several dissimilar items into a single item. A SIEM can collect data from multiple sources, such as firewalls, intrusion detection systems, proxy servers, and more. Each of these devices formats the logs differently. However, the SIEM can aggregate the data and store it in such a way that it is easy to analyze and search.
- **Correlation engine.** A correlation engine is a software component used to collect and analyze event log data from various systems within the network. It typically aggregates the data looking for common attributes. It then uses advanced analytic tools to detect patterns of potential security events and raises alerts. System administrators can then investigate the alert.
- **Automated alerting.** A SIEM typically comes with predefined alerts, which provide notifications of suspicious events. For example, if it detects a port scan on a server, it might send an email to an administrator group or display the alert on a heads-up display. SIEMs also include the ability to create new alerts.
- **Automated triggers.** Triggers cause an action in response to a predefined number of repeated events. As an example, imagine a trigger for failed logons is set at five. If an attacker repeatedly tries to log on to a server using Secure Shell (SSH), the server's log will show the failed logon attempts. When the SIEM detects more than five failed SSH logons, it can change the environment and stop the attack. It might modify a firewall to block these SSH logon attempts or send a script to the server to temporarily disable SSH. A SIEM includes the ability to modify predefined triggers and create new ones.
- **Time synchronization.** All servers sending data to the SIEM should be synchronized with the same time. This becomes especially important when investigating an incident so that security investigators know when events occurred. Additionally, large organizations can have locations in different time zones. Each of these locations might have servers sending data to a single centralized SIEM. If the server logs use their local time, the SIEM needs to ensure that it compensates for the time offset. One method

is to convert all times to Greenwich Mean Time (GMT), which is the time at the Royal Observatory in Greenwich, London.

- **Event deduplication.** Deduplication is the process of removing duplicate entries. As an example, imagine 10 users receive the same email and choose to save it. An email server using deduplication processing will keep only one copy of this email, but make it accessible to all 10 users. Imagine a NIDS collects data from a firewall and a SIEM collects data from the NIDS and the firewall. The SIEM will store only a single copy of any duplicate log entries, but also ensure that the entries are associated with both devices.
- **Logs/WORM.** A SIEM typically includes methods to prevent anyone from modifying log entries. This is sometimes referred to as write once read many (WORM). As logs are received, the SIEM will aggregate and correlate the log entries. After processing the logs, it can archive the source logs with write protection.

The location of the SIEM (and the location of its correlation engine) varies based on how the SIEM is used. However, it's common to locate the SIEM within the private network, even if it is collecting some data from the demilitarized zone (DMZ). The internal network will provide the best protection for the log data. In very large organizations, aggregation processes and the correlation engine can consume a lot of processing power, so organizations sometimes off-load these processes to another server. The primary SIEM appliance can then focus on alerts and triggers.

Continuous Monitoring

It's important to realize that there is never a time that security professionals can say, "Now that we've implemented this security measure, we can sit back knowing that we're safe." In other words, security is never finished. Instead, security professionals must continuously monitor their environment for emerging threats and new vulnerabilities.

Continuous security monitoring includes monitoring all relevant security controls, with the goal of ensuring that they help an organization maintain a strong security posture. There are many methods of monitoring, including performing periodic threat assessments, vulnerability assessments, and risk assessments. Many organizations perform routine vulnerability scans, such as once a week, and infrequent penetration tests. Additionally, organizations perform routine audits and reviews, such as usage auditing reviews and permission auditing reviews, which are discussed in the next section.

Remember this

A security information and event management (SIEM) system provides a centralized solution for collecting, analyzing, and managing data from multiple sources. It typically includes aggregation and correlation capabilities to collect and organize log data from multiple sources. It also provides continuous monitoring with automated alerts and triggers.

Usage Auditing and Reviews

Usage auditing refers to logging information on what users do. For example, if Homer accesses a file on a network server, the log entry would show his identity, when he accessed the file, what file he accessed, and what computer he used to access the file. He would not be able to refute the recorded action because auditing provides non-repudiation.

Determining Actions from Auditing

Reality Leigh Winner was arrested in 2017 on suspicion that she leaked an intelligence report to a news web site. She allegedly printed the document and sent it to The Intercept. The Intercept scanned the document, creating a five-page PDF file and included it in a story they published. The file was slightly redacted, but still gave investigators enough information to arrest Winner shortly after The Intercept published the story.

How did investigators identify Winner?

The PDF showed creases, indicating it was printed. After a little investigation, they discovered the file was printed by only six people. This indicates that the file likely had advanced auditing set on it. Advanced auditing can record any access on the file, including if the file is printed.

Ms. Winner was one of those six people. The PDF also included printer steganography tracking dots that provide another method of auditing. These coded dots identified the date and time when the file was printed and the printer model and serial number where it was printed. Access to this printer likely made it easy for investigators to rule out the other five people.

Auditing can include much more than when a user accessed a file. It can also include when a user logs on, accesses a network share, reads a file, modifies a file, creates a file, prints a file, accesses a web site via a proxy server, and much more.

Configuring logging of logon attempts is an important security step for system monitoring. After configuring logging, a system records the time and date when users log on, and when they access systems within a network. When users first log on to their account, it's recorded as a logon action. Additionally, when users access a resource over the network (such as a file server), it is also recorded as a logon action. Many systems utilize single sign-on (SSO), so users don't have to provide their credentials again. However, their access is still recorded as a logon action.

A usage auditing review looks at the logs to see what users are doing. For example, an organization might have a network share filled with files on a proprietary project. A usage auditing review might look at audit logs for these files to see who is accessing the files and what they are doing with the files.

Logs create an audit trail of what happened. Usage auditing reviews are often done to re-create the audit trail, or reconstruct what happened in the past. For example, if someone leaks proprietary information outside the organization, investigators can look at the auditing files to see who accessed the information, what they did with it (such as printing it), and when they did so.

Permission Auditing and Review

A **permission auditing review** looks at the rights and permissions assigned to users and helps ensure the principle of least privilege is enforced. Chapter 2, "Understanding Identity and Access Management," discusses the principle of least privilege in more depth, but in short it simply means that users have the rights and permissions they need, but no more. This includes ensuring users can access only the resources they need to perform their job.

Permission auditing reviews identify the privileges (rights and permissions) granted to users, and compares them against what the users need. It can detect privilege creep, a common problem that violates the principle of least privilege.

Privilege creep (or permission bloat) occurs when a user is granted more and more privileges due to changing job requirements, but unneeded privileges are never removed. For example, imagine Lisa is working in the Human Resources (HR) department, so she has access to HR data. Later, she transfers to the Sales department and administrators grant her access to sales data. However, no one removes her access to HR data even though she doesn't need it to perform her job in the Sales department.

Organizations commonly use a role-based access control model with group-based privileges, as described in Chapter 2. For example, while Lisa is working in the HR department, her account would be in appropriate HR department security groups to grant her appropriate privileges for the HR job. When she transfers to the Sales department, administrators would add her to the appropriate Sales department groups, granting her privileges for her new job. An organization should also have account management controls in place to ensure that administrators remove her account from the HR department security groups. The permission auditing review verifies that these account management practices are followed.

Most organizations ensure that permission auditing reviews are performed at least once a year, and some organizations perform them more often. The goal is to do them often enough to catch potential problems and prevent security incidents. However, unless they can be automated, they become an unnecessary burden if security administrators are required to do them too often, such as daily or even once a week.

> ### *Remember this*
>
> Usage auditing records user activity in logs. A usage auditing review looks at the logs to see what users are doing and it can be used to re-create an audit trail. Permission auditing reviews help ensure that users have only the access they need and no more and can detect privilege creep issues.

Chapter 8 Exam Topic Review

When preparing for the exam, make sure you understand these key concepts covered in this chapter.

Understanding Risk Management

- A risk is the likelihood that a threat will exploit a vulnerability. A threat is a potential danger that can compromise confidentiality, integrity, or availability of data or a system. A vulnerability is a weakness.
- Impact refers to the magnitude of harm that can be caused if a threat exercises a vulnerability.
- Threat assessments help an organization identify and categorize threats. An environmental threat assessment evaluates the likelihood of an environmental threat, such as a natural disaster, occurring. Manmade threat assessments evaluate threats from humans.
- Internal threat assessments evaluate threats from within an organization. External threat assessment evaluates threats from outside an organization.
- A vulnerability is a flaw or weakness in software or hardware, or a weakness in a process that a threat could exploit, resulting in a security breach.

- Risk management attempts to reduce risk to a level that an organization can accept, and the remaining risk is known as residual risk. Senior management is responsible for managing risk and the losses associated from residual risk.
- You can avoid a risk by not providing a service or participating in a risky activity. Purchasing insurance, such as fire insurance, transfers the risk to another entity. Security controls mitigate, or reduce, risks. When the cost of a control outweighs a risk, it is common to accept the risk.
- A risk assessment quantifies or qualifies risks based on different values or judgments. It starts by identifying asset values and prioritizing high-value items.
- Quantitative risk assessments use numbers, such as costs and asset values. The single loss expectancy (SLE) is the cost of any single loss. The annual rate of occurrence (ARO) indicates how many times the loss will occur annually. You can calculate the annual loss expectancy (ALE) as SLE × ARO.
- Qualitative risk assessments use judgments to prioritize risks based on likelihood of occurrence and impact. These judgments provide a subjective ranking.
- Risk assessment results are sensitive. Only executives and security professionals should be granted access to risk assessment reports.
- A risk register is a detailed document listing information about risks. It typically includes risk scores along with recommended security controls to reduce the risk scores.
- A supply chain assessment evaluates a supply chain needed to produce and sell a product. It includes raw materials and all the processes required to create and distribute a finished product.

Comparing Scanning and Testing Tools

- A port scanner scans systems for open ports and attempts to discover what services and protocols are running.
- Network mapping identifies the IP addresses of hosts within a network. Network scanners expand on network mapping. They identify the operating system running on each host. They can also identify services and protocols running on each host.
- Wireless scanners can detect rogue access points (APs) in a network. Many can also crack passwords used by the APs.
- Banner grabbing queries remote systems to detect their operating system, along with services, protocols, and applications running on the remote system.
- Vulnerability scanners passively test security controls to identify vulnerabilities, a lack of security controls, and common misconfigurations. They are effective at discovering systems susceptible to an attack without exploiting the systems.
- A false positive from a vulnerability scan indicates the scan detected a vulnerability, but the vulnerability doesn't exist. Credentialed scans run under the context of an account and can be more accurate than non-credentialed scans, giving fewer false positives.
- Penetration testers should gain consent prior to starting a penetration test. A rules-of-engagement document identifies the boundaries of the test.
- A penetration test is an active test that attempts to exploit discovered vulnerabilities. It starts with a vulnerability scan and then bypasses or actively tests security controls to exploit vulnerabilities.

- Passive reconnaissance gathers information from open-source intelligence. Active reconnaissance uses scanning techniques to gather information.
- After initial exploitation, a penetration tester uses privilege escalation techniques to gain more access. Pivoting during a penetration test is the process of using an exploited system to access other systems.
- In black box testing, testers perform a penetration test with zero prior knowledge of the environment. White box testing indicates that the testers have full knowledge of the environment, including documentation and source code for tested applications. Gray box testing indicates some knowledge of the environment.
- Scans can be either intrusive or non-intrusive. Penetration testing is intrusive (also called invasive) and can potentially disrupt operations. Vulnerability testing is non-intrusive (also called non-invasive).
- Exploitation frameworks store information about security vulnerabilities. They are often used by penetration testers (and attackers) to detect and exploit software.

Using Security Tools

- Protocol analyzers (sniffers) can capture and analyze data sent over a network. Testers (and attackers) use protocol analyzers to capture cleartext data sent across a network.
- Administrators use protocol analyzers for troubleshooting communication issues by inspecting protocol headers to detect manipulated or fragmented packets.
- Captured packets show the type of traffic (protocol), source and destination IP addresses, source and destination MAC addresses, and flags.
- Tcpdump is a command-line protocol analyzer. Captured packet files can be analyzed in a graphical protocol analyzer such as Wireshark.
- Nmap is a sophisticated network scanner run from the command line. Netcat is a command-line tool used to remotely administer servers. Netcat can also be used for banner grabbing.
- Logs record events and by monitoring logs, administrators can detect event anomalies. Security logs track logon and logoff activity on systems. System logs identify when services start and stop.
- Firewall and router logs identify the source and destination of traffic.
- A security information and event management (SIEM) system can aggregate and correlate logs from multiple sources in a single location. A SIEM also provides continuous monitoring and automated alerting and triggers.
- Continuous security monitoring helps an organization maintain its security posture, by verifying that security controls continue to function as intended.
- User auditing records user activities. User auditing reviews examine user activity. Permission auditing reviews help ensure that users have only the rights and permissions they need to perform their jobs, and no more.

Online References

- Don't forget to check out the online resources at *http://gcgapremium.com/501-extras*. It includes additional free practice test questions, labs, and other resources to help you pass.

Chapter 8 Practice Questions

1. A security expert is performing a risk assessment. She is seeking information to identify the number of times a specific type of incident occurs per year. Which of the following BEST identifies this?
   A. ALE
   B. ARO
   C. SLE
   D. WORM

2. Lisa needs to calculate the ALE for a group of servers used in the network. During the past two years, five of the servers failed. The hardware cost to repair or replace each server was $3,500 and the downtime resulted in $2,500 of additional losses for each outage. What is the ALE?
   A. $7,000
   B. $8,000
   C. $15,000
   D. $30,000

3. Martin is performing a risk assessment on an e-commerce web server. While doing so, he created a document showing all the known risks to this server, along with the risk score for each risk. What is the name of this document?
   A. Quantitative risk assessment
   B. Qualitative risk assessment
   C. Residual risk
   D. Risk register

4. Your organization includes an e-commerce web site used to sell digital products. You are tasked with evaluating all the elements used to support this web site. What are you performing?
   A. Quantitative assessment
   B. Qualitative assessment
   C. Threat assessment
   D. Supply chain assessment

5. A penetration tester is running several tests on a server within your organization's DMZ. The tester wants to identify the operating system of the remote host. Which of the following tools or methods are MOST likely to provide this information?
   A. Banner grabbing
   B. Vulnerability scan
   C. Password cracker
   D. Protocol analyzer

6. You need to perform tests on your network to identify missing security controls. However, you want to have the least impact on systems that users are accessing. Which of the following tools is the BEST to meet this need?
    A. A syn stealth scan
    B. Vulnerability scan
    C. Ping scan
    D. Penetration test

7. You periodically run vulnerability scans on your network, but have been receiving many false positives. Which of the following actions can help reduce the false positives?
    A. Run the scans as credentialed scans.
    B. Run the scans as non-credentialed scans.
    C. Run the scans using passive reconnaissance.
    D. Run the scans using active reconnaissance.

8. Your organization has a legacy server running within the DMZ. It is running older software that is not compatible with current patches, so management has decided to let it remain unpatched. Management wants to know if attackers can access the internal network if they successfully compromise this server. Which of the following is the MOST appropriate action?
    A. Perform a vulnerability scan.
    B. Perform a port scan.
    C. Perform a black box test.
    D. Perform a penetration test.

9. A penetration tester has successfully attacked a single computer within the network. The tester is now attempting to access other systems within the network via this computer. Which of the following BEST describes the tester's current actions?
    A. Performing reconnaissance
    B. Performing the initial exploitation
    C. Pivoting
    D. Escalating privileges

10. You are troubleshooting issues between two servers on your network and need to analyze the network traffic. Of the following choices, what is the BEST tool to capture and analyze this traffic?
    A. Network mapper
    B. Protocol analyzer
    C. Network scanner
    D. SIEM

11. A penetration tester is tasked with gaining information on one of your internal servers and he enters the following command:
    echo "" | nc -vv -n -w1 72.52.206.134 80

    What is the purpose of this command?
    A. Identify if a server is running a service using port 80 and is reachable.
    B. Launch an attack on a server sending 80 separate packets in a short period of time.
    C. Use Netcat to remotely administer the server.
    D. Use Netcat to start an RDP session on the server.

12. You suspect that an attacker has been sending specially crafted TCP packets to a server trying to exploit a vulnerability. You decide to capture TCP packets being sent to this server for later analysis and you want to use a command-line tool to do so. Which of the following tools will BEST meet your need?
    A. Wiredump
    B. Tcpdump
    C. Netcat
    D. Nmap

13. You suspect someone has been trying a brute force password attack on a Linux system. Which of the following logs should you check to view failed authentication attempts by users?
    A. /var/log/btmp
    B. /var/log/fail
    C. var/log/httpd
    D. /var/log/kern

14. An organization has a large network with dozens of servers. Administrators are finding it difficult to review and analyze the logs from all the network devices. They are looking for a solution to aggregate and correlate the logs. Which of the following choices BEST meets this need?
    A. Nmap
    B. Netcat
    C. Wireshark
    D. SIEM

15. Lisa has recently transferred from the HR department to payroll. While browsing file shares, Lisa notices she can access the HR files related to her new coworkers. Which of the following could prevent this scenario from occurring?
    A. Permission auditing and review
    B. Continuous monitoring
    C. Vulnerability scan
    D. Penetration testing

Chapter 8 Practice Question Answers

1. **B.** The annual rate of occurrence (ARO) is the best choice to identify how many times a specific type of incident occurs in a year. Annual loss expectancy (ALE) identifies the expected monetary loss for a year and single loss expectancy (SLE) identifies the expected monetary loss for a single incident. ALE = SLE × ARO and if you know any two of these values, you can identify the third value. For example, ARO = ALE / SLE. Write once read many (WORM) is a term sometimes used with archived logs indicating they cannot be modified.

2. **C.** The annual loss expectancy (ALE) is $15,000. The single loss expectancy (SLE) is $6,000 ($3,500 to repair or replace each server plus $2,500 in additional losses for each outage). The annual rate of occurrence (ARO) is 2.5 (five failures in two years or 5 / 2). You calculate the ALE as SLE × ARO ($6,000 × 2.5).

3. **D.** A risk register lists all known risks for an asset, such as a web server, and it typically includes a risk score (the combination of the likelihood of occurrence and the impact of the risk). Risk assessments (including quantitative and qualitative risk assessments) might use a risk register, but they aren't risk registers. Residual risk refers to the remaining risk after applying security controls to mitigate a risk.

4. **D.** A supply chain assessment evaluates all the elements used to create, sell, and distribute a product. Risk assessments (including both quantitative and qualitative risk assessments) evaluate risks, but don't evaluate the supply chain required to support an e-commerce web site. A threat assessment evaluates threats.

5. **A.** Banner grabbing is a technique used to gain information about a remote server and it will identify the operating system of the system in the demilitarized zone (DMZ). A vulnerability scanner checks for vulnerabilities. A password cracker attempts to discover passwords. A protocol analyzer collects packets sent across a network and can be used to analyze the packets.

6. **B.** A vulnerability scanner is passive and has the least impact on systems, and it can detect systems that are lacking specific security controls. Network scanners use methods such as a syn stealth scan and a ping scan to discover devices on a network, but they don't identify missing security controls. A penetration test is invasive and does not have the least impact on systems.

7. **A.** Running the scans as credentialed scans (within the context of a valid account) allows the scan to see more information and typically results in fewer false positives. Non-credentialed scans run without any user credentials and can be less accurate. Passive reconnaissance collects information on a target using open-source intelligence. All vulnerability scans use active reconnaissance techniques.

8. **D.** A penetration test attempts to exploit a vulnerability and can determine if a successful attack will allow attackers into the internal network. A vulnerability scan is passive. It does not attempt to compromise a system, so it cannot verify if an attacker can access the internal network. A port scan only identifies open ports. A black box test only refers to the knowledge of the testers and indicates they have zero knowledge prior to starting a test.

9. **C.** Pivoting is the process of accessing other systems through a single compromised system. Reconnaissance techniques are done before attacking a system. A successful attack on a single computer is the initial exploitation. Escalating privileges attempts to gain higher privileges on a target.

10. **B.** A protocol analyzer (also called a sniffer) is the best choice to capture and analyze network traffic. A network mapper can detect all the devices on a network, and a network scanner can detect more information about these devices, but neither of these tools is the best choice to capture and analyze traffic for troubleshooting purposes. A security information and event management (SIEM) system aggregates and correlates logs from multiple sources, but does not capture network traffic.

11. **A.** This command sends a query to the server over port 80 and if the server is running a service on port 80, it will connect. This is a common beginning command for a banner

grabbing attempt. It does not send 80 separate packets. Netcat is often used to remotely administer servers, but not using port 80. Remote Desktop Protocol (RDP) uses port 3389 and is not relevant in this scenario.

12. **B.** The tcpdump command-line tool is the best choice of the given answers. It is a command-line packet analyzer (or protocol analyzer) and its primary purpose is to capture packets. Wiredump isn't a valid tool name. Wireshark (not included as an answer choice) is a graphic-based packet analyzer that can be started from the command line, but tcpdump includes more command-line options than Wireshark. Netcat is useful for remotely accessing systems and can be used for banner grabbing, but it doesn't capture packets. Nmap analyzes packets during a scan. It can also use Npcap, the Nmap Project's packet sniffing library, but Nmap isn't the best choice to capture packets.

13. **A.** The /var/log/btmp log contains information on user failed login attempts. While not available as an answer, /var/log/auth also includes information on failed login attempts. While the /var/log/faillog log includes information on failed logins, /var/log/fail isn't a valid log name in Linux. The /var/log/httpd directory includes logs from the Apache web server, when it's installed. The /var/log/kern log contains information logged by the system kernel.

14. **D.** A security information and event management (SIEM) system provides a centralized solution for collecting, analyzing, and managing data from multiple sources and can aggregate and correlate logs. None of the other choices aggregate and correlate logs. Nmap is a network scanner that can discover and map devices on a network. Netcat is a command-line tool that can be used to connect to servers. Wireshark is a graphical-based protocol analyzer.

15. **A.** A permission auditing and review process verifies that the principle of least privilege is followed. This includes ensuring users can access only the resources they need to perform their job. Continuous monitoring includes monitoring all relevant security controls, but isn't the best choice for this specific scenario. A vulnerability scan will discover vulnerabilities on a system or network and a penetration test will scan a system or network and attempt to exploit vulnerabilities. However, vulnerability scans and penetration tests cannot verify a user has the appropriate privileges.

Chapter 9

Implementing Controls to Protect Assets

CompTIA Security+ objectives covered in this chapter:

1.2 Compare and contrast types of attacks.
- Social engineering (Tailgating)

1.6 Explain the impact associated with types of vulnerabilities.
- Vulnerable business processes, System sprawl/undocumented assets, Architecture/design weaknesses

2.1 Install and configure network components, both hardware- and software-based, to support organizational security.
- Load balancer (Scheduling [Affinity, Round-robin], Active-passive, Active-active, Virtual IPs)

2.2 Given a scenario, use appropriate software tools to assess the security posture of an organization.
- Backup utilities

2.3 Given a scenario, troubleshoot common security issues.
- Asset management

3.1 Explain use cases and purpose for frameworks, best practices and secure configuration guides.
- Defense-in-depth/layered security (Vendor diversity, Control diversity [Administrative, Technical], User training)

3.8 Explain how resiliency and automation strategies reduce risk.
- Distributive allocation, Redundancy, Fault tolerance, High availability, RAID

3.9 Explain the importance of physical security controls.
- Lighting, Signs, Fencing/gate/cage, Security guards, Alarms, Safe, Secure cabinets/enclosures, Protected distribution/Protected cabling, Airgap, Mantrap, Faraday cage, Lock

types, Biometrics, Barricades/bollards, Tokens/cards, Environmental controls (HVAC, Hot and cold aisles, Fire suppression), Cable locks, Cameras, Motion detection, Logs, Infrared detection, Key management

4.3   Given a scenario, implement identity and access management controls.
- Physical access control (Proximity cards, Smart cards)

5.2   Summarize business impact analysis concepts.
- RTO/RPO, MTBF, MTTR, Mission-essential functions, Identification of critical systems, Single point of failure, Impact (Life, Property, Safety, Finance, Reputation), Privacy impact assessment, Privacy threshold assessment

5.6   Explain disaster recovery and continuity of operation concepts.
- Recovery sites (Hot site, Warm site, Cold site), Order of restoration, Backup concepts (Differential, Incremental, Snapshots, Full), Geographic considerations (Off-site backups, Distance, Location selection, Legal implications, Data sovereignty), Continuity of operation planning (Exercises/tabletop, After-action reports, Failover, Alternate processing sites, Alternate business practices)

**

You can't eliminate risk to an organization's assets. However, you can reduce the impact of many threats by implementing security controls. It's common to implement several controls using a defense-in-depth strategy. Physical security controls help protect access to secure areas. Redundancy and fault-tolerance strategies help eliminate single points of failure for critical systems. Backups ensure that data remains available even after data is lost. More in-depth business continuity strategies help ensure mission-critical functions continue to operate even if a disaster destroys a primary business location. This chapter covers these concepts.

Implementing Defense in Depth

Defense in depth (also known as layered security) refers to the security practice of implementing several layers of protection. You can't simply take a single action, such as implementing a firewall or installing antivirus software, and consider yourself protected. You must implement security at several different layers. This way, if one layer fails, you still have additional layers to protect you.

If you drive your car to a local Walmart, put a five-dollar bill on the dash, and leave the keys in the car and the car running, there is a very good chance the car won't be there when you come out of the store. On the other hand, if you ensure nothing of value is visible from the windows, the car is locked, it has an alarm system, and it has stickers on the windows advertising the alarm system, it's less likely that someone will steal it. Not impossible, but less likely.

You've probably heard this as "there is no silver bullet." If you want to kill a werewolf, you can load your gun with a single silver bullet and it will find its mark. The truth is that there is no such thing as a silver bullet. (Of course, there is no such thing as a werewolf either.)

Applied to computers, it's important to implement security at every step, every phase, and every layer. Information technology (IT) professionals can never rest on their laurels with the thought they have done enough and no longer need to worry about security.

Control diversity is the use of different security control types, such as technical controls, administrative controls, and physical controls. For example, technical security controls such as firewalls, intrusion detection systems (IDSs), and proxy servers help protect a network. Physical security controls can provide extra protection for the server room or other areas where these devices are located. Administrative controls such as vulnerability assessments and penetration tests can help verify that these controls are working as expected.

Vendor diversity is the practice of implementing security controls from different vendors to increase security. As an example, Chapter 3, "Exploring Network Technologies and Tools," describes a demilitarized zone (DMZ). Many DMZs use two firewalls and vendor diversity dictates the use of firewalls from different vendors. For example, one firewall could be a Cisco firewall and the other one could be a Check Point firewall. If a vulnerability is discovered in one of these firewalls, an attacker might be able to exploit it. However, it's unlikely that both firewalls would develop a vulnerability at the same time.

User training also helps provide defense in depth. If users engage in risky behaviors, such as downloading and installing files from unknown sources or responding to phishing emails, they can give attackers a path into an organization's network. However, providing regular training to users on common threats, and emerging threats, helps them avoid these types of attacks.

> ### Remember this
>
> Layered security, or defense-in-depth practices, uses control diversity, implementing administrative, technical, and physical security controls. Vendor diversity utilizes controls from different vendors. User training informs users of threats, helping them avoid common attacks.

Comparing Physical Security Controls

A physical security control is something you can physically touch, such as a hardware lock, a fence, an identification badge, and a security camera. Physical security access controls attempt to control entry and exits, and organizations commonly implement different controls at different boundaries, such as the following:

- **Perimeter.** Military bases and many other organizations erect a fence around the entire perimeter of their land. They often post security guards at gates to control access. In some cases, organizations install barricades to block vehicles.
- **Buildings.** Buildings commonly have additional controls for both safety and security. For example, guards and locked doors restrict entry so only authorized personnel enter. Many buildings include lighting and video cameras to monitor the entrances and exits.
- **Secure work areas.** Some companies restrict access to specific work areas when employees perform classified or restricted access tasks. In some cases, an organization restricts access to all internal work areas. In other words, visitors can enter the lobby of a building, but they are not able to enter internal work areas without an escort.
- **Server and network rooms.** Servers and network devices such as routers and switches are normally stored in areas where only the appropriate IT personnel can access them. These spaces may be designated as server rooms or wiring closets. It's common for an organization to provide additional physical security for these rooms to prevent attackers from accessing the equipment. For example, locking a wiring closet prevents an attacker from installing illicit monitoring hardware, such as a protocol analyzer, to capture network traffic.
- **Hardware.** Additional physical security controls protect individual systems. For example, server rooms often have locking cabinets to protect servers and other equipment

installed in the equipment bays. Cable locks protect laptop computers, and smaller devices can be stored in safes.

- **Airgap.** An *airgap* is a physical security control that ensures that a computer or network is physically isolated from another computer or network. As an example, you can isolate a computer from a network by ensuring that it is not connected to any other system in the network. This lack of connectivity provides an airgap. This is often done to separate classified networks from unclassified networks.

Using Signs

A simple physical security control is a sign. For example, an "Authorized Personnel Only" sign will deter many people from entering a restricted area. Similarly, "No Trespassing" signs let people know they shouldn't enter. Of course, these signs won't deter everyone, so an organization typically uses additional physical security measures.

Comparing Door Lock Types

It's common to secure access to controlled areas of a building with door locks, and there are many different lock types. A door access system is one that only opens after some access control mechanism is used. Some common door access systems are cipher locks, proximity cards, and biometrics.

When implementing door access systems, it's important to limit the number of entry and exit points. As an example, if a data center has only one entrance and exit, it is much easier to monitor this single access point. You can control it with door locks, video surveillance, and guards. On the other hand, if the data center has two entry/exit points, you need another set of controls to control access in both places.

Another important consideration with door access systems is related to personnel safety and fire. In the event of a fire, door access systems should allow personnel to exit the building without any form of authentication.

> **Remember this**
>
> In the event of a fire, door access systems should allow personnel to exit the building without any form of authentication. Access points to data centers and server rooms should be limited to a single entrance and exit whenever possible.

Securing Door Access with Cipher Locks

Cipher locks often have four or five buttons labeled with numbers. Employees press the numbers in a certain order to unlock the door. For example, the cipher code could be 1, 3, 2, 4. Users enter the code in the correct order to gain access. Cipher locks can be electronic or manual. An electronic cipher lock automatically unlocks the door after you enter the correct code into the keypad. A manual cipher lock requires the user to turn a handle after entering the code.

To add complexity and reduce brute force attacks, many manual cipher locks include a code that requires two numbers entered at the same time. Instead of just 1, 3, 2, 4, the code could be 1/3 (entered at the same time), then 2, 4, 5.

One challenge with cipher locks is that they don't identify the users. Further, uneducated users can give out the cipher code to unauthorized individuals without understanding the risks. Shoulder surfers might attempt to discover the code by watching users as they enter. Security awareness training can help reduce these risks.

Securing Door Access with Cards

It's also possible to secure access to areas with proximity cards or smart cards. **Proximity cards** are small credit card-sized cards that activate when they are in close proximity to a card reader. Many organizations use these for access points, such as the entry to a building or the entry to a controlled area within a building. The door uses an electronic lock that only unlocks when the user passes the proximity card in front of a card reader.

Similarly, it's possible to use smart cards or physical tokens (described in Chapter 2, "Understanding Identity and Access Management") for door access. In some scenarios, the smart cards include proximity card electronics. In other scenarios, users must insert the smart card into a smart card reader to gain access.

You've probably seen proximity card readers implemented with credit card readers. Many self-serve gasoline stations and fast-food restaurants use them. Instead of swiping your credit card through a magnetic reader, you simply pass it in front of the reader (in close proximity to the reader), and the reader extracts your credit card's information.

These are becoming popular elsewhere, too. For example, if you stay at a Walt Disney World property, they can issue you a bracelet that includes the functionality of a proximity card. To enter your hotel room, you wave your bracelet in front of the door. If you want to buy food or souvenirs or pay for almost anything, you can simply wave your bracelet in front of a card reader to complete your purchase.

The card (and bracelet) doesn't require its own power source. Instead, the electronics in the card include a capacitor and a coil that can accept a charge from the proximity card reader. When you pass the card close to the reader, the reader excites the coil and stores a charge in the capacitor. Once charged, the card transmits the information to the reader using a radio frequency.

When used with door access systems, the proximity card can send just a simple signal to unlock the door. Some systems include details on the user and record when the user enters or exits the area. When used this way, it's common to combine the proximity card reader with a keypad requiring the user to enter a personal identification number (PIN). This identifies and authenticates the user with multifactor authentication. The user has something (the proximity card) and knows something (a PIN).

Many organizations use proximity cards with turnstiles to provide access for a single person at a time. These are the same type of turnstiles used as entry gates in subways, stadiums, and amusement parks.

> ### Remember this
> Proximity cards are credit card-sized access cards. Users pass the card near a proximity card reader and the card reader then reads data on the card. Some access control points use proximity cards with PINs for authentication.

Securing Door Access with Biometrics

It's also possible to use biometric methods as an access control system. One of the benefits is that some biometric methods provide both identification and authentication. When connected to a back-end database, these systems can easily record the activity, such as who entered the area and when.

For example, you can install a retina scanner at the entrance to a secure server room. When individuals want to enter, the biometric scanner identifies and authenticates them. It's important to ensure you use an accurate biometric system and configure it to use a low false acceptance rate, as described in Chapter 2. Otherwise, it might falsely identify unauthorized individuals and grant them access.

> **Remember this**
>
> Door access systems include cipher locks, proximity cards, and biometrics. Cipher locks do not identify users. Proximity cards can identify and authenticate users when combined with a PIN. Biometrics can also identify and authenticate users.

Tailgating

Chapter 6, "Comparing Threats, Vulnerabilities, and Common Attacks," discusses several types of social engineering attacks and tailgating is another one. *Tailgating* (also called piggybacking) occurs when one user follows closely behind another user without using credentials. For example, if Lisa opens a door with her proximity card and Bart follows closely behind her without using a proximity card, Bart is tailgating. If authorized users routinely do this, it indicates the environment is susceptible to a social engineering attack where an unauthorized user follows closely behind an authorized user.

As an example, an organization hired a security company to perform a vulnerability assessment. The company sent one of its top security professionals (who happened to be an attractive woman) to see if she could get into the building. She saw that employees were using proximity cards to get into the building, but she didn't have one. Instead, she loaded herself up with a book bag and a laptop—ensuring her hands weren't free. She timed her approach carefully and followed closely behind an employee with a proximity card. She flashed a friendly smile, and sure enough, the employee held the door open for her.

Most of us learn to be polite and courteous and social engineers take advantage of this. It's polite to hold a door open for people who have their hands full. In contrast, it's rude to slam the door in the face of someone following behind us. However, most users don't want to help criminals. Security awareness programs and training help users understand how criminals use tactics such as tailgating. Educated users are less likely to be tricked, even by a friendly smile from an attractive woman.

High-traffic areas are most susceptible to tailgating attacks. Security guards can be an effective preventive measure at access points, but they need to be vigilant to ensure that tailgating does not occur. The best solution is a mantrap.

Preventing Tailgating with Mantraps

A *mantrap* is a physical security mechanism designed to control access to a secure area through a buffer zone. Personnel use something like a proximity card to gain access, and the mantrap allows one person, and only one person, to pass through. Because they only allow one person through at a time, mantraps prevent tailgating. Mantraps get their name due to their ability to lock a person between two areas, such as an open access area and a secure access area, but not all of them are that sophisticated.

An example of a simple mantrap is a turnstile similar to what you see in many public transport systems. Even if you've never ridden the subway in one of many U.S. cities or the Tube in London, you've probably seen turnstiles in movies such as *While You Were Sleeping*. When customers present a token, the turnstile unlocks and allows a single person through at a time. Similarly, users unlock the turnstile mantrap with something like a proximity card.

A sophisticated mantrap is a room, or even a building, that creates a large buffer area between the secure area and the unsecured area. Access through the entry door and the exit door is tightly controlled, either with guards or with an access card such as a proximity card.

It's also possible to require identification and authentication before allowing passage through a mantrap. For example, a retina scanner can identify individuals and restrict access to only authorized individuals. Similarly, some card reader systems support the use of unique PINs assigned to the user. Users present their card and enter their PIN to gain access before the mantrap opens.

> ### Remember this
>
> Tailgating is a social engineering tactic that occurs when one user follows closely behind another user without using credentials. Mantraps allow only a single person to pass at a time. Sophisticated mantraps can identify and authenticate individuals before allowing access.

Increasing Physical Security with Guards

Many organizations use security guards to control access to buildings and secure spaces. If employees have ID badges, guards can check these badges prior to granting the employees access. Even if ID badges aren't used, guards can still verify people's identity using other identification. Similarly, the security guards can restrict access by checking people's identity against a preapproved access control list. In some cases, guards record all access in an access log.

Security guards can also take a less-active role to deter security incidents. For example, a security guard can deter tailgating incidents by observing personnel when they use their proximity card to gain access to a secure area.

Monitoring Areas with Cameras

Organizations are increasingly using security cameras in the workplace and surrounding areas for video surveillance. This includes areas outside of a building, such as a parking lot, and all building entrances and exits. Additionally, many organizations use cameras to monitor internal entrances of high-security areas, such as the entrance of a data center or server room.

Cameras are connected to a closed-circuit television (CCTV) system, which transmits signals from video cameras to monitors that are similar to TVs. In addition to providing security, CCTV can also enhance safety by deterring threats.

Organizations often use video cameras within a work environment to protect employees and enhance security in the workplace. In addition to live monitoring, most systems include a recording element, and they can verify if someone is stealing the company's assets. By recording activity, videos can be played back later for investigation and even prosecution.

Video surveillance provides the most reliable proof of a person's location and activity.

Access logs provide a record, but it's possible to circumvent the security of an access log. For example, if Bart used your proximity card to gain access to a secure space, the log will indicate you entered, not Bart. In contrast, if the video shows that Bart entered the room at a certain time of day, it's not easy for Bart to refute the video.

> ### Remember this
>
> Video surveillance provides reliable proof of a person's location and activity. It can identify who enters and exits secure areas and can record theft of assets.

When using video surveillance in a work environment, it's important to respect privacy and to be aware of privacy laws. Some things to consider are:

- **Only record activity in public areas.** People have a reasonable expectation of privacy in certain areas, such as locker rooms and restrooms, and it is often illegal to record activity in these areas.
- **Notify employees of the surveillance.** If employees aren't notified of the surveillance, legal issues related to the video surveillance can arise. This is especially true if the recordings are used when taking legal and/or disciplinary actions against an employee.
- **Do not record audio.** Recording audio is illegal in many jurisdictions, without the express consent of all parties being recorded. Many companies won't even sell surveillance cameras that record audio.

Fencing, Lighting, and Alarms

Fences provide a barrier around a property and deter people from entering. When using a fence, it's common to control access to the area via specific gates. Guards often monitor these gates and ensure only authorized individuals can enter. When additional security is required, organizations sometimes configure dual gates, allowing access into one area where credentials are checked before allowing full access. This effectively creates a cage preventing full access, but also prevents unauthorized individuals from escaping.

Installing lights at all the entrances to a building can deter attackers from trying to break in. Similarly, lighting at the entrances of any internal restricted areas can deter people from trying to enter. Many organizations use a combination of automation, light dimmers, and motion sensors to save on electricity costs without sacrificing security. The lights automatically turn on at dusk, but in a low, dimmed mode. When the motion sensors detect any movement, the lights turn on at full capacity. They automatically turn off at dawn.

It's important to protect the lights. For example, if an attacker can remove the light bulbs, it defeats the control. Either place the lights high enough so that they can't be easily reached, or protect them with a metal cage.

Alarms provide an additional physical security protection. This includes alarms that detect fire and alarms that detect unauthorized access. Fire alarms detect smoke and/or heat and trigger fire suppression systems. Burglary prevention systems monitor entry points such as doors and windows, detecting when someone opens them.

You can also combine motion detection systems with burglary prevention systems. They detect movement within monitored areas and trigger alarms. Obviously, you wouldn't have motion detection systems turned on all the time. Instead, you'd turn them on when people will not be working in the area, such as during nights or weekends.

You might have noticed that fencing, lighting, and alarms can all be combined with motion detection. At the most basic level, motion detection methods detect moving objects. Many motion detectors use microwave technologies to detect movement. This is like the technology used in some police radar speed guns.

A more advanced method is infrared detection. Infrared detectors sense infrared radiation, sometimes called infrared light, which effectively sees a difference between objects of different temperatures. As an example, a person is much warmer than objects in a room and easily stands out using an infrared detector. This can help eliminate false alarms by sensing more than just motion, but motion from objects of different temperatures.

> ### Remember this
>
> Fencing, lighting, and alarms all provide physical security. They are often used together to provided layered security. Motion detection methods are also used with these methods to increase their effectiveness. Infrared detectors detect movement by objects of different temperatures.

Securing Access with Barricades

In some situations, fencing isn't enough to deter potential attackers. To augment fences and other physical security measures, organizations erect stronger barricades. As an example, military bases often erect strong, zigzag barricades that require vehicles to slow down to navigate through them. This prevents attackers from trying to ram through the gates.

Businesses and organizations need to present an inviting appearance, so they can't use such drastic barricades. However, they often use *bollards*, which are short vertical posts, composed of reinforced concrete and/or steel. They often place the bollards in front of entrances about three or four feet apart. They typically paint them with colors that match their store. You've probably walked through a set of bollards multiple times without giving them a second thought. However, thieves who are contemplating driving a car or truck through the entrance see them.

Many thieves have driven vehicles right through the front of buildings, and then proceeded to steal everything in sight. Depending on the strength of the walls, criminals might even be able to drive through a wall with a truck. Strategically placed bollards will prevent these types of attacks.

> ### Remember this
>
> Barricades provide stronger barriers than fences and attempt to deter attackers. Bollards are effective barricades that can block vehicles.

Using Hardware Locks

You can implement simple physical security measures to prevent access to secure areas. For example, you can use hardware locks—similar to what you use to secure your home—to secure buildings as well as rooms within buildings. Companies that don't have the resources to employ advanced security systems often use these types of hardware locks.

Instead of allowing free access to wiring closets or small server rooms, small organizations use these types of locks to restrict access. Although these locks aren't as sophisticated as the ones used by large organizations, they are much better than leaving the rooms open and the equipment exposed.

Key management is an important concept to consider when using hardware locks. Proper key management ensures that only authorized personnel can access the physical keys. This might be done by locking keys within a safe or locking cabinet.

Securing Mobile Computers with Cable Locks

Cable locks are a great theft deterrent for mobile computers, and even many desktop computers at work. Computer cable locks work similar to how a bicycle cable lock works. However, instead of securing a bicycle to a bike rack or post, a computer cable lock secures a computer to a piece of furniture.

The user wraps the cable around a desk, table, or something heavy, and then plugs it into an opening in the laptop specifically created for this purpose. Most cable locks have a four-digit combo. If you (or anyone) remove the cable lock without the combo, it will likely destroy the laptop.

Another common use of cable locks is for computers in unsupervised labs. For example, you can secure laptop or desktop computers with cable locks in a training lab. This allows you to leave the room open so that students can use the equipment, but the cable locks prevent thieves from stealing the equipment.

Securing Servers with Locking Cabinets

Larger companies often have large server rooms with advanced security to restrict access. Additionally, within the server room, administrators use locking cabinets or enclosures to secure equipment mounted within the bays. An equipment bay is about the size of a large refrigerator and can hold servers, routers, and other IT equipment. These bays have doors in the back and many have doors in the front, too. Administrators lock these doors to prevent unauthorized personnel from accessing the equipment.

Offices often have file cabinets that lock, too, so it's important to pay attention to the context when referring to locking cabinets. For example, if you want to secure equipment within a server room, a locking cabinet is one of many physical security controls you can use. If you want to secure unattended smartphones in an office space, you can also use a locking cabinet, but this is an office file cabinet that locks.

> ### Remember this
>
> Cable locks are effective threat deterrents for small equipment such as laptops and some workstations. When used properly, they prevent losses due to theft of small equipment. Locking cabinets in server rooms provide an added physical security measure. A locked cabinet prevents unauthorized access to equipment mounted in server bays.

Securing Small Devices with a Safe

Locking file cabinets or safes used in many offices help prevent the theft of smaller devices. For example, you can store smaller devices such as external USB drives or USB flash drives in an office safe or locking cabinet when they aren't in use. Depending on the size of the office safe and office cabinet, you might also be able to secure laptops within them.

Asset Management

Asset management is the process of tracking valuable assets throughout their life cycles. For example, organizations commonly implement processes to track hardware such as servers, desktop computers, laptop computers, routers, and switches. An effective asset management system can help reduce several vulnerabilities:

- **Architecture and design weaknesses.** Asset management helps reduce architecture and design weaknesses by ensuring that purchases go through an approval process. The approval process does more than just compare costs. It also evaluates the purchase to ensure it fits in the overall network architecture. Unapproved assets often weaken security by adding in additional resources that aren't managed.
- **System sprawl and undocumented assets.** *System sprawl* occurs when an organization has more systems than it needs, and systems it owns are underutilized. Asset management begins before the hardware is purchased and helps prevent system sprawl by evaluating the purchase. Additionally, after the purchase is completed, asset management processes ensure hardware is added into the asset management tracking system. This ensures that the assets are managed and tracked from cradle to grave.

Many organizations use automated methods for inventory control. For example, radio-frequency identification (RFID) methods can track the movement of devices. These are the same types of devices used in stores to prevent shoplifting. If someone exits without paying, the RFID device transmits when the shoplifter gets close to the exit door and sounds an alarm. Organizations won't necessarily have an alarm, but they can track the movement of devices.

Mobile devices are easy to lose track of, so organizations often use asset-tracking methods to reduce losses. For example, when a user is issued a mobile device, asset-tracking methods record it. Similarly, if the user leaves the company, asset-tracking methods ensure the user returns the device.

Implementing Environmental Controls

Although environmental controls might not seem security related, they directly contribute to the availability of systems. This includes ensuring temperature and humidity controls are operating properly, fire suppression systems are in place, and proper procedures are used when running cables.

Heating, Ventilation, and Air Conditioning

Heating, ventilation, and air conditioning (**HVAC**) systems are important physical security controls that enhance the availability of systems. Quite simply, computers and other electronic equipment can't handle drastic changes in temperatures, especially hot temperatures. If systems overheat, the chips can actually burn themselves out.

The cooling capacity of HVAC systems is measured as tonnage. This has nothing to do with weight, but instead refers to cooling capacity. One ton of cooling equals 12,000 British thermal units per hour (Btu/hour), and typical home HVAC systems are three-ton units. Higher-tonnage HVAC systems can cool larger areas or areas with equipment generating more heat.

The amount of air conditioning needed to cool a massive data center is much greater than you need to cool your home, primarily because of all the heat generated by the equipment. If your home air conditioner fails in the middle of summer, you might be a little uncomfortable for a while, but if the data center HVAC system fails, it can result in loss of availability and a substantial loss of money.

I worked in several environments where we had a policy of shutting down all electronics when the room temperature reached a certain threshold. When we didn't follow the policy, the systems often developed problems due to the heat and ended up out of commission for a lot longer than the AC.

Most servers aren't in cases like a typical desktop computer. Instead, they are housed in rack-mountable cases. These rack-mountable servers are installed in equipment cabinets (also called racks or bays) about the size of tall refrigerators. A large data center will have multiple cabinets lined up beside each other in multiple rows.

These cabinets usually have locking doors in the front and rear for physical security. The doors are perforated with cold air coming in the front, passing over and through the servers to keep them cool, and warmer air exiting out the rear. Additionally, a server room has raised flooring with air conditioning pumping through the space under the raised floor.

> **Remember this**
>
> Higher-tonnage HVAC systems provide more cooling capacity. This keeps server rooms at lower operating temperatures and results in fewer failures.

Hot and Cold Aisles

Hot and cold aisles help regulate the cooling in data centers with multiple rows of cabinets. The back of all the cabinets in one row faces the back of all the cabinets in an adjacent row. Because the hot air exits out the back of the cabinet, the aisle with the backs facing each other is the hot aisle.

Similarly, the front of the cabinets in one row is facing the front of the cabinets in the adjacent row. Cool air is pumped through the floor to this cool aisle using perforated floor tiles in the raised flooring. This is the cold aisle. In some designs, cool air is also pumped through the base of the cabinets. This depends on the design of the cabinets and the needs of the equipment.

Consider what happens if all the cabinets had their front facing the same way without a hot/cold aisle design. The hot air pumping out the back of one row of cabinets would be sent to the front of the cabinets behind them. The front row would have very cold air coming in the front, but other rows would have warmer air coming in the front.

Of course, an HVAC also includes a thermostat as a temperature control and additional humidity controls. The thermostat ensures that the air temperature is controlled and maintained. Similarly, humidity controls ensure that the humidity is controlled. High humidity can cause condensation on the equipment, which causes water damage. Low humidity allows a higher incidence of electrostatic discharge (ESD).

HVAC and Fire

HVAC systems are often integrated with fire alarm systems to help prevent a fire from spreading. One of the core elements of a fire is oxygen. If the HVAC system continues to operate normally while a fire is active, it continues to pump oxygen, which feeds the fire. When the HVAC system is integrated with the fire alarm system, it controls the airflow to help prevent the rapid spread of the fire. Many current HVAC systems have dampers that can control airflow to specific areas of a building. Other HVAC systems automatically turn off when fire suppression systems detect a fire.

> ### Remember this
> HVAC systems increase availability by controlling temperature and humidity. Temperature controls help ensure a relatively constant temperature. Humidity controls reduce the potential for damage from electrostatic discharge and damage from condensation. HVAC systems should be integrated with the fire alarm systems and either have dampers or the ability to be turned off in the event of a fire.

Fire Suppression

You can fight fires with individual fire extinguishers, with fixed systems, or both. Most organizations included fixed systems to control fires and place portable fire extinguishers in different areas around the organization. A fixed system can detect a fire and automatically activate to extinguish the fire. Individuals use portable fire extinguishers to extinguish or suppress small fires.

The different components of a fire are heat, oxygen, fuel, and a chain reaction creating the fire. Fire suppression methods attempt to remove or disrupt one of these elements to extinguish a fire. You can extinguish a fire using one of these methods:

- **Remove the heat.** Fire extinguishers commonly use chemical agents or water to remove the heat. However, water should never be used on an electrical fire.
- **Remove the oxygen.** Many methods use a gas, such as carbon dioxide (CO_2) to displace the oxygen. This is a common method of fighting electrical fires because CO_2 and similar gasses are harmless to electrical equipment.
- **Remove the fuel.** Fire-suppression methods don't typically fight a fire this way, but of course, the fire will go out once all the material is burned.
- **Disrupt the chain reaction.** Some chemicals can disrupt the chain reaction of fires to stop them.

When implementing any fire suppression system, it's important to consider the safety of personnel. As an example, if a fire suppression system uses a gas such as carbon dioxide (CO_2) to displace the oxygen, it's important to ensure that personnel can get out before the oxygen is displaced.

Similarly, consider an exit door secured with a proximity card. Normally, employees open the door with the proximity card and the system records their exit. What happens if a fire starts and power to the building is lost? The proximity card reader won't work, and if the door can't open, employees will be trapped. It's important to ensure that an alternative allows personnel to exit even if the proximity card reader loses power. Of course, this might introduce a vulnerability to consider. You don't want an attacker to access a secure data center just by removing power to the proximity reader.

Environmental Monitoring

Environmental monitoring includes temperature and humidity controls. From a very basic perspective, an HVAC system monitors the current temperature and humidity and makes adjustments as necessary to keep the temperature and humidity constant.

Large-scale data centers often have sophisticated logging capabilities for environmental monitoring. The HVAC system still attempts to keep the temperature and humidity constant. However, the logs record the actual temperature and humidity at different times during the day. This allows administrators to review the performance of the HVAC system, to see if it is able to keep up with the demands within the data center.

Shielding

Shielding helps prevent electromagnetic interference (EMI) and radio frequency interference (RFI) from interfering with normal signal transmissions. It also protects against unwanted emissions and helps prevent an attacker from capturing network traffic.

Although you might see EMI and RFI in the same category as EMI/RFI, they are different. EMI comes from different types of motors, power lines, and even fluorescent lights. RFI comes from radio frequency (RF) sources such as AM or FM transmitters. However, shielding used to block interference from both EMI and RFI sources is often referred to as simply EMI shielding.

Attackers often use different types of eavesdropping methods to capture network traffic. If the data is emanating outside of the wire or outside of an enclosure, attackers may be able to capture and read the data. EMI shielding fulfills the dual purpose of keeping interference out and preventing attackers from capturing network traffic.

Protected Cabling

Twisted-pair cable, such as CAT5e and CAT6 cable, comes in both shielded twisted-pair (STP) and unshielded twisted-pair (UTP) versions. The shielding helps prevent an attacker from capturing network traffic and helps block interference from corrupting the data.

When data travels along a copper wire (such as twisted-pair), it creates an induction field around the wire. If you have the right tools, you can simply place the tool around the wire and capture the signal. The shielding in STP cable blocks this. Fiber-optic cable is not susceptible to this type of attack. Signals travel along a fiber-optic cable as light pulses, and they do not create an induction field.

Protected Distribution of Cabling

Physical security includes planning where you route cables and how you route them. Skilled network administrators can cut a twisted-pair cable, attach an RJ-45 connector to each end, and connect them back together with an adapter in less than 5 minutes. Experienced fiber-optic cable technicians can do the same thing with a fiber-optic cable within 10 minutes.

If an attacker did this, he could connect the cut cable with a hub, and then capture all the traffic going through the hub with a protocol analyzer. This represents a significant risk.

One method of reducing this risk is to run cables through cable troughs or wiring ducts. A cable trough is a long metal container, typically about 4 inches wide by 4 inches high. If you run data cables through the cable trough, they aren't as accessible to potential attackers. In contrast, many organizations simply run the cable through a false ceiling or a raised floor.

In addition to considering physical security, it's important to keep the cables away from EMI sources. As an example, if technicians run cables over or through fluorescent lighting fixtures, the EMI from the lights can disrupt the signals on the cables. The result is intermittent connectivity for users.

Faraday Cage

A *Faraday cage* is typically a room that prevents signals from emanating beyond the room. It includes electrical features that cause RF signals that reach the boundary of the room to be reflected back, preventing signal emanation outside the Faraday cage. A Faraday cage can also be a small enclosure.

In addition to preventing signals from emanating outside the room, a Faraday cage also provides shielding to prevent outside interference such as EMI and RFI from entering the room.

At a very basic level, some elevators act as a Faraday cage (though I seriously doubt the designers were striving to do so). You might have stepped into an elevator and found that your cell phone stopped receiving and transmitting signals. The metal shielding around the elevator prevents signals from emanating out or signals such as the cell phone tower signal from entering the elevator.

On a smaller scale, electrical devices such as computers include shielding to prevent signals from emanating out and block interference from getting in.

> ### Remember this
>
> EMI shielding prevents outside interference sources from corrupting data and prevents data from emanating outside the cable. Cable troughs protect cables distributed throughout a building in metal containers. A Faraday cage prevents signals from emanating beyond the cage.

Adding Redundancy and Fault Tolerance

One of the constants with computers, subsystems, and networks is that they will fail. It's one of the few things you can count on. It's not a matter of *if* they will fail, but *when*. However, by adding redundancy into your systems and networks, you can increase the reliability of your systems even when they fail. By increasing reliability, you increase one of the core security goals: availability.

Redundancy adds duplication to critical system components and networks and provides *fault tolerance*. If a critical component has a fault, the duplication provided by the redundancy allows the service to continue as if a fault never occurred. In other words, a system with fault tolerance can suffer a fault, but it can tolerate it and continue to operate. Organizations often add redundancies to eliminate single points of failure.

You can add redundancies at multiple levels:
- Disk redundancies using RAID
- Server redundancies by adding failover clusters
- Power redundancies by adding generators or an UPS
- Site redundancies by adding hot, cold, or warm sites

Single Point of Failure

A *single point of failure* is a component within a system that can cause the entire system to fail if the component fails. When designing redundancies, an organization will examine different components to determine if they are a single point of failure. If so, they take steps to provide a redundancy or fault-tolerance capability. The goal is to increase reliability and availability of the systems.

Some examples of single points of failure include:

- **Disk.** If a server uses a single drive, the system will crash if the single drive fails. Redundant array of inexpensive disks (RAID) provides fault tolerance for hard drives and is a relatively inexpensive method of adding fault tolerance to a system.
- **Server.** If a server provides a critical service and its failure halts the service, it is a single point of failure. Failover clusters (discussed later in this chapter) provide fault tolerance for critical servers.
- **Power.** If an organization only has one source of power for critical systems, the power is a single point of failure. However, elements such as uninterruptible power supplies (UPSs) and power generators provide fault tolerance for power outages.

Although IT personnel recognize the risks with single points of failure, they often overlook them until a disaster occurs. However, tools such as business continuity plans (covered later in this chapter) help an organization identify critical services and address single points of failure.

Remember this

A single point of failure is any component whose failure results in the failure of an entire system. Elements such as RAID, failover clustering, UPSs, and generators remove many single points of failure. RAID is an inexpensive method used to add fault tolerance and increase availability.

Disk Redundancies

Any system has four primary resources: processor, memory, disk, and the network interface. Of these, the disk is the slowest and most susceptible to failure. Because of this, administrators often upgrade disk subsystems to improve their performance and redundancy.

Redundant array of inexpensive disks (**RAID**) subsystems provide fault tolerance for disks and increase the system availability. Even if a disk fails, most RAID subsystems can tolerate the failure and the system will continue to operate. RAID systems are becoming much more affordable as the price of drives steadily falls and disk capacity steadily increases. While it's expected that you are familiar with RAID subsystems, the following sections provide a short summary to remind you of the important details.

RAID-0

RAID-0 (striping) is somewhat of a misnomer because it doesn't provide any redundancy or fault tolerance. It includes two or more physical disks. Files stored on a RAID-0 array are spread across each of the disks.

The benefit of a RAID-0 is increased read and write performance. Because a file is spread across multiple physical disks, the different parts of the file can be read from or written to each of the disks at the same time. If you have three 500 GB drives used in a RAID-0, you have 1,500 GB (1.5 TB) of storage space.

RAID-1

RAID-1 (mirroring) uses two disks. Data written to one disk is also written to the other disk. If one of the disks fails, the other disk still has all the data, so the system can continue to operate without any data loss. With this in mind, if you mirror all the drives in a system, you can actually lose half of the drives and continue to operate.

You can add an additional disk controller to a RAID-1 configuration to remove the disk controller as a single point of failure. In other words, each of the disks also has its own disk controller. Adding a second disk controller to a mirror is called disk duplexing.

If you have two 500 GB drives used in a RAID-1, you have 500 GB of storage space. The other 500 GB of storage space is dedicated to the fault-tolerant, mirrored volume.

RAID-2, RAID 3, and RAID-4 are rarely used.

RAID-5 and RAID-6

A RAID-5 is three or more disks that are striped together similar to RAID-0. However, the equivalent of one drive includes parity information. This parity information is striped across each of the drives in a RAID-5 and is used for fault tolerance. If one of the drives fails, the system can read the information on the remaining drives and determine what the actual data should be. If two of the drives fail in a RAID-5, the data is lost.

RAID-6 is an extension of RAID-5, and it includes an additional parity block. A huge benefit is that the RAID-6 disk subsystem will continue to operate even if two disk drives fail. RAID-6 requires a minimum of four disks.

> ### Remember this
>
> RAID subsystems, such as RAID-1, RAID-5, and RAID-6, provide fault tolerance and increased data availability. RAID-5 can survive the failure of one disk. RAID-6 can survive the failure of two disks.

RAID-10

A RAID-10 configuration combines the features of mirroring (RAID-1) and striping (RAID-0). RAID-10 is sometimes called RAID 1+0. A variation is RAID-01 or RAID 0+1 that also combines the features of mirroring and striping but implements the drives a little differently.

The minimum number of drives in a RAID-10 is four. When adding more drives, you add two (or multiples of two such as four, six, and so on). If you have four 500 GB drives used in a RAID-10, you have 1 TB of usable storage.

Server Redundancy and High Availability

High availability refers to a system or service that needs to remain operational with almost zero downtime. Utilizing different redundancy and fault-tolerance methods, it's possible to achieve 99.999 percent uptime, commonly called five nines. This equates to less than 6 minutes of downtime a year: 60 minutes × 24 hours × 365 days × .00001 = 5.256 minutes. Failover clusters are a key component used to achieve five nines.

Although five nines is achievable, it's expensive. However, if the potential cost of an outage is high, the high cost of the redundant technologies is justified. For example, some web sites generate a significant amount of revenue, and every minute a web site is unavailable represents lost money. High-capacity failover clusters ensure the service is always available even if a server fails.

Distributive allocation is another option to provide both high availability and scalability, though it is typically used primarily in scientific applications. In a distributed application model, multiple computers (often called nodes) are configured to work together to solve complex problems. These computers are configured within a local network. A central processor divides the complex problem into smaller tasks. It then coordinates tasking of the individual nodes and collecting the results. If any single nodes fail, the central processor doesn't task it anymore, but overall processing continues, providing high availability. This also provides high scalability because it is relatively easy to add additional nodes and task them when they come online.

Failover Clusters for High Availability

The primary purpose of a failover cluster is to provide high availability for a service offered by a server. Failover clusters use two or more servers in a cluster configuration, and the servers are referred to as nodes. At least one server or node is active and at least one is inactive. If an active node fails, the inactive node can take over the load without interruption to clients.

Consider Figure 9.1, which shows a two-node active-passive failover cluster. Both nodes are individual servers, and they both have access to external data storage used by the active server. Additionally, the two nodes have a monitoring connection to each other used to check the health or heartbeat of each other.

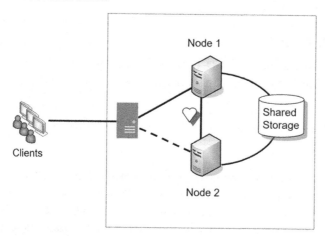

Figure 9.1: Failover cluster

Imagine that Node 1 is the active node. When any of the clients connect, the cluster software (installed on both nodes) ensures that the clients connect to the active node. If Node 1 fails, Node 2 senses the failure through the heartbeat connection and configures itself as the active node. Because both nodes have access to the shared storage, there is no loss of data for the client. Clients may notice a momentary hiccup or pause, but the service continues.

You might notice that the shared storage in Figure 9.1 represents a single point of failure. It's not uncommon for this to be a robust hardware RAID-10. This ensures that even if a hard drive in the shared storage fails, the service will continue. Additionally, if both nodes are plugged into the same power grid, the power represents a single point of failure. They can each be protected with a separate UPS, and use a separate power grid.

It's also possible to configure the cluster as an active-active cluster. Instead of one server being passive, the cluster balances the load between both servers.

Cluster configurations can include many more nodes than just two. However, nodes need to have close to identical hardware and are often quite expensive, but if a company truly needs to achieve 99.999 percent uptime, it's worth the expense.

Load Balancers for High Availability

A **load balancer** can optimize and distribute data loads across multiple computers or multiple networks. For example, if an organization hosts a popular web site, it can use multiple servers hosting the same web site in a web farm. Load-balancing software distributes traffic equally among all the servers in the web farm, typically located in a DMZ.

The term load balancer makes it sound like it's a piece of hardware, but a load balancer can be hardware or software. A hardware-based load balancer accepts traffic and directs it to servers based on factors such as processor utilization and the number of current connections to the server. A software-based load balancer uses software running on each of the servers in the load-balanced cluster to balance the load.

Load balancing primarily provides scalability, but it also contributes to high availability. Scalability refers to the ability of a service to serve more clients without any decrease in performance. Availability ensures that systems are up and operational when needed. By spreading the load among multiple systems, it ensures that individual systems are not overloaded, increasing overall availability.

Consider a web server that can serve 100 clients per minute, but if more than 100 clients connect at a time, performance degrades. You need to either scale up or scale out to serve more clients. You scale the server up by adding additional resources, such as processors and memory, and you scale out by adding additional servers in a load balancer.

Figure 9.2 shows an example of a load balancer with multiple web servers configured in a web farm. Each web server includes the same web application. A load balancer uses a scheduling technique to determine where to send new requests. Some load balancers simply send new requests to the servers in a **round-robin** fashion. The load balancer sends the first request to Server 1, the second request to Server 2, and so on. Other load balancers automatically detect the load on individual servers and send new clients to the least used server.

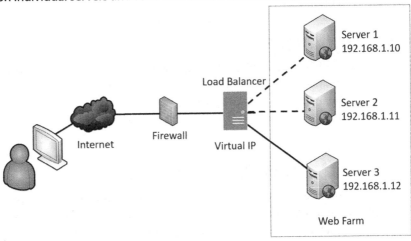

Figure 9.2: Load balancing

Some load balancers use source address *affinity* to direct the requests. Source affinity sends requests to the same server based on the requestor's IP address. As an example, imagine that Homer sends a request to retrieve a web page. The load balancer records his IP address and sends his request to Server 3. When he sends another request, the load balancer identifies his IP address and sends his request to Server 3 again. Source affinity effectively sticks users to a specific server for the duration of their sessions.

A software-based load balancer uses a virtual IP. For example, imagine the IP address of the web site is 72.52.206.134. This IP address isn't assigned to a specific server. Instead, clients send requests to this IP address and the load-balancing software redirects the request to one of the three servers in the web farm using their private IP addresses. In this scenario, the actual IP address is referred to as a virtual IP.

An added benefit of many load balancers is that they can detect when a server fails. If a server stops responding, the load-balancing software no longer sends clients to this server. This contributes to overall high availability for the load balancer.

> ### Remember this
>
> Failover clusters are one method of server redundancy and they provide high availability for servers. They can remove a server as a single point of failure. Load balancing increases the overall processing power of a service by sharing the load among multiple servers. Configurations can be active-passive, or active-active. Scheduling methods include round-robin and source IP address affinity. Source IP address affinity scheduling ensures clients are redirected to the same server for an entire session.

Clustering Versus Load Balancing

It's worth mentioning that CompTIA has grouped both clustering and load balancing into the same category of load balancing in the objectives. Many IT professionals do the same thing, though technically they are different concepts. In general, failover clusters are commonly used for applications such as database applications. Load balancers are often used for services, such as web servers in a web farm.

Power Redundancies

Power is a critical utility to consider when reviewing redundancies. For mission-critical systems, you can use uninterruptible power supplies and generators to provide both fault tolerance and high availability. An UPS provides fault tolerance for power and can protect against power fluctuations. It provides short-term power. Generators provide long-term power in extended outages.

Protecting Data with Backups

Backups are copies of data created to ensure that if the original data is lost or corrupted, it can be restored. Maybe I should restate that. Backups are copies of data created to ensure that *when* the original data is lost or corrupted, it can be restored. The truth is, if you work with computers long enough, you will lose data. The difference between a major catastrophe and a minor inconvenience is the existence of a usable backup.

A Backup Horror Story

A friend of mine was a consultant for small businesses and was once hired to help a small business owner recover some lost data. The owner had been growing his business for about five years and had just about everything related to his business (client lists, billing information, proposals, agreements, and more) on one system. The system crashed.

The consultant tried to restore information from the disk but wasn't successful. The business owner panicked, knowing he simply needed the information. If he couldn't get the data back, his business might fail.

Although it's expensive, it is possible to have a clean-room facility take a hard drive apart and read the data at the bit level to restore at least some of the data. At this point, the owner was willing to try anything, so he paid the high price and they sent the disk to a recovery facility. Unfortunately, the disk suffered a catastrophic failure, and they weren't able to retrieve any meaningful data even in the clean room.

My friend visited the owner to relay the bad news. He said that when he left, the owner had his head in his hands and was literally crying. The business he had built for five years was close to ruins without much chance for recovery.

The worst part of this story is that it's repeated over and over with many different people in many different environments. Too many people don't recognize the importance of backups until they've lost their data. Unfortunately, by then, it's too late.

It's important to realize that redundancy and backups are not the same thing. Protecting data with a RAID-1 or RAID-10 does not negate the need for backups. If a fire destroys a server, it also destroys the data on the RAID. Without a backup, all of the data is gone. Forever.

Comparing Backup Types

Backup utilities support several different types of backups. Even though third-party backup programs can be quite sophisticated in what they do and how they do it, you should have a solid understanding of the basics.

The most common media used for backups is tape. Tapes store more data and are cheaper than other media, though some organizations use hard drives for backups. However, the type of media doesn't affect the backup type.

The following backup types are commonly used:

- **Full backup.** A full (or normal backup) backs up all the selected data.
- **Differential backup.** This backs up all the data that has changed or is different since the last full backup.
- **Incremental backup.** This backs up all the data that has changed since the last full or incremental backup.
- **Snaphots.** A snapshot backup captures the data at a point in time. It is sometimes referred to as an image backup.

Full Backups

A *full backup* backs up all data specified in the backup. For example, you could have several folders on the D: drive. If you specify these folders in the backup program, the backup program backs up all the data in these folders.

Although it's possible to do a full backup on a daily basis, it's rare to do so in most production environments. This is because of two limiting factors:

- **Time.** A full backup can take several hours to complete and can interfere with operations. However, administrators don't always have unlimited time to do backups and other system maintenance. For example, if a system is online 24/7, administrators might need to limit the amount of time for full backups to early Sunday morning to minimize the impact on users.
- **Money.** Backups need to be stored on some type of media, such as tape or hard drives. Performing full backups every day requires more media, and the cost can be prohibitive.

Instead, organizations often combine full backups with differential or incremental backups. However, every backup strategy must start with a full backup.

Restoring a Full Backup

A full backup is the easiest and quickest to restore. You only need to restore the single full backup and you're done. If you store backups on tapes, you only need to restore a single tape. However, most organizations need to balance time and money and use either a full/differential or a full/incremental backup strategy.

Differential Backups

A *differential backup* strategy starts with a full backup. After the full backup, differential backups back up data that has changed or is different since the last full backup.

For example, a full/differential strategy could start with a full backup on Sunday night. On Monday night, a differential backup would back up all files that changed since the last full backup on Sunday. On Tuesday night, the differential backup would again back up all the files that changed since the last full backup. This repeats until Sunday, when another full backup starts the process again. As the week progresses, the differential backup steadily grows in size.

Order of Restoration for a Full/Differential Backup Set

Assume for a moment that each of the backups was stored on different tapes. If the system crashed on Wednesday morning, how many tapes would you need to recover the data?

The answer is two. You would first recover the full backup from Sunday. Because the differential backup on Tuesday night includes all the files that changed after the last full backup, you would restore that tape to restore all the changes up to Tuesday night.

Incremental Backups

An *incremental backup* strategy also starts with a full backup. After the full backup, incremental backups then back up data that has changed since the last backup. This includes either the last full backup, or the last incremental backup.

As an example, a full/incremental strategy could start with a full backup on Sunday night. On Monday night, an incremental backup would back up all the files that changed since the last full backup. On Tuesday night, the incremental backup would back up all the files that changed since the incremental backup on Monday night. Similarly, the Wednesday night backup would back up all files that changed since the last incremental backup on Tuesday night. This repeats until Sunday when another full backup starts the process again. As the week progresses, the incremental backups stay about the same size.

Order of Restoration for a Full/Incremental Backup Set

Assume for a moment that each of the backups were stored on different tapes. If the system crashed on Thursday morning, how many tapes would you need to recover the data?

The answer is four. You would first need to recover the full backup from Sunday. Because the incremental backups would be backing up different data each day of the week, each of the incremental backups must be restored—and must be restored in chronological order.

Sometimes, people mistakenly think the last incremental backup would have all the relevant data. Although it might have some relevant data, it doesn't have everything.

As an example, imagine you worked on a single project file each day of the week, and the system crashed on Thursday morning. In this scenario, the last incremental backup would hold the most recent copy of this file. However, what if you compiled a report every Monday but didn't touch it again until the following Monday? Only the incremental backup from Monday would include the most recent copy. An incremental backup from Wednesday night or another day of the week wouldn't include the report.

Choosing Full/Incremental or Full/Differential

A logical question is, "Why are there so many choices for backups?" The answer is that different organizations have different needs. For example, imagine two organizations perform daily backups to minimize losses. They each do a full backup on Sunday, but are now trying to determine if they should use a full/incremental or a full/differential strategy.

The first organization doesn't have much time to perform maintenance throughout the week. In this case, the backup administrator needs to minimize the amount of time required to complete backups during the week. An incremental backup only backs up the data that has changed since the last backup. In other words, it includes changes only from a single day. In contrast, a differential backup includes all the changes since the last full backup. Backing up the changes from a single day takes less time than backing up changes from multiple days, so a full/incremental backup is the best choice.

In the second organization, recovery of failed systems is more important. If a failure requires restoring data, they want to minimize the amount of time needed to restore the data. A full/differential is the best choice in this situation because it only requires the restoration of two backups, the full and the most recent differential backup. In contrast, a full/incremental can require the restoration of several different backups, depending on when the failure occurs.

> **Remember this**
>
> If you have unlimited time and money, the full backup alone provides the fastest recovery time. Full/incremental strategies reduce the amount of time needed to perform backups. Full/differential strategies reduce the amount of time needed to restore backups.

Snapshot Backup

A snapshot backup captures the data at a moment in time. It is commonly used with virtual machines and sometimes referred to as a checkpoint. Chapter 1, "Mastering Security Basics," discusses virtual machines (VMs) and administrators often take a snapshot of a VM before a risky operation such as an update. If the update causes problems, it's relatively easy to revert the VM to the state it was in before the update.

Testing Backups

I've heard many horror stories in which personnel are regularly performing backups thinking all is well. Ultimately, something happens and they need to restore some data. Unfortunately, they discover that none of the backups hold valid data. People have been going through the motions, but something in the process is flawed.

The only way to validate a backup is to perform a test restore. Performing a test restore is nothing more than restoring the data from a backup and verifying its integrity. If you want to verify that you can restore the entire backup, you perform a full restore of the backup. If you want to verify that you can restore individual files, you perform a test restore of individual files. It's common to restore data to a different location other than the original source location, but in such a way that you can validate the data.

As a simple example, an administrator can retrieve a random backup and attempt to restore it. There are two possible outcomes of this test, and both are good:

- **The test succeeds.** Excellent! You know that the backup process works. You don't necessarily know that every backup tape is valid, but at least you know that the process is sound and at least some of your backups work.
- **The test fails.** Excellent! You know there's a problem that you can fix before a crisis. If you discovered the problem after you actually lost data, it wouldn't help you restore the data.

An additional benefit of performing regular test restores is that it allows administrators to become familiar with the process. The first time they do a restore shouldn't be in the middle of a crisis with several high-level managers peering over their shoulders.

Protecting Backups

If data is important enough to be backed up, it's important enough to protect. Backup media should be protected at the same level as the data that it holds. In other words, if proprietary data enjoys the highest level of protection within an organization, then backups of this data should also have the highest level of protection.

Protecting backups includes:

- **Storage.** This includes using clear labeling to identify the data and physical security protection to prevent others from easily accessing it while it's stored.
- **Transfer.** Data should be protected any time it is transferred from one location to another. This is especially true when transferring a copy of the backup to a separate geographical location.
- **Destruction.** When the backups are no longer needed, they should be destroyed. This can be accomplished by degaussing the media, shredding or burning the media, or scrubbing the media by repeatedly writing varying patterns of 1s and 0s onto the media.

Backups and Geographic Considerations

Organizations typically create a backup policy to answer critical questions related to backups. The backup policy is a written document and will often identify issues such as what data to back up, how often to back up the data, how to test the backups, and how long to retain the backups.

Additionally, it's important to address special geographic considerations, such as the following:

- **Off-site backups.** A copy of a backup should be stored in a separate geographic location. This protects against a disaster such as a fire or flood. Even if a disaster destroys the site, the organization will still have another copy of the critical data.
- **Distance.** Many organizations have specific requirements related to the distance between the main site and the off-site location. In some scenarios, the goal is to have the off-site location relatively close so that backups can be easily retrieved. However, in other scenarios, the off-site location must be far away, such as 25 miles or further away.
- **Location selection.** The location is often dependent on environmental issues. As an example, consider an organization located in California near the San Andreas fault. The off-site backup location should be far enough away that an earthquake at the primary location doesn't affect the off-site location.
- **Legal implications.** The legal implications related to backups depends on the data stored in the backups. For example, if the backups include Personally Identifiable Information (PII) or Protected Health Information (PHI), the backups need to be protected according to governing laws.
- **Data sovereignty.** *Data sovereignty* refers to the legal implications when data is stored off-site. If the backups are stored in a different country, they are subject to the laws of that country. This can be a concern if the backups are stored in a cloud location, and the cloud servers are in a different country. For example, imagine that an organization is located in the United States. It routinely does backups and stores them with a cloud provider. The cloud provider has some servers in the United States, some in Canada, and some in Mexico. If the organization's backups are stored in the other countries, it can be subject to additional laws and regulations.

> ### *Remember this*
> Test restores are the best way to test the integrity of a company's backup data. Backup media should be protected with the same level of protection as the data on the backup. Geographic considerations for backups include storing backups off-site, choosing the best location, and considering legal implications and data sovereignty.

Comparing Business Continuity Elements

Business continuity planning helps an organization predict and plan for potential outages of critical services or functions. The goal is to ensure that critical business operations continue and the organization can survive the outage. Organizations often create a business continuity plan (BCP). This plan includes disaster recovery elements that provide the steps used to return critical functions to operation after an outage.

Disasters and outages can come from many sources, including:

- Fires
- Attacks
- Power outages
- Data loss from any cause
- Hardware and software failures
- Natural disasters, such as hurricanes, floods, tornadoes, and earthquakes

Addressing all of these possible sources takes a lot of time and effort. The goal is to predict the relevant disasters, their impact, and then develop recovery strategies to mitigate them. One of the first things an organization completes is a business impact analysis.

Business Impact Analysis Concepts

A *business impact analysis (BIA)* is an important part of a BCP. It helps an organization identify critical systems and components that are essential to the organization's success. These critical systems support mission-essential functions. The BIA also helps identify vulnerable business processes. These are processes that support mission-essential functions.

As an example, imagine an organization has an online e-commerce business. Some basic mission-essential functions might include serving web pages, providing a shopping cart path, accepting purchases, sending email confirmations, and shipping purchases to customers. The shopping cart path alone is a business process and because it is essential to the mission of e-commerce sales, management will likely consider it a vulnerable business process to protect. The customer needs to be able to view products, select a product, enter customer information, enter credit card data, and complete the purchase. Some critical systems that support the web site are web servers and a back-end database application hosted on one or more database servers.

If critical systems and components fail and cannot be restored quickly, mission-essential functions cannot be completed. If this lasts too long, it's very possible that the organization will not survive the disaster.

For example, if a disaster such as a hurricane hit, which services must the organization restore to stay in business? Imagine a financial institution. It might decide that customers must have uninterrupted access to account data through an online site. If customers can't access their funds online, they might lose faith with the company and leave in droves.

However, the company might decide to implement alternate business practices in other elements of the business. For example, management might decide that accepting and processing loan applications is not important enough to continue during a disaster. Loan processing is still important to the company's bottom line, but a delay will not seriously affect its ability to stay in business. In this scenario, continuous online access is a mission-essential function, but processing loan applications during a disaster is not mission-essential.

The time to make these decisions is not during a crisis. Instead, the organization completes a BIA in advance. The BIA involves collecting information from throughout the organization and documenting the results. This documentation identifies core business or mission requirements. The BIA does not recommend solutions. However, it provides management with valuable information so that they can focus on critical business functions. It helps them address some of the following questions:

- What are the critical systems and functions?
- Are there any dependencies related to these critical systems and functions?
- What is the maximum downtime limit of these critical systems and functions?
- What scenarios are most likely to impact these critical systems and functions?
- What is the potential loss from these scenarios?

As an example, imagine an organization earns an average of $5,000 an hour through online sales. In this scenario, management might consider online sales to be a mission-essential function and all systems that support online sales are critical systems. This includes web servers and back-end database servers. These servers depend on the network infrastructure connecting them, Internet access, and access to payment gateways for credit card charges.

After analysis, they might determine that the maximum allowable outage for online sales is five hours. Identifying the maximum downtime limit is extremely important. It drives decisions related to recovery objectives and helps an organization identify various contingency plans and policies.

Impact

The BIA evaluates various scenarios, such as fires, attacks, power outages, data loss, hardware and software failures, and natural disasters. Additionally, the BIA attempts to identify the impact from these scenarios.

When evaluating the impact, a BIA looks at multiple items. For example, it might attempt to answer the following questions related to any of the scenarios:

- Will a disaster result in loss of life? Is there a way to minimize the risk to personnel?
- Will a disaster result in loss of property?
- Will a disaster reduce safety for personnel or property?
- What are the potential financial losses to the organization?
- What are the potential losses to the organization's reputation?

For example, a database server might host customer data, including credit card information. If an attacker was able to access this customer data, the cost to the organization might exceed millions of dollars.

You might remember the attack on retail giant Target during November and December 2013. Attackers accessed customer data on more than 110 million customers, resulting in significant losses for Target. Estimates of the total cost of the incident have ranged from $600 million to over $1 billion. This includes loss of sales—Target suffered a 46 percent drop in profits during the last quarter of 2013, compared with the previous year. Customers were afraid to use their credit cards at Target and simply stayed away. It also includes the cost to repair their image, the cost of purchasing credit monitoring for affected customers, fines from the payment-card industry, and an untold number of lawsuits. Target reportedly has $100 million in cyber insurance that helped them pay claims related to the data breach.

> ### Remember this
>
> The BIA identifies mission-essential functions and critical systems that are essential to the organization's success. It also identifies maximum downtime limits for these systems and components, various scenarios that can impact these systems and components, and the potential losses from an incident.

Privacy Impact and Threshold Assessments

Two tools that organizations can use when completing a BIA are a privacy threshold assessment and a privacy impact assessment. National Institute of Standards and Technology (NIST) Special Publication (SP) 800-122, "Guide to Protecting the Confidentiality of Personally Identifiable Information (PII)," covers these in more depth, but refers to a privacy threshold assessment as a privacy threshold analysis.

The primary purpose of the ***privacy threshold assessment*** is to help the organization identify PII within a system. Typically, the threshold assessment is completed by the system owner or data owner by answering a simple questionnaire.

If the system holds PII, then the next step is to conduct a ***privacy impact assessment***. The impact assessment attempts to identify potential risks related to the PII by reviewing how the information is handled. The goal is to ensure that the system is complying with applicable laws, regulations, and guidelines. The impact assessment provides a proactive method of addressing potential risks related to PII throughout the life cycle of a computing system.

> ### Remember this
>
> A privacy threshold assessment is typically a simple questionnaire completed by system or data owners. It helps identify if a system processes data that exceeds the threshold for PII. If the system processes PII, a privacy impact assessment helps identify and reduce risks related to potential loss of the PII.

Recovery Time Objective

The recovery time objective (***RTO***) identifies the maximum amount of time it can take to restore a system after an outage. Many BIAs identify the maximum acceptable outage or maximum tolerable outage time for mission-essential functions and critical systems. If an outage lasts longer than this maximum time, the impact is unacceptable to the organization.

For example, imagine an organization that sells products via a web site generates $10,000 in revenue an hour. It might decide that the maximum acceptable outage for the web server is five minutes. This results in an RTO of five minutes, indicating any outage must be limited to less than five minutes. This RTO of five minutes only applies to the mission-essential function of online sales and the critical systems supporting it.

Imagine that the organization has a database server only used by internal employees, not online sales. Although the database server may be valuable, it is not critical. Management might decide they can accept an outage for as long as 24 hours, resulting in an RTO of less than 24 hours.

Recovery Point Objective

A recovery point objective (***RPO***) identifies a point in time where data loss is acceptable. As an example, a server may host archived data that has very few changes on a weekly basis. Management might decide that some data loss is acceptable, but they always want to be able to recover data from at least the previous week. In this case, the RPO is one week.

With an RPO of one week, administrators would ensure that they have at least weekly backups. In the event of a failure, they will be able to restore recent backups and meet the RPO.

In some cases, the RPO is up to the minute of the failure. For example, any data loss from an online database recording customer transactions might be unacceptable. In this case, the organization can use a variety of techniques to ensure administrators can restore data up to the moment of failure.

Comparing MTBF and MTTR

When working with a BIA, experts often attempt to predict the possibility of a failure.

> ### Remember this
>
> The recovery time objective (RTO) identifies the maximum amount of time it should take to restore a system after an outage. It is derived from the maximum allowable outage time identified in the BIA. The recovery point objective (RPO) refers to the amount of data you can afford to lose.

For example, what is the likelihood that a hard disk within a RAID configuration will fail? The following two terms are often used to predict potential failures:

- **Mean time between failures (MTBF).** The mean time between failures (*MTBF*) provides a measure of a system's reliability and is usually represented in hours. More specifically, the MTBF identifies the average (the arithmetic mean) time between failures. Higher MTBF numbers indicate a higher reliability of a product or system. Administrators and security experts attempt to identify the MTBF for critical systems with a goal of predicting potential outages.
- **Mean time to recover (MTTR).** The mean time to recover (*MTTR*) identifies the average (the arithmetic mean) time it takes to restore a failed system. In some cases, people interpret MTTR as the mean time to repair, and both mean essentially the same thing. Organizations that have maintenance contracts often specify the MTTR as a part of the contract. The supplier agrees that it will, on average, restore a failed system within the MTTR time. The MTTR does not provide a guarantee that it will restore the system within the MTTR every time. Sometimes, it might take a little longer and sometimes it might be a little quicker, with the average defined by the MTTR.

Continuity of Operations Planning

Continuity of operations planning focuses on restoring mission-essential functions at a recovery site after a critical outage. For example, if a hurricane or other disaster prevents the company from operating in the primary location, the organization can continue to operate the mission-essential functions at an alternate location that management previously identified as a recovery site. Failover is the process of moving mission-essential functions to the alternate site.

Recovery Sites

A *recovery site* is an alternate processing site that an organization can use after a disaster. The three primary types of recovery sites are hot sites, cold sites, and warm sites. These alternate locations could be office space within a building, an entire building, or even a group of buildings. Two other types of recovery sites are mobile sites and mirrored sites. The following sections provide more details on these sites.

Hot Site

A *hot site* would be up and operational 24 hours a day, seven days a week and would be able to take over functionality from the primary site quickly after a primary site failure. It would include all the equipment, software, and communication capabilities of the primary site, and all the data would be up to date. In many cases, copies of backup tapes are stored at the hot site as the off-site location.

In many cases, a hot site is another active business location that has the capability to assume operations during a disaster. For example, a financial institution could have locations in two separate cities. The second location provides noncritical support services, but also includes all the resources necessary to assume the functions of the first location.

Some definitions of hot sites indicate they can take over instantaneously, though this isn't consistent. In most cases, it takes a little bit of time to transfer operations to the hot site, and this can take anywhere from a few minutes to an hour.

Clearly, a hot site is the most effective disaster recovery solution for high-availability requirements. If an organization must keep critical systems with high-availability requirements, the hot site is the best choice. However, a hot site is the most expensive to maintain and keep up to date.

> ### Remember this
>
> A hot site includes personnel, equipment, software, and communication capabilities of the primary site with all the data up to date. A hot site provides the shortest recovery time compared with warm and cold sites. It is the most effective disaster recovery solution, but it is also the most expensive to maintain.

Cold Site

A *cold site* requires power and connectivity but not much else. Generally, if it has a roof, electricity, running water, and Internet access, you're good to go. The organization brings all the equipment, software, and data to the site when it activates it.

I often take my dogs for a walk at a local army base and occasionally see soldiers activate an extreme example of a cold site. On most weekends, the fields are empty. Other weekends, soldiers have transformed one or more fields into complete operational sites with tents, antennas, cables, generators, and porta-potties.

Because the army has several buildings on the base, they don't need to operate in the middle of fields, but what they're really doing is testing their ability to stand up a cold site wherever they want. If they can do it in the field, they can do it in the middle of a desert, or anywhere else they need to.

A cold site is the cheapest to maintain, but it is also the most difficult to test.

Warm Site

You can think of a *warm site* as the Goldilocks solution—not too hot and not too cold, but just right. Hot sites are generally too expensive for most organizations, and cold sites sometimes take too long to configure for full operation. However, the warm site provides a compromise that an organization can tailor to meet its needs.

For example, an organization can place all the necessary hardware at the warm site location but not include up-to-date data. If a disaster occurs, the organization can copy the data to the warm site and take over operations. This is only one example, but there are many different possibilities of warm site configurations.

Site Variations

Although hot, cold, and warm sites are the most common, you might also come across two additional alternate site types: mobile and mirrored.

A mobile site is a self-contained transportable unit with all the equipment needed for specific requirements. For example, you can outfit a semitrailer with everything needed for operations, including a satellite dish for connectivity. Trucks, trains, or ships haul it to its destination and it only needs power to start operating.

Mirrored sites are identical to the primary location and provide 100 percent availability. They use real-time transfers to send modifications from the primary location to the mirrored site. Although a hot site can be up and operational within an hour, the mirrored site is always up and operational.

> ### Remember this
>
> A cold site will have power and connectivity needed for a recovery site, but little else. Cold sites are the least expensive and the hardest to test. A warm site is a compromise between a hot site and a cold site. Mobile sites do not have dedicated locations, but can provide temporary support during a disaster.

Order of Restoration

After the disaster has passed, you will want to return all the functions to the primary site. As a best practice, organizations return the least critical functions to the primary site first. Remember, the critical functions are operational at the alternate site and can stay there as long as necessary.

If a site has just gone through a disaster, it's very likely that there are still some unknown problems. By moving the least critical functions first, undiscovered problems will appear and can be resolved without significantly affecting mission-essential functions.

Disaster Recovery

Disaster recovery is a part of an overall business continuity plan. Often, the organization will use the business impact analysis to identify the critical systems and components and then develop disaster recovery strategies and disaster recovery plans (DRPs) to address the systems hosting these functions.

In some cases, an organization will have multiple DRPs within a BCP, and in other cases, the organization will have a single DRP. For example, it's possible to have individual DRPs that identify the steps to recover individual critical servers and other DRPs that detail the recovery steps after different types of disasters such as hurricanes or tornadoes. A smaller organization might have a single DRP that simply identifies all the steps used to respond to any disruption.

A DRP or a BCP will include a hierarchical list of critical systems. This list identifies what systems to restore after a disaster and in what order. For example, should a server hosting an online web site be restored first, or a server hosting an internal application? The answer is dependent on how the organization values and uses these servers. In some cases, systems have interdependencies requiring systems to be restored in a certain order.

If the DRP doesn't prioritize the systems, individuals restoring the systems will use their own judgment, which might not meet the overall needs of the organization. For example, Nicky New Guy might not realize that a web server is generating $5,000 an hour in revenue but does know that he's responsible for keeping a generic file server operational. Without an ordered list of critical systems, he might spend his time restoring the file server and not the web server.

This hierarchical list is valuable when using alternate sites such as warm or cold sites, too.

When the organization needs to move operations to an alternate site, the organization will want the most important systems and functions restored first.

Similarly, the DRP often prioritizes the services to restore after an outage. As a rule, critical business functions and security services are restored first. Support services are restored last.

The different phases of a disaster recovery process typically include the following steps:

- **Activate the disaster recovery plan.** Some disasters, such as earthquakes or tornadoes, occur without much warning, and a disaster recovery plan is activated after the disaster. Other disasters, such as hurricanes, provide a warning, and the plan is activated when the disaster is imminent.
- **Implement contingencies.** If the recovery plan requires implementation of an alternate site, critical functions are moved to these sites. If the disaster destroyed on-site backups, this step retrieves the off-site backups from the off-site location.
- **Recover critical systems.** After the disaster has passed, the organization begins recovering critical systems. The DRP documents which systems to recover and includes detailed steps on how to recover them. This also includes reviewing change management documentation to ensure that recovered systems include approved changes.
- **Test recovered systems.** Before bringing systems online, administrators test and verify them. This may include comparing the restored system with a performance baseline to verify functionality.
- **After-action report.** The final phase of disaster recovery includes a review of the disaster, sometimes called an after-action review. This often includes a lessons learned review to identify what went right and what went wrong. After reviewing the after-action report, the organization often updates the plan to incorporate any lessons learned.

> **Remember this**
>
> A disaster recovery plan (DRP) includes a hierarchical list of critical systems and often prioritizes services to restore after an outage. Testing validates the plan. The final phase of disaster recovery includes a review to identify any lessons learned and may include an update of the plan.

Testing Plans with Exercises

Business continuity plans and disaster recovery plans include testing. Testing validates that the plan works as desired and will often include testing redundancies and backups. There are several different types of testing used with BCPs and DRPs.

NIST SP 800-34, "Guide to Test, Training, and Exercise Programs for IT Plans and Capabilities," provides detailed guidance on testing BCP and DRP plans. SP 800-34 identifies two primary types of exercises: tabletop exercises and functional exercises.

A *tabletop exercise* (also called a desktop exercise or a structured walk-through) is discussion-based. A coordinator gathers participants in a classroom or conference room, and leads them through one or more scenarios. As the coordinator introduces each stage of an incident, the participants identify what they'll do based on the plan. This generates discussion about team members' roles and responsibilities and the decision-making process during an incident. Ideally, this validates that the plan is valid. However, it sometimes reveals flaws. The BCP coordinator ensures the plans are rewritten if necessary.

Functional exercises provide personnel with an opportunity to test the plans in a simulated operational environment. There is a wide range of functional exercises, from simple simulations to full-blown tests. In a simulation, the participants go through the steps in a controlled manner without affecting the actual system. For example, a simulation can start by indicating that a server failed. Participants then follow the steps to rebuild the server on a test system. A full-blown test goes through all the steps of the plan. In addition to verifying that the test works, this also shows the amount of time it will take to execute the plan.

Some of the common elements of testing include:

- **Backups.** Backups are tested by restoring the data from the backup, as discussed in the "Testing Backups" section earlier in this chapter.
- **Server restoration.** A simple disaster recovery exercise rebuilds a server. Participants follow the steps to rebuild a server using a test system without touching the live system.
- **Server redundancy.** If a server is within a failover cluster, you can test the cluster by taking a primary node offline. Another node within the cluster should automatically assume the role of this offline node.
- **Alternate sites.** You can test an alternate site (hot, cold, or warm) by moving some of the functionality to the alternate site and ensuring the alternate site works as desired. It's also possible to test individual elements of an alternate site, such as Internet connectivity, or the ability to obtain and restore backup media.

> ## Remember this
>
> You can validate business continuity plans through testing. Tabletop exercises are discussion-based only and are typically performed in a classroom or conference setting. Functional exercises are hands-on exercises.

Chapter 9 Exam Topic Review

When preparing for the exam, make sure you understand these key concepts covered in this chapter.

Implementing Defense in Depth

- Layered security (or defense in depth) employs multiple layers of security to protect against threats. Personnel constantly monitor, update, add to, and improve existing security controls.
- Control diversity is the use of different security control types, such as technical controls, administrative controls, and physical controls.
- Vendor diversity is the practice of implementing security controls from different vendors to increase security.

Comparing Physical Security Controls

- Physical security controls are controls you can physically touch. They often control entry and exit points, and include various types of locks.
- An airgap is a physical security control that ensures that a computer or network is physically isolated from another computer or network.
- Controlled areas such as data centers and server rooms should only have a single

entrance and exit point. Door lock types include cipher locks, proximity cards, and biometrics.

- A proximity card can electronically unlock a door and helps prevent unauthorized personnel from entering a secure area. By themselves, proximity cards do not identify and authenticate users. Some systems combine proximity cards with PINs for identification and authentication.
- Tailgating occurs when one user follows closely behind another user without using credentials. A mantrap can prevent tailgating.
- Security guards are a preventive physical security control and they can prevent unauthorized personnel from entering a secure area. A benefit of guards is that they can recognize people and compare an individual's picture ID for people they don't recognize.
- Cameras and closed-circuit television (CCTV) systems provide video surveillance. They provide reliable proof of a person's identity and activity.
- Fencing, lighting, and alarms are commonly implemented with motion detection systems for physical security. Infrared motion detection systems detect human activity based on the temperature.
- Barricades provide stronger physical security than fences and attempt to deter attackers. Bollards are effective barricades that allow people through, but block vehicles.
- Cable locks secure mobile computers such as laptop computers in a training lab. Server bays include locking cabinets or enclosures within a server room. Small devices can be stored in safes or locking office cabinets to prevent the theft of unused resources.
- Asset management processes protect against vulnerabilities related to architecture and design weaknesses, system sprawl, and undocumented assets.
- Heating, ventilation, and air conditioning (HVAC) systems control airflow for data centers and server rooms. Temperature controls protect systems from damage due to overheating.
- Hot and cold aisles provide more efficient cooling of systems within a data center.
- EMI shielding prevents problems from EMI sources such as fluorescent lighting fixtures. It also prevents data loss in twisted-pair cables. A Faraday cage prevents signals from emanating beyond a room or enclosure.

Adding Redundancy and Fault Tolerance

- A single point of failure is any component that can cause the entire system to fail if it fails.
- RAID disk subsystems provide fault tolerance and increase availability. RAID-1 (mirroring) uses two disks. RAID-5 uses three or more disks and can survive the failure of one disk. RAID-6 and RAID-10 use four or more disks and can survive the failure of two disks.
- Load balancers spread the processing load over multiple servers. In an active-active configuration, all servers are actively processing requests. In an active-passive configuration, at least one server is not active, but is instead monitoring activity ready to take over for a failed server. Software-based load balancers use a virtual IP.
- Affinity scheduling sends client requests to the same server based on the client's IP address. This is useful when clients need to access the same server for an entire online session. Round-robin scheduling sends requests to servers using a predefined order.

Protecting Data with Backups

- Backup strategies include full, full/differential, full/incremental, and snapshot strategies. A full backup strategy alone allows the quickest recovery time.
- Full/incremental backup strategies minimize the amount of time needed to perform daily backups.
- Test restores verify the integrity of backups. A test restore of a full backup verifies a backup can be restored in its entirety.
- Backups should be labeled to identify the contents. A copy of backups should be kept off-site.
- It's important to consider the distance between the main site and the off-site location.
- The data contained in the backups can have legal implications. If it includes Personally Identifiable Information (PII) or Protected Health Information (PHI), it must be protected according to governing laws.
- The location of the data backups affects the data sovereignty. If backups are stored in a different country, the data on the backups is now subject to the laws and regulations of that country.

Comparing Business Continuity Elements

- A business impact analysis (BIA) is part of a business continuity plan (BCP) and it identifies mission-essential functions, critical systems, and vulnerable business processes that are essential to the organization's success.
- The BIA identifies maximum downtimes for these systems and components. It considers various scenarios that can affect these systems and components, and the impact to life, property, safety, finance, and reputation from an incident.
- A privacy threshold assessment identifies if a system processes data that exceeds the threshold for PII. If the system processes PII, a privacy impact assessment helps identify and reduce risks related to potential loss of the PII.
- A recovery time objective (RTO) identifies the maximum amount of time it should take to restore a system after an outage. The recovery point objective (RPO) refers to the amount of data you can afford to lose.
- Mean time between failures (MTBF) identifies the average (the arithmetic mean) time between failures. The mean time to recover (MTTR) identifies the average (the arithmetic mean) time it takes to restore a failed system.
- Continuity of operations planning identifies alternate processing sites and alternate business practices. Recovery sites provide alternate locations for business functions after a major disaster.
- A hot site includes everything needed to be operational within 60 minutes. It is the most effective recovery solution and the most expensive. A cold site has power and connectivity requirements and little else. It is the least expensive to maintain. Warm sites are a compromise between hot sites and cold sites.
- Periodic testing validates continuity of operations plans. Exercises validate the steps to restore individual systems, activate alternate sites, and document other actions within a plan. Tabletop exercises are discussion-based only. Functional exercises are hands-on exercises.

Online References

- Do you know how to answer performance-based questions? Check out the online extras at *http://gcgapremium.com/501-extras*.

Chapter 9 Practice Questions

1. After a recent attack on your organization's network, the CTO is insisting that the DMZ uses two firewalls and they are purchased from different companies. Which of the following BEST describes this practice?
     A. Single-layer security
     B. Vendor diversity
     C. Control diversity
     D. Redundancy

2. Management within your organization wants to create a small network used by executives only. They want to ensure that this network is completely isolated from the main network. Which of the following choices BEST meets this need?
     A. Airgap
     B. Mantrap
     C. Control diversity
     D. Infrared motion detectors

3. A security professional has reported an increase in the number of tailgating violations into a secure data center. Which of the following can prevent this?
     A. CCTV
     B. Mantrap
     C. Proximity card
     D. Cipher lock

4. Lisa is the new chief technology officer (CTO) at your organization. She wants to ensure that critical business systems are protected from isolated outages. Which of the following would let her know how often these systems will experience outages?
     A. MTTR
     B. MTBF
     C. RTO
     D. RPO

5. Thieves recently rammed a truck through the entrance of your company's main building. During the chaos, their partners proceeded to steal a significant amount of IT equipment. Which of the following choices can you use to prevent this from happening again?
     A. Bollards
     B. Guards
     C. CCTV
     D. Mantrap

6. You are a technician at a small organization. You need to add fault-tolerance capabilities within the business to increase the availability of data. However, you need to keep costs as low as possible. Which of the following is the BEST choice to meet these needs?
    A. Alternate processing site
    B. RAID-10
    C. Backups
    D. Faraday cage

7. Flancrest Enterprises recently set up a web site utilizing several web servers in a web farm. The web farm spreads the load among the different web servers. Visitor IP addresses are used to ensure that clients always return to the same server during a web session. Which of the following BEST describes this configuration?
    A. Affinity
    B. Round-robin
    C. Virtual IP
    D. Active-passive

8. Your organization is planning to deploy a new e-commerce web site. Management anticipates heavy processing requirements for a back-end application. The current design will use one web server and multiple application servers. Which of the following BEST describes the application servers?
    A. Load balancing
    B. Clustering
    C. RAID
    D. Affinity scheduling

9. Flancrest Enterprises recently set up a web site utilizing several web servers in a web farm. The web farm spreads the load among the different web servers by sending the first request to one server, the next request to the second server, and so on. Which of the following BEST describes this configuration?
    A. Affinity
    B. Round-robin
    C. Airgap
    D. Mantrap

10. Flancrest Enterprises recently set up a web site utilizing several web servers in a web farm. The web servers access a back-end database. The database is hosted by a database application configured on two database servers. Web servers can access either of the database servers. Which of the following BEST describes the configuration of the database servers?
    A. Active-passive
    B. Round-robin
    C. Affinity
    D. Active-active

11. Your organization has decided to increase the amount of customer data it maintains and use it for targeted sales. However, management is concerned that they will need to comply with existing laws related to PII. Which of the following should be completed to determine if the customer data is PII?

    A. Privacy threshold assessment
    B. Privacy impact assessment
    C. Tabletop exercise
    D. Affinity scheduling

12. Your backup policy for a database server dictates that the amount of time needed to perform backups should be minimized. Which of the following backup plans would BEST meet this need?

    A. Full backups on Sunday and full backups on the other six days of the week
    B. Full backups on Sunday and differential backups on the other six days of the week
    C. Full backups on Sunday and incremental backups on the other six days of the week
    D. Differential backups on Sunday and incremental backups on the other six days of the week

13. You are helping implement your company's business continuity plan. For one system, the plan requires an RTO of five hours and an RPO of one day. Which of the following would meet this requirement?

    A. Ensure the system can be restored within five hours and ensure it does not lose more than one day of data.
    B. Ensure the system can be restored within one day and ensure it does not lose more than five hours of data.
    C. Ensure the system can be restored between five hours and one day after an outage.
    D. Ensure critical systems can be restored within five hours and noncritical systems can be restored within one day.

14. A security analyst is creating a document that includes the expected monetary loss from a major outage. She is calculating the potential impact on life, property, finances, and the organization's reputation. Which of the following documents is she MOST likely creating?

    A. BCP
    B. BIA
    C. MTBF
    D. RPO

15. A security expert at your organization is leading an on-site meeting with key disaster recovery personnel. The purpose of the meeting is to perform a test. Which of the following BEST describes this test?

    A. Functional exercise
    B. Full-blown test
    C. Tabletop exercise
    D. Simulation to perform steps of a plan

Chapter 9 Practice Question Answers

1. **B.** The chief technology officer (CTO) is recommending vendor diversity for the demilitarized zone (DMZ). Firewalls from different companies (vendors) provide vendor diversity. This also provides defense in depth or layered security, but not single-layer security. Control diversity is the use of different controls such as technical, administrative, and physical. Redundancy is the use of duplicate components for fault tolerance, but the two firewalls work together in the DMZ.

2. **A.** An airgap ensures that a computer or network is physically isolated from another computer or network. A mantrap helps prevent unauthorized entry and is useful for preventing tailgating. Control diversity is the use of different controls such as technical, administrative, and physical, but it doesn't necessarily isolate networks. Infrared motion detectors sense motion from infrared light, but they don't isolate networks.

3. **B.** A mantrap is highly effective at preventing unauthorized entry and can also be used to prevent tailgating. CCTV uses cameras for video surveillance and it can record unauthorized entry, but it can't prevent it. A proximity card is useful as an access control mechanism, but it won't prevent tailgating, so it isn't as useful as a mantrap. A cipher lock is a door access control, but it can't prevent tailgating.

4. **B.** The mean time between failures (MTBF) provides a measure of a system's reliability and would provide an estimate of how often the systems will experience outages. The mean time to recover (MTTR) refers to the time it takes to restore a system, not the time between failures. The recovery time objective (RTO) identifies the maximum amount of time it can take to restore a system after an outage. The recovery point objective (RPO) identifies a point in time where data loss is acceptable.

5. **A.** Bollards are effective barricades that can block vehicles. Guards can restrict access for personnel, but they cannot stop trucks from ramming through a building. Closed-circuit television (CCTV) or a similar video surveillance system can monitor the entrance, but it won't stop the attack. Mantraps prevent tailgating, but they most likely won't stop a truck.

6. **B.** A redundant array of inexpensive disks 10 (RAID-10) subsystem provides fault tolerance for disks and increases data availability. An alternate processing site might be used for a mission-essential function, but it is expensive and does much more than increase the availability of data. Backups help ensure data availability, but they do not help with fault tolerance. A Faraday cage is a room or enclosure that prevents signals from emanating beyond the room.

7. **A.** Source address IP affinity scheduling allows a load balancer to direct client requests to the same server during a web session. Round-robin scheduling simply sends each request to the next server. Load balancers can use a virtual IP, but this refers to the IP address of the web server, not the IP address of a visitor. An active-passive configuration has at least one server that is not actively serving clients, but the scenario doesn't indicate any of the servers are in a passive mode.

8. A. The design is using load balancing to spread the load across multiple application servers. The scenario indicates the goal is to use multiple servers because of heavy processing requirements, and this is exactly what load balancing does. Clustering is typically used to provide high availability by failing over to another server if one server fails. RAID provides fault tolerance for disk drives, not servers. Affinity scheduling helps ensure clients go to the same server during a session, but this isn't relevant to this scenario.

9. B. A round-robin scheduling scheme allows a load balancer to send requests to servers one after another. Affinity scheduling directs user requests to a specific server based on the user's IP address to ensure that the user accesses the same server during a web session. An airgap ensures that computing systems are physically separated from each other and is unrelated to this question. A mantrap prevents unauthorized entry using the social engineering tactic of tailgating.

10. D. The database servers are in an active-active load-balancing configuration because web servers can query both database servers. In an active-passive configuration, only one of the database servers would be answering queries at any given time. Round-robin and affinity are two methods of scheduling the load balancing in an active-active configuration.

11. A. A privacy threshold assessment helps an organization identify Personally Identifiable Information (PII) within a system, and in this scenario, it would help the organization determine if the customer data is PII. A privacy impact assessment is done after you have verified that the system is processing PII, not to determine if the data is PII. A tabletop exercise is a discussion-based exercise used to talk through a continuity of operations plan. Affinity scheduling is a load-balancing scheduling scheme using the client's IP address and is unrelated to PII.

12. C. A full/incremental backup strategy is the best option with one full backup on one day and incremental backups on the other days. The incremental backups will take a relatively short time compared with the other methods. A full backup every day would require the most time every day. Differential backups become steadily larger as the week progresses and take more time to back up than incremental backups. Backups must start with a full backup, so a differential/incremental backup strategy is not possible.

13. A. The recovery time objective (RTO) identifies the maximum amount of time it should take to restore a system after an outage. The recovery point objective (RPO) refers to the amount of data you can afford to lose. RTO only refers to time, not data. RPO refers to data recovery points, not time to restore a system.

14. B. A business impact analysis (BIA) includes information on potential monetary losses along with the impact on life, property, and the organization's reputation. It is the most likely document of those listed that would include this information. A business continuity plan (BCP) includes a BIA, but the BIA is more likely to include this information than the BCP is. The mean time between failures (MTBF) provides a measure of a system's reliability. The recovery point objective (RPO) refers to the amount of data you can afford to lose, but it does not include monetary losses.

15. **C.** A tabletop exercise is discussion-based and is typically performed in a classroom or conference room setting. Because this is a meeting that includes disaster recovery personnel, it is a tabletop exercise. Functional exercises are hands-on exercises and include simulations and full-blown tests.

Chapter 10

Understanding Cryptography and PKI

CompTIA Security+ objectives covered in this chapter:

1.2   Compare and contrast types of attacks.
- Cryptographic attacks (Downgrade, Weak implementations)

1.6   Explain the impact associated with types of vulnerabilities.
- Weak cipher suites and implementations, Improper certificate and key management

2.2   Given a scenario, use appropriate software tools to assess the security posture of an organization.
- Steganography tools

2.3   Given a scenario, troubleshoot common security issues.
- Certificate issues

2.6   Given a scenario, implement secure protocols.
- Protocols (S/MIME)

6.1   Compare and contrast basic concepts of cryptography.
- Symmetric algorithms, Modes of operation, Asymmetric algorithms, Hashing, Salt, IV, nonce, Elliptic curve, Weak/deprecated algorithms, Key exchange, Digital signatures, Diffusion, Confusion, Steganography, Obfuscation, Stream vs. block, Key strength, Session keys, Ephemeral key, Secret algorithm, Data-in-transit, Data-at-rest, Data-in-use, Random/ pseudo-random number generation, Key stretching, Implementation vs. algorithm selection (Crypto service provider, Crypto modules), Perfect forward secrecy, Security through obscurity, Common use cases (Low power devices, Low latency, High resiliency)

6.2   Explain cryptography algorithms and their basic characteristics.
- Symmetric algorithms (AES, DES, 3DES, RC4, Blowfish/Twofish), Cipher modes (CBC, GCM, ECB, CTM, Stream vs. block), Asymmetric algorithms (RSA, DSA, Diffie-Hellman [Groups, DHE, ECDHE], Elliptic curve, PGP/GPG)
- Hashing algorithms (MD5, SHA, HMAC, RIPEMD)
- Key stretching algorithms (BCRYPT, PBKDF2)
- Obfuscation (XOR, ROT13, Substitution ciphers)

6.4 Given a scenario, implement public key infrastructure.
- Components (CA, Intermediate CA, CRL, OCSP, CSR, Certificate, Public key, Private key, Object identifiers [OID]), Concepts (Online vs. offline CA, Stapling, Pinning, Trust model, Key escrow, Certificate chaining)
- Types of certificates (Wildcard, SAN, Code signing, Self-signed, Machine/computer, Email, User, Root, Domain validation, Extended validation)
- Certificate formats (DER, PEM, PFX, CER, P12, P7B)

**

Although cryptography and Public Key Infrastructure (PKI) are only 12 percent of the exam, you might find that many of these topics aren't as familiar to you as other topics, and you might have to spend more than 12 percent of your study time here. When tackling these topics, don't lose sight of the basics. The first section in this chapter, "Introducing Cryptography Concepts," outlines and summarizes these basics. Other sections dig into the details of hashing, encryption, and Public Key Infrastructure (PKI) components.

Introducing Cryptography Concepts

Cryptography has several important concepts that you need to grasp for the CompTIA Security+ exam, but the topics are often new to many information technology (IT) professionals. Two core topics are integrity and confidentiality, introduced in Chapter 1, "Mastering Security Basics."

As an introduction, the following points identify the important core cryptography concepts. Remember, this is only an overview. If these bullets don't make sense to you now, they should after you complete this chapter:

- **Integrity** provides assurances that data has not been modified. Hashing ensures that data has retained integrity.
  - A **hash** is a number derived from performing a calculation on data, such as a message, patch, or file.
  - Hashing creates a fixed-size string of bits or hexadecimal characters, which cannot be reversed to re-create the original data.
  - Common hashing algorithms include MD5 and Secure Hash Algorithm (SHA).
- **Confidentiality** ensures that data is only viewable by authorized users. Encryption protects the confidentiality of data.
  - **Encryption** scrambles, or ciphers, data to make it unreadable if intercepted. Encryption normally includes an algorithm and a key.
  - Symmetric encryption uses the same key to encrypt and decrypt data.
  - Asymmetric encryption uses two keys (public and private) created as a matched pair.
    - o Asymmetric encryption requires a Public Key Infrastructure (PKI) to issue certificates.
    - o Anything encrypted with the public key can only be decrypted with the matching private key.
    - o Anything encrypted with the private key can only be decrypted with the matching public key.

- Stream ciphers encrypt data 1 bit at a time. Block ciphers encrypt data in blocks.
- Steganography provides a level of confidentiality by hiding data within other files. For example, it's possible to embed data within the white space of a picture file.
- A *digital signature* provides authentication, non-repudiation, and integrity.
  - *Authentication* validates an identity.
  - *Non-repudiation* prevents a party from denying an action.
  - Users sign emails with a digital signature, which is a hash of an email message encrypted with the sender's private key.
  - Only the sender's public key can decrypt the hash, providing verification it was encrypted with the sender's private key.

Providing Integrity with Hashing

You can verify integrity with hashing. Hashing is an algorithm performed on data such as a file or message to produce a number called a hash (sometimes called a checksum). The hash is used to verify that data is not modified, tampered with, or corrupted. In other words, you can verify the data has maintained integrity.

A key point about a hash is that no matter how many times you execute the hashing algorithm against the data, the hash will always be the same if the data is the same.

Hashes are created at least twice so that they can be compared. For example, imagine a software company is releasing a patch for an application that customers can download. They can calculate the hash of the patch and post both a link to the patch file and the hash on the company site. They might list it as:

- **Patch file.** Patch_v2_3.zip
- **SHA-1 checksum.** d4723ac6f72daea2c7793ac113863c5082644229

The Secure Hash Algorithm 1 (SHA-1) checksum is the calculated hash displayed in hexadecimal. Customers can download the file and then calculate the hash on the downloaded file. If the calculated hash is the same as the hash posted on the web site, it verifies the file has retained integrity. In other words, the file has not changed.

> ### Remember this
> Hashing verifies integrity for data such as email, downloaded files, and files stored on a disk. A hash is a number created with a hashing algorithm, and is sometimes listed as a checksum.

MD5

Message Digest 5 (*MD5*) is a common hashing algorithm that produces a 128-bit hash. Hashes are commonly shown in hexadecimal format instead of a stream of 1s and 0s. For example, an MD5 hash is displayed as 32 hexadecimal characters instead of 128 bits. Hexadecimal characters are composed of 4 bits and use the numbers 0 through 9 and the characters a through f.

MD5 has been in use since 1992. Experts discovered significant vulnerabilities in MD5 in 2004 and later years. As processing power of computers increased, it became easier and easier to exploit these vulnerabilities. Security experts now consider it cracked and discourage its use.

However, it is still widely used to verify the integrity of files. This includes email, files stored on disks, files downloaded from the Internet, executable files, and more. The "Hashing Files" section shows how you can manually calculate hashes.

SHA

Secure Hash Algorithm (**SHA**) is another hashing algorithm. There are several variations of SHA grouped into four families—SHA-0, SHA-1, SHA-2, and SHA-3:

- SHA-0 is not used.
- SHA-1 is an updated version that creates 160-bit hashes. This is similar to the MD5 hash except that it creates 160-bit hashes instead of 128-bit hashes.
- SHA-2 improved SHA-1 to overcome potential weaknesses. It includes four versions. SHA-256 creates 256-bit hashes and SHA-512 creates 512-bit hashes. SHA-224 (224-bit hashes) and SHA-384 (384-bit hashes) create truncated versions of SHA-256 and SHA-512, respectively.
- SHA-3 (previously known as Keccak) is an alternative to SHA-2. The U.S. National Security Agency (NSA) created SHA-1 and SHA-2. SHA-3 was created outside of the NSA and was selected in a non-NSA public competition. It can create hashes of the same size as SHA-2 (224 bits, 256 bits, 384 bits, and 512 bits).

Just as MD5 is used to verify the integrity of files, SHA also verifies file integrity. As an example, it's rare for executable files to be modified. However, some malware modifies executable files by adding malicious code into the file. Rootkits will often modify system-level files.

Some host-based intrusion detection systems (HIDSs) and antivirus software capture hashes of files on a system when they first scan it and include valid hashes of system files in signature definition files. When they scan a system again, they can capture hashes of executable and system files and compare them with known good hashes. If the hashes are different for an executable or system file, it indicates the file has been modified, and it may have been modified by malware.

HMAC

Another method used to provide integrity is with a Hash-based Message Authentication Code (**HMAC**). An HMAC is a fixed-length string of bits similar to other hashing algorithms such as MD5 and SHA-1 (known as HMAC-MD5 and HMAC-SHA1). However, HMAC also uses a shared secret key to add some randomness to the result and only the sender and receiver know the secret key.

For example, imagine that one server is sending a message to another server using HMAC-MD5. It starts by first creating a hash of a message with MD5 and then uses a secret key to complete another calculation on the hash. The server then sends the message and the HMAC-MD5 hash to the second server. The second server performs the same calculations and compares the received HMAC-MD5 hash with its result. Just as with any other hash comparison, if the two hashes are the same, the message retained integrity, but if the hashes are different, the message lost integrity.

The HMAC provides both integrity and authenticity of messages. The MD5 portion of the hash provides integrity just as MD5 does. However, because only the server and receiver know the secret key, if the receiver can calculate the same HMAC-MD5 hash as the sender, it knows that the sender used the same key. If an attacker was trying to impersonate the sender, the message wouldn't pass this authenticity check because the attacker wouldn't have the secret key. Internet Protocol security (IPsec) and Transport Layer Security (TLS) often use a version of HMAC such as HMAC-MD5 and HMAC-SHA1.

Remember this

Two popular hashing algorithms used to verify integrity are MD5 and SHA. HMAC verifies both the integrity and authenticity of a message with the use of a shared secret. Other protocols such as IPsec and TLS use HMAC-MD5 and HMAC-SHA1.

RIPEMD

RACE Integrity Primitives Evaluation Message Digest (**RIPEMD**) is another hash function used for integrity, though it isn't as widely used as MD5, SHA, and HMAC. Different versions create different size hashes. RIPEMD-160 creates 160-bit, fixed-size hashes. Other versions create hash sizes of 128 bits, 256 bits, and 320 bits.

Hashing Files

Many applications calculate and compare hashes automatically without any user intervention. For example, digital signatures (described later) use hashes within email, and email applications automatically create and compare the hashes.

Additionally, there are several applications you can use to manually calculate hashes. As an example, *sha1sum.exe* is a free program anyone can use to create hashes of files. A Google search on "download sha1sum" will show several locations. It runs the SHA-1 hashing algorithm against a file to create the hash.

If you downloaded a Kali Linux distribution image from the lab mentioned in Chapter 1, you would have seen hashes of the different images posted on the web site. The web site indicates that the SHA-1 hash for the file I downloaded is: 93AEB16A1A9A5D6E94A9AE6AF105573C7CB3357B.

By running the sha1sum command against the file, I can calculate the hash of the file I downloaded. I first used the dir command to list the files in the directory. I then ran sha1sum against the Kali Linux file three times. Each time, sha1sum created the same hash 93aeb16a1a9a5d6e94a9ae6af105573c7cb3357b, as shown in Figure 10.1

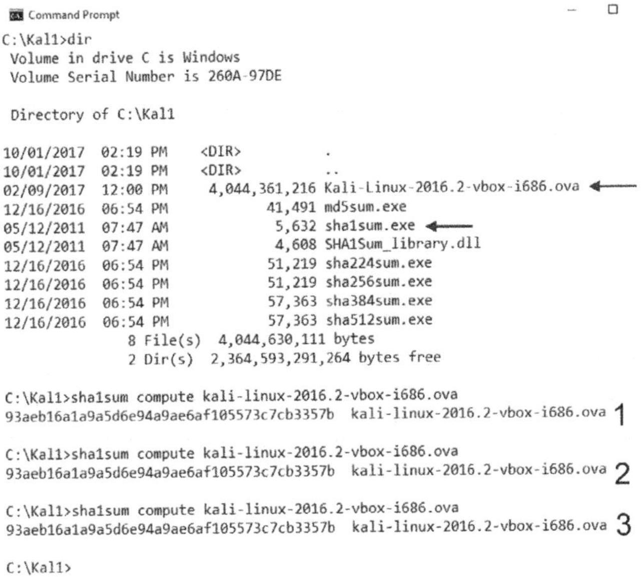

```
Command Prompt                                        —  □  ×
C:\Kali>dir
 Volume in drive C is Windows
 Volume Serial Number is 260A-97DE

 Directory of C:\Kali

10/01/2017  02:19 PM    <DIR>          .
10/01/2017  02:19 PM    <DIR>          ..
02/09/2017  12:00 PM     4,044,361,216 Kali-Linux-2016.2-vbox-i686.ova ◄──
12/16/2016  06:54 PM            41,491 md5sum.exe
05/12/2011  07:47 AM             5,632 sha1sum.exe ◄──
05/12/2011  07:47 AM             4,608 SHA1Sum_library.dll
12/16/2016  06:54 PM            51,219 sha224sum.exe
12/16/2016  06:54 PM            51,219 sha256sum.exe
12/16/2016  06:54 PM            57,363 sha384sum.exe
12/16/2016  06:54 PM            57,363 sha512sum.exe
               8 File(s)  4,044,630,111 bytes
               2 Dir(s)   2,364,593,291,264 bytes free

C:\Kali>sha1sum compute kali-linux-2016.2-vbox-i686.ova
93aeb16a1a9a5d6e94a9ae6af105573c7cb3357b  kali-linux-2016.2-vbox-i686.ova 1

C:\Kali>sha1sum compute kali-linux-2016.2-vbox-i686.ova
93aeb16a1a9a5d6e94a9ae6af105573c7cb3357b  kali-linux-2016.2-vbox-i686.ova 2

C:\Kali>sha1sum compute kali-linux-2016.2-vbox-i686.ova
93aeb16a1a9a5d6e94a9ae6af105573c7cb3357b  kali-linux-2016.2-vbox-i686.ova 3

C:\Kali>
```

Figure 10.1: Calculating a hash with sha1sum

Figure 10.1 demonstrates two important points:

- **The hash will always be the same no matter how many times you calculate it.**
  In the figure, I ran sha1sum three times, but it would give me the same result if I ran it 3,000 times.
- **Hashing verifies the file has retained integrity.**
  Because the calculated hash is the same as the hash posted on the download site, it verifies the file has not lost integrity.

In contrast, if sha1sum created a different hash than the one posted on the web site, I'd know that the file lost integrity. I wouldn't necessarily know *why* the file lost integrity. An attacker might have infected it with malware, or it might have lost a bit or two during the transfer. However, I would know that the integrity of the file was lost and the file should not be trusted.

It's worth stressing that hashes are one-way functions. In other words, you can calculate a hash on a file or a message, but you can't use the hash to reproduce the original data. The hashing algorithms always create a fixed-size bit string regardless of the size of the original data. The hash doesn't give you a clue about the size of the file, the type of the file, or anything else.

As an example, the SHA-1 hash from the message "I will pass the Security+ exam" is: *765591c4611be5e03bea41882ffdaa159352cf49*. However, you can't look at the hash and identify the message, or even know that it is a hash of a six-word message. Similarly, you can't look at the hash shown in Figure 10.1 and know that it was calculated from a 3.8 GB executable file.

If you want to work with hashes yourself, check out the hashing and checksum labs in the online resources for this book at *http://gcgapremium.com/501labs/*.

Hashing Passwords

Passwords are often stored as hashes. When a user creates a new password, the system calculates the hash for the password and then stores the hash. Later, when the user authenticates by entering a username and password, the system calculates the hash of the entered password, and then compares it with the stored hash. If the hashes are the same, it indicates that the user entered the correct password.

> **Remember this**
>
> Hashing is a one-way function that creates a string of characters. You cannot reverse the hash to re-create the original file. Passwords are often stored as hashes instead of storing the actual password. Additionally, applications often salt passwords with extra characters before hashing them.

Key Stretching

As mentioned in Chapter 7, "Protecting Against Advanced Attacks," many password attacks attempt to discover a password by calculating a hash on a guessed password, and then comparing it with the stored hash of the password. Using complex passwords goes a long way toward preventing these types of attacks but doesn't prevent them all.

Key stretching (sometimes called key strengthening) is a technique used to increase the strength of stored passwords and can help thwart brute force and rainbow table attacks. Key stretching techniques *salt* the passwords with additional random bits to make them even more complex. Two common key stretching techniques are bcrypt and Password-Based Key Derivation Function 2 (PBKDF2).

Bcrypt is based on the Blowfish block cipher and is used on many Unix and Linux distributions to protect the passwords stored in the shadow password file. Bcrypt salts the password by adding additional random bits before encrypting it with Blowfish. Bcrypt can go through this process multiple times to further protect against attempts to discover the password. The result is a 60-character string.

As an example, if your password is IL0ve$ecurity, an application can encrypt it with bcrypt and a random salt. It might look like this, which the application stores in a database:

$2b$12$HXIKtJr93DH59BzzKQhehOl9pGjRA/03ENcFRby1jH7nXwt1Tn0kG

Later, when a user authenticates with a username and password, the application runs bcrypt on the supplied password and compares it with the stored bcrypt-encrypted password. If the bcrypt result of the supplied password is the same as the stored bcrypt result, the user is authenticated.

As an added measure, it's possible to add some pepper to the salt to further randomize the bcrypt string. In this context, the pepper is another set of random bits stored elsewhere.

PBKDF2 uses salts of at least 64 bits and uses a pseudo-random function such as HMAC to protect passwords. Many algorithms such as Wi-Fi Protected Access II (WPA2), Apple's iOS mobile operating system, and Cisco operating systems use PBKDF2 to increase the security of passwords. Some applications send the password through the PBKDF2 process as many as 1,000,000 times to create the hash. The size of the resulting hash varies with PBKDF2 depending on how it is implemented. Bit sizes of 128 bits, 256 bits, and 512 bits are most common.

Some security experts believe that PBKDF2 is more susceptible to brute force attacks than bcrypt. A public group created the Password Hashing Competition (PHC). They received and evaluated 24 different hashing algorithms as alternatives. In July 2015, the PHC selected Argon2 as the winner of the competition and recommended it be used instead of legacy algorithms such as PBKDF2.

> ### Remember this
> Bcrypt and PBKDF2 are key stretching techniques that help prevent brute force and rainbow table attacks. Both salt the password with additional random bits.

Hashing Messages

Hashing provides integrity for messages. It provides assurance to someone receiving a message that the message has not been modified. Imagine that Lisa is sending a message to Bart, as shown in Figure 10.2. The message is "The price is $75." This message is not secret, so there is no need to encrypt it. However, we do want to provide integrity, so this explanation is focused only on hashing.

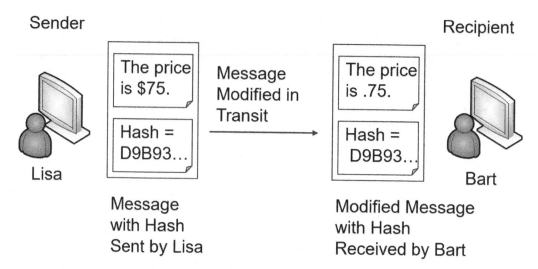

Figure 10.2: Simplified hash process

An application on Lisa's computer calculates the MD5 hash as:
D9B93C99B62646ABD06C887039053F56.

In the figure, I've shortened the full hash down to just the first five characters of "D9B93." Lisa then sends both the message and the hash to Bart.

In this example, something modified the message before it reaches Bart. When Bart receives the message and the original hash, the message is now "The price is .75." Note that the message is modified in transit, but the hash is *not* modified.

A program on Bart's computer calculates the MD5 hash on the received message as 564294439E1617F5628A3E3EB75643FE. It then compares the received hash with the calculated hash:

- Hash created on Lisa's computer, and received by Bart's computer:
  D9B93C99B62646ABD06C887039053F56
- Hash created on Bart's computer:
  564294439E1617F5628A3E3EB75643FE

Clearly, the hashes are different, so you know the message lost integrity. The program on Bart's computer would report the discrepancy. Bart doesn't know what caused the problem. It could have been a malicious attacker changing the message, or it could have been a technical problem. However, Bart does know the received message isn't the same as the sent message and he shouldn't trust it.

Using HMAC

You might have noticed a problem in the explanation of the hashed message. If an attacker can change the message, why can't the attacker change the hash, too? In other words, if Hacker Harry changed the message to "The price is .75," he could also calculate the hash on the modified message and replace the original hash with the modified hash. Here's the result:

- Hash created on Lisa's computer:

D9B93C99B62646ABD06C887039053F56
- Modified hash inserted by attacker after modifying the message:
  564294439E1617F5628A3E3EB75643FE
- Hash created for modified message on Bart's computer:
  564294439E1617F5628A3E3EB75643FE

The calculated hash on the modified message would be the same as the received hash. This erroneously indicates that the message maintained integrity. HMAC helps solve this problem.

With HMAC, both Lisa and Bart's computers would know the same secret key and use it to create an HMAC-MD5 hash instead of just an MD5 hash. Figure 10.3 shows the result.

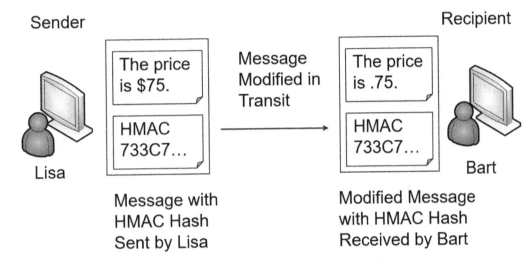

Figure 10.3: Using HMAC

Lisa is still sending the same message.

The MD5 hash is *D9B93C99B62646ABD06C887039053F56*. However, after applying the HMAC secret key, the HMAC-MD5 hash is *733C70A54A13744D5C2C9C4BA3B15034*. For brevity, I shortened this to only the first five characters (733C7) in the figure.

An attacker can modify the message in transit just as before. However, the attacker doesn't know the secret key, so he can't calculate the HMAC hash.

Bart's computer calculates the HMAC-MD5 hash on the received message using the shared secret key. It then compares the calculated hash with the hash received from Lisa:
- HMAC-MD5 hash created on Lisa's computer:
  733C70A54A13744D5C2C9C4BA3B15034
- HMAC-MD5 hash created on Bart's computer:
  1B4FF0F6C04434BF97F1E3DDD4B6C137

Again, you can see that the hashes are different and the message has lost integrity. If the messages weren't modified, the HMAC-MD5 hash would be the same.

Table 10.1 summarizes the important hashing protocols covered on the CompTIA Security+ exam.

Algorithm	Type	Comments
MD5	Hashing - Integrity	Creates 128-bit hashes
SHA-1	Hashing - Integrity	Creates 160-bit hashes
SHA-2	Hashing - Integrity	Creates 224-, 256-, 384-, or 512-bit hashes
SHA-3	Hashing - Integrity	Creates 224-, 256-, 384-, or 512-bit hashes
HMAC-MD5	Integrity/Authenticity	Creates 128-bit hashes
HMAC-SHA1	Integrity/Authenticity	Creates 160-bit hashes

Table 10.1: Hashing protocols

> **Remember this**
>
> If you can recognize the hashing algorithms such as MD5, SHA, and HMAC, it will help you answer many exam questions. For example, if a question asks what you would use to encrypt data and it lists hashing algorithms, you can quickly eliminate them because hashing algorithms don't encrypt data.

Providing Confidentiality with Encryption

Encryption provides confidentiality and prevents unauthorized disclosure of data. Encrypted data is in a ciphertext format that is unreadable. Attackers can't read encrypted traffic sent over a network or encrypted data stored on a system. In contrast, if data is sent in cleartext, an attacker can capture and read the data using a protocol analyzer.

Data-at-rest refers to any data stored on media and it's common to encrypt sensitive data. For example, it's possible to encrypt individual fields in a database (such as the fields holding customer credit card data), individual files, folders, or a full disk.

Data-in-transit refers to any data sent over a network and it's common to encrypt sensitive data-in-transit. For example, e-commerce web sites commonly use Hypertext Transfer Protocol Secure (HTTPS) sessions to encrypt transactions that include credit card data. If attackers intercept the transmissions, they only see ciphertext.

Data-in-use refers to data being used by a computer. Because the computer needs to process the data, it is not encrypted while in use. If the data is encrypted, an application will decrypt it and store it in memory while in use. If the application changes the data, it will encrypt it again before saving it. Additionally, applications usually take extra steps to purge memory of sensitive data after processing it.

The two primary encryption methods are symmetric and asymmetric. Symmetric encryption encrypts and decrypts data with the same key. Asymmetric encryption encrypts and decrypts data using a matched key pair of a public key and a private key.

These encryption methods include two elements:

- **Algorithm.** The algorithm performs mathematical calculations on data. The algorithm is always the same.

- **Key.** The key is a number that provides variability for the encryption. It is either kept private and/or changed frequently.

> ### Remember this
>
> Encryption provides confidentiality and helps ensure that data is viewable only by authorized users. This applies to any data-at-rest (such as data stored in a database) or data-in-transit being sent over a network.

Encryption Terms

There are several terms within cryptography that are important to grasp. Understanding these terms makes it much easier to understand many of the more advanced concepts:

- **Random and pseudo-random numbers.** Many encryption schemes require a random or pseudo-random number as an input. If you're able to pick a number completely by chance, it is a random number. However, computers don't do things by chance, so it's often difficult to get a true random number. Instead, computers often use techniques to obtain pseudo-random numbers. A pseudo-random number appears to be random, but it is created by a deterministic algorithm. In other words, given the same input, a pseudo-random number generator will produce the same output.
- **IV.** An initialization vector (IV) provides a starting value for a cryptographic algorithm. It is a fixed-size random or pseudo-random number that helps create random encryption keys. Ideally, the IV should be large enough so that the algorithm doesn't reuse the same IV and re-create the same encryption keys.
- **Nonce.** A *nonce* is a number used once. For example, an IV should be large enough so that it is only used once. Many cryptographic algorithms use a random or pseudo-random nonce as a seed or a starting number.
- **XOR.** XOR is a logical operation used in some encryption schemes. *XOR* operations compare two inputs. If the two inputs are the same, it outputs True (or a binary 1). If the two inputs are different, it outputs False (or a binary 0).
- **Confusion.** In the context of encryption, *confusion* means that the ciphertext is significantly different than the plaintext. As an example, when encrypting the words "I passed!" with Advanced Encryption Standard (AES), it results in the following text: nkm6olLdchB049LbrCpL5Q.
- **Diffusion.** Effective *diffusion* techniques ensure that small changes in the plaintext result in large changes in the ciphertext. Just changing a single character in the plaintext results in completely different ciphertext. As an example, when encrypting "I passed." with AES, it results in the following text: k/ljn+j6WBxAIKHN6IONBA. Compare this with the ciphertext from "I passed!" and you can see how changing only one character in the plaintext completely changed the ciphertext, indicating that AES is using strong diffusion techniques.
- **Secret algorithm.** A secret algorithm is one that is kept private. Security experts discourage this practice because it prevents a review of the algorithm by experts and mathematicians. Vigorous reviews can discover any flaws or potential weaknesses. In contrast, most algorithms are published and known.

- **Weak/deprecated algorithms.** A weak algorithm can be cracked, allowing an attacker to easily convert ciphertext back to plaintext. When flaws are discovered in algorithms, experts and authorities recommend deprecating the weak algorithm. As an example, web sites commonly used Secure Sockets Layer (SSL) to encrypt HTTPS sessions on the Internet. However, experts discovered flaws in SSL and most authorities have deprecated the use of SSL and recommend the use of TLS instead.
- **High resiliency.** A common use case for encryption algorithms is to provide high resiliency. Within cryptography, high resiliency refers to the security of an encryption key even if an attacker discovers part of the key. Ideally, keys are not susceptible to leakage, preventing attackers from gaining information on any part of a key. However, there are many situations that can cause leakage. A strong algorithm implements high-resiliency techniques that ensure this leakage does not compromise the encryption key.

Remember this

Random numbers are picked by chance. Pseudo-random numbers appear to be random but are created by deterministic algorithms, meaning that given the same input, a pseudo-random number generator will create the same output. In cryptology, confusion indicates that the ciphertext is significantly different than the plaintext. Diffusion cryptographic techniques ensure that small changes in the plaintext result in significant changes in the ciphertext.

Block Versus Stream Ciphers

Most symmetric algorithms use either a block cipher or a stream cipher. They are both symmetric, so they both use the same key to encrypt or decrypt data. However, they divide data in different ways.

A **block cipher** encrypts data in specific-sized blocks, such as 64-bit blocks or 128-bit blocks. The block cipher divides large files or messages into these blocks and then encrypts each individual block separately. A **stream cipher** encrypts data as a stream of bits or bytes rather than dividing it into blocks.

In general, stream ciphers are more efficient than block ciphers when the size of the data is unknown or sent in a continuous stream, such as when streaming audio and video over a network. Block ciphers are more efficient when the size of the data is known, such as when encrypting a file or a specific-sized database field.

An important principle when using a stream cipher is that encryption keys should never be reused. If a key is reused, it is easier to crack the encryption.

Remember this

Stream ciphers encrypt data a single bit, or a single byte, at a time in a stream. Block ciphers encrypt data in a specific-sized block such as 64-bit or 128-bit blocks. Stream ciphers are more efficient than block ciphers when encrypting data in a continuous stream.

Cipher Modes

Block ciphers can use a variety of different modes of operation. It's important to have a basic understanding of these modes when choosing cipher suites.

The Electronic Codebook (**ECB**) mode of operation is the simplest cipher mode mentioned in this section. Algorithms that use ECB divide the plaintext into blocks and then encrypt each block using the same key. This represents a significant weakness. If any of the plaintext blocks are the same, the resulting ciphertext is the same, making it much easier to crack. ECB is not recommended for use in any cryptographic protocols today.

Cipher Block Chaining (**CBC**) mode is used by some symmetric block ciphers. It uses an IV for randomization when encrypting the first block. It then combines each subsequent block with the previous block using an XOR operation. Because encryption of each block is dependent on the encryption of all previous blocks, CBC sometimes suffers from pipeline delays, making it less efficient than some other modes.

Counter (**CTM**) mode effectively converts a block cipher into a stream cipher. It combines an IV with a counter and uses the result to encrypt each plaintext block. Each block uses the same IV, but CTM combines it with the counter value, resulting in a different encryption key for each block. Multiprocessor systems can encrypt or decrypt multiple blocks at the same time, allowing the algorithm to be quicker on multiprocessor or multicore systems. CTM is widely used and respected as a secure mode of operation.

It's worthwhile noting that the CompTIA objectives list CTM and include CTM in the acronym list as Counter-Mode. However, it's much more common to see it listed as CTR or CM.

Galois/Counter Mode (**GCM**) is a mode of operation used by many block ciphers. It combines the Counter mode of operation with the Galois mode of authentication. Note that it doesn't authenticate users or systems, but instead provides data authenticity (integrity) and confidentiality. In addition to encrypting the data for confidentiality, it includes hashing techniques for integrity. It is widely used due to its efficiency and performance, allowing systems to quickly encrypt and decrypt data.

> **Remember this**
>
> The Electronic Codebook (ECB) mode of operation is deprecated and should not be used. Cipher Block Chaining (CBC) mode combines each block with the previous block when encrypting data and sometimes suffers from pipeline delays. Counter (CTM) mode combines an IV with a counter to encrypt each block. Galois/Counter Mode (GCM) combines Counter mode with hashing techniques for integrity.

Symmetric Encryption

Symmetric encryption uses the same key to encrypt and decrypt data. In other words, if you encrypt data with a key of three, you decrypt it with the same key of three. Symmetric encryption is also called secret-key encryption or session-key encryption.

As a simple example, when I was a child, a friend and I used to pass encoded messages back and forth to each other. Our algorithm was:

- **Encryption algorithm.** Move __X__ spaces forward to encrypt.
- **Decryption algorithm.** Move __X__ spaces backward to decrypt.

On the way to school, we would identify the key (X) we would use that day. For example, we may have used the key of three one day. If I wanted to encrypt a message, I would move each character three spaces forward, and he would decrypt the message by moving three spaces backward.

Imagine the message "PASS" needs to be sent:

- Three characters past "P" is "S"—Start at P (Q, R, S)
- Three characters past "A" is "D"—Start at A (B, C, D)
- Three characters past "S" is "V"—Start at S (T, U, V)
- Three characters past "S" is "V"—Start at S (T, U, V)

The encrypted message is SDVV. My friend decrypted it by moving backward three spaces and learned that "PASS" was the original message.

We were using a simple substitution cipher. A **substitution cipher** replaces **plaintext** with **ciphertext** using a fixed system. In the example, "PASS" is the plaintext, "SDVV" is the ciphertext, and the fixed system is three letters.

The **ROT13** (short for rotate 13 places) cipher uses the same substitution algorithm, but always uses a key of 13. To encrypt a message, you would rotate each letter 13 spaces. To decrypt a message, you would rotate each letter 13 spaces. However, because ROT13 uses both the same algorithm and the same key, it doesn't provide true encryption but instead just obfuscates the data.

Obfuscation methods attempt to make something unclear or difficult to understand. This is sometimes referred to as security through obscurity. However, this is rarely a reliable method of maintaining security.

Rotating letters with a different key shows how symmetric encryption uses the same key for encryption and decryption. If I encrypted the message with a key of three, my friend wouldn't be able to decrypt it with anything but a key of three. It also helps to demonstrate an algorithm and a key, though it is admittedly simple.

Sophisticated symmetric encryption techniques use the same components of an algorithm and a key. However, the algorithms and keys are much more complex. For example, the Advanced Encryption Standard (AES) symmetric algorithm typically uses 128-bit keys, but can use keys with 256 bits.

Imagine two servers sending encrypted traffic back and forth to each other using AES symmetric encryption. They both use the same AES algorithm and the same key for this data. The data is encrypted on one server with AES and a key, sent over the wire or other transmission medium, and the same key is used to decrypt it on the other server. Similarly, if a database includes encrypted data, the key used to encrypt data is the same key used to decrypt data.

However, symmetric encryption doesn't use the same key to encrypt and decrypt all data. For example, my friend and I used a different key each day. On the way to school, we decided on a key to use for that day. The next day, we picked a different key. If someone cracked our code yesterday, they couldn't easily crack our code today.

Symmetric encryption algorithms change keys much more often than once a day. For example, imagine an algorithm uses a key of 123 to encrypt a project file. It could then use a key of 456 to encrypt a spreadsheet file. The key of 123 can only decrypt the project file and the key of 456 can only decrypt the spreadsheet file.

On the other hand, if symmetric encryption always used the same key of 123, it would add vulnerabilities. First, when keys are reused, the encryption is easier to crack. Second, once the key is cracked, all data encrypted with this key is compromised. If attackers discover the key of

Comparing Symmetric Encryption to a Door Key

Occasionally, security professionals compare symmetric keys to a house key and this analogy helps some people understand symmetric encryption a little better. For example, imagine Marge moves into a new home. She'll receive a single key that she can use to lock and unlock her home. Of course, Marge can't use this key to unlock her neighbor's home.

Later, Marge marries Homer, and Homer moves into Marge's home. Marge can create a copy of her house key and give it to Homer. Homer can now use that copy of the key to lock and unlock the house. By sharing copies of the same key, it doesn't matter whether Marge or Homer is the one who locks the door; they can both unlock it.

Similarly, symmetric encryption uses a single key to encrypt and decrypt data. If a copy of the symmetric key is shared, others who have the key can also encrypt and decrypt data.

123, not only would they have access to the project file, but they would also have access to the spreadsheet file and any other data encrypted with this same key.

As a more realistic example, Chapter 4, "Securing Your Network," describes how Remote Authentication Dial-In User Service (RADIUS) encrypts password packets. RADIUS uses shared keys for symmetric encryption. When users authenticate, RADIUS servers and clients use the shared key to encrypt and decrypt data exchanged in a challenge/response session. Without the shared key, clients are unable to decrypt the data and respond appropriately.

Remember this

Symmetric encryption uses the same key to encrypt and decrypt data. For example, when transmitting encrypted data, symmetric encryption algorithms use the same key to encrypt and decrypt data at both ends of the transmission media. RADIUS uses symmetric encryption.

AES

The Advanced Encryption Standard (*AES*) is a strong symmetric block cipher that encrypts data in 128-bit blocks. The National Institute of Standards and Technology (NIST) adopted AES from the Rijndael encryption algorithm after a lengthy evaluation of several different algorithms. NIST is a U.S. agency that develops and promotes standards. They spent about five years conducting a review of 15 different symmetric algorithms and identified AES as the best of the 15.

AES can use key sizes of 128 bits, 192 bits, or 256 bits, and it's sometimes referred to as AES-128, AES-192, or AES-256 to identify how many bits are used in the key. When more bits are used, it makes it more difficult to discover the key and decrypt the data. AES-128 provides strong protection, but AES-256 provides stronger protection.

In general, the size of the key for any encryption directly corresponds to the key strength. Longer keys for a specific algorithm result in stronger key strength.

Because of its strengths, AES has been adopted in a wide assortment of applications. For example, many applications that encrypt data on USB drives use AES. Some of the strengths of AES are:

- **Fast.** AES uses elegant mathematical formulas and only requires one pass to encrypt

and decrypt data. In contrast, 3DES (mentioned later in this chapter) requires multiple passes to encrypt and decrypt data.
- **Efficient.** AES is less resource intensive than other encryption algorithms such as 3DES. AES encrypts and decrypts quickly even when ciphering data on small devices, such as USB flash drives.
- **Strong.** AES provides strong encryption of data, providing a high level of confidentiality.

DES

Data Encryption Standard (**DES**) is a symmetric block cipher that was widely used for many years, dating back to the 1970s. It encrypts data in 64-bit blocks. However, it uses a relatively small key of only 56 bits and can be broken with brute force attacks. In the '70s, the technology required to break 56-bit encryption wasn't easily available, but with the advances in computer technology, a 56-bit key is now considered trivial. DES is not recommended for use today.

3DES

3DES (pronounced as "Triple DES") is a symmetric block cipher designed as an improvement over the known weaknesses of DES. In basic terms, it encrypts data using the DES algorithm in three separate passes and uses multiple keys. Just as DES encrypts data in 64-bit blocks, 3DES also encrypts data in 64-bit blocks.

Although 3DES is a strong algorithm, it isn't used as often as AES today. AES is much less resource intensive. However, if hardware doesn't support AES, 3DES is a suitable alternative. 3DES uses key sizes of 56 bits, 112 bits, or 168 bits.

Remember this

AES is a strong symmetric block cipher that encrypts data in 128-bit blocks. AES uses 128-bit, 192-bit, or 256-bit keys. DES and 3DES are block ciphers that encrypt data in 64-bit blocks. 3DES was originally designed as a replacement for DES, but NIST selected AES as the current standard. However, 3DES is still used in some applications, such as when legacy hardware doesn't support AES.

RC4

Ron Rivest invented several versions of RC, which are sometimes referred to as Ron's Code or Rivest Cipher. The most commonly used version is **RC4** (also called ARC4), which is a symmetric stream cipher and it can use between 40 and 2,048 bits.

RC4 has enjoyed a long life as a strong cipher. For many years, it has been the recommended encryption mechanism in SSL and TLS, when encrypting HTTPS connections on the Internet.

However, experts have speculated since 2013 that agencies such as the U.S. National Security Agency (NSA) can break RC4, even when implemented correctly such as in TLS. Because of this, companies such as Microsoft recommend disabling RC4 and using AES instead. Even though AES is a block cipher and RC4 is a stream cipher, TLS can implement either one.

Blowfish and Twofish

Blowfish is a strong symmetric block cipher that is still widely used today. It encrypts data in 64-bit blocks and supports key sizes between 32 and 448 bits. Bruce Schneier (a widely respected voice in IT security) designed Blowfish as a general-purpose algorithm to replace DES.

Interestingly, Blowfish is actually faster than AES in some instances. This is especially true when comparing Blowfish with AES-256. Part of the reason is that Blowfish encrypts data in smaller 64-bit blocks, whereas AES encrypts data in 128-bit blocks.

Twofish is related to Blowfish, but it encrypts data in 128-bit blocks and it supports 128-, 192-, or 256-bit keys. It was one of the finalist algorithms evaluated by NIST for AES. However, NIST selected Rijndael as AES instead.

> ### Remember this
>
> RC4 is a strong symmetric stream cipher, but most experts recommend using AES instead today. Blowfish is a 64-bit block cipher and Twofish is a 128-bit block cipher. Although NIST recommends AES as the standard, Blowfish is faster than AES-256.

Symmetric Encryption Summary

Table 10.2 summarizes the important symmetric algorithms and their basic characteristics. The items marked with an asterisk (RC4 and DES) are no longer recommended for use, but are still included in the CompTIA Security+ objectives.

Algorithm	Type	Method	Key Size
AES	Symmetric encryption	128-bit block cipher	128-, 192-, or 256-bit key
3DES	Symmetric encryption	64-bit block cipher	56-, 112-, or 168-bit key
Blowfish	Symmetric encryption	64-bit block cipher	32- to 448-bit key
Twofish	Symmetric encryption	128-bit block cipher	128-, 192-, or 256-bit key
RC4*	Symmetric encryption	Stream cipher	40- to 2,048-bit key
DES*	Symmetric encryption	64-bit block cipher	56-bit key

Table 10.2: Symmetric encryption protocols

> ### Remember this
>
> If you can recognize the symmetric algorithms such as AES, DES, 3DES, Blowfish, and Twofish, it will help you answer many exam questions. For example, if a question asks what you would use to hash data and it lists encryption algorithms, you can quickly eliminate them because encryption algorithms don't hash data. You should also know the size of the blocks and the size of the keys listed in Table 10.2.

Asymmetric Encryption

Asymmetric encryption uses two keys in a matched pair to encrypt and decrypt data—a public key and a private key. There are several important points to remember with these keys:

- If the ***public key*** encrypts information, only the matching private key can decrypt the same information.
- If the ***private key*** encrypts information, only the matching public key can decrypt the same information.

- Private keys are always kept private and never shared.
- Public keys are freely shared by embedding them in a shared certificate.

> **Remember this**
>
> Only a private key can decrypt information encrypted with a matching public key. Only a public key can decrypt information encrypted with a matching private key. A key element of several asymmetric encryption methods is that they require a certificate and a PKI.

Although asymmetric encryption is very strong, it is also very resource intensive. It takes a significant amount of processing power to encrypt and decrypt data, especially when compared with symmetric encryption. Most cryptographic protocols that use asymmetric encryption only use it for key exchange. Key exchange is any cryptographic method used to share cryptographic keys between two entities. In this context, asymmetric encryption uses key exchange to share a symmetric key. The cryptographic protocol then uses the symmetric encryption to encrypt and decrypt data because symmetric encryption is much more efficient.

Some of the more advanced topics related to asymmetric encryption become harder to understand if you don't understand the relationship of matched public and private key pairs. However, because you can't actually see these keys, the concepts are hard to grasp for some people. The Rayburn box demonstrates how you can use physical keys for the same purposes as these public and private keys.

The Rayburn Box

I often talk about the Rayburn box in the classroom to help people understand the usage of public and private keys. A Rayburn box is a lockbox that allows people to securely transfer items over long distances. It has two keys. One key can lock the box, but can't unlock it. The other key can unlock the box, but can't lock it.

Both keys are matched to one box and won't work with other boxes:

- Only one copy of one key exists—think of it as the private key.
- Multiple copies of the other key exist, and copies are freely made and distributed— think of these as public keys.

The box comes in two different versions. In one version, it's used to send secrets in a confidential manner to prevent unauthorized disclosure. In the other version, it's used to send messages with authentication, so you know the sender sent the message and that the message wasn't modified in transit.

The Rayburn Box Used to Send Secrets

Imagine that I wanted you to send some proprietary information and a working model of an invention to me. Obviously, we wouldn't want anyone else to be able to access the information or the working model. I could send you the empty open box with a copy of the key used to lock it.

You place everything in the box and then lock it with the public key I've sent with the box. This key can't unlock the box, so even if other people had copies of the public key that I sent to you, they couldn't use it to unlock the box. When I receive the box from you, I can unlock it with the only key that will unlock it—my private key.

This is similar to how public and private keys are used to send encrypted data over the Internet to ensure confidentiality. The public key encrypts information. Information encrypted with a public key can only be decrypted with the matching private key. Many copies of the public key are available, but only one private key exists, and the private key always stays private. The "Encrypting HTTPS Traffic with TLS" section later in this chapter shows this process in more depth.

The Rayburn Box Used for Authentication

With a little rekeying of the box, I can use it to send messages while giving assurances to recipients that I sent the message. In this context, the message isn't secret and doesn't need to be protected. Instead, it's important that you know I sent the message.

When used this way, the private key will lock the Rayburn box, but it cannot unlock the box. Instead, only a matching public key can unlock it. Multiple copies of the public key exist and anyone with a public key can unlock the box. However, after unlocking the box with a matching public key, it isn't possible to lock it with the public key.

Imagine that you and I are allies in a battle. I want to give you a message of "SY0-501," which is a code telling you to launch a specific attack at a specific time. We don't care if someone reads this message because it's a code. However, we need you to have assurances that I sent the message.

I write the message, place it in the box, and lock it with my private key. When you receive it, you can unlock it with the matching public key. Because the public key opens it, you know this is my box and it was locked with my private key—you know I sent the message.

If an enemy spy intercepted the box and opened it with the public key, the spy wouldn't be able to lock it again using the public key, so you'd receive an open box. However, the spy could replace the message with something else. An open box with a message inside it doesn't prove I sent it. The only way you know that I sent it is if you receive a locked box that you can unlock with the matching public key.

This is similar to how digital signatures use public and private keys. The "Signing Email with Digital Signatures" section later in this chapter explains digital signatures in more depth. In short, I can send you a message digitally signed with my private key. If you can decrypt the digital signature with my matching public key, you know it was encrypted, or signed, with my private key. Because only one copy of the private key exists, and I'm the only person who can access it, you know I sent the message.

The Rayburn Box Demystified

Before you try to find a Rayburn box, let me clear something up. The Rayburn box is just a figment of my imagination. Rayburn is my middle name.

I haven't discovered a real-world example of how public/private keys work, so I've created the Rayburn box as a metaphor to help people visualize how public/private keys work. Feel free to build one if you want.

Certificates

A key element of asymmetric encryption is a certificate. A **certificate** is a digital document that typically includes the public key and information on the owner of the certificate. Certificate Authorities (CAs, explored in greater depth later in this chapter) issue and manage certificates. Certificates are used for a variety of purposes beyond just asymmetric encryption, including authentication and digital signatures.

Figure 10.4 shows a sample certificate with the public key selected. Users and applications share the certificate file to share the public key. They do not share the private key.

Figure 10.4: Certificate with public key selected

There is much more information in the certificate than just the public key, but not all of it is visible in the figure. Common elements within a certificate include:

- **Serial number.** The serial number uniquely identifies the certificate. The CA uses this serial number to validate a certificate. If the CA revokes the certificate, it publishes this serial number in a certificate revocation list (CRL).
- **Issuer.** This identifies the CA that issued the certificate.
- **Validity dates.** Certificates include "Valid From" and "Valid To" dates. This ensures a certificate expires at some point.
- **Subject.** This identifies the owner of the certificate. In the figure, it identifies the subject as Google, Inc and indicates this is a wildcard certificate used for all web sites with the *google.com* root domain name.
- **Public key.** RSA asymmetric encryption uses the public key in combination with the matching private key.
- **Usage.** Some certificates are only for encryption or authentication, whereas other certificates support multiple usages.

> **Remember this**
>
> Certificates are an important part of asymmetric encryption. Certificates include public keys along with details on the owner of the certificate and on the CA that issued the certificate. Certificate owners share their public key by sharing a copy of their certificate.

If you want to view a certificate, check out the View a Certificate Lab in the online labs for this book at *http://gcgapremium.com/501labs/*.

RSA

Ron Rivest, Adi Shamir, and Leonard Adleman developed RSA in 1977 and the *RSA* acronym uses their last names (Rivest, Shamir, Adleman). It is an asymmetric encryption method using both a public key and a private key in a matched pair, and it is widely used on the Internet and elsewhere due to its strong security.

As an example, email applications often use RSA to privately share a symmetric key between two systems. The application uses the recipient's public key to encrypt a symmetric key, and the recipient's private key decrypts it. The "Protecting Email" section later in this chapter discusses this process in more detail.

The RSA algorithm uses the mathematical properties of prime numbers to generate secure public and private keys. Specifically, RSA relies on the fact that it is difficult to factor the product of two large prime numbers. The math is complex and intriguing to mathematicians, but you don't have to understand the math to understand that RSA is secure if sufficient key sizes are used.

What is a sufficient key size? RSA laboratories recommend a key size of 2,048 bits to protect data through the year 2030. If data needs to be protected beyond 2030, they recommend a key size of 3,072 bits.

> **Remember this**
>
> RSA is widely used to protect data such as email and other data transmitted over the Internet. It uses both a public key and a private key in a matched pair.

Static Versus Ephemeral Keys

The two primary categories of asymmetric keys are static and ephemeral. In general, a static key is semipermanent and stays the same over a long period of time. In contrast, an *ephemeral key* has a very short lifetime and is re-created for each session.

RSA uses static keys. A certificate includes an embedded public key matched to a private key and this key pair is valid for the lifetime of a certificate, such as a year. Certificates have expiration dates and systems continue to use these keys until the certificate expires. A benefit of static keys is that a CA can validate them as discussed in the "Certificate Issues" section later in this chapter.

An ephemeral key pair includes a private ephemeral key and a public ephemeral key. However, systems use these key pairs for a single session and then discard them. Some versions of Diffie-Hellman (discussed later in this section) use static keys and some versions use ephemeral keys.

Perfect forward secrecy is an important characteristic that ephemeral keys comply with in asymmetric encryption. Perfect forward secrecy indicates that a cryptographic system generates random public keys for each session and it doesn't use a deterministic algorithm to do so. In other words, given the same input, the algorithm will create a different public key. This helps ensure that systems do not reuse keys. The result is that the compromise of a long-term key does not compromise any past keys.

Elliptic Curve Cryptography

Elliptic curve cryptography (ECC) doesn't take as much processing power as other cryptographic methods. Because of this, ECC is often considered with common use cases of low-power devices. For example, ECC is often used with small wireless devices because it doesn't take much processing power to achieve the desired security. It uses mathematical equations to formulate an elliptical curve. It then graphs points on the curve to create keys. This is mathematically easier and requires less processing power, while also being more difficult to crack.

The U.S. NSA previously endorsed the use of ECC for digital signatures and Diffie-Hellman key agreements. However, they announced in late 2015 their intent to move away from its use. Since then, they have deprecated the use of various ECC versions for government agencies.

Diffie-Hellman

Diffie-Hellman (DH) is a key exchange algorithm used to privately share a symmetric key between two parties. Once the two parties know the symmetric key, they use symmetric encryption to encrypt the data.

Whitfield Diffie and Martin Hellman first published the Diffie-Hellman scheme in 1976. Interestingly, Malcolm J. Williamson secretly created a similar algorithm while working in a British intelligence agency. It is widely believed that the work of these three provided the basis for public-key cryptography.

Diffie-Hellman methods support both static keys and ephemeral keys. RSA is based on the Diffie-Hellman key exchange concepts using static keys. Two Diffie-Hellman methods that use ephemeral keys are:

- **DHE.** Diffie-Hellman Ephemeral (DHE) uses ephemeral keys, generating different keys for each session. Some documents list this as Ephemeral Diffie-Hellman (EDH).
- **ECDHE.** Elliptic Curve Diffie-Hellman Ephemeral (ECDHE) uses ephemeral keys generated using ECC. Another version, Elliptic Curve Diffie-Hellman (ECDH), uses static keys.

When Diffie-Hellman is used, the two parties negotiate the strongest group that both parties support. There are currently more than 25 DH (Diffie Hellman) groups in use and they are defined as DH Group 1, DH Group 2, and so on. Higher group numbers indicate the group is more secure. For example, DH Group 1 uses 768 bits in the key exchange process and DH Group 15 uses 3,072 bits.

> **Remember this**
>
> Diffie-Hellman is a secure method of sharing symmetric encryption keys over a public network. Elliptic curve cryptography is commonly used with small wireless devices. ECDHE is a version of Diffie-Hellman that uses elliptic curve cryptography to generate encryption keys.

Steganography

Steganography hides data inside other data, or, as some people have said, it hides data in plain sight. The goal is to hide the data in such a way that no one suspects there is a hidden message. It doesn't actually encrypt the data, so it can't be classified as either symmetric or asymmetric. However, it can effectively hide information using obfuscation, so it is included with encryption topics. As mentioned in Chapter 1, obfuscation methods attempt to make something unclear or difficult to understand.

There are a variety of steganography tools available that make the process easier. Additionally, these tools attempt to resist detection by forensic methods. For example, Kali Linux includes Steghide and StegoSuite, two tools you can use to embed data into graphic files.

Some common examples of steganography are:

- **Hide data by manipulating bits.** It's possible to manipulate some bits within an image or sound file to embed a message. One method of embedding data in large files is modifying the least significant bit in some bytes. By modifying the least significant bit in some of the individual bytes of a JPEG file, it embeds a message, but the changes are so small that they are difficult to detect. However, if people know the file includes a message, they can easily retrieve it.
- **Hide data in the white space of a file.** Many files have unused space (called white space) at the end of file clusters. Imagine a small 6 KB file stored in two 4 KB clusters. It has an extra 2 KB of unused space and it's possible to fill this white space with a message. For example, you can embed a message into the white space of a GIF or JPEG file without altering the file size.

Security professionals use steganalysis techniques to detect steganography, and the most common method is with hashing. If a single bit of a file is modified, the hashing algorithm creates a different hash. By regularly taking the hashes of different files and comparing them with previous hashes, it's easy to detect when a file has been modified.

If you want to see how to embed a text file in an image file, check out the Steganography Lab mentioned in Chapter 1 at *http://gcgapremium.com/501labs*.

> ### Remember this
>
> Steganography hides messages or other data within a file. For example, you can hide messages within the white space of a JPEG or GIF file. Security professionals use hashing to detect changes in files that may indicate the use of steganography.

Using Cryptographic Protocols

With a basic understanding of hashing, symmetric encryption, and asymmetric encryption, it's easier to grasp how cryptography is used. Many applications use a combination of these methods, and it's important to understand how they're intertwined.

When describing public and private keys earlier, it was stressed that one key encrypts and the other key decrypts. A common question is "which one encrypts and which one decrypts?" The answer depends on what you're trying to accomplish. The following sections describe the details, but as an overview, these are the important points related to these keys:

- Email digital signatures
  - The *sender's private key* encrypts (or signs).
  - The *sender's public key* decrypts.
- Email encryption
  - The *recipient's public key* encrypts.
  - The *recipient's private key* decrypts.
- Web site encryption
  - The *web site's public key* encrypts.
  - The *web site's private key* decrypts.
  - The *symmetric key* encrypts data in the web site session.

Email and web site encryption commonly use a combination of both asymmetric and symmetric encryption. They use asymmetric encryption for key exchange, privately sharing a symmetric key. Symmetric encryption encrypts the data.

> ### Remember this
>
> Knowing which key encrypts and which key decrypts will help you answer many questions on the exam. For example, just by knowing that a private key is encrypting, you know that it is being used for a digital signature.

Protecting Email

Cryptography provides two primary security methods you can use with email: digital signatures and encryption. These are separate processes, but you can digitally sign and encrypt the same email.

Signing Email with Digital Signatures

Digital signatures are similar in concept to handwritten signatures on printed documents that identify individuals, but they provide more security benefits. The digital signature algorithm (**DSA**) uses an encrypted hash of a message. The hash is encrypted with the sender's private key. If the recipient of a digitally signed email can decrypt the hash, it provides the following three security benefits:

- **Authentication.** This identifies the sender of the email. Email recipients have assurances the email actually came from who it appears to be coming from. For example, if an executive digitally signs an email, recipients know it came from the executive and not from an attacker impersonating the executive.
- **Non-repudiation.** The sender cannot later deny sending the message. This is sometimes required with online transactions. For example, imagine Homer sends an order to sell stocks using a digitally signed email. If the stocks increase after his sale completes, he can't deny the transaction.
- **Integrity.** This provides assurances that the message has not been modified or corrupted. Recipients know that the message they received is the same as the sent message.

Digital signatures are much easier to grasp if you understand some other cryptography concepts discussed in this chapter. As a short review, these concepts are:

- **Hashing.** Digital signatures start by creating a hash of the message. A hash is simply a number created by executing a hashing algorithm on the message.
- **Certificates.** Digital signatures need certificates, and certificates include the sender's public key.
- **Public/private keys.** In a digital signature, the sender uses the sender's private key to encrypt the hash of the message. The recipient uses the sender's public key to decrypt the hash of the message. The public key is often distributed in an *S/MIME.p7s* formatted file.

Figure 10.5 shows an overview of this process. In the figure, Lisa is sending a message to Bart with a digital signature. Note that the message "I passed" is not secret. If it was, Lisa would encrypt it, which is a separate process. The focus in this explanation is only the digital signature.

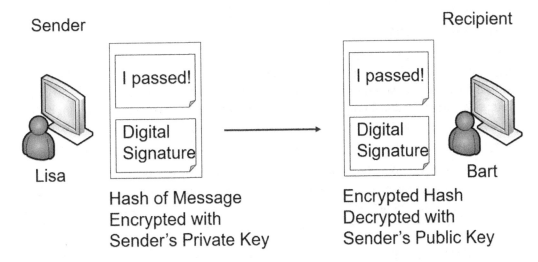

Sender   Recipient

Lisa   Bart

Hash of Message   Encrypted Hash
Encrypted with   Decrypted with
Sender's Private Key   Sender's Public Key

Figure 10.5: Digital signature process

Lisa creates her message in an email program, such as Microsoft Outlook. Once Microsoft Outlook is configured, all she does is click a button to digitally sign the message. Here is what happens when she clicks the button:

1. The application hashes the message.
2. The application retrieves Lisa's private key and encrypts the hash using this private key.
3. The application sends both the encrypted hash digital signature (the digital signature) and the unencrypted message to Bart.

When Bart's system receives the message, it verifies the digital signature using the following steps:

1. Bart's system retrieves Lisa's public key, which is in Lisa's public certificate. In some situations, Lisa may have sent Bart a copy of her certificate with her public key. In domain environments, Bart's system can automatically retrieve Lisa's certificate from a network location.
2. The email application on Bart's system decrypts the encrypted hash with Lisa's public key.
3. The application calculates the hash on the received message.
4. The application compares the decrypted hash with the calculated hash.

If the calculated hash of the received message is the same as the encrypted hash of the digital signature, it validates several important checks:

- **Authentication.** Lisa sent the message. The public key can only decrypt something encrypted with the private key, and only Lisa has the private key. If the decryption succeeded, Lisa's private key must have encrypted the hash. On the other hand, if another key was used to encrypt the hash, Lisa's public key could not decrypt it. In this case, Bart will see an error indicating a problem with the digital signature.
- **Non-repudiation.** Lisa cannot later deny sending the message. Only Lisa has her private key and if the public key decrypted the hash, the hash must have been encrypted with her private key. Non-repudiation is valuable in online transactions.
- **Integrity.** Because the hash of the sent message matches the hash of the received message, the message has maintained integrity. It hasn't been modified.

> ### Remember this
>
> A digital signature is an encrypted hash of a message. The sender's private key encrypts the hash of the message to create the digital signature. The recipient decrypts the hash with the sender's public key. If successful, it provides authentication, non-repudiation, and integrity. Authentication identifies the sender. Integrity verifies the message has not been modified. Non-repudiation prevents senders from later denying they sent an email.

At this point, you might be thinking, if we do all of this, why not just encrypt the message, too? The answer is resources. It doesn't take much processing power to encrypt 256 bits in a SHA-256 hash. In contrast, it would take quite a bit of processing power to encrypt a lengthy email and its attachments. However, if you need to ensure confidentiality of the email, you can encrypt it.

Encrypting Email

There are times when you want to ensure that email messages are only readable by authorized users. You can encrypt email and just as any other time encryption is used, encryption provides confidentiality.

Encrypting Email with Only Asymmetric Encryption

Imagine that Lisa wants to send an encrypted message to Bart. The following steps provide a simplified explanation of the process if only asymmetric encryption is used:

1. Lisa retrieves a copy of Bart's certificate that contains his public key.
2. Lisa encrypts the email with Bart's public key.
3. Lisa sends the encrypted email to Bart.
4. Bart decrypts the email with his private key.

This works because Bart is the only person who has access to his private key. If attackers intercepted the email, they couldn't decrypt it without Bart's private key. It's important to remember that when you're encrypting email contents, the recipient's public key encrypts and the recipient's private key decrypts. The sender's keys are not involved in this process. In contrast, a digital signature only uses the sender's keys but not the recipient's keys.

In most cases, the public key doesn't actually encrypt the message, but instead encrypts a symmetric key used to encrypt the email. The recipient then uses the private key to decrypt the symmetric key, and then uses the symmetric key to decrypt the email.

> ### Remember this
>
> The recipient's public key encrypts when encrypting an email message and the recipient uses the recipient's private key to decrypt an encrypted email message.

Encrypting Email with Asymmetric and Symmetric Encryption

The previous description provides a simplistic explanation of email encryption used by some email applications. However, most email applications combine both asymmetric and symmetric encryption. You may remember from earlier in this chapter that asymmetric encryption is slow and inefficient, but symmetric encryption is very quick.

Instead of using only symmetric encryption, most email applications use asymmetric encryption to privately share a session key. They then use symmetric encryption to encrypt the data. For example, imagine that Lisa is sending Bart an encrypted message. Figure 10.6 shows the process of encrypting the message and the symmetric key. Figure 10.7 shows the process of sending the encrypted message and encrypted session key, and identifies how the recipient can decrypt the data:

1. Lisa identifies a symmetric key to encrypt her email. For this example, assume it's a simplistic symmetric key of 53, though a symmetric algorithm like AES would use 128-bit or larger keys.
2. Lisa encrypts the email contents with the symmetric key of 53.
3. Lisa retrieves a copy of Bart's certificate that contains his public key.
4. She uses Bart's public key to encrypt the symmetric key of 53.
5. Lisa sends the encrypted email and the encrypted symmetric key to Bart.
6. Bart decrypts the symmetric key with his private key.
7. He then decrypts the email with the decrypted symmetric key.

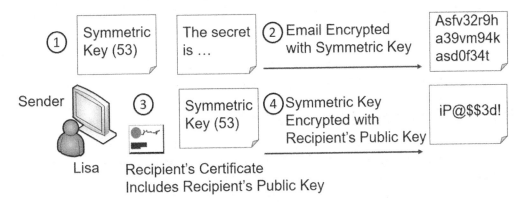

Figure 10.6: Encrypting email

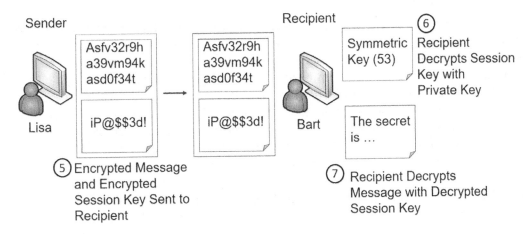

Figure 10.7: Decrypting email

Unauthorized users who intercept the email sent by Lisa won't be able to read it because it's encrypted with the symmetric key. Additionally, they can't read the symmetric key because it's encrypted with Bart's public key, and only Bart's private key can decrypt it.

S/MIME

Secure/Multipurpose Internet Mail Extensions (**S/MIME**) is one of the most popular standards used to digitally sign and encrypt email. Most email applications that support encryption and digital signatures use S/MIME standards.

S/MIME uses RSA for asymmetric encryption and AES for symmetric encryption. It can encrypt email at rest (stored on a drive) and in transit (data sent over the network). Because S/MIME uses RSA for asymmetric encryption, it requires a PKI to distribute and manage certificates.

PGP/GPG

Pretty Good Privacy (PGP) is a method used to secure email communication. It can encrypt, decrypt, and digitally sign email. Phillip Zimmerman designed PGP in 1991, and it has gone through many changes and improvements over the years. Symantec Corporation purchased it in June 2010.

OpenPGP is a PGP-based standard created to avoid any conflict with existing licensing. In other words, users have no obligation to pay licensing fees to use it. Some versions of PGP follow S/MIME standards. Other versions follow OpenPGP standards. GNU Privacy Guard (GPG) is free software that is based on the OpenPGP standard.

Each of the PGP versions uses the RSA algorithm and public and private keys for encryption and decryption. Just like S/MIME, PGP uses both asymmetric and symmetric encryption.

HTTPS Transport Encryption

Transport encryption methods encrypt data-in-transit to ensure transmitted data remains confidential. This includes data transmitted over the Internet and on internal networks. As an example, Chapter 3, "Exploring Network Technologies and Tools," discusses the use of Secure Shell (SSH) to encrypt traffic, such as Secure File Transfer Protocol (SFTP). This section focuses on transport encryption methods used with HTTPS.

SSL Versus TLS

Secure Sockets Layer (SSL) and Transport Layer Security (TLS) are encryption protocols that have been commonly used to encrypt data-in-transit. For example, it is common to encrypt HTTPS with either SSL or TLS to ensure confidentiality of data transmitted over the Internet. They can also be used to encrypt other transmissions such as File Transfer Protocol Secure (FTPS).

Netscape created SSL for its web browser and updated it to version SSL 3.0. This was before organizations such as the Internet Engineering Task Force (IETF) created and maintained standards. Netscape's success waned and there wasn't a standardization process to update SSL, even though all web browsers were using it. The IETF created TLS to standardize improvements with SSL.

Both SSL and TLS provide certificate-based authentication and they encrypt data with a combination of both symmetric and asymmetric encryption during a session. They use asymmetric encryption for the key exchange (to privately share a session key) and symmetric encryption to encrypt data displayed on the web page and transmitted during the session. The next section shows this process.

Transport Layer Security (TLS) is a replacement for SSL and is widely used in many different applications. The IETF has updated and published several TLS documents specifying the standard. TLS 1.0 is based on SSL 3.0 and is referred to as SSL 3.1. Similarly, each update to TLS indicates it is an update to SSL. For example, TLS 1.1 is called SSL 3.2 and TLS 1.2 is called SSL 3.3.

As mentioned in Chapter 3, SSL has been deprecated by most organizations in favor of TLS. However, many people commonly refer to TLS as SSL/TLS as if they are the same. Even the CompTIA Security+ objectives list many topics as SSL or SSL/TLS. In this context, you can consider any reference to SSL on the exam as a reference to TLS.

It's important to remember that TLS and SSL require certificates. Certificate Authorities (CAs) issue and manage certificates, so a CA is required to support TLS and SSL. These CAs can be internal or external third-party CAs.

> ### Remember this
>
> TLS is the replacement for SSL. Both TLS and SSL require certificates issued by Certificate Authorities (CAs). TLS encrypts HTTPS traffic, but it can also encrypt other traffic.

Encrypting HTTPS Traffic with TLS

HTTP Secure (HTTPS) is commonly used on the Internet to secure web traffic. HTTPS commonly uses TLS to encrypt the traffic, with both asymmetric and symmetric encryption. If you're able to grasp the basics of how HTTPS combines both asymmetric and symmetric encryption, you'll have what you need to know for most protocols that use both encryptions.

Because asymmetric encryption isn't efficient to encrypt large amounts of data, symmetric encryption is used to encrypt the session data. However, both the client and the server must know what this symmetric key is before they can use it. They can't whisper it to each other over the Internet. That's like an actor on TV using a loud whisper, or stage whisper, to share a secret. Millions of TV viewers can also hear the secret.

Instead, HTTPS uses asymmetric encryption to transmit a symmetric key using a secure key exchange method. It then uses the symmetric key with symmetric encryption to encrypt all the data in the HTTPS session.

Figure 10.8 and the following steps show the overall process of establishing and using an HTTPS session. As you read these steps, try to keep these two important concepts in mind:

- TLS uses *asymmetric* encryption to securely share the symmetric key.
- TLS uses *symmetric* encryption to encrypt the session data.

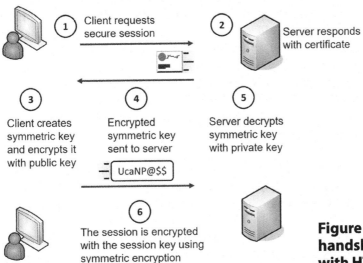

Figure 10.8: Simplified TLS handshake process used with HTTPS

1. The client begins the process by requesting an HTTPS session. This could be by entering an HTTPS address in the URL or by clicking on an HTTPS link.
2. The server responds by sending the server's certificate. The certificate includes the server's public key. The matching private key is on the server and only accessible by the server.
3. The client creates a symmetric key and encrypts it with the server's public key. As an example, imagine that the symmetric key is 53 (though it would be much more complex in a live session). The client encrypts the symmetric key of 53 using the web server's public key creating ciphertext of UcaNP@$$. This symmetric key will be used to encrypt data in the HTTPS session, so it is sometimes called a session key.
4. The client sends the encrypted session key (UcaNP@$$) to the web server. Only the server's private key can decrypt this. If attackers intercept the encrypted key, they won't be able to decrypt it because they don't have access to the server's private key.
5. The server receives the encrypted session key and decrypts it with the server's private key. At this point, both the client and the server know the session key.
6. All the session data is encrypted with this symmetric key using symmetric encryption.

The amazing thing to me is that this happens so quickly. If a web server takes as long as five seconds, many of us wonder why it's taking so long. However, a lot is happening to establish this session.

Cipher Suites

Cipher suites are a combination of cryptographic algorithms that provide several layers of security for TLS and SSL, though most organizations have deprecated the use of SSL. When two systems connect, they identify a cipher suite that is acceptable to both systems and then use the protocols within that suite. The protocols within the suite provide three primary cryptographic solutions. They are:

- **Encryption.** Encryption provides confidentiality of data. TLS uses asymmetric cryptography to privately exchange a symmetric key and then encrypts the data with a symmetric algorithm. TLS supports several types of symmetric encryption, including 3DES and AES.
- **Authentication.** TLS uses certificates for authentication. Clients can verify the authenticity of the certificate by querying the CA that issued the certificate.
- **Integrity.** TLS uses a message authentication code (MAC) for integrity. For example, it can use HMAC-MD5 or HMAC-SHA256.

There are over 200 named cipher suites, and systems identify them with a cipher identifier as a string of hexadecimal characters and a coded name. Here are two examples:

- **0x00C031.** TLS_ECDH_RSA_WITH_AES_128_GCM_SHA256
- **0x00003C.** TLS_RSA_WITH_AES_128_CBC_SHA256

If you're familiar with the acronyms, you can get a good idea of what each cipher suite is using. Here are some notes for clarification:

- **Protocol.** Both are using TLS.
- **Key exchange method.** The first one is using ECDH and the second one is using RSA.
- **Authentication.** Both are using RSA, though, they shortened the code in the second one. Instead of listing RSA twice (for both the key exchange method and authentication), it is only listed once.
- **Encryption.** Both are using 128-bit AES, though in different modes of operation. Galois/Counter Mode (GCM) and Cipher Block Chaining (CBC) are the two modes identified here. The next section discusses cipher modes in more depth.

- **Integrity.** Both are using the SHA-256 hashing algorithm.

Some cipher suites are very old and include encryption algorithms such as DES. Clearly, they shouldn't be used and are disabled by default in most systems today. When necessary, administrators configure systems and applications to disable older specific cipher suites.

When two systems connect, they negotiate to identify which cipher suite they use. Each system passes a prioritized list of cipher suites it is willing to use. They then choose the cipher suite that is highest on their lists and common to both lists.

Implementation Versus Algorithm Selection

As you read about different algorithms and different modes of operation, you might have been wondering how this is relevant. It really depends on your job. Two terms are relevant here:

- **Crypto module.** A *crypto module* is a set of hardware, software, and/or firmware that implements cryptographic functions. This includes algorithms for encryption and hashing, key generation, and authentication techniques such as a digital signature.
- **Crypto service providers.** A *crypto service provider* is a software library of cryptographic standards and algorithms. These libraries are typically distributed within crypto modules.

As an example, software developers access software libraries when implementing cryptographic functions in their programs. If they need to encrypt data, they don't start from nothing. Instead, they access a crypto service provider, or cryptographic service provider, which is a library of different implementations of cryptographic standards and algorithms.

Crypto service providers are typically distributed within crypto modules. As an example, Python is a popular application used by web developers to create dynamic web sites. Python includes a rich assortment of crypto modules developers can use. The Python Cryptography Toolkit includes a library of both hashing functions and encryption algorithms. Developers simply follow the syntax defined within the library to implement these hashing functions and encryption algorithms.

Developers should know about the different cryptographic algorithms, along with the different modes of operation. As an example, although it's possible to select DES for encryption, this would be a mistake because DES has been deprecated. Similarly, it's possible for a developer to implement an algorithm using the ECB mode of operation. However, ECB has known weaknesses, so this would also be a mistake.

Administrators implement algorithms via cipher suites on servers. Their responsibility is to ensure that deprecated and weak cipher suites are disabled on servers. If administrators leave weak or deprecated algorithms functioning on servers, it makes the servers susceptible to attacks such as downgrade attacks.

Downgrade Attacks on Weak Implementations

A *downgrade attack* is a type of attack that forces a system to downgrade its security. The attacker then exploits the lesser security control. It is most often associated with cryptographic attacks due to weak implementations of cipher suites.

The common example is with Transport Layer Security (TLS) and Secure Sockets Layer (SSL). SSL has known vulnerabilities and has been replaced with TLS in most implementations. However, many servers have both SSL and TLS installed. If a client is unable to use TLS, the server will downgrade its security and use SSL.

Attackers exploit this vulnerability by configuring their systems so that they cannot use TLS. When they communicate with the server, the server downgrades security to use SSL instead of TLS. This allows attackers to launch SSL-based attacks such as the well-known Padding Oracle On Downgraded Legacy Encryption (POODLE) attack.

One way to ensure that SSL isn't used on a site is to modify the server's protocol list and ensure that SSL is disabled. Typically, a web site server will have the following five options: SSL 2, SSL 3, TLS 1.0, TLS 1.1, and TLS 1.2. You can prevent SSL-based downgrade attacks by disabling SSL 2 and SSL 3 on the web site server.

Similarly, cipher suites with known vulnerabilities should be disabled. If weak cipher suites are enabled on a server, it increases the vulnerabilities.

> **Remember this**
>
> Administrators should disable weak cipher suites and weak protocols on servers. When a server has both strong and weak cipher suites, attackers can launch downgrade attacks bypassing the strong cipher suite and exploiting the weak cipher suite.

Exploring PKI Components

A **Public Key Infrastructure (PKI)** is a group of technologies used to request, create, manage, store, distribute, and revoke digital certificates. Asymmetric encryption depends on the use of certificates for a variety of purposes, such as protecting email and protecting Internet traffic with SSL and TLS. For example, HTTPS sessions protect Internet credit card transactions, and these transactions depend on a PKI.

A primary benefit of a PKI is that it allows two people or entities to communicate securely without knowing each other previously. In other words, it allows them to communicate securely through an insecure public medium such as the Internet.

For example, you can establish a secure session with Amazon.com even if you've never done so before. Amazon purchased a certificate from Symantec. As shown in the "Encrypting HTTPS Traffic with TLS" section previously, the certificate provides the ability to establish a secure session.

A key element in a PKI is a Certificate Authority.

Certificate Authority

A Certificate Authority (**CA**) issues, manages, validates, and revokes certificates. In some contexts, you might see a CA referred to as a Certification Authority, but they are the same thing. CAs can be very large, such as Comodo or Symantec, which are public CAs. A CA can also be very small, such as a single service running on a server within a private network.

Public CAs make money by selling certificates. For this to work, the public CA must be trusted. If the CA is trusted, all certificates issued by the CA are trusted.

This is similar to how a driver's license is trusted. The Department of Motor Vehicles (DMV) issues driver's licenses after validating a person's identity. If you want to cash a check, you might present your driver's license to prove your identity. Businesses trust the DMV, so they trust the driver's license. On the other hand, if you purchased an ID from Gibson's Instant IDs, businesses might not trust it.

Although we might trust the DMV, why would a computer trust a CA? The answer is based on the certificate trust path.

Certificate Chaining and Trust Models

CAs are trusted by placing a copy of their root certificate into a trusted root CA store. The **root certificate** is the first certificate created by the CA that identifies it, and the store is just a collection of these root certificates. If the CA's root certificate is placed in this store, all certificates issued by this CA are trusted.

Figure 10.9 shows the Trusted Root Certification Authority store on a Windows computer. You can see that there are many certificates from many different CAs. In the figure, I've selected one of the certificates from COMODO Certification Authority. One of the labs for this chapter (available at *http://gcgapremium.com/501labs*) shows how to access this on a Windows computer.

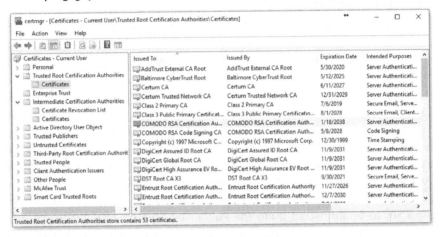

Figure 10.9: Trusted Root Certification Authorities

Public CAs such as Symantec and Comodo negotiate with web browser developers to have their certificates included with the web browser. This way, any certificates that they sell to businesses are automatically trusted.

Figure 10.10: Certificate chain

The most common trust model is the hierarchical trust model, also known as a centralized trust model. In this model, the public CA creates the first CA, known as the root CA. If the organization is large, it can create intermediate and child CAs. If you look back at Figure 10.9, you can see that it includes a section used to store intermediate CA certificates. A large trust chain works like this:

- The root CA issues certificates to intermediate CAs.
- Intermediate CAs issue certificates to child CAs.
- Child CAs issue certificates to devices or end users.

Certificate chaining combines all the certificates from the root CA down to the certificate issued to the end user. For example, Figure 10.10 shows the certificate chain for a wildcard certificate issued to google.com. A certificate chain would include all three certificates.

In a small organization, the root CA can simply issue certificates to the devices and end users. It's not necessary to have intermediate and child CAs.

Another type of trust model is a web of trust or decentralized trust model, sometimes used with PGP and GPG. A web of trust uses self-signed certificates, and a third party vouches for these certificates. For example, if five of your friends trust a certificate, you can trust the certificate. If the third party is a reliable source, the web of trust provides a secure alternative. However, if the third party does not adequately verify certificates, it can result in the use of certificates that shouldn't be trusted.

Registration and CSRs

Users and systems request certificates from a CA using a registration process. In some cases, a user enters information manually into a web site form. In other cases, a user sends a specifically formatted file to the CA. Within a domain, the system handles much of the process automatically.

As an example, imagine I wanted to purchase a certificate for *GetCertifiedGetAhead.com* for secure HTTPS sessions. I would first create a public and private key pair. Many programs are available to automate this process. For example, OpenSSL is a command-line program included in many Linux distributions. It creates key pairs in one command and allows you to export the public key to a file in a second command. Technically, OpenSSL and similar applications create the private key first. However, these applications appear to create both keys at the same time.

I would then put together a certificate signing request (**CSR**) for the certificate, including the purpose of the certificate and information about the web site, the public key, and me. Most CAs require CSRs to be formatted using the Public-Key Cryptography Standards (PKCS) #10 specification. The CSR includes the public key, but not the private key. A CA typically publishes a certificate template showing exactly how to format the CSR.

After receiving the CSR, the CA validates my identity and creates a certificate with the public key. The validation process is different based on the usage of the certificate. In some cases, it includes extensive checking, and in other cases, verification comes from the credit card I use to purchase it.

I can then register this certificate with my web site along with the private key. Any time someone initiates a secure HTTPS connection, the web site sends the certificate with the public key and the TLS/SSL session creates the session.

Certificates use object identifiers (OIDs) to identify specific objects within the certificates and some CAs require OIDs within the CSR for certain items. The OID is a string of numbers separated by dots. OIDs can be used to name almost every object type in certificates.

As an example, while looking at a Google certificate, I noticed a certificate with this OID on the General tab, 1.3.6.1.4.1.11129.2.5.1:

- The first 1 indicates that it is an International Organization for Standardization (ISO) OID.
- 1.3 indicates it is an identified organization.
- 1.3.6.1.4.1 indicates it is using an IANA enterprise number.
- 1.3.6.1.4.1.11129 indicates the organization is Google.
- The additional numbers (2.5.1) are specifically defined within Google's enterprise.

In large organizations, a registration authority (RA) can assist the CA by collecting registration information. The RA never issues certificates. Instead, it only assists in the registration process.

If the CA is online, meaning it is accessible over a network, it's possible to submit the CSR using an automated process. However, an organization may choose to keep some CAs offline to protect them from attacks. Offline CAs can only accept CSRs manually.

> ### Remember this
>
> You typically request certificates using a certificate signing request (CSR). The first step is to create the RSA-based private key, which is used to create the public key. You then include the public key in the CSR and the CA will embed the public key in the certificate. The private key is not sent to the CA.

Revoking Certificates

Normally, certificates expire based on the Valid From and Valid To dates. However, there are some instances when a CA will revoke a certificate before it expires.

For example, if a private key is publicly available, the key pair is compromised. It no longer provides adequate security because the private key is no longer private. Similarly, if the CA itself is compromised through a security breach, certificates issued by the CA may be compromised, so the CA can revoke certificates.

In general, any time a CA does not want anyone to use a certificate, the CA revokes it. Although the most common reasons are due to compromise of a key or the CA, there are others. A CA can use any of the following reasons when revoking a certificate:

- Key compromise
- CA compromise
- Change of affiliation
- Superseded
- Cease of operation
- Certificate hold

CAs use certificate revocation lists (CRLs, pronounced "crill") to revoke a certificate. The **CRL** is a version 2 certificate that includes a list of revoked certificates by serial number. For example, Figure 10.11 shows a copy of a CRL. One of the labs for this chapter shows you how to download and view a CRL.

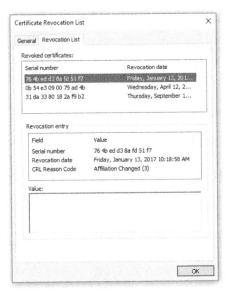

Figure 10.11: Certificate revocation list

Certificate Issues

Before clients use a certificate, they first verify it is valid with some checks. There are many different certificate issues that can result in an invalid certificate. Browsers typically display an error describing the issue and encouraging users not to use the certificate. Applications that detect a certificate issue might display an error using a certificate, but they are typically coded to not use it. Some of the common issues are:

- **Expired.** The first check is to ensure that it isn't expired. If the certificate is expired, the computer system typically gives the user an error indicating the certificate is not valid.
- **Certificate not trusted.** The next check is to see if the certificate was issued by a trusted CA. For example, a Windows system will look in the Trusted Root Certification Authority store and the Intermediate Certification Authorities store shown previously in Figure 10.9. If the system doesn't have a copy of the CA's certificate, it will indicate the certificate is not trusted. Users can override this warning, though there are often warnings encouraging users not to continue.
- **Improper certificate and key management.** Private keys should remain private. They are typically stored in an encrypted format and never shared publicly. If the certificates holding the private keys aren't managed properly, it can compromise the certificate.

Clients also validate certificates through the CA to ensure they haven't been revoked. First, they verify that the certificate was issued by a trusted CA. Next, they query the CA to verify the CA hasn't revoked the certificate. A common method of validating a certificate is by requesting a copy of the CRL, as shown in Figure 10.12. The following steps outline the process:

1. The client initiates a session requiring a certificate, such as an HTTPS session.
2. The server responds with a copy of the certificate that includes the public key.
3. The client queries the CA for a copy of the CRL.
4. The CA responds with a copy of the CRL.

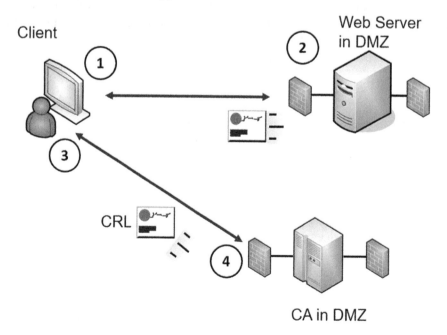

Figure 10.12: Validating a certificate

The client then checks the serial number of the certificate against the list of serial numbers in the CRL. If the certificate is revoked for any reason, the application gives an error message to the user.

CRLs are typically cached after being downloaded the first time. Instead of requesting another copy of the CRL, clients use the cached copy. This generates a lot of traffic between clients and the CA.

Another method of validating a certificate is with the Online Certificate Status Protocol (**OCSP**). OCSP allows the client to query the CA with the serial number of the certificate. The CA then responds with an answer of "good," "revoked," or "unknown." A response of "unknown" could indicate the certificate is a forgery.

Because OCSP provides a real-time response, it is an excellent example of supporting a common use case of low latency. If a CA revokes a certificate, clients using OCSP will know immediately. In contrast, if clients are using a cached CRL, they will be unaware of the revoked certificate until another copy of the CRL is downloaded.

Over time, authorities realized that OCSP was generating a lot of real-time traffic to the CA because it requires a CA to respond to every request. OCSP **stapling** solves this problem. The certificate presenter (such as the web server in Figure 10.12) obtains a timestamped OCSP response from the CA. Before sending it, the CA signs it with a digital signature. The certificate presenter then appends (or metaphorically staples) a timestamped OCSP response to the certificate during the TLS handshake process. This eliminates the need for clients to query the CA.

Remember this

CAs revoke certificates for several reasons such as when the private key is compromised or the CA is compromised. The certificate revocation list (CRL) includes a list of revoked certificates and is publicly available. An alternative to using a CRL is the Online Certificate Status Protocol (OCSP), which returns answers such as good, revoked, or unknown. OCSP stapling appends a digitally signed OCSP response to a certificate.

Public Key Pinning

Public key **pinning** is a security mechanism designed to prevent attackers from impersonating a web site using fraudulent certificates. When configured on a web site server, the server responds to client HTTPS requests with an extra header. This extra header includes a list of hashes derived from valid public keys used by the web site. It also includes a max-age field specifying how long the client should store and use the data.

When clients connect to the same web site again, they recalculate the hashes and then compare the recalculated hashes with the stored hashes. If the hashes match, it verifies that the client is connected to the same web site.

Web site administrators create hashes of one or more certificates used by the web site. This can be the public key used by the web site's certificate. It can also include any public keys from certificates in the certificate chain such as the public key from the root CA certificate, and/or the public key from intermediate CA certificates. Last, it must include a backup key that can be used if the current key becomes invalid.

> ### Remember this
>
> Certificate stapling is an alternative to OCSP. The certificate presenter (such as a web server) appends the certificate with a timestamped digitally signed OCSP response from the CA. This reduces OCSP traffic to and from the CA. Public key pinning helps prevent attackers from impersonating a web site with a fraudulent certificate. The web server sends a list of public key hashes that clients can use to validate certificates sent to clients in subsequent sessions.

Key Escrow

Key escrow is the process of placing a copy of a private key in a safe environment. This is useful for recovery. If the original is lost, the organization retrieves the copy of the key to access the data. Key escrow isn't required, but if an organization determines that data loss is unacceptable, it will implement a key escrow process.

In some cases, an organization provides a copy of the key to a third party. Another method is to designate employees within the organization who will be responsible for key escrow. These employees maintain and protect copies of the key, and if the original key is lost, they check out a copy of the key to an administrator or user.

Recovery Agent

A key recovery agent is a designated individual who can recover or restore cryptographic keys. In the context of a PKI, a recovery agent can recover private keys to access encrypted data. The recovery agent may be a security professional, administrator, or anyone designated by the company.

In some cases, the recovery agent can recover encrypted data using a different key. For example, Microsoft BitLocker supports encryption of entire drives. It's possible to add a data recovery agent field when creating a BitLocker encrypted drive. In this case, BitLocker uses two keys. The user has one key and uses it to unlock the drive during day-to-day use. The second key is only accessible by the recovery agent and is used for recovery purposes if the original key is lost or becomes inaccessible.

Comparing Certificate Types

Certificates are sometimes identified based on their usage. The following bullets describe some common certificate types:

- **Machine/Computer.** Certificates issued to a device or a computer are commonly called machine certificates or computer certificates. The certificate is typically used to identify the computer within a domain.
- **User.** Certificates can also be issued to users. They can be used for encryption, authentication, smart cards, and more. For example, Microsoft systems can create user certificates allowing the user to encrypt data using Encrypting File System (EFS).
- **Email.** The two uses of email certificates are for encryption of emails and digital signatures.
- **Code signing.** Developers often use code signing certificates to validate the

authentication of executable applications or scripts. The code signing certificate verifies the code has not been modified.

- **Self-signed.** A self-signed certificate is not issued by a trusted CA. Private CAs within an enterprise often create self-signed certificates. They aren't trusted by default. However, administrators can use automated means to place copies of the self-signed certificate into the trusted root CA store for enterprise computers. Self-signed certificates from private CAs eliminate the cost of purchasing certificates from public CAs.

- **Wildcard.** A *wildcard certificate* starts with an asterisk (*) and can be used for multiple domains, but each domain name must have the same root domain. For example, Google uses a wildcard certificate issued to *.google.com. This same certificate can be used for other Google domains, such as *accounts.google.com* and *support.google.com*. Wildcard certificates can reduce the administrative burden associated with managing multiple certificates.

- **SAN.** A Subject Alternative Name (SAN) is used for multiple domains that have different names, but are owned by the same organization. For example, Google uses SANs of *.google.com, *.android.com, *.cloud.google.com, and more. It is most commonly used for systems with the same base domain names, but different top-level domains. For example, if Google used names such as google.com and google.net, it could use a single SAN certificate for both domain names. Similarly, a SAN certificate can be used for *google.com* and *www.google.com*.

- **Domain validation.** A domain-validated certificate indicates that the certificate requestor has some control over a DNS domain. The CA takes extra steps to contact the requestor such as by email or telephone. The intent is to provide additional evidence to clients that the certificate and the organization are trustworthy.

- **Extended validation.** Extended validation certificates use additional steps beyond domain validation. If you visit a domain with an extended validation certificate, the address bar includes the name of the company before the actual URL. This helps prevent impersonation from phishing attacks. For example, PayPal uses an extended validation certificate. If you visit, you'll see that it shows PayPal, Inc [US] | before the URL. Imagine an attacker sends a phishing email with a link to paypa1.com (with 1 in paypa1 instead of the letter). If a user clicks the link, she will be able to see that the site isn't truly a PayPal site, assuming she understands extended validation certificates.

Certificate Formats

Most certificates use one of the X.509 v3 formats. The primary exception is certificates used to distribute certificate revocation lists (described later in this chapter), which use the X.509 v2 format.

Certificates are typically stored as binary files or as BASE64 American Standard Code for Information Interchange (ASCII) encoded files. Binary files are stored as 1s and 0s. BASE64 encoding converts the binary data into an ASCII string format. Additionally, some certificates are also encrypted to provide additional confidentiality.

The base format of certificates is Canonical Encoding Rules (**CER**) or Distinguished Encoding Rules (**DER**). CER and DER formats are defined by the International Telegraph Union Telecommunication Standardization Sector (ITU-T) in the X.690 standard. They use a variant of the Abstract Syntax Notation One (ASN.1) format, which defines data structures commonly used in cryptography. CER is a binary format and DER is an ASCII format.

DER-based certificates include headers and footers to identify the contents. As an example, the following text shows a header and a footer for a certificate:

```
-----BEGIN CERTIFICATE-----
MIIDdTCCAl2gAwIBAgILBAAAAAABFUtaw5QwDQYJKoZIhvcNAQEFBQAwVzELMAkG
... additional ASCII Characters here...
HMUfpIBvFSDJ3gyICh3WZlXi/EjJKSZp4A==
-----END CERTIFICATE-----
```

Each header starts with five dashes (-----), BEGIN, a label, and five more dashes. The footer starts with five dashes, End, the same label, and five more dashes. In the previous example, the label is CERTIFICATE. Other labels include PUBLIC KEY, PRIVATE KEY, ENCRYPTED PRIVATE KEY, CERTIFICATE REQUEST, and X509 CRL. CER-based certificates are binary encoded so they do not have headers and footers.

Certificate files can have many extensions, such as .crt, .cer, .pem, .key, .p7b, .p7c, .pfx, and .p12. However, it's worth stressing that a certificate with the .cer extension doesn't necessarily mean that it is using the CER format.

When comparing the different formats, it's important to know what they can contain and how to identify them. Table 10.3 provides an overview of the primary formats and the following sections describe these in more depth.

Type	Common Extensions	Format	Common Purpose	Can Contain
CER	.cer	Binary	Used for binary certificates	Varies
DER	.der	ASCII	Used for ASCII certificates	Varies
PEM	.pem, .cer, .crt, .key	Binary (CER) or ASCII (DER)	Can be used for almost any certificate purpose	Server certificates, certificate chains, keys, CRL
P7B	.p7b, .p7c	ASCII (DER)	Used to share the public key	Certificates, certificate chains, CRL, but never the private key
P12 PFX	.p12, .pfx	Binary (CER)	Commonly used to store private keys with a certificate	Certificates, certificate chains, and private keys

Table 10.3: Certificate formats

PEM is derived from the Privacy Enhanced Mail format, but that is misleading. It implies that PEM-based certificates are used for email only. However, PEM-based certificates can be used for just about anything. They can be formatted as CER (binary files) or DER (ASCII files). They can also be used to share public keys within a certificate, request certificates from a CA as a CSR, install a private key on a server, publish a CRL, or share the full certificate chain.

You might see a PEM-encoded certificate with the .pem extension. However, it's more common for the certificate to use other extensions. For example, a PEM-encoded file holding the certificate with the public key typically uses the .cer or .crt extension. A PEM file holding just the private key typically uses the .key extension.

P7B certificates use the PKCS version 7 (PKCS#7) format and they are DER-based (ASCII). They are commonly used to share public keys with proof of identity of the certificate holder. Recipients use the public keys to encrypt or decrypt data. For example, a web server might use a

P7B certificate to share its public key. P7B certificates can also contain a certificate chain or a CRL. However, they never include the private key.

P12 certificates use the PKCS version 12 (PKCS#12) format and they are CER-based (binary). They are commonly used to hold certificates with the private key. For example, when installing a certificate on a server to supports HTTPS sessions, you might install a P12 certificate with the private key. Because it holds the private key, it's common to encrypt P12 certificates. It's also possible to include the full certificate chain in a P12 certificate.

Personal Information Exchange (*PFX*) is a predecessor to the P12 certificate and it has the same usage. Administrators often use this format on Windows systems to import and export certificates.

Remember this

CER is a binary format for certificates and DER is an ASCII format. PEM is the most commonly used certificate format and can be used for just about any certificate type. P7B certificates are commonly used to share public keys. P12 and PFX certificates are commonly used to hold the private key.

Chapter 10 Exam Topic Review

When preparing for the exam, make sure you understand these key concepts covered in this chapter.

Introducing Cryptography Concepts

- Integrity provides assurances that data has not been modified. Hashing ensures that data has retained integrity.
- Confidentiality ensures that data is only viewable by authorized users. Encryption protects the confidentiality of data.
- Symmetric encryption uses the same key to encrypt and decrypt data.
- Asymmetric encryption uses two keys (public and private) created as a matched pair.
- A digital signature provides authentication, non-repudiation, and integrity.
  - Authentication validates an identity.
  - Non-repudiation prevents a party from denying an action.
  - Users sign emails with a digital signature, which is a hash of an email message encrypted with the sender's private key.
  - Only the sender's public key can decrypt the hash, providing verification it was encrypted with the sender's private key.

Providing Integrity with Hashing

- Hashing verifies the integrity of data, such as downloaded files and email messages.
- A hash (sometimes listed as a checksum) is a fixed-size string of numbers or hexadecimal characters.
- Hashing algorithms are one-way functions used to create a hash. You cannot reverse the process to re-create the original data.
- Passwords are often stored as hashes instead of the actual password. Salting the password thwarts many password attacks.

- Two commonly used key stretching techniques are bcrypt and Password-Based Key Derivation Function 2 (PBKDF2). They protect passwords against brute force and rainbow table attacks.
- Common hashing algorithms are Message Digest 5 (MD5), Secure Hash Algorithm (SHA), and Hash-based Message Authentication Code (HMAC). HMAC provides both integrity and authenticity of a message.

Providing Confidentiality with Encryption

- Confidentiality ensures that data is only viewable by authorized users.
- Encryption provides confidentiality of data, including data-at-rest (any type of data stored on disk) or data-in-transit (any type of transmitted data).
- Block ciphers encrypt data in fixed-size blocks. Advanced Encryption Standard (AES) and Twofish encrypt data in 128-bit blocks.
- Stream ciphers encrypt data 1 bit or 1 byte at a time. They are more efficient than block ciphers when encrypting data of an unknown size or when sent in a continuous stream. RC4 is a commonly used stream cipher.
- Cipher modes include Electronic Codebook (ECB), Cipher Block Chaining (CBC), Counter (CTM) mode, and Galois/Counter Mode (GCM). ECB should not be used. GCM is widely used because it is efficient and provides data authenticity.
- Data Encryption Standard (DES), Triple DES (3DES), and Blowfish are block ciphers that encrypt data in 64-bit blocks. AES is a popular symmetric block encryption algorithm, and it uses 128, 192, or 256 bits for the key.
- Asymmetric encryption uses public and private keys as matched pairs.
    - If the public key encrypted information, only the matching private key can decrypt it.
    - If the private key encrypted information, only the matching public key can decrypt it.
    - Private keys are always kept private and never shared.
    - Public keys are freely shared by embedding them in a certificate.
- RSA is a popular asymmetric algorithm. Many cryptographic protocols use RSA to secure data such as email and data transmitted over the Internet. RSA uses prime numbers to generate public and private keys.
- Elliptic curve cryptography (ECC) is an encryption technology commonly used with small wireless devices.
- Diffie-Hellman provides a method to privately share a symmetric key between two parties. Elliptic Curve Diffie-Hellman Ephemeral (ECDHE) is a version of Diffie-Hellman that uses ECC to re-create keys for each session.
- Steganography is the practice of hiding data within a file. You can hide messages in the white space of a file without modifying its size. A more sophisticated method is by modifying bits within a file. Capturing and comparing hashes of files can discover steganography attempts.

Using Cryptographic Protocols

- When using digital signatures with email:
    - The sender's private key encrypts (or signs).
    - The sender's public key decrypts.

- A digital signature provides authentication (verified identification) of the sender, non-repudiation, and integrity of the message.
  - Senders create a digital signature by hashing a message and encrypting the hash with the sender's private key.
  - Recipients decrypt the digital signature with the sender's matching public key.
- When encrypting email:
  - The recipient's public key encrypts.
  - The recipient's private key decrypts.
  - Many email applications use the public key to encrypt a symmetric key, and then use the symmetric key to encrypt the email contents.
- S/MIME and PGP secure email with encryption and digital signatures. They both use RSA, certificates, and depend on a PKI. They can encrypt email at rest (stored on a drive) and in transit (sent over the network).
- TLS is the replacement for SSL. SSL is deprecated and should not be used.
- When encrypting web site traffic with TLS:
  - The web site's public key encrypts a symmetric key.
  - The web site's private key decrypts the symmetric key.
  - The symmetric key encrypts data in the session.
- Weak cipher suites (such as those supporting SSL) should be disabled to prevent downgrade attacks.

Exploring PKI Components

- A Public Key Infrastructure (PKI) is a group of technologies used to request, create, manage, store, distribute, and revoke digital certificates. A PKI allows two entities to privately share symmetric keys without any prior communication.
- Most public CAs use a hierarchical centralized CA trust model, with a root CA and intermediate CAs. A CA issues, manages, validates, and revokes certificates.
- Root certificates of trusted CAs are stored on computers. If a CA's root certificate is not in the trusted store, web users will see errors indicating the certificate is not trusted or the CA is not recognized.
- You request a certificate with a certificate signing request (CSR). You first create a private/public key pair and include the public key in the CSR.
- CAs revoke certificates when an employee leaves, the private key is compromised, or the CA is compromised. A CRL identifies revoked certificates as a list of serial numbers.
- The CA publishes the CRL, making it available to anyone. Web browsers can check certificates they receive from a web server against a copy of the CRL to determine if a received certificate is revoked.
- Public key pinning provides clients with a list of hashes for each public key it uses.
- Certificate stapling provides clients with a timestamped, digitally signed OCSP response. This is from the CA and appended to the certificate.
- User systems return errors when a system tries to use an expired certificate.
- A key escrow stores a copy of private keys used within a PKI. If the original private key is lost or inaccessible, the copy is retrieved from escrow, preventing data loss.
- Wildcard certificates use a * for child domains to reduce the administrative burden of managing certificates. Subject Alternative Name (SAN) certificates can be used for multiple domains with different domain names.

- A domain validated certificate indicates that the certificate requestor has some control over a DNS domain. Extended validation certificates use additional steps beyond domain validation to give users a visual indication that they are accessing the site.
- CER is a binary format for certificates and DER is an ASCII format.
- PEM is the most commonly used certificate format and can be used for just about any certificate type.
- P7B certificates are commonly used to share public keys. P12 and PFX certificates are commonly used to hold the private key.

Online References

- Remember, there are additional resources at *http://gcgapremium.com/501-extras*. They include labs, sample performance-based questions, and more.

Chapter 10 Practice Questions

1. Bart recently sent out confidential data via email to potential competitors. Management suspects he did so accidentally, but Bart denied sending the data. Management wants to implement a method that would prevent Bart from denying accountability in the future. Which of the following are they trying to enforce?

    A. Confidentiality

    B. Encryption

    C. Access control

    D. Non-repudiation

2. A software company occasionally provides application updates and patches via its web site. It also provides a checksum for each update and patch. Which of the following BEST describes the purpose of the checksum?

    A. Availability of updates and patches

    B. Integrity of updates and patches

    C. Confidentiality of updates and patches

    D. Integrity of the application

3. A one-way function converts data into a string of characters. It is not possible to convert this string of characters back to the original state. What type of function is this?

    A. Symmetric encryption

    B. Asymmetric encryption

    C. Stream cipher

    D. Hashing

4. An application developer is working on the cryptographic elements of an application. Which of the following cipher modes should NOT be used in this application?

    A. CBC

    B. CTM

    C. ECB

    D. GCM

5. The following text shows the ciphertext result of encrypting the word "passed" with an uppercase P and a lowercase p:
   - Passed!—xnBKcndl+25mHjnafwi6Jw
   - passed!—RqMbHJqLdPE3RCuUU17FtA

   Which of the following BEST describes the cryptography concept demonstrated by comparing the resulting ciphertext of both words?
   - A. Confusion
   - B. Diffusion
   - C. Key stretching
   - D. Security through obscurity

6. Which of the following is a symmetric encryption algorithm that encrypts data 1 bit at a time?
   - A. Block cipher
   - B. Stream cipher
   - C. AES
   - D. DES
   - E. MD5

7. A supply company has several legacy systems connected within a warehouse. An external security audit discovered the company is using DES for data-at-rest. It mandated the company upgrade DES to meet minimum security requirements. The company plans to replace the legacy systems next year, but needs to meet the requirements from the audit. Which of the following is MOST likely to be the simplest upgrade for these systems?
   - A. S/MIME
   - B. HMAC
   - C. 3DES
   - D. TLS

8. Bart wants to send a secure email to Lisa, so he decides to encrypt it. Bart wants to ensure that Lisa can verify that he sent it. Which of the following does Lisa need to meet this requirement?
   - A. Bart's public key
   - B. Bart's private key
   - C. Lisa's public key
   - D. Lisa's private key

9. Bart wants to send a secure email to Lisa, so he decides to encrypt it. He wants to ensure that only Lisa can decrypt it. Which of the following does Lisa need to decrypt Bart's email?
   - A. Bart's public key
   - B. Bart's private key
   - C. Lisa's public key
   - D. Lisa's private key

10. An organization requested bids for a contract and asked companies to submit their bids via email. After winning the bid, Acme realized it couldn't meet the requirements of the contract. Acme instead stated that it never submitted the bid. Which of the following would provide proof to the organization that Acme did submit the bid?

   A. Digital signature
   B. Integrity
   C. Repudiation
   D. Encryption

11. Application developers are creating an application that requires users to log on with strong passwords. The developers want to store the passwords in such a way that it will thwart brute force attacks. Which of the following is the BEST solution?

   A. 3DES
   B. MD5
   C. PBKDF2
   D. Database fields

12. Administrators have noticed a significant amount of OCSP traffic sent to an intermediate CA. They want to reduce this traffic. Which of the following is the BEST choice to meet this need?

   A. Pinning
   B. Digital signatures
   C. Stapling
   D. Hashing

13. A web site is using a certificate. Users have recently been receiving errors from the web site indicating that the web site's certificate is revoked. Which of the following includes a list of certificates that have been revoked?

   A. CRL
   B. CA
   C. OCSP
   D. CSR

14. An organization recently updated its security policy. One change is a requirement for all internal web servers to only support HTTPS traffic. However, the organization does not have funds to pay for this. Which of the following is the BEST solution?

   A. Create code signing certificates for the web servers.
   B. Create one wildcard certificate for all the web servers.
   C. Create a public CA and issue certificates from it.
   D. Create certificates signed by an internal private CA.

15. An administrator is installing a certificate with a private key on a server. Which of the following certificate types is he MOST likely installing?

   A. DER
   B. P12
   C. P7B
   D. CRT

Chapter 10 Practice Question Answers

1. **D.** Non-repudiation methods such as digital signatures prevent users from denying they took an action. Encryption methods protect confidentiality. Access control methods protect access to data.

2. **B.** The checksum (also known as a hash) provides integrity for the updates and patches so that users can verify they have not been modified. Installing updates and patches increases the availability of the application. Confidentiality is provided by encryption. The checksums are for the updates and patches, so they do not provide integrity for the application.

3. **D.** A hash function creates a string of characters (typically displayed in hexadecimal) when executed against a file or message, and hashing functions cannot be reversed to re-create the original data. Encryption algorithms (including symmetric encryption, asymmetric encryption, and stream ciphers) create ciphertext from plaintext data, but they include decryption algorithms to re-create the original data.

4. **C.** The Electronic Codebook (ECB) mode of operation encrypts blocks with the same key, making it easier for attackers to crack. The other cipher modes are secure and can be used. Cipher Block Chaining (CBC) mode is used by some symmetric block ciphers, though it isn't as efficient. Counter (CTM) mode combines an initialization vector (IV) with a counter and effectively converts a block cipher into a stream cipher. Galois/Counter Mode (GCM) combines the Counter mode with hashing techniques for data authenticity and confidentiality.

5. **B.** This demonstrates diffusion because a small change in the plaintext results in a large change in the ciphertext. Confusion indicates that the ciphertext is significantly different than the plaintext. Although this is true for both results, the question is asking you to compare the two results. Key stretching techniques add salts to passwords before hashing them to thwart password cracking attacks. Security through obscurity methods use obfuscation methods to hide data, but they don't necessarily encrypt data.

6. **B.** A stream cipher encrypts data a single bit or a single byte at a time and is more efficient when the size of the data is unknown, such as streaming audio or video. A block cipher encrypts data in specific-sized blocks, such as 64-bit blocks or 128-bit blocks. Advanced Encryption Standard (AES) and Data Encryption Standard (DES) are block ciphers. Message Digest 5 (MD5) is a hashing algorithm.

7. **C.** The best choice is Triple Data Encryption Standard (3DES). None of the other answers are valid replacements for the symmetric encryption algorithm Data Encryption Standard (DES). Secure/Multipurpose Internet Mail Extensions (S/MIME) is used to digitally sign and encrypt email. Hash-based Message Authentication Code (HMAC) is a hashing algorithm used to verify the integrity and authenticity of messages. Transport Layer Security (TLS) uses both symmetric and asymmetric encryption to encrypt data-in-transit, not data-at-rest.

8. **A.** Lisa would decrypt the digital signature with Bart's public key and verify the public key is valid by querying a Certificate Authority (CA). The digital signature provides verification that Bart sent the message, non-repudiation, and integrity for the message. Bart encrypts the digital signature with his private key, which can only be decrypted with his public key. Lisa's keys are not used for Bart's digital signature, but might be used for the encryption of the email. Although not part of this scenario, Bart would encrypt the email with Lisa's public key and Lisa would decrypt the email with Lisa's private key.

9. **D.** Lisa would decrypt the email with her private key and Bart would encrypt the email with Lisa's public key. Although not part of this scenario, if Bart wanted Lisa to have verification that he sent it, he would create a digital signature with his private key and Lisa would decrypt the private key with Bart's public key. Bart does not use his keys to encrypt email sent to someone else.

10. **A.** If Acme submitted the bid via email using a digital signature, it would provide proof that the bid was submitted by Acme. Digital signatures provide verification of who sent a message, non-repudiation preventing them from denying it, and integrity verifying the message wasn't modified. Integrity verifies the message wasn't modified. Repudiation isn't a valid security concept. Encryption protects the confidentiality of data, but it doesn't verify who sent it or provide non-repudiation.

11. **C.** Password-Based Key Derivation Function 2 (PBKDF2) is a key stretching technique designed to protect against brute force attempts and is the best choice of the given answers. Another alternative is bcrypt. Both salt the password with additional bits. Triple DES (3DES) is an encryption protocol. Passwords stored using Message Digest 5 (MD5) are easier to crack because they don't use salts. Storing the passwords in encrypted database fields is a possible solution, but just storing them in unencrypted database fields does not protect them at all.

12. **C.** Online Certificate Status Protocol (OCSP) stapling reduces OCSP traffic sent to a Certificate Authority (CA). Certificate presenters append a timestamped, digitally signed OCSP response to a certificate. Public key pinning includes a list of public key hashes in HTTPS responses from the web server. While pinning helps validate certificates, it is unrelated to OCSP. Digital signatures won't reduce traffic. Hashing is used for integrity and it won't reduce OCSP traffic.

13. **A.** A certificate revocation list (CRL) is a list of certificates that a Certificate Authority (CA) has revoked. The CA stores a database repository of revoked certificates and issues the CRL to anyone who requests it. The Online Certificate Status Protocol (OCSP) validates trust with certificates, but only returns short responses such as good, unknown, or revoked. A certificate signing request (CSR) is used to request certificates.

14. **D.** The best solution is to use certificates signed by an internal private Certificate Authority (CA). This ensures connections use Hypertext Transfer Protocol Secure (HTTPS) instead of HTTP. Even if the organization doesn't have an internal CA, it is possible to create one on an existing server without incurring any additional costs. A code signing certificate provides a digital signature for an application or script, not an entire web server. A wildcard certificate is used for a single domain with multiple subdomains. It is not used for multiple

web servers unless they all share the same root domain name, but the scenario doesn't indicate the web servers share the same root domain name. You would not create a public CA to support internal private servers. While it is feasible to purchase certificates from a public CA, that would cost money, but the scenario indicates money isn't available.

15. **B.** P12 (PKCS #12) certificates commonly include a private key and they are used to install a private key on a server. A Distinguished Encoding Rules (DER)–based certificate is an ASCII encoded file, but P12 certificates are Canonical Encoding Rules (CER) binary encoded files. A P7B (PKCS #7) certificate never includes the private key. CRT isn't a valid certificate type, though many certificates do use the .crt extension.

Chapter 11

Implementing Policies to Mitigate Risks

CompTIA Security+ objectives covered in this chapter:

2.2 **Given a scenario, use appropriate software tools to assess the security posture of an organization.**
- Data sanitization tools

2.3 **Given a scenario, troubleshoot common security issues.**
- Personnel issues (Policy violation, Personal email)

4.4 **Given a scenario, differentiate common account management practices.**
- General Concepts (Onboarding/offboarding)

5.1 **Explain the importance of policies, plans and procedures related to organizational security.**
- Standard operating procedure, Agreement types (BPA, SLA, ISA, MOU/MOA), Personnel management (Mandatory vacations, Job rotation, Separation of duties, Clean desk, Background checks, Exit interviews, Role-based awareness training [Data owner, System administrator, System owner, User, Privileged user, Executive user], NDA, Onboarding, Continuing education, Acceptable use policy/rules of behavior, Adverse actions), General security policies (Social media networks/applications, Personal email)

5.4 **Given a scenario, follow incident response procedures.**
- Incident response plan (Documented incident types/category definitions, Roles and responsibilities, Reporting requirements/escalation, Cyber-incident response teams, Exercise), Incident response process (Preparation, Identification, Containment, Eradication, Recovery, Lessons learned)

5.5 **Summarize basic concepts of forensics.**
- Order of volatility, Chain of custody, Legal hold, Data acquisition (Capture system image, Network traffic and logs, Capture video, Record time offset, Take hashes, Screenshots, Witness interviews), Preservation, Recovery, Strategic intelligence/counterintelligence gathering (Active logging), Track man-hours

5.8   Given a scenario, carry out data security and privacy practices.
- Data destruction and media sanitization (Burning, Shredding, Pulping, Pulverizing, Degaussing, Purging, Wiping), Data sensitivity labeling and handling (Confidential, Private, Public, Proprietary, PII, PHI), Data roles (Owner, Steward/custodian, Privacy officer), Data retention, Legal and compliance

**

Organizations often develop written security policies. These provide guiding principles to the professionals who implement security throughout the organization. These policies include personnel management policies and data protection policies. Combined with training for personnel to raise overall security awareness, they help mitigate risk and reduce security incidents. However, security incidents still occur, and incident response policies provide the direction on how to handle them.

Exploring Security Policies

Security policies are written documents that lay out a security plan within a company. They are one of many administrative controls used to reduce and manage risk. When created early enough, they help ensure that personnel consider and implement security throughout the life cycle of various systems in the company. When the policies and procedures are enforced, they help prevent incidents, data loss, and theft.

Policies include brief, high-level statements that identify goals based on an organization's overall beliefs and principles. After creating the policy, personnel within the organization create plans and procedures to support the policies. Although the policies are often high-level statements, the plans and procedures provide details on policy implementation.

As an example, organizations often create **standard operating procedures (SOPs)** to support security policies. These typically include step-by-step instructions employees can use to perform common tasks or routine operations. Security controls such as those covered in Chapter 1, "Mastering Security Basics," enforce the requirements of a security policy. For example, a security policy may state that internal users must not use peer-to-peer (P2P) applications. A firewall with appropriate rules to block these applications provides a technical implementation of this policy. Similarly, administrators can use port-scanning tools to detect applications running on internal systems that are violating the security policy.

A security policy can be a single large document or divided into several smaller documents, depending on the needs of the company. The following sections identify many of the common elements of a security policy.

Personnel Management Policies

Companies frequently develop policies to specifically define and clarify issues related to personnel management. This includes personnel behavior, expectations, and possible consequences. Personnel learn these policies when they are hired and as changes occur. Some of the policies directly related to personnel are acceptable use, mandatory vacations, separation of duties, job rotation, and clean desk policies. The following sections cover these and other personnel policies in more depth.

> **Remember this**
>
> Written security policies are administrative controls that identify a security plan. Personnel create plans and procedures to implement security controls and enforce the security policies.

Acceptable Use Policy

An *acceptable use policy (AUP)* defines proper system usage or the rules of behavior for employees when using information technology (IT) systems. It often describes the purpose of computer systems and networks, how users can access them, and the responsibilities of users when they access the systems.

Many organizations monitor user activities, such as what web sites they visit and what data they send out via email. For example, a proxy server typically logs all web sites that a user visits. The AUP may include statements informing users that systems are in place monitoring their activities.

In some cases, the AUP might include privacy statements informing users what computer activities they can consider private. Many users have an expectation of privacy when using an organization's computer systems and networks that isn't justified. The privacy policy statement helps to clarify the organization's stance.

The AUP often includes definitions and examples of unacceptable use. For example, it might prohibit employees from using company resources to access P2P sites or social media sites.

It's common for organizations to require users to read and sign a document indicating they understand the acceptable use policy when they're hired and in conjunction with annual security training. Other methods, such as logon banners or periodic emails, help reinforce an acceptable use policy.

Mandatory Vacations

Mandatory vacation policies help detect when employees are involved in malicious activity, such as fraud or embezzlement. As an example, employees in positions of fiscal trust, such as stock traders or bank employees, are often required to take an annual vacation of at least five consecutive workdays.

For embezzlement actions of any substantial size to succeed, an employee would need to be constantly present in order to manipulate records and respond to different inquiries. On the other hand, if an employee is forced to be absent for at least five consecutive workdays, someone else would be required to answer any queries during the employee's absence. This increases the likelihood of discovering illegal activities by employees. It also acts as an effective deterrent.

Mandatory vacations aren't limited to only financial institutions, though. Many organizations require similar policies for administrators. For example, an administrator might be the only person required to perform sensitive activities such as reviewing certain logs. A malicious administrator can overlook or cover up certain activities revealed in the logs. However, a mandatory vacation policy would require someone else to perform these activities, which increases the chance of discovery.

Of course, mandatory vacations by themselves won't prevent fraud. Most companies will implement the principle of defense in depth by using multiple layers of protection. Additional policies may include separation of duties and job rotation to provide as much protection as possible.

> ### Remember this
>
> Mandatory vacation policies require employees to take time away from their job. These policies help to deter fraud and discover malicious activities while the employee is away.

Separation of Duties

Separation of duties is a principle that prevents any single person or entity from being able to complete all the functions of a critical or sensitive process. It's designed to prevent fraud, theft, and errors.

Accounting provides a classic example. It's common to divide Accounting departments into two divisions: Accounts Receivable and Accounts Payable. Personnel in the Accounts Receivable division review and validate bills. They then send the validated bills to the personnel in the Accounts Payable division, who pay the bills. Similarly, this policy would ensure personnel are not authorized to print and sign checks. Instead, a separation of duties policy separates these two functions to reduce the possibility of fraud.

If Homer were the only person doing all these functions, it would be possible for him to create and approve a bill from Homer's Most Excellent Retirement Account. After approving the bill, Homer would then pay it. If Homer doesn't go to jail, he may indeed retire early at the expense of the financial health of the company.

Separation of duties policies also apply to IT personnel. For example, it's common to separate application development tasks from application deployment tasks. In other words, developers create and modify applications and then pass the compiled code to administrators. Administrators then deploy the code to live production systems. Without this policy in place, developers might be able make quick, untested changes to code, resulting in unintended outages. This provides a high level of version control and prevents potential issues created through uncontrolled changes.

> ### Remember this
>
> Separation of duties prevents any single person or entity from controlling all the functions of a critical or sensitive process by dividing the tasks between employees. This helps prevent potential fraud, such as if a single person prints and signs checks.

As another example, a group of IT administrators may be assigned responsibility for maintaining a group of database servers. However, they would not be granted access to security logs on these servers. Instead, security administrators regularly review these logs, but these security administrators will not have access to data within the databases.

Imagine that Bart has been working as an IT administrator but recently changed jobs and is now working as a security administrator. What should happen? Based on separation of duties, Bart should now have access to the security logs, but his access to the data within the databases should be revoked. If his permissions to the data are not revoked, he will have access to more than he needs, violating the principle of least privilege. A user rights and permissions review often discovers these types of issues.

Job Rotation

Job rotation is a concept that has employees rotate through different jobs to learn the processes and procedures in each job. From a security perspective, job rotation helps to prevent or expose dangerous shortcuts or even fraudulent activity. Employees might rotate through jobs temporarily or permanently.

For example, your company could have an Accounting department. As mentioned in the "Separation of Duties" section, you would separate accounting into two divisions—Accounts Receivable and Accounts Payable. Additionally, you could rotate personnel in and out of jobs in the two divisions. This would ensure more oversight over past transactions and help ensure that employees are following rules and policies.

In contrast, imagine a single person always performs the same function without any expectation of oversight. This increases the temptation to go outside the bounds of established policies.

Job rotation policies work well together with separation of duties policies. A separation of duties policy helps prevent a single person from controlling too much. However, if an organization only used a separation of duties policy, it is possible for two people to collude in a scheme to defraud the company. If a job rotation policy is also used, these two people will not be able to continue the fraudulent activity indefinitely.

Job rotation policies also apply to IT personnel. For example, the policy can require administrators to swap roles on a regular basis, such as annually or quarterly. This prevents any single administrator from having too much control over a system or network.

> ### Remember this
>
> Job rotation policies require employees to change roles on a regular basis. Employees might change roles temporarily, such as for three to four weeks, or permanently. This helps ensure that employees cannot continue with fraudulent activity indefinitely.

Clean Desk Policy

A *clean desk policy* directs users to keep their areas organized and free of papers. The primary security goal is to reduce threats of security incidents by ensuring the protection of sensitive data. More specifically, it helps prevent the possibility of data theft or inadvertent disclosure of information.

Imagine an attacker goes into a bank and meets a loan officer. The loan officer has stacks of paper on his desk, including loan applications from various customers. If the loan officer steps out, the attacker can easily grab some of the documents, or simply take pictures of the documents with a mobile phone.

Beyond security, organizations want to present a positive image to customers and clients. Employees with cluttered desks with piles of paper can easily turn off customers.

However, a clean desk policy doesn't just apply to employees who meet and greet customers. It also applies to employees who don't interact with customers. Just as dumpster divers can sort through trash to gain valuable information, anyone can sort through papers on a desk to learn information. It's best to secure all papers to keep them away from prying eyes. Some items left on a desk that can present risks include:

- Keys
- Cell phones

I'll Go to Jail Before I Give You the Passwords!

The city of San Francisco had an extreme example of the dangers of a single person with too much explicit knowledge or power. A network administrator with one of Cisco's highest certifications—Cisco Certified Internetwork Expert (CCIE)—made changes to the city's network, changing passwords so that only he knew them and ensuring that he was the only person with administrative access.

It could be that he was taking these actions to protect the network that he considered his "baby." He was the only CCIE, and it's possible he thought others did not have the necessary knowledge to maintain the network adequately. Over the years, fewer and fewer people had access to what he was doing, and his knowledge became more and more proprietary. Instead of being malicious in nature, he might have simply been protective, even if overly protective.

At some point, his supervisor recognized that all the proverbial information eggs were in the basket of this lone CCIE. It was just too risky. What if a bus, or one of San Francisco's famous trolleys, hit him? What would the organization do? His supervisor asked him for some passwords and he refused, even when faced with arrest. Later, he gave law enforcement personnel passwords that didn't work.

Law enforcement personnel charged him with four counts of tampering with a computer network and courts kept him in custody with a $5 million bail. Ultimately, a court convicted him of one felony count and sentenced him to four years in prison. This is a far fall from his reported annual salary of $127,735.

The city of San Francisco had to bring in experts from Cisco and the city reported costs of $900,000 to regain control of their network. Following his conviction, the court also ordered the administrator to pay $1.5 million in restitution.

What's the lesson here? Internal security controls, such as creating and enforcing policies related to rotation of duties, separation of duties, and cross-training, might have been able to avoid this situation completely. If this CCIE truly did have good intentions toward what he perceived as his network, these internal controls might have prevented him from going over the line into overprotection and looking at the world through the bars of a jail cell.

- Access cards
- Sensitive papers
- Logged-on computer
- Printouts left in printer
- Passwords on Post-it notes
- File cabinets left open or unlocked
- Personal items such as mail with Personally Identifiable Information (PII)

Some people want to take a clean desk policy a step further by scrubbing and sanitizing desks with antibacterial cleaners and disinfectants on a daily basis. They are free to do so, but that isn't part of a security-related clean desk policy.

Remember this

A clean desk policy requires users to organize their areas to reduce the risk of possible data theft. It reminds users to secure sensitive data and may include a statement about not writing down passwords.

Background Check

It's common for organizations to perform background checks on potential employees and even after employees are hired. A ***background check*** checks into a potential employee's history with the intention of discovering anything about the person that might make him a less-than-ideal fit for a job.

A background check will vary depending on job responsibilities and the sensitivity of data that person can access. For example, a background check for an associate at Walmart will be significantly less than a background check for a government employee who will handle Top Secret Sensitive Compartmented Information.

However, background checks will typically include a query to law enforcement agencies to identify a person's criminal history. In some cases, this is only to determine if the person is a felon. In other cases, it checks for all potential criminal activity, including a review of a person's driving records.

Many organizations check a person's financial history by obtaining a credit report. For example, someone applying for a job in an Accounting department might not be a good fit if his credit score is 350 and he has a string of unpaid loans.

It is also common for employers to check a person's online activity. This includes social media sites, such as Facebook, LinkedIn, and Twitter. Some people say and do things online that they would rarely do in public. One reason is a phenomenon known as the online disinhibition effect. Just as a beer or glass of wine releases inhibitions in many people, individuals are often less inhibited when posting comments online. And what they post often reflects their true feelings and beliefs. Consider a person who frequently posts hateful comments about others. A potential employer might think that this person is unlikely to work cohesively in a team environment and hire someone else.

Note that some background checks require the written permission from the potential employee. For example, the Fair Credit Reporting Act (FCRA) requires organizations to obtain written permission before obtaining a credit report on a job applicant or employee. However, other background checks don't require permission. For example, anyone can look at an individual's social media profile.

NDA

A non-disclosure agreement (**NDA**) is used between two entities to ensure that proprietary data is not disclosed to unauthorized entities. For example, imagine BizzFad wants to collaborate with Costington's on a project. BizzFad management realizes they need to share proprietary data with Costington's personnel, but they want to ensure that distribution of the data is limited. The NDA is a legal document that BizzFad can use to hold Costington's legally responsible if the proprietary data is shared.

Similarly, many organizations use an NDA to prohibit employees from sharing proprietary data either while they are employed, or after they leave the organization. It's common to remind employees of an existing NDA during an exit interview.

Exit Interview

An ***exit interview*** is conducted with departing employees just before they leave an organization. Note that an exit interview isn't only conducted when employees are fired from their job. They are also done when employees leave voluntarily. The overall purpose is for the employer to gain information from the departing employee. Some common questions asked during an exit interview are:

- What did you like most (and/or least) about your job here?
- Do you think you had adequate training to do your job here?
- Can you tell me what prompted you to leave your current position?
- Can you describe the working relationship you had with your supervisor(s)?
- What skills and qualification does your replacement need to excel in this position?

Exit interviews are commonly conducted by an employee in the Human Resources (HR) department. In addition to seeking feedback from the employee, departing employees are sometimes required to sign paperwork, such as a reminder about a previously signed NDA. The NDA prevents the employee from sharing proprietary information with personnel outside the organization.

From a security perspective, it's also important to ensure other things occur during or before the exit interview. For example, the user's account should be disabled (or deleted depending on company policy). Ideally, this should occur during the interview. One way organizations do this is by informing the IT department of the time of the scheduled interview a day before. An administrator then disables the account after the interview starts. The key is that a departing employee should not have access to computing and network resources after the interview.

It's also important to collect any equipment (such as smartphones, tablets, or laptops), security badges, or proximity cards the organization issued to the employee. This is more than just a cost issue. Equipment very likely has proprietary data on it and the company needs to take steps to protect the data. Additionally, smart cards and proximity cards can allow individuals access to protected areas.

> ### Remember this
>
> Background checks investigate the history of an individual prior to employment and, sometimes, during employment. They may include criminal checks, credit checks, and an individual's online activity. An exit interview is conducted when an individual departs an organization. User accounts are often disabled or deleted during the exit interview and everything issued to the employee is collected.

Onboarding

Onboarding is the process of granting individuals access to an organization's computing resources after being hired. This includes providing the employee with a user account and granting access to appropriate resources. One of the key considerations during the onboarding process is to follow the principle of least privilege. Grant the new employees access to what they need for their job, but no more.

Offboarding is the process of removing their access. When employees leave the company, it's important to revoke their access. This is often done during the exit interview.

Policy Violations and Adverse Actions

What do you do if an employee doesn't follow the security policy? What adverse actions should a supervisor take? Obviously, that depends on the severity of the policy violation.

Imagine that an employee sends out an email to everyone in the organization inviting them to his church. The supervisor might decide to verbally counsel the employee and make it clear that sending out personal emails like this is unacceptable. Based on how well the conversation goes, the supervisor might choose to document this as written counseling and place the warning in the employee's HR folder.

Some incidents require more severe responses. Imagine that an employee begins a cyberbullying campaign against another employee. He has been sending her hateful emails and posting hateful messages on social media pages. In most organizations, this bully will be looking for employment elsewhere once his activity is discovered.

Although it's possible to document specific adverse actions within a security policy, this is rarely recommended. Actual policy violations aren't always the same and if the policy requires a specific action in response to a policy violation, it doesn't always allow supervisors or managers to respond appropriately to a violation.

Other General Security Policies

From a more general perspective, an organization may implement personnel management policies that affect other areas of an employee's life. Some examples include behavior on social media networks and the use of email.

As a simple example, employees of a company should not post adverse comments about other employees or customers. Employees who engage in cyberbullying against fellow employees are typically fired. Similarly, employees who post derogatory comments about customers quickly find themselves looking for other employment.

You might think that people would know that what they post on the Internet can be seen by anyone, including their employer. However, if you do a quick Google search on "employee fired after Facebook post" or "employee fired after tweet," you'll find many examples where people ignored the possibility that their words would be seen by their employer.

Another consideration is personal email. Some organizations allow employees to use the organization's IT infrastructure to send and receive personal email, while other organizations forbid it. The key here is ensuring that employees understand the policy.

Social Media Networks and Applications

Millions of people interact with each other using social media networks and applications, such as Facebook and Twitter. Facebook allows people to share their lives with friends, family, and others. Twitter allows people to tweet about events as they are happening. From a social perspective, these technologies allow people to share information about themselves with others. A user posts a comment and a wide group of people instantly see it.

However, from a security perspective, they present some significant risks, especially related to inadvertent information disclosure. Attackers can use these sites to gain information about individuals and then use that information in an attack. Organizations typically either train users about the risks or block access to the social media sites to avoid the risks.

Users often post personal information, such as birth dates, their favorite colors or books, the high school they graduated from, graduation dates, and much more. Some sites use this personal information to validate users when they forget or need to change their password. Imagine Maggie needs to reset her password for a bank account. The web site may challenge her to enter her birth date, favorite book, and graduation date for validation. This is also known as a cognitive password and, theoretically, only Maggie knows this information. However, if Maggie posts all this information on Facebook, an attacker can use it to change the password on the bank account.

As an example, David Kernell used Yahoo!'s cognitive password account recovery process to change former Alaska Governor Sarah Palin's password for her email account. At the time, Yahoo! asked questions such as her high school and birth date and Kernell obtained all the information from online searches. Of course, it didn't turn out well for him. A jury convicted him of a felony and he served more than a year in prison.

In some cases, attackers have used personal information from social networking sites to launch scams. For example, attackers first identify the name of a friend or relative using the social networking site. The attackers then impersonate the friend or relative in an email, claiming to have been robbed and stuck in a foreign country. Attackers end the email with a plea for help asking the victim to send money via wire transfer.

It's also worth considering physical security. While vacationing in Paris, Kim Kardashian West was regularly posting her status and location on social media. She also stressed that she didn't wear fake jewelry. Thieves robbed her at gunpoint in her Paris hotel room. They bound and gagged her and took one of her rings (that is worth an estimated $4.9 million) and a jewelry box (with jewelry worth an estimated $5.6 million). After being caught and arrested, one of the thieves later admitted that it was relatively easy to track her just by watching her online activity.

> **Remember this**
>
> Social media sites allow people to share personal comments with a wide group of people. However, improper use of social networking sites can result in inadvertent information disclosure. Attackers can also use information available on these sites to launch attacks against users or in a cognitive password attack to change a user's password. Training helps users understand the risks.

Banner Ads and Malvertisements

Attackers have been delivering malware through malicious banner ads for several years now. These look like regular ads, but they contain malicious code. Many of these are Flash applets with malicious code embedded in them, but others just use code to redirect users to another server, such as one with a drive-by download waiting for anyone who clicks.

Although these malvertisements have been on many social media sites, they've also appeared on mainstream sites. For example, attackers installed a malvertisement on the *New York Times* web site where it ran for about 24 hours before webmasters discovered and disabled it.

Similarly, malvertising has appeared on the Yahoo! web site. Users who clicked on some Yahoo! ads were taken to sites hosting fake antivirus software. These sites included pop-ups indicating that users' systems were infected with malware and encouraging the users to download and install it. Users who took the bait installed malware onto their systems. Some of these ads sent users to sites in Eastern Europe that were hosting CryptoWall, according to research by Blue Coat Systems, Inc. CryptoWall is a malicious form of ransomware that encrypts user files and demands payment to decrypt them.

Attackers have used two primary methods to get these malvertisements installed on legitimate web sites. One method is to attack a web site and insert ads onto that web site. The second method is to buy ads. They often represent an ad agency pretending to represent legitimate clients. For example, one attacker convinced Gawker Media to run a series of Suzuki advertisements, which were actually malvertisements. Similarly, it's unlikely that Yahoo! was aware that it was hosting malvertising, but instead, these ads likely appeared as a result of attacks or by being tricked.

Social Networking and P2P

Peer-to-peer (P2P or file sharing) applications allow users to share files, such as music, video, and data, over the Internet. Instead of a single server providing the data to end users, all computers in the P2P network are peers, and any computer can act as a server to other clients.

The first widely used P2P network was Napster, an online music-sharing service that operated between 1999 and 2001. Users copied and distributed MP3 music files among each other, and these were often pirated music files. The files were stored on each user's system, and as long as the system was accessible on the Internet, other users could access and download the files. A court order shut down Napster due to copyright issues, but it later reopened as an online music store. Other P2P software and P2P networks continue to appear and evolve.

Organizations usually restrict the use of P2P applications in networks, but this isn't because of piracy issues. One reason is because the P2P applications can consume network bandwidth, slowing down other systems on the network. Worse, a significant risk with P2P applications is data leakage. Users are often unaware of what data they are sharing. Another risk is that users are often unaware of what data the application downloads and stores on their systems, causing them to host inappropriate data. Two examples help illustrate these data leakage risks.

Information concentrators search P2P networks for information of interest and collect it. Investigators once discovered an information concentrator in Iran with over 200 documents containing classified and secret U.S. government data. This included classified information about Marine One, the helicopter used by the president. Although the information about Marine One made the headlines, the attackers had much more information. For example, this concentrator included Iraq status reports and lists of soldiers with privacy data.

How did this happen? Investigations revealed that a defense contractor installed a P2P application on a computer. The computer had access to this data, and the P2P application shared it.

The media latched onto the news about Marine One, so this story was widely published. However, it's widely believed that much more data is being mined via P2P networks. Most end users don't have classified data on their systems, but they do have PII, such as banking information or tax data. When an attacker retrieves data on a user's system and empties a bank account, it might be a catastrophe to the user, but it isn't news.

Organizations can restrict access to P2P networks by blocking access in firewalls. Additionally, port scanners can scan open ports of remote systems to identify P2P software. Organizations often include these checks when running a port scanner as part of a vulnerability scan.

> **Remember this**
>
> Data leakage occurs when users install P2P software and unintentionally share files. Organizations often block P2P software at the firewall.

Agreement Types

Organizations often utilize different types of agreements to help identify various responsibilities. Many are used when working with other organizations, but they can often be used when working with different departments within the same organization. These include:

- **Interconnection security agreement (ISA).** An *ISA* specifies technical and security requirements for planning, establishing, maintaining, and disconnecting a secure connection between two or more entities. For example, it may stipulate certain types of encryption for all data-in-transit. NIST SP 800-47, "Security Guide for Interconnecting Information Technology Systems," includes more in-depth information on ISAs.
- **Service level agreement (SLA).** An *SLA* is an agreement between a company and a vendor that stipulates performance expectations, such as minimum uptime and maximum downtime levels. Organizations use SLAs when contracting services from service providers such as Internet Service Providers (ISPs). Many SLAs include a monetary penalty if the vendor is unable to meet the agreed-upon expectations.
- **Memorandum of understanding (MOU) or memorandum of agreement (MOA).** An *MOU/MOA* expresses an understanding between two or more parties indicating their intention to work together toward a common goal. An MOU/MOA is often used to support an ISA by defining the purpose of the ISA and the responsibilities of both parties. However, it doesn't include any technical details. You can also compare an MOU/MOA with an SLA because it defines the responsibilities of each of the parties. However, it is less formal than an SLA and does not include monetary penalties. Additionally, it doesn't have strict guidelines in place to protect sensitive data.
- **Business partners agreement (BPA).** A *BPA* is a written agreement that details the relationship between business partners, including their obligations toward the partnership. It typically identifies the shares of profits or losses each partner will take, their responsibilities to each other, and what to do if a partner chooses to leave the partnership. One of the primary benefits of a BPA is that it can help settle conflicts when they arise.

> ### Remember this
>
> A memorandum of understanding or memorandum of agreement (MOU/MOA) defines responsibilities of each party, but it is not as strict as a service level agreement (SLA) or interconnection security agreement (ISA). If the parties will be handling sensitive data, they should include an ISA to ensure strict guidelines are in place to protect the data while in transit. An MOU/MOA often supports an ISA.

Protecting Data

Every company has secrets. Keeping these secrets can often make the difference between success and failure. A company can have valuable research and development data, customer databases, proprietary information on products, and much more. If the company cannot keep private and proprietary data secret, it can directly affect its bottom line.

Data policies assist in the protection of data and help prevent data leakage. This section covers many of the different elements that may be contained in a data policy.

Information Classification

As a best practice, organizations take the time to identify, classify, and label data they use. Data classifications ensure that users understand the value of data, and the classifications help protect sensitive data. Classifications can apply to hard data (printouts) and soft data (files).

As an example, the U.S. government uses classifications such as Top Secret, Secret, Confidential, and Unclassified to identify the sensitivity of data. Private companies often use terms such as Proprietary, Private, Confidential, or Public. Note that while the U.S. government has published standards for these classifications, there isn't a published standard that all private companies use.

For comparison, the following statements identify the typical meaning of these public classifications:

- **Public data** is available to anyone. It might be in brochures, press releases, or on web sites.
- **Confidential data** is information that an organization intends to keep secret among a certain group of people. For example, most companies consider salary data confidential. Personnel within the Accounting department and some executives have access to salary data, but they keep it secret among themselves. Many companies have specific policies in place telling people that they shouldn't even tell anyone else their salary amount.
- A proprietor is an owner and **proprietary data** is data that is related to ownership. Common examples are information related to patents or trade secrets.
- **Private data** is information about an individual that should remain private. Two classic examples within IT security are Personally Identifiable Information (PII) and Personal Health Information (PHI). Both PII and PHI are covered in more depth later in this chapter.

The labels and classifications an organization uses are not as important as the fact that they use labels and classifications. Organizations take time to analyze their data, classify it, and provide training to users to ensure the users recognize the value of the data. They also include these classifications within a data policy.

Data Sensitivity Labeling and Handling

Data *labeling* ensures that users know what data they are handling and processing. For example, if an organization classified data as confidential, private, proprietary, and public, it would also use labeling to identify the data. These labels can be printed labels for media such as backup tapes. It's also possible to label files using metadata, such as file properties, headers, footers, and watermarks.

Consider a company that spends millions of dollars on research and development (R&D) trying to develop or improve products. The company values this proprietary data much more than data publicly available on its web site, and needs to protect it. However, if employees have access to the R&D data and it's not classified or labeled, they might not realize its value and might not protect it.

For example, a web content author might write an article for the company's web site touting its achievements. If the R&D data isn't classified and labeled, the author might include some of this R&D data in the article, inadvertently giving the company's competitors free access to proprietary data. Although the R&D employees will easily recognize the data's value, it's not safe to assume that everyone does. In contrast, if the data is labeled, anyone would recognize its value and take appropriate steps to protect it.

Chapter 9, "Implementing Controls to Protect Assets," presents information on backups. As a reminder, it's important to protect backups with the same level of protection as the original data. Labels on backup media help personnel easily identify the value of the data on the backups.

Remember this

Public data is available to anyone. Confidential data information is kept secret among a certain group of people. Proprietary data is data related to ownership, such as patents or trade secrets. Private data is information about individuals that should remain private. Data classifications and data labeling help ensure personnel apply the proper security controls to protect information.

Data Destruction and Media Sanitization

When computers reach the end of their life cycles, organizations donate them, recycle them, or sometimes just throw them away. From a security perspective, you need to ensure that the computers don't include any data that might be useful to people outside your organization or damaging to your organization if unauthorized people receive it.

It's common for organizations to have a checklist to ensure that personnel *sanitize* a system prior to disposing of it. The goal is to ensure that personnel remove all usable data from the system.

Hard drives represent the greatest risk because they hold the most information, so it's important to take additional steps when decommissioning old hard drives. Simply deleting a file on a drive doesn't actually delete it. Instead, it marks the file for deletion and makes the space available for use. Similarly, formatting a disk drive doesn't erase the data. There are many recovery applications available to recover deleted data, file remnants, and data from formatted drives.

Data destruction isn't limited to only hard drives. Organizations often have a policy related to paper containing any type of sensitive data. Shredding or incinerating these papers prevents them from falling into the wrong hands. If personnel just throw this paper away, dumpster divers can sift through the trash and gain valuable information. An organization also takes steps to destroy other types of data, such as backup tapes, and other types of devices, such as removable media.

Some common methods used to destroy data and sanitize media are:

- **Purging.** *Purging* is a general sanitization term indicating that all sensitive data has been removed from a device.
- **File shredding.** Some applications remove all remnants of a file using a *shredding* technique. They do so by repeatedly overwriting the space where the file is located with 1s and 0s.
- **Wiping.** *Wiping* refers to the process of completely removing all remnants of data on a disk. A disk wiping tool might use a bit-level overwrite process that writes different patterns of 1s and 0s multiple times and ensures that the data on the disk is unreadable.
- **Erasing and overwriting.** Solid-state drives (SSDs) require a special process for sanitization. Because they use flash memory instead of magnetic storage platters, traditional drive wiping tools are not effective. Some organizations require personnel to physically destroy SSDs as the only acceptable method of sanitization.
- **Burning.** Many organizations burn materials in an incinerator. Obviously, this can be done with printed materials, but isn't as effective with all materials.

> ### *Cluster Tip Wiping*
>
> Cluster tip wiping is a special process that removes the random data stored at the end of a file. It is useful when you want to keep a file, but remove the random data.
>
> Files are stored in clusters and cluster sizes are typically about 4 KB. Files use as many clusters as they need, but the last cluster has some unused space that the operating system pads with random data.
>
> As an example, imagine you are saving a 6 KB file. It will use two 4 KB clusters and the last 2 KB in the second cluster isn't used to store information for your file. However, this last 2 KB isn't empty. Instead, it contains random data pulled from memory. If someone was recently working with proprietary data, the last 2 KB might hold some of that data. Cluster tip wiping tools can sanitize files stored on a system, and eliminate this issue.

- **Paper shredding.** You can physically shred papers by passing them through a shredder. When doing so, it's best to use a cross-cut shredder that cuts the paper into fine particles. Large physical shredders can even destroy other hardware, such as disk drive platters removed from a disk drive.
- **Pulping.** *Pulping* is an additional step taken after shredding paper. It reduces the shredded paper to mash or puree.
- **Degaussing.** A degausser is a very powerful electronic magnet. Passing a disk through a *degaussing* field renders the data on tape and magnetic disk drives unreadable.
- **Pulverizing.** *Pulverizing* is the process of physically destroying media to sanitize it, such as with a sledge hammer (and safety goggles). Optical media is often pulverized because it is immune to degaussing methods and many shredders can't handle the size of optical media. It's also possible to remove disk platters from disk drives and physically destroy them.

It's also worth mentioning that hard drives and other media can be in devices besides just computers. For example, many copy machines include disk drives, and they can store files of anything that employees recently copied or printed. If personnel don't sanitize the drives before disposing of these devices, it can also result in a loss of confidentiality.

Data Retention Policies

A *data retention policy* identifies how long data is retained, and sometimes specifies where it is stored. This reduces the amount of resources, such as hard drive space or backup tapes, required to retain the data. Retention policies also help reduce legal liabilities. For example, imagine if a retention policy states that the company will only keep email for one year. A court order requiring all email from the company can only expect to receive email from the last year.

On the other hand, if the organization doesn't have a retention policy, it might need to provide email from the past 10 years or longer in response to a court order. This can require an extensive amount of work by administrators to recover archives or search for specific emails. Additionally, investigations can uncover other embarrassing evidence from previous years. The retention policy helps avoid these problems.

Some laws mandate the retention of data for specific time frames, such as three years or longer. For example, laws mandate the retention of all White House emails indefinitely. If a law applies to an organization, the retention policy reflects the same requirements.

PII and PHI

Personally Identifiable Information (**PII**) is personal information that can be used to personally identify an individual. Personal Health Information (**PHI**) is PII that includes health information.

Some examples of PII are:

- Full name
- Birthday and birth place
- Medical and health information
- Street or email address information
- Personal characteristics, such as biometric data
- Any type of identification number, such as a Social Security number (SSN) or driver's license number

In general, you need two or more pieces of information to make it PII. For example, "John Smith" is not PII by itself because it can't be traced back to a specific person. However, when you connect the name with a birth date, an address, medical information, or other data, it is PII.

When attackers gain PII, they often use it for financial gain at the expense of the individual. For example, attackers steal identities, access credit cards, and empty bank accounts. Whenever possible, organizations should minimize the use, collection, and retention of PII. If it's not kept, it can't be compromised. On the other hand, if they collect PII and attackers compromise the data, the company is liable.

The number of security breach incidents resulting in the loss of PII continues to rise. For example, a Veteran's Affairs (VA) employee copied a database onto his laptop that contained PII on over 26 million U.S. veterans. He took the laptop home and a burglar stole it. The VA then went through the painful and expensive process of notifying all of the people who were vulnerable to identity theft, and the affected individuals spent countless hours scouring their records for identity theft incidents. Even though police later recovered the laptop, the VA paid $20 million to settle a lawsuit in the case.

This is not an isolated incident. The Identity Theft Resource Center tracks data breaches and lists them on their site (*http://www.idtheftcenter.org/*). Their 2015 report reported the number of known U.S. data breaches at 780, exposing more than 177 million records containing PII and/or PHI. Some data breaches were small, affecting only a few hundred people. Others were large such as the attack on Scottrade, accessing more than 4.6 million records. Many times, the companies don't even report how many records were accessed, so the number of data records in the hands of criminals is very likely much higher.

Each of these instances resulted in potential identity theft and the loss of goodwill and public trust of the company. Both customers and employees were negatively impacted, and the companies were forced to spend time and energy discussing the incident, and spend money trying to repair their reputations.

Protecting PII and PHI

Organizations have an obligation to protect PII. There are many laws that mandate the protection of PII, including international laws, federal laws, and local regulations. Organizations often develop policies to identify how they handle, retain, and distribute PII, and these policies help ensure they are complying with relevant regulations. When a company doesn't use a specific

PII policy, it usually identifies methods used to protect PII in related data policies.

Many laws require a company to report data losses due to security breaches. If an attack results in the loss of customer PII data, the company is required to report it and notify affected individuals. As an example, Arizona enacted a security breach notification law that requires any company doing business in Arizona to notify customers of security breaches. Most states in the United States have similar laws, and similar international laws exist.

One of the common reasons data seems to fall into the wrong hands is that employees don't understand the risks involved. They might not realize the value of the data on a laptop, or they might casually copy PII data onto a USB flash drive. As mentioned previously, data classification and labeling procedures help employees recognize the data's value and help protect sensitive data.

Training is also important. One of the goals of security professionals is to reinforce the risks of not protecting PII. When employees understand the risks, they are less likely to risk customer and employee data to identity theft.

Additionally, if employees need to transmit PII over a network, they can ensure it's protected by using encryption. As mentioned previously in this book, encrypting data-in-transit provides strong protection against loss of confidentiality.

Many governments have enacted laws mandating the protection of both PII and PHI. Also, there are many documents that provide guidance on how to protect it. The National Institute of Standards and Technology (NIST) created Special Publication (SP) 800-122 "Guide to Protecting the Confidentiality of Personally Identifiable Information (PII)." It identifies many specific safeguards that organizations can implement to protect PII along with steps to take in response to a data breach involving PII. You can access all the NIST publications at *http://csrc.nist. gov/publications/PubsSPs.html*.

> ### Remember this
>
> Personally Identifiable Information (PII) includes information such as a full name, birth date, biometric data, and identifying numbers such as a SSN. PHI is PII that includes medical or health information. Organizations have an obligation to protect PII and PHI and often identify procedures for handling and retaining PII in data policies.

Legal and Compliance Issues

Organizations have a responsibility to follow all laws that apply to them, and ensure that they remain in compliance. Within the context of data security and privacy, the following laws are often a key concern:

- **Health Insurance Portability and Accountability Act of 1996 (HIPAA).** HIPAA mandates that organizations protect PHI. This includes any information directly related to the health of an individual that might be held by doctors, hospitals, or any health facility. It also applies to any information held by an organization related to health plans offered to employees. Fines for not complying with the law have been as high as $4.3 million.
- **Gramm-Leach Bliley Act (GLBA).** This is also known as the Financial Services Modernization Act and includes a Financial Privacy Rule. This rule requires financial institutions to provide consumers with a privacy notice explaining what information

they collect and how that information is used.

- **Sarbanes-Oxley Act (SOX).** SOX was passed after several accounting scandals by major corporations, such as Enron and WorldCom. Companies were engaging in accounting fraud to make their financial condition look better than it was and prop up their stock price. For example, Enron's stock value was over $90 in 2000, but executives knew of problems and began selling their stock. As the scandal emerged, the stock crashed to $42 a year later, and $15 in October of 2001. In December 2002, the stock was worthless at six cents a share, effectively wiping out $60 billion in investments. SOX requires that executives within an organization take individual responsibility for the accuracy of financial reports. It also includes specifics related to auditing, and identifies penalties to individuals for noncompliance.
- **General Data Protection Regulation (GDPR).** This European Union (EU) directive supersedes the Data Protection Directive (also known as Directive 95/46/EC). Both mandate the protection of privacy data for individuals within the EU.

While this section outlined four specific laws related to data, there are others. The key is that organizations have a responsibility to know which laws apply to them and remain in compliance with the laws.

Data Roles and Responsibilities

Many people within the organization handle data. However, an organization often assigns specific roles to some people. Each of these roles has specific responsibilities as outlined in the following list:

- **Owner.** The data owner is the individual with overall responsibility for the data. It is often a high-level position such as the chief executive officer (CEO) or a department head. The data owner is responsible for identifying the classification of the data, ensuring the data is labeled to match the classification, and ensuring security controls are implemented to protect the data.
- **Steward/custodian.** A data steward or data custodian handles the routine tasks to protect data. For example, a data custodian would ensure data is backed up in accordance with a backup policy. The custodian would also ensure that backup tapes are properly labeled to match the classification of the data and stored in a location that provides adequate protection for the classification of the data. Data owners typically delegate tasks to the data custodian.
- **Privacy officer.** A privacy officer is an executive position within an organization. This person is primarily responsible for ensuring that the organization is complying with relevant laws. For example, if the organization handles any PHI, the privacy officer ensures the organization complies with HIPAA. If SOX applies to the organization, the privacy officer ensures that the organization is complying with SOX.

Remember this

Key data roles within an organization are responsible for protecting data. The owner has overall responsibility for the protection of the data. A steward or custodian handles routine tasks to protect data. A privacy officer is an executive responsible for ensuring the organization complies with relevant laws.

Responding to Incidents

Many organizations create **incident response** policies to help personnel identify and respond to incidents. A **security incident** is an adverse event or series of events that can negatively affect the confidentiality, integrity, or availability of data or systems within the organization, or that has the potential to do so.

Some examples include attacks, release of malware, security policy violations, unauthorized access of data, and inappropriate usage of systems. For example, an attack resulting in a data breach is a security incident. Once the organization identifies a security incident, it will respond based on the incident response policy.

Organizations regularly review and update the policy. Reviews might occur on a routine schedule, such as annually, or in response to an incident after performing a lessons learned review of the incident.

As an example, in the early days of computers, one hacker broke into a government system and the first thing he saw was a welcome message. He started poking around, but authorities apprehended him. Later, when the judge asked him what he was doing, he replied that when he saw the welcome message, he thought it was inviting him in. The lesson learned here was that a welcome message can prevent an organization from taking legal action against an intruder. Government systems no longer have welcome messages. Instead, they have warning banners stressing that only authorized personnel should be accessing the system. It's common to see similar warning banners when logging on to any system today.

NIST SP 800-61 Revision 2, "Computer Security Incident Handling Guide," provides comprehensive guidance on how to respond to incidents. It is 79 pages so it's obviously more in-depth than this section, but if you want to dig deeper into any of these topics, it's an excellent resource. Use your favorite search engine and search for "NIST SP 800-61."

> ### Remember this
>
> An incident response policy defines a security incident and incident response procedures. Incident response procedures start with preparation to prepare for and prevent incidents. Preparation helps prevent incidents such as malware infections. Personnel review the policy periodically and in response to lessons learned after incidents.

Incident Response Plan

An **incident response plan (IRP)** provides more detail than the incident response policy. It provides organizations with a formal, coordinated plan personnel can use when responding to an incident. Some of the common elements included with an incident response plan include:

- **Definitions of incident types.** This section helps employees identify the difference between an event (that might or might not be a security incident) and an actual incident. Some types of incidents include attacks from botnets, malware delivered via email, data breach, and a ransom demand after a criminal encrypts an organization's data. The plan may group these incident types using specific category definitions, such as attacks, malware infections, and data breaches.
- **Cyber-incident response teams.** A cyber-incident response team is composed of employees with expertise in different areas. Organizations often refer to the team as a

cyber-incident response team, a computer incident response team (CIRT), or a security incident response team. Combined, they have the knowledge and skills to respond to an incident. Due to the complex nature of incidents, the team often has extensive training. Training includes concepts, such as how to identify and validate an incident, how to collect evidence, and how to protect the collected evidence.

- **Roles and responsibilities.** Many incident response plans identify specific roles for an incident response team along with their responsibilities. For example, an incident response team might include someone from senior management with enough authority to get things done, a network administrator or engineer with the technical expertise necessary to understand the problems, a security expert who knows how to collect and analyze evidence, and a communication expert to relay information to the public if necessary.

- **Escalation.** After identifying an incident, personnel often need to escalate it. Escalation can require a technician to inform his supervisor that he discovered a malware infection and is resolving it. If critical servers are under attack from a protracted distributed denial-of-service (DDoS) attack, escalation can require all members of the incident response team to get involved in responding to the incident.

- **Reporting requirements.** Depending on the severity of the incident, security personnel might need to notify executives within the company of the incident. Obviously, they wouldn't notify executives of every single incident. However, they would notify executives about serious incidents that have the potential to affect critical operations. If the incident involves a data breach, personnel need to identify the extent of the loss, and determine if outside entities are affected. For example, if attackers successfully attacked a system and collected customer data such as credit information, the organization has a responsibility to notify customers of the data breach as soon as possible. The incident response plan outlines who needs to be notified and when.

- **Exercises.** One method of preparing for incident response is to perform exercises. These can test the response of all members of the team. For example, a technical exercise can test the administrator's ability to rebuild a server after a simulated attack. Mock interviews or press conferences can test the team's responses to the media. NIST SP 800-84, "Guide to Test, Training, and Exercise Programs for IT Plans and Capabilities," provides much more in-depth information about performing exercises.

Incident Response Process

Incident response includes multiple phases. It starts with creating an incident response policy and an incident response plan. With the plan in place, personnel are trained and given the tools necessary to handle incidents. Ideally, incident response preparation will help an organization prevent an incident. However, this isn't realistic for most organizations, but with an effective plan in place, the organization will be able to effectively handle any incidents that occur.

Some of the common phases of an *incident response process* are:

- **Preparation.** This phase occurs before an incident and provides guidance to personnel on how to respond to an incident. It includes establishing and maintaining an incident response plan and incident response procedures. It also includes establishing procedures to prevent incidents. For example, preparation includes implementing security controls to prevent malware infections.

- **Identification.** All events aren't security incidents so when a potential incident is reported, personnel take the time to verify it is an actual incident. For example, intrusion detection systems (IDSs) might falsely report an intrusion, but administrators would investigate it and verify if it is a false positive or an incident. If the incident is verified, personnel might try to isolate the system based on established procedures.
- **Containment.** After identifying an incident, security personnel attempt to isolate or contain it. This might include quarantining a device or removing it from the network. This can be as simple as unplugging the system's network interface card to ensure it can't communicate on the network. Similarly, you can isolate a network from the Internet by modifying access control lists on a router or a network firewall. This is similar to how you'd respond to water spilling from an overflowing sink. You wouldn't start cleaning up the water until you first turn off the faucet. The goal of isolation is to prevent the problem from spreading to other areas or other computers in your network, or to simply stop the attack.
- **Eradication.** After containing the incident, it's often necessary to remove components from the attack. For example, if attackers installed malware on systems, it's important to remove all remnants of the malware on all hosts within the organization. Similarly, an attack might have been launched from one or more compromised accounts. Eradication would include deleting or disabling these accounts.
- **Recovery.** During the recovery process, administrators return all affected systems to normal operation and verify they are operating normally. This might include rebuilding systems from images, restoring data from backups, and installing updates. Additionally, if administrators have identified the vulnerabilities that caused the incident, they typically take steps to remove the vulnerabilities.
- **Lessons learned.** After personnel handle an incident, security personnel perform a lessons learned review. It's very possible the incident provides some valuable lessons and the organization might modify procedures or add additional controls to prevent a reoccurrence of the incident. A review might indicate a need to provide additional training to users, or indicate a need to update the incident response policy. The goal is to prevent a future reoccurrence of the incident.

Remember this

The first step in the incident response process is preparation. After identifying an incident, personnel attempt to contain or isolate the problem. This is often as simple as disconnecting a computer from a network. Eradication attempts to remove all malicious components from an attack and recovery returns a system to normal operation. Reviewing lessons learned allows personnel to analyze the incident and the response with a goal of preventing a future occurrence.

Implementing Basic Forensic Procedures

A forensic evaluation helps the organization collect and analyze data as evidence it can use in the prosecution of a crime. In general, forensic evaluations proceed with the assumption that the data collected will be used as evidence in court. Because of this, forensic practices protect evidence to prevent modification and control evidence after collecting it.

Once the incident has been contained or isolated, the next step is a forensic evaluation. What do you think of when you hear forensics? Many people think about the TV program *CSI* (short for "crime scene investigation") and all of its spin-offs. These shows demonstrate the phenomenal capabilities of science in crime investigations.

Computer forensics analyzes evidence from computers to determine details on computer incidents, similar to how CSI personnel analyze evidence from crime scenes. It uses a variety of different tools to gather and analyze computer evidence. Computer forensics is a growing field, and many educational institutions offer specialized degrees around the science. Although you might not be the computer forensics expert analyzing the evidence, you should know about some of the basic concepts related to gathering and preserving the evidence.

Forensic experts use a variety of forensic procedures to collect and protect data after an attack. A key part of this process is preserving the evidence during the data acquisition phase. In other words, they ensure that they don't modify the data as they collect it, and they protect it after collection. A rookie cop wouldn't walk through a pool of blood at a crime scene, at least not more than once. Similarly, employees shouldn't access systems that have been attacked or power them down.

For example, files have properties that show when they were last accessed. However, in many situations, accessing the file modifies this property. If the file is evidence, then accessing it has modified the evidence. This can prevent an investigation from identifying when an attacker accessed the file. Additionally, data in a system's memory includes valuable evidence, but turning a system off deletes this data. In general, an incident response team does not attempt to analyze evidence until they have taken the time to collect and protect it.

Forensic experts have specialized tools they can use to capture data. For example, many experts use EnCase Forensic by Guidance Software or Forensic Toolkit (FTK) by AccessData. These tools can capture data from memory or disks. This includes documents, images, email, webmail, Internet artifacts, web history, chat sessions, compressed files, backup files, and encrypted files. They can also capture data from smartphones and tablets.

Kali Linux includes a wide variety of forensic tools. Feel free to dig into any of them to learn more. They are available via the Applications > Forensics menu.

Order of Volatility

Order of volatility refers to the order in which you should collect evidence. Volatile doesn't mean it's explosive, but rather that it is not permanent. In general, you should collect evidence starting with the most volatile and moving to the least volatile.

For example, random access memory (RAM) is lost after powering down a computer. Because of this, it is important to realize you shouldn't power a computer down if you suspect it has been involved in a security incident and might hold valuable evidence.

A processor can only work on data in RAM, so all the data in RAM indicates what the system was doing. This includes data users have been working on, system processes, network processes, application remnants, and much more. All of this can be valuable evidence in an investigation, but if a rookie technician turns the computer off, the evidence is lost.

Many forensic tools include the ability to capture volatile data. For example, Kali Linux includes the application Volatility (available in Applications > Forensics > Volatility) that can capture the contents of RAM. Once it's captured, experts can analyze it and gain insight into what the computer and user were doing.

In contrast, data on a disk drive remains on the drive even after powering a system down.

This includes any files and even low-level data such as the Master Boot Record on a drive. However, it's important to protect the data on the disk before analyzing it, and a common method is by capturing an image of the disk.

The order of volatility from most volatile to least volatile is:

- Data in cache memory, including the processor cache and hard drive cache
- Data in RAM, including system and network processes
- A paging file (sometimes called a swap file) on the system disk drive
- Data stored on local disk drives
- Logs stored on remote systems
- Archive media

In case you don't remember from your CompTIA A+ days, the page file is an extension of RAM and it is stored on the hard drive. However, the page file isn't a typical file and it's rebuilt when the system is rebooted, making it more volatile than other files stored on hard drives.

> ### Remember this
>
> When collecting data for a forensic analysis, you should collect it from the most volatile to the least volatile. The order of volatility is cache memory, regular RAM, swap or paging file, hard drive data, logs stored on remote systems, and archived media.

Data Acquisition and Preservation of Evidence

When performing data acquisition for evidence, it's important to follow specific procedures to ensure that the evidence is not modified. The following sections provide more information on these procedures.

Capture System Image

A forensic image of a disk captures the entire contents of the drive. Some tools use bit-by-bit copy methods that can read the data without modifying it. Other methods include hardware devices connected to the drive to write-protect it during the copy process.

Chapter 5, "Securing Hosts and Data," introduces disk images as a common method used to deploy systems. These system disk images include mandatory security configurations and help ensure a system starts in a secure state. A distinct difference between standard system images and forensic images is that a forensic image is an exact copy and does not modify the original. This isn't always true with system imaging tools.

One of the oldest disk imaging tools used for forensics is the dd command available in Linux systems, including Kali Linux. It can also be installed on Windows systems. To see how dd works, check out the labs for this chapter at *http://gcgapremium.com/501labs/*.

These methods capture the entire contents of the disk, including system files, user files, and files marked for deletion but not overwritten. Similarly, many tools include the ability to capture data within volatile memory and save it as an image.

After capturing an image, experts create a copy and analyze the copy. They do not analyze the original disk and often don't even analyze the original image. They understand that by analyzing the contents of a disk directly, they can modify the contents. By creating and analyzing forensic copies, they never modify the original evidence.

Take Hashes

Hashing is an important element of forensic analysis to provide proof that collected data has retained integrity. Chapter 10, "Understanding Cryptography and PKI," covers hashes and hashing. As a reminder, a hash is simply a number. You can execute a hashing algorithm against data as many times as you want, and as long as the data is the same, the hash will be the same. The focus in Chapter 10 is on using hashes with files and messages. A captured forensic image (from RAM or a disk) is just a file, and you can use hashing with forensic images to ensure image integrity.

If you do the dd lab mentioned previously, it includes steps to create a copy of the image. After creating the copy, you also have a chance to use the sha1sum command to create and compare hashes.

For example, after capturing an image of a disk, an expert can create a hash of the image. The expert can then write-protect the image to prevent accidental modifications during the analysis. Later, the expert can take another hash of the image and compare it with the original hash. As long as both hashes are the same, it provides proof that the image is the same and the analysis did not modify it.

Forensic analysts sometimes make a copy of the image to analyze, instead of analyzing the first image they capture. If they ever need to verify the integrity of the copy, they run the same hashing algorithm against it. Again, as long as the hash is the same, they know the analyzed data is the same as the captured data.

Similarly, some tools allow you to create a hash of an entire drive. These verify that the imaging process has not modified data. For example, you can create a hash of a drive before capturing the image and after capturing the image. If the hashes are the same, it verifies that the imaging process did not modify the drive.

Remember this

A forensic image is a bit-by-bit copy of the data and does not modify the data during the capture. Experts capture an image of the data before analysis to preserve the original and maintain its usability as evidence. Hashing provides integrity for captured images, including images of both memory and disk drives. You can take a hash of a drive before and after capturing an image to verify that the imaging process did not modify the drive contents.

Network Traffic and Logs

A forensic investigation often includes an analysis of network traffic and available logs. This information helps the investigators re-create events leading up to and during an incident.

As an example, an organization might want to prove that a specific computer was involved in an attack. One way is to match the media access control (MAC) address used by the attacking computer with an existing computer. The MAC address is permanently assigned to a network interface card, and even though the operating system can be manipulated to use a different MAC, the actual MAC isn't changed. In contrast, the IP address and name of the computer are not permanently assigned, and it is relatively easy to change them.

Chapter 8, "Using Risk Management Tools," covers protocol analyzers used to analyze data packets. Data within packets identifies the computers involved in a conversation based on their

IP address and their MAC address. If a data capture shows a MAC address matches the actual MAC address of a suspected computer, it provides a strong indication the computer was involved in the attack.

Similarly, if the attack came from the Internet, you can trace the IP address back to the Internet Service Provider (ISP). ISPs issue IP addresses to users and the ISP logs identify exactly who was issued an IP address at any given time. This is often effective at catching amateur hackers, but professional criminals use a variety of tools to mask their actual address.

Chapter 8 presents information on logs. Logs record what happened during an event, when it happened, and what account was used during the event. You might remember that a Security log records logon and logoff events. Similarly, many applications require users to authenticate, and applications log authentication events. All of these logs can be invaluable in re-creating the details of an event after a security incident, including the identity of the account used in the attack.

Capture Video

Video surveillance methods such as closed-circuit television (CCTV) systems are often used as a detective control during an investigation. If a person is recorded on video, the video provides reliable proof of the person's location and activity. For example, if a person is stealing equipment or data, video might provide proof.

As an example, I remember a high school student was working nights at a local grocery store. The store had a delivery of beer in a tractor-trailer that hadn't been unloaded yet but was kept backed up to the store loading dock overnight. The student stole several cases of beer thinking the crime was undetectable. However, the entire scene was recorded on video. When he showed up for work the next evening, the store promptly called the police and provided a copy of the video. The video provided reliable proof that simply couldn't be disputed.

Record Time Offset

In some cases, it's easy to identify the time of an event such as in Figure 11.1. In the figure, you can easily identify the exact dates and times when someone created, modified, last saved, and last accessed the file. However, in some cases, you need to consider a time offset.

Figure 11.1: File Explorer showing exact dates and times

For example, Greenwich Mean Time (GMT) identifies the time at the Royal Observatory in Greenwich, London. Other times are often expressed as a relationship to GMT. For example, I live in the Eastern Standard Time (EST) zone, which has a four-hour offset. You can express the Date Accessed time as 5:10 p.m. EST. Using GMT, you can express the same time as 9:10 p.m. GMT. One benefit of using GMT is that it doesn't change for daylight saving time, so it stays constant.

Many video recorders use a *record time offset* to identify times on tape recordings rather than the actual time. For example, a recording might use a displayed counter to identify the time that has passed since the recording started. Imagine that the counter advances 1,000 ticks or counts per hour. If the counter indicates an event occurred at an offset time of 1,500 and the recording started at midnight, then the time of the event was 1:30 a.m.

When analyzing timestamps of any evidence, it's important to understand that these times are often based on an offset. If you can't identify the offset, you might not be able to identify the actual time.

Screenshots

Screenshots are simply pictures of what you can see displayed on a computer screen. If you want to capture exactly what a user was doing, or specific displays, a screenshot is the perfect solution.

For example, Figure 11.1, shown previously, is a screenshot of File Explorer. You can save screenshots as graphics files and embed these graphics into documents. Many operating systems include the ability to capture the screen and save it to the Clipboard. For example, you can capture the screen of almost any system by pressing the PrtScn key found on most keyboards. Many applications such as the Windows Snipping Tool or Snagit by TechSmith allow you to capture screenshots from specific windows or applications, any region of the screen, and even scrolling windows such as a long web page.

Witness Interviews

Another element of an investigation is interviewing witnesses. Witnesses provide firsthand reports of what happened and when it happened. However, witnesses won't necessarily come forward with relevant information unless someone asks them. Often witnesses don't recognize what information is valuable.

For example, imagine a tailgating incident where an attacker follows closely behind an employee. The employee uses a proximity card to get in, but the attacker just walks right in behind the employee. The employee might notice, but not give it much thought, especially if tailgating is common in the organization. If the attack resulted in loss of equipment or data, an investigator might get a good description of the attacker just by interviewing witnesses.

Chain of Custody

A key part of incident response is collecting and protecting evidence. A ***chain of custody*** is a process that provides assurances that evidence has been controlled and handled properly after collection. Forensic experts establish a chain of custody when they first collect evidence.

Security professionals use a chain of custody form to document this control. The chain of custody form provides a record of every person who was in possession of a physical asset collected as evidence. It shows who had custody of the evidence and where it was stored the entire time since collection. Additionally, personnel often tag the evidence as part of a chain of custody process. A proper chain of custody process ensures that evidence presented in a court of law is the same evidence that security professionals collected.

As an example, imagine that Homer collected a hard drive as part of an investigation. However, instead of establishing a chain of custody, he simply stores the drive on his desk with the intention of analyzing it the next day. Is it possible that someone could modify the contents of the drive overnight? Absolutely. Instead, he should immediately establish a chain of custody and lock the drive in a secure storage location.

If evidence is not controlled, someone can modify, tamper, or corrupt it. Courts will rule the evidence inadmissible if there is a lack of adequate control, or even a lack of documentation showing that personnel maintained adequate control. However, the chain of custody provides proof that personnel handled the evidence properly.

Legal Hold

A *legal hold* refers to a court order to maintain different types of data as evidence. As an example, imagine that Ziffcorp is being sued for fraud and is being investigated by the Securities and Exchange Commission. A court orders them to maintain digital and paper documents for the past three years related to the case. Ziffcorp now needs to take steps to preserve the data.

This data may include emails; databases; backup tapes; data stored on servers in file shares and document libraries; and data stored on desktop computers, laptops, tablets, and smartphones owned by the company. The first step management needs to take is to direct the data custodians to preserve this data. On the surface, this might sound easy, but it can be tremendously complex, especially if it is not clear to data custodians what data should be maintained. They might preserve too much data, resulting in a significant cost to store it. They might preserve too little data, subjecting the company to more litigation in a suspected cover-up.

Data retention policies also apply here. As an example, imagine that the data retention policy states that email older than six months is deleted. If administrators rigorously followed the policy, the company wouldn't have any emails from more than six months ago. That's OK if the policy is in writing and administrators are following it.

What if the administrators didn't follow the data retention policy? What if they have email from as long as two years ago? In this scenario, administrators need to maintain these emails. If they take steps to delete the emails after receiving the court order, it looks like they are trying to withhold evidence and puts the organization into legal jeopardy for a cover-up.

> **Remember this**
>
> A chain of custody provides assurances that evidence has been controlled and handled properly after collection. It documents who handled the evidence and when they handled it. A legal hold is a court order to preserve data as evidence.

Recovery of Data

Generically, data recovery refers to restoring lost data, such as restoring a corrupt file from a backup. In the context of forensics, data recovery goes further. Even without backups, it's often possible to recover data that has been intentionally or accidentally deleted.

When a user deletes a file, the operating system typically just marks it for deletion and makes the space the file is consuming available to use for other files. However, the file is still there. Many file systems place the file in a recycle bin or trash can and you can just retrieve it from there. Even if the user empties the trash after deleting a file, forensic experts can use tools to undelete the files.

Formatting a drive appears as though it has overwritten all the data on the drive. However, just as forensic experts have tools to undelete files, they also have tools they can use to unformat drives. It's worth noting that criminals have access to these same tools, too, and can recover data from systems that haven't been sanitized.

Active Logging for Intelligence Gathering

It's often appropriate for organizations to engage in strategic intelligence or counterintelligence gathering by increasing the amount of data that they collect. For example, an active logging strategy can help an organization gather a significant amount of data on attackers.

Typically, a network infrastructure is configured to log only the data needed for daily operations. If the network is under attack, administrators might increase the logging capabilities at some point while the attack is happening. However, they might not have valuable data if they had those same logging capabilities enabled when the attack began.

An active logging strategy increases the amount of logged data collected on a routine basis. Ideally, network administrators will have filters available so that they can view only the data they need for daily operations. However, if an attack begins, security professionals can view all the logged data.

Track Man-Hours and Expense

Investigations can take an extraordinary amount of time and, for any business, time is money. When budget time rolls around, the departments that can accurately identify how much time and money they spent are more likely to get their requested budget approved.

Additionally, quantitative risk assessments base decisions on using specific monetary amounts, such as cost and asset values. If an incident required involvement by security professionals on an incident response team, the man-hours and expenses incurred by the incident response team need to be included in the assessment. Including this data improves the accuracy of the cost values used in the quantitative risk assessment.

Providing Training

Organizations commonly provide training to users on a variety of issues. This includes training personnel on security policies and continuing education training to help ensure personnel remain up to date with current technologies.

Role-Based Awareness Training

Role-based awareness training is targeted to personnel based on their roles. The primary goal is to minimize the risk to the organization, and by giving users the training they need, they are better prepared to avoid threats. The following roles often require role-based training:

- **Data owner.** Data owners need to understand their responsibilities related to data that they own. This includes ensuring that the data is classified correctly and ensuring that the data is labeled to match the classification. They are also responsible for ensuring adequate security controls are implemented to protect the data. While they often delegate day-to-day tasks to data custodians, they cannot delegate their responsibility.
- **System administrator.** System administrators are responsible for the overall security of a system. They often need technical training so that they understand the software capabilities and vulnerabilities, and how to ensure the system is operating in a secure state. As a simple example, if an organization purchases a new hardware firewall, system administrators need training to ensure they know how to implement it securely.
- **System owner.** A system owner is typically a high-level executive or department head who has overall responsibility for the system. While system owners won't perform

daily maintenance on their systems, they are responsible for ensuring that system administrators have the skills and knowledge to maintain them.

- **User.** Regular end users need to understand common threats, such as malware and phishing attacks. They also need to understand the risk posed by clicking an unknown link and how drive-by downloads can infect their system. Training can include a wide variety of topics depending on the organization and can be delivered via different methods. For example, security experts can send emails informing users of current threats. Some training is delivered via web sites, in a classroom, or informally by supervisors. Training is often included when users review and sign an organization's AUP.
- **Privileged user.** A privileged user is any user with more rights and permissions than typical end users. Privileged users need training on the classification and labeling of data that they handle. Administrators are often required to use two accounts, one for regular use and one for administrative use. For administrators to follow this policy, they need to understand why it's implemented and the potential repercussions if the administrator always uses the administrator account.
- **Executive user.** Executives need high-level briefings related to the risks that the organization faces, along with information on the organization's overall information security awareness program. Additionally, executives should be trained on whaling attacks because attackers target executives with malicious phishing emails.
- **Incident response team.** An incident response team needs detailed training on how to respond to incidents. Even within the team, personnel might require different training. For example, security personnel responsible for forensic investigations need specialized forensic training.

The success of any security awareness and training plan is directly related to the support from senior management. If senior management supports the plan, middle management and employees will also support it. On the other hand, if senior management does not show support for the plan, it's very likely that personnel within the organization will not support it either.

Remember this

Role-based training ensures that employees receive appropriate training based on their roles in the organization. Common roles that require role-based training are data owners, system administrators, system owners, end users, privileged users, and executive users.

Continuing Education

Training is rarely a once and done event. Instead, personnel need to regularly receive additional training to ensure they are up to date on current threats, vulnerabilities, and technologies. If network administrators are still using the same practices and technologies they learned 10 years ago, their networks are very likely vulnerable to a multitude of attacks.

This concept is used in many different professions. For example, your doctor is required to regularly attend continuing education to update her knowledge. That's a good thing. When you're receiving medical treatment and advice, you don't want treatment and advice that was valid a decade ago, but might not be valid today. Similarly, many certifications (including the CompTIA Security+ certification) have formal continuing education requirements.

Continuing education within an organization can take many forms. It's often possible to send personnel to classes to update their knowledge. When many people need the same training, an organization will often bring in a trainer to teach a class in-house.

Training and Compliance Issues

There are many situations where training is required to maintain compliance with existing laws, best practices, and standards. As an example, many laws exist covering PII. Although these laws have many similarities, there can be minor differences in different localities. It's important for personnel handling any PII to understand the laws that apply.

Best practices often prevent a wide range of incidents when users understand and follow them. This book has covered many best practices, including developing and following a security policy, ensuring users do not share accounts, using strong passwords, following the principle of least privilege, and much more. Unless personnel know about them, and understand them, they might not be implementing them.

Additionally, many organizations should abide by certain standards. For example, organizations handling credit card information need to comply with the Payment Card Industry Data Security Standard (PCI DSS). PCI DSS includes six control objectives and 12 specific requirements that help prevent fraud.

Administrators might understand how to implement many of these without any additional training. However, some of the requirements might require additional training to maintain compliance. PCI DSS isn't foolproof, but it has helped reduce many of the risks associated with credit card fraud.

Troubleshooting Personnel Issues

One of the objectives for the CompTIA exam is to troubleshoot common security issues, including personnel issues. While I've covered these topics in different chapters, I am summarizing them here. The personnel issues are insider threat, personal email, policy violation, social engineering, and social media.

The way to detect an insider threat depends on the activity. Imagine Bart is trying to copy proprietary data onto an external drive or send proprietary data outside the network via email. Data loss prevention (DLP) techniques provide the best method to detect these activities. DLP systems typically send notifications to security personnel, who can then take steps to stop Bart.

Audits and reviews can often detect insider threats, too. As an example, usage auditing will detect what users are doing. This includes showing what files and folders they're accessing, and how they are using their rights and permissions. If they're doing things outside their job role, it should be investigated.

Two of these issues (personal email and social media) refer to users not following the security policy. For example, a policy might say that users can't use email for personal purposes and can't associate themselves with the organization when posting to social media. These activities are often detected by other employees and reported to management. A training program reminding users of the policies can minimize these incidents.

When policy violations are detected, management acts based on the organization's policies. This can include anything from verbal counseling to termination.

The best way to detect social engineering tactics is to educate personnel on common tactics.

When they detect a social engineer, employees should report them. Security personnel can take additional steps to raise the awareness of these incidents through training and awareness programs.

Chapter 11 Exam Topic Review

When preparing for the exam, make sure you understand these key concepts covered in this chapter.

Exploring Security Policies

- Written security policies are administrative controls that identify an overall security plan for an organization and help to reduce overall risk. Plans and procedures identify security controls used to enforce security policies.
- An acceptable use policy defines proper system usage for users and spells out rules of behavior when accessing systems and networks. It often provides specific examples of unacceptable usage, such as visiting certain web sites, and typically includes statements informing users that the organization monitors user activities. Users are required to read and sign an acceptable use policy when hired, and in conjunction with refresher training.
- Mandatory vacation policies require employees to take time away from their job. These policies help to reduce fraud and discover malicious activities by employees.
- A separation of duties policy separates individual tasks of an overall function between different entities or different people, and helps deter fraud. For example, a single person shouldn't be able to approve bills and pay them, or print checks and then sign them.
- Job rotation policies require employees to change roles on a regular basis. Employees might swap roles temporarily, such as for three to four weeks, or permanently. These policies help to prevent employees from continuing with fraudulent activities, and help detect fraud if it occurs.
- Clean desk policies require users to organize their desks and surrounding areas to reduce the risk of possible data theft and password compromise.
- Background checks are performed before hiring an employee. Once hired, onboarding processes give employees access to resources. An exit interview is conducted before an employee departs the organization, and the account is typically disabled during the interview.
- Improper use of social networking sites can result in inadvertent information disclosure. Attackers gather information from these sites to launch attacks against users, such as cognitive password attacks to change users' passwords. Training reduces these risks.
- A non-disclosure agreement helps ensure that proprietary data is not shared.
- A service level agreement (SLA) is an agreement between a company and a vendor that stipulates performance expectations, such as minimum uptime and maximum downtime levels.
- An interconnection security agreement (ISA) specifies technical and security requirements for connections and ensures data confidentiality while data is in transit.
- A memorandum of understanding or memorandum of agreement (MOU/MOA) supports an ISA, but doesn't include technical details.

Protecting Data

- Information classification practices help protect sensitive data by ensuring users understand the value of data. Data labeling ensures that users know what data they are handling and processing.
- Public data is available to anyone. Confidential data is information that an organization intends to keep secret among a certain group of people. Proprietary data is data that is related to ownership, such as patents or trade secrets. Private data includes PII and PHI.
- Destruction and sanitization methods ensure that sensitive data is removed from decommissioned systems. File shredders remove all remnants of a file. Wiping methods erase disk drives.
- Degaussing a disk magnetically erases all the data. Physically destroying a drive is the most secure method of ensuring unauthorized personnel cannot access proprietary information.
- Retention policies identify how long data is retained. They can limit a company's exposure to legal proceedings and reduce the amount of labor required to respond to court orders.
- Personally Identifiable Information (PII) is used to personally identify an individual. Examples include the full name, birth date, address, and medical information of a person. Personal Health Information (PHI) is PII that includes medical or health-related information.
- PII/PHI requires special handling for data retention. Many laws mandate the protection of both, and require informing individuals when an attack results in the compromise of PII or PHI.
- A data owner has overall responsibility for data. A steward or custodian handles routine tasks to protect data. A privacy officer is responsible for ensuring an organization complies with relevant laws to protect privacy data, such as PII or PHI.

Responding to Incidents

- An incident response policy defines an incident and response procedures. Organizations review and update incidents periodically and after reviewing lessons learned after actual incidents.
- The first step in incident response is preparation. It includes creating and maintaining an incident response policy and includes prevention steps such as implementing security controls to prevent malware infections.
- Before acting, personnel verify an event is an actual incident. Next, they attempt to contain or isolate the problem. Disconnecting a computer from a network will isolate it.
- Eradication attempts to remove all malicious components left after an incident. Recovery restores a system to its original state. Depending on the scope of the incident, administrators might completely rebuild the system, including applying all updates and patches.
- A review of lessons learned helps an organization prevent a reoccurrence of an incident.
- The order of volatility for data from most volatile to least volatile is cache memory, regular RAM, a paging file, hard drive data, logs stored on remote systems, and archived media.
- Forensic experts capture an image of the data before analysis to preserve the original and maintain its usability as evidence.

- Hard drive imaging creates a forensic copy and prevents the forensic capture and analysis from modifying the original evidence. A forensic image is a bit-by-bit copy of the data and does not modify the data during the capture.
- Hashing provides integrity for images, including images of both memory and disk drives. Taking a hash before and after capturing a disk image verifies that the capturing process did not modify data. Hashes can reveal evidence tampering or, at the very least, that evidence has lost integrity.
- A chain of custody provides assurances that personnel controlled and handled evidence properly after collecting it. It may start with a tag attached to the physical item, followed by a chain of custody form that documents everyone who handled it and when they handled it.
- A legal hold requires an organization to protect existing data as evidence.

Providing Training

- Security awareness and training programs reinforce user compliance with security policies and help reduce risks posed by users.
- Role-based training ensures that personnel receive the training they need. For example, executives need training on whaling attacks.
- Common roles that require role-based training are data owners, system administrators, system owners, end users, privileged users, and executive users.
- Continuing education programs ensure that personnel are kept up to date on current technologies, threats, and vulnerabilities.

Online References

- Do you know how to answer performance-based questions? Check out the online extras at *http://gcgapremium.com/501-extras.*

Chapter 11 Practice Questions

1. Management within your organization wants to ensure that users understand the rules of behavior when they access the organization's computer systems and networks. Which of the following BEST describes what they would implement to meet this requirement?
   A. AUP
   B. NDA
   C. BYOD
   D. DD

2. Martin has worked as a network administrator for several years within your organization. Over time, he has been tasked with performing several jobs, including database administration and application development. Security personnel are concerned that his level of access represents a serious risk. Which of the following is the BEST solution to reduce this risk?
   A. Mandatory vacations
   B. Exit interview
   C. Change management
   D. Separation of duties

3. After a recent security audit, management has decided to upgrade the security policy. Among other items, they want to identify a policy that will reduce the risk of personnel within an organization colluding to embezzle company funds. Which of the following is the BEST choice to meet this need?
   A. AUP
   B. Training
   C. Mandatory vacations
   D. Background check

4. After a major data breach, Lisa has been tasked with reviewing security policies related to data loss. Which of the following is MOST closely related to data loss?
   A. Clean desk policy
   B. Legal hold policy
   C. Job rotation policy
   D. Background check policy

5. An organization is preparing to hire additional network administrators. They decide to perform background checks on all personnel after obtaining written permission. Which of the following items is NOT appropriate to include in a background check?
   A. Social media presence
   B. Criminal background
   C. Financial history
   D. Medical history

6. Dan has been working at your company as an accountant. However, after a disagreement with an executive, he decides to leave the company and work at the local mall. He has a user account allowing him to access network resources. Which of the following is the MOST appropriate step to take?
   A. Ensure his account is disabled when he announces that he will be leaving the company.
   B. Immediately terminate his employment.
   C. Force him to take a mandatory vacation.
   D. Ensure his account is disabled during his exit interview.

7. Your organization is planning to implement an incident response plan in response to a new incident response security policy. Which of the following items is the FIRST step in an incident response process?
   A. Preparation
   B. Identification
   C. Containment
   D. Eradication

8. Waylon reported suspicious activity on his computer. After investigating, you verify that his computer is infected with malware. Which of the following steps should you take NEXT?
   A. Identification
   B. Preparation
   C. Containment
   D. Eradication

9. After a recent incident, a forensic analyst was given several hard drives to analyze. Which of the following should the analyst do FIRST?

    A. Take screenshots and capture drive images.

    B. Take hashes and screenshots.

    C. Take hashes and capture drive images.

    D. Perform antivirus scans and create chain of custody documents.

10. You need to create an image of a large hard drive for forensic analysis from a Linux system. Which of the following will you MOST likely use?

    A. hashing

    B. screenshots

    C. dd

    D. logs

11. The BizzFad company decides to partner with Costington's to bid on a contract. Management in both companies realize that they need to share proprietary data. However, they want to ensure that distribution of this data is limited within each of the companies. Which of the following will BEST meet this need?

    A. MOU

    B. BPA

    C. NDA

    D. ISA

12. You are reviewing incident response procedures related to the order of volatility. Which of the following is the LEAST volatile?

    A. Hard disk drive

    B. Memory

    C. RAID-10 cache

    D. CPU cache

13. After learning that an employee had unauthorized material on his computer, management directed security personnel to confiscate his computer. Later, a security expert captured a forensic image of the system disk. However, he reported that the computer was left unattended for several hours before he captured the image. Which of the following is a potential issue if this incident goes to court?

    A. Chain of custody

    B. Order of volatility

    C. Time offset

    D. Screenshot

14. Your organization is involved in a lawsuit. A judge issued a court order requiring your organization to keep all emails from the last three years. Your data retention policy states that email should only be maintained from the last 12 months. After investigating, administrators realize that backups contain email from the last three years. What should they do with these backups?

    A. Backups older than 12 months should be deleted to comply with the data retention policy.

    B. Backups for the last 12 months should be protected to comply with the legal hold.

    C. Backups for the last two years should be protected to comply with the legal hold.

    D. Backups for the last three years should be protected to comply with the legal hold.

15. Your organization has decided to implement a more aggressive training and continuing education program using role-based training. Management wants to ensure that each role gets the necessary training based on the role. Which of the following BEST describes the responsibilities of data owners and indicates what training they need?

    A. Ensuring data is backed up in accordance with the data policy

    B. Ensuring data is classified and labeled correctly

    C. Complying with laws related to privacy

    D. Understanding common threats, such as malware and phishing attacks

Chapter 11 Practice Question Answers

1. **A.** An acceptable use policy (AUP) informs users of company expectations when they use computer systems and networks, and it defines acceptable rules of behavior. A non-disclosure agreement (NDA) ensures that individuals do not share proprietary data with others. A bring your own device (BYOD) policy identifies requirements for employee-owned mobile devices. The dd command (short for data duplicator) is available on Linux systems to copy files or entire disk images. Forensic analysts use it to create an image of a disk without modifying the original disk.

2. **D.** A separation of duties policy prevents any single person from performing multiple job functions that might allow the person to commit fraud. In this scenario, the administrator has accumulated privileges across several job functions, which represents the risk. A mandatory vacation policy is useful to discover fraud committed by an individual, but this scenario clearly indicates this individual controls too many job functions. An exit interview is performed when an employee leaves the organization. Change management ensures changes are reviewed before being implemented.

3. **C.** Mandatory vacations help to reduce the possibility of fraud and embezzlement. An acceptable use policy informs users of company policies and even though users sign them, they don't deter someone considering theft by embezzling funds. Training can help reduce incidents by ensuring personnel are aware of appropriate policies. A background check is useful before hiring employees, but it doesn't directly reduce risks related to employees colluding to embezzle funds.

4. **A.** A clean desk policy requires users to organize their areas to reduce the risk of possible data theft and password compromise. A legal hold refers to a court order to protect data

that might be needed as evidence. A legal hold policy may state that the organization will comply with the court order, but it isn't related to data theft. Job rotation policies require employees to change roles on a regular basis and can expose fraudulent activity. A background check policy typically identifies what to check for when hiring an employee.

5. **D.** Medical history is not appropriate to include in a background check. However, it is common to check a potential employee's social media presence, criminal background, and financial history.

6. **D.** His account should be disabled (or deleted if that is the company policy) during the exit interview. It's appropriate to conduct an exit interview immediately before an employee departs. Employees often give a two-week or longer notice. If their access is revoked immediately, they won't be able to do any more work. While some companies do terminate employment when someone gives notice, from a security perspective, it's best to take action related to the user account. The purpose of a mandatory vacation is to detect fraud, but if the employee is leaving, any potential fraud will be detected when that employee leaves.

7. **A.** The first step in an incident response process is preparation. When a potential incident occurs, the next step is identification. If the event is a security incident, the next step is containment to isolate the incident and limit the damage. Next, personnel take steps to eradicate all elements that caused the incident, such as malware or compromised accounts.

8. **C.** After identifying an incident, the next step is containment. The scenario indicates you have identified the incident as a malware infection. Preparation is the first step in an incident response process. Eradication attempts to remove all elements of the incident after first containing it.

9. **C.** Forensic analysts capture drive images and take hashes before beginning analysis, and they only analyze the imaged copies, not the original drive. Screenshots are taken when a computer is running. An antivirus scan might modify the drive and chain of custody documents are created when evidence is collected.

10. **C.** The dd command is available on Linux systems and it is used to copy files for analysis. As an example, the dd if=/dev/sda2 of=sd2disk.img command creates an image of a disk without modifying the original disk. None of the other choices creates an image of a drive. Hashing algorithms create a hash of a file. Screenshots create a graphic from a computer screen. Logs record log entries in files.

11. **C.** A non-disclosure agreement (NDA) helps ensure that proprietary data is not shared. It can be written to ensure that employees don't share proprietary data or business partners don't share proprietary data. A memorandum of understanding (MOU) expresses an understanding between two or more parties indicating their intention to work together toward a common goal. A business partners agreement (BPA) details the relationship between business partners, including their obligations toward the partnership. An interconnection security agreement (ISA) specifies the technical and security requirements for planning, establishing, maintaining, and disconnecting a secure connection between two or more entities.

12. **A.** Data on a hard disk drive is the least volatile of those listed. All other sources are some type of memory, which will be lost if a system is turned off. This includes data in normal memory, a redundant array of inexpensive disks 10 (RAID-10) cache, and the central processing unit's (CPU's) cache.

13. **A.** Chain of custody is the primary issue here because the computer was left unattended for several hours. It's difficult to prove that the data collected is the same data that was on the employee's computer when it was confiscated. Data captured from a disk is not volatile, so volatility is not an issue in this scenario. The time offset refers to logged times and is not related to this question. Screenshots are pictures of a screen at a moment in time, but are not related to this question.

14. **D.** The court order specified a legal hold on email from the last three years, so all the backups for the last three years should be kept. If the backups had been destroyed before the court order, they wouldn't be available, so the legal hold wouldn't apply to them. Deleting them after the court order is illegal. Protecting only the backups from the last 12 months or the last two years doesn't comply with the court order.

15. **B.** Owners are responsible for identifying the proper classification of data, ensuring it is labeled correctly, and ensuring security controls are implemented to protect the data. A data steward is responsible for routine daily tasks such as backing up data. A privacy officer is responsible for ensuring the organization is complying with relevant laws. End users need to be trained on common threats, such as malware and phishing attacks.

Post-Assessment Exam

Use this practice exam as an additional study aid before taking the live exam. An answer key with explanations is available at the end of the practice exam.

1. Homer needs to send an email to his supervisor with an attachment that includes proprietary data. He wants to maintain the confidentiality of this data. Which of the following choices is the BEST choice to meet his needs?
   A. Digital signature
   B. Encryption
   C. Steganography
   D. Hashing

2. You are the security administrator in your organization. You want to ensure that a file maintains integrity. Which of the following choices is the BEST solution to meet your goal?
   A. Steganography
   B. Encryption
   C. Hash
   D. AES

3. Which of the following accurately identifies primary security control types?
   A. Role-based and discretionary
   B. Technical and administrative
   C. Confidentiality and availability
   D. Encryption and hashing

4. You recently started a new job in information technology security. Your primary responsibilities are to monitor security logs, analyze trend reports, and install CCTV systems. Which of the following choices BEST identifies your responsibilities? (Select TWO.)
   A. Hardening systems
   B. Detecting security incidents
   C. Preventing incidents
   D. Implementing monitoring controls

5. A security expert is identifying and implementing several different physical deterrent controls to protect an organization's server room. Which of the following choices would BEST meet this objective?
    A. Using hardware locks
    B. Utilizing data encryption
    C. Performing a vulnerability assessment
    D. Training users

6. An organization is implementing a feature that allows multiple servers to operate on a single physical server. Which of the following is the feature being implemented?
    A. Virtualization
    B. IaaS
    C. Cloud computing
    D. DLP

7. Lisa is using a Linux computer to monitor network traffic. She connected the computer to the mirror port of a switch and started the logging software. However, she found that the only traffic being collected is traffic to or from the Linux computer. She wants to collect all traffic going through the switch. Which of the following actions should she take?
    A. Run the command ipconfig eth0 promisc.
    B. Run the command ifconfig eth0 promisc.
    C. Reconfigure the switch.
    D. Connect the computer to a router.

8. Management has updated the security policy and it has changed the requirements for the password policy. The password policy needs to ensure that users change their passwords regularly and they cannot reuse their passwords. Which of the following settings need to be configured? (Select THREE.)
    A. Maximum password age
    B. Password length
    C. Password history
    D. Password complexity
    E. Minimum password age

9. Your organization has implemented a system that stores user credentials in a central database. Users log on once with their credentials. They can then access other systems in the organization without logging on again. Which of the following does this describe?
    A. Federation
    B. SAML
    C. Single sign-on
    D. Biometrics

10. You are modifying a configuration file used to authenticate Linux accounts against an external server. The file includes phrases such as DC=Server1 and DC=Com. Which authentication service is the external server MOST likely using?
    - A. Diameter
    - B. RADIUS
    - C. LDAP
    - D. SAML

11. A network includes a ticket-granting ticket server. Which of the following choices is the primary purpose of this server?
    - A. Authentication
    - B. Identification
    - C. Authorization
    - D. Access control

12. Your organization has a strict policy requiring administrators to disable user accounts during the exit interview. This provides several security benefits. Which of the following choices BEST identifies a security benefit of this practice?
    - A. Ensures that user security keys are retained
    - B. Ensures that user files are retained
    - C. Ensures that the account can be enabled again if the employee returns
    - D. Ensures that users cannot log on remotely

13. An administrator needs to grant users access to different servers based on their job functions. Which access control model is the BEST choice to use?
    - A. Discretionary access control
    - B. Mandatory access control
    - C. Role-based access control
    - D. Rule-based access control

14. You configure access control for users in your organization. Some departments have a high employee turnover, so you want to simplify account administration. Which of the following is the BEST choice?
    - A. User-assigned privileges
    - B. Group-based privileges
    - C. Domain-assigned privileges
    - D. Network-assigned privileges

15. The Mapple organization is creating a help-desk team to assist employees with account issues. Members of this team need to create and modify user accounts and occasionally reset user passwords. Which of the following is the BEST way to accomplish this goal?
    - A. Give each help-desk employee appropriate privileges individually.
    - B. Add members of the help-desk team to a security group that has the appropriate privileges.
    - C. Add each member of the help-desk team to the administrator group within the domain.
    - D. Assign attributes to members of the group and give these attributes appropriate privileges.

16. Lisa wants to manage and monitor the switches and routers in her network. Which of the following protocols would she use?
    A. NAT
    B. SRTP
    C. SNMPv3
    D. DNSSEC

17. Your organization has several switches within the network. You need to implement a security control to prevent unauthorized access to these switches. Which of the following choices BEST meets this need?
    A. Disable unused ports.
    B. Implement an implicit deny rule.
    C. Disable STP.
    D. Enable SSH.

18. You are troubleshooting a network connectivity issue and find that when you try to ping a remote server, it fails. You suspect that an ACL within a router may be blocking some traffic. Which of the following would give you this symptom?
    A. The router is blocking DNS traffic.
    B. The router is blocking ICMP traffic.
    C. The router is blocking SSH traffic.
    D. The router is blocking SFTP traffic.

19. Your network currently has a dedicated firewall protecting access to a web server. It is currently configured with only the following two rules in the ACL:

    PERMIT TCP ANY ANY 443

    PERMIT TCP ANY ANY 80

    You have detected DNS requests and zone transfer requests coming through the firewall and you need to block them. Which of the following would meet this goal? (Select TWO. Each answer is a full solution.)
    A. Add the following rule to the firewall: DENY TCP ALL ALL 53.
    B. Add the following rule to the firewall: DENY UDP ALL ALL 53.
    C. Add the following rule to the firewall: DENY TCP ALL ALL 25.
    D. Add the following rule to the firewall: DENY IP ALL ALL 53.
    E. Add an implicit deny rule at the end of the ACL.

20. Your organization wants to combine some of the security controls used to control incoming and outgoing network traffic. At a minimum, the solution should include malware inspection, content inspection, and a DDoS mitigator. Which of the following BEST meets this goal?
    A. VLAN
    B. NAT
    C. UTM
    D. DNSSEC

21. Your email server is getting overloaded with spam and much of it is malicious. You need to implement a solution that can help reduce the amount of spam reaching the email server. Which of the following is the BEST choice?

    A. Reverse proxy

    B. Media gateway

    C. Web application firewall

    D. Mail gateway

22. Your organization has a dedicated classroom used for teaching computer classes. Students include internal employees and visiting guests. Security administrators recently discovered that students were unplugging the network cable from some classroom computers and plugging the network cable into their laptop computers, giving them access to network resources. Which of the following is the BEST solution to prevent this activity?

    A. Flood guard

    B. VLAN

    C. Port security

    D. Loop protection

23. A HIDS reported a vulnerability on a system based on a known attack. After researching the alert from the HIDS, you identify the recommended solution and begin applying it. What type of HIDS is in use?

    A. Network-based

    B. Signature-based

    C. Heuristic-based

    D. Anomaly-based

24. After recently adding additional network devices, administrators noticed an increased workload related to their IDS. Which of the following can cause an increased workload from incorrect reporting?

    A. False negatives

    B. False positives

    C. Signature-based IDS

    D. Behavioral-based IDS

25. Lenny noticed a significant number of logon failures for administrator accounts on the organization's public web site. After investigating it further, he notices that most of these attempts are from IP addresses assigned to foreign countries. He wants to implement a solution that will detect and prevent similar attacks. Which of the following is the BEST choice?

    A. Add a flood guard to the network.

    B. Block all traffic from foreign countries.

    C. Implement an IPS.

    D. Disable the administrator accounts.

26. You are assisting a small business owner in setting up a public wireless hot spot for her customers. Which of the following actions is MOST appropriate for this hot spot?
    A. Using Open mode
    B. Enabling MAC filtering
    C. Disabling SSID broadcast
    D. Installing directional antennas

27. Jasper is setting up an 802.11ac network at the Retirement Castle. He wants to provide the highest level of security. Which of the following would BEST meet his needs?
    A. WPA2 with AES
    B. WPA2 with TKIP
    C. WPA2 with SSL
    D. WPA2 with MD5

28. You are planning a wireless network for a business. A core requirement is to ensure that the solution encrypts user credentials when users enter their usernames and passwords. Which of the following BEST meets this requirement?
    A. WPA2-PSK
    B. WPA2 using CCMP
    C. WPS with EAP-FAST
    D. WPA2 with EAP-TTLS

29. An attacker can access email contact lists on your smartphone. What type of attack is this?
    A. Bluesnarfing
    B. Bluejacking
    C. Captive portal
    D. WPS

30. An organization is hosting a VPN. Management wants to ensure that all VPN clients are using up-to-date operating systems and antivirus software. Which of the following would BEST meet this need?
    A. NAT
    B. NAC
    C. VLAN
    D. DMZ

31. A network administrator needs to update the operating system on switches used within the network. Assuming the organization is following standard best practices, what should the administrator do first?
    A. Submit a request using the baseline configuration process.
    B. Submit a request using the incident management process.
    C. Submit a request using the change management process.
    D. Submit a request using the application patch management process.

32. What functions does an HSM include?
    A. Reduces the risk of employees emailing confidential information outside the organization
    B. Provides webmail to clients
    C. Provides full drive encryption
    D. Generates and stores keys used with servers

33. The Shelbyville Nuclear Power Plant stores some data in the cloud using its own resources. The Springfield school system also has a cloud using its own resources. Later, the two organizations decide to share some of the educational data in both clouds. Which of the following BEST describes the cloud created by these two organizations?
    A. Community
    B. Private
    C. Public
    D. PaaS

34. Ziffcorp is planning to eliminate its current BYOD policy and instead implement a COPE deployment model. You're asked to provide input for the new policy. Which of the following concepts are appropriate for this policy?
    A. Encryption on employee-owned devices
    B. HSM
    C. ISA
    D. Remote wipe

35. Your organization is planning to implement a CYOD policy. Which of the following security controls will help protect data by isolating it?
    A. Encrypt sensitive data
    B. Storage segmentation
    C. Full device encryption
    D. Rooting

36. Bart recently launched an attack on a company web site using scripts he found on the Internet. Which of the following BEST describes Bart as a threat actor?
    A. Insider
    B. Hacktivist
    C. Script kiddie
    D. Nation-state

37. Recently, malware on a computer at the Monty Burns Casino destroyed several important files after it detected that Homer was no longer employed at the casino. Which of the following BEST identifies this malware?
    A. Logic bomb
    B. Rootkit
    C. Backdoor
    D. Adware

38. A security administrator at a shopping mall discovered two wireless cameras pointing at an automatic teller machine. These cameras were not installed by mall personnel and are not authorized. What is the MOST likely goal of these cameras?
    A. Tailgating
    B. Dumpster diving
    C. Vishing
    D. Shoulder surfing

39. Maggie reports that she keeps receiving unwanted emails about mortgages. What does this describe?
    A. Phishing
    B. Spear phishing
    C. Spam
    D. Vishing

40. Your organization has been receiving a significant amount of spam with links to malicious web sites. You want to stop the spam. Of the following choices, which provides the BEST solution?
    A. Add the domain to a block list.
    B. Use a URL filter.
    C. Use a MAC filter.
    D. Add antivirus software.

41. Lisa received an email advertising the newest version of a popular smartphone. She's been looking for this smartphone, but can't find it anywhere else. This email includes a malicious link. Which of the following principles is the email sender employing?
    A. Authority
    B. Intimidation
    C. Scarcity
    D. Trust

42. An IDS alerts on increased traffic. Upon investigation, you realize it is due to a spike in network traffic from several sources. Assuming this is malicious, which of the following is the MOST likely explanation?
    A. A smurf attack
    B. A spoofing attack
    C. A DoS attack
    D. A DDoS attack

43. An application on one of your database servers has crashed several times recently. Examining detailed debugging logs, you discover that just prior to crashing, the database application is receiving a long series of x90 characters. What is MOST likely occurring?
    A. SQL injection
    B. Buffer overflow
    C. XML injection
    D. Zero-day

44. A review of a web application discovered that the application is not performing boundary checking. Which of the following should the web developer add to this application to resolve this issue?

    A. XSRF

    B. XSS

    C. Input validation

    D. Fuzzing

45. Web developers are implementing error handling in a web site application. Which of the following represents a best practice for this?

    A. Displaying a detailed error message but logging generic information on the error

    B. Displaying a generic error message but logging detailed information on the error

    C. Displaying a generic error message and logging generic information on the error

    D. Displaying a detailed error message and logging detailed information on the error

46. Developers have created an application that users can download and install on their computers. Management wants to provide users with a reliable method of verifying that the application has not been modified. Which of the following methods provides the BEST solution?

    A. Code signing

    B. Input validation

    C. Code obfuscation

    D. Stored procedures

47. Some protocols include timestamps and sequence numbers. These components help protect against what type of attacks?

    A. Amplification

    B. Replay

    C. SYN flood

    D. Salting

48. Looking at logs for an online web application, you see that someone has entered the following phrase into several queries:

    ' or '1'='1' --

    Which of the following provides the BEST protection against this attack?

    A. Normalization

    B. Proper error handling

    C. Removing dead code

    D. Stored procedures

49. You need to calculate the ALE for a server. The value of the server is $3,000 and it has failed 10 times in the past year. Each time it failed, it resulted in a 10 percent loss. What is the ALE?
    A. $300
    B. $500
    C. $3,000
    D. $30,000

50. A recent vulnerability scan reported that a web application server is missing some patches. However, after inspecting the server, you realize that the patches are for a protocol that administrators removed from the server. Which of the following is the BEST explanation for this disparity?
    A. False negative
    B. False positive
    C. Lack of patch management tools
    D. The patch isn't applied

51. You suspect that a database server used by a web application does not have current patches. Which of the following is the BEST action to take to verify the server has up-to-date patches?
    A. Network mapping
    B. Port scan
    C. Protocol analyzer
    D. Vulnerability scan

52. You suspect that a user is running an unauthorized AP within the organization's building. Which of the following tools is the BEST choice to see if an unauthorized AP is operating on the network?
    A. Rogue system
    B. Wireless scanner
    C. Password cracker
    D. Penetration test

53. Your organization outsourced development of a software module to modify the functionality of an existing proprietary application. The developer completed the module and is now testing it with the entire application. What type of testing is the developer performing?
    A. White box
    B. Black box
    C. Gray box
    D. Black hat

54. Your coworker tells you how recent attacks on the network have been disrupting services and network connectivity. He suggests that you use Nmap to run a vulnerability scan on the network and identify vulnerabilities. Which of the following should you do FIRST?
    A. Create a network map.
    B. Locate a network map.
    C. Obtain an administrative account to run a credentialed scan.
    D. Obtain authorization.

55. Your organization's security policy states that administrators should follow the principle of least privilege. Which of the following tools can ensure that administrators are following the policy?
    A. Permission auditing review
    B. Risk assessment
    C. Vulnerability assessment
    D. Threat assessment

56. You need to secure access to a data center. Which of the following choices provides the BEST physical security to meet this need? (Select THREE.)
    A. Biometrics
    B. Cable locks
    C. Mantrap
    D. CCTV

57. Your company wants to control access to a restricted area of the building by adding an additional physical security control that includes facial recognition. Which of the following provides the BEST solution?
    A. Bollards
    B. Guards
    C. Retina scanners
    D. Cameras

58. An organization needs to improve fault tolerance to increase data availability. However, the organization has a limited budget. Which of the following is the BEST choice to meet the organization's needs?
    A. RAID
    B. Backup system
    C. Hot and cold aisles
    D. UPS

59. You need to modify the network infrastructure to increase availability of web-based applications for Internet clients. Which of the following choices provides the BEST solution?
    A. Load balancing
    B. Proxy server
    C. UTM
    D. Content inspection

60. Your backup policy for a database server dictates that the amount of time needed to restore backups should be minimized. Which of the following backup plans would BEST meet this need?
    A. Full backups on Sunday and incremental backups on the other six days of the week
    B. Full backups on Sunday and differential backups on the other six days of the week
    C. Incremental backups on Sunday and differential backups on the other six days of the week
    D. Differential backups on Sunday and incremental backups on the other six days of the week

61. After a recent attack causing a data breach, an executive is analyzing the financial losses. She determined that the attack is likely to cost at least $1 million. She wants to ensure that this information is documented for future planning purposes. In which of the following is she MOST likely to document it?
    A. DRP
    B. BIA
    C. HVAC
    D. RTO

62. An organization is considering an alternate location as part of its continuity of operations plan. It wants to identify a solution that provides the shortest recovery time. Which of the following is the BEST choice?
    A. Cold site
    B. Warm site
    C. Hot site
    D. Off-site backups

63. You need to identify a method that can be used for data integrity. Which of the following choices will meet your needs?
    A. AES
    B. DES
    C. RC4
    D. SHA

64. Users in your organization sign their emails with digital signatures. Which of the following provides integrity for these digital signatures?
    A. Hashing
    B. Encryption
    C. Non-repudiation
    D. Private key

65. Network administrators in your organization need to administer firewalls, security appliances, and other network devices. These devices are protected with strong passwords, and the passwords are stored in a file listing these passwords. Which of the following is the BEST choice to protect this password list?
    A. File encryption
    B. Database field encryption
    C. Full database encryption
    D. Whole disk encryption

66. An application developer needs to use an encryption protocol to encrypt credit card data within a database used by the application. Which of the following would be the FASTEST, while also providing strong confidentiality?
    A. AES-256
    B. DES
    C. Blowfish
    D. SHA-2

67. A developer is creating an application that will encrypt and decrypt data on mobile devices. These devices don't have a lot of processing power. Which of the following cryptographic methods has the LEAST overhead and will work with these mobile devices?
    A. Elliptic curve
    B. 3DES
    C. PBKDF2
    D. Bcrypt

68. Your organization hosts a web site used only by employees. The web site uses a certificate issued by a private CA and the network downloads a CRL from the CA once a week. However, after a recent compromise, security administrators want to use a real-time alternative to the CRL. Which of the following will BEST meet this need?
    A. DSA
    B. HMAC
    C. CSR
    D. OCSP

69. You need to request a certificate for a web server. Which of the following would you MOST likely use?
    A. CA
    B. CRL
    C. CSR
    D. OCSP

70. Your organization recently updated a security policy. It states that duties of network administrators and application developers must be separated. Which of the following is the MOST likely result of implementing this policy?
    A. One group develops program code and the other group deploys the code.
    B. One group develops program code and the other group modifies the code.
    C. One group deploys program code and the other group administers databases.
    D. One group develops databases and the other group modifies databases.

71. Your organization wants to prevent damage from malware. Which of the following phases of common incident response procedures is the BEST phase to address this?
    A. Preparation
    B. Identification
    C. Containment
    D. Lessons learned

72. A forensic expert is preparing to analyze a hard drive. Which of the following should the expert do FIRST?
    A. Capture an image.
    B. Identify the order of volatility.
    C. Create a chain of custody document.
    D. Take a screenshot.

73. An administrator recently learned of a suspected attack on a Florida-based web server from IP address 72.52.206.134 at 01:45:43 GMT. However, after investigating the logs, he doesn't see any traffic from that IP at that time. Which of the following is the MOST likely reason why the administrator was unable to identify the traffic?

    A. He did not account for time offsets.

    B. He did not capture an image.

    C. The IP address has expired.

    D. The logs were erased when the system was rebooted.

74. Social engineers have launched several successful phone-based attacks against your organization resulting in several data leaks. Which of the following would be MOST effective at reducing the success of these attacks?

    A. Implement a BYOD policy.

    B. Update the AUP.

    C. Provide training on data handling.

    D. Implement a program to increase security awareness.

75. Security personnel recently released an online training module advising employees not to share specific personal information on social media web sites that they visit. Which of the following is this advice MOST likely trying to prevent?

    A. Spending time on non-work-related sites

    B. Phishing attack

    C. Cognitive password attacks

    D. Rainbow table attack

Assessment Exam Answers

When checking your answers, take the time to read the explanation. Understanding the explanations will help ensure you're prepared for the live exam. The explanations also show the chapter or chapters where you can get more detailed information on the topic.

1. **B.** Encryption is the best choice to provide confidentiality of any type of information, including proprietary data. A digital signature provides integrity, non-repudiation, and authentication. Steganography provides a level of confidentiality, but it is not as strong as encryption. Hashing provides integrity. See Chapter 1.

2. **C.** A hash provides integrity for files, emails, and other types of data. Steganography provides confidentiality by hiding data within other data, and encryption provides confidentiality by ciphering the data. Advanced Encryption Standard (AES) is an encryption protocol. See Chapter 1.

3. **B.** Security controls are classified as technical (implemented by technical means) and administrative (implemented via administrative or management methods). The other combinations are not security control classifications. Access control models include role-based access control (role-BAC) and discretionary access control (DAC). Confidentiality and availability are common security goals. Encryption is a method used to ensure confidentiality, and hashing is a method used to ensure integrity. See Chapter 1.

4. **B, D.** Monitoring security logs and analyzing trend reports are detective controls with the goal of detecting security incidents. Installing closed-circuit television (CCTV) systems is one example of implementing a monitoring control. Hardening a system is a preventive control that includes several steps such as disabling unnecessary services, but the scenario doesn't describe any hardening steps. Preventive controls attempt to prevent incidents, but the scenario doesn't specifically describe any preventive controls. See Chapter 1.

5. **A.** A hardware lock is a physical security control. It's also a deterrent control because it would deter someone from entering. Data encryption is a technical control designed to protect data and is not a physical security control. A vulnerability assessment is a management control designed to discover vulnerabilities, but it is not a physical control. Training users is an effective preventive control, but it is not a physical control. See Chapter 1.

6. **A.** Virtualization allows multiple virtual servers to exist on a single physical server. Infrastructure as a Service (IaaS) is a cloud computing option where the vendor provides access to a computer, but customers manage it. Cloud computing refers to accessing computing resources via a different location than your local computer. Data loss prevention (DLP) techniques examine and inspect data looking for unauthorized data transmissions. See Chapter 1.

7. **B.** She should run the command ifconfig eth0 promisc to enable promiscuous mode on eth0, the network interface card (NIC). Promiscuous mode allows a NIC to process all traffic it receives, instead of only traffic addressed to it. The ipconfig command doesn't support this feature. Port mirroring on a switch sends a copy of all traffic received by the switch to the mirror port. The scenario indicates this is configured, so the switch doesn't need to be reconfigured. The scenario indicates she wants to collect traffic going through the switch, so connecting to a router isn't necessary. See Chapter 1.

8. **A, C, E.** The maximum password age ensures users change their passwords regularly. The password history records previously used passwords (such as the last 24 passwords) to prevent users from reusing the same passwords. The minimum password age prevents users from changing their password repeatedly to get back to their original password and should be used with the password history setting. Password length requires a minimum number of characters in a password. Password complexity requires a mix of uppercase and lowercase letters, numbers, and special characters. See Chapter 2.

9. **C.** This describes a single sign-on (SSO) solution in which users only log on once. Although a federation supports SSO, not all SSO systems use a federation. Security Assertion Markup Language (SAML) is an SSO solution used for web-based applications, but not all SSO solutions use SAML. Biometrics is a method of authentication, such as a fingerprint, but it isn't an SSO solution. See Chapter 2.

10. **C.** Lightweight Directory Access Protocol (LDAP) uses X.500-based phrases to identify components such as the domain component (DC). Diameter is an alternative to Remote Authentication Dial-In User Service (RADIUS), but neither of these use X.500-based phrases. Security Assertion Markup Language (SAML) is an Extensible Markup Language (XML) used for web-based single sign-on (SSO) solutions. See Chapter 2.

11. **A.** Kerberos uses a ticket-granting ticket (TGT) server for authentication. Users claim an identity with a username for identification. They prove their identity with credentials for authentication and Kerberos incorporates these credentials in tickets. Users are authorized access to resources with permissions, but only after they have been authenticated by an authentication service such as Kerberos. Access controls restrict access to resources after users are identified and authenticated. See Chapter 2.

12. **A.** This ensures that user security keys (also known as cryptographic keys) are retained. These cryptographic keys can encrypt and decrypt files and if the keys are deleted (such as when the account is deleted), it might not be possible to access files that the user encrypted. By disabling the account, it helps ensure that access to the files is retained, but it does not directly retain user files. Employees who leave are not expected to return, so this policy has nothing to do with making it easier to enable an account when they return. Users will not be able to use the accounts locally or remotely if they are disabled or deleted, which is a primary reason to have a disablement policy. See Chapter 2.

13. **C.** The role-based access control (role-BAC) model is the best choice for assigning access based on job functions. A discretionary access control (DAC) model specifies that every object has an owner and owners have full control over objects, but it isn't related to job functions. A mandatory access control (MAC) model uses labels and a lattice to grant access rather than job functions. A rule-based access control (rule-BAC) model uses rules that trigger in response to events. See Chapter 2.

14. **B.** Group-based privileges are a form of role-based access control and they simplify administration. Instead of assigning permissions to new employees individually, you can just add new employee user accounts into the appropriate groups to grant them the rights and permissions they need for the job. User-assigned privileges require you to manage privileges for each user separately, and they increase the account administration burden. Domain-assigned and network-assigned privileges are not valid administration practices. See Chapter 2.

15. **B.** The best solution of the available choices is to add members of the help-desk team to a security group that has the appropriate privileges. Assigning permissions to users individually adds to the administrative workload. Giving members administrator privileges violates the principle of least privilege by giving them too many privileges. An attribute-based access control model can use attributes to grant access, but you don't assign attributes. See Chapter 2.

16. **C.** Simple Network Management Protocol version 3 (SNMPv3) monitors and manages network devices. None of the other choices is related to managing and monitoring network devices. Network Address Translation (NAT) translates public IP addresses to private IP addresses and private addresses back to public. The Secure Real-time Transport Protocol (SRTP) secures voice and other streaming media transmissions. Domain Name System Security Extensions (DNSSEC) helps prevent DNS cache poisoning attacks. See Chapter 3.

17. **A.** You can prevent unauthorized access by disabling unused physical ports on the switches. This prevents the connection if someone plugs their computer into an unused disabled

port. An implicit deny rule is placed at the end of an access control list on a router to deny traffic that hasn't been explicitly allowed, but it doesn't affect physical ports differently. Spanning Tree Protocol (STP) prevents switching loop problems and should be enabled. Secure Shell (SSH) encrypts traffic but doesn't protect a switch. See Chapter 3.

18. **B.** The most likely cause of this symptom is that the router is blocking Internet Control Message Protocol (ICMP) traffic, which is used by ping. None of the other protocols listed use pint. Domain Name System (DNS) traffic is used to resolve domain names to IP addresses. Secure Shell (SSH) encrypts traffic sent over a network. Secure File Transfer Protocol (SFTP) is used to transfer encrypted files over a network and uses SSH for encryption. See Chapter 3.

19. **D, E.** The easiest way is to add an implicit deny rule at the end of the access control list (ACL) and all firewalls should have this to block all unwanted traffic. You can also deny all IP traffic using port 53 with DENY IP ALL ALL 53. Domain Name System (DNS) requests use UDP port 53, and DNS zone transfers use TCP port 53, so blocking only TCP 53 or UDP 53 does not block all DNS traffic. Port 25 is for Simple Mail Transfer Protocol (SMTP) and unrelated to this question. See Chapter 3.

20. **C.** A unified threat management (UTM) device combines multiple security controls into a single device and typically includes malware inspection, content inspection, and a distributed denial-of-service (DDoS) mitigator. None of the other answers includes these components. You can configure a virtual local area network (VLAN) on a switch to group computers together logically. Network Address Translation (NAT) translates public IP addresses to private IP addresses and private addresses back to public IP addresses. Domain Name System Security Extensions (DNSSEC) is a suite of extensions for DNS that provides validation for DNS responses. See Chapter 3.

21. **D.** A mail gateway is placed between an email server and the Internet and it can filter out spam. None of the other solutions includes a spam filter. A reverse proxy protects an internal web server. A media gateway converts data from one format to another, such as telephony traffic to IP-based traffic. A web application firewall protects a web server. See Chapter 3.

22. **C.** Port security is the best solution. More specifically, the switch ports used by the classroom computers should be configured to only allow the media access control (MAC) addresses of the corresponding classroom computers. A flood guard blocks MAC flood attacks, but this scenario doesn't indicate any attack is in progress. A virtual local area network (VLAN) segments traffic, but wouldn't prevent students from connecting to the network in this scenario. Loop protection protects against switching loop problems, but this is unrelated to this question. See Chapter 3.

23. **B.** If the host-based intrusion detection system (HIDS) identified a known issue, it is using signature-based detection. A HIDS is not network-based. Heuristic-based or anomaly-based (sometimes called behavioral-based) detection systems identify issues by comparing current activity against a baseline. They can identify issues that are not previously known. See Chapter 4.

24. **B.** False positives from an intrusion detection system (IDS) can cause an increased workload because they falsely indicate an alert has occurred. A false negative doesn't report an actual attack, so it doesn't increase the workload because administrators are unaware of the attack. Signature-based IDSs don't necessarily cause an increased workload unless they have a high incidence of false positives. The scenario indicates the network has a behavioral-based IDS. It is likely sending more false positives after additional network devices were added because the IDS baseline wasn't upgraded after adding the devices. See Chapter 4.

25. **C.** An intrusion prevention system (IPS) can dynamically detect, react, and prevent attacks. In this scenario, it can be configured to detect the logon attempts and block the traffic from the offending IP addresses. A flood guard blocks flood attacks (such as a SYN flood attack) but is unrelated to this scenario. If you block all traffic from foreign countries, you will likely block legitimate traffic. You should disable administrator accounts if they're not needed. However, if you disable all administrator accounts, administrators won't be able to do required work. See Chapter 4.

26. **A.** Open mode is the best choice of those given for a public wireless hot spot. It is used with Wired Equivalent Privacy (WEP), doesn't require users to enter a pre-shared key or passphrase, and doesn't require the business owner to give out this information. It's also possible to disable security for the hot spot. Media access control (MAC) address filtering would be very difficult to maintain. Disabling service set identifier (SSID) broadcasting would make it difficult to find the wireless network. An omnidirectional antenna (not a directional antenna) is best for a public wireless hot spot. See Chapter 4.

27. **A.** Wi-Fi Protected Access II (WPA2) with Advanced Encryption Standard (AES) is the best choice to secure the 802.11n wireless network. This uses Counter Mode with Cipher Block Chaining Message Authentication Code Protocol (CCMP) required by the Wi-Fi Alliance to meet the WI-FI CERTIFIED logo. Temporal Key Integrity Protocol (TKIP) is an older encryption protocol used with Wi-Fi Protected Access (WPA). IEEE has deprecated both WPA and TKIP due to different security issues. Secure Sockets Layer (SSL) has been replaced with Transport Layer Security (TLS) in most implementations and is not used with wireless protocols. Message Digest 5 (MD5) is a hashing protocol and it isn't used to secure 802.11n networks. See Chapter 4.

28. **D.** Wi-Fi Protected Access II (WPA2) with Extensible Authentication Protocol-Tunneled Transport Layer Security (EAP-TTLS) encrypts user credentials when users enter their usernames and passwords. EAP-TTLS is implemented in Enterprise mode and would use an 802.1x server. WPA2-pre-shared key (PSK) does not authenticate users based on their usernames. WPA2 with Counter Mode Cipher Block Chaining Message Authentication Code Protocol (CCMP) is strong, but it only uses a PSK, not usernames. Wi-Fi Protected Setup (WPS) is a standard designed to simplify the setup of a wireless network, but it does not implement usernames. EAP-Flexible Authentication via Secure Tunneling (EAP-FAST) is a lightweight version of EAP, but it is not used with WPS. See Chapter 4.

29. **A.** A successful bluesnarfing attack allows attackers to access data (including email contact lists) on a smartphone. Bluejacking is the practice of sending unsolicited messages to other Bluetooth devices. A captive portal is not an attack. Instead, it forces users to acknowledge

a usage policy or pay for access. A Wi-Fi Protected Setup (WPS) attack attempts to discover an access point WPS PIN by guessing PIN numbers. See Chapter 4.

30. **B.** Network access control (NAC) technologies can inspect virtual private network (VPN) clients for health status, including having up-to-date operating systems and antivirus software. None of the answers will inspect VPN clients. Network Address Translation (NAT) allows multiple users with private IP addresses to share a single public IP address. A virtual local area network (VLAN) can segment clients, but not inspect them. A demilitarized zone (DMZ) provides a layer of protection for Internet-facing servers, putting them in a buffer zone between the Internet and an internal network. See Chapter 4.

31. **C.** The network administrator should submit a request using the change management process, which is the same process that is typically used for changes to any devices or systems. A baseline configuration identifies the starting configuration. Incident management addresses security incidents. A regular patch management process typically includes following change management, but application patch management does not apply to devices. See Chapter 5.

32. **D.** A hardware security module (HSM) is a removable device that can generate and store RSA keys used with servers for data encryption. A data loss prevention (DLP) device is a device that can reduce the risk of employees emailing confidential information outside the organization. Software as a Service (SaaS) provides software or applications, such as webmail, via the cloud. A Trusted Platform Module (TPM) provides full drive encryption and is included in many laptops. See Chapter 5.

33. **A.** They created a community cloud. In the scenario, the two organizations have a common goal of sharing educational materials. The individual clouds created by each organization are private clouds, but the resources in the shared community cloud are not private. A public cloud would be available to anyone, but these are restricted. Platform as a Service (PaaS) provides an easy-to-configure operating system and on-demand computing for customers, but is unrelated to this question. See Chapter 5.

34. **D.** Remote wipe sends a remote signal to the device to wipe or erase all the data and is appropriate for a corporate-owned, personally enabled (COPE) deployment model. None of the other answers are relevant for a COPE deployment model. The company is eliminating the bring your own device (BYOD) policy so employee-owned devices should not be used. A hardware security module (HSM) is a security device typically used with servers to manage, generate, and securely store cryptographic keys. An interconnection security agreement (ISA) specifies technical and security requirements for planning, establishing, maintaining, and disconnecting a secure connection between two or more entities. See Chapter 5.

35. **B.** Storage segmentation is one way to protect company data on mobile devices owned by users and allowed under a choose your own device (CYOD) policy. It isolates data (and sometimes applications) in a secure area of a user's device. Encrypting sensitive data or using full device encryption (FDE) will help protect the confidentiality of data, but it doesn't isolate it. Rooting is the process of modifying an Android device to give the user root-level access to the device. Rooting is not a security control. See Chapter 5.

36. **C.** In this scenario, Bart is acting as a script kiddie because he is using existing scripts. An insider works for an organization, but there isn't any indication that Bart is an employee of the company he attacked. A hacktivist launches attacks as part of an activist movement, but this scenario doesn't indicate Bart's actions are trying to increase awareness about a cause. A nation-state refers to a government, but Bart is working alone in this scenario. See Chapter 6.

37. **A.** A logic bomb executes in response to an event. In this scenario, the logic bomb is delivering its payload when it detects that Homer is no longer employed at the company. A rootkit doesn't respond to an event. A backdoor provides another method of accessing a system, but it does not delete files. Adware uses advertising methods, such as pop-up windows. See Chapter 6.

38. **D.** Shoulder surfing is the practice of peering over a person's shoulder to discover information. In this scenario, the attacker is using the wireless cameras to discover PINs as users enter them. Tailgating is the practice of following closely behind someone else without using credentials. Dumpster diving is the practice of searching trash dumpsters for information. Vishing is a form of phishing using the phone. See Chapter 6.

39. **C.** Spam is unwanted emails from any source. Phishing and spear phishing are types of attacks using email. Vishing is similar to phishing, but it uses telephone technology. See Chapter 6.

40. **A.** You can block emails from a specific domain sending spam by adding the domain to a block list. While the question doesn't indicate that the spam is coming from a single domain, this is still the best answer of the given choices. A URL filter blocks outgoing traffic and can be used to block the links to the malicious web sites in this scenario, but it doesn't stop the email. Routers and switches use MAC filters to restrict access within a network. Antivirus software does not block spam. See Chapter 6.

41. **C.** The attacker is using scarcity to entice the user to click the link. A user might realize that clicking on links from unknown sources is risky, but the temptation of getting the new smartphone might cause the user to ignore the risk. There isn't any indication that the email is from any specific authority. It isn't trying to intimidate the recipient and there isn't any indication it is trying to build trust. See Chapter 6.

42. **D.** A distributed denial-of-service (DDoS) attack causes spikes in network traffic as multiple systems attempt to connect to a server and deplete the target's resources. A smurf attack is an attack using directed broadcasts, and this might be a smurf attack if routers aren't blocking directed broadcasts, but it could also be another type of DDoS attack. A spoofing attack attempts to hide the source of the attack by changing the source IP address or the source MAC address, but the scenario doesn't indicate spoofing. A DoS attack comes from a single system. See Chapter 7.

43. **B.** Buffer overflow attacks include a series of no operation (NOP) commands, such as hexadecimal 90 (x90). When successful, they can crash applications and expose memory, allowing attackers to run malicious code on the system. SQL injection attacks and

Extensible Markup Language (XML) injection attacks do not use NOP commands. Zero-day attacks are unknown or undocumented, but attacks using NOP commands are known. See Chapter 7.

44. **C.** The lack of input validation is a common coding error and it includes boundary or limit checking to validate data before using it. Proper input validation prevents many problems, such as cross-site request forgery (XSRF), cross-site scripting (XSS), buffer overflow, and command injection attacks. Fuzzing injects extra data and tests the effectiveness of input validation. See Chapter 7.

45. **B.** You should display a generic error message but log detailed information on the error. Detailed error messages to the user are often confusing to them and give attackers information they can use against the system. Logging generic information makes it more difficult to troubleshoot the problem later. See Chapter 7.

46. **A.** Code signing provides a digital signature for the code, verifies the publisher of the code, and verifies that it hasn't been modified since the publisher released it. None of the other answers verify the application hasn't been modified. Input validation verifies data is valid before using it. Code obfuscation makes the code more difficult to read. Stored procedures are used with SQL databases and can be used for input validation. See Chapter 7.

47. **B.** Timestamps and sequence numbers act as countermeasures against replay attacks. None of the other answer choices are thwarted by timestamps and sequence numbers. Amplification attacks increase the amount of traffic sent to a victim. SYN (synchronize) flood attacks disrupt the TCP three-way handshake. Salting isn't an attack, but it does protect against brute force attacks on passwords. See Chapter 7.

48. **D.** The phrase (' or '1'='1' --) is commonly used in SQL injection attacks and stored procedures are an effective method of preventing SQL injection attacks. Normalization techniques organize tables and columns in a database to reduce redundant data, but don't block SQL injection attacks. This phrase won't cause an error, so proper error-handling techniques won't help. Dead code is code that is never executed and it should be removed, but dead code is unrelated to a SQL injection attack. See Chapter 7.

49. **C.** The annual loss expectancy (ALE) is $3,000. It is calculated as single loss expectancy (SLE) × annual rate of occurrence (ARO). Each failure has resulted in a 10 percent loss (meaning that it cost 10 percent of the asset value to repair it). The SLE is 10 percent of $3,000 ($300) and the ARO is 10. 10 × $300 is $3,000. See Chapter 8.

50. **B.** A false positive on a vulnerability scan indicates that a vulnerability is positively detected, but the vulnerability doesn't actually exist. A false negative indicates that the vulnerability scan did not detect a vulnerability that does exist on a system. False positives can occur even if an organization has a strong patch management process in place. Although it's true that the patch isn't applied, it's also true that the patch cannot be applied because it is for a protocol that administrators removed. See Chapter 8.

51. **D.** A vulnerability scan determines if the system has current patches. None of the other answers will detect missing patches. Network mapping discovers devices on the network,

but it only focuses on connectivity. A port scan identifies open ports. A protocol analyzer (sniffer) captures traffic for analysis. See Chapter 8.

52. **B.** A wireless scanner can detect all of the wireless access points (APs) running on a network. By comparing this with a list of authorized APs, you can detect unauthorized APs. A rogue system is an unauthorized system, but it isn't used to detect unauthorized APs. A password cracker can often crack passwords used by APs, but it isn't used to detect rogue APs. A penetration test attempts to exploit known vulnerabilities, but it isn't used to detect rogue APs. See Chapter 8.

53. **C.** The developer is performing a gray box test. A gray box tester has some knowledge of the application. In this scenario, the tester needs some knowledge of the application (such as input and output data) to develop and test the module. White box testers have full knowledge about the product or network they are testing, but because this is a proprietary application, it is unlikely the tester has full knowledge. Black box testers do not have any knowledge about the product or network they are testing, but this isn't feasible for a developer who needs to develop and test a module to modify an existing application. Black hat refers to a malicious attacker. See Chapter 8.

54. **D.** Before performing any type of network scan, you should first ensure you have authorization to do so. Without authorization, you might be perceived as an attacker. Nmap will create a network map during the scan. You could locate a network map to compare it with the map Nmap creates, but you should still obtain permission first. You might run a credentialed scan, but again, you need to obtain permission first. See Chapter 8.

55. **A.** A permission auditing review verifies users have the permissions they need for their job, and no more, which verifies the principle of least privilege is being followed. Risk, vulnerability, and threat assessments assess current risks. While they might verify the principle of least privilege is being followed, they do much more. See Chapter 8.

56. **A, C, D.** A biometric reader used for access control, a mantrap, and a closed-circuit television (CCTV) system all provide strong physical security for accessing a data center. Cable locks are effective theft deterrents for mobile devices such as laptops, but they don't protect data centers. See Chapter 9.

57. **B.** Security guards can protect access to restricted areas with facial recognition and by checking identities of personnel before letting them in. In some cases, the guards might recognize people and in other situations, they might compare people's faces with their security badge. Bollards are effective barricades to block vehicles, but they do not block personnel. Retina scanners are effective biometric access devices, but they do not use facial recognition. Cameras can monitor who goes in and out of an area, but they do not control the access. See Chapter 9.

58. **A.** A redundant array of inexpensive disks (RAID) system would provide fault tolerance for disk drives and increase data availability if drives fail. A backup system improves data availability because you can restore data after data is lost or corrupt. However, a backup system does not provide fault tolerance. Hot and cold aisles help regulate cooling in a data center, but they don't directly increase data availability unless the data center is experiencing failures

due to heat. An uninterruptible power supply (UPS) provides short-term power after a power failure, but it does not directly increase data availability. See Chapter 9.

59. **A.** Load-balancing solutions increase the availability of web-based solutions by spreading the load among multiple servers. A proxy server is used by internal clients to access Internet resources and does not increase availability of a web server. A unified threat management (UTM) security appliance protects internal resources from attacks, but does not directly increase the availability of web-based applications. Content inspection is one of the features of a UTM, and it protects internal clients but does not directly increase the availability of web-based applications. See Chapter 9.

60. **B.** A full/differential backup strategy is best with one full backup on one day and differential backups on the other days. A restore would require only two backups, making it quicker than the other options. A full/incremental backup would typically require you to restore more than two backups. For example, data loss on Friday would require you to restore the full backup, plus four incremental backups. Backups must start with a full backup, so neither an incremental/differential nor a differential/incremental backup strategy is possible. See Chapter 9.

61. **B.** A business impact analysis (BIA) includes information on potential losses and is the most likely document of those listed where this loss would be documented. A disaster recovery plan (DRP) includes methods used to recover from an outage. Heating, ventilation, and air conditioning systems regulate temperature and humidity; it is not a document. The recovery time objective (RTO) identifies the time period when you plan to restore a system after an outage; it is not a document. See Chapter 9.

62. **C.** A hot site has the shortest recovery time, but it is also the most expensive. Cold sites have the longest recovery time, and warm sites are shorter than cold sites but not as quick as hot sites. While a copy of backups should be stored off-site, that is not an alternate location considered in a continuity of operations plan. See Chapter 9.

63. **D.** Secure Hash Algorithm (SHA) is one of many available hashing algorithms used to verify data integrity. None of the other options are hashing algorithms. Advanced Encryption Standard (AES), Data Encryption Standard (DES), and Rivest Cipher 4 (RC4) are symmetric encryption algorithms. See Chapter 10.

64. **A.** Hashing provides integrity for digital signatures and other data. A digital signature is a hash of the message encrypted with the sender's private key, but the encryption doesn't provide integrity. The digital signature provides non-repudiation, but non-repudiation does not provide integrity. The private key and public key are both needed, but the private key does not provide integrity. See Chapter 10.

65. **A.** The best choice is file encryption to protect the passwords in this list. If the passwords were stored in a database, it would be appropriate to encrypt the fields in the database holding the passwords. It's rarely desirable to encrypt an entire database. Whole disk encryption is appropriate for mobile devices. See Chapters 5 and 10.

66. **C.** Blowfish would be the fastest in this scenario. Blowfish provides strong encryption, so it would provide strong confidentiality. Advanced Encryption Standard-256 (AES-256) is

a strong encryption protocol, but Blowfish is faster than AES in some situations, such as when comparing it against AES-256. Data Encryption Standard (DES) is not secure and is not recommended today. Secure Hash Algorithm version 2 (SHA-2) is a hashing algorithm used for integrity. See Chapter 10.

67. **A.** Elliptic curve cryptography (ECC) has minimal overhead and is often used with mobile devices for encryption. Triple Data Encryption Standard (3DES) consumes a lot of processing time and isn't as efficient as ECC. Password-Based Key Derivation Function 2 (PBKDF2) and bcrypt are key stretching techniques that salt passwords with additional bits to protect against brute force attempts. See Chapter 10.

68. **D.** The Online Certificate Status Protocol (OCSP) provides real-time responses to validate certificates issued by a Certificate Authority (CA). A certificate revocation list (CRL) includes a list of revoked certificates, but if it is only downloaded once a week, it can quickly be out of date. None of the other answers validates certificates. A digital signature algorithm (DSA) creates a digital signature. A Hash-based Message Authentication Code (HMAC) creates a hash. A certificate signing request (CSR) is used to request a certificate. See Chapter 10.

69. **C.** A certificate signing request (CSR) uses a specific format to request a certificate. You submit the CSR to a Certificate Authority (CA), but the request needs to be in the CSR format. A certificate revocation list (CRL) is a list of revoked certificates. The Online Certificate Status Protocol (OCSP) is an alternate method of validating certificates and indicates if a certificate is good, revoked, or unknown. See Chapter 10.

70. **A.** This describes a separation of duties policy where the application developers create and modify the code, and the administrators deploy the code to live production systems, but neither group can perform both functions. Developers would typically develop the original code as well as modify it when necessary. This scenario does not mention databases. See Chapter 11.

71. **A.** The preparation phase is the first phase of common incident response procedures, and attempts to prevent security incidents. Incident identification occurs after a potential incident occurs and verifies it is an incident. Containment attempts to limit the damage by preventing an incident from spreading, but it doesn't prevent the original incident. Lessons learned occurs later and involves analysis to identify steps that will prevent a future occurrence. See Chapter 11.

72. **A.** Before analyzing a hard drive, a forensic expert should capture an image of the hard drive and then analyze the image. This protects it from accidental modifications and preserves it as usable evidence. The order of volatility identifies which data is most volatile (such as cache) and which is least volatile (such as hard drives). A chain of custody document should be created when evidence is first collected. A screenshot is taken when a system is operational. See Chapter 11.

73. **A.** The most likely reason is that he did not account for the time offset. The attack occurred at 01:45:43 Greenwich Mean Time (GMT) and the web server is in the Eastern Standard

Time (EST) zone in Florida, which is five hours different from GMT. There is no need to capture an image to view logs. IP addresses on the Internet do not expire. Logs are written to a hard drive or a central location; they are not erased when a system is rebooted. See Chapter 11.

74. **D.** The best choice of the available answers is to implement a program to increase security awareness, and it could focus on social engineering attacks. A bring your own device (BYOD) policy or an acceptable use policy (AUP) doesn't apply in this scenario. Training is useful, but training users on data handling won't necessarily educate them on social engineering attacks. See Chapter 11.

75. **C.** A cognitive password attack utilizes information that a person would know, such as the name of a first pet or favorite color. If this information is available on Facebook or another social media site, attackers can use it to change the user's password. This advice has nothing to do with employees visiting the sites, only with what they post. Although attackers may use this information in a phishing attack, they can also launch phishing attacks without this information. A rainbow table attack is a password attack, but it uses a database of precalculated hashes. See Chapter 11.

Appendix A—Glossary

3DES—Triple Digital Encryption Standard. A symmetric algorithm used to encrypt data and provide confidentiality. It is a block cipher that encrypts data in 64-bit blocks.

A

AAA—Authentication, authorization, and accounting. A group of technologies used in remote access systems. Authentication verifies a user's identification. Authorization determines if a user should have access. Accounting tracks a user's access with logs. Sometimes called AAAs of security.

ABAC—Attribute-based access control. An access control model that grants access to resources based on attributes assigned to subjects and objects.

acceptable use policy (AUP)—A policy defining proper system usage and the rules of behavior for employees. It often describes the purpose of computer systems and networks, how users can access them, and the responsibilities of users when accessing the systems.

access point (AP)—A device that connects wireless clients to wireless networks. Sometimes called wireless access point (WAP).

accounting—The process of tracking the activity of users and recording this activity in logs. One method of accounting is audit logs that create an audit trail.

ACLs—Access control lists. Lists of rules used by routers and stateless firewalls. These devices use the ACL to control traffic based on networks, subnets, IP addresses, ports, and some protocols.

active reconnaissance—A penetration testing method used to collect information. It sends data to systems and analyzes responses to gain information on the target. Compare with *passive reconnaissance*.

ad hoc—A connection mode used by wireless devices without an AP. When wireless devices connect through an AP, they are using infrastructure mode.

administrative controls—Security controls implemented via administrative or management methods.

AES—Advanced Encryption Standard. A strong symmetric block cipher that encrypts data in 128-bit blocks. AES can use key sizes of 128 bits, 192 bits, or 256 bits.

affinity—A scheduling method used with load balancers. It uses the client's IP address to ensure the client is redirected to the same server during a session.

aggregation switch—A switch used to connect multiple switches together into a network. Switches connect to the aggregation switch and it connects to a router.

agile—A software development life cycle model that focuses on interaction between customers, developers, and testers. Compare with *waterfall*.

AH—Authentication Header. An option within IPsec to provide authentication and integrity.

airgap—A physical security control that provides physical isolation. Systems separated by an airgap don't typically have any physical connections to other systems.

ALE—Annual (or annualized) loss expectancy. The expected loss for a year. It is used to measure risk with ARO and SLE in a quantitative risk assessment. The calculation is SLE × ARO = ALE.

amplification attack—An attack that increases the amount of bandwidth sent to a victim.

anomaly—A type of monitoring on intrusion detection and intrusion prevention systems. It detects attacks by comparing operations against a baseline. It is also known as heuristic detection.

ANT—A proprietary wireless protocol used by some mobile devices. It is not an acronym.

antispoofing—A method used on some routers to protect against spoofing attacks. A common implementation is to implement specific rules to block certain traffic.

antivirus—Software that protects systems from malware. Although it is called antivirus software, it protects against most malware, including viruses, Trojans, worms, and more.

application blacklist—A list of applications that a system blocks. Users are unable to install or run any applications on the list.

application cell—Also known as application containers. A virtualization technology that runs services or applications within isolated application cells (or containers). Each container shares the kernel of the host.

application whitelist—A list of applications that a system allows. Users are only able to install or run applications on the list.

APT—Advanced persistent threat. A group that has both the capability and intent to launch sophisticated and targeted attacks.

ARO—Annual (or annualized) rate of occurrence. The number of times a loss is expected to occur in a year. It is used to measure risk with ALE and SLE in a quantitative risk assessment.

arp—A command-line tool used to show and manipulate the Address Resolution Protocol (ARP) cache.

ARP poisoning—An attack that misleads systems about the actual MAC address of a system.

asset value—An element of a risk assessment. It identifies the value of an asset and can include any product, system, resource, or process. The value can be a specific monetary value or a subjective value.

asymmetric encryption—A type of encryption using two keys to encrypt and decrypt data. It uses a public key and a private key. Compare with *symmetric encryption.*

attestation—A process that checks and validates system files during the boot process. TPMs sometimes use remote attestation, sending a report to a remote system for attestation.

audit trail—A record of events recorded in one or more logs. When security professionals have access to all the logs, they can re-create the events that occurred leading up to a security incident.

authentication—The process that occurs when a user proves an identity, such as with a password.

authorization—The process of granting access to resources for users who prove their identity (such as with a username and password), based on their proven identity.

availability—One of the three main goals of information security known as the CIA security triad. Availability ensures that systems and data are up and operational when needed. Compare with *confidentiality* and *integrity.*

B

backdoor—An alternate method of accessing a system. Malware often adds a backdoor into a system after it infects it.

background check—A check into a person's history, typically to determine eligibility for a job.

banner grabbing—A method used to gain information about a remote system. It identifies the operating system and other details on the remote system.

bcrypt—A key stretching algorithm. It is used to protect passwords. Bcrypt salts passwords with additional bits before encrypting them with Blowfish. This thwarts rainbow table attacks.

BIOS—Basic Input/Output System. A computer's firmware used to manipulate different settings such as the date and time, boot drive, and access password. UEFI is the designated replacement for BIOS.

birthday—A password attack named after the birthday paradox in probability theory. The paradox states that for any random group of 23 people, there is a 50 percent chance that 2 of them have the same birthday.

black box test—A type of penetration test. Testers have zero knowledge of the environment prior to starting the test. Compare with *gray box test* and *white box test.*

block cipher—An encryption method that encrypts data in fixed-sized blocks. Compare with *stream cipher.*

Blowfish—A strong symmetric block cipher. It encrypts data in 64-bit blocks and supports key sizes between 32 and 448 bits. Compare with *Twofish*.

bluejacking—An attack against Bluetooth devices. It is the practice of sending unsolicited messages to nearby Bluetooth devices.

bluesnarfing—An attack against Bluetooth devices. Attackers gain unauthorized access to Bluetooth devices and can access all the data on the device.

bollards—Short vertical posts that act as a barricade. Bollards block vehicles but not people.

bots—Software robots that function automatically. A botnet is a group of computers that are joined together. Attackers often use malware to join computers to a botnet, and then use the botnet to launch attacks.

BPA—Business partners agreement. A written agreement that details the relationship between business partners, including their obligations toward the partnership.

bridge—A network device used to connect multiple networks together. It can be used instead of a router in some situations.

brute force—A password attack that attempts to guess a password. Online brute force attacks guess passwords of online systems. Offline attacks guess passwords contained in a file or database.

buffer overflow—An error that occurs when an application receives more input, or different input, than it expects. It exposes system memory that is normally inaccessible.

business impact analysis (BIA)—A process that helps an organization identify critical systems and components that are essential to the organization's success.

BYOD—Bring your own device. A mobile device deployment model. Employees can connect their personally owned device to the network. Compare with *COPE* and *CYOD*.

C

CA—Certificate Authority. An organization that manages, issues, and signs certificates. A CA is a main element of a PKI.

CAC—Common Access Card. A specialized type of smart card used by the U.S. Department of Defense. It includes photo identification and provides confidentiality, integrity, authentication, and non-repudiation.

captive portal—A technical solution that forces wireless clients using web browsers to complete a process before accessing a network. It is often used to ensure users agree to an acceptable use policy or pay for access.

carrier unlocking—The process of unlocking a mobile phone from a specific cellular provider.

CBC—Cipher Block Chaining. A mode of operation used for encryption that effectively converts a block cipher into a stream cipher. It uses an IV for the first block and each subsequent block is combined with the previous block.

CCMP—Counter Mode with Cipher Block Chaining Message Authentication Code Protocol. An encryption protocol based on AES and used with WPA2 for wireless security. It is more secure than TKIP, which was used with the original release of WPA.

CER—Canonical Encoding Rules. A base format for PKI certificates. They are binary encoded files. Compare with *DER*.

certificate—A digital file used for encryption, authentication, digital signatures, and more. Public certificates include a public key used for asymmetric encryption.

certificate chaining—A process that combines all certificates within a trust model. It includes all the certificates in the trust chain from the root CA down to the certificate issued to the end user.

chain of custody—A process that provides assurances that evidence has been controlled and handled properly after collection. Forensic experts establish a chain of custody when they first collect evidence.

change management—The process used to prevent unauthorized changes. Unauthorized changes often result in unintended outages.

CHAP—Challenge Handshake Authentication Protocol. An authentication mechanism where a server challenges a client. Compare with *MS-CHAPv2* and *PAP*.

chroot—A Linux command used to change the root directory. It is often used for sandboxing.

ciphertext—The result of encrypting plaintext. Ciphertext is not in an easily readable format until it is decrypted.

clean desk policy—A security policy requiring employees to keep their areas organized and free of papers. The goal is to reduce threats of security incidents by protecting sensitive data.

clickjacking—An attack that tricks users into clicking something other than what they think they're clicking.

cloud access security broker (CASB)—A software tool or service that enforces cloud-based security requirements. It is placed between the organization's resources and the cloud, monitors all network traffic, and can enforce security policies.

cloud deployment models—Cloud model types that identify who has access to cloud resources. Public clouds are for any organization. Private clouds are for a single organization. Community clouds are shared among community organizations. A hybrid cloud is a combination of two or more clouds.

code signing—The process of assigning a certificate to code. The certificate includes a digital signature and validates the code.

cold site—An alternate location for operations. A cold site will have power and connectivity needed for activation, but little else. Compare with *hot site* and *warm site*.

collision—A hash vulnerability that can be used to discover passwords. A hash collision occurs when two different passwords create the same hash.

compensating controls—Security controls that are alternative controls used when a primary security control is not feasible.

compiled code—Code that has been optimized by an application and converted into an executable file. Compare with *runtime code*.

confidential data—Data meant to be kept secret among a certain group of people. As an example, salary data is meant to be kept secret and not shared with everyone within a company.

confidentiality—One of the three main goals of information security known as the CIA security triad. Confidentiality ensures that unauthorized entities cannot access data. Encryption and access controls help protect against the loss of confidentiality. Compare with *availability* and *integrity*.

configuration compliance scanner—A type of vulnerability scanner that verifies systems are configured correctly. It will often use a file that identifies the proper configuration for systems.

confusion—A cryptography concept that indicates ciphertext is significantly different than plaintext.

containerization—A method used to isolate applications in mobile devices. It isolates and protects the application, including any data used by the application.

context-aware authentication—An authentication method using multiple elements to authenticate a user and a mobile device. It can include identity, geolocation, the device type, and more.

continuity of operations planning—The planning process that identifies an alternate location for operations after a critical outage. It can include a hot site, cold site, or warm site.

control diversity—The use of different security control types, such as technical controls, administrative controls, and physical controls. Compare with *vendor diversity*.

controller-based AP—An AP that is managed by a controller. Also called a thin AP. Compare with *fat AP*.

COPE—Corporate-owned, personally enabled. A mobile device deployment model. The organization purchases and issues devices to employees. Compare with *BYOD* and *CYOD*.

corrective controls—Security controls that attempt to reverse the impact of a security incident.

CRL—Certificate revocation list. A list of certificates that a CA has revoked. Certificates are commonly revoked if they are compromised, or issued to an employee who has left the organization.

crossover error rate—The point where the false acceptance rate (FAR) crosses over with the false rejection rate (FRR). A lower CER indicates a more accurate biometric system.

cross-site request forgery (XSRF)—A web application attack. XSRF attacks trick users into performing actions on web sites, such as making purchases, without their knowledge.

cross-site scripting (XSS)—A web application vulnerability. Attackers embed malicious HTML or JavaScript code into a web site's code, which executes when a user visits the site.

crypto-malware—A type of ransomware that encrypts the user's data.

crypto module—A set of hardware, software, and/or firmware that implements cryptographic functions. Compare with *crypto service provider*.

crypto service provider—A software library of cryptographic standards and algorithms. These libraries are typically distributed within crypto modules.

CSR—Certificate signing request. A method of requesting a certificate from a CA. It starts by creating an RSA-based private/public key pair and then including the public key in the CSR.

CTM—Counter mode. A mode of operation used for encryption that combines an IV with a counter. The combined result is used to encrypt blocks.

custom firmware—Mobile device firmware other than the firmware provided with the device. People sometimes use custom firmware to root Android devices.

cyber-incident response team—A group of experts who respond to security incidents. Also known as *CIRT*.

CYOD—Choose your own device. A mobile device deployment model. Employees can connect their personally owned device to the network as long as the device is on a preapproved list. Compare with *BYOD* and *COPE*.

D

DAC—Discretionary access control. An access control model where all objects have owners and owners can modify permissions for the objects (files and folders). Microsoft NTFS uses the DAC model.

data-at-rest—Any data stored on media. It's common to encrypt sensitive data-at-rest.

data execution prevention (DEP)—A security feature that prevents code from executing in memory regions marked as nonexecutable. It helps block malware.

data exfiltration—The unauthorized transfer of data outside an organization.

data-in-transit—Any data sent over a network. It's common to encrypt sensitive data-in-transit.

data-in-use—Any data currently being used by a computer. Because the computer needs to process the data, it is not encrypted while in use.

data retention policy—A security policy specifying how long data should be kept (retained).

data sovereignty—A term that refers to the legal implications of data stored in different countries. It is primarily a concern related to backups stored in alternate locations via the cloud.

DDoS—Distributed denial-of-service. An attack on a system launched from multiple sources intended to make a computer's resources or services unavailable to users. DDoS attacks typically include sustained, abnormally high network traffic. Compare with *DoS*.

dead code—Code that is never executed or used. It is often caused by logic errors.

defense in depth—The use of multiple layers of security to protect resources. Control diversity and vendor diversity are two methods organizations implement to provide defense in depth.

degaussing—The process of removing data from magnetic media using a very powerful electronic magnet. Degaussing is sometimes used to remove data from backup tapes or to destroy hard disks.

DER—Distinguished Encoding Rules. A base format for PKI certificates. They are BASE64 ASCII encoded files. Compare with *CER*.

DES—Data Encryption Standard. A legacy symmetric encryption standard used to provide confidentiality. It has been compromised and AES or 3DES should be used instead.

detective controls—Security controls that attempt to detect security incidents after they have occurred.

deterrent controls—Security controls that attempt to discourage individuals from causing a security incident.

dictionary—A password attack that uses a file of words and character combinations. The attack tries every entry within the file when trying to guess a password.

differential backup—A type of backup that backs up all the data that has changed or is different since the last full backup.

Diffie-Hellman (DH)—An asymmetric algorithm used to privately share symmetric keys. DH Ephemeral (DHE) uses ephemeral keys, which are re-created for each session. Elliptic Curve DHE (ECDHE) uses elliptic curve cryptography to generate encryption keys.

diffusion—A cryptography concept that ensures that small changes in plaintext result in significant changes in ciphertext.

dig—A command-line tool used to test DNS on Linux systems. Compare with *nslookup*.

digital signature—An encrypted hash of a message, encrypted with the sender's private key. It provides authentication, non-repudiation, and integrity.

disablement policy—A policy that identifies when administrators should disable user accounts.

disassociation attack—An attack that removes wireless clients from a wireless network.

dissolvable agent—A NAC agent that runs on a client, but deletes itself later. It checks the client for health. Compare with *permanent agent*.

DLL injection—An attack that injects a Dynamic Link Library (DLL) into memory and runs it. Attackers rewrite the DLL, inserting malicious code.

DLP—Data loss prevention. A group of technologies used to prevent data loss. They can block the use of USB devices, monitor outgoing email to detect and block unauthorized data transfers, and monitor data stored in the cloud.

DMZ—Demilitarized zone. A buffer zone between the Internet and an internal network. Internet clients can access the services hosted on servers in the DMZ, but the DMZ provides a layer of protection for the internal network.

DNS—Domain Name System. A service used to resolve host names to IP addresses. DNS zones include records such as A records for IPv4 addresses and AAAA records for IPv6 addresses.

DNSSEC—Domain Name System Security Extensions. A suite of extensions to DNS used to protect the integrity of DNS records and prevent some DNS attacks.

DNS poisoning—An attack that modifies or corrupts DNS results. DNSSEC helps prevent DNS poisoning.

domain hijacking—An attack that changes the registration of a domain name without permission from the owner.

DoS—Denial-of-service. An attack from a single source that attempts to disrupt the services provided by the attacked system. Compare with *DDoS*.

downgrade attack—A type of attack that forces a system to downgrade its security. The attacker then exploits the lesser security control.

DSA—Digital signature algorithm. An encrypted hash of a message used for authentication, non-repudiation, and integrity. The sender's private key encrypts the hash of the message.

dumpster diving—The practice of searching through trash looking to gain information from discarded documents. Shredding or burning papers helps prevent the success of dumpster diving.

E

EAP—Extensible Authentication Protocol. An authentication framework that provides general guidance for authentication methods. Variations include PEAP, EAP-TLS, EAP-TTLS, and EAP-FAST.

EAP-FAST—EAP-Flexible Authentication via Secure Tunneling (EAP-FAST). A Cisco-designed replacement for Lightweight EAP (LEAP). EAP-FAST supports certificates, but they are optional.

EAP-TLS—Extensible Authentication Protocol-Transport Layer Security. An extension of EAP sometimes used with 802.1x. This is one of the most secure EAP standards and is widely implemented. It requires certificates on the 802.1x server and on the clients.

EAP-TTLS—Extensible Authentication Protocol-Tunneled Transport Layer Security. An extension of EAP sometimes used with 802.1x. It allows systems to use some older authentication methods such as PAP within a TLS tunnel. It requires a certificate on the 802.1x server but not on the clients.

ECB—Electronic Codebook. A legacy mode of operation used for encryption. It is weak and should not be used.

embedded system—Any device that has a dedicated function and uses a computer system to perform that function. It includes a CPU, an operating system, and one or more applications.

EMI—Electromagnetic interference. Interference caused by motors, power lines, and fluorescent lights. EMI shielding prevents outside interference sources from corrupting data and prevents data from emanating outside the cable.

EMP—Electromagnetic pulse. A short burst of energy that can potentially damage electronic equipment. It can result from electrostatic discharge (ESD), lightning, and military weapons.

encryption—A process that scrambles, or ciphers, data to make it unreadable. Encryption normally includes a public algorithm and a private key. Compare with *asymmetric* and *symmetric encryption*.

Enterprise—A wireless mode that uses an 802.1x server for security. It forces users to authenticate with a username and password. Compare with *Open* and *PSK* modes.

ephemeral key—A type of key used in cryptography. Ephemeral keys have very short lifetimes and are re-created for each session.

error handling—A programming process that handles errors gracefully.

ESP—Encapsulating Security Payload. An option within IPsec to provide confidentiality, integrity, and authentication.

evil twin—A type of rogue AP. An evil twin has the same SSID as a legitimate AP.

exit interview—An interview conducted with departing employees just before they leave an organization.

exploitation frameworks—Tools used to store information about security vulnerabilities. They are often used by penetration testers (and attackers) to detect and exploit software.

extranet—The part of an internal network shared with outside entities. Extranets are often used to provide access to authorized business partners, customers, vendors, or others.

F

facial recognition—A biometric method that identifies people based on facial features.

false negative—A security incident that isn't detected or reported. As an example, a NIDS false negative occurs if an attack is active on the network but the NIDS does not raise an alert.

false positive—An alert on an event that isn't a security incident. As an example, a NIDS false positive occurs if the NIDS raises an alert but activity on the network is normal.

FAR—False acceptance rate. Also called the false match rate. A rate that identifies the percentage of times a biometric authentication system incorrectly indicates a match.

Faraday cage—A room or enclosure that prevents signals from emanating beyond the room or enclosure.

fat AP—An AP that includes everything needed to connect wireless clients to a wireless network. Fat APs must be configured independently. Sometimes called a stand-alone AP. Compare with *thin AP*.

fault tolerance—The capability of a system to suffer a fault, but continue to operate. Said another way, the system can tolerate the fault as if it never occurred.

FDE—Full disk encryption. A method to encrypt an entire disk. Compare with *SED*.

federation—Two or more members of a federated identity management system. Used for single sign-on.

fingerprint scanners—Biometric systems that scan fingerprints for authentication.

firewall—A software or a network device used to filter traffic. Firewalls can be application-based (running on a host), or a network-based device. Stateful firewalls filter traffic using rules within an ACL. Stateless firewalls filter traffic based on its state within a session.

firmware OTA updates—Over-the-air updates for mobile device firmware that keep them up to date. These are typically downloaded to the device from the Internet and applied to update the device.

flood guard—A method of thwarting flood attacks. On switches, a flood guard thwarts MAC flood attacks. On routers, a flood guard prevents SYN flood attacks.

framework—A structure used to provide a foundation. Cybersecurity frameworks typically use a structure of basic concepts and provide guidance to professionals on how to implement security.

FRR—False rejection rate. Also called the false nonmatch rate. A rate that identifies the percentage of times a biometric authentication system incorrectly rejects a valid match.

FTPS—File Transfer Protocol Secure. An extension of FTP that uses TLS to encrypt FTP traffic. Some implementations of FTPS use TCP ports 989 and 990.

full backup—A type of backup that backs up all the selected data. A full backup could be considered a normal backup.

full tunnel—An encrypted connection used with VPNs. When a user is connected to a VPN, all traffic from the user is encrypted. Compare with *split tunnel*.

G

GCM—Galois/Counter Mode. A mode of operation used for encryption. It combines the Counter (CTM) mode with hashing techniques for data authenticity and confidentiality.

geofencing—A virtual fence or geographic boundary. It uses GPS to create the boundary. Apps can then respond when a mobile device is within the virtual fence.

geolocation—The location of a device identified by GPS. It can help locate a lost or stolen mobile device.

GPO—Group Policy Object. A technology used within Microsoft Windows to manage users and computers. It is implemented on a domain controller within a domain.

GPS—Global Positioning System. A satellite-based navigation system that identifies the location of a device or vehicle. Mobile devices often incorporate GPS capabilities.

GPS tagging—A process of adding geographical data to files such as pictures. It typically includes latitude and longitude coordinates of the location where the picture was taken or the file was created.

gray box test—A type of penetration test. Testers have some knowledge of the environment prior to starting the test. Compare with *black box test* and *white box test*.

group-based access control—A role-based access control method that uses groups as roles.

Guest account—A pre-created account in Windows systems. It is disabled by default.

H

hacktivist—An attacker who launches attacks as part of an activist movement or to further a cause.

hardware root of trust—A known secure starting point. TPMs have a private key burned into the hardware that provides a hardware root of trust.

hash—A number created by executing a hashing algorithm against data, such as a file or message. Hashing is commonly used for integrity. Common hashing algorithms are MD5, SHA-1, and HMAC.

heuristic/behavioral—A type of monitoring on intrusion detection and intrusion prevention systems. It detects attacks by comparing traffic against a baseline. It is also known as anomaly detection.

HIDS—Host-based intrusion detection system. Software installed on a system to detect attacks. It protects local resources on the host. A host-based intrusion prevention system (HIPS) is an extension of a HIDS. It is software installed on a system to detect and block attacks.

high availability—A term that indicates a system or component remains available close to 100 percent of the time.

HMAC—Hash-based Message Authentication Code. A hashing algorithm used to verify integrity and authenticity of a message with the use of a shared secret. It is typically combined with another hashing algorithm such as SHA.

hoax—A message, often circulated through email, that tells of impending doom from a virus or other security threat that simply doesn't exist.

home automation—Smart devices used within the home that have IP addresses. These are typically accessible via the Internet and are part of the Internet of things (IoT).

honeypot—A server designed to attract an attacker. It typically has weakened security encouraging attackers to investigate it.

honeynet—A group of honeypots in a network. Honeynets are often configured in virtual networks.

hot and cold aisles—A method commonly used in data centers to keep equipment cool. Cool air flows from the front of the cabinets to the back, making the front aisle cooler and the back aisle warmer.

HOTP—HMAC-based One-Time Password. An open standard used for creating one-time passwords. It combines a secret key and a counter, and then uses HMAC to create a hash of the result.

hot site—An alternate location for operations. A hot site typically includes everything needed to be operational within 60 minutes. Compare with *cold site* and *warm site*.

HSM—Hardware security module. A removable or external device that can generate, store, and manage RSA keys used in asymmetric encryption. Compare with *TPM*.

HTTPS—Hypertext Transfer Protocol Secure. A protocol used to encrypt HTTP traffic. HTTPS encrypts traffic with TLS using TCP port 443.

HVAC—Heating, ventilation, and air conditioning. A physical security control that increases availability by regulating airflow within data centers and server rooms.

I

IaaS—Infrastructure as a Service. A cloud computing model that allows an organization to rent access to hardware in a self-managed platform. Compare with *PaaS* and *SaaS*.

ICS—Industrial control system. A system that controls large systems such as power plants or water treatment facilities. A SCADA system controls the ICS.

identification—The process that occurs when a user claims an identity, such as with a username.

IEEE 802.1x—An authentication protocol used in VPNs and wired and wireless networks. VPNs often implement it as a RADIUS server. Wired networks use it for port-based authentication. Wireless networks use it in Enterprise mode. It can be used with certificate-based authentication.

ifconfig—A command-line tool used on Linux systems to show and manipulate settings on a network interface card (NIC). Similar to ipconfig used on Windows systems.

IMAP4—Internet Message Access Protocol version 4. A protocol used to store and manage email on servers. IMAP4 uses TCP port 143. Secure IMAP4 uses TLS to encrypt IMAP4 traffic.

impact—The magnitude of harm related to a risk. It is the negative result of an event, such as the loss of confidentiality, integrity, or availability of a system or data. Compare with *likelihood of occurrence*.

implicit deny—A rule in an ACL that blocks all traffic that hasn't been explicitly allowed. The implicit deny rule is the last rule in an ACL.

Incident response. The process of responding to a security incident. Organizations often create an incident response plan that outlines the procedures to be used when responding to an incident.

incident response plan (IRP)—The procedures documented in an incident response policy.

incident response process—The phases of incident response, including preparation, identification, containment, eradication, recovery, and lessons learned.

incremental backup—A type of backup that backs up all the data that has changed since the last full or incremental backup.

injection attack—An attack that injects code or commands. Common injection attacks are DLL injection, command injection, and SQL injection attacks.

inline—A configuration that forces traffic to pass through a device. A NIPS is placed inline, allowing it to prevent malicious traffic from entering a network. Sometimes called in-band. Compare with *out-of-band*.

input validation—A programming process that verifies data is valid before using it.

insider—An attacker who launches attacks from within an organization, typically as an employee.

integer overflow—An application attack that attempts to use or create a numeric value that is too big for an application to handle. Input handling and error handling thwart the attack.

integrity—One of the three main goals of information security known as the CIA security triad. Integrity provides assurance that data or system configurations have not been modified. Audit logs and hashing are two methods used to ensure integrity. Compare with *availability* and *confidentiality*.

intranet—An internal network. People use an intranet to communicate and share content with each other.

IoT—Internet of things. The network of physical devices connected to the Internet. It typically refers to smart devices with an IP address, such as wearable technology and home automation systems.

ip—A command-line tool used on Linux systems to show and manipulate settings on a network interface card (NIC). Developers created this to replace ifconfig.

ipconfig—A command-line tool used on Windows systems to show the configuration settings on a NIC.

IPsec—Internet Protocol security. A suite of protocols used to encrypt data-in-transit that can operate in both Tunnel mode and Transport mode. It uses Tunnel mode for VPN traffic and Transport mode in private networks.

IP spoofing—An attack that changes the source IP address.

iris scanners—Biometric systems that scan the iris of an eye for authentication.

ISA—Interconnection security agreement. An agreement that specifies technical and security requirements for connections between two or more entities. Compare with *MOU/MOA*.

IV (initialization vector) attack—A wireless attack that attempts to discover the IV. Legacy wireless security protocols are susceptible to IV attacks.

J

jailbreaking—The process of modifying an Apple mobile device to remove software restrictions. It allows a user to install software from any third-party source. Compare with *rooting*.

jamming—A DoS attack against wireless networks. It transmits noise on the same frequency used by a wireless network.

job rotation—A process that ensures employees rotate through different jobs to learn the processes and procedures in each job. It can sometimes detect fraudulent activity.

K

KDC—Key Distribution Center. Also known as a TGT server. Part of the Kerberos protocol used for network authentication. The KDC issues timestamped tickets that expire.

Kerberos—A network authentication mechanism used with Windows Active Directory domains and some Unix environments known as realms. It uses a KDC to issue tickets.

kernel—The central part of the operating system. In container virtualization, guests share the kernel.

key escrow—The process of placing a copy of a private key in a safe environment.

keylogger—Software or hardware used to capture a user's keystrokes. Keystrokes are stored in a file and can be manually retrieved or automatically sent to an attacker.

key stretching—A technique used to increase the strength of stored passwords. It adds additional bits (called salts) and can help thwart brute force and rainbow table attacks.

known plaintext—A cryptographic attack that decrypts encrypted data. In this attack, the attacker knows the plaintext used to create ciphertext.

L

labeling—The process of ensuring data is tagged clearly so that users know its classification. Labels can be physical labels, such as on backup tapes, or digital labels embedded in files.

LDAP—Lightweight Directory Access Protocol. A protocol used to communicate with directories such as Microsoft Active Directory. It identifies objects with query strings using codes such as CN=Users and DC=GetCertifiedGetAhead.

LDAPS—Lightweight Directory Access Protocol Secure. A protocol used to encrypt LDAP traffic with TLS.

least functionality—A core principle of secure systems design. Systems should be deployed with only the applications, services, and protocols needed to meet their purpose.

least privilege—A security principle that specifies that individuals and processes are granted only the rights and permissions needed to perform assigned tasks or functions, but no more.

legal hold—A court order to maintain data for evidence.

likelihood of occurrence—The probability that something will occur. It is used with impact in a qualitative risk assessment. Compare with *impact*.

load balancer—Hardware or software that balances the load between two or more servers. Scheduling methods include source address IP affinity and round-robin.

location-based policies—Policies that prevent users from logging on from certain locations, or require that they log on only from specific locations.

logic bomb—A type of malware that executes in response to an event. The event might be a specific date or time, or a user action such as when a user launches a specific program.

loop prevention—A method of preventing switching loop or bridge loop problems. Both STP and RSTP prevent switching loops.

M

MAC—Mandatory access control. An access control model that uses sensitivity labels assigned to objects (files and folders) and subjects (users). MAC restricts access based on a need to know.

MAC—Media access control. A 48-bit address used to identify network interface cards. It is also called a hardware address or a physical address.

MAC filtering—A form of network access control to allow or block access based on the MAC address. It is configured on switches for port security or on APs for wireless security.

MAC spoofing—An attack that changes the source MAC address.

mail gateway—A server that examines and processes all incoming and outgoing email. It typically includes a spam filter and DLP capabilities. Some gateways also provide encryption services.

malware—Malicious software. It includes a wide range of software that has malicious intent, such as viruses, worms, ransomware, rootkits, logic bombs, and more.

mandatory vacation—A policy that forces employees to take a vacation. The goal is to deter malicious activity, such as fraud and embezzlement, and detect malicious activity when it occurs.

man-in-the-browser—An attack that infects vulnerable web browsers. It can allow the attacker to capture browser session data, including keystrokes.

man-in-the-middle (MITM)—An attack using active interception or eavesdropping. It uses a third computer to capture traffic sent between two other systems.

mantrap—A physical security mechanism designed to control access to a secure area. A mantrap prevents tailgating.

MD5—Message Digest 5. A hashing function used to provide integrity. MD5 creates 128-bit hashes, which are also referred to as MD5 checksums. Experts consider MD5 cracked.

MDM—Mobile device management. A group of applications and/or technologies used to manage mobile devices. MDM tools can monitor mobile devices and ensure they are in compliance with security policies.

memory leak—An application flaw that consumes memory without releasing it.

MFDs—Multi-function devices. Any device that performs multiple functions. As an example, many printers are MFDs because they can print, scan, and copy documents. Many also include faxing capabilities.

MMS—Multimedia Messaging Service. A method used to send text messages. It is an extension of SMS and supports sending multimedia content.

MOU/MOA—Memorandum of understanding or memorandum of agreement. A type of agreement that defines responsibilities of each party. Compare with *ISA*.

MS-CHAPv2—Microsoft Challenge Handshake Authentication Protocol version 2. Microsoft implementation of CHAP. MS-CHAPv2 provides mutual authentication. Compare with *CHAP* and *PAP*.

MTBF—Mean time between failures. A metric that provides a measure of a system's reliability and is usually represented in hours. The MTBF identifies the average time between failures.

MTTR—Mean time to recover. A metric that identifies the average time it takes to restore a failed system. Organizations that have maintenance contracts often specify the MTTR as a part of the contract.

multifactor authentication—A type of authentication that uses methods from more than one factor of authentication.

N

NAC—Network access control. A system that inspects clients to ensure they are healthy. Agents inspect clients and agents can be permanent or dissolvable (also known as agentless).

NAT—Network Address Translation. A service that translates public IP addresses to private IP addresses and private IP addresses to public IP addresses.

NDA—Non-disclosure agreement. An agreement that is designed to prohibit personnel from sharing proprietary data. It can be used with employees within the organization and with other organizations.

Netcat—A command-line tool used to connect to remote systems.

netstat—A command-line tool used to show network statistics on a system.

network mapping—A process used to discover devices on a network, including how they are connected.

network scanner—A tool used to discover devices on a network, including their IP addresses, their operating system, along with services and protocols running on the devices.

NFC attack—An attack against mobile devices that use near field communication (NFC). NFC is a group of standards that allow mobile devices to communicate with nearby mobile devices.

NIDS—Network-based intrusion detection system. A device that detects attacks and raises alerts. A NIDS is installed on network devices, such as routers or firewalls, and monitors network traffic.

NIPS—Network-based intrusion prevention system. A device that detects and stops attacks in progress. A NIPS is placed inline (also called in-band) with traffic so that it can actively monitor data streams.

NIST—National Institute of Standards and Technology. NIST is a part of the U.S. Department of Commerce, and it includes an Information Technology Laboratory (ITL). The ITL publishes special publications related to security that are freely available to anyone.

Nmap—A command-line tool used to scan networks. It is a type of network scanner.

nonce—A number used once. Cryptography elements frequently use a nonce to add randomness.

non-persistence—A method used in virtual desktops where changes made by a user are not saved. Most (or all) users have the same desktop. When users log off, the desktop reverts to its original state.

non-repudiation—The ability to prevent a party from denying an action. Digital signatures and access logs provide non-repudiation.

normalization—The process of organizing tables and columns in a database. Normalization reduces redundant data and improves overall database performance.

nslookup—A command-line tool used to test DNS on Microsoft systems. Compare with *dig*.

NTLM—New Technology LAN Manager. A suite of protocols that provide confidentiality, integrity, and authentication within Windows systems. Versions include NTLM, NTLMv2, and NTLM2 Session.

O

OAuth—An open source standard used for authorization with Internet-based single sign-on solutions.

obfuscation—An attempt to make something unclear or difficult to understand. Steganography methods use obfuscation to hide data within data.

OCSP—Online Certificate Status Protocol. An alternative to using a CRL. It allows entities to query a CA with the serial number of a certificate. The CA answers with good, revoked, or unknown.

onboarding—The process of granting individuals access to an organization's computing resources after being hired. It typically includes giving the employee a user account with appropriate permissions.

Open—A wireless mode that doesn't use security. Compare with *Enterprise* and *PSK* modes.

OpenID Connect—An open source standard used for identification on the Internet. It is typically used with OAuth and it allows clients to verify the identity of end users without managing their credentials.

open-source intelligence—A method of gathering data using public sources, such as social media sites and news outlets.

order of volatility—A term that refers to the order in which you should collect evidence. For example, data in memory is more volatile than data on a disk drive, so it should be collected first.

out-of-band—A configuration that allows a device to collect traffic without the traffic passing through it. Sometimes called passive. Compare with *inline*.

P

P7B—PKCS#7. A common format for PKI certificates. They are DER-based (ASCII) and commonly used to share public keys.

P12—PKCS#12. A common format for PKI certificates. They are CER-based (binary) and often hold certificates with the private key. They are commonly encrypted.

PaaS—Platform as a Service. A cloud computing model that provides cloud customers with a preconfigured computing platform they can use as needed. Compare with *IaaS* and *SaaS*.

PAP—Password Authentication Protocol. An older authentication protocol where passwords or PINs are sent across the network in cleartext. Compare with *CHAP* and *MS-CHAPv2*.

passive reconnaissance—A penetration testing method used to collect information. It typically uses open-source intelligence. Compare with *active reconnaissance*.

pass the hash—A password attack that captures and uses the hash of a password. It attempts to log on as the user with the hash and is commonly associated with the Microsoft NTLM protocol.

password cracker—A tool used to discover passwords.

patch management—The process used to keep systems up to date with current patches. It typically includes evaluating and testing patches before deploying them.

PBKDF2—Password-Based Key Derivation Function 2. A key stretching technique that adds additional bits to a password as a salt. It helps prevent brute force and rainbow table attacks.

PEAP—Protected Extensible Authentication Protocol. An extension of EAP sometimes used with 802.1x. PEAP requires a certificate on the 802.1x server.

PEM—Privacy Enhanced Mail. A common format for PKI certificates. It can use either CER (ASCII) or DER (binary) formats and can be used for almost any type of certificates.

penetration testing—A method of testing targeted systems to determine if vulnerabilities can be exploited. Penetration tests are intrusive. Compare with *vulnerability scanner*.

perfect forward secrecy—A characteristic of encryption keys ensuring that keys are random. Perfect forward secrecy methods do not use deterministic algorithms.

permanent agent—A NAC agent that is installed on a client. It checks the client for health. Compare with *dissolvable agent*.

permission auditing review—An audit that analyzes user privileges. It identifies the privileges (rights and permissions) granted to users, and compares them against what the users need.

PFX—Personal Information Exchange. A common format for PKI certificates. It is the predecessor to P12 certificates.

PHI—Personal Health Information. PII that includes health information.

phishing—The practice of sending email to users with the purpose of tricking them into revealing personal information or clicking on a link.

physical controls—Security controls that you can physically touch.

PII—Personally Identifiable Information. Information about individuals that can be used to trace a person's identity, such as a full name, birth date, biometric data, and more.

ping—A command-line tool used to test connectivity with remote systems.

pinning—A security mechanism used by some web sites to prevent web site impersonation. Web sites provide clients with a list of public key hashes. Clients store the list and use it to validate the web site.

PIV—Personal Identity Verification card. A specialized type of smart card used by U.S. federal agencies. It includes photo identification and provides confidentiality, integrity, authentication, and non-repudiation.

pivot—One of the steps in penetration testing. After escalating privileges, the tester uses additional tools to gain additional information on the exploited computer or on the network.

plaintext—Text displayed in a readable format. Encryption converts plaintext to ciphertext.

pointer dereference—A programming practice that uses a pointer to reference a memory area. A failed dereference operation can corrupt memory and sometimes even cause an application to crash.

POP3—Post Office Protocol version 3. A protocol used to transfer email from mail servers to clients.

port mirror—A monitoring port on a switch. All traffic going through the switch is also sent to the port mirror.

preventive controls—Security controls that attempt to prevent a security incident from occurring.

privacy impact assessment—An assessment used to identify and reduce risks related to potential loss of PII. Compare with *privacy threshold assessment*.

privacy threshold assessment—An assessment used to help identify if a system is processing PII. Compare with *privacy impact assessment*.

private data—Information about an individual that should remain private. Personally Identifiable Information (PII) and Personal Health Information (PHI) are two examples.

private key—Part of a matched key pair used in asymmetric encryption. The private key always stays private. Compare with *public key*.

privilege escalation—The process of gaining elevated rights and permissions. Malware typically uses a variety of techniques to gain elevated privileges.

privileged account—An account with elevated privileges, such as an administrator account.

proprietary data—Data that is related to ownership. Common examples are information related to patents or trade secrets.

protocol analyzer—A tool used to capture network traffic. Both professionals and attackers use protocol analyzers to examine packets. A protocol analyzer can be used to view data sent in clear text.

proximity cards—Small credit card-sized cards that activate when they are in close proximity to a card reader. They are often used by authorized personnel to open doors.

proxy/proxies—A server (or servers) used to forward requests for services such as HTTP or HTTPS. A forward proxy server forwards requests from internal clients to external servers. A reverse proxy accepts requests from the Internet and forwards them to an internal web server. A transparent proxy does not modify requests, but nontransparent proxies include URL filters. An application proxy is used for a specific application, but most proxy servers are used for multiple protocols.

PSK—Pre-shared key. A wireless mode that uses a pre-shared key (similar to a password or passphrase) for security. Compare with *Enterprise* and *Open* modes.

public data—Data that is available to anyone. It might be in brochures, in press releases, or on web sites.

public key—Part of a matched key pair used in asymmetric encryption. The public key is publicly available. Compare with *private key*.

Public Key Infrastructure (PKI)—A group of technologies used to request, create, manage, store, distribute, and revoke digital certificates.

pulping—A process that is performed after shredding papers. It reduces the shredded paper to a mash or puree.

pulverizing—A process used to physically destroy items such as optical discs that aren't erased by a degausser.

purging—A general sanitization term indicating that all sensitive data has been removed from a device.

push notification services—The services that send messages to mobile devices.

Q

qualitative risk assessment—A risk assessment that uses judgment to categorize risks. It is based on impact and likelihood of occurrence.

quantitative risk assessment—A risk assessment that uses specific monetary amounts to identify cost and asset value. It then uses the SLE and ARO to calculate the ALE.

R

race condition—A programming flaw that occurs when two sets of code attempt to access the same resource. The first one to access the resource wins, which can result in inconsistent results.

RADIUS—Remote Authentication Dial-In User Service. An authentication service that provides central authentication for remote access clients. Alternatives are TACACS+ and Diameter.

RAID—Redundant array of inexpensive disks. Multiple disks added together to increase performance or provide protection against faults. Common types include RAID-1, RAID-5, RAID-6, and RAID-10.

rainbow table—A file containing precomputed hashes for character combinations. Rainbow tables are used to discover passwords. PBKDF2 and bcrypt thwart rainbow table attacks.

ransomware—A type of malware used to extort money from individuals and organizations. Ransomware typically encrypts the user's data and demands a ransom before decrypting the data.

RAT—Remote access Trojan. Malware that allows an attacker to take control of a system from a remote location.

RC4—A symmetric stream cipher that can use between 40 and 2,048 bits. Experts consider it cracked and recommend using stronger alternatives.

record time offset—An offset used by recorders to identify times on recordings. If you know when the recording started, you can use the offset to identify the actual time at any point in the recording.

recovery site—An alternate location for business functions after a major disaster.

redundancy—The process of adding duplication to critical system components and networks to provide fault tolerance.

refactoring—A driver manipulation method. Developers rewrite the code without changing the driver's behavior.

remote wipe—The process of sending a signal to a remote device to erase all data. It is useful when a mobile device is lost or stolen.

replay attack—An attack where the data is captured and replayed. Attackers typically modify data before replaying it.

resource exhaustion—The malicious result of many DoS and DDoS attacks. The attack overloads a computer's resources (such as the processor and memory), resulting in service interruption.

retina scanners—Biometric systems that scan the retina of an eye for authentication.

RFID attacks—Attacks against radio-frequency identification (RFID) systems. Some common RFID attacks are eavesdropping, replay, and DoS.

RIPEMD—RACE Integrity Primitives Evaluation Message Digest. A hash function used for integrity. It creates fixed-length hashes of 128, 160, 256, or 320 bits.

risk—The possibility or likelihood of a threat exploiting a vulnerability resulting in a loss. Compare with *threat* and *vulnerability*.

risk assessment—A process used to identify and prioritize risks. It includes quantitative risk assessments and qualitative risk assessments.

risk management—The practice of identifying, monitoring, and limiting risks to a manageable level. It includes risk response techniques, qualitative risk assessments, and quantitative risk assessments.

risk mitigation—The process of reducing risk by implementing controls. Security controls reduce risk by reducing vulnerabilities associated with a risk, or by reducing the impact of a threat.

risk register—A document listing information about risks. It typically includes risk scores along with recommended security controls to reduce the risk scores.

risk response techniques—Methods used to manage risks. Common risk response techniques are accept, transfer, avoid, and mitigate.

rogue AP—An unauthorized AP. It can be placed by an attacker or an employee who hasn't obtained permission to do so.

role-BAC—Role-based access control. An access control model that uses roles based on jobs and functions to define access. It is often implemented with groups (providing group-based privileges).

root certificate—A PKI certificate identifying a root CA.

rooting—The process of modifying an Android device, giving the user root-level, or administrator, access. Compare with *jailbreaking*.

rootkit—A type of malware that has system-level access to a computer. Rootkits are often able to hide themselves from users and antivirus software.

ROT13—A substitution cipher that uses a key of 13. To encrypt a message, you would rotate each letter 13 spaces. To decrypt a message, you would rotate each letter 13 spaces.

round-robin—A scheduling method used with load balancers. It redirects each client request to servers in a predetermined order.

router—A network device that connects multiple network segments together into a single network. They route traffic based on the destination IP address and do not pass broadcast traffic. Routers use ACLs.

RPO—Recovery point objective. A term that refers to the amount of data you can afford to lose by identifying a point in time where data loss is acceptable. It is often identified in a BIA.

RSA—Rivest, Shamir, and Adleman. An asymmetric algorithm used to encrypt data and digitally sign transmissions. It is named after its creators, Rivest, Shamir, and Adleman.

RSTP—Rapid Spanning Tree Protocol. An improvement of STP to prevent switching loop problems.

RTO—Recovery time objective. The maximum amount of time it should take to restore a system after an outage. It is derived from the maximum allowable outage time identified in the BIA.

RTOS—Real-time operating system. An operating system that reacts to input within a specific time. Many embedded systems include an RTOS.

rule-BAC—Rule-based access control. An access control model that uses rules to define access. Rule-based access control is based on a set of approved instructions, such as an access control list, or rules that trigger in response to an event, such as modifying ACLs after detecting an attack.

runtime code—Code that is interpreted when it is executed. Compare with *compiled code.*

S

SaaS—Software as a Service. A cloud computing model that provides applications over the Internet. Webmail is an example of a cloud-based technology. Compare with *IaaS* and *PaaS.*

salt—A random set of data added to a password when creating the hash. PBKDF2 and bcrypt are two protocols that use salts.

SAML—Security Assertion Markup Language. An XML-based standard used to exchange authentication and authorization information between different parties. SAML provides SSO for web-based applications.

sandboxing—The use of an isolated area on a system, typically for testing. Virtual machines are often used to test patches in an isolated sandbox. Application developers sometimes use the chroot command to change the root directory creating a sandbox.

sanitize—The process of destroying or removing all sensitive data from systems and devices. Data sanitization methods include burning, shredding, pulping, pulverizing, degaussing, purging, and wiping.

SATCOM—Satellite communications. A communication system that allows devices to connect to a satellite for communications. Many cars include satellite communication capabilities.

SCADA—Supervisory control and data acquisition. A system used to control an ICS such as a power plant or water treatment facility. Ideally, a SCADA is within an isolated network.

screen filter—A physical security device used to reduce visibility of a computer screen. Screen filters help prevent shoulder surfing.

script kiddie—An attacker with little expertise or sophistication. Script kiddies use existing scripts to launch attacks.

SDN—Software defined network. A method of using software and virtualization technologies to replace hardware routers. SDNs separate the data and control planes.

secure boot—A process that checks and validates system files during the boot process. A TPM typically uses a secure boot process.

secure DevOps—A software development process using an agile-aligned methodology. It considers security through the lifetime of the project.

security incident—An adverse event or series of events that can negatively affect the confidentiality, integrity, or availability of an organization's information technology (IT) systems and data.

SED—Self-encrypting drive. A drive that includes the hardware and software necessary to encrypt a hard drive. Users typically enter credentials to decrypt and use the drive.

separation of duties—A security principle that prevents any single person or entity from controlling all the functions of a critical or sensitive process. It's designed to prevent fraud, theft, and errors.

service account—An account used by a service or application.

session hijacking—An attack that attempts to impersonate a user by capturing and using a session ID. Session IDs are stored in cookies.

SFTP—Secure File Transfer Protocol. An extension of Secure Shell (SSH) used to encrypt FTP traffic. SFTP transmits data using TCP port 22.

SHA—Secure Hash Algorithm. A hashing function used to provide integrity. Versions include SHA-1, SHA-2, and SHA-3.

Shibboleth—An open source federated identity solution.

shimming—A driver manipulation method. It uses additional code to modify the behavior of a driver.

shoulder surfing—The practice of looking over someone's shoulder to obtain information, such as on a computer screen. A screen filter placed over a monitor helps reduce the success of shoulder surfing.

shredding—A method of destroying data or sanitizing media. Cross-cut paper shredders cut papers into fine particles. File shredders remove all remnants of a file by overwriting the contents multiple times.

sideloading—The process of copying an application package to a mobile device. It is useful for developers when testing apps, but can be risky if users sideload unauthorized apps to their device.

SIEM—Security information and event management. A security system that attempts to look at security events throughout the organization.

signature-based—A type of monitoring used on intrusion detection and intrusion prevention systems. It detects attacks based on known attack patterns documented as attack signatures.

single point of failure—A component within a system that can cause the entire system to fail if the component fails.

SLA—Service level agreement. An agreement between a company and a vendor that stipulates performance expectations, such as minimum uptime and maximum downtime levels.

SLE—Single loss expectancy. The monetary value of any single loss. It is used to measure risk with ALE and ARO in a quantitative risk assessment. The calculation is SLE × ARO = ALE.

smart card—A credit card-sized card that has an embedded microchip and a certificate. It is used for authentication in the something you have factor of authentication.

S/MIME—Secure/Multipurpose Internet Mail Extensions. A popular standard used to secure email. S/MIME provides confidentiality, integrity, authentication, and non-repudiation.

SMS—Short Message Service. A basic text messaging service. Compare with *MMS*.

snapshot—A copy of a virtual machine (VM) at a moment in time. If you later have problems with the VM, you can revert it to the state it was in when you took the snapshot. Some backup programs also use snapshots to create a copy of data at a moment in time.

SNMPv3—Simple Network Management Protocol version 3. A protocol used to monitor and manage network devices such as routers and switches.

SoC—System on a chip. An integrated circuit that includes a computing system within the hardware. Many mobile devices include an SoC.

social engineering—The practice of using social tactics to gain information. Social engineers attempt to gain information from people, or get people to do things they wouldn't normally do.

something you are—An authentication factor using biometrics, such as a fingerprint scanner.

something you do—An authentication factor indicating action, such as gestures on a touch screen.

something you have—An authentication factor using something physical, such as a smart card or token.

something you know—An authentication factor indicating knowledge, such as a password or PIN.

somewhere you are—An authentication factor indicating location, often using geolocation technologies.

spam—Unwanted or unsolicited email. Attackers often launch attacks using spam.

spam filter—A method of blocking unwanted email. By blocking email, it often blocks malware.

spear phishing—A targeted form of phishing. Spear phishing attacks attempt to target specific groups of users, such as those within a specific organization, or even a single user.

split tunnel—An encrypted connection used with VPNs. A split tunnel only encrypts traffic going to private IP addresses used in the private network. Compare with *full tunnel*.

spyware—Software installed on users' systems without their awareness or consent. Its purpose is often to monitor the user's computer and the user's activity.

SRTP—Secure Real-time Transport Protocol. A protocol used to encrypt and provide authentication for Real-time Transport Protocol (RTP) traffic. RTP is used for audio/video streaming.

SSH—Secure Shell. A protocol used to encrypt network traffic. SSH encrypts a wide variety of traffic such as SFTP. SSH uses TCP port 22.

SSID—Service set identifier. The name of a wireless network. SSIDs can be set to broadcast so users can easily see it. Disabling SSID broadcast hides it from casual users.

SSL—Secure Sockets Layer. The predecessor to TLS. SSL is used to encrypt data-in-transit with the use of certificates.

SSL decryptors—Devices used to create separate SSL (or TLS) sessions. They allow other security devices to examine encrypted traffic sent to and from the Internet.

SSL/TLS accelerators—Devices used to handle TLS traffic. Servers can off-load TLS traffic to improve performance.

SSO—Single sign-on. An authentication method where users can access multiple resources on a network using a single account. SSO can provide central authentication.

standard operating procedures (SOPs)—A document that provides step-by-step instructions on how to perform common tasks or routine operations.

stapling—The process of appending a digitally signed OCSP response to a certificate. It reduces the overall OCSP traffic sent to a CA.

STARTTLS—A command (not an acronym) used to upgrade an unencrypted connection to an encrypted connection on the same port.

steganography—The practice of hiding data within data. For example, it's possible to embed text files within an image, hiding them from casual users. It is one way to obscure data to hide it.

storage segmentation—A method used to isolate data on mobile devices. It allows personal data to be stored in one location and encrypted corporate data to be stored elsewhere.

stored procedures—A group of SQL statements that execute as a whole, similar to a mini-program. Developers use stored procedures to prevent SQL injection attacks.

STP—Spanning Tree Protocol. A protocol enabled on most switches that protects against switching loops. A switching loop can be caused if two ports of a switch are connected.

stream cipher—An encryption method that encrypts data as a stream of bits or bytes. Compare with *block cipher*.

substitution cipher—An encryption method that replaces characters with other characters.

supply chain assessment—An evaluation of the supply chain needed to produce and sell a product. It includes raw materials and all the processes required to create and distribute a finished product.

switch—A network device used to connect devices. Layer 2 switches send traffic to ports based on their MAC addresses. Layer 3 switches send traffic to ports based on their IP addresses and support VLANs.

symmetric encryption—A type of encryption using a single key to encrypt and decrypt data. Compare with *asymmetric encryption*.

system sprawl—A vulnerability that occurs when an organization has more systems than it needs, and systems it owns are underutilized. Compare with *VM sprawl*.

T

tabletop exercise—A discussion-based exercise where participants talk through an event while sitting at a table or in a conference room. It is often used to test business continuity plans.

TACACS+—Terminal Access Controller Access-Control System Plus. An authentication service that provides central authentication for remote access clients. It can be used as an alternative to RADIUS.

tailgating—A social engineering attack where one person follows behind another person without using credentials. Mantraps help prevent tailgating.

taps—Monitoring ports on a network device. IDSs use taps to capture traffic.

tcpdump—A command-line protocol analyzer. Administrators use it to capture packets.

technical controls—Security controls implemented through technology.

tethering—The process of sharing an Internet connection from one mobile device to another.

thin AP—An AP that is managed by a controller. Sometimes called a controller-based AP. Compare with *fat AP*.

third-party app store—An app store other than the primary source for mobile device apps. It refers to an app store other than the App Store or Google Play for Apple and Android devices, respectively.

threat—Any circumstance or event that has the potential to compromise confidentiality, integrity, or availability. Compare with *risk* and *vulnerability*.

threat assessment—An evaluation of potential threats. Some common types of threat assessments are environmental, manmade, internal, and external.

time-of-day restrictions—An account restriction that prevents users from logging on at certain times.

TKIP—Temporal Key Integrity Protocol. A legacy wireless security protocol. CCMP is the recommended replacement.

TLS—Transport Layer Security. The replacement for SSL. TLS is used to encrypt data-in-transit. Like SSL, it uses certificates issued by CAs.

token—An authentication device or file. A hardware token is a physical device used in the something you have factor of authentication. A software token is a small file used by authentication services indicating a user has logged on.

TOTP—Time-based One-Time Password. An open source standard similar to HOTP. It uses a timestamp instead of a counter. One-time passwords created with TOTP expire after 30 seconds.

TPM—Trusted Platform Module. A hardware chip on the motherboard included with many laptops and some mobile devices. It provides full disk encryption. Compare with *HSM*.

tracert—A command-line tool used to trace the route between two systems.

transitive trust—An indirect trust relationship created by two or more direct trust relationships.

Trojan—Malware also known as a Trojan horse. A Trojan often looks useful, but is malicious.

trusted operating system—An operating system that is configured to meet a set of security requirements. It ensures that only authorized personnel can access data based on their permissions.

Twofish—A symmetric key block cipher. It encrypts data in 128-bit blocks and supports 128-, 192-, or

256-bit keys. Compare with *Blowfish*.

Type I hypervisors—A virtualization technology. Type I hypervisors (or bare-metal hypervisors) run directly on the system hardware. They don't need to run within an operating system.

Type II hypervisors—A virtualization technology. Type II hypervisors run as software within a host operating system. The Microsoft Hyper-V hypervisor runs within a Microsoft operating system to host VMs.

typo squatting—The purchase of a domain name that is close to a legitimate domain name. Attackers often try to trick users who inadvertently use the wrong domain name. Also called URL hijacking.

U

UAVs—Unmanned aerial vehicles. Flying vehicles piloted by remote control or onboard computers.

UEFI—Unified Extensible Firmware Interface. A method used to boot some systems and intended to replace Basic Input/Output System (BIOS) firmware.

URL hijacking—The purchase of a domain name that is close to a legitimate domain name. Attackers often try to trick users who inadvertently use the wrong domain name. Also called typo squatting.

USB OTG—Universal Serial Bus On-The-Go. A cable used to connect mobile devices to other devices. It is one of many methods that you can use to connect a mobile device to external media.

use case—A methodology used in system analysis and software engineering to identify and clarify requirements to achieve a goal. For example, a use case of supporting confidentiality can help an organization identify the steps required to protect the confidentiality of data.

UTM—Unified threat management. A group of security controls combined in a single solution. UTM appliances can inspect data streams for malicious content and block it.

V

VDI/VDE—A virtual desktop infrastructure or virtual desktop environment. Users access a server hosting virtual desktops and run the desktop operating system from the server.

vendor diversity—The practice of implementing security controls from different vendors to increase security. Compare with *control diversity*.

version control—A method of tracking changes to software as it is updated.

virtualization—A technology that allows you to host multiple virtual machines on a single physical system. Different types include Type I, Type II, and application cell/container virtualization.

virus—Malicious code that attaches itself to a host application. The host application must be executed to run, and the malicious code executes when the host application is executed.

VLAN—Virtual local area network. A method of segmenting traffic. A VLAN logically groups several different computers together without regard to their physical location.

VM escape—An attack that allows an attacker to access the host system from within a virtual machine. The primary protection is to keep hosts and guests up to date with current patches.

VM sprawl—A vulnerability that occurs when an organization has many VMs that aren't properly managed. Unmanaged VMs are not kept up to date with current patches. Compare with *system sprawl*.

voice recognition—A biometric method that identifies who is speaking using speech recognition methods to identify different acoustic features.

VPN—Virtual private network. A method that provides access to a private network over a public network such as the Internet. VPN concentrators are dedicated devices used to provide VPN access to large groups of users.

vulnerability—A weakness. It can be a weakness in the hardware, the software, the configuration, or even the users operating the system. Compare with *risk* and *threat*.

vulnerability scanner—A tool used to detect vulnerabilities. A scan typically identifies vulnerabilities, misconfigurations, and a lack of security controls. It passively tests security controls.

W

warm site—An alternate location for operations. A compromise between an expensive hot site and a cold site. Compare with *cold site* and *hot site*.

waterfall—A software development life cycle model using a top-down approach. It uses multiple stages with each stage starting after the previous stage is complete. Compare with *agile*.

watering hole attack—An attack method that infects web sites that a group is likely to trust and visit.

wearable technology—Smart devices that a person can wear or have implanted.

web application firewall (WAF)—A firewall specifically designed to protect a web application, such as a web server. A WAF inspects the contents of traffic to a web server and can detect malicious content, such as code used in a cross-scripting attack, and block it.

whaling—A form of spear phishing that attempts to target high-level executives. When successful, attackers gain confidential company information that they might not be able to get anywhere else.

white box test—A type of penetration test. Testers have full knowledge of the environment prior to starting the test. Compare with *black box test* and *gray box test*.

Wi-Fi Direct—A standard that allows devices to connect without a wireless access point.

wildcard certificate—A certificate that can be used for multiple domains with the same root domain. It starts with an asterisk.

wiping—The process of completely removing all remnants of data on a disk. A bit-level overwrite writes patterns of 1s and 0s multiple times to ensure data on a disk is unreadable.

wireless scanners—A network scanner that scans wireless frequency bands. Scanners can help discover rogue APs and crack passwords used by wireless APs.

worm—Self-replicating malware that travels through a network. Worms do not need user interaction to execute.

WPA—Wi-Fi Protected Access. A legacy wireless security protocol. It has been superseded by WPA2.

WPA2—Wi-Fi Protected Access II. A wireless security protocol. It supports CCMP for encryption, which is based on AES. It can use Open mode, a pre-shared key, or Enterprise mode.

WPS—Wi-Fi Protected Setup. A method that allows users to easily configure a wireless network, often by using only a PIN. WPS brute force attacks can discover the PIN.

WPS attack—An attack against an AP. A WPS attack discovers the eight-digit WPS PIN and uses it to discover the AP passphrase.

X

XML—Extensible Markup Language. A language used by many databases for inputting or exporting data. XML uses formatting rules to describe the data.

XOR—A logical operation used in some encryption schemes. XOR operations compare two inputs. If the two inputs are the same, it outputs True. If the two inputs are different, it outputs False.

Z

zero-day vulnerability—A vulnerability or bug that is unknown to trusted sources but can be exploited by attackers. Zero-day attacks take advantage of zero-day vulnerabilities.

Index

35862505R00338

Made in the USA
Middletown, DE
08 February 2019